CHILDREN WITH EXCEPTIONALITIES IN CANADIAN CLASSROOMS

EIGHTH EDITION

CHILDREN WITH EXCEPTIONALITIES IN CANADIAN CLASSROOMS

EIGHTH EDITION

MARGRET WINZER
University of Lethbridge

PEARSON
Prentice Hall

Toronto

Library and Archives Canada Cataloguing in Publication

Winzer, Margret, 1940–
    Children with exceptionalities in Canadian classrooms / Margret
Winzer.—8th ed.

ISBN-13: 978-0-13-222394-2
ISBN-10: 0-13-222394-5

    1. Special education—Canada—Textbooks.   I. Title.

LC3984.W56 2008   371.90971   C2006-904871-1

ISBN-13: 978-0-13-222394-2
ISBN-10: 0-13-222394-5

Editor-in-Chief, Vice-President of Sales: Kelly Shaw
Acquisitions Editors: Christine Cozens, Kathleen McGill
Marketing Manager: Toivo Pajo
Supervising Developmental Editor: Suzanne Schaan
Production Editor: Katie Hearn
Copy Editor: Allegra Robinson
Proofreader: Joe Zingrone
Production Coordinator: Andrea Falkenberg
Composition: Integra
Photo Research: Amanda McCormick
Art Director: Julia Hall
Cover Design: Chris Tsintziras
Interior Design: Chris Tsintziras
Cover Image: Masterfile/David Nardini

Photo credits appear on page p. 641, which constitutes an extension of this copyright page.

6   12 11

Printed and bound in the United States of America.

Contents

Chapter 5   **Children with Learning Disabilities   128**

Chapter 6   Children with Intellectual Disabilities   169

Section 3   Children with Behavioural Disorders   205

Chapter 8   **Children with Attention Deficit Hyperactivity Disorder (ADHD)   253**

Section 4   Children Who Are Gifted, Creative, and Talented 277

Chapter 9   **Children Who Are Gifted, Creative, and Talented   279**

Section 5   Children with Sensory Impairments   319

Chapter 10   Children with Hearing Impairments   321

Chapter 11   **Children with Visual Impairments   359**

Section 6   Children with Low-Incidence Disabilities   391

Section 7   Infants, Preschoolers, Families, and Young Adults   515

Preface

Children with Exceptionalities in Canadian Classrooms, Eighth Edition, is designed to serve as a comprehensive introduction to children with exceptionalities in Canada and to Canadian special education. It is intended to be a practical and readily understandable guide for those who, for the first time, are studying children with exceptionalities, their special needs, and their education, as well as a resource for more advanced students. The text is written for a broad audience. It will interest students involved in special education, general education, early childhood education, and early childhood special education. Students in psychology; rehabilitation; nursing; social work; and allied child-care disciplines such as audiology, speech therapy, and language pathology will also find *Children with Exceptionalities* relevant.

The overarching theme of this text is an examination of students with exceptionalities within Canadian special education. We stress the psychological, cognitive, social, and physical differences that more and less able learners bring to the teaching/learning situation, the unique difficulties faced by children who are exceptional, the developmental consequences of various disabilities, and the multiple types of interventions necessary to accommodate these students effectively in local schools. The age range of the students with exceptionalities spans infants to young adults.

Founding an introductory text on children and their needs follows the general tenor of different strands of research in the field of special education, as well as recent standards presented by the Council for Exceptional Children (CEC) for educators' basic knowledge and skills. One research strand shows that most general educators do not have a thorough understanding of students with exceptionalities and their skills and needs. It becomes important, therefore, to know specific things about specific students, because the reason a child with a severe behaviour disorder is not learning is different from the reason a child with severe intellectual disabilities is not learning. Such knowledge is vital for professionals if they are to successfully identify, diagnose, prescribe treatment for, teach, remediate, motivate, or generally improve the lives of individuals with exceptional conditions.

Another research strand demonstrates that knowledge changes attitudes toward both people with disabilities as well as their education and place in society. The beliefs of school personnel can be a conservative force that impedes or obstructs change; teacher beliefs about the value of disability and professional responsibilities correlate with teaching practices in serving children who are exceptional. Teachers and others who hold a clear understanding of exceptional conditions tend to be more tolerant and accepting of the students themselves and of the special education placements and interventions than teachers and others who know little about the conditions and the way they affect students' development.

All of those involved in any way with children and education require knowledge of the philosophies, practices, and policies that determine the care and education of children and youth with special needs. The CEC guidelines, for example, point out that educators dealing with students with exceptionalities require a background in the professional, ethical, legal, historical, and philosophical aspects of the field; knowledge of the characteristics of children with exceptionalities and the ways that these characteristics may interact with culture and environment; assessment procedures for program implementation; and knowledge of effective instructional procedures and programs (see O'Shea, Hammitte, Mainzer, & Crutchfield, 2000). Each of these aspects is treated thoroughly in this text.

This book also aims to open a window on the Canadian experience and to capture the flavour of Canadian services. While Canadian special education shares much with that of other nations in both its historical development and contemporary practice, there is also much that is unique and special to our situation. It is important to provide recognition of the considerable Canadian achievements in the field and detail the exciting new advances that are occurring, so that readers may discover the depth of the concern and care in Canada for children and youth with exceptionalities and their families.

Of particular importance and relevance is an understanding of the ideology and subsequent implementation of major movements in contemporary special education. In this age of greater teacher accountability and increased teacher decision-making, it is vital that those within the profession and those aspiring to join it fully understand the debates circulating in the field so that they can justify their own practices and explain them to others.

For example, inclusive education has been a critical aspect of the Canadian educational vista for 20 years; today, inclusive schooling for students with special needs is policy right across the country. Although the debates and counter-debates that characterized the 1990s have muted, the issue of inclusive schooling remains one of the most controversial and even contentious debates in contemporary special education and one with fluid and rapidly changing parameters. Another important topic is how best to handle students displaying serious and pervasive behavioural disorders. New and exciting themes are emerging, but no one is quite sure about the most effective methods.

No text on special education is ever going to win universal assent. Every author brings to a text opinions formed by experience and practice, as well as conclusions based on research. However, when discussing inclusion or behavioural regimes—indeed, any new movements and trends—we would be uncomfortable presenting a single philosophical stance, adopting a single model as an unvarying theme, or promoting a particular service model. In the context of controversial issues, the author adopts a non-evaluative, neutral position as far as possible and attempts to present all the arguments based on the newest research and findings drawn from the special education literature and supported by relevant work from child development, educational psychology, and so on, and elaborated via styles of organization and models of best practice. Hence, in discussions about inclusion, as an example, we outline the theory of inclusive schooling, detail the workable necessary technology, pinpoint barriers to successful implementation, and discuss current placement issues, service delivery models, and best practices in the field. Given the research base, the text discussions, the dynamic nature of reform, and the teachers' and students' own readings and observations, we hope that they will arrive at their own reasoned and flexible positions on these issues.

Throughout this text a categorical approach is adopted. Not only is this the most practical and logical manner in which to organize such a huge body of information, but it allows a focus on the specific needs of diverse groups of children and the medical, therapeutic, psychological, sociological, and educational aspects of the various categories of exceptionality. Within each chapter, the reader will find material dealing with etiology; developmental consequences; definitions and classification; prevalence; identification and measurement; and educational, medical, and technical interventions for each type of condition.

Such a categorical approach does not overlook the fact that there is much overlap between categories and that many environmental, technological, communicative, and instructional strategies are suitable for a range of learners. Common themes are found throughout the text, particularly in relation to classroom interventions and service delivery models.

NEW TO THIS EDITION

In this eighth edition, many of the features of earlier editions have been retained and expanded. The presentation includes highly current topics, events, and relationships from various fields, since these affect what does—or does not—happen in the lives of children and youth who are exceptional.

There are, however, many new improvements and revisions that distinguish the eighth edition. Readers will find the following changes and revisions:

- An entirely new chapter (Chapter 8) dealing with students with Attention Deficit Hyperactivity Disorder (ADHD).
- A greatly expanded chapter (Chapter 14) on pervasive developmental disorders, with a focus on Autism Spectrum Disorders.
- New sections in each categorical chapter on children's play.
- New material and sections that reflect the realities of mounting numbers of students within a particular classification. For example, readers of this edition will find new and expanded information on non-specific learning disabilities; new genetic findings relevant to persons with intellectual disabilities; an expanded section on Fetal Alcohol Spectrum disorders; and new information on Functional Behavioural Assessment, wraparound, and Positive Behavioural Supports.

Other features are new or expanded in this edition. These are

- Debates designed to present both sides of certain critical issues have been revised for clarity and ease of reference.
- Research Notes boxes that present new findings or directions have been expanded. The extensive research and thorough discussions of important research findings and key theories provide a strong foundation of issues, knowledge, and skills in seminal areas of contemporary special education.
- Revised and expanded Case Studies are provided to elaborate various aspects required to instruct a particular student representing a classification of exceptionality. While the Case Studies are simplified versions of actual events, intended only to highlight particular aspects, they are integrated into the material presented to help readers translate the ideas into the parameters of classrooms and present approaches, models, techniques, and strategies that assist in accommodating students with exceptionalities in general classrooms and other settings. Case Studies include extracts from Individual Education Plans presented in varied formats.
- Sections on creating accessible classrooms have been expanded and revised for clarity.

ORGANIZATIONAL FEATURES

- Learning Outcomes located at the opening of each section
- New tables and figures that enhance and illustrate the text
- Glossary terms set in bold type and highlighted in the margins for ease of reference

SUPPLEMENTAL TEACHING AND LEARNING AIDS

A Companion Website accompanies the text. It is designed as a study guide for students and contains an overview and general information. Users will find

- General information—key terms, concepts and names, and summaries of each chapter
- Reflective and review questions in various formats
- Reflections based on the Case Studies in the text
- Additional reflective assignments that offer students and instructors sources for term papers, discussion questions, and term assignments
- Study options—reliable sources for further study that include related texts and journals
- Weblinks that guide students to relevant online journals, newspapers, agencies, and other resources

An Instructor's Resource CD-ROM (0-13-243988-3) includes an Instructor's Manual, which is also available for download from a password-protected section of Pearson Education Canada's online catalogue (vig.pearsoned.ca). Navigate to your book's catalogue page to view a list of those supplements that are available. See your local sales representative for details and access.

The CD-ROM also includes a test item file in TestGen format. The Pearson TestGen is a testing software that enables instructors to view and edit the existing questions, add questions, generate tests, and distribute the tests in a variety of formats. Powerful search and sort functions make it easy to locate questions and arrange them in any order desired. TestGen also enables instructors to administer tests on a local area network, have the tests graded electronically, and have the results prepared in electronic or printed reports. TestGen is compatible with Windows and Macintosh operating systems, and can be downloaded from the TestGen website located at **www.pearsoned.com/testgen**. Contact your local sales representative for details and access.

ACKNOWLEDGMENTS

I would like to express gratitude to Jamie Wilde, my graduate student, for her input and interest in the text, particularly the research background for a number of chapters. Of particular importance is my friend and colleague, Professor Kas Mazurek, who was invaluable in his assistance and support of this edition. I am grateful to the following reviewers for their thoughtful comments and suggestions: Cheryll Duquette, University of Ottawa; Caron Fitzpatrick, Algonquin College; Fred French, Mount Saint Vincent University; Tom McNorton, University of Windsor; and others who chose to remain anonymous.

About the Author

Margret Winzer is a professor (emerita) in the Faculty of Education at the University of Lethbridge. She teaches in the areas of special education and early childhood education. Professor Winzer has wide experience in the schools in both general education and special education, specifically as a teacher of deaf children. Her academic writing and research covers broad areas of special education with a particular focus on the history of special education and comparative studies in special education. Dr. Winzer was awarded the Ingrid Speaker research medal in 2003 and the Lifelong Achievement Award in 2004 from the International Special Education division of the Council for Exceptional Children.

SECTION 1

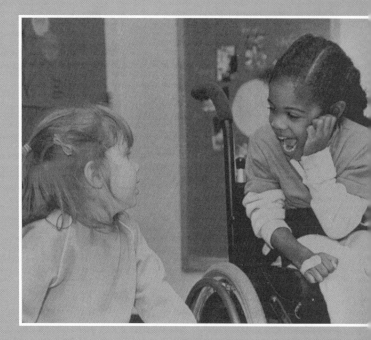

Foundations of
Special Education

In a philosophical and humanitarian sense, all children are special. They all have certain strengths and weaknesses and their own particular patterns of inter- and intra-individual differences. In most children, the strengths outweigh the weaknesses. In this text, however, we are concerned with children and youth for whom the balance of strengths and weaknesses may tip a different way.

This book is about children with exceptionalities, those who have difficulty in realizing their full human potential. Their intellectual, emotional, physical, or social performance falls below that of other children. The differences may be related to physical, language, psychological, cognitive, emotional, or social factors, or a combination of these. Children who are gifted and talented are also included, although their patterns do not fall below but rather rise above those of average children.

In the past few decades, Canadian society in general has made such major gains in its ability to provide sophisticated services for individuals who are exceptional that the prospects for these children and adults have altered dramatically. In the wide social arena, an emphasis on the dignity and worth of each person has brought greater acceptance of individuals who are exceptional. Together with a significant increase in public awareness and understanding, current social philosophy aims to provide such individuals with a lifestyle as close to normal as possible. Throughout Canada, the rights of persons with disabilities have emerged as key priorities, and public policies appear promising as the federal, provincial, and territorial governments increasingly seek to develop the potential of individuals who are disabled and to make better use of their aptitudes.

Medicine has made great strides in the prevention of disabling conditions, interventions to ameliorate them, and the care of children who must live with them. There is growing excitement in the field of molecular genetics; genetic investigation and diagnosis of the causes of some disabilities are racing ahead. In the technological field, dramatic advances provide a variety of adaptive devices and aids to help individuals with disabilities in learning and day-to-day living.

In education, significant philosophical and program changes are ongoing. Special education is no longer something apart and separate from general education. Rather, every school district, every school, and every teacher must now consider the individual learning needs of all students and rethink their understanding of exceptionality and special programs.

The opening section of this text is designed to introduce children and youth with exceptionalities, special education, and some general principles and practices that are germane to the care and education of individuals who are exceptional. Chapter 1 introduces the topic of exceptionality. We consider the recognized exceptionalities; issues in classification, labelling, and prevalence; and the ways in which students with special needs are educated.

Educational services and the ideas that stimulate and direct their growth are never static. Changing needs lead to the formulation of new policies, legislation, and other administrative arrangements and practices. Nowhere is this more true than in the field of special education. In areas such as legislation, school placements, assessment, and teaching methodologies and approaches, today's special education is in a state of flux. Nearly all advocates for students with disabilities want "appropriate education in the least restrictive environment; public education that accommodates students with special problems; labels that carry the least possible social stigma; parental participation in decisions to provide special services; and collaboration among all service providers" (Kauffman, 1993, p. 10). How these ends are to be achieved remains the subject of intense debate. Special education is grappling with new and intriguing philosophies, innovative practices and approaches, and new forms of collaboration.

Chapter 2 explores some of the major issues, trends, and movements that surround contemporary special education and exceptionality. We place particular emphasis on inclusive schooling for students with special needs. As systems increasingly move toward integrating children who are exceptional, it is important for educators, parents, and others to recognize the complexity of the issues and understand what they mean to classroom teachers, parents, and students, both those with disabilities and their typical peers.

Considerations of etiology (causes) are generally the domain of medical personnel. Nevertheless, teachers need a working knowledge of causes and their consequences for learning and behaviour if they are to instruct children adequately. In Chapter 3, we outline some of the major etiologies and look at a huge group of children subsumed within the generic category of "at risk."

Learning Outcomes

This section is designed to provide a broad overview of special education, the clientele it serves, the professionals involved, and the manner in which it is implemented. After reading this section, you should be able to

People and Foundations

1. Outline how special education developed and evolved and how new underlying philosophies such as normalization and inclusive schooling have brought dramatic changes to the field.
2. Understand the major debates in contemporary special education, how they relate to reforms in general education, and the status of the reform movement in Canada today.

Issues

3. Explain some of the major trends and movements in contemporary special education.
4. Recognize the differences that occur in the practice of special education across Canada.
5. Understand the importance of legislation and litigation in the area of special education in both Canada and the United States and make clear distinctions between how the two countries treat these issues.
6. Understand and describe the difficulties inherent in defining, classifying, and estimating prevalence rates for children and youth with disabilities in Canada.
7. Detail the pros and cons of the use of labels in special education.
8. Understand the many familial and extra-familial factors that can place students at risk for learning and behavioural problems, particularly the potential difficulties associated with cultural and linguistic differences.

Knowledge

9. Explain the various modes of intervention with children who are exceptional, the personnel involved, the continuum of educational services available, and the service delivery models found in current special education in Canada.
10. Distinguish between established, biological, and environmental risk and have a working knowledge of major risk factors and how they affect development.
11. Understand the different stages of the assessment process and some of the procedures used.

Skills

12. Explain the process and practice of Individual Education Plans (IEPs).
13. Detail the common components of an IEP and provide examples of each one.
14. Be aware of accommodations, adaptations, and modifications that can be used in a classroom.

CHAPTER 1

INTRODUCTION TO CHILDREN WHO ARE EXCEPTIONAL

CHAPTER OUTLINE

INTRODUCTION

All children differ from one another to varying degrees. The colour of their eyes, hair, and skin differs; the way they dress and speak differs; and their physical, cognitive, social and emotional development and skills differ. Every child possesses a unique combination of abilities and problems, interests and fears, successes and failures. These individual differences fall along a continuum and are characteristic of all humans.

We all have certain strengths, we all have some limitations on our mental and physical ability, and we all have some disabilities, however minor, when it comes to learning. Most of these problems fall into common areas—a tendency to be easily bored, distractibility, poor study habits, poor memory, inadequate motor control, family interference, and so on. Some of us have problems learning a foreign language; others forget directions or people's names. For most of us, a perfect backhand is an unreachable goal.

The assumption that there is a core homogeneous group of learners in the classroom is flawed. Common sense, and increasingly neuroscience, tell us that learners considered to be within the so-called "normal" group are at least as diverse along various dimensions affecting learning as learners considered to be in different groups (Rose & Meyer, 2002). There are myriad subtle differences that make each child unique, and classroom teachers see minor differences and problems all the time. As they take these varied learning aptitudes and styles into account, teachers do not expect every student to learn the same things at the same pace, with the same materials, in the same time, and with the same amount of instruction. Good teachers always adapt to learning differences and minor learning difficulties.

In some students, the learning difficulties are more serious, and the children deviate more significantly in one way or another. These are students who are exceptional, whose learning and behaviour deviates significantly from the norm.

THE STUDY OF EXCEPTIONALITY

The study of exceptionality, closely related to special education, can be viewed through a number of lenses. One emerging lens, generally referred to as *disability studies*, is an innovative and complex multidisciplinary field with an extensive professional and academic foundation. The field of disability studies addresses exceptionality in its social and political garb. The main focus is the dynamic interaction between bodily impairments, people's social and physical environments, and the factors that influence the participation of people with disabilities in society.

Another way of looking at exceptionality is to study the characteristics of students with exceptionalities. We find that they are an extraordinarily diverse group when compared to the general population. Indeed, every child with an exceptional condition is different from every other child as far as symptoms, needs, and teachability. It follows that the complexities of studying people with exceptionalities lie in the differences, similarities, and diversity of the population. Because the individual with an exceptionality is different from the average person in some or many areas of functioning, the study of persons with exceptionalities is the study of differences. Individuals who are exceptional demonstrate differences in the physical, intellectual, communicative, social, or emotional domain, or in some combination of these areas.

However, we are often unable to make definitive statements about groups of children with the same exceptionality or even about a single child. Psychologists have not yet unravelled all the mysteries of normal child development, so it is not surprising that understanding and explaining the course of development for children with disabilities poses a unique challenge to developmental researchers. Many aspects of atypical child development still remain unclear.

A textbook such as this is bound by its expository structure. By its nature, it cannot capture the joy and dignity of all children, but has to focus on the differences that we find in children who are exceptional. Nevertheless, it is not desirable or acceptable to look only at children's limitations; a preoccupation with failings makes it difficult to notice strengths. Even as we examine the differences, it is equally important to give significant emphasis to the similarities. Children with exceptionalities do not differ in every way from their typical peers. They are children first and exceptional second. Individuals with exceptionalities share many attitudes, needs, and perceptions with everyone else. They desire acceptance, approval, and affection as much as all children. These similarities are important, and we must always be aware of the danger of seeing only the disability and losing sight of how much children with exceptional conditions resemble other children.

SPECIAL EDUCATION

A dominant commonality found in children and youth with exceptionalities is the need for skilled intervention and special care from trained professionals. Intervention may take many forms—medical, technical, therapeutic, and educational. In an educational context, children are considered exceptional only when their educational program must be altered to meet their unique needs. It must be clearly demonstrated that these students need special educational support to reach their full potential.

Special education means instruction that is specially designed to meet the unique needs of children and youth who are exceptional. Special education is provided for many students who

special education

display disparate characteristics. It encompasses students who are having problems adjusting to the regular school curriculum and those who encounter difficulties in conforming to the social needs of the classroom. Some pupils who are exceptional may require specific physical accommodations in the classroom and the school environment, such as a hearing aid or a wheelchair ramp. Children who are gifted and talented are recognized as exceptional because they too need specialized help from professionals to fully develop their unique abilities.

Until quite recently, special education was chiefly identified with the school system and with school-aged children and their teachers. This is no longer true. In the past three decades, special education has expanded dramatically. It now includes infants and preschoolers and reaches up to encompass adolescents and young adults. Today, special education could include a mother using sign language with her deaf infant at home, a caregiver in a nursery school modifying an activity for a preschooler, a classroom teacher using remedial techniques in the schoolroom, or a counsellor setting up a work experience program for a young adult with a disability.

Special education is founded on the proposition that all children can reach their full potential if given the opportunity to do so, along with effective teaching and proper resources. As the Historical Notes feature at the end of this chapter shows, special education has been traditionally undertaken and is also being currently conducted by different personnel in different settings. While the current ideology in North America emphasizes inclusive settings (see Chapter 2), a few children may be placed in special schools or classrooms with specially trained teachers. Others may be in the general classroom, supported by paraeducators, or may be provided with adapted or modified instruction; still others may receive part-time special

Table 1-1 Sampling of disciplines involved with children who are exceptional

Medical	Paramedical	Educational	Psychological, social
dental surgeon	audiologist	educational consultant	intervenor
neurologist	optometrist	home visiting teacher	social worker
ophthalmologist	public health nurse	interpreter (sign and oral)	school social worker
otolaryngologist	school nurse	itinerant teacher	child care worker
pediatrician		paraeducator	guidance counsellor
physician		pripatologist (orientation	psychologist
psychiatrist		and mobility teacher)	
		school counsellor	
		support services	
		occupational therapist	
		physical therapist	
		speech/language therapist	
		or pathologist	

assistance in a resource room. Today, however, the majority of students with exceptionalities are in general classrooms, with instruction presented by teachers who are increasingly required to tailor classroom instruction to the individual, not the group.

Although the onus for classroom instruction is increasingly being placed on general education teachers, these teachers are not alone in their efforts. Psychologists, speech therapists, physical and occupational therapists, counsellors, and other professionals consult and collaborate with teachers to help them plan the best possible education for each student who is exceptional. These people form part of what is referred to as related services, ancillary services, auxiliary services, the interdisciplinary team, or the inclusion team. We use the broad term **support services** to refer to those services that assist a child who is exceptional to benefit from special education.

support services

The disciplines most closely aligned to education are shown in Table 1-1. Throughout the text, the contributions of many of the people working in these disciplines are explained more fully.

DEFINITIONS IN THE FIELD OF EXCEPTIONALITY

Children and youth who have differences that substantially change the way they learn, respond, or behave have been described in many ways. You will find these children referred to as children with exceptionalities, children with exceptional conditions, children with special needs, children with disabilities or disabling conditions, and children who are challenged.

We use the descriptor *children with exceptionalities* because it tends to be the most encompassing and most acceptable. For example, in one study (Hastings, Sonuga-Barke, & Remington, 1993) that examined college students' attitudes toward descriptors, researchers found that, although new terms such as *learning disability* were evaluated more positively than old ones such as *mental handicap*, most of the labels were still evaluated negatively. The only term that received a positive evaluation was *exceptional*.

To define a name or a term is to explain it precisely. Precise definitions of individual disabling conditions are vital. Definitions provide the basis for theories and hypotheses, for classifying disorders, communicating with others, and obtaining accurate prevalence figures. Nevertheless, even though a definition should communicate succinctly a conceptual framework that has direct implications for practitioners, the search for universal or specific features of various conditions is ongoing and the results remain futile and frustrating. Terms are particularly problematic in areas of overlap between illness and disability.

Even today, the entire area of disability is characterized by conceptual chaos. Children who are exceptional are constantly being reconceptualized, reconsidered, and renamed. Yet perhaps such chaos is inevitable. It arises from the broad range of disciplines providing information and input, the various classification systems, the ongoing changes in terminology, and the continuing discovery of new etiologies (causes).

Many disciplines contribute to research and intervention for children who are exceptional. Alongside the expected areas of education, disability studies, social work, medicine, and psychology, varied fields such as genetics, sociology, economics, law, ethics, and politics provide new insight. Many of the professionals involved have different ways of looking at exceptionalities and use slightly different frameworks for defining and classifying them. This means that people working in medicine, psychology, social work, or other disciplines may perceive different connotations of the term exceptional than people in education.

Some people, for example, assess differences according to how far development deviates from the norm: a psychologist may report that a child's score on an IQ test is three standard deviations below the mean. Others classify differences in terms of some underlying organic or functional cause; for example, medical personnel determine whether a child has spastic or athetoid cerebral palsy. Educators, of course, describe exceptional conditions in terms of educational functioning and achievement. If a child with athetoid cerebral palsy or a mild cognitive delay is in a classroom, the teacher is more likely to be concerned with the activities and techniques that will help the child learn than with the etiology of his or her condition or an exact IQ score.

SOME IMPORTANT TERMINOLOGY

Language, terms, and definitions are powerful tools that gird the formation of concepts and ideas about persons who are exceptional. Little wonder that the terminology in contemporary special education is dynamic. It constantly changes as researchers and practitioners search for language that is appropriate and non-stigmatizing but still descriptive and helpful.

Contemporary society sees a disorder or disability as only one part of the total person. The terms we use today reflect a transformation in the way people with disabilities are viewed. Even 30 years ago, you could hear such emotionally laden and essentially incorrect terms such as "deaf and dumb" or "handicapped child." These terms have now been almost completely abandoned. We know that people who are deaf are not "dumb" in any way. "Handicapped" is not usually an acceptable descriptor.

The major thrust in today's terminology is toward non-stigmatizing language. We use terms and language that place the child first, the disability second. Hence, we speak of *children with Down syndrome* or *children with intellectual disabilities* rather than of "Down syndrome children" and "intellectually disabled children." Or by simply saying *a person who uses a wheelchair* (rather than "wheelchair-bound") we communicate information without using emotionally charged terms (McCrindle, 1995).

As we mentioned, *exceptional* is not the only generic term in place. Other terms are used synonymously, although their meanings may be more restricted and slightly different. The World Health Organization (WHO) is a leader in harmonizing international terminology and statistics on disability. The WHO's definitions of impairment and disability (2001), outlined in part below, are accepted by governments and medical practitioners in many nations, including Canada.

impairments

- **Impairments** are abnormalities of body structure and system function resulting from any cause.

disabilities

- **Disabilities** reflect the consequences of impairments in terms of functional performance and activity by the individual; an individual who is disabled suffers from a disability or impairment of function in one or more areas, such as vision, hearing, or mobility. In other words, a disability refers to the behaviour relevant to the completion of a task and obviously implies a limited aptitude in that task.

- **Handicaps** are the disadvantages experienced by individuals as a result of impairments or disability and reflect an interaction of the individual with the environment. A handicap, then, refers to environmental or functional demands in a *particular situation* that are placed on a person who is disabled. A disability is always connected with a person; a handicap is not. A disability becomes a handicap when the person who is disabled is unable to meet environmental demands and achieve personal goals. For example, a bright child with spina bifida could function well in math class but would be handicapped on the ball field.

handicaps

- **Atypical** refers to youngsters who either do not reach the norm in some functional area or areas, or who rise above the norm.

atypical

- **Special needs** is an educational term that arose from legislation in the United Kingdom. It is used to designate pupils who require special education.

special needs

- **High risk** or **at risk** are synonymous terms increasingly found in contemporary education and special education. **Risk status** is a mechanism for describing the likelihood that a particular individual will experience a specific outcome given certain conditions (Planta, 1990). When the term at risk is used, children are seen to be vulnerable to some future condition. Some children are at risk for exceptional conditions that affect their functioning and achievement. Or a child may be at risk for learning and behavioural problems as a result of factors such as poverty or abuse, psychological disorders, or generally having an unproductive and unrewarding childhood. Older students may be at risk for dropping out of school or delinquency. At-risk status is discussed in Chapter 3.

high risk/at risk

risk status

- **Developmental disability** is a broad and encompassing term referring to conditions that represent a significant delay in the process of development. The presence of a developmental delay is an indication that the process of development is significantly affected and that, without special intervention, educational performance at school age will likely be affected.

developmental disability

- **Developmental delay** implies that a child is lagging in one or more areas of development but may catch up with normally developing children (unlike the child with a developmental disability). Today, the term developmental delay is often used instead of specific terms such as learning disability or intellectual disability when dealing with very young children.

developmental delay

- **Medically fragile** refers to persons with extremely fragile physiological conditions who require ongoing medical support and care.

medically fragile

- **Dually diagnosed** is a relatively new term that refers to children with two disabilities such as deafness and blindness. The term multiple disabilities or co-occurring disabilities is also used here.

dually diagnosed

- **Comorbidity** (used synonymously with *co-occurring disabilities*) is the simultaneous occurrence of two or more conditions. Although the term may seem to relate more to children with significant disabilities, among all children who are exceptional comorbidity is the rule rather than the exception. Disabling conditions rarely appear in a pure form, untainted by other problems and disabilities. For example, children with behavioural

comorbidity

disorders typically display more than one type of disorder; more than 70 percent of children with learning disabilities have accompanying problems; and children with mild intellectual problems have high rates of secondary disabilities.

CLASSIFICATION AND MAJOR CATEGORIES OF EXCEPTIONALITY

A classification system is a means of organizing information. To be useful, a classification system must be based on reliably observed phenomena and the classification of a given disorder should have a clear relationship to its nature, origin, course, and treatment (Kauffman, 2005).

But as with definitions, classification systems used in special education remain imprecise. The current classification systems evolved gradually, haphazardly, and inconsistently over the decades, and today there is relatively little standardization in the study of children who are exceptional. A single consistent and universally accepted method of describing and grouping different groups of children with certain exceptional conditions does not exist.

mildly disabled

Considerable overlap occurs in the classification of disabling conditions. As pointed out, many children who are exceptional have more than one difficulty; because these children do not fall easily into one specific category, they are difficult to classify. Furthermore, children who have been traditionally classified and grouped as **mildly disabled**—those described as learning disabled, mildly intellectually disabled, and mildly behaviourally disordered—tend to share a variety of academic and behavioural characteristics that transcend traditional approaches to classification.

This overlap of categories is particularly relevant to general classroom teachers as these children will be the bulk of those included. The overlap is discussed in the accompanying Research Notes box and readdressed in Chapters 5, 6, and 7.

RESEARCH NOTES

Approaching Categories of Mild Disability

Students with mild disabilities—those labelled as learning disabled, mildly intellectually disabled, and mildly behaviourally disordered—form more than 70 percent of those classified as disabled. Interest in these groups—specifically in whether there are differences or an overlap among the categories—has long been a flourishing field. Since 1977, there have been more than 150 articles, studies, chapters, and monographs that discuss the similarities and differences between categories (Sabornie, Cullinan, Osborne, & Brock, 2005).

The overlap or difference between the categories of learning disabilities, mild intellectual disabilities, and mild behavioural disorders is more than just an item of passing interest. It has implications for prevalence estimates, funding, parent perceptions, and classroom instruction.

Traditionally, special education held that children with mild disabilities did not share common etiological factors and behavioural characteristics. Among the three groups mentioned above, differences were said to exist in the level of cognitive ability, academic achievement, patterns of cognitive performance, degree of underachievement, and adaptiveness of social and emotional development. With different developmental characteristics, children therefore required education matched to their particular area of deficit. During the 1980s, research indicated that in many respects these students could not be reliably distinguished from one another. Multiple studies confirmed the overlap and the similar characteristics displayed between students. Specific domains of development in behaviour and learning are shown in table form below and remain reasonably valid.

Recently, however, sophisticated meta-analyses and ongoing research indicate that students with high-incidence disabilities can be separated categorically on measures of IQ, academic achievement, and behaviour. Sabornie and colleagues (2005), for example, used a meta-analysis that showed these differences. One of the major findings revolves around students with behavioural disorders. Studies show that these children appear to have more serious academic achievement deficits than those with learning disabilities (Nelson, Stage, Epstein, & Pierce, 2005). Furthermore, students with behavioural disorders do not respond to instruction as favourably as students with learning disabilities. Whereas students with learning disabilities improve their reading performance over time, students with behavioural disorders do not demonstrate the same growth (Anderson, Kutash, & Duchnowski, 2001). Inevitably, this leads to another difference. Typically, inclusion in general classrooms is significantly lower for students with behavioural disorders than it is for children with learning disabilities or mild intellectual disabilities.

For classroom considerations, you should be aware of three defining points in the contemporary educational arena. First of all, there is a kind of hydraulic relationship between learning disabilities and mild intellectual disabilities. There is evidence that school personnel often bend the rules and apply the label of learning disabled rather than the more stigmatizing one of mentally retarded (MacMillan & Siperstein, 2001) so that many students who were previously labelled as mildly mentally retarded are being propelled into the classification of learning disabled. For example, one study (Gottlieb, Alter, Gottlieb, & Wishner, 1994) reported that urban students identified as learning disabled had an average IQ of 81.4. Gresham and MacMillan (1996) found that students with IQ scores lower than 75 and as low as 58 had been classified as learning disabled.

At the same time, pupils identified as mildly intellectually disabled tend to have greater disabilities than pupils in previous years and their average ability level is lower than that of previous students. Included in the category of mildly intellectually disabled today are children with Down syndrome and those previously classified as trainable mentally retarded (TMR) (Robinson, Palton, Polloway, & Sargent, 1989).

Finally, as far as classroom instruction goes, the contention that students with one disability should be taught differently from students with another mild disability is flawed. Similar instructional practices are effective in promoting student learning regardless of diagnostic category. Intense interventions for students with behavioural disorders are discussed in Chapters 7 and 8.

	LEARNING DISABLED	MILD INTELLECTUAL DISABILITIES	BEHAVIOURALLY DISORDERED
Cognitive	Average or above average IQ	IQ below 75	Average IQ, mean around 90
Learning	Deficits in attention, memory, achievement	Deficits in memory, attention, and achievement	Deficits in memory, attention, and achievement
	Significantly more off-task behaviour	Significantly more off-task behaviour	Significantly more off-task behaviour
Social	Ignored or rejected by peers	Ignored or rejected by peers	Often actively disliked by peers
Physical	No physical anomalies	No physical anomalies	No physical anomalies
Communication	Speech and language difficulties	Speech and language difficulties	High rates of speech and language problems
Self-concept	Poor self-concept, outward locus of control	Poor self-concept, outward locus of control	Often outward locus of control, poor self-concept
Gender	4:1 boys to girls	5:1 boys to girls	6–12:1 boys to girls

Keeping these caveats in mind, we use the following categories in this text to group the special traits of children who are exceptional.

- *Children and youth with mild disorders to learning.* Included in this category are students with intellectual differences—those who are intellectually disabled, those with learning disabilities, and those with communication disorders—and children who have speech difficulties and language problems. Such a grouping reflects the contemporary movement toward inclusive schools, the overlap among categories, and the changing foci in dealing with students with mild disabilities in particular.

- *Children and youth with behavioural disorders.* Behavioural disorders include a wide variety of problems—conduct disorders, anxiety and withdrawal, Attention Deficit Hyperactivity Disorder, and socialized aggression.

- *Children and youth who are intellectually superior.* This category includes children who are gifted, creative, and talented.

- *Children and youth who have sensory disabilities.* Included here are children with auditory impairments (deaf and hard of hearing) and those with visual problems (blind and visually impaired).

- *Children and youth who have significant or pervasive disabilities.* This category encompasses a large and disparate population. Among physical disabilities and impaired health are included neurological defects, orthopedic conditions, birth defects, and conditions that are a result of infection and disease (not all of which are significant or pervasive). There are also children and youth who have developmental disabilities—those with pervasive disorders such as severe mental retardation and infantile autism, and those with multiple disabilities such as cerebral palsy and mental retardation, or deafness and blindness.

The above classifications are arbitrary, and since many disorders cover a spectrum, additional qualifiers are used to provide more specificity to these general classifications. Degrees of severity—mild, moderate, severe, and profound—are the most commonly used qualifiers. For example, when we speak of a child with a mild intellectual disability, we mean that the child has an IQ somewhere in the range of 55 to 70 and demonstrates deficits in **adaptive behaviour**—the ability to respond to and function in the environment according to age and social standards. On the other hand, a child with profound intellectual disabilities would have an IQ below 25 and extreme difficulties in any form of adaptive behaviour.

adaptive behaviour

LOOKING AT LABELS

Naming, defining, and classifying are three distinct processes. We have just pointed out the problems with definitions and classification. These meld with and contribute to the intense difficulties in the naming or labelling process in special education.

Labelling refers to the categorizing of children on the basis of their primary disability. The practice evolved gradually; no one really planned it. Labels are products of the human mind—in special education they grew from a psychomedical model that encompassed diagnosis, classification, and placement. (The Historical Notes at the end of Chapter 3 explain the medical model and its genesis and development.) Once the quest for labels began in earnest in the 1850s, the labelling industry never stopped. In fact, it has grown since the late 1980s (see Winzer, 2007).

labelling

For a long time, there has been distrust of the labels and the effectiveness of the discrete compartmentalization that permeates special education. In the early 1970s, Nicholas Hobbs (1975) led a research team from Vanderbilt University on a quest to examine the value of labels and the stigma attached to them. The conclusions then were as ambiguous and inconclusive as they are today. For example, the researchers looked at *labelling bias*—the expectations that others may develop for a person with a certain label—but could not determine its impact. The broad conclusion was, and still is, that while there is always the potential that children will suffer adverse effects from labelling, in some cases the practice may prove advantageous.

The labelling debate in special education continues and is chiefly concerned with whether or not to label, the validity of the practice, the type of labels, and whether labelling creates stigma. Some of the many pros and cons of the dilemma are shown in A Matter of Debate on pages 14 and 15.

In the United States and Canada, discrete categories of exceptionality and specific labels for particular conditions still abound. In Canada, a number of provinces (for example, Ontario, Saskatchewan, Newfoundland and Labrador, and Alberta) still include definitions and categories of exceptionality in special education policies.

What do persons with disabilities themselves say about labelling? *The Disability Rag*, a U.S. disability activist publication, periodically editorializes against euphemisms created by non-disabled people. Articles point out that disabilities are real, and that policies to enable real choice are necessary, rather than euphemistic terms that gloss over the need for action (Sleeter & Grant, 1994). Kate McCrindle also notes that many people with disabilities object to "sugar-coated euphemisms" such as *handi-capable* and

A MATTER OF DEBATE

Labels in Special Education

USEFULNESS/UTILITY

Pros	Cons
A field cannot have any coherence without a common understanding of the limits of the phenomenon.	Labels are subversive disempowerment, part of the maintenance of social and symbolic order. They expel things that are different and divide normal and acceptable from deviant and unacceptable.
Problems cannot be identified or discussed if they lack a descriptor or label.	Labels describe only problems and deficiencies and how persons differ from the norm.
There can be no public policy or research without names and labels.	Labels assume something wrong either in the family, the child, or the culture.
Labels promote effective communication and provide a common language for professionals in clinical work, science, human services, education, and funding.	Labelling renders people voiceless and untrustworthy. They have to live up to their deviancy.
A carefully considered label simplifies information for all involved.	Conditions do not represent dichotomous variables, allowing neat classification.
Labels are "necessary conceptual shorthand in a busy world" (McCrindle, 1995, p. 16).	

SERVICE DELIVERY

Pros	Cons
We cannot prevent or ameliorate disabilities without singling out children for special treatment.	No necessary connection exists between labels of impairment and labels of service delivery.
Labels have diagnostic, legal, and entitlement perspectives that affect research, service provision, and funding.	Labels do not automatically result in better services.
Labels identify children who require differentiated instruction.	Teachers confer alphabet labels (ADHD, ODD) on students without appropriate facts and diagnoses.
Parents are aware that labels are essential passports to additional services.	

CONSEQUENCES OF LABELS

Pros	Cons
Labels make others more tolerant of a disability and provide explanations for behaviour or appearance.	Labels can be arbitrary and permanently assign a child to a specific category of exceptionality.
Labels bring increased visibility for people with special needs.	A child's functional level, not the label, should be the critical component driving intervention.
	Labels seldom adequately reflect a child's educational and therapeutic needs.

STIGMA

Pros	Cons
Teachers react to a child's classroom behaviour, not the label.	A labelled person is viewed differently than a non-labelled one.
Students' damage to self-esteem is a consequence of learning and behavioural problems, not of labels.	Deviant behaviour is expected from labelled individuals.
Stigma precedes a label, not the other way around.	Teachers may hold lowered or negative expectations for those who are labelled.
Concern for the negative effects of labelling appears to have little foundation in research evidence.	Students may be misclassified and placed in unsuitable educational environments.

Sources: Curci & Gottlieb, 1990; Prewitt, 2005; Singer, 1988; Thomas & Loxely, 2001.

physically challenged because "they are condescending and reinforce the idea that a disability can't be dealt with in a straightforward manner" (1995, p. 22). For many people, the word *challenged* has already joined an unacceptable lexicon. In a segment of *60 Minutes*, Rick Curry, himself disabled, laughed at "challenged" because it sounds "as if we're not trying hard enough."

Some people have adopted *disability* as a proud label used in asserting their struggle for rights. Others have reclaimed *disabled person* to convey the message that the person is disabled by his or her social and physical environments (UNICEF, 2005). Many activists, however, feel that expressions that emphasize abilities and mirror advances are more constructive. These include words such as *choice, empowerment, inclusion, self-determination, independence, capabilities, normalized environment, equity,* and *individual support systems.*

PREVALENCE OF EXCEPTIONAL CONDITIONS

United Nations surveys estimate that there are more than 290 million people with moderate to severe physical and mental disabilities in the world today; however, there are no reliable international estimates that single out the rates for children only (UNICEF, 2005). In developing countries, the numbers may be even greater than the present catastrophic figures suggest. When we consider how many people are affected by largely preventable diseases, such as water-borne blindness, tuberculosis, and leprosy, and by chronic debilitating conditions that stem from malnutrition, impure water, and inadequate sanitation, the rates are simply staggering (Mazurek & Winzer, 1994). Also note that the number of children with disabilities in central and eastern Europe, republics in the former Soviet Union, and the Baltic States has tripled since 1990 (UNICEF, 2005).

In the United States, approximately 35 million people are considered exceptional. More than 6.4 million school-aged children are receiving special education services.

Canadian statistics on people with disabilities are based on the WHO definitions of disability. The first cycle of the 1994–1995 National Longitudinal Survey of Children and Youth (NLSCY), as well as research based on the National Population Health Survey (1996–1997), shed some light on national data on children with special needs. It appears that approximately 7.7 percent of all children from birth to 19 years of age have a limitation or disability (see Valentine, 2001).

School-related figures tend to be far higher. They stress the children and youth receiving special education services and may include such things as severe reading disabilities and behavioural disorders. When rates are juxtaposed to the need for special education, anywhere from 12 to 15.5 percent of the Canadian school-aged population is considered to be exceptional. In Ontario, for example, an estimated 12.5 percent of the student population receives special education programs and services (ETFO, 2002).

Moreover, numbers are on the rise. From 1998 to 2004, the proportion of special needs children in Ontario's schools more than doubled; more than 50 000 children were identified between 2001 and 2004 (Urquhart, 2005). In Alberta, 1998 to 2003 saw a 64 percent increase in identification of students with severe disabilities and a 140 percent increase in students with mild/moderate disabilities, compared to a general increase in the school population of 5 percent (Pyryt, 2003).

The four most common disability areas are learning disabilities, speech and language impairments, intellectual disabilities, and behavioural disorders. The least common areas are visual impairments, Traumatic Brain Injury, pervasive developmental disorders, and deaf-blindness.

Severity levels are critical. Of the children reported as disabled, about 89 percent have a mild disability, 8 percent a moderate disability, and 3 percent a severe disability. Figure 1-1 shows severity levels. Among these children and adolescents, boys are more likely to be classified as exceptional than girls.

incidence

Estimates of the numbers of individuals who are exceptional are generally reported as either incidence or prevalence. **Incidence** refers to the number of new cases of a particular condition identified over a given period of time, usually a year. Incidence is important for

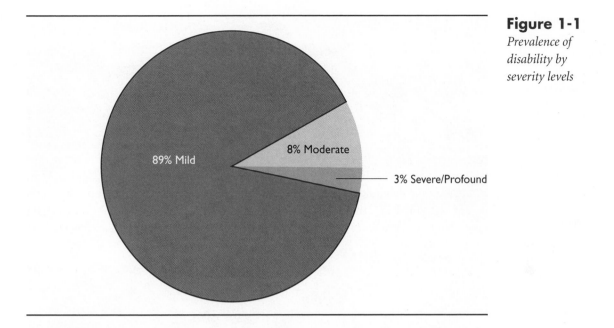

Figure 1-1
Prevalence of disability by severity levels

89% Mild

8% Moderate

3% Severe/Profound

seeing trends, but for special education purposes prevalence has far more meaning, since disabilities often last throughout a lifetime.

Prevalence applies to the total number of existing cases, old and new. The term prevalence is also used to refer to the percentage or proportion of the population that falls into a given category. The prevalence statistic tells teachers and others the total number of children in a category. Table 1-2 shows the approximate proportions of various types of

prevalence

Table 1-2 Estimated prevalence of selected exceptional conditions

Exceptionality	General child population (%)	Special education population (%)
All exceptional conditions	12–15.5	
Speech/language problems	2–4	19
Learning disabilities	2–4	48
Intellectual disabilities	1–3	10
Behavioural disorders	1–6	10
Gifted and talented	2–5	3
Hearing impaired	0.5–0.7	2
Visually impaired	0.08–0.12	1
Health disabled	0.4–0.6	2
Neurological disorders	0.2–1.5	2
Pervasive developmental disorders	0.5–0.7	2

Approximately 15.5 percent of the Canadian school-aged population is considered to be exceptional

exceptional conditions drawn from the data on percentages and numbers that are presented throughout this text.

View the list in Table 1-2 with great caution. A precise determination of the incidence and prevalence rates for exceptional children and adolescents with specific conditions in Canada is very difficult. In general, estimates of the number of children with some identifiable special condition vary widely, particularly for those with high-incidence disabilities such as learning disabilities and behavioural disorders. For example, the proposed rates for behavioural disorders vary from about 0.5 to 20 percent or more of the school-aged population (Kauffman, 2005). It is easier to obtain accurate figures for low-incidence disabilities such as severe visual impairment.

Prevalence estimates are influenced by a complex set of interacting factors. Some of the major factors are outlined below. The subsequent categorical chapters offer further cautions regarding accurate prevalence figures.

Definitional Problems

The search for definitions is ongoing in most areas of special education. In part, this is attributable to new information about children who are exceptional and the best ways to teach them. It is also related in part to the range of professional disciplines—medical, psychological, therapeutic, and educational—that intervene. These necessary services sometimes confound prevalence rates, simply because each discipline brings its own definitions and characterizations of what is exceptional.

In the educational system, students are considered exceptional only when their educational program must be altered to meet their unique needs. For example, although heart disease is a serious condition, it may not have any impact on a student's learning, so a child with a heart disorder may not be counted among the special education population. On the other hand, a medical condition such as pediatric AIDS has major effects on learning, and an affected child would very likely require special education services.

Moreover, special education itself uses many vague and inconsistent definitions and, lacking clear definitions, it is almost impossible to estimate prevalence. School systems tend to interpret a child's condition according to services provided; therefore a child may be called learning disabled in one school district and counted as a low achiever in another. To make it even more confusing, there are differences in categorization across Canada. For example, in broad terms, Ontario uses the categories found in this text. In contrast, the Northwest Territories make no mention of what constitutes an exceptionality. As another instance, Ontario uses the term Traumatic Brain Injury (TBI) whereas Newfoundland and Labrador does not (Dworet & Bennett, 2002).

Changing Diagnoses

The diagnosis of a disabling condition is not, nor should it be, immutable. A diagnosis that is correct today could easily be inappropriate tomorrow. Sometimes, children diagnosed with behavioural disorders or learning disabilities—and especially speech defects—improve to such an extent that they are no longer considered disabled.

Another factor that confounds efforts to estimate prevalence is ongoing research that changes diagnoses by bringing new ways of looking at disabling conditions. For example, recent discoveries in neurology and genetics have altered traditional conceptions of the causes and nature of Autism Spectrum Disorders; the conditions are no longer classified as severe emotional disturbances but as neurological disabilities within the framework of pervasive developmental disorders.

Co-occurring and Multiple Disabilities

Confusion arises about the classification of children with dual or multiple disabilities. When children have more than one pertinent condition, such as intellectual disability, cerebral palsy, and hearing impairment, or a speech disorder and visual impairment, classification often depends on the major condition (called the **primary disability**). For example, a child who is deaf with an emotional problem may be classified as hearing impaired and receive services designed for deaf children; the emotional problem is

primary disability

presumed to be a secondary condition or secondary disability. Or the child may be numbered in both categories, or simply described as multiply disabled. Obviously, such varied counting and categorization makes rates unstable.

Early Identification

Low-incidence conditions, such as severe intellectual disabilities, serious physical impairment, or blindness, are usually identified early in a child's life and involve more professional intervention than high-incidence conditions, such as mild intellectual disability. A mild intellectual disability, for example, may not be identified until the child confronts the complexities of reading and writing in the classroom. As a result, low-incidence disabilities are more likely to be reported.

Changing Rates

Difficulties also arise from different prevalence figures at different points in a person's life cycle. Data from the Canadian Institute of Child Health (1994) shows that the rate of disability varies by age and gender. Numbers are higher among older rather than younger children, partly because many conditions, particularly learning disabilities and mild intellectual disabilities, are often not identified until a child reaches school. For children with intellectual problems, prevalence tends to show a sharp increase during the school years. But since many of the adults who function in this range achieve personal and vocational independence, the estimated prevalence decreases substantially as they enter the working world and assume their places as productive citizens.

Distribution Factors

Disability is not randomly distributed in the population. Families that live in poverty and minority families are more likely to have a child with a disability (see Chapters 3 and 15). School-related risks are most heavily concentrated among visible minorities, people who are poor, residents of the inner city and poor rural regions, and individuals who are not fluent in English (Wotherspoon & Schissel, 2001).

The Stigma of Identification

The Canadian Office for Disability Issues (1997) states, "Attitudes can be the most difficult barrier persons with disabilities must face in gaining full integration, acceptance and participation in society" (p. 1). In the face of stereotypes and negative attitudes, it is not surprising that some parents are reluctant to have their children identified as exceptional. Parents may fail to report a condition, or they may opt for a different category of classification. Parents appear to see labels that specify a particular problem as less stigmatizing than those that imply a global developmental impairment. For example, many parents find the term *learning disabilities* more palatable than *intellectual disabilities* or *mild mental retardation*.

Survey Problems and Sampling Errors

Epidemiology refers to the study of the distribution and determinants of diseases and disabling conditions in a population. Survey problems result when epidemiologists and other researchers use varied definitions of an exceptionality. Surveys can also be misleading when figures from a small area are extrapolated to the rest of the country. Newfoundland and Labrador, for example, has a high rate of spina bifida, and to apply figures from this province to the rest of Canada would clearly be unwise.

epidemiology

INTERVENTION WITH CHILDREN AND YOUTH WHO ARE EXCEPTIONAL

Intervention is a general term that refers to the application of professional skills to maintain or improve an individual's potential and functioning. **Early intervention**, a major trend in current special education practice, refers to the establishment of educational and support services for young children who have disabilities or who are at risk for them, and their families. Although intervention is strongly associated with active educational programming, the term also includes medical intervention, mental health services, and welfare provisions for the family and the child.

intervention

early intervention

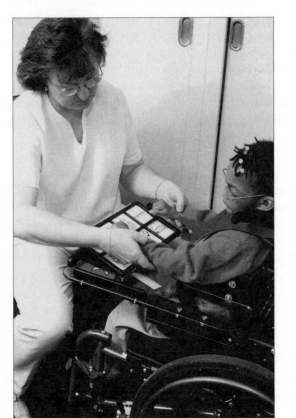

Intervention with children who are exceptional can involve a variety of specialties.

habilitation

rehabilitation
remediation

A number of processes and terms are subsumed under the general rubric of intervention. First of all, there is **habilitation**, which comes from the Latin habilitare, "to make skilled." In habilitation, people in medical, social, psychological, and educational fields support and assist individuals with disabilities in their development and daily lives. Closely aligned to habilitation is **rehabilitation**, a therapeutic term for procedures that endeavour to restore an individual to normal or optimal functioning. **Remediation** is an educational term that refers to helping a child to overcome, or compensate for, specific deficits in learning and development.

For the child who is exceptional, the basic approaches to care and education include four major forms of intervention—medical, therapeutic, educational, and social. A broad outline of some basic intervention techniques is provided here; these are expanded upon in later chapters.

Medical Intervention

Medical intervention and treatment for children who are exceptional is a complex, varied, and highly sophisticated process that involves a variety of specialists with unique skills. The most common forms of medical intervention involve surgery; treatment that is life saving, such as insulin; the controlled use of medication; and supportive therapy.

Sub-specialties within the field of pediatric surgery account for the many forms of surgical treatment. Widely used surgical interventions include reconstructive surgery for repair of physical anomalies such as a cleft lip or palate; neurosurgery for disabling conditions of the brain and spinal cord; and orthopedic surgery for problems of the skeletal system that occur in youngsters with cerebral palsy or multiple physical anomalies. Other sophisticated techniques have been developed to help children with Down syndrome, to insert cochlear implants in deaf individuals, and to transplant organs in children with cystic fibrosis. Of all the medical treatments for children with exceptional conditions, psychopharmacology, or drug therapy, is the one that teachers are most likely to come into contact with, particularly in relation to children with ADHD, which is today the most commonly diagnosed disorder of childhood (see Snider, Busch, & Arrowood, 2003). We discuss drug therapy fully in Chapter 8.

therapy

Therapy

Therapy, the treatment of an illness or disabling condition, consists of a broad range of interventions to help children adapt to their particular disabilities. Physical, occupational, and speech/language therapists provide many essential treatments. Some of the tasks undertaken by therapists are shown in Table 1-3.

There are different types of therapeutic intervention. In *direct therapy*, therapeutic techniques are used with treatment that only the therapist can safely carry out. In monitoring (sometimes called *consultative therapy*), therapists watch and check treatment carried out by parents, teachers, or paraeducators (Dunn, 1989).

Educational Intervention

Education for children who are exceptional is provided through a variety of educational arrangements, settings, and instructional alternatives. Programs vary, often quite dramatically, across the country, the provinces, and even the school districts. The two major differences are

Table 1-3 Therapy and Therapists

Therapists	What they do	Focus
Physical Therapists	Work to improve overall muscle strength; use assistive devices designed to teach skills; develop, improve, or restore more efficient muscular functioning; maintain maximum motor functioning; provide information on positioning and handling; show the use of adaptive equipment	Prosthetic management training; wheelchair mobility training; gross motor skill exercise
Occupational Therapists	Focus on motor development, attention to aspects of the sensory environment, and the achievement of functional daily tasks; develop arm and wrist strength; improve the ability to reach, grasp, and release objects of different sizes, textures, and weights	Vestibular balance; tactile, kinesthetic, and perceptual motor coordination; self-help skills
Speech/Language Therapists/ Pathologists	Provide remedial treatment; develop augmentative communication; identify potential communication disorders; assess and diagnose problems; plan and recommend intervention activities	Speech and language problems; cannot talk; eating problems

the *organizational context*—the legislation and policy underlying special education—and the **service delivery models**—plans for bringing together students, teachers, instruction, and learning that are individual to schools. For example, Alberta manages inclusion differently from New Brunswick. New Brunswick includes all children in general classrooms; Alberta uses a continuum of educational services.

service delivery models

Again, we introduce some broad ideas here. Chapter 2 examines policy and legislation. Each categorical chapter further explores educational intervention for specific populations.

Service Delivery Models

When it comes to service delivery models and **educational settings**—the places where students who are exceptional receive instruction—the alternatives are determined by the unique needs of each child. Many different kinds and combinations of programs are required to accommodate the wide range of conditions that occur in varying degrees of severity and the need for different types and degrees of assistance at various age levels.

educational settings

The general classroom is the prime location for service delivery. However, many experts in the field recommend the provision of a cascade, or **continuum of services**—an ordered

continuum of services

Figure 1-2

Continuum of educational services

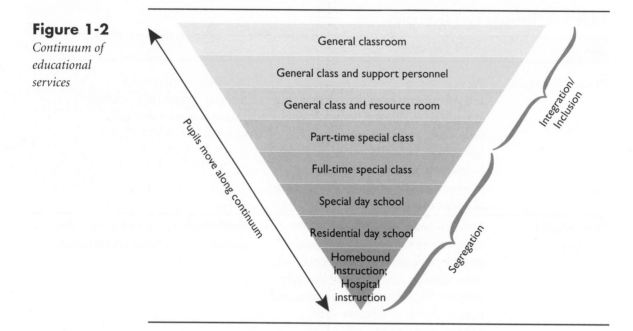

sequence of placements that vary according to their degree of restrictiveness. The continuum is represented in Figure 1-2.

The continuum of educational services has been an important blueprint for special education since 1975. It reflects a number of facets important in serving students who are exceptional.

least restrictive environment

The continuum manifests the concept of the **least restrictive environment** (LRE)—the most appropriate placement in which a student can receive instruction and services. Settings on the continuum involve a series of options that move from contrived to more natural arrangements. As shown in Figure 1–2, the wider the band of the pyramid, the more children are encompassed. As we move down the inverted pyramid, environments become increasingly restrictive, with the point of the pyramid generally considered the most restrictive because it denotes children in homebound instruction who have little opportunity for social interaction with their peers. We discuss the various settings below, moving from the point of the pyramid up to the top.

The continuum also reflects the intensity of a child's needs and the type and severity of his or her disability. With a full continuum of services, educators base placement decisions on potential student outcomes, determining in which setting the child will succeed and be prepared to become a productive and active citizen. Whether this means receiving educational services in the general classroom; moving out of the classroom for remedial help for short periods of time; or working in a resource room, self-contained class, or even a separate setting must be determined on a child-by-child basis.

At the moment, children and youth with mild disabilities are more likely to be in general classrooms, and those with more significant disabilities, in special classes, schools, or facilities. Students who are deaf-blind, who have multiple disabilities, or who have serious emotional disorders comprise the largest proportions in separate schools (McLeskey, Henry, & Hodges, 1999).

The percentage of time students spend in a setting defines what the primary placement is. Data from the United States in reports to Congress provide clarity. General education placement is defined as a setting where students receive special education and related services outside the general classroom for less than 21 percent of the school day. The resource room is a setting for children who are outside of the general classroom 21 to 60 percent of the time. A separate class is a place where students spend more than 60 percent of the school day. Finally, in a separate school placement, students receive education and services in separate schools, residential facilities, or homebound/hospital environments for more than 50 percent of the school day.

The less common the child's condition, the more adults are usually needed to help with his or her care. Students with pervasive developmental disorders, for example, form only a minuscule part of the population with special needs but generally require intensive support from a range of people—teachers, therapists, medical personnel, and paraeducators.

The resources needed or available are an integral, if tacit, component of the LRE and the continuum. If the student lacks appropriate supports, the general classroom may not be able to provide the best education. Take, for example, a child with a profound hearing loss who uses American Sign Language as the primary mode of communication. Without amplification and access to an interpreter, the child would likely flounder in a general setting.

Settings for Service Delivery

Home/Hospital Instruction

Homebound and hospital instruction are provided by local school boards for children who are confined because of illness, physical injury, or other problems (excluding suspension or expulsion). Intervention is initiated if students' absences begin to seriously affect their progress in school.

Residential Schools

Special education in Canada began with residential institutions designed to serve the special needs of students who were blind, deaf, and intellectually disabled. Provincially funded residential schools for children who have significant physical, learning, or emotional disorders still function across Canada. In these settings, children live with other youngsters who have the same exceptional conditions and are instructed by specialist teachers. One of the problems with residential schools is that they separate the child from the home. However, the concept of full-time residential placement has changed substantially in recent years and many of these schools could more correctly be termed residential/day schools as more students are encouraged to commute.

Special Schools

During the late 1940s, the special school, designed and equipped to meet the needs of discrete populations of students who were exceptional, was considered to be a logical extension of the special class. Day schools allowed a core of specially trained teachers and professionals to guide a child's education while he or she continued to live at home. A few special day schools still provide special education services, usually to specific groups of children with exceptionalities and often at the preschool level, particularly for young children who are deaf. Examples of schools for school-aged students are the Horizon School in Olds, Alberta, which specializes in assisting children with severe physical disabilities, and the Christine Meikle School for children with mental disabilities in Calgary.

Special Classes

Traditionally, the full-time special class functioned as the most popular vehicle for serving students with exceptional conditions. During the late 1960s, the notion of special classes was critically examined, and the resulting debates and evidence added impetus to the movement toward inclusion. Nevertheless, special classes remain a setting for a small number of students who are exceptional. In special classrooms, which are staffed by specially trained teachers and located within a regular school, children with similar disabilities are brought together for instruction and social interplay. Partial integration is a major aim.

Resource Rooms

Before the advent of resource rooms in the mid-1970s, children with mild learning difficulties either floundered in general classrooms, were placed in special classes, or were sent to special schools. Today, resource rooms stand at the point between self-contained and general classrooms. Pupils receive part of their education in the general classroom and part of it in the resource room. This allows some learning to take place in an environment that is less distracting, intense, and competitive than the general milieu. The classroom teacher still carries primary responsibility for program design, but works in close coordination with resource room personnel, who design, alter, and present instruction across a number of curriculum areas and address elements that facilitate students' success in the general environment. They may provide support in academic learning of both the core and remedial curricula, and training in social and communication skills that help a student to interact better in the general classroom.

General Classroom

It is the general classroom that provides the student who is exceptional with the least restrictive environment and the opportunity for maximum social integration with normally developing peers. The classroom teacher holds primary responsibility for the child and ensures that appropriate programs and curriculum adaptations or modifications are made. The teacher also works with a number of professionals to tailor education to the needs of the individual child. An outline of the entire process is shown graphically in Figure 1-3.

Providing Supports

Inclusion won't work very well unless supports are in place for both teacher and student. Supports vary according to the needs of the child, the type of program espoused by the school, and the resources available. In very general terms, supports can be examined in two groupings—personnel and administrative arrangements.

Personnel A principal has prime responsibility for a school; his or her leadership is seen as the key factor to success (Hipp & Huffman, 2000). The principal's vision (or lack of vision) of what the school could and should be is likely the single most salient factor affecting the school norms that teachers then internalize and follow. As the instructional leader, the principal fosters the learning climate and **school culture**—the beliefs, habits, and assumed ways of doing things among a school community. Supportive principals have

school culture

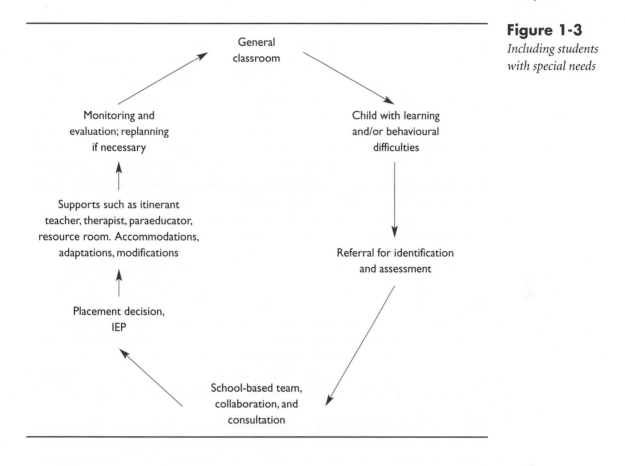

Figure 1-3
*Including students
with special needs*

General
classroom

Monitoring and
evaluation; replanning
if necessary

Child with learning
and/or behavioural
difficulties

Supports such as itinerant
teacher, therapist, paraeducator,
resource room. Accommodations,
adaptations, modifications

Referral for identification
and assessment

Placement decision,
IEP

School-based team,
collaboration, and
consultation

been found to significantly increase teacher commitment, satisfaction, job retention, and feelings of professional trust and autonomy.

Principals are expected to design, lead, manage, and implement programs for all students, including those who are exceptional (Praisner, 2003). The administrator must facilitate the interface of general and special education in such a way that special education philosophies and instructional methods are accommodated as part of an integrated system in a general education environment (Lipp, 1992). For inclusion to be successful, the principal must display positive attitudes and commitment. Continuous encouragement from the principal has been mentioned in many studies as being instrumental in creating positive attitudes to inclusion (e.g., Janney, Snell, & Beers, 1995).

Itinerant teachers are specially trained educators who give individual assistance to a child for specific periods during the normal school schedule. The clientele are often children such as students with severe visual impairments or those who are deaf. The type and intensity of itinerant intervention depend on the needs of the child. Some children may simply need tutoring to keep up in regular school subjects; others may require a specific program in one area, such as speech and auditory training. Itinerant teachers may work with classroom teachers on program preparation and offer in-service training. They may also help prepare the special child's classmates by explaining his or her disabling condition. In some instances, the itinerant teacher serves as an advocate, ensuring that the special child receives the best education possible in the most appropriate environment.

itinerant teachers

educational
consultants

Educational consultants, sometimes referred to as support facilitators or inclusion specialists, usually do not have instructional responsibilities but serve to assist classroom teachers throughout a school district to keep children who are exceptional in their general school programs. As an indirect service provider, the consultant may function as a diagnostician, a materials specialist, an administrator of various services, and an advocate.

paraeducators

Paraeducators (variously referred to as teacher's aides, teaching assistants, classroom assistants, child-care workers, or paraprofessionals) are the fastest-growing personnel segment in special education. The Canadian Education Association (1975) reported that there were approximately 12 000 paraeducators in 1967. This number increased to nearly 6000 by 1974. In 1998, there were a reported 58 000 paraeducators in Canadian schools (Human Resources and Skills Development Canada, 2000).

Paraeducators form an integral part of the instructional team that shares responsibility for facilitating learning and overseeing behaviour. For example, working under the direction of the teacher, a paraeducator may be involved in developing and/or selecting daily elements of the curriculum as defined in an individualized educational plan, delivering individual or small-group instruction, providing remedial experiences, monitoring a child's progress, making individual educational assessments, and recording behaviour.

The speech/language, physical, and occupational therapists that we mentioned earlier are critical in providing special services. Often, the therapeutic services will be brought to the child in the classroom rather than remove the child in order to access services.

School counsellors are a critical part of children's scholastic experience, assisting them with a variety of academic and personal and social developmental tasks (See Chapter 16).

Administrative Arrangements Ideally, when children with exceptionalities are in general classrooms, teachers receive support in the form of training, help, consultation, and collaboration with special education teachers and other personnel, paraeducators, therapists, and so on. There are subtle differences between consultation and collaboration.

consultation

collaboration

Consultation occurs when two equals work together to discuss or solve a problem. **Collaboration** involves an interdependent relationship among two or more people to achieve a common goal (Salisbury, Evans, & Palombaro, 1997). An extensive anecdotal literature supports the advantages of collaborative relationship-building; many scholars view the process where teachers work together to achieve common goals to be a central element of major school reform efforts (see Niles & Mercellino, 2004). Collaboration allows educators and others with diverse expertise to construct effective alternatives to traditional educational approaches. Teachers can discuss skills such as assessing learning styles and abilities, adapting or modifying curriculum, and using various teaching strategies to meet student needs.

Teams are the concrete manifestation of the collaborative process. The names for school-based teams vary considerably. They may be referred to as teacher assistance teams, staff support teams, student assistance teams, intervention assistance teams, child study teams, peer intervention teams, building-level assistance teams, school-based problem-solving teams, school consultation committees, instructional support teams, or inclusion teams.

Teaming is not easy for professionals trained to conduct their teaching responsibilities autonomously within the walls of their own classrooms. In fact, many teachers feel that the hardest part of inclusion is making plans with another person (Roach, 1995). Yet working in isolation rarely produces the kind of innovative instructional methods needed to keep students with special needs in general classrooms.

Teaming requires regular face-to-face interaction, performance monitoring, a structure for addressing issues, and clear individual accountability once responsibilities are agreed upon. Team collaboration not only provides a forum for educators to share ideas and concerns; research suggests that teams increase the appropriateness of special education referrals, reduce referrals for special education, and produce positive changes in student academic and behavioural performance (e.g., Ingalls & Hammond, 1996; Safran & Safran, 1996; see also Chapter 15).

The organization of a team is largely determined by the child's needs and school policy. To assist a child who is deaf, for example, a teacher may work on a school-based team with the school principal, itinerant teachers, a psychologist, a speech therapist, a language therapist, and such allied child-care personnel as audiologists and school nurses. The parents of the child should be part of the team; older students should have input into their own individual plans.

Teams undertake a number of decisions (supplemented by extensive official documentation in relation to assessment, placement, and funding). At the simplest level, the team first considers a student's difficulties in school and determines whether he or she is eligible for special education. Next, the team carefully considers placement. Finally (and often following further assessment), the team discusses and documents the accommodations, adaptations, and modifications that a student requires in order to succeed. The process is formalized in the preparation of an Individual Education Plan (IEP).

Individual Education Plans

The signature feature of special education is its focus on the individual student as the unit for planning. That is, the essence of special education is individualization: goals and methods are formulated in response to individual needs and documented in an individual plan. See Figure 1-4 on the next page for a representation of this process.

Some people think that individualizing programs for pupils who are exceptional means that the teacher must work with that child on a one-to-one basis at all times. This is patently untrue. By individualizing the program, we attempt to fit the curriculum and the program to the child, rather than vice versa. The individualization is in the planning, not necessarily the instruction. Hence, individualization is not a teaching method but a plan for instructional organization that may incorporate many methods. The defining characteristic of *individual instruction* is that each student works within learning plans designed to match his or her needs, interests, abilities, and pace of learning.

The process of adapting or modifying the regular curriculum and classroom environment often begins with an Individual Education Plan (IEP). In the United States, Individual Education Plans are mandated under federal special education legislation. Canadian jurisdictions are less prescriptive but still carefully document how students with exceptionalities are to be instructed.

Each student's IEP is a broad statement that assists teachers by pre-specifying the goals and objectives of instruction and ensuring that the educational program is appropriate to the child's specific needs. The plan of action outlines long-term goals and short-term objectives or benchmarks, touches on the methods and techniques that will be used to achieve

Figure 1-4

Representation of the IEP process

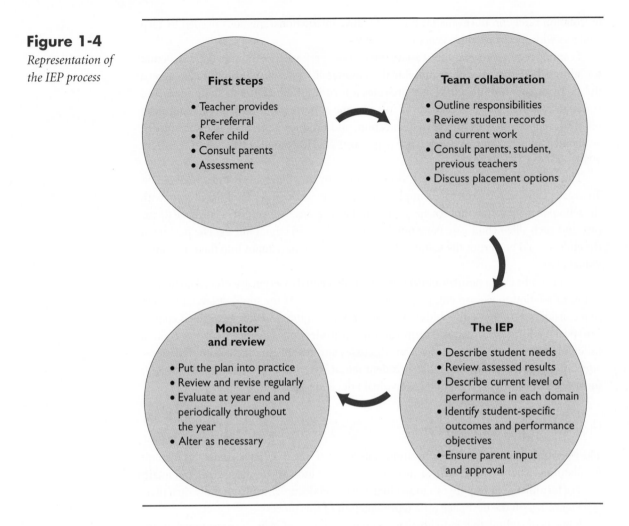

them, and details the responsibilities of various people who will help the child along the way, such as the classroom teacher, the resource room teacher, or the speech therapist.

The IEP is a personalized program that is prepared annually, usually at an early point in the year. Because it is put together before programming begins, the first Individual Education Plan for a child with a disability is largely guesswork. The goals and objectives are hypotheses about what a child can and cannot do and about his or her critical needs. Moreover, the process of programming for needs is a dynamic one. An IEP is not a static document or a performance contract. Nor is it written in stone. It is rather a communication document that is constantly modified to match a child's progress and needs. A child who is visually impaired, for example, may be so for life, but his or her needs will change, not merely each year but perhaps each week or even each day.

The major problem confronting teachers is determining and prioritizing the skills that are important to teach. Skill determination is easier for children with mild disabilities, who generally follow the curriculum designed for typical peers. The IEPs for these students show the degree of involvement in the general program as well as adaptations. These students may need only minor changes that can be documented on one page. On the other hand, the most complex IEPs are for children with communication disorders, because language comprises so many interdependent functions.

Writing an IEP requires not only knowledge of the plan's format. Teachers must also be knowledgeable about the following areas: curriculum for a number of grade levels, normal child development and how it relates to the curriculum, task analysis, diverse strategies for effective learning, incorporating the skills of support personnel, and employing the skills of paraeducators effectively.

Format of Individual Education Plans

Throughout Canada, the document used to individualize student learning goes by a number of different names: Individual Program Plan (IPP) in Alberta, Individual Support Services Plan in Newfoundland and Labrador, and Individual Education Plan in Ontario and the Northwest Territories. As well, the actual formats of the plans differ markedly. Most, however, contain standard components.

1. Child data such as name, date of birth, chronological age, school, grade, and teacher.

2. Many plans contain information about the preparation of the IEP, including the names and positions of those who attended the team meeting when the document was drawn up and whether it is an initial IEP, a second IEP, or an evaluation document.

3. A statement of the educational setting considered the most appropriate placement for the student with special needs.

4. Many plans include the results of psycho-educational assessment that is designed to discover a child's strengths and weaknesses in different domains, such as cognitive development, language, physical and motor development, socio-emotional development, adaptive behaviour, and academic performance and progress. In the broadest sense, a child's strengths are any aspect of his or her personality or abilities that are perceived positively by others. Weaknesses are areas that require intervention.

5. With a record of a child's performance based on information derived from assessment, those preparing the IEP can pinpoint a student's present levels of performance (functioning) across a range of domains and academic areas. For example, an assessment of reading ability may show that Kim, although in grade 3, is reading at a beginning grade 1 level.

   The present levels of functioning should provide a list of a child's strengths and weaknesses. These are divided into skills that need remediation, skills that are delayed, and skills that are within the normal ranges. From this list of levels of functioning, the team can then determine the skills the child needs to acquire. Present levels of functioning also apply to deviant and antisocial behaviour. For a child with a behavioural disorder, present levels would include a description of the intensity, duration, and frequency of a behaviour.

6. Long-term or annual goals. A **goal** may be defined as a stated outcome desired as the result of some action. On an IEP, goals are broad general statements used to estimate what outcomes can be expected in an academic year, based on the student's present level of functioning. Goals focus on the general areas for which individualized programming is to be provided. They indicate the *priorities for intervention*—the major learning experiences the child will have and the broad range of skills that he or she can

goal

be expected to attain. Long-range goals are usually made for one year, except in the case of children with significant disabilities, who may have long-range goals that cover a longer period, up to five years.

The priorities for intervention (long-term goals) are drawn from the list of skills that need remediation, as shown in the determination of present levels of functioning. (A good rule of thumb here is to move back about 6 months from the present level of functioning. If Jimmy, for example, is reading at a mid–grade 2 level, instruction should start at the beginning grade 2 level to ensure greater initial success).

Typically, 5 to 10 goals are identified in the domains where the child is showing the greatest lag. When written down, goals should represent specific expectations or skills (as opposed to vague generic statements). For example, "Will learn to read" is not specific enough, whereas "Will read books at grade 1 level" is.

7. Short-term objectives or benchmarks are derived from long-term goals; they describe meaningful intermediate and measurable outcomes between the student's current performance and the annual goal. **Objectives** are clear statements of exactly what a teacher wants a child to be able to do as a result of instruction. They refer to increments in the progress of learning from the child's present level of functioning to the annual goals—that is, the amount of progress a child is expected to make within a specified period. Objectives then are essentially the steps toward achieving the goals, and they help to direct instruction and learning on a day-to-day basis. Objectives are used when goals can be divided into discrete skill components. **Benchmarks** describe the amount of progress the child is expected to make within a specified period.

objectives

benchmarks

There is no set rule, but generally three or four objectives are provided for each long-range goal. The way to turn long-range goals into short-term objectives or benchmarks is through **task analysis**—analyzing the behavioural components and prerequisite skills of a task. When a teacher task-analyzes an objective, the elements of the task a child must master are clearly identified. For example, reading skills are broken down into the smallest possible steps; skills are taught one at a time.

task analysis

Good behavioural objectives are written as brief action statements using verbs that lend themselves to observation and measurement. Appropriate verbs include *apply*, *describe*, *recognize*, *repeat*, *copy*, *reproduce*, *choose*, *draw*, *classify*, *match*, *identify*, and *select*. They often contain a condition—"When presented with 20 CVC words on flashcards . . ."—and a criterion—"80 percent of the time."

8. Once goals and objectives have been identified, the next step is to select and sequence the most appropriate learning experiences to achieve those aims and objectives. However, in a sense an IEP represents a philosophy of what should be taught rather than illustrations of how teaching should happen. Examples of how to accomplish an objective may appear, but every approach, activity, or group interaction will not.

9. Specific educational and support services to attain each goal are listed, including the personnel who will hold primary responsibility for specific goals and objectives. In addition to indicating the responsibilities of various people, the IEP shows the kinds of services required (such as speech therapy), the type of instruction (individual or group), and the time to be spent on each activity (for example, half an hour a day).

10. The anticipated duration of the services.

11. Specific evaluation procedures—the criteria for determining whether the objectives have been attained.

12. Procedures for re-evaluating the total IEP document.

13. Parent input and consent. Parents should be involved in the IEP process, particularly placement decisions. Parents give informed consent, which means they have a clear understanding of the activity for which they are granting consent. The IEP is signed by all participants.

14. Older students should be invited to participate in the meeting and set their own goals.

Instructional Practices

It would be nice if there were a single correct approach to educating students with exceptionalities, a sort of encompassing "theory of instruction." But although we know a great deal more about how to deal with exceptional learners than we did even 20 years ago, no universal conviction exists about how to teach these children. There is no such thing as a panacea. Research does not tell us what works and what does not, or supply foolproof prescriptions for effective instruction. At the same time, there is scant research on how teachers develop the competencies that enable them to teach diverse students effectively in the classroom.

Of course, there are some very critical things that we do know. These include the following:

- Effective practices do not consist of a number of particular strategies added onto overall mediocre teaching competence. Teachers must set out with effective teaching skills. Good teachers in inclusive settings tend to be flexible, able to adopt and adapt new curricula, and able to change strategies readily.

- For students with mild disabilities, the changes in teaching methods are often not that obvious or different. In general, specialized competencies and teaching methods are extensions and refinements of core competencies rather than new sets of teaching behaviour and skills (Ysseldyke & Algozzine, 1990).

- Multiple strategies are necessary to accommodate the differences in learning that exist between students with disabilities and their typical peers, as well as to help everyone achieve classroom membership and social belonging among peers.

- Teachers use a variety of strategies and approaches. These include individualized programming, Direct Instruction, small-group instruction, intermittent tutoring, precision teaching, cognitive strategy training, focused questions, monitoring of children's on-task behaviour, and activities matched to the particular needs of their students. They also employ differentiated instruction and **multilevel instruction**, in which a main lesson is prepared and taught with variations included for individual student needs. Three broad general approaches of great relevance to inclusive classrooms are direct instruction, co-operative learning, and peer tutoring (see Chapter 5).   **multilevel instruction**

- No matter how compelling the argument given, none of the above strategies are appropriate to all students and all teachers at all times. For example, research on the various peer tutoring and co-operative learning strategies mentioned above suggest that they may be extremely helpful for some students but virtually useless for others (Hallahan & Kauffman, 2003; Winzer & Mazurek, 1998).

co-teaching

- **Co-teaching** involves collaboration between general and special education teachers who take responsibility for an entire class of children. It allows educators to share planning, presentation, and classroom management and develop a differentiated curriculum that meets the needs of all children.

- Traditional instructional arrangements and lesson formats include lectures, demonstration, practice, whole-class discussion, games and simulations, and experiential learning, and range from large-group instruction to co-operative learning groups and peer partners to individual and independent seat work. Many of the traditional techniques that work with typical students may be unsuccessful with those who are exceptional. However, conversely, many of the instructional strategies that work with students with special needs work with all students. Therefore, when teachers find innovative ways to enhance the learning environment to accommodate the learning differences and behavioural difficulties of pupils who are exceptional, they are enhancing the teaching/learning process for everyone in the classroom.

One element that teachers will use in their planning consists of procedures and techniques that, for purposes of clarity, we arbitrarily refer to as accommodations, adaptations, and modifications in the physical, instructional, and psychosocial environments. The distinctions among these terms are subtle and there is much overlap. We can say that

accommodation

- An **accommodation** is a change that assists a child's functioning in the environment, a technique that eliminates or minimizes the learning differences by offering alternate ways of handling a task. Examples include an FM system for a child with a hearing impairment; seating close to the teacher for the child with a behavioural disorder; increased lighting, but no glare, for the child with a visual disability; or extra space between desks for the child with a physical disability.

adaptation

- **Adaptations** are procedures, changes, or enhancements that enable a student who is exceptional to undertake tasks that he or she would not otherwise be able to accomplish easily. *Material adaptations* are alterations made in the materials that the student uses to learn or that the teacher uses to teach. *Instructional adaptations* refer to how teachers change instruction within the regular curriculum so that the same outcomes as those for typical children are achieved.

modifications

- **Modifications** step away from the general curriculum and have learning outcomes that are substantially different from those of the prescribed curriculum. Modifications generally apply to children with significant disabilities. In a modified setting, more than 50 percent of the general outcomes of a grade level curriculum have been altered.

The array of adaptations from which a teacher may choose is huge. In each of the categorical chapters of this text, you will find lists of adaptations and modifications in the boxes on Creating Accessible Classrooms. As you read these, you will notice than many of the ideas and approaches are suitable for a broad array of learners with special needs. You should also be aware that selecting skills from a menu of adaptations entails a great deal of advance planning, assessment of student ability and skill, consideration of resources, and curriculum knowledge.

Social Intervention

Social intervention covers a spectrum of services that can be grouped under the general category of child welfare. A primary concern is the care and treatment of the child within the family environment. A wide range of personnel are involved in **social service delivery**—giving assistance to people who need it. Included among personnel are social workers, family counsellors, foster parents, child advocates, child-care workers, probation officers, and others who try to ensure that the child develops under the care of the family or surrogate family.

social service delivery

Advocacy—the act of pleading the cause of another—must be foregrounded. As a means of promoting and defending the interests and welfare of children and youth with diverse needs, advocacy has a long history. Those involved in it today include parent groups, educators, and community agencies.

advocacy

Often vigorous parental advocacy has been needed in order to obtain services. Parent advocacy has been able to ensure appropriate programming in the least restrictive environment; facilitate successful vocational/special education programs through collaborative consultation with the schools; alter the standards of treatment in institutions; promote the development of community-based living facilities; stimulate research in prevention and amelioration of disabling conditions; and bring to the courts the plight of children who are exceptional.

SUMMARY

1. Children who are exceptional are those who deviate in some way from what society calls normal. However, the norm itself encompasses a wide range of behaviours from which everyone deviates to some degree so that there is really no such thing as a homogeneous classroom.

2. Over the years, the way professionals and society in general have described persons with exceptionalities has changed in a positive way. In the past, the terms used to describe people who were exceptional were value-laden and tended to emphasize the person's disorder or disability. Today's terms are non-stigmatizing and as clear and unambiguous as possible.

3. Dilemmas and paradoxical effects exist in labelling. Many professionals see the traditional system of labelling children by their primary disability as more stigmatizing than useful. Others counter that categories and labels are essential to human communication; they are inescapable; and they open the door to special programs, technology, and funding. Not surprisingly, the research on labelling remains unclear and inconsistent.

4. In general, incidence addresses the question of how often a disorder occurs; prevalence looks at how many individuals are affected. Difficulties in obtaining accurate rates are related to the varying definitions and descriptions of disabilities, the methods of data collection, the interpretation of data, and social factors related to stigmatization and public perceptions.

5. Many children with special needs require various types of therapy. A child with poor articulation may require help from a speech therapist; a child who has lost a limb will need physical therapy; an adolescent with cerebral palsy may benefit from occupational therapy.

HISTORICAL NOTES

Society's attitude toward persons with disabilities has always been complex, fashioned at any given time by the prevailing culture, religion, government, and economic conditions. Because the care, training, and education of individuals with exceptionalities has tended to mirror societal attitudes, the history of disability and the history of special education can be seen as following historical trends, rather than creating them.

The history of disability extends far back in time. Persons with disabilities were mentioned by the ancient Egyptians, Greeks, and Romans, as well as in the Bible. The greatest attention was directed toward those considered mad or insane, a population that traditionally included persons with intellectual disabilities and those with epilepsy. Hippocrates and the Roman physicians Galen and Celsus intervened in cases of deafness, blindness, and overt physical disabilities.

Although the historical record is murky, it seems that from humanity's earliest beginnings and throughout the ages persons with disabilities were grossly mistreated. Their conditions were considered hopeless, and in most cultures they were scorned as degraded and inferior beings. A more humane climate emerged in the mid-1700s with the development of treatment and the beginnings of special education. In France, a new social philosophy, ushered in by Enlightenment thought, brought about major educational advances made manifest by pioneer French educators such as Michel de l'Épée, Jacob Periere, Valentin Huay, and Edouard Seguin. With their advances in establishing permanent schools and delineating specific methodologies, particularly for students who were deaf, blind, or mentally disabled, these French educators emerged as the founders of special education as we know it today (Winzer, 1993).

In North America, special education began in 1817 with the founding of an institution for deaf students at Hartford, Connecticut. The first Canadian special school, again for persons who were deaf, opened near Montreal in 1831, but lack of funds forced it to close within five years. It was not until 1848 that permanent residential schools were established in British North America, the first ones being in Halifax and Montreal.

For reasons of economy and convenience, students who were exceptional were chiefly educated in institutional settings. However, very few children were actually served. Differentiation among exceptional conditions was murky, and energies were directed to those with obvious and overt disabilities. Schooling was open to children with sensory impairments (those who were deaf and blind); those with intellectual problems (known then as idiotic and feeble-minded); and those considered to be socially at risk (vagrant, neglected, and delinquent children). A concern for children with mild disabilities and the emergence of categories such as emotional disturbed, behavioural disorders, physical and health disabilities, and learning disabilities was largely a phenomenon of the first half of the 20th century.

Segregated classes began in serious in the public schools in 1910 and expanded rapidly in the following decades. Placement in institutions, special classes, and special schools remained the common mode of education for students with disabilities right into the 1960s.

But for many years controversy in the field had been simmering, revolving around the tension between training students with disabilities to fit into so-called normal society and training them in regard to their unique needs. The most salient manifestation of this tension was (and continues to be) the often acrimonious debate about students' school address—that is, their educational placement.

The 1960s was the benchmark era. It brought the philosophy of normalization (see Chapter 2), mounting and vexatious questioning of the value of special education, a series of efficacy studies that provided pessimistic evidence of just what special education was achieving, and shocking exposés of the conditions in institutions for persons with intellectual disabilities. Throughout the 1970s, intensive scrutiny of the knowledge and practices of special education continued, and simultaneously, discontent with special classes peaked. Many questioned the need for a dual system of education, particularly the high proportion of educational funding directed toward special education, the fragmentary nature of so much service delivery, the potential stigmatization of children identified, and the inherently discriminatory and unequal nature of segregated classes.

Agitation by parent and professional groups led to new legislation and many of the changes that are apparent in special education today. With enabling legislation passed in the United States in 1975 (Public Law 94-142), the way opened for large numbers of students with exceptional conditions to move into local schools and general classrooms.

The ripples of the 1970s turned into a strong tide in the 1980s; there were dramatic increases in the number of students mainstreamed into general classrooms. Today we see continuing efforts by boards of education and other agencies to increase the universality of special education services. The dominant philosophy is *inclusive schooling*. This term emerged in the professional literature in 1984 and has become the major discourse in special education. Inclusion in its various facets is addressed in every chapter of this text.

6. Children requiring special education may be taught in a range or continuum of settings from the general classroom to a residential school or hospital program.

7. To fully accomplish the aim of individualizing instruction for children with exceptionalities, special education teachers and those involved in educationally integrating these students combine their resources with a varied group of support personnel. Teamwork demands collaboration, a style of interacting in which persons with diverse expertise voluntarily agree to work together to generate creative solutions to mutually defined problems.

8. Educational teams tend to be multidisciplinary in nature, with their major duties consisting of planning, implementation, and evaluation of educational programs for special students. The team prepares an Individual Education Plan (IEP), a written planning document that outlines educational services and learning objectives to meet the specific needs of a child. It aims to coordinate plans and services, personalize and individualize a child's program, and integrate the individual plan with the overall plans for the classroom group.

9. There is no question that teaching students with special needs involves a wider range of organizational and instructional materials and alternatives than general teaching. Children may need special attention because of limited ability, poor motivation, sensory or physical impairments, or specific learning disabilities. To effectively instruct students with special needs, teachers must meet individual learning needs through appropriate changes in the environment, instruction, and content.

CHAPTER 2

ISSUES AND TRENDS IN CANADIAN SPECIAL EDUCATION

INTRODUCTION

Social attitudes toward the education, care, and training of individuals who are exceptional usually reflect more general cultural attitudes toward the obligations of a society to its individual citizens. It is only recently that the creation of societies where persons who are exceptional can live productive and fulfilling lives has become an imperative, not just a dream. In today's climate of heightened social identity, justice and equity are perceived in fundamentally different ways than in the past. As a newly evolving social philosophy has emphasized the value of the individual and the rights of every citizen, the prospects for people who are exceptional have altered positively in the social, occupational, and educational arenas.

In the past 40 years, education has seen a dramatic swing in ideas regarding educational placement as educators, officials, legislators, and parents attempt to reform, revamp, and generally improve services for students with special needs. Such reform efforts are not new—they have characterized special education from its beginnings. As the Historical Notes at the end of Chapter 1 show, the history of special education reveals a plethora of changes and reforms, all reflective of a gradual humanizing of attitudes toward persons with exceptionalities.

A field as historically complex and as diverse as special education is bound to reveal controversial issues and unsolved dilemmas and to reflect major social trends and movements. Over the years, both generic and category-specific controversies and dilemmas have emerged. The aim of this chapter is to familiarize readers with broad general issues that are currently under debate within special education and to present some of the relevant arguments. Dilemmas related to specific groups of students such as bilingual education for those who are deaf or acceleration practices in gifted education are reserved for the categorical chapters.

We give the greatest attention to issues that directly affect the teacher in the classroom. Of these, inclusion still tops the list. It is important to understand the varied parameters of the movement, which include the development, the terminology, the debates, and the ways in which inclusion can be best implemented. Other current topics include legislation and litigation, early identification and intervention, transition services for adolescents, assessment practices and procedures, and students with cultural and linguistic differences.

To do justice to these issues would take an entire book for each one. We can discuss only some of the major issues quite briefly in this chapter in an attempt to alert readers to the movements and trends and to lay the groundwork for later chapters in this text. Throughout the discussion, it should be kept in mind that reforms in education are continuous and that this text is a document written in a particular place at a particular time. It represents only a snapshot of special education and cannot faithfully reproduce the dynamic shifts that are occurring in the field. In addition, changes in special education are not always neat and may require many detours. Policy implementation is not so much an event but a process that is slow, multifaceted, and incremental, one that is ongoing and influenced by many external forces that include legislation, politics, medicine, ethics, and economics, to mention only a few.

CHANGING VIEWS OF EXCEPTIONALITY

As the Historical Notes on pages 66 and 67 of this chapter point out, North American society has not traditionally shown a high tolerance for persons who are exceptional. A gradual humanizing expression throughout the last century has manifested today in significant increases in public awareness and understanding of individuals who are exceptional.

Supporters of normalization argue that all people who are exceptional deserve an educational and living environment that is as close to normal as possible

The decade of the 1960s was a potent crucible for changes in public perceptions and portrayals of persons with disabilities. Some quite diverse trends and events melded together. To mention only a few, there was the civil rights movement in general society; agitation for the rights of oppressed groups; and U.S. President Lyndon Johnson's War on Poverty and its offshoot, ameliorative programs for young children, such as Head Start. In special education, there was the President's Panel on Mental Retardation in 1963, exposés of conditions in institutions for those intellectually disabled, and the birth of the field of learning disabilities.

normalization

A critical and specific movement arrived from the Scandinavian countries under the mantle of normalization. Essentially, **normalization** refers to the philosophical belief that all individuals who are exceptional, no matter what their level and type of disability, should be provided with an education and living environment as close to normal as possible. Normalization and its corollary, *deinstitutionalization*, are discussed in the accompanying Research Notes feature.

RESEARCH NOTES

Normalization and Changes in Perceptions

The civil rights movement of the 1960s saw new conceptions of traditionally oppressed groups. One theme held that persons with disabilities had a civil right to live, attend school, and work in the same environment as others. In Scandinavia, Bank-Mikkleson operationalized the concept and incorporated the principle of what was called *normalization* into Danish law in 1959. Benge Nirje, then Secretary General of the Swedish Association for Retarded Children, began to apply the ideas in about 1967.

Normalization, as defined by Nirje, was "making available to all mentally retarded people patterns of life and conditions of everyday living which are as close as possible to the regular circumstances of society" (1979, p. 173). The principles of normalization were rapidly translated to North America and Canada and soon expanded beyond a single category to include all persons with disabilities.

The major aim of normalization is for society to regard persons with disabilities as individuals and to treat them fairly and humanely. This translates into a normal family and community life for all.

People who are exceptional can fill a variety of roles in general society and are offered the chance of a normal life routine, normal developmental experiences, independent choices, and the right to live, work, and play in normal surroundings. Ultimately, normalization will have occurred when individuals who are exceptional live with members of the cultural group in a normal domicile within the community and have access to all the privileges and services that are available to others, including education in neighbourhood schools and general education classes.

An obvious sidebar to normalization is the process of deinstitutionalization. An *institution* is defined as a publicly supported, professionally managed facility housing 15 or more people with similar disabilities. In the physical sense, *deinstitutionalization* means the movement of individuals from large institutions into community-based living arrangements such as group homes and halfway houses. In the broader social context, deinstitutionalization addresses a return to the community, maintenance in the community, the respect of other citizens, and acceptance by peers and others in the culture.

Canada readily accepted the principles of normalization. In fact, Munby, Hutchinson, and Chin (1999) point out that "Canada was the first country to guarantee constitutionally the rights of persons with a disability to legal equality" (p. 45). Nevertheless, changes are slow and stilted. In the general social arena, Canada usually gets an excellent report card from the United Nations Development Index, which measures income, education, and life expectancy. But full legal and political rights for all Canadians with disabilities were not attained until the 1990s. Valentine and Vickers (1996) note that it was only in 1991 that Canadians with a psychiatric or mental disability were able to vote, and full access to voting stations for persons with mobility and sensory limitations were only guaranteed in 1992.

Within Canada, legislation such as the Canadian Human Rights Act and the Charter of Rights and Freedoms prohibit discrimination in the workplace because of disability. Programs such as the Canada Assistance Plan and the Vocational Rehabilitation of Disabled Persons Act are joint federal and provincial initiatives that provide vocational learning and upgrading. Despite these grand schemes, people with disabilities are disproportionately poor across the board.

On the theme of employment opportunities, in its 1998 Annual Report, the Canadian Human Rights Commission chided that "Canadians with disabilities continue to be denied equal opportunities to jobs and services and full participation in our society" ("Access denied . . ." 1999, p. 12). According to the Report, the situation of people with disabilities in the workforce remains poor. (See also Chapter 17).

REFORMS IN EDUCATION

The school reform movement began with its focus entirely on general education practices and outcomes. Therefore, changes and reforms in contemporary special education cannot be fully appreciated without a digression into reforms within the entire educational arena.

The outcomes of general education were brought into focus in 1983 with the U.S. publication of *A Nation at Risk*. It caused a groundswell of societal indignation at the lack of educational accountability. Parents, legislators, the general public, and educators themselves pointed to the gaps and deficiencies in the current educational system. Some critics went so far as to assert that education was teetering on the brink of chaos and failure and that educational reform had to be a major objective in North American education. Reform became a key concern and a top political priority.

Canada elevated school reform to a major movement for all levels and all populations, and a myriad of initiatives were proposed to change the structure and culture of schools. Two main threads could be discerned woven into the fabric of the multiple reform proposals. One thread stressed improving educational outcomes such as greater accountability from schools and teachers; advanced academic achievement from students, especially in mathematics and science; improvement in literacy skills; and a halting or lessening of dropout rates. The other focused on equity. It called for the incorporation of multi-ethnic and multicultural perspectives into classrooms and schools; ways to promote bilingualism and teach students with limited English proficiency; and the promotion of educational equality and opportunity for all students.

One of the overarching objectives of the focus on equity was the creation of socially just and democratic communities that began by transforming schools into places where all students belong and learn together. The term that emerged to describe educational systems where equity was in place for all students was *inclusion*, or *inclusive schooling*. In this general sense, inclusion is concerned with a wide swath of students—those of multi-racial, ethnic, and linguistic backgrounds, gay and lesbian students, francophone students in a minority context, students at risk, and students with disabilities.

REFORMS IN SPECIAL EDUCATION

The reform movement did not pass special education by. On the contrary. In the late1980s, special education became deeply embroiled in reform efforts and was subjected to enormous pressures for change. Rhetoric called for special education to "break the mould," for "revolution," a "paradigm shift," a "fundamental reconceptualization," and "radical restructuring" (Kauffman, 1993, p. 10).

Reform in special education, though loudly articulated in the 1980s, actually began earlier. As we pointed out, it was during the 1960s that the influence of the civil rights movement melded with pressure for normalization, and a disenchantment with special education as it was then practised led to the formulation of new policies.

From the late1960s on, students with exceptionalities were increasingly drawn into the orbit of the public schools. The responsibility to provide equal access to an education in a manner most appropriate to these students' needs gradually became embedded in legislation and supported by ethical and philosophical precepts. Placement and instructional procedures that used terms such as *integration*, the *least restrictive environment* (LRE), and *mainstreaming* emerged and were practised.

Today, efforts to restructure schools, bring about basic changes in the fundamental operating mode of special education, improve educational practice, and operationalize a closer merger between general and special education are encompassed under a concept and practice variously termed *inclusion*, *inclusive schooling*, *inclusive education*, and, occasionally, *progressive* inclusion.

Development of the Inclusionary Movement

Over the past four decades, the gradual process of more and more children with exceptionalities receiving their special education while enrolled in general education classes and schools has been described in a number of ways. In the 1950s and 1960s, *integration* was the common term. It remains popular today.

Mainstreaming, often used as a synonym for integration, emerged in the 1970s. The basic goal of mainstreaming was the provision of free, appropriate education in the most suitable setting for all youngsters with exceptionalities. Philosophically, mainstreaming focused on the integration of children with exceptionalities with their typical peers in the context of the neighbourhood school. As a process, mainstreaming provided services along a continuum—the range of educational options and support services described in Chapter 1. The continuum allowed pupils to be integrated in the least restrictive environment in the manner best suited to their individual needs, supported by individual programming in the form of an Individual Education Plan (IEP).

The next giant step was inclusion, or inclusive schooling, which connotes subtle but real differences from integration or mainstreaming. Advocates of inclusive schooling argue that the social-cultural realities of mainstreaming and integration are that one group is viewed as the "mainstream" and one group is not; hence, one group has to "push in" to the activities and settings occupied by the other (Salisbury, 1991). In other words, integration and mainstreaming sought to change individuals to fit the existing system; inclusion seeks to change the system so that exclusion and marginalization are avoided.

Under the principles of inclusion, children do not push into the mainstream, because the underlying supposition in inclusive programs is that all children will be based in the classrooms they would attend if they did not have a disability. Promoters insist that inclusive education is the most enlightened system since it alters classroom and school structures to allow all children to gain an education there.

Defining Inclusive Schooling

A single, universal. or generally accepted version of inclusion simply does not exist. If we held a meeting, say, of teachers from Newfoundland and Labrador, the Northwest Territories, and Manitoba, we would probably find similar philosophies but quite different interpretations of the way to handle implementation. The lack of clarity and agreement about inclusion has not only exacerbated the controversies surrounding reform, but has also created great difficulties in terms of interpreting the research on the topic (Simpson, 2005).

We can say that in the current climate it is probably more apt to talk about inclusions rather than a single inclusion. As well, today there is little debate about the "why" of inclusive schooling, but many about the "how." The field has moved to what may be seen as second generation questions—what works? for whom? in what settings? under what circumstances? with what supports? That is, the issue is no longer whether most students with special needs should or should not be included but what support is needed for inclusion to be successful. People argue about who should be targeted for inclusion, the nature of the general educational provision, and the manner in which supports are provided.

Even if the overarching philosophical issues see consensus, the area is fluid and changing rapidly. Inclusive schooling defies easy interpretation, definitions abound, and implementation sees a variety of models and programs. To reconcile different interpretations, we define inclusion in this text broadly. We see inclusive education

> as a system of equity for students with exceptionalities that expresses a commitment to educate each child to the maximum extent through placement, instruction, and support in the most heterogeneous and appropriate environment.

Each phrase in this conception of inclusive schooling is important:

- *Equity.* Equal opportunity implies equal educational rights for all children and youth. As Smith (1994) notes, "Young people with disabilities have an equal right to be in school and to have something meaningful happen once they are inside" (p. 7).

- *Heterogeneous.* Students of varied abilities and strengths will be in all classrooms. In such heterogeneous settings, the learning/teaching bond is forged in normalized ways instead of in segregated settings, where a disability classification is the common denominator.

- *Placement.* The general classroom is the least restrictive environment. But the movement toward inclusion involves considerably more than the placement of children in general education classes. Each child should be treated individually, and many educators hold that a continuum of services is necessary to accommodate the diverse needs of students with exceptionalities. Location is not the key; the provision of supports and effective services and instruction is. While the ultimate goal is integration in the general classroom with normally developing peers, placement issues should not trump those of the most effective instruction.

- *Supported.* The settings in which students are placed are strengthened and supported by an infusion of specially trained personnel and other appropriate supportive practices according to the individual needs of the child. Resources and supports include access to specialists, collaborative planning and decision-making, appropriate equipment, individual planning, and the availability of paraeducators.

Operationalizing the Inclusive Philosophy

Inclusion is a radically different way of conceptualizing schools and the children they serve. For schools, inclusion is a proxy for school restructuring. For teachers and pupils, inclusion represents a fundamental change in who does what, to whom it is done, where it is done, and how resources support what is done.

Although the concept that school systems should provide for students with a wide range of needs can be supported from a relatively coherent set of basic assumptions, many barriers continue to exist. The overall larger question of whether inclusion is appropriate has been answered. We are now at the level of details—how to find the most effective means to educate all children with disabilities.

The remaining barriers are troubling, but are nevertheless characteristic of the long-standing dilemma in special education about students' school addresses. If we step far back to the 1880s, for example, we see teachers in institutional settings throwing up their hands in horror when reformers such as Alexander Graham Bell and Samuel Gridley Howe promoted the movement of special children from the institutions into regular schools. Then, almost as soon as special segregated classes got under way after 1910, an acrimonious debate on movement into normalized settings began. It accelerated in the 1940s, became very loud in the 1960s, and has continued unabated through mainstreaming, a movement in the 1980s known as the Regular Education Initiative, and into today's inclusive climate.

The school restructuring that is inherent to inclusion will not occur without fundamental changes in the *culture of schools*—the ideas, commitments, and order that determine rules and daily operations. But, as with most reforms in education, inclusion is all about making changes within a system as the system is in motion. In the sense that an old system rarely ceases completely to make way for a new one, some barriers will likely remain. The fundamental impediments to restructuring schools can be classified in many ways. Some of the most salient are outlined below.

- *Teacher attitudes.* Public education depends on teachers' willingness to commit themselves to serving the public good, believing that they can make an important difference in the lives of children, particularly those traditionally marginalized by virtue of social class, gender, cultural or linguistic difference, or disability (Strouse, 1997). Indeed, the great strength of Canadian schools is the motivation and dedication of its professional teachers.

Many educators have one foot on either side of the paradigm shift. Most teachers recognize that they have an ethical responsibility to accommodate the inherent dignity and worth of every student. It is when implementation is broached that a consensus is not reached, and there are often contradictions between espoused policy and actual practice. For example, a national study of 1492 Canadian teachers found that more than two-thirds of teachers believe that inclusion is academically beneficial to children with special needs and their peers in regular classrooms, and 90 percent of teachers cite social benefits (Galt, 1997; "Resistance . . ." 1997). Nevertheless, support is tempered: teachers also articulate the weaknesses in the shifting propositions, identify critical problems in implementation, and show a persistent uneasiness about the practice. In British Columbia, Naylor (2002) found that teachers showed general approval of the philosophy of inclusion, but also had a level of disillusionment and frustration with the lack of support for integrating students with special needs.

- *Restricted knowledge.* General educators often do not have a thorough understanding of the nature and characteristics of students with exceptionalities (see Chang, Early, & Winton, 2005).

- *Lack of skills.* Perhaps the most commonly cited source of teacher resistance is a lack of skills necessary to teach students who are exceptional. A body of research has indicated that preservice teachers leave their teacher preparation programs having received limited training and experience in integrating students with disabilities and do not feel adequately prepared to teach such students in general classrooms (e.g., Cook, 2002; Shippen, Crites, Houchins, Ramsey, & Simon, 2005; Walther-Thomas, Korinek, McLaughlin, & Williams, 2000). Considerable evidence further suggests that many general education teachers are not well versed in the skills necessary to adapt curriculum for special learners (McLeskey & Waldron, 2002). For example, Alan Edmunds (2003) from the University of Western Ontario examined the perspectives of 186 teachers in Nova Scotia and reported that the teachers felt that they were not professionally prepared to teach students with special needs. An earlier large-scale study of 725 teachers in the same province (Edmunds, Halsall, MacMillan, & Edmunds, 2000) found that 80 percent of the respondents felt they did not have adequate professional training for inclusion. In a survey of U.S. teachers (Futrell, Gomez, & Bedden, 2003), 80 percent of classroom teachers reported that they felt unprepared to teach diverse learners.

- *Adapting instruction.* Lacking the required skills, teachers are often unwilling to make the pilgrimage toward meeting the needs of special learners. Studies find that teachers vary significantly in their willingness to make adaptations.

- *Conflicting principles.* Inclusion is not the only principle driving contemporary education. The day-in and day-out activity of teachers is often fraught with dilemmas that demand both reasoning and knowledge. Despite earnest applications, some teachers find themselves performing a sort of academic triage, prioritizing teaching students in heterogeneous groups versus individualized programs for students with special needs. Even if they are sensitive and well committed, teachers may claim that the prevailing pressures of today's schools preclude the implementation of individualized practices.

Finally, the values of inclusion may come into conflict with other values teachers hold dear, such as achievement and merit, and also with the dual restraints of heightened responsibilities and accountability. Hence, whether inclusion is right or wrong, effective or ineffective, may not be as moot as how it merges with other principles.

- *Lack of supports.* For a substantial number of educators, the controlling factors are concerns about workload and supports. Implicitly, inclusion demands that supports be brought to the classroom to the child, not that the child be removed to the supports. Supports for children are varied, such as adaptive equipment and speech therapy. Supports for teachers include additional personnel assistance, such as a paraeducator or daily contact with special education teachers for collaborative teaming and teaching and shared planning.

  In Nova Scotia, Edmunds and colleagues (2000) found that 77 percent of teachers did not think that they had adequate resources to properly carry out their teaching duties. A school principal in Alberta stated, "If you can't support them in the classroom, then they shouldn't be included in the classroom. Because you can't take the learning of 24 kids and set it to the side for the learning of one kid" (Fieber & Winzer, 2006). In the British Columbia study mentioned earlier (Naylor, 2002), respondents were asked to identify the supports most important to them. The great majority (74 percent) chose reduced class sizes. A substantial number of studies agree and tell us that class size is a factor in efficient individualization for students with special needs and one that deters teachers from making adaptations (e.g., Coleman, 2001; Fisher, Grove, & Sax, 2000; Fondacaro, 2001).

- *Outside forces.* The resolution of special education and inclusive education for learners with special needs will not emerge in a social vacuum; rather, it will depend upon an interplay of interests, politics, economics, and so on.

- *Funding*—and who should provide it—forms a major roadblock. Contextual features such as cost and economic restraint cause tension between school administrators and parents, disability rights advocates and general educators, and districts and provinces as they try to balance aid for general education and also ensure that students with special needs receive the necessary supports. A major complaint is that time and effort is being wasted complying with funding requirements. British Columbia researchers (Siegel, Lam, & Ladyman, 2000) found that "the existing funding system requires categorization that consumes valuable time and resources for assessment to secure funding" (p. 25).

- *Research evidence.* Many disagreements about the progress of inclusion hinge on the lack of empirical research. There is not yet a solid research base to show the effectiveness (or ineffectiveness) of any type of inclusive model. As well, we still have little information about how students with disabilities are progressing compared to general norms or how education reforms are affecting them. So far, there are no comprehensive data available on special education students' academic gains, graduation rates, preparation for post-secondary schooling or work, involvement in community living, or progress with paraeducator support.

The social integration of children who are exceptional is essential to the success of inclusion.

Making Inclusion Work

You would think that making inclusion work means just knocking down the barriers mentioned above. They are substantial, to be sure, and it will not be easy to undo counter-productive actions and change course. But there is more to it than that. In a very important way, inclusion is a mindset. A commitment to the principles and a willingness to place them in practice to change the entire culture of schools is more basic than surface changes such as classroom adaptations or parent involvement. Table 2-1 lists some of the varied factors that contribute to successful inclusion.

Table 2-1 Making inclusion work

School	More unified educational system created by restructuring to merge special education and regular education
	School personnel committed to accepting responsibility
	Accommodations made to the physical plant and environment
	Supportive principal
Teachers	Positive attitudes; believe students can succeed
	Appropriate expectations
	Willingness to collaborate, adapt, and modify

Table 2-1 continued

	Tolerance of diverse student levels
	Real and perceived knowledge of students with disabilities
	Knowledge about and acceptance of students' problems and requirements
	Willingness to plan learning experiences individualized to students' needs
Team approaches	Co-operation, consultation, and collaboration
	Development of shared responsibility for students: general and special education teachers and other allied disciplines working side by side
	Team planning
Individualization	Individual Education Plan (IEP)
	Environmental accommodations
	Instructional and materials adaptations
	Specialized devices and equipment (assistive technology, augmentative communication, etc.)
Curriculum	Curriculum that is adapted and matched to each student's needs
	Modified special curriculum that is developmentally and age-appropriate
	Strategies such as co-operative learning, direct instruction, peer tutoring, and independent studies
	Different groupings and lesson formats
Evaluation	Policies for monitoring progress
	Accurate and ongoing assessment
	Adapted tests and grading practices
Supports	Appropriate teacher training
	Paraeducator assistance
	Support from therapists and other support services
Social	Peer supports for students
	Social skills training for students with special needs
Parents	Parental support of program goals
	Parental involvement in IEP process

TYPICAL SERVICES IN CANADA

A *policy* may be defined as a course of action chosen from alternatives that are formulated to guide and determine present and future decisions. All the Canadian provinces and territories have policies regarding special education but it is difficult to make any broad statements about inclusive schooling across the whole of Canada. Not only is education a provincial responsibility, but on the Canadian vista the literature and research sources offering national perspectives on inclusion remain quite limited.

Across Canada, the form and process of inclusion depends on provincial policy and the individual school district. Therefore, the implementation of inclusionary practices varies widely from province to province and even among neighbouring school boards. Note that this variation is not unique to Canada. In the United States, dramatic differences exist across states in the degree to which students with disabilities are educated in general classrooms. Some states have made significant progress toward serving students with disabilities in less restrictive settings; other less than stellar systems are notorious laggards with inclusion. Australia tends to mirror Canada, with each Australian state approaching inclusion differently (Winzer, Altieri, Jacobs, & Mellor, 2003).

It is true to say that in Canada all systems support inclusive schooling and have made fundamental changes. New Brunswick and Nova Scotia, for example, have adopted full inclusion. British Columbia does not have a target group in the sense that all children and youth are to be included and every student is treated as unique. Other jurisdictions treat inclusion programs as one more choice, albeit the most important one, on the education menu. They have chosen to maintain a continuum of services and typically approach inclusion on a one-to-one basis. It is held that case-by-case decisions are consistent with the essence of special education; rather than a blanket policy, the special needs of each pupil must be carefully assessed and the most appropriate educational placement for that child judged. Opting for participation in any program is justified only if such programming meets the needs, wishes, and interests of a student.

The reality of different policies and ways of approaching inclusion across Canada should not be seen in terms of right or wrong, best practice or flawed model, or in any type of hierarchal fashion. There is not an indisputable "best" form of provision. Rather, provinces and territories have tailored programs to suit their particular philosophies and resources.

With the flux and change that is characteristic of the area, it is virtually impossible to pinpoint exactly where individual provinces and territories are in their progress toward inclusive schooling. Table 2-2 presents a snapshot of what the provinces and territories are trying to accomplish in inclusive schooling for students with exceptionalities.

Table 2-2 Snapshot of inclusive policies in Canada

British Columbia	Promotes equitable access to learning by all students and the opportunity for all students to pursue their goals in all aspects of their education. In British Columbia, "The practice of inclusion transcends the idea of physical location, and incorporates basic values that promote participation, friendship and interaction" (British Columbia Ministry of Education, 1995).
Alberta	Students should have the opportunity to acquire the knowledge, skills and attitudes needed to be self-reliant, responsible, caring, and contributing members of society. The individual school is responsible to decide how best to organize to meet children's learning needs (Alberta Learning, 2000). In Alberta, "Inclusion, by definition, refers not merely to setting but to specially

Table 2-2 continued

	designed instruction for students with special needs in regular classrooms and neighbourhood schools. Instruction, rather than setting, is the key to success and decisions related to the placement of students are best made on an individual basis in a manner that maximizes their opportunity to participate fully in the experience of schooling" (Alberta Learning, 2002, p. 13).
Saskatchewan	Saskatchewan Learning broadly defies inclusion by focusing on the integration of the philosophy of inclusion with community education principles and practices to create a learning community in which integrated, community-based schools are the core agencies to deliver all services to all children and youth. The purpose of mandatory special education legislation is to provide appropriate educational opportunities and equitable benefits for all children and youth with exceptional needs.
Manitoba	Manitoba embraces inclusion as a means of enhancing the well-being of every member of the community. Teachers are expected to "create classroom learning environments that can address a broad range of diverse learning styles and educational needs" (Manitoba Education, Training and Youth, 2002). For special education, Manitoba has a mandatory all-inclusive programming policy under Bill 17, the Public Schools Amendment Act.
Ontario	Founded on the Education Amendment Act (1980), Ontario remains committed to the principle that the integration of exceptional pupils should be the normal practice when such a placement meets the student's needs and is in accordance with parental wishes.
Quebec	All students with disabilities or difficulties have access to quality educational services in the most normal environment approach possible. Special education in Quebec is founded on a mandatory, human rights approach.
New Brunswick	Bill 85 (1986) established a policy of mandatory inclusion that gave New Brunswick the strongest inclusive policy in the country. The guidelines on integration are directive about how schools should operate. The law requires the inclusion of all children with disabilities within general classrooms. All children are special and, accordingly, each child is to have an individual learning plan (New Brunswick, 2002).
Nova Scotia	The school's function is to do all it can to inspire its students with the desire to achieve the highest degree of excellence that is possible for them: each school has a responsibility to provide each students with a learning environment that encourages growth and development in all aspects of learning. Nova Scotia enacted non-categorical full inclusion in 1996. The official policy on special education is to "facilitate the membership, participation and learning of all students in school programs and activities." The general classroom is the first choice, rather than an optional choice, for placement
Newfoundland and Labrador	Schooling provides students the opportunity to acquire the knowledge, skills, and attitudes needed to be self-reliant, responsible, caring, and contributing

Table 2-2 continued

	members of society. There are no specific statutes governing special education although the Schools Act (1997) appears to be a significant piece of legislation for students with special needs (Edmunds, 2003). Programming is delivered with age peers "except where compelling reasons exist." The service delivery model includes *Pathways*, the provincially prescribed regular curriculum, *Pathways to Programming and Graduation* then maps out five different curriculum pathways.
Prince Edward Island	Public education provides for the development of children so that each may take a meaningful place in society. Special education is mandatory and non-categorical.
Yukon	The aim is to develop the intellectual, physical, social, emotional, cultural, and aesthetic potential of all students to the limits of their abilities so that they may become productive, responsible, and independent members of society who can lead personally rewarding lives in a rapidly changing world. Yukon promotes mandatory and non-categorical special education.
Northwest Territories	In order for each student to learn and grow, education must be based on individual strengths and needs and be relevant and meaningful for each person. Policy promotes education in the general classroom.

LEGISLATION

Law may be defined as a system of rules and regulations relating to the behaviour of individuals and society as a whole (Warren, 1988). A regulation is a rule of order having the force of law. **School law** is the legislation, regulations, by-laws, and judicial decisions that apply primarily to all or part of the public school system (Nicholls & Martin, 1983). School law is designed to support teachers, school administrators, and parents and includes providing appropriate interventions for students in need of assistance in general and special education (Cole & Brown, 1996).

school law

The relationship between legislation and the quality of services is not a direct correlation. Attitudes cannot be legislated, nor can responsibility. In the final analysis, the measure of responsible education will not be the number and length of laws, court cases, and interpretative regulations. The quality of education will be determined by the nature of the direction provided by educational leaders and the commitment of teachers and others to quality as they attempt to implement the intent of the directions provided. Legislation therefore may not reshape special education, but it reflects the efforts that special educators have been working for years to achieve.

Canadian special education has tended to follow the U.S. model. Canadian educational issues—legislative, administrative, and curricular—are directly influenced by events, philosophies, and pedagogy from the United States. As a result, Canadians have a touchstone against which to critically assess their progress and greater freedom to meld practices and philosophies into Canada's unique educational system.

Probably the most critical and pervasive difference between special education in Canada and the United States relates to legislation. Canada does not have a federal office of education and therefore has no equivalent to the federal mandates in the United States.

Legislation in the United States

The United States has a long history of relying on legislative and judicial remedies for social issues, including special education. During the 1950s, federal commitment to special education truly began. Since then, the participation of the federal government has steadily increased and today Washington plays a prominent role in special education.

A number of important pieces of legislation related to individuals with disabilities—adults, school-aged, and preschool-aged children—have been passed and then amended in various ways. Four particular laws work together to ensure that persons with exceptionalities are not discriminated against, receive a free and appropriate public education, and have access to facilities.

A particularly important piece of legislation is the Americans with Disabilities Act (ADA) of 1990, which relates to people in general society. The ADA guarantees equal opportunity and access to all persons with disabilities, in and out of the school system. Essentially, the ADA forces employers and others to recognize the abilities of persons with disabilities.

An early and crucial educational law is Title V of the Rehabilitation Act, more commonly called Section 504, passed originally in 1974. Section 504 is a civil rights law that protects children and adults against discrimination. In the schools, it ensures that students can participate in educational programs. However, it compels schools only to make reasonable accommodations, not to provide substantial or expensive services. Students not included under other laws, such as those with Attention Deficit Hyperactivity Disorder, are served under Section 504. (Note that the Individuals with Disabilities Education Act [IDEA] amendments in 1997 allowed that Attention Deficit Hyperactivity Disorder and Attention Deficit Disorder may result in eligibility for special education under the category of "other health impairment.")

The Education for All Handicapped Children Act (EHA), often simply referred to as Public Law 94–142, the seminal legislation, came about in 1975. It was prompted by the civil rights movement, efficacy studies in special education, parent activism, professional pressure, and reports that more than half of all children with disabilities were not receiving any educational services at all (Douvanis & Hulsey, 2002). When President Gerald Ford signed PL 94–142 into law in November 1975, these children were ensured a free and appropriate education in the least restrictive environment. (Note that the numbers refer to the 142nd bill in the 94th Congress of the United States.)

As a legislative remedy to some of the past failures of schools to provide appropriate education, Public Law 94–142 had a tremendous impact on the provision of services to children who were in some way exceptional. It represented official recognition by the U.S. Congress of a growing dissatisfaction with placing students with disabilities in special classes. The Act and its amendments legitimized the notion of placing such students in the public schools and in general classroom settings. The legislation also promoted individualized instruction, increased the role of parents in the instruction of their children, and made education possible for previously unserved, seriously disabled children.

The least restrictive environment (LRE) was the cornerstone of Public Law 94–142. The law mandates that children with special needs must be educated in the LRE with an

Individual Education Plan (IEP) developed, maintained, and evaluated for each child. States must assume non-discriminatory testing and confidentiality, and must ensure due process procedures for all children with disabilities and their parents or guardians. As well, the states must actively attempt to identify children in need of special services and must provide a complete system of personnel development.

PL 94–142 was a grant-in-aid law, which means that financial responsibility for its implementation is shared by local, state, and federal governments. To be eligible for federal funds, state and local agencies must comply with the requirements of the law. All states chose to participate, so all were provided federal funds to support the education of students with disabilities.

PL 94–142 and its amendments adopt a categorical approach. While 13 specific groups of students are now included, the law did not automatically apply to gifted and talented students. Their needs for financial assistance and programs were originally addressed in PL 95–561, the Gifted and Talented Children's Education Act of 1978. The Jacob K. Javits Gifted and Talented Students Education Act assists disadvantaged children; the Omnibus Education Bill of 1987 provides modest support.

Amendments

Although deeply significant, PL 94–142 was not model legislation. Like other comprehensive federal laws in the United States, PL 94–142 periodically undergoes reauthorization and amendments in response to changing circumstances. Under the original legislation, all states were mandated to serve children between the ages of 6 and 18. Ongoing amendments have extended the rights to preschool exceptional children and initiated transition programs for adolescents.

The first amendment was PL 99–457 in 1986, which provided full services for 3-year-olds by 1992 and dramatically increased funding for preschool programs. PL 99–457 divided the preschool population into two groups—infants and toddlers (birth to 3 years) and preschoolers (3 to 6 years). Part H of PL 99–457 refers to infants; Part B refers to preschoolers. Early intervention is fully addressed in Chapter 16 of this book.

In 1990, the Individuals with Disabilities Education Act (IDEA) (PL 101–476) again amended PL 94–142. The IDEA retained all the basic provisions of the original legislation but expanded to include 13 types of disability when it added autism and traumatic brain injury as categories. The title of the law was also changed to stress people-first terminology—that is, to say "a child with a disability," rather than "a handicapped child."

The IDEA was amended on June 4, 1997, as PL 105–17. While most of the general requirements of the 1997 IDEA had been in the law since 1975, the amendment refined the basics and addressed the issues of school discipline and the authority of school personnel to handle children who could be a danger to themselves and others. It put new discipline provisions in place, strengthened the role of parents, and added a new variable to the formula by changing the notion of a separate curriculum for individual children. The 1997 reauthorization required that the general education curriculum be a starting place for all students and that outcome measures on IEPs (goals and objectives) be tied directly to the general education curriculum goals and objectives. As students with special needs become more involved in the regular school curriculum, it is expected that most children with IEPs will take the standard proficiency tests beginning as early as grade 4 (see Yell & Shriner, 1997).

The most recent amendment was the Individuals with Disabilities Education Improvement Act (IDIEA) of 2004, PL 108–446, passed into law on June 19, 2004. The regulations that accompany the law and explain how it is to be implemented are still being prepared.

You should also be aware of the No Child Left Behind Act (NCLB) passed in January 2002, an amendment to the Elementary and Secondary Education Act. The NCLB, though not directed toward children with special needs, pulls them further into high stakes testing, discussed later in this chapter.

In the United States, *inclusion* is a state-of-the art term; it is not mentioned in federal law or in state statutes. The IDEA of 1990 stipulated that children with disabilities must be provided with a free, appropriate public education in the least restrictive environment, but it requires a full continuum of services, which includes such environments as residential schools. Students can be placed in special settings only when the use of supplementary aids and services in the general classroom cannot achieve a satisfactory education (Culross, 1997). The next IDEA in 1997 did not mandate inclusion but strongly encouraged consideration of educational placements in general classrooms.

Legislation in Canada

In the Canadian federal arena, it cannot be said that the law clearly and unequivocally obliges the publicly supported school system to provide appropriate forms of education for all students, exceptionality notwithstanding. Except for the Declaration of Human Rights, there is no federal law to outline or guarantee the rights of children who are exceptional; the right of every child to education is not entrenched by any constitutional provision. The 1867 British North America Act (Sec. 93) was chiefly concerned with protecting the educational rights of linguistic and religious minorities.

The responsibility for education in Canada rests almost entirely with provincial legislation. Each of the 10 provinces and 3 territories has its own school system based upon provincial or territorial education legislation that springs from diverse sources—federal and provincial constitutional provisions, federal and provincial statutory law, administrative rules and regulations, and case law.

Since 1969, all of the provinces and territories have enacted legislation guaranteeing education to all children, including those who are exceptional (Goguen, 1993). Within these guaranteed services, each government has developed its own legislation, regulations, policies, and procedures to ensure that all children receive a free and appropriate education. Provincial legislation is found in the Education Act of each province and territory. There are important differences between legislative provisions across the country; some legislation is detailed and prescriptive while some place more stress on philosophy. For students who are exceptional, the specificity of the law in each province varies from the minimal right for most students to attend school to the right of full inclusion in the general classroom (Crealock, 1996).

Educational goals and priorities occur in policy documents, the most relevant of which are issued by the various ministries of education. Only a few schools, such as provincial resource centres for the deaf, are controlled directly by the provincial government. The rest are administered through local school boards, each of which is responsible for a geographical school district.

Funding stems from a combination of property taxes and provincial government grants, according to formulae that vary from province to province. For the purposes of special education, the Maritime provinces tend to fund on a block-per-pupil basis. The Western provinces provide a basic instruction block (or core grant) supplemented with specific (categorical) funding for special education pupils. In other Canadian jurisdictions, there is a trend to provide categorical funding based on student needs rather than labels (see Manitoba Department of Education, 1998).

Legislation makes school boards implement fair and equitable provisions for special education assessment, placement, and programming. As pointed out, Canadian provinces and territories have recognized the right to an education for all children in different ways, which can be broadly categorized as mandatory and permissive. Mandatory legislation says that boards "must" include students with special needs; permissive legislation allows, but does not require, the integration of such students.

Legislative activity has tended to focus on students with disabilities. Although gifted youngsters are considered to be exceptional in their need for special education, they have not fared as well in the legislative arena, perhaps because legal arguments for students who are gifted are different from those for children with disabilities; they are not fought on denial of access but denial of appropriate programs (see Chapter 9).

LITIGATION

Litigation, a process that occurs through the court system, is one of the principal means by which society exerts pressure over, and provides direction to, public schools. Litigious influence has altered public policy and the functioning of the school system in areas as diverse as architectural barriers, residential facilities, custody of children, life management and sterilization, inclusion, assessment and classification, and appropriate educational practices.

Litigation involves an individual or a small group of people filing a suit against another group. The suit represents a complaint against the status quo. For example, a parent of a child who is intellectually disabled may sue a school board on behalf of the child or as a class action for all children who are intellectually disabled.

In Canada, the emphasis on using the power of the courts to settle disputes of an educational nature is less pronounced than in the United States, but nevertheless does occur with some regularity. At the moment, judicial activity in Canada seems to be stimulated by three connected factors. These are the principles of the inclusion movement, the willingness of advocacy groups to support parents, and interpretations of the Canadian Charter of Rights and Freedoms.

Much of the litigation is initiated by parents. Sometimes, parents ask that a school district provide special educational services to a child or extend the amount of services. In other cases, parents view the general school as the most appropriate educational setting for the special child and disagree with the decisions regarding his or her placement in, or exclusion from, a particular program. Other Canadian litigation has involved the rights of people with disabilities, sometimes brought by individuals or sometimes brought on their behalf. As examples over time, in the 1978 Carriere case in Alberta, it was ruled that it is the responsibility of local school jurisdictions to provide an educational program for all children. In 1982 the Adult Mental Incompetency Act came under close scrutiny in the case of Clark vs. Clark, heard in County Court, Lanark, Ontario. In this case, Justin Clark, a young person with cerebral palsy, won his rights. In British Columbia, the Stephen Dawson case involving sustaining life support was brought forward on Stephen's account. In Eldridge vs. the Attorney General of British Columbia, a deaf appellant objected to the failure of the province to provide interpretation services free of charge.

The Charter of Rights and Freedoms is the federal and supreme law of Canada; it can override all provincial legislation. Section 15 of the Charter states that every individual is "equal before and under the law and has the right to equal protection of the law without discrimination and in particular, without discrimination based on mental or physical disability" (s. 15 (1)).

Interpretations of the Charter mean that the courts are making complex and difficult decisions that ultimately influence educational policy and practice. A number of challenges to the existing educational structure heard under the Charter have occurred. Cases under the equality rights include Elwood (1986), Rowett (1989), and Robichaud (1989). A critical seminal case that passed through the Ontario Court of Appeals and on to the Supreme Court of Canada was that of Eaton versus the Brant County Board of Education, decided in 1997.

In the Eaton case, the Supreme Court decided that an individual child's needs are to be considered to determine the most appropriate placement from a range of options. As well, when an exceptional pupil has been placed in a general education class with appropriate supports and modifications and where objective evidence demonstrates that the child's needs are not being met, there is no violation of the Ontario Human Rights Code or the federal Charter of Rights and Freedoms in placing the child in a special class (Makin, 1997). Therefore, excluding some children from mainstream classes is an acceptable form of discrimination, provided that it is done in the best interests of the child. Unanimously, the Court rejected the idea of there being an automatic assumption that children with disabilities should gain entry into general classrooms if that is the wish of the parents. Instead, decisions should be made on a one-to-one basis, using the yardstick of the best interests of an individual child (Bogie, 1997; Makin, 1997).

The Eaton ruling parallels many in the United States. There, court actions have confirmed the rights of children who are exceptional to an appropriate education and have mandated public schools to provide that education. However, federal rulings about inclusion have also determined that the focus of an intervention should be on where a child can receive an appropriate education that meets his or her needs and that this may be a segregated or a regular setting. (For more on U.S. litigation, see McLaughlin & Henderson, 2000.)

TRENDS AND MOVEMENTS

We pointed out at the opening of this chapter that myriad issues are germane to current special education. Most of them either directly or peripherally revolve around the notion of school restructuring and inclusion for students who are exceptional. In the following section we outline some of the broadest and most influential general trends.

Expansion of Services

As educational programming is provided for all children and youth, whatever the type and degree of their disability, there have been increasing pressures on special education to assume responsibility for the education of a greater proportion of the school population and a concomitant expansion of services. Programs are reaching down to encompass infants and preschoolers and up to provide transition programs and post-secondary education for students who are exceptional.

Expansion of the scope of special education is also related to the increasing number of students with cultural and linguistic differences. Recent demographic data suggest that public schools are faced with an increasingly diverse population. One result of demographic change is that the special education system is increasingly serving students who are in the process of acquiring a second language or who come from home backgrounds that differ culturally or linguistically from the Canadian majority.

Multicultural Special Education

Culture is "a broad concept that reflects a wide range of beliefs, practices, and attitudes that make up an individual" (Harry, Kalyanpur, & Day, 1999, p. 4). Cultural issues pose important implications for research and practice. Children do not shed their cultural differences at the school door; rather, they bring their socialization patterns, linguistic backgrounds, modes of communication, social mores, learning styles, and the manifestations of their culture and language to the classroom with them (Winzer & Mazurek, 1998).

One solution to the needs of students with cultural differences that simultaneously builds tolerance and understanding in other students is the process of multicultural education. Children with special needs also need to understand their own culture and those of others, develop positive understandings of their own cultural heritage, and explore similarities and differences. They need multicultural special education that celebrates the first language and culture while building a second language and accommodating to the new culture.

Multicultural special education can be defined as

> a set of perspectives and skills that change the climate, curriculum, and interactions in schools and classrooms so that all students, whatever their cultural and linguistic background or type and degree of disability, have equal respect, the opportunity to learn, and are given the skills to develop cross-cultural sensitivity and the competencies necessary to function in a pluralistic society. Multicultural perspectives and skills meld with special education practices, are infused throughout the curriculum, and are tailored to the unique strengths and needs of each child who is exceptional. (Winzer & Mazurek, 1998, pp. 104–105)

In an overarching sense, multicultural education systematically prepares students to live and thrive in a world characterized by mixed cultures and various frames of reference. It is interesting to note that the education of students with disabilities draws upon, reflects, and echoes the same concerns as multicultural education—equity, justice, quality of life, and full participation in a pluralistic and democratic society.

Early Intervention

Early identification and early intervention are two of the most promising areas of contemporary special education. **Early identification** is used to identify children with established disabilities, those who are at risk for problems, and those experiencing lags and delays. **Early intervention** refers to the establishment of educational and support services for preschool children and infants who are at risk for disabilities, and their families.

early identification

early intervention

As examples, many studies have reported impressive gains for some children with autism as a result of very specialized early intervention. Children with Down syndrome are typically engaged in early intervention soon after birth.

Early identification and intervention are part of the broader construct of *early childhood special education*. This new direction truly emerged in 1986 with the passage of PL 99–457, an amendment to PL 94–142. The principles and practices of early childhood special education are discussed in Chapter 16.

Transition

Many adults with disabilities do not fare well once they leave school. Increasingly, educators are becoming concerned with job placements, acquisition of a job, and maintenance of the job for these young people. To ease the passage from school to work, transition programs are now viewed as important elements of secondary special education.

Transition programs rest on the premise that the quality of life and the extent to which youth with disabilities achieve the desired goals of employment, community living, and social and leisure opportunities depend on the effectiveness and appropriateness of secondary school experiences as well as on co-operative service planning and the availability of needed adult services. The area of secondary programming and transitions is discussed in Chapter 17.

Parent Involvement

Reform efforts in general education stress the greater involvement of parents, mirrored in recent Canadian policy and the amendments to the IDEA in the United States. Schooling simply works better when parents are involved. With parents as partners, the educational experience for all children is enhanced. Parent involvement has been consistently related to students' cognitive development and academic achievement. For students with disabilities, parent input assists them to make educational gains in a planned and coordinated manner. For example, children with learning disabilities fare better with parental assistance with reading or math homework (Cooper & Nye, 1994; Salend & Garia, 1995). Again, when parents are taught ways to help their children who are having difficulty learning to read, their children have been shown to perform better on standardized tests of reading than comparable children who received tutoring in school but no home help (see Hewison, 1988).

Technological Advances

Technology and science are driving forces in modern society; they are changing the world in which we live and work. Today, for example, students use word processors to prepare written assignments and have access to electronic mail that instantly puts them in touch with people anywhere in the world. Teachers maintain databases of their students' achievements and can use the internet to catalogue shop anywhere. Administrators effectively track, maintain, and produce paperwork, and have portable telephones that keep them accessible at all times.

The explosive growth of technology and the current proliferation of computer programs, CD-ROMs, and Web-based activities that provide swift access to multimedia (such as graphics, video, text, and sound) provide both teachers and students unlimited possibilities to experience novel and creative learning environments. Technological advances are also a boon to persons with disabilities. Today, there is wide availability of devices that enhance communication, mobility, and learning. These can be grouped generally as **instructional technology**—various types of hardware and software—and **assistive technology**—various devices used to help students with disabilities function in their environments. The roots of special education technology are in the latter—assistive technology (AT).

instructional technology

assistive technology

As an aside, it is interesting to note that many assistive technologies are becoming mainstream as tech giants incorporate AT solutions into regular products for universal application. Meyer and Rose (2000) point out that television captioning first appeared for deaf persons who had to retrofit their TVs with decoder boxes. Now, with decoder chips built into every TV, the universal design feature benefits not only the deaf but exercisers in health clubs, people working on their language skills, and couples who go to sleep at different times.

The technology can also be seen on a continuum from high- to low-tech. High-tech solutions involve the use of sophisticated devices, such as computers, interactive multimedia systems, and high-technology communication aids that have speech output, printed output, or sometimes both output modes. Medium-tech solutions use less complicated electronic or mechanical devices, such as videocassette players and wheelchairs. Low-tech solutions are less sophisticated, such as adapted spoon handles, Velcro fasteners, or raised desks that can accommodate a wheelchair (see Maddux, 2000). Further examples are found in Table 2-3.

Table 2-3 Examples of assistive and instructional technology

Level	Organization	Reading/language	Math
Low-tech	print schedule picture schedule highlighted text picture communication board page turners pencil gripper	predictable books pocket dictionary word wall	enlarged work sheets graph paper number line abacus

Mid-tech	recorded material	dictionary
		tape recorder
		semantic
		mapping software
		optical character recognition
		    (ORC) scanner
			electronic calculator
			    with printout
			talking clock

High-tech	alternative keyboard
	closed-circuit television
		electronic books
		software for concept
		    development
		hand-held computer
		voice recognition software
		voice output device with
		    speech synthesis
			software for drill and
			    practice, concept
			    development, etc.

Computers are perhaps the technology that most obviously affects the lives of people who are disabled. Add to this the advent of the internet, the World Wide Web, and CD-ROM technology in the late 1990s. With these services, the perceptions of computers as information sources grew tremendously. As technology continues to improve lifestyles, computers provide sensory input, enhance mobility, develop cognitive and language skills, strengthen motor and perceptual functioning, and facilitate communication. Computer technology can provide reading for blind students, language for those who are deaf, and speech for students deprived by serious disabilities.

In the classroom, computers are an effective supplement to classroom instruction—a tool that helps students learn more and have fun doing so. In special education, computer-assisted instruction (CAI) has proven effective in influencing the educational outcomes of students of all ages. After a review of 133 research reports on the effectiveness of computer technology, one team (Sivin-Kachala & Bialo, 1995) reported that educational technologies have a significant and positive effect on achievement, self-concept, and attitudes in both general and special education.

Assistive technology devices help children with disabilities to undertake tasks they could not do otherwise. These devices can be as simple as a pair of eyeglasses or as complex as a speech synthesizing program or a book that lets a child turn the pages with a puff of air.

Assessment Practices

Diagnosis is a term derived from the Greek root *dia* (apart) and *gignoskien* (to know). By definition, diagnosis is the art of identifying disease from its symptoms. In education, the word **assessment**, which comes from the Latin *assidere*, to sit beside, has largely replaced diagnosis. Assessment is more relevant to instruction because it stresses the current level of developmental functioning. The term refers to a multifaceted process of gathering valid evidence to specify and verify problems, make decisions about students, guide decisions about curriculum and instruction, and evaluate the outcomes of instruction.

assessment

Every day, teachers use *continuous assessment*—they daily observe children and their performance. They also take note of children who appear to be making an inadequate adjustment in some aspect of their development, whether it be behavioural, social, emotional, or communicative, or some combination of these.

Effective classroom assessment is guided by three fundamental principles—assessment should promote learning, use multiple sources of information, and provide fair, valid, and reliable information. The process is not intended to label a child or to propel him or her toward special education. Rather, the basic purpose is to collect information, to clarify the "whys" of a child's performance and behaviour. Assessment targets behaviours to determine how a child learns best, the behavioural characteristics that will affect learning, and whether there are any sensory or motor impairments relevant to achievement and performance. Moreover, there is no clear line between assessment and intervention. The assessment process is vital in making decisions about the best educational placement for a child and is a first step toward preparing an IEP.

Over the years, the responsibility for assessing students with disabilities has come to be viewed as substantially different from assessment in general education. This is not correct. Assessment in the field of special needs is best viewed as an extension of the measurement (putting a number on) and evaluation (what does it mean?) techniques used by all teachers to assess student learning. The special education process, however, tends to be more varied and complex. Here assessment is not a one-time or single procedure. A single test, person, or occasion is not a sufficient source of information; instead, a valid description of a child's status is generated from data collected from several sources, instruments, and settings, and on multiple occasions.

There is no such thing as a flawless diagnostic system, and quite a bit of controversy surrounds the assessment of students with exceptionalities. One of the major arguments concerns the utility of traditional diagnostic models—that is, assessment based on the underlying assumption that a diagnosis can be formed on the basis of observations and tests of the individual and that there is a corresponding treatment for a rehabilitating effect. We can find out what is "wrong" with a person and then "fix" it. Diagnostic models feed into labelling (Chapter 1), categorical approaches (Chapter 2), and medical models (Chapter 3).

As the field moves past medical models, practices in assessment for learning problems show many paradigm shifts. There are changes in the preferred types of tools and measures, the environment used for assessment, the flexibility of the procedures, and the greater involvement of general and special education personnel in the processes. No longer is assessment the sole responsibility of a psychologist in a clinic setting. There is increasing recognition of the importance of assessing student performance and learning outcomes in the context of the classroom and home environment.

As this occurs, interest is being generated around new methods and approaches. In the following chapters in this book, you will encounter, for example, the use of portfolios (Chapter 9), functional behaviour analysis (Chapter 7), curriculum-based measurement (Chapter 5), and vocational evaluations (Chapter 17). In this short section, we overview the assessment process to lay the groundwork for the discussions of assessment for special populations, which are embedded in the next chapters.

Stages in Assessment

A good way to conceptualize the actual assessment process is as three interrelated stages: survey, or screening; specific, or direct; and intensive, or medical and allied disciplines. Each of these stages involves different strategies and is undertaken by different professionals. All, however, focus on developing efficient treatment and educational programs for an individual child. The primary goal is to gather and analyze enough pertinent information to teach a child effectively.

Screening

The term *screening* originated in the medical literature. It is now used in medicine and education to refer to developmental and health activities that are intended to identify those children who have a high probability of exhibiting delayed or abnormal development.

Screening in education refers to a classroom activity that generally occurs prior to direct testing. The procedures look at large groups of children and begin to identify those who may have difficulties in behaviour and learning. In this way, screening is a first step in determining whether a child may need intervention or special services for a condition that could prove disabling, or whether the child might profit from an adapted or individualized educational program due to disabilities or giftedness. Effective screening similarly eliminates problems that are not cause for serious concern or that will resolve themselves without intervention.

screening

The widespread practice of screening children for school readiness is generally done in an attempt to identify children who will experience difficulty in school and intervene early. For example, as early as age four, young children can be screened to show who is at risk for reading difficulties. The procedures used are broad. Included are interviews with parents, first-hand observations, child interviews, past records, developmental checklists, behaviour rating scales, inventories, teacher-made tests, criterion-referenced tests, group achievement tests, and error analysis.

Although screening is widely used and there are many tests on the market, the accuracy of most measures is unknown, as is the percentage of children with and without problems accurately identified. One early research team (Lerner, Mardell-Czudnowski, & Goldenberg, 1981) said that, on average, most educational screening identifies about 85 percent of children with exceptionalities. An exception is students who are gifted, where screening procedures are less successful (see Chapter 9). Note, too, that many students with severe or multiple disabilities do not pass through the screening process since they are obviously disabled; the assessment process for them begins with psycho-educational testing. In the case of children with cultural and linguistic differences, teachers often need guidance in how to evaluate the information about student behaviour. What may look like a language disability, for example, may be only a stage of second language acquisition.

Specific Assessment

psycho-educational assessment

Specific assessment includes **psycho-educational assessment** (direct testing), which is examining children across a variety of domains relevant to social and educational performance. The aim is to gather further information on children who were identified through screening. Direct testing confirms or discounts the existence of a problem and helps determine what types of intervention are needed.

tests

Psycho-educational assessment relies heavily on testing. In general, the term *testing* means that explicit criteria for performance are established in advance. **Tests** are defined as controlled and structured procedures that attempt to elicit particular responses that the child might not demonstrate spontaneously (Bailey & Brochin, 1989). Many tests are standardized—they use standard materials, administrative procedures, scoring procedures, and score interpretation. The purpose of standardization is to ensure that all children taking the test receive essentially the same experience, are expected to perform the same tasks with the same set of materials, receive the same amount of assistance from the evaluator, and are evaluated according to a standard set of criteria. The overwhelming majority

norm-referenced

of standardized tests are **norm-referenced**—they indicate a child's developmental level in relation to that of other children of the same age, the normative group.

intelligence quotient

IQ tests (measures of mental ability) are probably the best known and the most controversial of the norm-referenced measures. They provide an **intelligence quotient** (IQ). Traditionally, this referred to the relationship between a child's mental age (MA) and chronological age (CA). Today it is more correct to say that IQ reflects the difference between the child's performance on the tests and the normative performance for the child's age level.

Certain assumptions underlie the definition of IQ. The most crucial is the notion that intelligence, as measured on standardized tests of mental ability, is normally distributed. A normal distribution is a continuum of scores that vary from the average score by predictable amounts. Figure 2-1 shows the normal curve of intelligence using an average score of 100 and a standard deviation of 15.

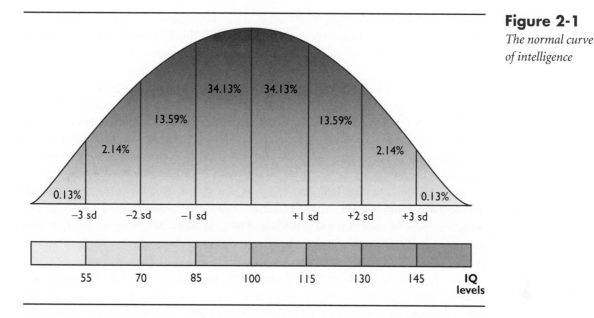

Figure 2-1

The normal curve of intelligence

Teachers are not usually involved in assessing intelligence and cognitive functioning. Because IQ tests are delicate instruments and need careful interpretation, their use is restricted to psychologists and others who have received special training. The teacher's role, as part of the IEP team, is to take the results of *a battery of* assessments (a range of measures that examine various domains of functioning), translate them into present levels of performance, and then use them in planning programming. The process is not as straightforward as it may seem at first. In fact, it is quite complicated and takes much careful thought.

Many educators query the need for IQ scores, which they deem as having limited value in determining the needs and styles of inclusive classrooms. Nevertheless, psychometric assessment is still widely used. Some jurisdictions demand intellectual assessment as a source of data in the designation and placement of students in special education. Advocates of IQ testing argue that an assessment of a child's cognitive skills is essential to a complete understanding of his or her development because cognitive skills are closely intertwined with skills in other domains, especially language, social functioning, and behaviour. Further, when properly used and interpreted, tests perform important functions. The greatest advantage of standardized tests is their potential for comparing a child's performance to that of other children (the norm group), and they can be used with considerable success to predict academic achievement. The downside is that these measures are more important for defining delays than for program planning. Standardized measures tap isolated intellectual and language abilities but do not yield intervention-relevant information on functional skills that can be included in an individual child's program and be easily integrated with daily activities.

Standards Testing Although there is no finely-tuned definition, *accountability* can be thought of as a system of informing those both inside and outside educational circles of the direction in which schools are moving (Westat, 1994). Accountability includes attainment of student goals and outcomes, often known as *standards testing*. Content standards define the knowledge, skills, and understanding that students should acquire in academic areas. Performance standards define the levels of achievement that students need to prove their proficiency.

In the United States, statewide and district assessments are known as high-stakes testing. Recent US documents and legislation such as the 1997 and 2004 versions of the IDEA; the federal law, No Child Left Behind Act of 2001; and the Quality Counts document of 2004 place enormous emphasis on accountability as manifested in testing. The United States has also moved to include more and more students with disabilities within general testing processes.

Canadian jurisdictions have adopted province-wide testing for various grade levels with somewhat different *test accommodations*—changes in the standard test conditions that remove sources of error that could be created by a disability. As examples only, in British Columbia students who receive special services, including those who have little or no language skills in English, and those who would, at the administrator's discretion, be under undue stress, are exempt from participation in the tests. Manitoba allows exemptions for students with significant cognitive delays or if there would be harm to the student, and allows accommodations such as extra time to other students with special needs. In Ontario, accommodations must not affect the level or content of the assessment, or its reliability or validity. Possible accommodations include adjustments in scheduling, changes in setting, the use of aids and equipment, and adjustments in the format of assessments.

High-stakes or standards testing is enormously controversial, with contradictory opinions emanating from legislators, educators, teachers' associations, the media, and parents. Some people argue that the testing provides an infallible reflection of a child's or school's achievement and that it leads to both excellence and equity, referred to as "raising the bar" or "closing the gap." Critics (e.g., Biriamah, 2005; Kohn, 2004) contend that they accomplish neither. Canadian researcher Bernie Froese-Germain (2004) observes, "When accountability is reduced to measuring, comparing and ranking students, teachers and schools on the basis of test results, special needs and other vulnerable students suffer most because they end up essentially being treated as academic liabilities" (p. 5).

Medical Assessment

Professionals involved at the medical level of assessment include school nurses, family doctors, pediatricians, neurologists, audiologists, and ophthalmologists, to mention only a few. The medical procedures are as varied as the personnel.

Screening may begin as early as the prenatal period with, for example, an ultrasound to determine the presence of certain disorders. Immediately following birth, screening occurs as physicians check for obvious disabilities or genetic and metabolic disorders. Later, a public health nurse uses a sweep test to check hearing or a Snellen chart for visual acuity.

For a school-aged child, a complete look at his or her health history and current medical status must form part of the total assessment. Suppose, for example, that a grade 1 child who appears bright and outgoing cannot seem to comprehend such sound-symbol associations as "S is for snake." Before any specific psycho-educational diagnosis is undertaken, the child should be referred to an audiologist for a complete assessment of hearing acuity.

SUMMARY

1. Special education is a dynamic field, its growth and change mediated by legislation, politics, economics, and ethics, as well as by education reform and innovations. Issues, trends, and movements apparent in the field are all designed ultimately to improve conditions of living and learning for persons who are exceptional.

2. Many of the changes in attitudes and perceptions toward persons who are exceptional can be dated to the 1960s and the birth of the normalization movement. This ideological shift argued that all people who are exceptional deserve an educational and living environment that is as close to normal as possible, and held that community settings were superior in their effects on social, vocational, and academic learning. The late 1970s and early 1980s was the period in which the practice of special education came of age and the true movement toward integration got underway. In the 1970s, enormous changes came about as a result of enabling legislation in both the United States and Canada. The dual philosophies of normalization and mainstreaming impelled many children with mild to severe disabilities into the orbit of the public schools.

3. Special education is deeply involved in reforming the system at various structural and theoretical levels. Probably no reform question has occupied professionals more in past decades than the effects of including children with disabilities within general classrooms. Even after 20 years of debate and practice, inclusion remains one of the most controversial issues in education, made more so by the divisive and widespread disagreement on the nature and meaning of the term.

4. Inclusive schooling emerged from the wave of educational reform that addressed the structural causes of inequity in terms of the massive student diversity characterizing contemporary classrooms. The philosophical ideal of inclusion is more accepted than the implementation. Many educators support inclusionary philosophies but dispute inclusion as a universal template that assumes that only one solution exists to the various challenges faced by children with special needs.

5. Law and public policy have had a profound effect on the type and quality of education offered to children and youth who are exceptional. In some cases, they decide whether exceptional students are educated at all; in others, they determine how such children are educated. Litigation and legislation underlie much of the process of educational integration witnessed today. Parent groups, court decisions, escalating educational costs, and the example set by the American PL 94–142 and its amendments have all exerted pressure on governments.

6. In the United States, overarching and prescriptive federal legislation such as the Individuals with Disabilities Education Act (IDEA) provides direction, impetus, and funding for special education. The actual term *inclusion* is not law in the United States; the least restrictive environment in which the most appropriate education can take place is law. The U.S. Department of Education has taken a middle road on inclusive schooling—it supports inclusion but also a continuum to ensure appropriate settings for individual learners.

7. In Canada over the past 10 years, there has been a remarkable commitment to inclusive ideals and the development of policies and practices aimed at meeting the needs of all students. However, across Canada, we do not find a consistent definition of *inclusion*. Provincial and territorial legislation speak to the idea of inclusion but differ in practice.

Some jurisdictions support full inclusive schooling; others opt for a model that allows for alternative placement when it is considered to be in the best interests of the student. To keep abreast of changing reforms, Canadian policies are in a state of perpetual revision.

8. Inclusion is more than simply the place where students with disabilities receive services. Rather, it is a way to deliver services effectively, where the opportunities made available by the setting, not the setting itself, become important.

9. Before teachers can help children who are exceptional, they must accurately pinpoint their problems. For each child, a detailed picture of strengths and weaknesses in a variety of domains is needed. Assessment serves little purpose if the process is undertaken merely to collect data. Data from screening and psycho-educational diagnosis are useful only when used to initiate more effective services and programming.

HISTORICAL NOTES

When special education began in North America, individuals with disabilities were believed to differ from the rest of the population in almost every domain. Because of this, and for reasons of economy and convenience, children with exceptionalities were educated chiefly in institutional settings designed as much to protect the rest of society from the so-called deviant children as to protect the children from an intolerant and prejudiced world.

Residential schools—variously referred to as *asylums, institutions, colonies,* or *training schools*—were first established in Canada in the mid-19th century to serve children described in the parlance of the day as deaf and dumb, blind, and idiotic or feeble-minded. In the United States and Canada these special schools were divorced from the general educational system and administered along with prisons, asylums, and public charities. Not until the early 1900s were special schools in most parts of Canada placed under provincial departments of education.

Schooling became the social norm for most children in Canada by the early 1900s. As the public schools assumed responsibility for socializing and educating huge numbers of children, they were faced with an unforeseen problem. How could they best provide for children who could not be handled in the regular classes? These difficult students, labelled as truant, delinquent, incorrigible, and feeble-minded, were those with mild disabilities in behaviour and learning. To keep order in the schools and protect the education of other students and the time of teachers, special segregated classes seemed the ideal solution. First known as ungraded or unruly classes, segregated programs were introduced in the United States in 1879, founded on German models.

In Canada, the first special day classes were started in 1906 for children with physical problems—those described as crippled, sickly, and malnourished. These were followed by provisions for pupils who were intellectually disabled, sight-saving classes, home instruction, speech correction, and lip-reading classes. There were also orthopedic classes, vocational and advancement classes, and remedial reading programs.

The late 1940s saw a huge expansion of special education due to simple demographics. The postwar baby boom increased the number of children with disabilities. The polio epidemic of the 1950s and the rubella epidemic of the 1960s generated still more demand for special education; more demand came from advances in medical technology, which kept more children alive and limited degrees of impairment. Parents' associations formed and spearheaded a social movement to extend educational and treatment services to the most severely disabled children. Sometimes, parents established schools for children with moderate and severe disabilities. The great majority of special education services were still provided in segregated settings—special classes or schools, clinics, hospitals, and so on.

The modern retelling of special education really began in the 1960s. Efforts to restructure special education, long-simmering and glacially paced, accelerated. As we mention in Chapter 1, parents, advocates, legislators, and educational systems began to reject the notion that students who were exceptional should be educated separately from their peers or that people with mental disabilities should be herded into large institutional settings. Grave dissatisfaction with special classes was bolstered by numerous efficacy studies that found that children performed no better in special classes than in general classrooms. People who were disabled themselves began to unite and question the ways they were understood and treated by the non-disabled majority, including those in the helping professions such as education, psychology, and social work.

The 1970s saw enabling legislation, Public Law 94–142, in the United States. In Canada, the Commission on Emotional and Learning disorders produced a report in 1970, *One Million Children*. This offered a new perspective on educational practices and provided the first real endorsement of the integration of students with exceptionalities into general classrooms.

Together, these factors prompted a radical reconsideration of the special education delivery system. In 1987, writers (Reynolds, Wang, and Walberg, 1987) called for "the joining of demonstrably effective practices from special, compensatory, and general education to establish a general educational system that is more inclusive, and better serves all students, particularly those who require greater-than-usual educational support" (p. 394).

Today we have a vibrant inclusion movement that seeks regular education advantages for all children with disabilities.

CHAPTER 3

RISK FACTORS AND CHILDREN AT RISK

INTRODUCTION

Dozens and dozens of factors surround children as they grow up. Some of them are related to the classroom; many more arise from familial or extra-familial conditions. If teachers are to truly understand the children in their charge, they must be aware of these children's social world and development; their social skills and self-esteem; their interactions with parents; and, in many cases, their cultural and linguistic backgrounds. This is even more crucial when a child has a disability. Not only must teachers be aware of the psychological, social, and educational factors related to a disability, but they must also have a working knowledge of biomedical causes and developmental consequences of the condition.

In recent years, the term *at risk* has become popular in educational parlance. The expression's initial use in the field of education did not emerge from worries about learners, but through criticism of schools. It was invoked most prominently in the United States in *A Nation at Risk* (National Commission, 1983), which shook the foundations of the educational system and led to the reform movement for accountability that we described in Chapter 2.

Today, the term *at risk* is somewhat confusing because it is used in different ways by different people, and applied to different groups with different outcomes. When the term was originally applied to children, it was used to describe children who have disabilities, may acquire disabilities, or may have unfortunate learning and behavioural outcomes in school. Recently, notions of risk have broadened to encompass more and more of children's lives and circumstances. At the same time, the research and literature on risk have expanded considerably. Wendy Cassidy and Anita Bates (2005) from Simon Fraser University explain that notions of risk tend to be divided into two categories. The first is an individual deficit category that sees students and their families as the sources of risk. The second takes a wider social justice approach and recognizes that difficulties faced by individuals, families, and cultural groups are inevitably bound up with larger social inequities of poverty, marginalization, and disadvantage.

In this chapter we examine both categories of risk. The discussion is organized around **risk factors**—essentially, the things that account for varied adverse outcomes. They include a huge range of agents that we group as established, biological, or environmental risks.

risk factors

When applied to children, the term *established risk* revolves chiefly around genetic and chromosomal factors. Today, more than 3500 genetic diseases have been identified. A second huge group of factors, referred to as *biological risk factors* (for example, prematurity), account for disabling or potentially disabling conditions in children. *Environmental* causes that place students at risk for developing problems that affect learning and/or behaviour are legion, although the most pervasive and important seem to be poverty, dysfunctional families, and cultural and linguistic differences. Types of risk, risk factors, and examples of potential outcomes are shown in Figure 3-1.

When you consider risk factors, keep in mind that every human life is a complex interplay of heredity and environment, and it is almost impossible to determine the relative influences of each variable on human behaviour. Genes alone cannot produce a human being; an environment that provides nourishment, warmth, stimulation, and protection is also necessary.

This chapter provides a general road map of biological and environmental conditions. Readers will find more explicit information in the categorical chapters of the book. This chapter focuses on ideas and conditions that are important for teachers.

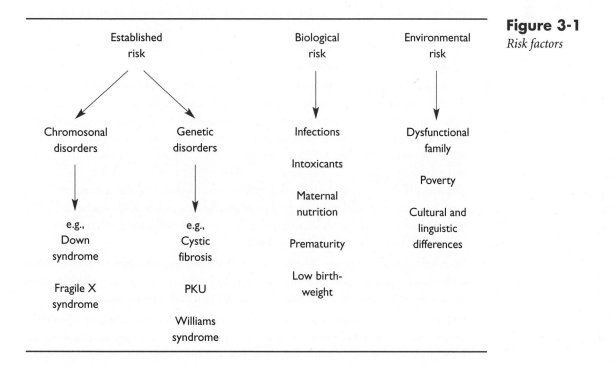

Figure 3-1
Risk factors

THE IMPORTANCE OF ETIOLOGICAL CONSIDERATIONS

etiology

Etiology refers to the process of finding causes to explain how a particular problem came into existence. Etiology includes within its purview *symptomology*, the study of symptoms and characteristics and the overt reactions or manifestations of the body to a certain condition. It also includes *teratology*. The word comes from the Greek *teros*, meaning "monster", and implies the study of the agents (teratogens) involved in causing malformations and how these impact on the long-term medical and psychological functioning of an affected individual.

Not so long ago, Kahn (1985) observed that "most special educators do not believe that etiology is pertinent to their functions" (p. 550). Certainly, disability-specific information provides limited information about the supports that students require in the classroom. Nevertheless, there is now compelling testimony that etiology cannot be ignored. Indeed, understanding and delineating the etiology that leads to behavioural phenotypes is essen-

behavioural phenotype

tial to understanding the competencies and needs of affected individuals. A **behavioural phenotype** refers to patterns of behaviour or the specific and characteristic behavioural repertoire exhibited by individuals with a certain condition.

Some of the many reasons education professionals should possess a basic knowledge of the etiology, symptomology, and treatment of exceptional conditions are summarized below.

- The causes of disabilities cannot easily be separated from the developmental consequences—the psychological, social, and educational implications that affect learning and behaviour.

- Recent genetic research provides dramatic evidence that students affected by different genetic conditions present quite different profiles (behavioural phenotypes). This is most evident in genetic causes of intellectual disability, which are outlined below and discussed more fully in Chapter 6.

- Etiological knowledge leads to a better appreciation of a disability. Understanding of medical conditions helps teachers to become sensitized to the social, emotional, and educational problems resulting from a child's disabilities. It enhances the teacher's relationship with the child and creates an atmosphere of acceptance among classmates and others. A child with spina bifida, for example, often requires an artificial bladder for urine drainage. The clinical manifestations of the student's urologic difficulties (incontinence) and the need for medical management (the bag worn on the stomach or flank) may create practical and psychological problems for him or her. If the teacher is unable to assist and reassure the child, then his or her medical problems may create learning difficulties (Freund, Casey, & Bradley, 1982).

- Knowledge breeds tolerance. Research attests that teachers and others who hold a clear understanding of exceptional conditions tend to be more tolerant and accepting than those who know little about etiologies and developmental consequences.

- Effective treatment requires an appropriate theoretical understanding of a problem. Teachers who have knowledge are confident in their ability to program effectively for individual children. One teacher wrote, "The scariest thing about integration is the medical aspect of it. We're looking at giving out medication, injections, changing diapers and always having to be on guard for handicapped children's frailties in case they get a reaction to something or stop breathing for some reason" (Alberta Teachers' Association, 1993, p. 12). Understanding a condition leads to greater confidence in handling its medical aspects.

- Some children with disabilities require medication on a regular basis, such as anticonvulsants for seizures, muscle relaxants for spasticity, stimulants for attention disorders, and a variety of medications for respiratory and cardiac problems. Depending on school-board policy, the teacher may be involved in the monitoring of drug dosages.

- Some children with disabilities have difficulty participating in certain physical activities. The teacher must know when to limit certain activities, when to restrict the duration of an activity, and when to recommend an alternative learning experience.

RISK FACTORS

The term **risk factors** refers to the biological and environmental conditions associated with an increased probability that an individual will develop problems in one or many domains of functioning. Risk factors may be intrinsic—involved with an individual's make-up—or extrinsic—involved with an environment that elevates risk. To some extent, this is an arbitrary distinction. As we pointed out in the introduction to this chapter, heredity and environment interact in complex ways.

risk factors

When individuals are exposed to risk factors, they become at risk—they have increased vulnerability for adverse outcomes. However, although risk connotes probability, it does not imply certainty. In other words, although the risk is higher, not all exposed individuals will be affected. In fact, the majority of children deemed to be within the traditionally accepted categories of biological and environmental risk, such as those who are born prematurely and those who are raised by young unmarried mothers with low incomes, will develop normally. Nevertheless, when compared to the general population, a greater proportion of children who are exposed to risk factors will develop difficulties. Present estimates indicate that between 30 and 70 percent of infants classified at birth as at risk eventually develop problems that require some form of intervention.

When we examine risk factors—the hazards—and *vulnerability*—an individual's susceptibility to a negative outcome—we have to wonder why some at-risk children are affected while others aren't. The answer is complex. One explanation is that, even with heightened risk, some children are simply more resilient. Recently, there has been growing attention to this concept of resilience, which suggests that "significant numbers of children raised in the most adverse circumstances develop into competent and productive adults" (Gardynik & McDonald, 2005, p. 206).

Resilience is not a unitary concept, but rather involves a number of personal capacities and conditions. The trait appears early in life in connection with adaptable, easy-tempered children and maternal warmth. At least average intelligence seems to act as a protective factor and may be the most important personal quality promoting resilience (Osofsky & Thompson, 2000). Associated traits include curiosity, enthusiasm, ability to set goals, and high self-esteem. Resilient children tend to be sociable and assertive, and well liked by peers and adults.

Thousands upon thousands of risk factors exist. These can be slotted into the major categories of established risk, biological risk, and environmental risk. There is a lot of overlap between the categories (see Figure 3-1 on page 69). Note too that the types of risk are constantly changing as new etiologies emerge and other diseases are eliminated. In the past, conditions such as Rh factor and diseases such as whooping cough, measles, smallpox, enteric fever, scarlet fever, and meningitis seriously impaired or even destroyed the vision and hearing of many children and left a range of other disabling conditions. Scarlet fever and other such diseases have been virtually eliminated, but a new group of disorders related to new etiologies has emerged. These new disorders include Attention Deficit Hyperactivity Disorder (ADHD), Traumatic Brain Injury (TBI), Fetal Alcohol Spectrum Disorders, and fragile X syndrome.

pediatric AIDS

Pediatric AIDS—AIDS contracted by children under the age of thirteen—and the potential impairments caused to infants by drug-abusing mothers is a matter of grave concern. Also included in this category of new morbidity are extremely premature babies. Although rescued by aggressive medical treatments, infants are at high risk for a number of neurological and physical impairments. As well, a significant proportion of children are being born with major disabilities that require lifelong support from professionals (see Carpenter, 1999). Many children with severe and profound disabilities or severe chronic illnesses can expect to live a normal lifespan.

Established Risk

established risk

Established risk refers to medical conditions and anomalies that invariably result in a disability or developmental delay. This means that certain causes are known to relate to certain conditions; a known etiology and known developmental outcomes exist. There is also a *continuum of reproductive casualty*; that is, the problems may range from relatively minor through to major difficulties.

Established risk, most often related to genetic and chromosomal problems, includes conditions such as Down syndrome, fragile X syndrome, and Tay-Sachs disease. In the following section, we examine the broad categories of established risk but only touch on specific conditions. Details of these disabilities are found in the following chapters and in Table 3-1.

Table 3-1 Sample of disabling conditions and sequelae

Condition	Classification	Timing	Major sequelae
CMV	Infection	Birth	Intellectual disabilities; can be fatal
Cystic fibrosis	Hereditary anomaly	Conception	Involvement of digestive and respiratory systems

Table 3-1 continued

Condition	Classification	Timing	Major sequelae
Down syndrome	Chromosomal aberration	Dysjunction at conception or soon after	Mental and physical anomalies
Fetal Alcohol Syndrome	Intoxication	Throughout pregnancy	Mental and physical anomalies
Fragile X syndrome	Chromosomal aberration	Conception	Mental and physical anomalies
Galactosemia	Hereditary anomaly	Conception	Untreated will result in intellectual disabilities
Herpes	Infection	Birth	Intellectual disabilities; often fatal
Muscular dystrophy	X-linked genetic anomaly	Conception	Muscle degeneration
Phenylketonuria (PKU)	Autosomal metabolic	Conception	Untreated will lead to intellectual disabilities disorder
Rh factor	Genetic	Conception	Jaundice, intellectual disabilities problem deafness
Rubella	Infection	First trimester	Deafness, blindness, Intellectual disabilities, multiple handicaps
Spina bifida	Perhaps multifactorial inheritance	Possibly throughout pregnancy	Neurological impairments of varying degrees
Syphilis	Infection	Second and third trimester	Physical handicaps, intellectual disabilities, sensory disabilities
Tay-Sachs disease	Autosomal hereditary anomaly	Conception	Fatal
Turner's syndrome	Chromosomal aberration	Conception	Mental and physical differences

Genetic and Chromosomal Differences

All individuals are born with a unique combination of genes that is theirs alone from the moment of conception. Nothing will ever change. Individuals will die with the same number and set of genes and share these same genes with their offspring. Almost every human cell contains a complete package of hereditary instructions for the characteristics that comprise the individual. These instructions are located in 46 chromosomes arranged in 23 pairs. Each pair carries one chromosome from each parent. The first 22 chromosomal pairs are autosomal (identical) and determine the thousands of traits that make up a human being, whether male or female. The 23rd pair determines the sex of the individual. Each chromosome consists of thousands of genes, and each gene is made up of deoxyribonucleic acid (DNA), which in turn consists of thousands of combinations of 4 chemical sub-units. The order in which these sub-units are joined together spells out the gene's message in the genetic code. Whether a particular cell will become facial skin or ankle bone depends on which genes are "switched on."

Just one misspelling in the DNA code throws off the entire process. This happens in the 3 to 5 percent of all babies born with a *chromosomal abnormality*—a clearly defined genetic disease—or a genetically influenced defect such as malformation of the spine.

In recent decades, massive research has been undertaken in the field of *cytogenetics,* the study of the location and organization of genetic material from chromosomes. The work on genetic and chromosomal abnormalities has focused on the location, organization, and regulation of the genetic materials of the chromosomes, and on detecting a marker or unusual DNA sequence that is associated with a disease-causing gene (Nelkin & Tancredi, 1989).

These advances culminated in February 2001 when researchers announced that they had successfully completed drafts of the entire human genome. The mapping of the human genome and the often dizzying pace of the genetic research that followed accelerated advances in a number of domains (Anderson & Nickerson, 2005). At the very least, new genetic syndromes are being discovered rapidly and our understanding of the known causes of disabilities is increasing.

Chromosomal Disorders

Chromosomal problems result from chromosomal dysjunction—a malfunction in cell division. Problems occur when there is an extra chromosome or when pieces or parts of chromosomes attach themselves to other chromosomes. About 1 newborn in 200 has a chromosomal abnormality (Plomin, De Fries, & McClearn, 1990).

Many different chromosomal disorders affect children. The effects of the damage vary greatly. Wide variations occur in the onset of symptoms, the parts of the body involved, the nature of the symptoms, the degree of severity, and the possible multiplicity of impairments.

The most commonly occurring chromosomal aberration—and the most deeply researched—is Down syndrome. Almost half (46 percent) of all studies on any genetic disorder have focused on this syndrome (Hodapp & Fidler, 1999). Another important chromosomal problem is fragile X syndrome, a relatively recent addition to the catalogue of causes of mental retardation. The fragile X chromosome was first reported in 1969, but the syndrome was not consistently diagnosed until the 1980s. Today fragile X syndrome is second only to Down syndrome among cytogenetic abnormalities associated with mental retardation (Simen & Rogers, 1989). Both conditions are fully explored in Chapter 6.

Genetic Disorders

As the embryo develops, DNA directs the chemical process within its cells. One tiny flaw in the genetic structure can have tragic results. A change in DNA may repair itself or lead to spontaneous abortion (miscarriage). The flaw may also create abnormalities present at birth, called **congenital abnormalities** or hereditary anomalies. Because hereditary anomalies exist in the genes, they may be passed on to subsequent generations. Whether an anomaly is passed on depends on the type of inheritance involved.

In the case of *dominant inheritance*, a child usually has parents with the same disorder. Confirmed or suspected dominant genetic disorders that can result in intellectual disabilities and other disabilities include achondroplasia, a form of dwarfism; Huntington's disease, a progressive nervous system degeneration; and polydactyly, extra fingers or toes. In the case of *recessive inheritance,* the child must inherit a gene from both parents, who carry the gene but may not manifest the condition. Under simple Mendelian inheritance, each child runs a four-to-one risk of manifesting a disorder. Recessive disorders include cystic fibrosis, galactosemia, and Tay-Sachs disease.

Some disorders are linked to the genes on the 23rd pair of chromosomes. In *x-linked inheritance,* sons have a 50–50 chance of inheriting a condition through their mother. Of the more than 250 types of X-linked inheritance disorders identified, colour blindness, hemophilia, and muscular dystrophy are probably the best known.

Multifactorial inheritance results from the interaction of many genes with other genes and/or environmental factors. Patterns of transmission are poorly defined; some conditions thought to be multifactorial are spina bifida, clubfoot, and cleft lip or palate.

In some cases, various types of transmission can account for a condition. For example, retinitis pigmentosa is a condition that affects the retina, the film-like layer in the back of the eye, and causes progressive visual loss. Retinitis pigmentosa is an inherited disease, transmitted through the generations by a gene that may be recessive, dominant, or sex-linked. An estimated 1 person in 80 carries the gene for recessive retinitis pigmentosa.

Down syndrome is the most common chromosomal aberration.

congenital abnormalities

Inborn Errors of Metabolism

One small group of genetic disorders causes metabolic problems; these problems are often the result of the action of a single pair of genes. In these cases, there are missing or defective enzymes, which are the proteins that help the body convert one substance into another as, for example, in the transformation of nutrients to chemicals usable by the cells. The absence of, or a defect in, one of the enzymes means that the normal chemistry of the cell is altered by the inability to provide or dispose of a critical chemical or protein, leading to unusual levels of particular chemicals in the body. Many of these conditions, such as phenylketonuria (PKU) can be treated or controlled; others, such as Tay-Sachs disease—a fatal deterioration of brain function—are untreatable.

We describe two specific types of inborn errors of metabolism below. Tay-Sachs disease may be seen as an example of the viability of genetic counselling. PKU is perhaps the most dramatic instance in which identification of a genetic disorder has resulted in successful prevention of a biological disorder (Wilson, 1998).

Tay-Sachs Disease   Tay-Sachs disease is named after its discoverers, Warren Tay, an English physician, and Bernard Sachs, an American physician, who identified the condition in 1877. Tay-Sachs results from an enzyme deficiency caused by a single autosomal recessive gene. Infants appear normal at birth, but their nervous system is gradually destroyed because of the missing enzyme hexosamidose A. When the child lacks this enzyme, various fatty substances build up in the body cells, including those of the brain. The excessive glycolipid in the cells of the nervous system causes the cells to swell, rupture, and finally die. As the nerve cells die, the child regresses dramatically in cognitive and motor ability, and becomes deaf and blind. Effects of the condition can be seen at 3 to 6 months after birth. Death is inevitable, usually between 4 and 6 years of age.

The parents, who are heterozygous carriers, each have only about half of the regular amount of the enzyme, but this is sufficient for normal development. About 1 in 30 Jews carries the defective gene. Tay-Sachs is also found in non-Jewish persons, but is 100 times less frequent.

Phenylketonuria (PKU)   PKU, a relatively rare genetically transmitted metabolic disorder, was discovered in 1934 by physician and biochemist Dr. Ashborn Folling of Norway (Henderson, 1989). Worldwide treatment began in the mid-1960s.

The genetic transmission of PKU is relatively well understood. The condition is carried on a double recessive gene by about 1 in every 600 people, so the chance of 2 carriers marrying is statistically 1 in every 36 000. The condition affects about 1 child in every 14 000. Phenylketonuria is primarily a condition that affects persons of northern European ancestry—about 1 in 4000 live births.

Essentially, PKU is a problem with modifier genes—genes that act on other genes and determine how these other genes express themselves. In PKU, the condition is marked by an inability to normally oxidize the amino acid phenylalanine, which is found in fish, dairy products, and most protein sources. Sustained hyperphenylalanine anemia in the early years is neurotoxic and almost invariably results in severe intellectual impairment (see Griffiths, Smith, & Harvie, 1997). Once in place, the effects are irreversible.

Early screening and a special diet eliminates or diminishes the effects of PKU. Screening procedures include urinalysis and blood tests shortly after birth. The most reliable test is the Guthrie blood test, developed by Dr. Robert Guthrie in 1961. It is performed between the third and sixth day after birth, with retesting after two weeks.

Early detection of PKU is vital, because the infant must immediately be restricted to a diet low in phenylalanine. Although phenylalanine cannot be completely eliminated from a child's diet, it can be severely restricted with a phenylalanine-deficient formula, Lofenalac, a prepared milk substitute. Low-phenylalanine foods include vegetables, fruits, juices, some cereals, breads, and starches. Milk and dairy foods are restricted and meat is eliminated from the child's daily intake.

Although the effects of phenylketonuria can be almost eliminated, some recent research has demonstrated mild problems, even in children on strict diets. One group of researchers found that some treated PKU children showed neurophysiological problems that interfered with academic functioning. Others discovered that in treated PKU children, their IQs were within normal limits but tended to be lower than those of parents, siblings, and non-sibling control subjects (see Ozanne, Kaimmer, & Murdoch, 1990). Many females fail to maintain the diet; when they bear children, the elevated levels of PKU increase the probability of having an impaired infant (Henderson, 1989).

Deletion Syndromes

In these rare diseases, it is not a case of aberrant genes. Rather, there is too little genetic material or there is at least one gene missing. Examples include Williams syndrome, Prader-Willi syndrome, cri du chat, and Angleman syndrome. As risk factors in intellectual disabilities, these deletion syndromes are discussed more fully in Chapter 6.

Syndromes with Abnormal Chromosome Numbers

The prevalence of disorders caused by an abnormal number of X or Y chromosomes is relatively high, about 1 in every 400 births. The most common variation is Klinefelter syndrome (XXY), which is found in about 1 in every 700 male births. Individuals, although seemingly normal at first, grow tall, but have little musculature and reduced sexual development. Although they have a wide range of intelligence, they almost universally show abnormal behaviour that includes language dysfunction, withdrawal, moroseness, and passive-aggressive behaviour.

In females with Turner's syndrome (XXX) there are varied effects. Girls may be short, tend to obesity, be at risk for middle-ear infections in childhood, have extreme difficulty with math and perceptual organization, and show very poor handwriting skills.

Biological Risk

Biological risk refers to specific factors that place an individual at high risk or at risk for physically, medically, or psychologically failing to thrive or developing some form of disabling condition. Most often, biological risk relates to infants and toddlers with a history of prenatal, perinatal, neonatal, or early developmental events that can result in biological insults to developing systems.

biological risk

Although significant biological conditions do not lead inevitably to developmental delay or disorder, they do carry a greater probability of delay or disability than that found in the general population. If we think of established risk as definitely causing a problem, then biological risk poses dangers.

For purposes of discussion, it is useful to group biological risk factors into some major categories and then discuss them in specific developmental periods: the *prenatal* or gestation period; the *perinatal* period, which extends from the seventh month of pregnancy and includes the delivery and birth period as well as the neonatal period, or first two weeks after birth; and the *postnatal* period.

Prenatal Period

Life begins not at birth, but at conception. At the beginning of life, a human being is smaller than the period at the end of this sentence. The individual is a single cell, barely visible to the naked eye, a tiny drop of fluid made up mainly of non-living material surrounding a minuscule nucleus of living matter. By the time of birth, some 38 weeks later, the individual weighs about 3.5 kilograms and contains 200 billion specialized cells (Montagu, 1977).

The prenatal period encompasses three stages. The first two weeks are known as the period of the *ovum,* or *zygote.* The next stage, the period of the *embryo,* lasts until the beginning of the third month. The remaining gestation time is known as the period of the *fetus.* The change of labels charts the organism's growth from a simple cell to a recognizable human creature. Specific changes occur to the developing human at specific times. Every cell, every tissue, and every organ has its own timetable for coming into existence, developing, and beginning to carry out its functions. So consistent are these functions that embryologists can determine them with great accuracy.

From the moment of conception until delivery nine months later, the human being is more susceptible to the environment than at any other time. The opening third of pregnancy, the first trimester, is the most important to development. Here the dye is cast, so to speak, in that the organism is immutably affected. During this time, major organs and basic tissues take shape and develop into their finished forms; after this stage, it is difficult to affect their growth in any fundamental way (Montagu, 1977).

Infections and Intoxicants

During pregnancy, the mother's health and adequate nutrition are vital to the development of the fetus. Any maternal condition that impairs the transport of oxygen and nutrients to the fetus or the exchange of metabolic waste products between mother and fetus has the potential to act deleteriously on fetal development.

critical period

Rubella Rubella (German measles) provides an example of a critical period when exposure to a certain teratogen is most harmful to the fetus. A **critical period** is a part of the life cycle during which the developing organism is particularly sensitive or responsive to specific environmental forces. Outside this period, the same event or influences are thought to have few if any lasting effects.

The rubella virus crosses the placenta and affects the developing fetus. The fetal organs likely to be affected are those whose development is underway when the mother contracts the virus. If this is during the first trimester of pregnancy, the eye, ear, nervous system, and heart are especially vulnerable. It is estimated that 50 percent of fetuses are damaged if rubella is contracted in the first month; 20 percent of embryos affected in the second month are born with defects (Rosenblith & Sims-Knight, 1985).

Severe sensorineural hearing loss is the major effect of maternal rubella; other major permanent features include cataracts, glaucoma, intellectual disabilities, congenital heart disease, and cerebral palsy. There is also a significant occurrence of late-onset defects of rubella (conditions that are not apparent at birth but occur later), including vascular disease, growth hormone deficiency, thyroid dysfunction, and diabetes mellitus.

Rubella often appears as epidemics that are estimated to occur in 25-year cycles. In 1964, the last major rubella epidemic created a phenomenal spike in the charts measuring the numbers of children who were left deaf and blind or with other multiple disabilities as a result of the disease. Vaccines developed in 1969 make a rubella baby rare today.

Syphilis Syphilis, one of the venereal diseases, is produced by the bacterium *Treponema pallidum* (also called *Spirocheta pallida*). Instead of affecting the developing organs as rubella does, syphilis produces destructive lesions (abnormal changes in structure) in already developed organs. While rubella is most critical during the first trimester of pregnancy, syphilis affects the fetus after the 16th or 18th week of gestation. If the disease is controlled by penicillin before that time, only about 2 percent of fetuses will contract it. After the 5th month, uncontrolled syphilis will affect about 40 percent of fetuses. Twenty-five percent of affected fetuses die before birth; 33 percent of babies who survive die in early childhood. Infants who survive may exhibit many disabilities, including intellectual disabilities, blindness, and deafness. Other affected infants show liver problems, peritonitis, central nervous system disorders, and pegged teeth (Montagu, 1977; Rosenblith & Sims-Knight, 1985).

Drugs When we talk about drugs, we are referring to a wide assortment of potentially harmful agents that range from hard drugs such as heroin, through prescription and over-the-counter drugs, to drugs widely used in Canadian society—nicotine and alcohol. The problem is significant, although the picture of overall numbers and effects is not as bleak as it was some years ago.

Because researchers are unable to conclusively identify a set of characteristics that represent prenatal drug exposure, a typical profile of children exposed to drugs prenatally does not exist. Two additional factors make generalizations about children exposed to drugs prenatally troublesome.

First, it is extremely difficult to attribute specific characteristics to certain drugs, since abuse of multiple drugs is common. It is known that mothers who are multi-drug (cocaine plus other drugs) users have children with the most adverse outcomes (Van Dyke & Fox, 1990). Infants of multi-drug users fare worse than infants exposed to single drugs in the areas of birth-weight, gestational age, withdrawal responses, and length of hospital stay (Kaye, Elkind, Goldberg, & Tytum, 1989).

Second, caregiving of the infant is vital in mitigating or exacerbating prenatal exposure effects. Prenatal exposure and later development is often compounded by the presence of a constellation of risk factors that include poverty, neglect, or drug use by others in the home. Mothers may be passive, lacking in emotional involvement and responsiveness, and more prone to abuse, which further compromises a child's development.

Prescription Drugs Prescription drugs have been shown to have an adverse effect on fetal development. Research has linked some antibiotic, anticonvulsant, and anticancer medications to fetal malformations (Batshaw & Perret, 1986). There is also evidence that pain-relieving drugs administered during labour and delivery can result in behavioural differences in infants (Rosenblith & Sims-Knight, 1985).

Cocaine The 1980s saw an increase in the use of cocaine in all socio-economic classes, races, ages, and sexes. Children exposed to cocaine prenatally are at risk for developmental delay. Cocaine use during the last trimester may cause fetal hyperactivity, premature placental detachment from the uterus, and a significant reduction in the weight of the fetus.

It is also associated with a higher malformation rate. Case histories of congenital abnormalities among cocaine-exposed children show missing fingers and forearm bones, cardiac anomalies, and microcephaly. Newborns may have deformed heads, lungs, digestive systems, or limbs. Later, in learning situations, children who were exposed to cocaine prenatally may demonstrate poor abstract reasoning and memory, poor judgement, inability to concentrate, inability to deal with stress, frequent tantrums, a wide variety of behaviour disorders, and violent acting out.

Despite these potentially serious consequences, recent investigations focus more carefully on environmental risk factors. They suggest that the environmental factors associated with prenatal cocaine exposure pose a greater risk for developmental delay than the possible teratogenic effects of the drug (Bono, Bolzani, Dinehart, Claussen, Scott, Murdy, & Katz, 2005).

In the late 1980s, crack, a relatively pure and inexpensive form of cocaine, emerged on the drug scene. As with cocaine, there is no single profile of an infant born to a crack-using mother. Some infants appear healthy. Others suffer neurological damage and are adversely affected, are more prone to having strokes and seizures, or are born with small heads, missing bowels, and malformed genitals. Crack babies are irritable, tremulous, and difficult to soothe for at least the first three months. They have a significantly higher rate of Sudden Infant Death Syndrome (SIDS) than babies who are not prenatally exposed to crack (see Rest, 1990).

As is the case with infants exposed to cocaine, too often the environment of the infant exposed to crack simply compounds the problems. Children born exposed to crack leave the hospital and enter homes often headed by poor, drug-addicted young mothers who are not able to cope with the demands of their own care, let alone the needs of a high-strung, difficult-to-soothe, unhealthy infant.

Heroin Heroin passes through the placenta so that the infants of addicted women are themselves born addicted. Withdrawal symptoms can prove fatal. Survivors suffer a number of difficulties, but it is not known whether these extend beyond infancy. Methadone, the substitute used to withdraw heroin addicts, may cause even more physiological damage to the fetus. Children are small and subject to high mortality. They suffer more seizures and central nervous system damage, and seem to have altered breathing responses that persist 20 to 40 days after methadone is no longer detected in their systems (Rosenblith & Sims-Knight, 1985).

Fetal Alcohol Spectrum Disorders (FASD) Together with nicotine, alcohol is the drug most likely to be used and abused by Canadians. In the past, alcohol in moderate amounts was thought to be safe during pregnancy. We now realize that even small amounts can damage the developing fetus. Alcohol ingestion by pregnant women can be more catastrophic to the growing fetus than illicit drugs such as crack cocaine or heroin (Phelp, 2000). A proportion of children of drinking mothers are born with a **syndrome**—a constellation of findings similar from patient to patient—now referred to collectively as FASD. The conditions and their developmental consequences are fully discussed in Chapter 12.

syndrome

Maternal Smoking When the mother smokes a cigarette, the fetus smokes it too. After the first few puffs its heart begins to beat faster, and it feels a drop in oxygen (hypoxia) and an increase in carbon dioxide. It stops moving and increases its fetal breathing to try to make up for the hypoxia. All these responses have a severe enough cumulative effect in heavy smokers to contribute to spontaneous abortions, bleeding during pregnancy, premature rupture of the amniotic sac, and deaths of fetuses and newborns (Salkind, 1990).

Smokers are twice as likely as non-smokers to have low-birth-weight babies. The infants of smokers weigh an average of 200 grams less than infants of non-smokers (Vorhees & Mollnow, 1987). Infants of smokers are shorter, have smaller head, chest, arm, and thigh circumferences and lower neurological scores than infants of non-smokers (Metcoff, Cristiloe, Crosby, Sandstread, & Milne, 1989).

Some studies have shown a possible connection between smoking and alcohol during pregnancy and the risk of ADHD. One team (Milberger, Biederman, Faraone, Chen, & Jones, 2002) investigated 140 6- to 17-year-old boys with ADHD and 120 normal subjects. The team's findings revealed that 72 percent of ADHD children had a maternal history of smoking during pregnancy, compared to 8 percent of normal subjects. When Rodriguez and Bohlin (2005) examined the relationship between stress and maternal smoking and ADHD symptoms in children, they also found that prenatal exposure to stress and smoking was associated with later symptoms of ADHD in the children, especially boys.

Maternal Nutrition Maternal nutritional deficiency covers a wide range of problems and developmental consequences. In general, malnourished women are much more likely to produce low-birth-weight babies, although it may be that low birthweight *per se* is not so much a problem as the fact that maternal malnutrition increases the fetus's vulnerability to other risk factors—the risk of congenital defects, prolonged labour, stillbirth, and infant mortality during the first year.

The period of intra-uterine development and the first 18 months after birth are crucial to the physiological development of every organ system. This is especially true for the brain. Inadequate prenatal nutrition can affect the relationship between the body's biochemistry and the functioning of the brain. Severe malnutrition can stunt brain growth and produce a significant lowering of intellectual ability. Nutrition in the mother seems to be particularly important in the third trimester, when the fetus should be making rapid gains in weight and its nervous system is developing rapidly.

Poor postnatal nutrition is a factor in child mortality and morbidity risks, but its relationship to disability is less straightforward. However, it is clear that poor diets are associated with congenital anomalies, immune system and vision problems, intellectual disabilities, and under-development (UNICEF, 2005).

Unknown Prenatal Influence There are a number of conditions present at or before birth for which there is no known cause. One is *microcephaly,* a rare phenomenon in which brain development is impaired by an abnormally small cranium. Another is *macrocephaly,* an enlargement of the head most frequently caused by **hydrocephalus**, a buildup of cerebrospinal fluid in the brain. Retardation may follow, but its severity can be reduced or eliminated by early diagnosis and treatment (see Chapter 12).

hydrocephalus

Birth and Neonatal Development

Birth takes place in 3 stages: labour, delivery, and afterbirth. It is a long process. An average first labour takes 14 hours; the average for later labours is 8 hours. In many areas of life, too much or too little is not a good thing. This is true of labour—labours that are too long or too short produce a greater likelihood of problems.

Birth can be dangerous for the child and/or the mother. The fetus may be in an unusual position, such as breech or transverse presentations. The membranes may rupture too early, leading to infection. An incorrectly placed placenta may mean excessive bleeding. Drugs and forceps used during delivery may cause harm to the fetus.

Neological Impairments

Before a child is born, he or she has no contact with the atmosphere. The oxygen that is necessary for survival and the orderly development of the body reaches the fetus by way of the mother's bloodstream. When the time of birth draws near, the oxygen level in the placenta and the child's circulatory system drops sharply. During the birth process, the human fetus is squeezed through the birth canal for several hours, during which time the head sustains considerable pressure and the infant is intermittently deprived of oxygen. Most infants tolerate this without difficulty; in spite of surface appearances, the stresses of normal delivery are usually not harmful (Lagercrantz & Slotkin, 1986).

Sometimes inadequate uterine environments pose additional risks, and the infant cannot tolerate the normal changes of labour. If the child is overly deprived of oxygen, the condition is called **anoxia**. Most birth injuries result from deprivation of oxygen to the immature brain, leading to abridgment of nervous system function. If supplies of oxygen to the nerve cells of the brain are too greatly reduced, brain damage or death can result. When a portion of the brain is damaged, the part of the individual that is controlled by that portion of the brain is also damaged.

anoxia

Damage to the brain may be so mild as to be undetectable, or so profound as to reduce the child to a very low level of functioning. There may be focal brain damage involving a very specific and delimited area of the brain, or diffuse brain damage involving a large or poorly defined area. Depending on the degree and location of the damage, the child's behaviour will be affected. For example, one of the traditional etiologies of learning disabilities is minimal brain dysfunction. On the other hand, generalized and diffuse brain damage results in mental retardation; damage to the motor areas causes cerebral palsy.

Preterm and Low-Birth-Weight Infants

Premature babies generally weigh 2500 grams or less, as compared to the usual birth weight of 3000 to 3500 grams. Advances in medical neonatology have dramatically improved the survival rates for premature infants. The greatest increases are for infants at very low (under 1500 grams) and extremely low (under 1000 grams) birth weights. In Canada, about 75 percent of infants at 25 weeks gestation now survive, about half at 24 weeks, and about one-quarter at 23 weeks. Surviving infants have a greater than 70 percent chance of being free of disability (Barrington, Papageorgiou, & Usher, 2001).

The most critical problem for preterm babies is lung immaturity and obtaining enough oxygen. A preterm baby has very little surfactin, a substance that normally coats the lungs during the last three or four weeks of gestation to prevent them from collapsing. Respiratory distress syndrome is responsible for about half of all newborn deaths in North America. Research has also established clearly that preterm infants have a higher incidence of developmental problems in childhood than full-term infants.

Preterm infants are often of low birth weight. Full-term infants may also be of low birth weight because of possible difficulties with placental nutrition. Both groups of infants are prone to a range of potentially dangerous conditions; for example, babies born weighing less than 2500 grams face increased risk of impaired immune function and diabetes and heart disease later in life. They are also more likely to grow up malnourished, and low birth weight has been directly linked to lower IQs and intellectual disabilities (see Chapman, Scott, & Mason, 2002; UNICEF, 2005). As they grow, small-for-term babies as a group tend to remain shorter and lighter than their age-mates, while preterm babies who survive are more likely to achieve normal heights and weights.

An overly long pregnancy can also be problematic. Infants born 2 weeks or more beyond the expected due date are said to be postmature. These children are in somewhat greater danger from anoxia and cerebral hemorrhage than children born at the normal 266 to 270 days. They also have a higher death rate and suffer more frequently from severe congenital abnormalities (Montagu, 1977).

CMV and Herpes

Some conditions are transmitted to the baby right at the time of delivery. Two potentially harmful or fatal conditions of this nature are cytomegalovirus (CMV) and herpes.

CMV, a form of herpes, is the most frequently occurring congenital virus among newborns. It affects about 3 percent of pregnant women. When babies are born to mothers who have infections in the active stages, the mortality rate is about 50 percent. Of children who survive, about half suffer from conditions such as microcephaly, spasticity, paralysis, seizures, deafness, or blindness (McIntosh, 1984).

Herpes (HVH), actually less prevalent than CMV, is potentially as damaging and can be fatal. Although it is a rare occurrence, babies are infected as they pass through the cervix or vagina. Affected infants are treated with an antiviral drug, but survivors are still at considerable risk for permanent damage (Hetherington & Parke, 1986).

Pediatric AIDS

AIDS in children may be the result of tainted blood transfusions or, in rare cases, the disease may be contracted through the mother's milk. Placental passage in utero and newborn contact with the mother's blood or vaginal fluids during the process of labour and delivery are the two major routes of perinatal HIV infection. Children infected with HIV will likely develop symptoms of AIDS; between 30 and 60 percent of children born to HIV-positive mothers will contract the disease (Dokecki, Baumeister, & Kupstas, 1989). Pediatric AIDS is readdressed in Chapter 12.

Postnatal Development

Postnatally, accidents are the most common cause of disabilities in children, followed by cancer in its various forms. As well, a variety of childhood diseases and infections can hinder children's progress. These are discussed in more detail in Chapters 12 and 13.

Infections

Both meningitis and encephalitis can result in intellectual disabilities, visual impairment, deafness, cerebral palsy, and other disabling conditions. Meningitis attacks the meninges, or coverings of the brain and spinal cord; it is accompanied by a high fever. Spinal meningitis has a mortality rate of about 10 percent in young children and is often an offshoot of influenza B. Recently, a new vaccine became available to protect children from spinal meningitis.

Encephalitis can be caused by viral, bacterial, or parasitic infections. More encephalitic children suffer retardation than meningitic children (see also Chapter 14).

Environmental Risk

In the classroom, teachers will meet many students who have not been identified as having disabilities, do not have IEPs, and are not designated for special assistance. Yet these students are not "getting" the curriculum, may be low achievers, or may understand some of the subject matter but not enough to develop competency in it. The achievement of these students falls just beyond the various categorical boundaries served by special education but is still problematic.

Such children and youth are described as at risk. In this usage, at-risk status includes young girls who become pregnant, adolescents involved in drugs and crime, those who have attempted suicide, school dropouts, and large groups of children for whom English is not the first language. Large numbers of students are potentially involved. U.S. studies find that between 25 and 35 percent of all students are seriously at risk (Frymier & Gansneder, 1989; Johnson, 1998). In Canada, various agencies suggest that as many as 30 to 40 percent of children could be deemed at risk (Wotherspoon & Schissel, 2001). Data from the National Longitudinal Study of Children and Youth (NLSCY) can be interpreted to mean that 27.6 percent of Canadian children under the age of 11 are considered "vulnerable" to emotional, behavioural, social, or academic problems (Zeesman, 2001, p 5.) Do be aware, however, that the NLSCY data highlight 11 major risk factors ranging from prenatal problems to caregiver well-being. For a lot of children, exposure to many of these factors is transitory and not likely to cause long-term problems. When we consider that at-risk status is defined as exposure to 4 or more of the 11 identified risk factors, the proportion of children under the age of 11 deemed to be at risk drops to 3.9 percent (Zeesman, 2001).

environmental risk

The risk factors affecting these children are grouped in the category of **environmental risk**. This term refers to conditions that occur when a child is biologically normal but is at risk for not developing age-appropriate behaviour at the typical rate.

For the very young child, environmental risk relates to factors such as maternal and family care, health care, nutrition, opportunities for expression of language, adaptive behaviour, and patterns of physical and social stimulation. For school-aged children, educators define *at risk* as "those in danger of failing to complete their education with the skills necessary to survive in a modern technological society" (Slavin, Karweit, & Madden, 1989).

The environmental variables that place children at risk are legion. We cannot possibly describe here all the factors that exist; rather, we briefly examine three major types of environmental risk that are particularly relevant to classroom learning and behaviour. We touch on family structures, poverty, and cultural and linguistic differences.

Family Structures

Students receive about 900 hours of instruction in school each year. However, they spend a great deal more time out of school; about 87 percent out of the classroom and only 13 percent in it (Monroe, 1991). What happens in the home, within the family, and in the neighbour-hood during that 87 percent of the time affects every aspect of a student's functioning and learning.

Teachers must be aware that the child population of today is different from that of ear-lier generations. Today's children are caught in the midst of rapid social changes. Many of the changes are positive; on the negative side are changing social and family structures that include everything from shortages in technical labour markets, to children living in poverty and homelessness, to the destabilization of the institution of the family as shown by mounting divorce rates and increases in the number of single-parent families.

High numbers of children are born to unmarried mothers. The number of single-parent families has increased at a rate 2.5 times faster than two-parent families to 14 percent in 1995. According to Statistics Canada (2000), the 1998 divorce rates indicate that 36 percent of marriages will end in divorce. Many children now have blended families that include stepbrothers and stepsisters moving in and out of children's lives.

The family is universally recognized as a fundamental influence on child behaviour. Family structure establishes the norms of behaviour and teaches, explicitly and implicitly, social, moral, and psychological lessons to the developing child. As families change, new problems emerge. This is not in any way to suggest that non-traditional, non-nuclear families are dysfunctional. However, research does support the contention that increasing family instability leads to dysfunctional relationships.

For children, family dysfunction during childhood and adolescence has been found to be related to verbal and physical aggression against others; school truancy and dropping out; behaviour disorders; learning disabilities; intellectual disabilities; juvenile crime and delinquency; social isolation and withdrawal; and bad-conduct discharges from the mili-tary (Bracken & Newman, 1994). The area of familial and non-familial influences on children's behaviour is readdressed in Chapter 7; the area of child abuse in Chapter 12.

Poverty

The heightened risks embedded in poverty are common themes in the dialogue of child welfare. Schorr (1988) observed that "Persistent and concentrated poverty virtually guar-antees the presence of a vast collection of risk factors and their continuing destructive impact over time" (p. 30).

The collection of risk factors accompanying poverty serve to compromise a child's development to an extraordinary extent. In fact, living in poverty is associated with adverse mental health outcomes in both children and adults. A Canadian study found that nearly 17 percent of children with disabilities live in families who depend on government income support, compared with only approximately 8 percent of non-disabled children. These findings are supported by the Canadian Council on Social Development, which reports that poor children are 2.5 times more likely than children living in high-income families to have vision, hearing, speech, or mobility impairments (see Ross & Roberts, 1999). A high percentage of preterm infants are born into high-risk social situations that may have led to early birth in the first place.

In the family setting, lower socio-economic status (SES) negatively correlates with eight adverse socializing factors—harsh discipline, lack of maternal warmth, exposure to aggres-sive adult models, maternal aggressive values, family life stressors, maternal lack of social support, peer group instability, and lack of cognitive stimulation (Dodge, Pettit, & Bates, 1994). Children of lower SES families are much more at risk for abuse than children from higher SES homes (Dodge, Bates, & Pettit, 1990).

Poor children can be adversely affected from the moment of conception. Poor families may not utilize adequate prenatal and postnatal health care. Children are more likely to suffer the consequences of poor maternal nutrition, complications of pregnancy and delivery, prematurity, and low birth weight. Within the school system, children of poverty are at high risk for reading and writing difficulties. They make up a disproportionately large percentage of those who repeat a grade, are placed in special education, or drop out before completing school (see Winzer & Mazurek, 1998). Parents may wish to help. But lower SES parents often lack the paid leave and flexibility to meet with school personnel and help their children with homework.

From another angle, it can be seen that raising a child with disabilities increases family expenditures while it tends to reduce the opportunity, especially for mothers, to earn income. In Canada, research shows that parents of children with disabilities spend 50 to 60 hours a week on tasks related to the disability— more than the equivalent of a full-time job (Roeher Institute, 2000). (See Chapter 16.)

One devastating effect of poverty is homelessness. A homeless child is any child who lacks a fixed, regular, and adequate nighttime residence. These children may be sharing the housing of others, living in cars, motels, campgrounds, homeless shelters, or bus stations, or they may be awaiting foster care placement (*"Exceptional and homeless,"* 2003, p. 1).

Cultural and Linguistic Differences

More than 200 000 immigrants arrive in Canada annually. Nowhere is the multi-racial/ethnic/linguistic character of Canada more evident than in large urban centres such as Vancouver, Montreal, and Toronto. The changing tapestry of Canada is then apparent in the diversity seen in our schools.

Every child views the world through culturally-tinted lenses that influence behaviour, social interactions, beliefs, and values. This translates into the huge impact that cultural and linguistic differences have on children's learning and achievement. We are certainly not suggesting any firm equation between school problems and cultural and linguistic differences, or that minority group status is necessarily a risk factor. But we must be aware of the cumulative effects when such variables as poverty, disability, limited English proficiency, and lack of appreciation of a child's cultural values and learning styles meld with cultural and linguistic diversity.

Culturally diverse students may be at risk because they are more likely than those from majority backgrounds to be poor. In general, children from minority families who have limited English proficiency and are impoverished have historically done poorly in school (Dao, 1991). In both the United States and Canada, these students show an unacceptable pattern of social separation and isolation, a growing gap between their achievement and that of majority-group children, disproportionate referrals to special education, tracking to lower streams, lower scores on tests, lower grades, high rates of school failure, high dropout rates, and lower rates of college attendance (Winzer & Mazurek, 1998).

Limited English proficiency places a child at risk for learning lags. Research in Canadian schools suggests that students learning English as a second language take between four to six years to match the achievement levels of first-language students on achievement tests (Klesner, 1994) (see Chapter 5).

In urban school populations we often find that minority children are met by a teaching force that continues to be predominantly white. Educators must be aware that children's success is dependent on the teachers' own willingness to cross cultural boundaries. Misunderstanding the values of a child's culture, ignoring unique learning styles, or lacking knowledge and appreciation of a culture can place students at risk.

In the same way that teachers may not understand students, minority students may not understand the classroom game as well as others, and teachers can then interpret this as a lack of ability or potential (Subsotnik, 1997). Children from different cultures interact with adults in different ways than those from the dominant culture. When teachers and students are out of sync, they clash and confront each other, both consciously and unconsciously, in matters concerning proxemics (use of interpersonal distance), paralanguage (behaviour accompanying speech, such as voice tone and pitch, or speech rate and length), and verbal behaviour (gestures, facial expressions, eye gaze) (Cartledge, Tillman, & Johnson, 2001). For example, Schneller (1989) found that although members of different cultures claim to recognize 70 to 100 percent of the gestures from the dominant culture groups, these members correctly interpreted the gestures at rates as low as 30 percent.

Further risk accrues when educational programs have little or no relevance to a child's family and community culture, language, and values. Or students may be threatened by unrealistic expectations for academic and behavioural performance. Other subtle biases may intrude. For example, misdiagnosis can occur when school psychologists are not trained or are at a loss when considering cultural and linguistic differences in their testing.

Culturally Different Students with Special Needs

To live and develop in two culturally different systems is sufficiently challenging for students without exceptional conditions. When special problems in cognitive functioning, sensory use, communication, mobility, or social and behavioural interactions combine with cultural and linguistic diversity, individual differences increase dramatically, as do the chances of school failure, even when special services are provided.

Culturally diverse students are represented in all categories of exceptionality and can experience any disability that is found in other children: disabilities of the same type affect children from diverse cultural backgrounds just as they do those of the dominant culture. However, demographic information on the number of children with exceptionalities who have diverse cultural and linguistic backgrounds is difficult to extrapolate from sources because of a lack of consistency in identifying, defining, and reporting these populations.

In the United States, Hardman and colleagues (1993) estimate that among students with disabilities, 41 percent are from culturally diverse backgrounds. In Canada, a partial picture emerges from national data compiled by the Canadian Council on Social Development (1999). These data suggest that of the 7.5 percent of children who speak neither French nor English as a first language, 5 percent were born in another country, and 5 percent are First Nations or Métis. Available data on children of Aboriginal ancestry with disabilities is limited. One major reason for the lack of figures lies in the fact that Native people are not a homogeneous group but are comprised of various nations with distinct values, customs, and beliefs. This leads to varied under-standings of disability within Native communities, which in turn affects data collection (Prince, 2001).

To accommodate culturally diverse students with disabilities, educators must place high priority on recognizing individual differences relating to cultural backgrounds and attitudes in a positive way. They must appreciate the values and beliefs, learning styles, communication and language patterns, behavioural and response mechanisms, and family and community roles and involvement that accompany these children to school.

PREVENTION

The levels *primary, secondary,* and *tertiary* are used to describe the prevention of disabilities and potentially disabling conditions and the elimination of risk factors. Each level has dif-ferent aims and approaches.

primary prevention

Primary prevention is concerned with establishing medical and social programs to reduce the occurrence of diseases and conditions that cause disabilities. The aim is to reduce the incidence of certain problems in the population, remove the causative factors that account for the initial occurrence of a disorder, and strengthen the well-being of individuals in the population as a form of inoculation against subsequent problems. For example, providing medical care and fluoridated water to all children prevents childhood diseases and tooth decay (Planta, 1990). Other examples of primary prevention include measures to counteract poor nutrition, poverty, and premature birth.

Genetic counselling and educational programs on conditions such as Down syndrome are also part of primary prevention. *Genetic counselling* deals with the human and medical problems associated with the occurrence of risk or recurrence of a genetic disorder in the family. The major goal is to convey an understanding of birth defects and genetic mecha-nisms to affected families in order for prospective parents to make informed decisions about child-bearing (see Roberts, Stough, & Parrish, 2002).

secondary prevention

Once a disorder has emerged, primary prevention is not possible. **Secondary prevention** refers to ascertaining, as early as possible, the evidence of disorders that may cause disabili-ties, as well as allied attempts to keep the disorder from increasing in intensity. Successful secondary prevention programs provide services for high-risk groups to keep problems from becoming debilitating and to diminish the effects of dysfunctions that are identified early (Planta, 1990).

In many cases, secondary prevention has proven very successful. For example, Tay-Sachs carriers are detected through a simple blood test. In North America, the rate of Tay-Sachs among Jewish infants decreased by 95 percent in the 20 years from 1970 to 1990. In the case of Down syndrome, prenatal testing led to a drop in the incidence from 1 in 600 in 1970 to 1 in 1000 in 1990 (Plomin, De Fries, & McClearn, 1990).

The major method used in the prenatal diagnosis of Down syndrome and other chro-mosomal or genetic disorders is amniocentesis. In this relatively safe procedure, amniotic fluid is extracted and checked for karyotypes (genetic patterns) that are typical of specific disabling conditions. Further procedures include percutaneous umbilical blood sampling, ultrasonography, fetoscopy, chorionic villi sampling (CVS), and the maternal serum alfale-toprotein test.

Included in secondary prevention are procedures to manage conditions in order to ameliorate their impact. For example, certain organic conditions that cause intellectual disabilities can be successfully managed when identified early. The effect of PKU can be prevented or diminished if a low-phenylalanine diet is introduced in infancy. Hydrocephalus can be surgically treated, even in the fetus, by the insertion of a shunt to remove excess cerebrospinal fluid. An example of secondary prevention in the schools includes dropout prevention programs. (See Chapter 7.)

Tertiary prevention consists of intervention strategies taken after a negative outcome has occurred. It is designed for disorders that have reached advanced stages and threaten to produce significant side effects or complications that may overwhelm the individual (Kauffman, 2005). The object of tertiary prevention is to minimize disabilities and maximize potential. Interventions may be medical, psychological, social, or educational.

tertiary prevention

SUMMARY

1. As increasing numbers of children with exceptional conditions move into general educational milieus, teachers will encounter students with problems such as epilepsy, Traumatic Brain Injury, visual and auditory impairment, and orthopedic and urologic difficulties. Fundamental to providing for the needs of these students is a basic understanding of etiology.

2. Medical research is bringing us a more complete understanding of the ways in which a child's psychological, social, and educational environments are related to learning. Teachers' knowledge of the etiology, developmental consequences, treatments, and prognoses of exceptional conditions will serve to increase their interactions with and understanding of children with disabilities. Without specific information, teachers will be able to engage in only the most cursory and superficial interactions with children with special needs.

3. Discourses related to notions of children and youth considered to be at risk have gained widespread currency in the educational world. Risk and resiliency may be opposites. Many children who should be deemed at risk avoid major difficulties.

4. A huge range of disabilities affect children as a result of multiple etiologies. Disorders and diseases may arise from chromosomal or genetic aberrations, infections and intoxicants, malnutrition, deprivation of oxygen, and environmental hazards. The causes of childhood disabling conditions are changing; with the rapid advances in medical science, certain conditions have disappeared, but others have filled their places. For example, premature babies are surviving, but a wide range of insults to the nervous and organic systems that can lead to intellectual and other disabilities can possibly affect these children.

5. The groupings of biological and environmental risk include children not currently identified as disabled but more likely than their peers to develop some type of problem. Difficulties may be overcome in a warm family environment; in unstable low-income families lacking decent housing and enough money, a child's growth can be seriously hampered by restricted sensory stimulation, deprivation, and impoverishment.

6. Teachers must be aware of the myriad economic, environmental, and geographic factors that influence the lives of children with exceptionalities. Linguistic, cultural,

socio-economic, and lifestyle differences are not of themselves disabling conditions, but their consequences may place children at higher risk.

7. In Canada, there is very little national data on disability as it relates to different groups, cultural differences, or socio-economic status. Nevertheless, the schools reflect the rapid demographic changes seen in society and student diversity is synonymous with today's classrooms. The difficulties multiply for students who are culturally and linguistically diverse and also disabled.

8. Language and colour barriers often separate students from the educational institutions they attend and place them at risk for educational and behavioural difficulties as well as for cultural bias and discrimination.

HISTORICAL NOTES

Throughout history, exceptional conditions have been bounded by medical paradigms. Those requiring medical treatment were the first to be addressed; the recognition and care of intellectually and sensorially deprived persons had to wait for more enlightened attitudes regarding social care, which historically tended to lag behind purely medical concerns. The medical stress largely determined societal attitudes and legal mandates for persons with disabilities.

In the mid-19th century enormous interest in human genetics and heredity was stimulated by Darwin's work (1859). Major advances occurred in the etiology of disabilities, particularly mental retardation. One of the most important advances came when John Langdon Down identified specific subcategories of retardation in 1866.

Our Victorian ancestors were fascinated with the world of natural science. It is not surprising that from about 1860 on constructs of disability shifted and evolved in concert with new scientific knowledge and spawned new beliefs about the nature of various conditions (especially mental retardation), the educability of affected children, and the type of training that should be offered. Many pioneer educators came from the medical profession and added a further medical slant. For example, all of the early superintendents of institutions for persons with

mental retardation were physicians. Today's American Association on Mental Retardation (AAMR) began as the Association of Medical Superintendents of American Institutions for the Feeble Minded (Winzer, 1993).

The normative categories of deaf, blind, and intellectual disabilities were the focus of 19th century special education. With the birth of special classes from about 1910, a plethora of categories of disability emerged. Medical models dominated and special education developed along the lines of a clinical individual service model attached to concepts of individual differences, intervention, and prevention.

Medical models conceptualized learning disorders as having distinct patterns of symptoms and signs that resulted from different disease entities and causes, and which responded to different treatments. In the schools, this translated to diagnostic-prescriptive approaches, where traits are diagnosed and then a prescription is written to address weaknesses. A child was diagnosed, labelled, slotted into a separate pigeonhole, placed in a class consonant with the label, and presented a particular treatment. Teachers were trained for specific conditions to serve a specific clientele.

Medical models still remain important in special education, reflected in the current categorical systems and the diagnostic-prescriptive IEP process. Nevertheless, as the ideas associated with disablement have shifted to broader conceptualizations, disability is also understood to have social causes in the forms of barriers placed by society. Educators prefer to focus on the learning styles and behaviours of a child rather than the presumed underlying etiology. Contemporary systems tend to describe or profile children's behaviour patterns and move the field closer to models in which descriptions of children's needs, not etiological labels, drive intervention efforts.

SECTION 2

Children with Mild Differences in Learning

In this first section of categorical chapters, we discuss children and youth with mild differences in learning. Traditionally, the area of mild differences has included communication disorders, learning disabilities, mild intellectual disabilities, and mild behavioural disorders. We discuss the first three categories in this section. The broad and complex area of behaviour disorders, including Attention Deficit Hyperactivity Disorder (ADHD) is reserved for Section 3.

It is important to begin by stressing one critical caveat and two main ideas that underlie the following chapters. First, the caveat: this revolves around the use of the qualifier *mild*. Although this is a traditional descriptor, any condition or disability that can seriously disrupt a student's educational career should not be considered in anything less than a serious light.

The first important underlying idea concerns the contemporary movement toward inclusive classrooms, which is particularly relevant to students with mild disabilities to learning. Most, if not all, of these students will be presented with the general curriculum in a general classroom as the responsibility of the general classroom teacher. Various methods can be put in place to support the teacher—collaboration with special education and other resource personnel, a paraeducator for in-class assistance, or part-time resource room assistance for the students.

Second, as we explained in Chapter 1, there is much overlap among these categories. The way these students learn, their manifested behaviours, and teachers' strategies and adaptations are similar. The generic adaptations found in each chapter's box on creating accessible classrooms should therefore be seen as useful for all these children and youth.

This section opens with Chapter 4 on speech and language problems. Language, behaviour, and social skills overlap in early development, each domain contributing to emergent competence in the others (Guralnick & Neville, 1997). And while speech and language problems are a separate category of exceptionality, they also cut across other areas. Many, if not most, children with other disabling conditions also manifest speech and language problems that further hinder their optimal development. At least 60 percent of young children with developmental delays and disabilities have delayed development in the area of language and communication (U.S. Department of Education, 1987). Children with hearing impairments, learning disabilities, intellectual disabilities, and severe emotional disturbance typically display speech and language problems.

If teachers are to intervene successfully with students who show speech and language disorders as primary disabilities, or with the larger number of students who show disorders as secondary conditions, they need a comprehensive footing. This includes an understanding of language development, the content of the language arts curriculum, and the use of augmentative and alternative communication systems. Therefore, it makes sense to understand normal speech and language development and the associated disorders before approaching other categories of exceptionality.

Chapter 5 examines the particular developmental consequences and the needs of students with learning disabilities. The common thread is the inability of these students to learn adequately in regular classrooms under traditional teaching approaches and methods. Youngsters who are learning disabled are sound in mind and body but still cannot seem to get the hang of reading, writing, and arithmetic, and therefore lag noticeably in school.

At the moment, the field concerned with intellectual disabilities is seeing some dramatic changes, brought about chiefly by the completion of the Human Genome Project, provocative genetic discoveries of specific behavioural phenotypes, new ways of conceptualizing disability, and emerging terminology. In Chapter 6 we glance at the full spectrum of intellectual disabilities to assure the continuity of the material; readers will find more explicit information about students with severe and profound disorders in Chapter 15.

Learning Outcomes

This section focuses on students who have mild disabilities in learning. After reading this section, you should be able to

People and Foundations

1. Explain the development and evolution of the fields of learning disabilities and intellectual disabilities.
2. Detail the contributions of pioneers in special education, particularly Jean Marc Itard, Samuel Kirk, and Alfred Strauss.
3. Appreciate the rapid changes in constructions of disability, new etiologies, and new terminology in the various areas.

Issues

4. Recognize the relationship between mild forms of disability, delineate the overlap between the categories, and explain the implications for classroom intervention.
5. Understand how issues of definition, classification, and prevalence impact on the fields concerned with mild disabilities.

Knowledge

6. Understand how concepts of language and its development in young children have evolved, as well as the major elements of language, its stages, the process of language acquisition and development in normally developing students, and the impact of delayed or deviant language and speech disorders.

7. Detail the major types of speech and language disorders, their developmental consequences, and the influence the various disorders have on children's behaviour and learning.

8. Understand the definitions of the different types of exceptionalities included in this section, the classification system employed in each area, the effects of the rapidly changing systems, etiological considerations, and developmental consequences.

9. Recognize the varied types of assessment procedures and tools that are used to determine status in cognition, language, and learning.

Skills

10. Understand the many forms of intervention in settings, approaches, and techniques used with students who have mild disabilities in learning.

11. Be aware of a sampling of accommodations, adaptations, and modifications that teachers can apply to assist learners with special needs and be able to apply adaptations to improve student functioning in memory, organization, attention, and academic achievement.

CHAPTER 4

CHILDREN WITH SPEECH AND LANGUAGE DIFFERENCES

INTRODUCTION

Of all the achievements of early childhood, the acquisition and development of speech and language is one of the most remarkable. Tiny infants, initially able to produce only vegetative sounds and reflexive cries, listen and respond to the language in their environments. Babies do not merely listen passively to the language around them; like miniature linguists, they recreate for themselves the language of their culture. Through exposure and experience, they quite unconsciously learn to produce an infinite variety of intelligible utterances.

The first three years of life are critical: about twice as much language growth occurs between the first and third years as between the third and fifth (Cratty, 1986). Without formal instruction, most children in those first three years develop a lexicon of spoken words and learn to form simple multilevel utterances.

The language explosion that occurs in the early years is most apparent in the growth of vocabulary—from about 110 words at 18 months to 300 words at age 2, to about 540 at 30 months (Fenson, Dale, Reznick, Bates, Thal, & Pethick, 1994). As children develop speech and language, they are also developing **communicative competence**—they know how to interact, how to communicate appropriately in various situations, and how to make sense of what others say and do in communicative interactions.

What happens in the early stages of acquisition of speech and language is critical: it reflects many aspects of development, is closely tied to cognitive development and self-concept, and affects a child's performance in the classroom later on. Problems can impair a child's functioning in play and with peers and can result in the development of secondary behavioural problems.

A basic understanding of the normal development of language and speech underlies an appreciation of the nature of communication disorders. We therefore begin this chapter with a brief overview of how speech and language is acquired and develops in young children.

OVERVIEW OF SPEECH AND LANGUAGE

In all the enormous repertoire of human skills and abilities, communication is one of the most critical tools. **Communication** may be seen as the process of exchanging information and ideas between participants. All living things communicate in some way and, in this sense, communication includes the entire spectrum of acts performed by living creatures in order to pass on and respond to messages. *Language* and *speech* are the typically human activities in communication.

Language is a system of symbols organized into conventional patterns to communicate meaning. **Speech** is essentially a mechanical production of language. Other methods than speech may be appropriately employed to express language—sign language and writing, for example. However, while it is possible to possess language and lack the ability to speak, it is not possible to have speech without language.

A number of important points characterize speech and language development. First, there are distinct stages. These should not be viewed as a set of discrete milestones through which children pass on the way to mastering adult communication. Rather, as language learning begins in infancy and continues throughout life, formal language use is one point on a continuum of communication behaviour that begins in non-verbal social exchanges during infancy and extends through the use of written language.

Another important aspect of language is the creativity involved. Children are not passive organisms into which language is poured; rather, they are catalytic agents. In other words, it is not so much that language develops, but that it is acquired. It is clear quite early that children do not put words together only if they have heard those words in combination before; instead, they produce utterances they have never heard. As children develop vocabulary and internalize a knowledge of the rules of their native language, they can potentially create an infinite number of unique utterances.

Finally, all children acquiring language do so in essentially the same order. In English, children learn *in* and *on* before other prepositions such as *under*, and they learn the progressive form using *-ing* before other verb endings such as *-ed*. After they learn regular plurals and past tenses, as in *horses* and *skated*, they create some forms of their own, like *mouses* and *eated* (Gleason, 1985).

Elements of Language

Language consists of interrelated and intertwined components, all of which must be present or developing for appropriate usage. Children must simultaneously learn the sound structure of the language (the *phonology*), the rules that govern the ordering of words within sentences (the *syntax* or *grammar*), and the meaning of words and phrases (*semantics*). If their usage is to attain appropriate meaning, children must employ *pragmatics*—the use of language in its social context.

Syntax is the network of organizational principles underlying linguistic expression. Syntactic rules govern what we call the grammar of language, which formalizes the conventions of language so that communication is consistent throughout a certain society. **Grammar** refers to the rules and to the word choices. The child who says, "I ain't gunna do it,"

communicative competence

communication

language

speech

syntax

grammar

has fine grammar but questionable word choice, whereas the child who talks about the "Ball, big red here" has incorrect grammar.

semantics

Semantics is concerned specifically with meaning. The acquisition of words, their meanings, and the links between them does not usually happen at once. Words are clearly comprehended before they are spoken, and the number of words comprehended continues to be greater all through life. Comprehension of the first word is about 3 months ahead of its production. Moreover, children learn to produce 50 words before they string them together into sentences. Vocabulary growth begins slowly, but there is a great spurt in word learning between 24 and 30 months (Reich, 1986).

morphology

Morphology is the system of word building in the language. *Morphemes* may be words or significant elements, such as prefixes and suffixes, called *bound morphemes*.

phonology

Phonology is the sound system of language; the smallest sound units are called *phonemes*. Phonology encompasses the rules for using the sounds of language, for combining phonemes in particular ways to form identifiable language units such as the /s/ that we add to make words plural. **Phonetics** is the description of the speech sounds of a language. There are only 26 letters—vowels and consonants—in the English alphabet, but they are pronounced in different ways. People who speak American or Canadian English use and recognize 44 phoneme combinations that produce every English word. Other languages use and recognize different sounds.

phonetics

pragmatics

Pragmatics is concerned with the social use of language. Pragmatics develops from the early stages as children use their language to query, request, deny, and declare. How they use language—the content of their interactions and the role of context in communicative interactions—changes with the interaction and the situation. Children can talk baby talk to infants, tell jokes and riddles, be rude to their friends and (usually) polite to their teachers and parents.

The Speech Mechanism

The act of speech is enormously complicated. English speakers talk at an average rate of 150 words per minute. A speaker produces 14 phonemes per second, using about 100 muscles that require 100 motor units apiece (Shames & Wiig, 1990).

The anatomical structures involved in the comprehension and production of language and speech include the nervous system, the respiratory system, the oral part of the digestive tract, and the auditory sense receptors. These physical structures function in a highly organized and integrated fashion. Each part is synchronized with others to produce a meaningful sequence of accurate speech sounds while maintaining proper levels of loudness and pitch and a pleasing voice quality.

In general terms, speech is produced in an airstream that is shaped and resonated by the lips, tongue, teeth, jaw, nasal cavity, larynx, and pharynx. Figure 4-1 shows the organs and musculature of speech.

Speech and Language Development

Language acquisition overlaps and relies upon social and cognitive growth. These aspects of development are closely intertwined, and really cannot be considered separately. Further, it is extremely difficult to separate speech and language development in the early years because language usage is expressed so cogently in speech forms in most children.

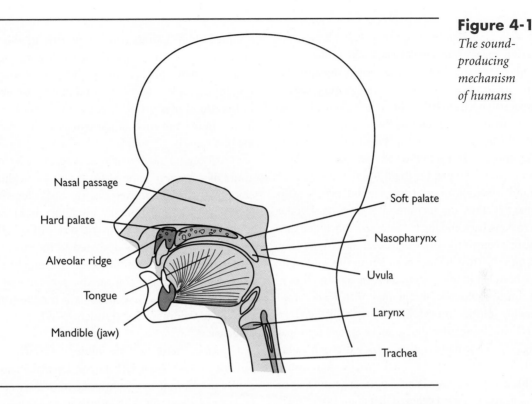

Figure 4-1
The sound-producing mechanism of humans

We can say that language is first and foremost a social behaviour. At the outset, the quality of adult-child interactions is the single most important influence on a child's language development. Adult–child communicative interaction is sometimes called *motherese*. When interacting with infants, both adults and children tend to use motherese (register changes)—a higher pitch, exaggerated intonation, clear enunciation, a slower rate with more pauses between utterances, simplified speech sounds, repeated syllables, and simplified syntax.

How important is adult–child interaction in the early months? One report (Begley, 1996) notes that infants whose mothers spoke to them a lot knew 131 more words at 20 months than babies of more taciturn, or less involved mothers. At 24 months, the gap widened to 295 words. When there is minimal or no social interaction, language acquisition will be severely hindered. Quite famous in the history of special education are Victor and his teacher, Jean Marc Itard. Their story, recounted in Case Study 4-1, illustrates what happens when a child is deprived of early stimulation.

CASE STUDY

Victor

Jean Marc Gaspard Itard (1755–1838), a French physician, is remembered for his intervention with the so-called wild boy of Aveyron. Caught in the woods, the boy was reported to have been raised by wolves. When the lad finally reached Paris on Bastille Day, 1800, he was placed in the school for the deaf because of his muteness. Itard named him Victor.

Victor was stunted in growth, with a light complexion and scarred, pockmarked skin, probably the result of the smallpox he had caught in captivity. A huge scar ran across his larynx, suggesting that his throat had been cut before he was abandoned in the forest. Instead of resembling Rousseau's "noble savage," the boy was dirty, incapable of focusing attention, and insensitive to the basic sensations of heat and cold. He lapped his food, uttered inarticulate sounds, fixated on empty space, bit people who came too close, and spent most of his time sleeping or rocking back and forth. Observers concluded that Victor's constitution was defective; the boy was not an idiot because he had been left in the wilds, but had been left in the wilds because he was an idiot.

Itard could not accept that Victor was irreversibly idiotic. Instead, he believed that the child was mentally arrested due to social and educational neglect; Victor had acquired idiocy through isolation, suffering a sort of mental atrophy from disuse of his senses. Despite Victor's appearance and lack of responsiveness, Itard believed that appropriate environmental conditions could humanize the boy and decided to try to educate him rather than send him to a lunatic hospital.

Itard began his work with little concept of the complexities involved in working with a severely disabled child. Using crude diagnostic methods, he determined that Victor's sense organs were intact, though "dull" or insensitive. Victor would not, for example, respond to loud noises, not even to the sound of a pistol shot. On the other hand, he would react to such subtle signals as the cracking of a walnut.

Itard used a variety of means to make Victor aware of sensation—hot baths, massages, tickling, emotional excitement, even electric shock. Together with sensory stimulation and discipline, Itard presented Victor with a systematic series of specific sense training activities designed to improve his visual, auditory, and motor skills. He taught the activities in order and at a variable rate tailored to fit Victor's progress. Especially, Itard tried to teach the boy to communicate through speech and sign language.

In time, Victor became moderately socialized but not, as Itard had naively hoped, normal. Victor's ability to communicate continued to increase, and he learned the basic skills of eating and dressing. Nevertheless, after five years, Itard concluded that his work had been a failure and left Victor in the care of a friendly housekeeper. It is said that Victor roamed the empty halls of the school until he died at about the age of 40.

Speech development begins with the first sound following the birth cry. Newborns have a limited range of vocalizations. They cry, burp, cough, and make a few other sounds. For the later development of language, *cooing*—the production of clear vowels, often in isolation— is the most important. By their eighth week, infants can usually produce a variety of these vowel sounds.

Because they require finer motor control of the tongue and lips, consonant sounds are more difficult to produce than vowel sounds. But as infants approach the six-month mark, the nature of cooing changes and consonant-vowel patterns begin to appear.

babbling

This incorporation of vowel and consonant sounds is known as **babbling**—random sound play of almost infinite variety. Babbling is a fairly universal response during infancy and does not seem to require exposure to language or other environmental auditory input. Even infants who are deaf babble, although they do not do so in the same way; their babbling is substantially delayed and sounds usually stop around one year of age (Pettito & Marenette, 1991). The exceptions to the universal nature of babbling behaviour are children who are autistic or neurologically damaged; they may not babble at all.

Early stimulation from parents and siblings aids in young children's language acquisition.

At the same time that infants begin to babble, they also show the first indications of comprehension. Babies at about six months of age begin to associate certain sounds with people, events, and objects in the environment. Their signals also take on a relatively consistent form, produced in the expectation that they will promote a consistent response from their parents and others.

There is considerable controversy over the relationship between babbling and later speech. Most researchers now believe that babbling and early speech are one continuous phenomenon, and that the babbling stage is a period of "tuning up" and establishing the necessary integrations between hearing/listening and sound production. Babbling also helps to develop the musculature of the lips and the mouth necessary for the later articulation of speech sounds. Further, children begin to babble the sounds unique to their own language. By six months of age, infants in English-speaking homes have different auditory maps than do those in Swedish-speaking homes (Begley, 1996).

Once infants are using consonants in their babbling, they attempt to imitate adult sounds. At about 8 months of age, they begin to use **echolalic speech**—speech that is an immediate imitation of that of some other speaker. Soon infants move into the jargon stage; they begin to imitate adults consistently and are able to reproduce the intonation patterns or melodies of the language they hear. By 10 or 11 months, children are babbling in sentences, combining several incomprehensible "words" and uttering them with correct inflections (Reich, 1986).

echolalic speech

At around 1 year of age, two new developments occur—first words and an increased ability to discern meaning from contextual as well as voice clues. First words emerge when an infant's motor system for speech production has become coordinated with breath control and the movements of lips and tongue. The age for first words ranges from 9 to 19 months for normal children. As children move into using single words, there is a corresponding decrease in babbling. Children also begin to comprehend words; they learn to follow simple directions and associate many environmental clues with speech that they have heard and with gestures.

holophrasic speech

Toddlers' first single-word utterances are called **holophrasic speech** because a single word is used to express a more complex idea. Single words are used for naming favourite toys or foods, family members, or pets, and to make requests, comments, and inquiries. Children also incorporate single-word approximations of frequently used adult phrases such as "all gone" or "bad boy." Although the first words may differ markedly from adult pronunciation, they are likely to be simplifications of adult usage involving the omission of final consonants, the reduction of consonant clusters, the omission of unstressed syllables, or the reduplication of syllables (Lindfors, 1987).

Several weeks after the first word, vocabulary begins to grow quite rapidly as new words are learned daily. Children learn to produce about 50 words before they string them together. Between 18 and 24 months of age, they begin to combine words. These early phrases (presentences) are the precursors of true sentences. For example, the child may say phrases such as "Daddy no," "Car now," or "No more milk." Children show a wide range of variation in the number of presentences they use. Some children use only a few; others as many as 1000.

telegraphic speech

The sentence, the landmark in language acquisition, emerges between about 19 and 23 months. The first true sentences used by small children are described as **telegraphic speech** because they resemble a telegram in that only the essential aspects of the message are included. In these utterances, children begin to use syntax and morphology; inflections to signify plurality; possession; verb tense and subject–verb agreement; and comparative and superlative forms of adjectives. Children at this stage also use function words such as *in* and *on*, and the articles *a*, *an*, and *the*.

At first, young children tend to regularize the language because they have not yet learned the exceptions. A small child is likely to say, "He runned," or "He hurt his self." As well, small children often reach beyond the borders of word meaning and overextend their word usage, as in the little boy who calls every animal a doggie.

By the time they are using simple sentences at about 2 years of age, children are about 70 to 80 percent intelligible in their speech. Yet the full development of all of the sounds of English is a slow process. It is not until they are about 8 years old that children are able to produce all the speech sounds: vowels, consonants, diphthongs, and blends. The last English sound that most children acquire is the /zh/, as in *leisure* and *measure*.

By 3 years of age, children are capable of understanding three quarters of the language that is the basis for all future understanding (Mellon, 2000). Most children demonstrate the construction of simple affirmative-declarative sentences. They put together a noun phrase for a subject and a verb phrase for a predicate. As syntax develops, the child learns how to change word order and add and replace words to express more complex grammatical relationships. These changes are called *transformations*; as syntax becomes more complex, many transformations are used within the same utterances.

Four-year-old children have mastered enough syntax, semantics, and pragmatics to be considered proficient language users (Mellon, 2000). They use the basic structures of their language and have developed an array of conversational skills that enable them to engage in extensive social and play interactions with their peers and others in the environment. They gain greater control over the speech mechanisms so that speech is now more than 90 percent intelligible. By the time they arrive at school at about 5 or 6 years of age, children are sophisticated language users with a mastery over language, developing metalinguistic skills, and a firm linguistic base on which teachers can formally build reading and writing.

When children enter grade 1, they bring with them an impressive store of background knowledge and a vocabulary of between 6000 and 14 000 words with which to talk about their experiences (Chall, Jacobs, & Baldwin, 1990). Children now use a variety of language functions, a greater variety of discourse styles and organization, more abstract vocabulary, and more complex syntax. The developmental emphasis moves from semantics and syntax to pragmatics and **metalinguistics** (the ability to reflect on all the aspects of language). Children learn to recognize **instructional discourse**—the language that gives them information about the curriculum and feedback on their efforts in mastering it.

During middle childhood, every subsystem of language improves. Children begin to use a number of complex grammatical forms that did not appear in their earlier speech, and correct many of their syntactical errors. They use past participles, such as *eaten*, and perfect tense, such as *has been*, personal pronouns, and passive voice. They develop wider metalinguistic skills: nine-year-olds are more likely than five-year-olds to recognize grammatical errors in sentences and to be able to correct them. They also use the prepositions *as*, *if*, *so*, and *because* more accurately than earlier, although full development does not occur until later.

An eleven-year-old-child has a vocabulary of about 20 000 words. Conjunctions such as *although* don't come until the late elementary years or early adolescence. There are further major developments in adolescence, such as the ability to understand abstractions as in metaphors and similes.

Obviously, language development is a lifelong process. It will continue to develop in conjunction with expanding cognitive skills and learning. But the critical syntactic, morphological, and phonological bases are in place by school age and later development is in metalinguistics, semantics, and pragmatics.

metalinguistics

instructional discourse

SPEECH AND LANGUAGE DIFFERENCES

Learning to communicate and understand the communication of others is one of the biggest challenges young children face. It is little surprise, then, that delays and disorders in speech and language are the most common and varied disabilities that teachers, especially those involved with young children, will encounter.

For many school-aged children, inferior communication skills inhibit learning and contribute to feelings of failure. We can see this in the signs and effects of communication disorders presented in Table 4-1 on the next page. The problems are also evident in Ashley, the child discussed in the Case Study on the next page. Rather than talking in school, Ashley is resorting to shrugs and gestures. His academic work is suffering and his social interactions are becoming more negative.

Defining, classifying, and estimating the prevalence of communication disorders and the two sub-categories of speech and language problems is challenging. Within the generic

Table 4-1 Signs and effects of communication disorders

Disorder	Signs	Effects
Language delay	More than six months behind norm in reaching language milestones	Slower in all the elements of language acquisition and usage
Language disorders	May show impaired comprehension and poor verbal expression	Failure to understand instructions; withdrawal from group situations
Aphasia	Impaired reception or production of oral language	Failure to understand speech or to produce meaningful sentences
Apraxia	Inability to sequence the muscle movements needed for speech	Failure to produce meaningful speech
Articulation disorders	Abnormal production of speech sounds; speech not typical of chronological age	May be ridiculed by peers; may have decoding and comprehension problems with respect to specific words
Dysfluency	Impaired fluency and rhythm	Peer ridicule, oral difficulties
Voice disorders	Abnormal vocal quality, pitch, loudness, or duration	Self-confidence may suffer; withdrawal
Orofacial defects	Variety of clefts, such as cleft lip or cleft palate	May have problems in feeding, speech, or respiration
Dysarthria	Paralysis of the muscles associated with speech	Distorted speech

CASE STUDY

Ashley

Ashley is seven-and-a-half years old and in a grade 2 class in a large school in Langley, a community just east of Vancouver in British Columbia. Ashley is small for his age and lags behind in academic work. Although the teacher describes him as a "dear child," she is increasingly frustrated with Ashley's lack of progress and his diminishing motivation.

Before referring Ashley for an assessment, the classroom teacher undertook some pre-referral interventions that included observations of his behaviour, interactions with peers, and on-task behaviour in the classroom. She also used some broad measures of reading achievement, particularly vocabulary and comprehension. Instructionally, she tried a more structured approach to beginning reading, stressing phonological awareness activities.

Little improvement was seen, and in her referral for a full assessment the teacher noted that Ashley's reading was poor, showing a marked academic delay of about a year. Writing and spelling also lagged badly. Math performance was at grade level or slightly below. Of all the areas that worried the teacher, oral language performance topped the list. Very often, Ashley's speech was difficult to understand, particularly when he was nervous, in a hurry, or attempting to read aloud. But Ashley did not talk a lot. The teacher observed that he often refused to speak, balked at reading orally, and would not join in during the morning opening exercises in songs, chants, or conversations. He answered questions with a shrug or a frown, and increasingly used gestures to express his wants.

The teacher tried to identify the mispronunciations in Ashley's speech. He appeared to be missing or substituting a number of consonant sounds. For example, a sentence such as "The little child sat under a tree," sounded to the teacher as "Ta wittle kild at una ta ree." Other children in the class were amused by Ashley's speech and called him Baby or other names.

At a meeting with the mother, the teacher became aware of Ashley's growing dislike of school. He complained at home that the work was too hard, that the teacher asked him too many questions, and that the other children did not like him. "They say I talk like a baby," he confided to his mother. "They laugh at me and call me names."

classification of *communication disorders*, we find *speech disorders* (as in Ashley's case), *language delays and disorders*, and *problems subsequent to hearing loss*.

Speech problems include delayed onset of speech, speech usage below age-level expectations, oddities in articulation, peculiar usage of grammar, stuttering, unusual intonations or voice quality, paucity of speech, inability to recall familiar words, poor self-expression, or total absence of speech. Language disorders include delayed language, different language, deviant language, or even no language. Typically, language disorders are more complex in identification, diagnosis, and remediation than speech problems. Hearing impairments, as we discuss in Chapter 10, are the most complex. Figure 4-2 on the next page shows the various problems under the communication disorders umbrella.

The overlap between speech and language is considerable. For clarity, however, we describe speech and language disorders separately.

Definitions of Language Problems

Language problems refer to a range of difficulties with the linguistic code, or with the rules for linking the symbols and the symbol sequences. When language problems occur as the sole disability, we find *language delays* and *language disorders* existing in the face of otherwise normal development.

Children who demonstrate significant lags but whose language is still progressing according to the stages of normal language development are said to have **language delays**. **Language disorders** are more complex than language delays. As defined by the American Speech-Language-Hearing Association (1982).

language delays

language disorders

> language disorders refer to impairment or deviant development of comprehension or of the use of a spoken, written, or other symbol system. These disorders may involve form (phonological, morphological, and syntactical elements), content (semantics), function (pragmatics) or any combination of these.

Figure 4-2

Classification of communication disorders

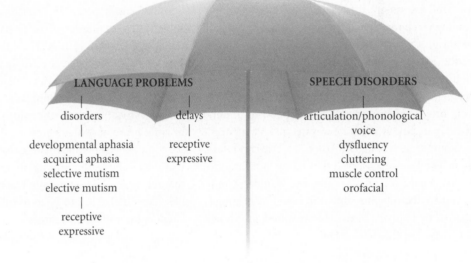

LANGUAGE PROBLEMS

disorders   delays

developmental aphasia
acquired aphasia
selective mutism
elective mutism

receptive
expressive

receptive
expressive

SPEECH DISORDERS

articulation/phonological
voice
dysfluency
cluttering
muscle control
orofacial

Classification of Language Differences

Language problems relate to disorders in the recognition and understanding of spoken language or in the ability to formulate well-organized grammatical sentences. Depending on the type, intensity, and duration of the difficulties, children may be characterized as having delayed or disordered language.

A further distinction is between receptive and expressive problems. **Receptive disorders** are those that interfere with the comprehension of spoken language; the more common **expressive disorders** are those that affect the formulation of grammatical utterances. Language disorders in children frequently combine both receptive and expressive problems. They range in severity from mild language learning difficulties to profoundly debilitating disorders.

receptive disorders

expressive disorders

Delayed Language Development

A child with delayed language development learns language in an orderly progression but more slowly and less proficiently than normal-aged peers. Children with language delays characteristically use language infrequently; by the time they reach preschool age, they talk approximately half as much as their peers and are much less responsive to inquiries from teachers and peers (McCabe, Jenkins, Mills, Dale, Cole, & Pepler, 1996).

Minor delays in language development may be caused by generalized immaturity rather than a pervasive language problem. Clinicians sometimes use the "rule of six" in defining language delays; that is, if a child's language development lags six months behind what is considered to be normal, the child is said to have a delay.

Children with minor speech and language disorders can often receive adequate assistance within the school from a special education teacher or speech-and-language clinician.

Many young children who show minor delays catch up with their peers by the time they are five or six. Others may not close the gap in functioning.

Language Disorders

Children who are language disordered show a developmental language difficulty that affects most or all aspects of expressive and receptive language. Some of these children meet such problems in developing language in a normal progression that they may never attain adult levels; others demonstrate bizarre language behaviour. The great majority of children meet difficulties with acquisition such that they require structured and systematic intervention. Another group shows deviant language secondary to other disabling conditions.

Aphasia

Of the many factors accounting for language problems, the most prominent are brain dysfunction and psychological problems. Neurological (brain) dysfunction underlies the most severe types of speech and language disorders. It follows that one of the most serious neurological language disorders is **aphasia**, a condition in which a child's primary impairment is the inability to communicate effectively with verbal language because of comprehension and/or production difficulties. Aphasia may be developmental (often referred to as *dysphasia*) or acquired.

aphasia

Children with developmental aphasia show severe delays in the development of receptive and expressive language but do not suffer from any apparent additional disabling conditions. *Acquired aphasia* refers to conditions (trauma) that occur after language has been developed. It is a loss in linguistic ability that usually results from brain damage arising from serious illness, trauma to the head, or stroke. Verbal output and understanding are diminished but not always altogether absent. Generally, children under 8 years of age make excellent recoveries from acquired aphasia (Zemlin, 1990; see also Chapter 13 on Traumatic Brain Injury).

Aphasia is also classified as receptive or expressive. *Receptive aphasia* is the inability to understand speech. *Expressive aphasia* manifests itself as trouble remembering words (**dysnomia**), blocking on a word, and hesitating often when speaking. *Severe global aphasia* means that both expressive and receptive aphasia are present to a severe degree, often associated with additional perceptual problems, such as with sight or hearing.

dysnomia

Mutism

aphonia

The condition where there is no voice is known as **aphonia**. This is different from *mutism*, the total absence of speech. Mutism is a rare condition, related to severe emotional, neurological, or sensory deficit.

elective mutism

The term **elective mutism** describes emotionally disturbed children who do not speak or speak only in certain circumstances. Elective mutism may be associated with a traumatic event and is always symptomatic of a deep disturbance of psychological functioning.

selective mutism

Selective mutism is different in intensity. The condition is seen in children who generally have normal language development yet talk to only a small group of relatives or peers (Powell & Dalley, 1995). DSM-IV (APA, 2000) classifies selective mutism as an anxiety-based disorder. It accounts for less than 1 percent of all mental health referrals. It is one of the few childhood disorders that is more common in girls than boys. It may be a variant of school phobia (see Chapter 7).

The failure to speak in certain social situations is not due to lack of knowledge of or comfort with spoken language, as the majority of children who show selective mutism speak at home with family members (Kristensen, 2001). However, in a study using a Canadian sample (Cunningham, 2004) the results indicated that children with selective mutism were less likely to join groups, introduce themselves, start conversations, or invite friends to their houses.

Prevalence of Language Problems

Questions about the prevalence of language delays and disorders are difficult. This is because

- Researchers disagree on definitional and classification systems. Many types of language disorders remain ambiguous and controversial; a consensus has not been reached about the patterns of subtypes of language impairments or the criteria for their classification.

- Varied terms are used to describe language disorders. These include *aphasia*, *dysphasia*, *communicatively impaired*, and *language learning disabled*. Some clinicians prefer the terms *aphasia* or *dysphasia* because they suggest fairly specific conditions; others opt for the general term *language disabled*.

- Surveys of language problems are often based on interviews of questionable validity, and there is likely a tendency to under-report the presence of communication disorders. In fact, Ripley and Yuill (2005) warn that the number of children who actually have speech and language impairments may be seriously underestimated.

- Children in other categories of exceptionality often have language problems. For example, students who are learning disabled more often than not demonstrate deviations or delays in language; children who are intellectually disabled do not develop language commensurate with their intellectual ability. Language problems are the chief difficulty of children who are hearing impaired; communication problems are the hallmark of autism spectrum disorders.
- Estimates combine speech problems with language difficulties.

The best current estimates of combined speech and language impairments set the rate at 7 to 10 percent of children (Lindsay & Dockrell, 2000). When language disorders alone are considered, they affect about 2 to 3 percent of preschoolers and 1 percent of the school-aged population (Matthews & Frattali, 1994). Of all children with language disabilities, about two-thirds are boys (Silva, 1980). As well, there is an increase in communication disorders in people over the age of 40 as a result of stroke and other conditions.

Etiology of Language Problems

As mentioned, damage to the speech/language centres of the brain can lead to aphasia or generalized communication disorders with varying characteristics depending on the site of the lesion. Head injuries, especially from motor vehicle accidents, and diseases such as encephalitis, are the most common causes of aphasia in children, with stroke the most common cause in adults (Holland, Swindell, & Ruinmuth, 1990).

Disruptions in early social interactions may contribute to the particular difficulties experienced by some children. That is, language delays or disorders may be exacerbated by the child's interactions with the family. Children who are neglected, for example, show delays in language development. We saw this in Victor's Case Study on pages 99 and 100. Parents also engage in fewer play and language activities with children who have language delays or disorders, unwittingly contributing to them. For example, studies have found that mothers of three-month-old infants with minor facial anomalies (cleft lip and palate) were less active during interactions with their infants than mothers of normal infants (Barden, Ford, Jensen, Rogers-Salyer, & Salyer, 1989). Other research indicates that in social interactions with their mothers, infants with Down syndrome show atypical interactive behaviours when compared with normal infants matched for mental age (Coggins & Morrison, 1981). As well, adults tend to speak less *to* non-verbal or low-verbal children but to talk more *for* them.

DEFINITIONS OF SPEECH PROBLEMS

Speech disorders are problems encountered in the oral production of language. Van Riper and Emerick (1990) observe that "Speech is abnormal when it deviates so far from the speech of other people that it calls attention to itself, interferes with communication, or causes the speaker or his listeners to be distressed" (p. 34).

speech disorders

Speech disorders should not be confused with the speech errors that all young children make when learning to talk. In small children, mispronunciations and dysfluencies are common; children are about 8 years old before they are relatively stable in the sounds of the

English language. Even then, about 10 percent of 8-year-old children still have some trouble with /s/, /z/, /v/, /th/, and /zh/ (Rathus, 1988).

Mispronunciations and dysfluencies become disorders only when they persist as characteristics in the speech of children who should have acquired certain sounds. We would worry more, for example, about the seven-year-old who talks about his "Wittle wellow wabbit" than about the child of the same age who could not get her tongue around the /zh/ sound in *leisure* and *measure*.

Classification of Speech Disorders

There are many ways to classify speech disorders. For the sake of clarity and simplicity, we focus on specific major areas—phonological and articulation problems; voice disorders; problems with speech flow (dysfluency); problems associated with muscle control; and orofacial defects.

Articulation Disorders

Therapists talk about phonological difficulties and articulation disorders. The differences are subtle, related to use and ability.

phonological difficulties

Phonological difficulties are related to use; they occur when a child has mastered a sound and pronounces it correctly in some contexts but not in others. Children with phonological impairments are aware of the effect of their errors on a listener's comprehension and will make adjustments to enhance verbal comprehension (Owens, 1991).

articulation problems

Articulation problems concern ability. With an articulation disorder, a child cannot actually make or produce a sound. Speech sounds are incorrect because of changes in the placement and manner of articulators. With a lisp, for example, the child's tongue is misplaced and says /th/ instead of /s/.

Some articulation errors result from problems such as cleft palate, but in the large majority of cases the disorders appear to result simply from deficiencies in learning. When the child was first learning speech, for example, there may have been inadequate coordination of oral and facial muscles, which eventually became habitual.

Articulation disorders are characterized by omissions, substitutions, distortions, and additions of speech sounds that may occur in the initial, medial, or final position in a word. The most commonly misarticulated sounds are /s/, /z/, voiceless /th/ as in *bath*, /r/, /l/, /sh/, and /j/ as in *judge* (Gearheart, Mullen, & Gearheart, 1993).

Omission errors, in which one or more sounds are left out of words, occur most frequently with blended sounds, such as /bl/, /pl/, /pr/, /st/, /dr/, and /tr/. When words begin with a blend, children may drop one sound so that *smell* becomes *mell, break* is *reak,* play is *pay,* and school is *kool.*

Substitutions of speech sounds occur when one phoneme is replaced by another: /b/ for /v/, /w/ for /r/, or /w/ for /l/, or as in *thunshine* for *sunshine* or *bake* for *cake.* A lisp is a substitution where /th/ is used for /s/ or /z/. Some children may substitute sounds in some words but not others. A child may be able to say the word *yes* correctly, but substitute /l/ for /y/ in the word *yellow.*

Distortions involve deviations from normal speech sounds and are often caused by placing the tongue or lips in the wrong position for the production of a particular sound, as *shoup* for *soup* or *ideer* for *idea*. *Addition of sounds* refers to the adding of a sound to a word. The extra sounds are usually added between blended sounds, such as *terain* for *train* or as the unstressed /u/ after the final consonant so that *safety* become *safe-u-ty* (see Case & Taylor, 2005).

Voice Disorders

Voice disorders are probably the least understood of all the various communication problems. In general, a voice that lacks power, is unpleasant, or abuses the vocal mechanism is likely to be considered defective.

Voice disorders include hoarseness (too nasal or rough a voice), breathiness, loudness (too loud or too soft), pitch (too high or too low), and sudden breaks in pitch. They are frequently combined with other speech problems to form a complex communication disorder. Deviations may impair both speaking and singing.

The most common deviations in pitch are levels that are too high or low and levels that are monotonous with little variation of pitch. Children who do not speak loudly enough for their needs may suffer from hearing loss, an organic disorder, or reticence about speaking. Some children do not know how to use a "big" voice without abusing the vocal mechanism (Moore, 1986).

In some people, pitch problems are caused by too small a larynx (too high a pitch) or too large a larynx (too low). Some may result from overall slow maturation. In children, most voice disorders are functional, related to poor learning of voice control. Children who scream or talk loudly are in danger of abusing their vocal cords. Vocal abuse can lead to vocal nodules or polyps, which may have to be removed surgically.

The child who "talks through the nose" has hypernasal speech. This may result from a cleft palate, or from partial paralysis of the soft palate rendering the necessary closure of the nasal passages impossible.

Dysfluency

Fluency is the smoothness with which sounds, syllables, words, and phrases flow together; the opposite, **dysfluency** (speech flow disorder) describes conditions in which the flow of speech is interrupted with blocking, repetitions, or prolongations of sounds, words, phrases, or syllables.

dysfluency

Stuttering, the major type of dysfluency, affects approximately 1 percent of the entire population. Two to ten times more males than females stutter. As it relates to school-aged children, stuttering affects about 5 percent during language development (Guitar, 1998), usually beginning between the ages of 2 and 5. This number may be low. It is estimated that teachers routinely identify only about one-half of the children who stutter in their classrooms because children hide the problem (see Williams, 1999).

stuttering

The condition is not related to social class or cognitive functioning; stuttering is found among all ethnic and socio-economic groups. Many famous people were stutterers, including Aesop, Aristotle, Demosthenes, Charles I, Winston Churchill, Charles Darwin, and George VI.

As a serious communication problem, stuttering is both complicated and multidimensional. In terms of severity, it should be seen on a continuum. At one end is normal dysfluency, which is not stuttering but a part of speech development in young children at about three years of age. Next on the continuum is *primary stuttering*, which is characterized by breaks in speech caused by repetitions of syllables and sounds, and sometimes prolongations, but is not usually accompanied by physical signs. The final stage is *secondary stuttering*, which is terse, non-fluent speech in which the rate and rhythm are severely affected. Secondary stutterers show symptoms such as eye blinking, head jerking, facial grimaces and tension, other types of body distortions, muscular tension, and forcing when they try to speak. Secondary stuttering is much harder to overcome than primary stuttering.

The earliest age of onset of stuttering is generally around 18 months, just when children begin to speak in short phrases. However, a child may begin to stutter at any time, usually beginning between the ages of 2 and 5 (Williams, 1999). The progression of stuttering is often episodic, with periods of increased fluency (Guitar, 1998). In some cases, stuttering progresses from a sporadic to a chronic problem. In others, it spontaneously disappears by adolescence; a greater number of females than males recover spontaneously. In another group, stuttering disappears only to resurface later. Stuttering often diminishes or disappears under specific conditions, including unison reading, singing, and speaking under noisy conditions (see Williams, 1999).

The likelihood of spontaneous recovery is inversely related to the age of the child. Children who stop stuttering are generally younger than 3 when they begin and usually recover within 12 to 14 months of onset (Curlee & Yairi, 1997; Yairi & Ambrose, 1992). On the other hand, if the problem persists until a child is 4 years old, the stuttering may have progressed beyond the point where there is little likelihood that it will disappear without intervention.

Cluttering

Cluttered speech should not be confused with stuttering. Cluttering involves rapid, jerky, stumbling speech with marked omissions. Speakers may clip off speech sounds, omit sounds, and have rapid-fire bursts of speech. Cluttered speech shows excessive speed combined with disorganized sentence structure and articulation problems. It lacks appropriate phrasing or grouping of words within an utterance and is difficult to understand. In severe cases, the speech is confused, disorganized, and even chaotic (Van Riper & Emerick, 1990).

Muscle Control

dysarthria

Dysarthria refers to a group of speech disorders resulting from disturbed muscular control over the speech mechanisms. The articulation of speech sounds is disturbed when there is a partial or complete paralysis of the muscles associated with speech. When a child with dysarthria tries to talk, consonant sounds are distorted and efforts at speech may not be successful. Indeed, the harder the child tries to speak, the more difficult speech becomes.

apraxia

Apraxia is the inability to program, position, and sequence the muscle movements involved in speech. The child with apraxia can produce the movements involved in articulation, but often fails to combine these movements into meaningful speech.

Orofacial Defects

Clefts are known as *midline defects*. They are only one of the wide variety of craniofacial anomalies. They are also one of the most common and generally least severe.

There are several patterns of clefting, including cleft mandible, double mouth, cleft tongue, cleft uvula, undeveloped tongue, cleft lip, cleft palate, and cleft lip and palate. Clefts vary in severity. A cleft lip can range from a slight notch in the vermilion (the coloured portion of the lip) to a complete separation of the lip extending up and into the nose. When there is a cleft lip, the alveolar ridge (the upper gum ridge) may also be separated. Lip clefts can occur on one or both sides of the lip. Clefts may also be part of a disorder such as Crouzon's disease or Treacher Collins syndrome, both of which are accompanied by facial anomalies.

Clefts occur in approximately 1 in every 750 live births (Moran & Pentz, 1995; Speltz, Endriga, Fisher, & Mason, 1997). Incidence varies by gender and ethnic group, but not by socio-economic status or maternal age. The condition is found more often among Native Americans and Asians; it is less common among Blacks (McWilliams, Morris, & Shelton, 1990). Usually more males than females are affected, except in the rare condition of a cleft palate only, in which case more females are affected.

The palate separates the respiratory and the digestive systems. Many children with clefts are born with a gap in the roof of the mouth (palate), which opens into the nasal cavity. Children with an unrepaired cleft lip/palate have difficulties in the feeding process because of interruptions in the rhythm of feeding, or in mastication, swallowing, choking, and regurgitation. There may be malocclusion (abnormality in the coming together of the teeth). As well, between 25 and 60 percent of children with cleft palates have a degree of hearing loss due to intermittent occurrence of middle-ear disease.

Children with clefts may exhibit delayed language development and are more likely to have language-based learning disabilities (Moran & Pentz, 1995). Delayed articulation is not uncommon because children may have difficulty building and sustaining enough air pressure in the mouth to make consonants such as /p/, /b/, /s/, /z/, and /ch/.

Prevalence of Speech Disorders

As with language problems, reliable figures on the prevalence of speech disorders among children are difficult to obtain. One reason is that the criteria and definitions of communication disorders vary. Another is that prevalence varies according to age. Many speech disorders, such as articulation problems, are due to general immaturity and simply disappear without special intervention.

About 10 to 15 percent of preschool children and about 6 percent of students in elementary and secondary grades have speech problems (Matthews & Frattali, 1994; Williams, 1999). Speech problems are more common among boys than girls, especially in the early grades; this is particularly true in the case of stuttering. Articulation problems are the most usual types of speech problem, accounting for approximately 75 percent of all disorders.

Etiology of Speech Disorders

Structural inadequacies are a major cause of speech disorders in children. Structural problems may be found in the vocal folds (larynx), tongue, teeth, lips, palate, and resonating cavities. Most defects of this type are of a developmental nature, although they can result from physical injury or disease.

Damage to or maldevelopment of the central and/or peripheral nervous system is another major cause of speech disorders. Dysarthria, for example, results from a fundamental disturbance in the movement or motoric function, brought about by damage to the nervous system. Dysarthria is common among children with cerebral palsy: the motor impairment that affects the lips, tongue, jaw, and soft palate hinders the intelligibility of their speech. Inadequacy of the hearing mechanism, causing hearing impairment, is a third major cause of speech disorders.

The precise causes of clefts are confusing. Some result from arrests of midline facial development during the first trimester of pregnancy. Other clefts of the lip and palate seem to have distinct genetic correlates. Still others seem to result from an interaction of genetic and environmental influences. Numerous villains have been suggested, including alcohol, acetylsalicylic acid, certain foods, and an excess or lack of vitamin A.

Stuttering is known to have both biochemical and physiological indicators. There is also clear evidence of genetic transmissions of susceptibility that has been reported since the 1960s. Analysis of pedigrees—family trees—has found that much stuttering is familial (Ambrose, Cox, & Yairi, 1997).

DEVELOPMENTAL CONSEQUENCES OF SPEECH AND LANGUAGE PROBLEMS

All types of speech and language disorders affect the ease with which children communicate with people in their environment. As language is inextricably intertwined with perceiving, remembering, attending, comprehending, and thinking—in short, all of our attempts to make sense of our experiences with the world—children who communicate poorly may be hindered in their academic performance and almost every aspect of functioning. Note that the outcomes for children with simultaneous speech and language impairments are generally worse than for children with only one of the impairments (Yoder, Camarata, & Gardner, 2005).

Cognitive Development

No correlation exists between speech and language disorders and poor cognitive functioning. However, many cognitive abilities are clearly language dependent, and children with language problems tend to be more rigid and literal in their thinking. They lack the flexibility required for pretending, playing word games, laughing at riddles and jokes, and effective social interaction.

Academic Achievement

As one would expect, children with language problems perform poorly in those aspects of learning that rely on language; indeed, competence with language has a direct influence on a child's ability to learn to read and write. Children with disabilities tend to acquire the skills of **emergent literacy**—the reading and writing knowledge and behaviour that precedes conventional literacy—at a rate slower than that of their same-aged peers. Delays are

emergent literacy

particularly prevalent in children with language impairments, either as a primary or a secondary disability (Snow, Burns, & Griffin, 1998).

Children who have difficulty understanding and using language when they are in kindergarten and grade 1 typically have problems learning to read and are likely to be clearly identified as poor readers by grade 3 (see Seidenberg, 1997). On this note, Catts (1993) found that as many as 83 percent of kindergarten children with speech and language delays eventually qualify for remedial reading services. In the later grades, literacy skills suffer. Not only do problems in language acquisition and use invariably produce difficulties in learning to read, but the abstract and symbolic material that becomes important by about grade 4 makes it increasingly difficult for children to cope with academic subjects.

Speech disorders bring their own set of difficulties. For example, students with articulation disorders, particularly those with multiple sound errors, also have difficulties with comprehension, syntax, and vocabulary (Bernthal & Bankston, 1981).

Clefts are not associated with lower cognitive ability. But there are problems related to their associated language deficits, and children who have clefts tend to show poorer self-perception and lower school achievement than peers (Speltz et al., 1997).

Behaviour

Any degree of disturbance in our communication with others in the environment has an impact on social adjustment. Although the link between language deficits and the development of behavioural problems is not well understood, it is known that there is a fairly strong relationship between communication disorders and emotional and behavioural disorders in children and adolescents.

Language problems can have both a direct and indirect impact on behaviour, perhaps blazing a pathway for later behaviour problems. Among children with identified language impairments, prevalence rates for behaviour problems have been reported from 29 to nearly 60 percent. Furthermore, the prevalence of behaviour problems increases over time. Those with pure language deficits, particularly receptive deficits, appear to be at higher risk for antisocial behaviour than those with speech disorders or speech/language disorders (Benner, Nelson, & Epstein, 2002; Nelson, Benner, & Cheney, 2005). As well, Speltz and colleagues (1997) reported on studies indicating that children with cranio-facial anomalies were two to three times more likely than peers to have parent and teacher reports of behavioural problems when they entered school.

Abnormal language development can disrupt the development of behavioural control. Teachers may observe behaviours such as short attention span, excitability, tantrums, and solitary behaviour. When children cannot understand a message or command, they cannot conform; this may then be perceived as a behavioural disorder. Some children find it so difficult to communicate that they become frustrated and depressed. They may withdraw from social contact and talk only when absolutely necessary because of the negative feedback they have received in the past. They use physical means to gain others' attention by relying on gesture and body language—a shake of the head or a shrug. We saw this with Ashley in his Case Study on pages 104 and 105. This tendency of children such as Ashley to respond but not to initiate conversation results in very limited participation in conversational exchanges that might otherwise promote sophisticated language behaviour.

Children who stutter are very aware of listeners' reactions and often feel embarrassed, guilty, frustrated, and angry. They may respond to their difficulties by becoming more anxious, less self-confident, and more socially withdrawn than non-stutterers. Some students become aggressive; others deny they have a problem.

The longer people stutter, the more likely they are to have associated emotional problems. The reactions of others in the environment add to the frustration. One UK study (Hugh-Jones & Smith, 1999) found suggestions that bullying and peer relationships are related to children's dysfluency. In this study, 83 percent of the sample reported being bullied in school. A second UK study (Mooney & Smith, 1995) found that 82 percent of the members of the Association for Stammerers in Great Britain were bullied in their school lives and bullying was often related to their stammer.

In some students, more serious problems emerge. Since disorders of the development of language are likely to be central to the development of human personality, researchers point out that "There appears to be a strong association between developmental language deficits and severe psychiatric disorders" (Gualtieri, Koriath, Van Bourgondien, & Saleeby, 1983, p. 168) (see Chapter 7).

Play Behaviours

Many researchers and practitioners hold that children's optimal learning is through play. They contend that play is the universal language of childhood; that curious children thrive in environments that encourage investigation and active learning; and that play is therefore not only a source of pleasure for children but also an important way to learn and practise new forms of behaviour.

Preschoolers' construction of collaborative (symbolic or dramatic) play is a powerful activity that is linked to the development of cognitive and language abilities. It is during play that language is most rapidly mastered, and complicated grammatical and pragmatic forms of language are often first used during play. But symbolic play in young children with language impairments is different from that of their peers, although the differences seem quite small (Casby, 1997). A cycle emerges—less interaction during play, less peer collaboration, and less language development.

Family Variables

Little data exists about the parents of children with speech and language difficulties and the impact these problems have on family functioning. In the case of clefts, parents often worry about the physical manifestations and social stigma, while the child's emotional and social development are harmed by parents' feelings of guilt that the deformity is their fault. Of particular concern to parents are the child's appearance; the need for immediate surgery and regular and protracted contact with physicians; the child's speech development; fears that the child may choke during feeding; the reaction of the spouse, siblings, family, and friends; the child's intellectual development; financial considerations; and a recurrence of the defect in future children. Very often, parents are anxious about possible cognitive delays in the child in addition to the physical defect (Vanpoelvoorde & Shaughnessy, 1991).

Cultural and Linguistic Differences

With the increasing linguistic and cultural diversity in our schools, the special education system is serving more students who are in the process of acquiring a second language or who come from home backgrounds where a language other than English is spoken. Certainly, some of these students have disabilities that require special intervention. But be aware that the distinction between actual disabilities and problems reflecting sociocultural differences is often blurred. Far too many minority group children who have linguistic difficulties within the general system are misconstrued as having problems that require special education intervention.

Within special education, language minority children are treated as a further differentiation from those with language problems. *Limited English proficient* (LEP) students make up an increasingly high proportion of special classes (Willig & Greenberg, 1986). For example, in the United States, Asian American children are over-represented in special education speech programs (Grossman, 1995).

Note that when students do have speech or language problems as well as being LEP, similar difficulties will emerge in both languages. For example, a Spanish-speaking child with substitutions in speech will make similar mistakes in English (see Winzer & Mazurek, 1998).

ASSESSMENT OF SPEECH AND LANGUAGE PROBLEMS

Because language and speech are so intimately connected, assessment usually includes both areas. However, language is far more complex both in assessment and remediation. Robert Owens, Jr. (1991) describes the evaluation of language as "part science and part art" (p. 290). This statement reflects the multiple contexts in which communication assessment should be implemented, the variability in children's functioning, the vast range of areas to be assessed, and the relative shortage of appropriate tools. Moreover, the types of measures used, the domains sampled, and the targeted skills are quite different for children with mild delays and for those with severe disabilities of which language is only one component. Students with severe or multiple disabilities may be functioning at prelinguistic or minimally linguistic levels (see Chapter 15). As well, since speech and language disorders affect other areas of development, impact negatively on social integration, and hinder educational and personal achievement, early identification and early intervention are vital.

Assessing Language Problems

Language problems are generally assessed by a team comprising a psychologist, a speech clinician, a physician, an educator, and possibly a neurologist. All physical and psychological disturbances to normal language development, such as hearing loss or low IQ, must first be ruled out. After that, assessment involves both linguistic and cognitive skills, since both are necessary for language competence. A comprehensive assessment uses a range of tools and procedures.

Assessing Speech Problems

Assessment of articulation, voice, and fluency disorders is undertaken by a speech/language therapist/pathologist in a school or clinic setting.

An example of the measures that may be used, articulation assessment is a rapid and effective way of obtaining a sample of a child's speech. In its crudest form, the articulation test examines a child's ability to pronounce correctly, in the view of the investigator, a certain number of words. Children under age four are usually tested on their ability to echo or imitate the clinician's model. Children over four are usually asked to name either objects or pictures. Older children may be asked to read words or sentences or to describe objects. We can see some of the procedures in the following Case Study.

CASE STUDY

Ashley (continued)

Once the teacher referred Ashley, a number of professionals using different tools and procedures assessed him. These included medical personnel, a psychologist, and a speech/language therapist. To rule out any hearing or physical problems, medical and audiological assessments were undertaken first. Results showed Ashley to have normal hearing and no deviations in his speech mechanisms.

When a psychologist assessed Ashley, his performance on standardized tests showed a child of average-level abilities whose competence exceeded his performance. His poor academic progress in the classroom did not correlate with his cognitive levels, so other factors were intervening.

It was the speech/language therapist who found the root of Ashley's problems. During an assessment, the therapist used a number of measures, beginning with language functioning and use and moving to speech production. She began with the Peabody Picture Vocabulary Test (PPVT) to assess receptive language. Ashley scored at the

84th percentile. However, he performed poorly on informal tests of phonological processing and auditory tasks involving discrimination, sequence, and memory.

When specifically assessing speech production, the clinician asked Ashley to name the objects in a series of pictures. Ashley correctly produced all the phonemes in the initial, medial, and final word positions up to approximately the developmental level of a four-year-old. He produced substitutions and distortions of certain sounds, such as /ts/, /s/, and /z/ in all positions.

The clinician also tried to determine whether there was a pattern in Ashley's errors. She found that he consistently mispronounced the sounds /s/, /th/, /l/ and blended sounds such as /tr/, /pr/, and /cl/. He could not correctly pronounce /th/ and usually substituted an /f/ sound. He also had problems with /r/ sounds, sometimes substituted /w/ for /l/, and did not have a clear /s/ in his conversational speech.

INTERVENTION WITH CHILDREN WHO HAVE SPEECH AND LANGUAGE DISORDERS

Language specialists and educators have developed many forms of treatment for children with speech and language disorders, both for the classroom and for the clinic. Nevertheless, a guaranteed method to correct speech and language difficulties simply does not exist, and diversity in remediation programs characterizes the status quo.

As with every type of disabling condition, the one thing that is clear is the critical nature of early intervention. For example, preschoolers who have grammatical impairments (such as lower utterance length than expected for their age) and speech intelligibility impairments are at particular risk for continued language impairment (Yoder, Camarata, & Gardner, 2005). Intervention during the early years is critical.

The actual methods selected depend on the needs of a particular child, the severity of the disability, the setting for intervention, the targeted skills, the guidance of the therapist, and the expertise of the teacher. Here we focus on natural approaches used in general settings. We return to the topic of intervention for children with severe speech and language disorders in Chapters 10 and 15.

Medical Intervention

When speech disorders result from structural defects or inadequacies, medical intervention is often the first step in habilitation. Surgery tries to correct defects of the respiratory, oral, and facial musculature involved in speech production.

Corrective and plastic surgery can largely prevent the wide-ranging speech problems associated with cleft palate and other orofacial defects. Clefts of the primary and secondary palates and velopharyngae (lip and palate) inefficiency require special examinations and treatments by a number of different professionals over many years. The lip is typically repaired early in the first year of life. The time for surgical repair of the cleft palate is more variable, but the procedure is most commonly performed before the child is two years of age (Moran & Pentz, 1995) When other facial-skeletal anomalies accompany the cleft palate, prostheses designed to facilitate speech are prescribed. Dental surgery may also be necessary.

Therapy

Speech/language pathologists or therapists are concerned with communication, its normal development, and its disorders. While remediation of speech problems is specifically the venue of therapists/pathologists, classroom teachers should work proactively with therapists to reinforce elements the child attains in therapy sessions. At the same time, therapists consider speech and language intervention within the context of the classroom and therefore stress the skills that teachers see as essential. These include areas such as using appropriate language in a variety of contexts; the ability to adjust language to a listener's needs; organizing a message cognitively prior to its verbal presentation; and speaking at a comfortable rate (Elksnin, 1997).

The therapist/pathologist works with individual children to teach them how to speak and listen effectively and how to overcome the effects of communication disorders. To treat articulation disorders, for example, therapists teach children to listen, recognize, and discriminate consonant sounds; to produce articulated speech sounds; and to retain the memory of speech sounds. Major areas of emphasis in voice therapy include listening and articulatory adjustments and breath-control training. Breath control includes training to relax and reduce laryngeal tension as well as other specialized techniques (Van Osdol & Shane, 1982).

Although the many studies of the symptoms and treatment of stuttering have not revealed all of its possible underlying causes, many effective therapeutic methods have been developed to treat the problem. Psychotherapy, behaviour modification, and biofeedback are used to reduce the intensity of stuttering or eliminate it (Perkins, 1990). Some therapists combine a variety of techniques, including therapies such as desensitization, parent-child verbal interaction, and fluency shaping.

Technical Aids

One successful use of computers in the classroom is to promote social interaction in children with language difficulties. Studies have found higher levels of social interaction and social play from delayed children, significantly more turn-taking, and cognitively complex and imaginative verbalizations during computer activities.

Technology is a boon for individuals unable to use speech. Elaborate computer-driven devices enable children and adults who have language disorders to communicate more complex and subtle messages. These devices offer multiple outputs, such as printout, screen, or speech-synthesized voice. They are easily activated by a variety of volitional movements, including eye control, finger contact, or sipping and puffing on a blow stick. Further technical devices are described in the section on augmentative communication in Chapter 15.

Educational Intervention

Language is the primary medium through which much classroom learning takes place, and the acquisition of socially and academically appropriate forms of both oral and written language in general is seen as one of the principal goals of education. As efficient speech and language underlie academic success, the goal of any language intervention effort is to enhance a child's ability to use language as an effective means of communication in everyday life and to develop academic skills.

A second goal is bolstering peer acceptance in school-aged children. Language training is important because various communication skills have been found to predict social acceptance in middle childhood (Dodge, Pettit, McCloskey, & Boron, 1986). Finally, "Understanding and correcting deficiencies of language can improve behaviour and help a child resolve at least some of his emotional dilemmas" (Gualtieri et al., 1983, p. 169).

Service Delivery Models

The key word in current language intervention is *natural*. Natural procedures take place in natural environments, involve all those close to the child—parents, peers, and teacher—and pay attention to functional communication and conversational skills. Hence, the general classroom is the most appropriate setting for children who have speech and language difficulties as their sole impairment.

Educational Approaches

Many theoretical explanations of how to teach language have emerged. However, the procedures used in language intervention vary extensively and research has not indicated which strategy for teaching communication is the most effective. In the broadest terms, approaches may be grouped as *grammatical* or *naturalistic.*

Grammatical Approaches

Grammatical approaches include programs that are very structured and rely on direct teaching. As an example, in syntax-based programs, specific language skills are identified and then activities are designed so students can use the skills. Instruction provides the child with specific language structures, such as subject, verb, and object, and word order relationships, such as question forms.

CASE STUDY

Ashley (continued)

The speech clinician, the psychologist, Ashley's teacher, and Ashley's parent met to discuss a program for Ashley. Ashley's mother pointed out that he was the baby of the family, the youngest of four children. His parents both work outside the home and are away all day.

The speech therapist then explained that phonological speech problems such as Ashley's are developmental rather than physiological and respond well to remedial instruction. She felt that Ashley's problems were caused by a combination of immaturity, lack of opportunity to practise speaking, and self-consciousness at school, which further deprives him of necessary practice. She also noted that Ashley knows he does not speak clearly. He told her that he tries hard, but that he was bashful about speaking because the children at school made fun of him. The anomalies in articulation may account for Ashley's failure to learn basic reading skills.

The team agreed that both the teacher and therapist would undertake intervention efforts. The ultimate goal is not absolutely correct grammar or pronunciation but to enhance Ashley's ability to use language as an effective means of communication in everyday life.

There are three main prongs to Ashley's program: individual speech therapy to learn new speech sounds and improve language, much practice in the broader context of academic and social communication, and remediation in academic areas. The therapist will teach Ashley how to correctly produce the misarticulated sounds and give him a great deal of speaking practice. As he attains new sounds, the teacher will promote correct use and reinforce it in the classroom. She will also ensure that Ashley has many opportunities to use oral language, and will use incidental teaching strategies to improve both his speech and his language. At the same time, she will implement strategies to help him catch up in the language arts, such as placing stress on a sight word vocabulary in order to circumvent the articulation problems.

Naturalistic Approaches

There are many limitations to highly structured didactic teaching approaches. They tend not to enhance the generalization of skills, their practice cannot be distributed across the school day, and drill on linguistic forms is separate from any real need to communicate. The pendulum has swung toward more naturalistic methods to increase language skills.

Natural environments provide the best settings for language training primarily because much language is learned in a social context. Language production is necessarily the result of an interaction between the skills of the speaker and events in the environment, and language is best taught through social interaction and naturally occurring events. And since training occurs in natural settings, the language is bound to be **functional language**—useful and relevant in a child's daily activities and environment. The problems of generalizing skills are circumvented and the likelihood that new language will be maintained and generalized is enhanced.

Naturalistic approaches occur in general classrooms where children learn what language is by learning what language can do. Much of the teaching is therefore **incidental teaching**—it comes up in normal classroom interactions, rather than in direct instruction. Incidental teaching stresses teachable moments when teachers respond to communicative attempts in order to encourage more elaborate speech and language. Ashley's intervention, as described in the last Case Study, is illustrative. The teacher may use many of the natural strategies shown in Table 4-3 on page 124 and ideas drawn from the generic approaches shown in Table 4-2 below.

(margin notes) **functional language**   **incidental teaching**

Table 4-2 Creating accessible classrooms

General

- Create language-rich classrooms in which children are deliberately exposed to high quality written and verbal input by adults and peers.
- Reinforce language usage by ensuring that adult-child verbal interactions are characterized by high levels of adult responsiveness.
- Stress the language arts curriculum of listening, expressive language, and reading.

Receptive language problems

- Speak clearly and at a moderate speed to be more easily understood. Use a normal pace and loudness and avoid over-enunciation. The exceptions are dysphasic children. Rapid sound changes may cause problems that impair their ability to identify and discriminate consonants. For these children, speak at a slower rate to improve comprehension.
- When possible, use hand gestures.
- Use directed questioning and responses. Make questions meaningful to activate a child's thinking and promote problemsolving. Wait patiently for an answer.
- Respond to the content rather than the correctness of the language; stress the answer, not the grammar.
- Before giving a message, say the student's name and wait for the child to look at you.

Table 4-2 continued

- Keep instructions short. "Laundry lists" confuse everybody.

- Be explicit with directions. A rapid strategy that assists children with poor receptive language and maintains control during transitions is to state the directive, such as "Take out your math book and turn to page 35." Then ask, "Mary, what did I say?" Move quickly to ask, "Pete, what did Mary say?"

Expressive language delays and disorders

- Avoid placing pressures on the child to use oral language.

- Use puppets; young children tend to be braver about poor performance or use of language when they are protected by the puppet.

- If a child is having therapy, work proactively with the therapist. Find out what sounds the child is *stimulable* for (ready to learn). Target these sounds in individual sessions and give the child real-life opportunities to produce them.

- Recognize and reinforce the child's use of correct forms; use formal reinforcement such as praise or stickers.

- For children with limited vocabulary, present new words with incidental teaching. Cazden (1988) suggests that word meanings are most easily learned through interactions and conversations with an adult who introduces new words.

- Present new words in many contexts. The likelihood that a child will learn the meaning of a new word from a single exposure in a meaningful context ranges from 5 to 20 percent.

- Use "Think, pair, share." After posing a question to the class, ask the students to find a partner, make eye contact, share their responses to the question, and remember their partner's response.

Children learning English as a second language

- Know the stages of second language acquisition.

- Be aware of cultural differences in order to understand the behaviours and learning styles of students from diverse cultures.

- Become familiar with features of students' dialects so as to understand better and distinguish miscues from errors.

- Try to get trained paraeducators who speak the child's language.

- Stress oral language and conversational skills before moving to reading and written language.

- Adapt English instruction to make it highly contextualized and multisensory, to be more easily understood by students.

- Assign students classroom roles that capitalize on their strengths and do not make unrealistic demands on their English skills.

- Use much oral language work. Garcia (1988) found that students learn math and literacy skills most effectively when student-student discussions take up to at least 50 percent of instructional time.

- Gain parental involvement and support and develop program models, goals, and objectives that are meaningful for the local culture.

Table 4-3 Examples of strategies to use in a natural approach to language intervention

Strategy	Description	Example
Imitation	Modelling	The teacher may say "Show me," or "You say this now."
Follow the child's responses	Maintaining conversational interaction	The child says, "I saw monkeys." This is related to "Monkeys are funny," not "Good talking."
Expansion	A restatement of what the child has just said, with information added	The child may say "Car go," and the teacher expands on it to "Yes, the car goes." Or if a child says, "Camera takes pictures," the teacher can expand to, "Yes, he has a camera to take pictures, like your grandma does."
Extension	Similar to expansions; follows a child's statement with different words	The child says "Cat in the Hat," and the adult responds, "Yes, that Cat in the Hat is making a big mess." Or if a child says, "I miss the bus," the teacher may respond with, "You missed the bus. Were you late for the dentist?"
Paraphrasing	Repeat a statement or question to elicit a reply	Responding, for example, to "Want ball," with "You want the ball."
Recast sentences	Repeat or restate a child's words in the correct form	If a child says a sentence such as "That boy hitted me," the teacher responds with "That boy hit you."
Open-ended questions	Genuine requests for information requiring more than a "yes" or "no" response	Examples include, "Why could the man be angry?" "Where is my book?" "Why did the man go to the store?" "Where is he going next?"
Indirect statements	Using third-person commands	As in "Tell Tommy what you want."
Systematic	Comments highlight the action/toy/work that is the focus of attention.	"What is the dolly's name?" "How many blocks will go in your tower?"
Praise	A statement describing a child's prior verbal or non-verbal communication as correct, acceptable, or good	"I like how you did that." "That's right!"
Directives	Comprehension check	After giving a direction, have the child repeat it to show comprehension.

Sources: McNeill & Fowler, 1996; Winzer, 1997.

SUMMARY

1. As an element of communication, language is a typically human activity. Human language is incredibly complex, bound by structured rules, and the product of all aspects of development—physical, sensory, social, and neurological. It includes written language and speech (essentially a mechanical production of language) as well as a variety of non-speech forms, such as sign language, and many non-verbal forms, such as gestures and body language.

2. Language development is neither random nor capricious. There are developmental milestones, all reached in infancy or early childhood. A linguistic environment, an intact cognitive/perceptual system, and normal social interaction all underlie normal development. Hence, if a child does not hear language, has some impairment of the cognitive/perceptual mechanism, or has a troubled family background, language development will reflect these problems.

3. Speech development depends on having something to say (language) and the opportunity to say it (social interaction). It also depends on the development of the speech mechanisms and articulators—the pharynx and larynx, the tongue, the palate, the lips and the teeth, and the production and modulation of breath flow.

4. Compared to language during the preschool years, language during the school years is complex and sophisticated. Children have a firm linguistic base, metalinguistic skills, a grasp of semantic and syntactic rules, and an ever-expanding vocabulary.

5. Speech and language disorders are manifested in a staggering array of distinct forms. Few, however, can be precisely labelled and many remain ambiguous in terms of etiology, prevalence, developmental consequences, and intervention. Speech disorders are problems in the articulation of language sounds, voice production, and fluency. Language disorders are problems of varied degress in the acquisition, comprehension, and formulation of language.

6. After learning disabilities, speech and language disorders are the most common problems seen in the schools. (In preschool children, speech and language disorders are the most common form of disability.) For some children, this is a short-term delay in acquiring articulation proficiency. Other children have chronic, recurrent speech and language difficulties, such as stuttering. For others, speech and language difficulties are part of a more complex constellation of disorders that may limit their lifetime options.

7. Because speech and language disabilities interfere with the ease with which a child interacts with the world, they can mean painful consequences for all aspects of a child's development. Speech and language disabilities socially isolate those who have them, impoverish their lives, and impact on their school success. When children with communication disorders are considered as a group, it is evident that they have an increased prevalence of learning problems and psychiatric disorders.

8. Academic functioning is affected with either minimal or major consequences, particularly the language arts. Children with speech and language disorders tend to be slower in acquiring emergent literacy skills. Behaviourally, children with language deficits are 10 times more likely to exhibit antisocial behaviour than those in the general population. The problems increase as the children age.

9. Children with language disorders require structured and systematic intervention. But since language develops in the framework of family associations, social interactions, and interpersonal relationships, the general classroom is generally the most appropriate setting. To promote communication, skilled teachers use descriptive feedback, directing, telling and explaining, question asking, modelling, and prompt and coaching statements. When necessary, they use teacher-mediated and peer-mediated strategies and direct teaching.

communicative behaviour

HISTORICAL NOTES

For centuries, parents, scholars, and teachers have been fascinated by the way children acquire and use language. Virtually all the major philosophers since Plato and Aristotle have considered the problems of the origin and role of human language. Debates centred on the role of language in the progressive differentiation of humans from other creatures and the way in which reason, if an original endowment of humans, manifested itself in language.

Eighteenth century empiricists were particularly intrigued by language development in humans. (See the profile on Victor in the Case Study on pages 99 and 100.) In the 19th century, the study of speech and language was known as *philology*; most of the research was in the form of diary studies. These soon gave way to an examination of children's vocabulary, which is perhaps the most traditional approach to the study of language acquisition.

In the early 20th century, the study of language development emphasized language form; these forms were identified and classified into language categories related to sentence types, parts of speech, and so on. By the 1930s and 1940s, data collection was more formalized. Then when psycholinguistics emerged as a discrete discipline in the early 1950s, language became a favourite research area.

Today, the study of language differences and how children learn language is like many other academic pursuits. Everyone agrees about what

children actually do, but considerable controversy remains about how children acquire a natural language. Different approaches and theories compete for acceptance and there are champions of every conceivable position. Occasionally one theory predominates, but generally portions of each are used to explain different aspects of development.

Behaviourists consider language a subset of other learned behaviours and stress reinforcement in language acquisition. A social learning view of language extends the behavioural position to include the processes of imitation. It is held that children learn to speak one language rather than another, and to speak it with particular vocabularies and idioms, because they imitate and are reinforced for imitating the language spoken in their homes and neighbourhoods.

Because children of all cultures learn language at about the same age and tend to learn it in similar ways, some question whether humans are born with a natural innate tendency to acquire language. Piaget believed that language acquisition is a direct result of cognitive development, that language is the handmaiden of thought. To Piaget, children cannot develop language skills until at least the last stage of sensorimotor development, because it is not until then that their mental apparatus allows them to represent symbolically an object that is no longer present. Noam Chomsky (1965), also holding a cognitive-biological position, believes that a sense of grammar is innate, or native, to the human brain. Chomsky postulates an innate language acquisition device unique to and present in all humans that enables us to learn language simply by being exposed to it.

Enormously complex and comprehensive research into the nature and acquisition of language continues apace. Studies include all the traditional topics and there is a new focus on **communicative behaviour**—any behaviour that conveys a social message from one person to another, such as American Sign Language (ASL) and augmentative communication.

CHAPTER 5

CHILDREN WITH LEARNING DISABILITIES

INTRODUCTION

In the very first edition of this text in 1987, the introduction to the chapter on learning disabilities noted, "Perhaps more than any other field of exceptionality, the field of learning disabilities (LD) has generated controversy, confusion, misconceptions, and polarization among concerned professionals." Further, we wrote that of all the problems, "the most challenging issue in the field of learning disabilities has been the search for an appropriate definition" (Winzer, Rogow, & David, 1987, p. 236).

Twenty years later, the field of learning disabilities remains beset with conceptual confusion. An effective definition remains elusive. Because of the lack of a coherent theory to explain the construct and the presence of many competing definitions, there is no single statement that describes the condition of learning disabilities (Kavale, Holdnack, & Mostert, 2005). This is largely due to the nature of the population being conceptualized. While some categories in special education can be easily identified by a common trait, such as hearing loss, visual impairment, or speech dysfunction, learning disabilities do not concern a single, easily identifiable disability, and children with learning disabilities do not form a unified, homogeneous group. On the contrary, *Learning disabilities* is a syndrome— a group of related and overlapping conditions that includes vastly different populations that reveal a wide variety of behavioural, learning, social, and interpersonal problems.

Although individuals who are learning disabled differ in many critical ways, they do share some common problems. Chiefly, these students seem unable to learn through traditional instructional methods and show academic lags, inconsistent performances, memory and attention problems, and perceptual deficits. Many students with learning disabilities appear bright and receptive in all sorts of ways, but they still fail in school. They earn report cards larded with comments such as "Could try harder," or "Should apply herself," or "He is not working up to his potential." But many of these young people are applying themselves, and the more they try and fail, the more unhappy and frustrated they become. They are eventually caught up in a cycle of frustration and failure that threatens their entire educational careers and engenders lack of motivation, social problems, increasingly less acceptable classroom behaviours, and dropping out, or even being subtly pushed out, of a school system that cannot accommodate their unique needs.

In the past, children with learning disabilities have been described as hyperactive, distractible, inattentive, brain damaged, slow learning, dyslexic, perceptually disabled, aggressive, and emotionally labile. More unsavoury terms have included *dull*, *lazy*, *inept*, and *disturbed*. Because of difficulties in identification, youngsters with learning disabilities were often shunted into classes for children either intellectually disabled or emotionally disturbed. Others were placed in non-stimulating settings where their problems and progress were improperly evaluated.

Students with learning disabilities are neither emotionally disturbed nor intellectually disabled. They stand in good company with similarly affected historical figures. Thomas Edison's teacher, for example, described him as "addled." Auguste Rodin's father complained that he had "an idiot for a son." Woodrow Wilson had severe problems with reading and writing (Thompson, 1971). Albert Einstein did not speak until age three; he found school so difficult that one teacher predicted that "nothing good" would come of him (Patten, 1973). Nelson Rockefeller, who became vice-president of the United States, encountered great difficulties with reading. Rockefeller later wrote that he "just struggled to understand words that seemed to garble before my eyes, numbers that came out backward, sentences that were hard to grasp" (Rockefeller, 1976). Suspected of having dyslexia, a specific reading disability, are figures such as Hans Christian Andersen, Winston Churchill, George Patton, Leonardo da Vinci, Galileo, Cher, and Tom Cruise (Spafford & Grosser, 1996).

DEFINITIONS OF LEARNING DISABILITIES

As you can see in the accompanying Case Study about Danny, learning disabilities is a puzzling condition—one of the least understood and the most difficult to deal with. As mentioned above, the lack of understanding results partly from the varied and contradictory

CASE STUDY

Danny

Eight-year-old Danny attends school in a small own in northern British Columbia. School is really hard for Danny. He tries and tries but just can't seem to learn as easily and quickly as his classmates. When he was younger, Danny loved going to school and was always eager and excited. Now he approaches each day with apprehension.

In the classroom, Danny is very passive, rarely responding to questions or participating at all. He attempts seat work but is often distractible and off-task. He then bothers other children and engages in minor misdemeanours.

In academic work, specifically reading, spelling, and arithmetic, Danny shows serious lags. He is far behind in math and has not yet really mastered rational counting skills, basic place value, or any number facts. He is further ahead in reading, and has quite a broad range of sight word knowledge. However, he needs much work in phonological awareness and phonics. His weaknesses here hinder his reading and make his spelling very much a hit or miss procedure. His printing is poor, as are his attempts at creative writing. He has problems generating ideas, understanding cause and effect relationships, and using sequential thought processes, which are compounded by his poor printing and spelling. Danny's social skill deficits are becoming more prominent; for example, he exhibits discomfort when given a compliment and has poor eye contact.

Early in his school career, the teachers suspected that Danny had learning problems, but it was not until the end of his grade 2 year that he was formally referred. In British Columbia, if students show a discrepancy between IQ test scores and achievement scores, they are placed in the category of Severe Learning Disability (Siegel, Lam, & Ladyman, 2000). Danny was adminis-

tered a battery of psycho-educational measures. On the WISC-III, he scored a little above the normal range (Full Scale score 112). In overall achievement measures on the Woodcock-Johnson 111 Test of Achievement Danny performed well below his age group on items of math calculation, math reasoning, oral expression, oral language, and listening comprehension. Other test results are shown on Danny's IEP, presented on page 164 in this chapter.

With the results in hand, the school principal called a team meeting that included the classroom teacher, the special education teacher, the psychologist, and Danny's mother. At the meeting, the psychologist spoke with some certainty. "Danny," she said, "is fairly typical of children with learning disabilities, who often enter into a cycle of frustration and failure." She went on to explain that production deficiencies, self-helplessness syndrome, and an outward locus of control all interact to produce learners who are passive, incapacitated with feelings of self-defeat, and have a fear of learning. Ineffective coping skills include not asking questions, resisting making choices, being poor risk takers, failing to use effective study skills, and failing to use self-monitoring strategies.

The suggestions generated to assist Danny and an extract from his IEP are shown later in this chapter.

manifestations of learning disabilities themselves. Additional points of confusion factors include the field's evolution, its accelerated growth, and its interdisciplinary nature.

Although the actual term *learning disabilities* did not emerge until 1963, practitioners and professionals were well aware of these children by the beginning of the 20th century. The genesis and development of the learning disabilities field is outlined in the Historical Notes feature at the end of this chapter.

From the outset, there has been lack of a clear definition for learning disabilities. This is more than an academic problem. Kavale and Forness (2000) observe that "the failure to produce a unified definition has meant that LD lacks two critical elements: understanding—a clear and unobscured sense of LD—and explanation—a rational exposition of the reasons why a particular student is LD" (p. 240). Further, lack of a clear definition creates confusion when we talk about prevalence, etiology, placement, strategies for intervention, and the design and use of tools and tests for assessment.

Many reasons contribute to the difficulties facing practitioners and professionals attempting to identify and define a child's learning disabilities. Chief among these are the following:

- The extremely heterogeneous nature of the identified population. Rather than existing as a single condition, learning disabilities is a syndrome of behaviours that manifests differently in different individuals although the components of the syndrome itself are varied and confused. Therefore, the implications of the condition are neither fully understood nor adequately conceptualized.

- Learning disabilities cannot be simply measured by a numerical designation, such as an IQ score or a decibel loss.

- *Learning disabilities* is often referred to as a socially constructed category. At the outset, it applied to children from middle-class backgrounds with no discernible mental or physical anomalies who were nevertheless failing in school (see this chapter's Historical Notes). As we pointed out in Chapter 1, there has recently been much movement among the categories of mild disability. The blurring of categories, combined with the disparate characteristics of the learning-disabled population, further muddies clarity between categories of exceptionality.

- The field of learning disabilities also reflects the thorny issue of terminology. The phrase *learning disabilities* is more socially desirable than slow learner or intellectually disabled. This is partly because it generally reflects the notion of an impairment that is specific rather than global in nature and is therefore less stigmatizing to the image of the child as a whole person. In light of this and the overlap among categories of mild disability, we find that *learning disabilities* is mutating into an encompassing category.

- Across Canada, there are differences in the definitions and major emphases of learning disabilities. There is considerable variability in the identification of learning disabilities from one province to the next, and even from one teacher to another.

- Taking a world view, we find that the term means rather different things in different nations. In the UK, for example, it is intimately tied to dyslexia. Some Asian nations use *learning disabilities* as a generic phrase to describe all children who are not performing well at school.

- Learning disabilities are considered the proper and legitimate concern of many disciplines and professions, including education, psychology, neuropsychology, speech and language pathology, neurology, psychiatry, ophthalmology, optometry, and occupational therapy. Which professional groups have the most influence has changed over the years.

With such confusion about definitions, perhaps no other area of special education has expended so much effort to define itself and its population. Many definitions of *learning disabilities* have emerged, and all have their advocates and their opponents. Most modern definitions echo Kirk's original model, quoted in the Historical Notes.

A current popular definition states that

> *Learning disabilities* is a general term that refers to a heterogeneous group of disabilities manifested by significant difficulties in the acquisition and use of listening, speaking, reading, writing, reasoning, and mathematical abilities. These disabilities are intrinsic to the individual, presumed to be due to central nervous system dysfunction, and may occur across the life span. Problems in self-regulatory behaviours, social perception, and social interactions may exist with learning disabilities but do not by themselves constitute a learning disability. Although learning disabilities occur concomitantly with other handicapping conditions (for example, sensory impairments, mental retardation, serious emotional disturbance), or with

extrinsic influences (such as cultural differences, insufficient or inappropriate instruction) they are not the result of these conditions or influences (National Joint Committee on Learning Disabilities, 2001, p. 31).

The essential tenets of this definition are echoed by other groups such as the Learning Disabilities Association of Canada (LDAC) (2002) and in provincial policy documents. As the varying definitions tend to be more similar than different, it makes sense to examine their common elements. Being clear about these will do much to dispel confusion about the discrete category of learning disabilities.

Neurological Dysfunction

Much of the theoretical understanding of learning disabilities grew out of work with children described as "brain damaged." In the 1930s and 1940s, Alfred Strauss argued that children with brain injuries are subject to major disorders in perception, thinking, and behaviour that reduce their ability to read, write, spell, and calculate.

Many theorists still attribute learning disabilities to some type of brain impairment or central nervous system (CNS) dysfunction. This pathological emphasis is particularly evident among medical professionals; in educational circles, the tendency over the years has been to de-emphasize pathological aspects of the problems and stress behavioural ones. It follows that many educators today would like to see the concept of presumed neurological impairment dropped entirely. They prefer to focus on each child's particular perceptual, cognitive, learning, and motor problems and skills so that appropriate educational programming can be developed.

Uneven Growth Pattern

Students with learning disabilities are presumed to have irregular or uneven development of the various domains of development. While some of the components mature quickly, others lag behind. Uneven development manifests as peaks and valleys in a student's performance. Some children, for example, are average in their motor abilities but far behind in their verbal abilities and lag behind their age group in the use of oral language.

Difficulty in Academic Tasks

Academic problems are perhaps the clearest indication of a learning disability. A child may encounter difficulties with a wide range of learning tasks. Specific problems may occur in the acquisition of speech and oral language, reading, written language, handwriting, spelling, or arithmetic. Depending on the definition, thinking, motor skills, perceptual skills, and psychosocial skills could be added.

Discrepancy between Potential and Performance

Traditionally, students with learning disabilities were most often described as those who manifest educationally significant discrepancies, usually seen as a substantial gap between potential and performance. Although the discrepancy did not in and of itself constitute a learning disability, it has been considered a prerequisite.

There are two main ways of looking at a discrepancy. It can be seen as a discrepancy between age or grade level expectations, such as reading two levels below grade placement. Or it can be seen in terms of differences among achievement areas such as reading comprehension versus listening comprehension. The most common discrepancy measure is the former—between a child's tested potential for academic tasks and the child's performance in academic domains (between what a child is capable of learning and what the child actually achieves). Potential is judged by the mental age obtained on a standardized test of mental ability, which is then compared to performance on achievement tests. A difference of two years between the estimated potential and the performance is frequently used as an indicator of academic retardation.

While the discrepancy criterion is still widely used (Overton, 2003), it is under attack, as we explain in the section on identification later in this chapter. By dispensing with the discrepancy criterion, the trend is to replace the generic definition of learning disabilities with definitions that specify the precise characteristics of an individual child's disability such as a learning disability in math, reading, or written expression.

Exclusion of Other Causes

Most definitions of learning disabilities exclude children whose exceptionality is primarily the result of other causes such as intellectual disability, behaviour disorders, visual or hearing impairment, or social and economic disadvantage. This is not to say that children with other disabilities cannot also be learning disabled. However, by excluding other disabilities, the field of learning disabilities gains clarity regarding its special population of learners.

Average or Above-Average Intelligence

Inherent in the whole concept of learning disabilities, and closely associated with the exclusionary clause, is the notion that the child who is learning disabled is of average or above-average intelligence. When we approach both exclusionary clauses and notions about average intelligence today, however, the movement among categories and the changing nature of children identified as learning disabled must be foregrounded. As stressed earlier, currently many students called learning disabled would have been classified previously as intellectually disabled.

Social Deficits

Some definitions define learning disabilities strictly in terms of intellect and achievement; others include emotional and social complications that may adversely affect school learning and achievement. Arguments for the latter rest on data that show that social interactions are often difficult for children with learning disabilities, particularly non-verbal learning disabilities, and that social skill deficits are common.

CLASSIFICATION OF LEARNING DISABILITIES

Efforts to define and then classify specific subtypes of learning disabilities can be traced back almost as far as the concept itself. After years of intense research, classification systems have changed quite dramatically, although a consensus has not been reached.

As we observe in this chapter's Historical Notes, the roots of the field of learning disabilities are embedded in the areas of neurology, ophthalmology, and other medical specialties. When the disabilities were attributed to various types of brain damage, terminology generally reflected a medical orientation. Common terms included *minimal brain dysfunction*, *brain crippled*, *cerebral disordered*, *neurologically impaired*, *dyslexic*, and *dysphasic*.

Although the terminology drawn from neurology is less popular today, some terms are still in general use and warrant explanation. In the following, the prefix *a-* means an absence of and *dys-* means a disturbance of.

- *Agnosia* is a lack of knowledge, an inability to recognize the significance of sensory stimuli.
- *Dysgraphia* means a disturbance in the ability to express thoughts in writing.
- *Dyscalculia* is a disturbance in the ability to use and remember numbers and do arithmetic.

dyslexia

- **Dyslexia** is the term that has become part of the common language. It is an old descriptor, first introduced by a German ophthalmologist, R. Berlin, in 1890, and concurrently referred to as *word blindness*. Today, precise definitions vary, but generally "dyslexia refers to a severe difficulty in learning to read" (Mercer, 1987, p. 374) or to "an inability to read normally as a result of damage to the brain" (Myers & Hammill, 1990, p. 63). The condition is characterized by impaired single word reading, deficits in phonological decoding, difficulty in differentiating symbols, problems with reading the printed page from left to right, and reversal of letters and shapes in printing and drawing.

Prevalence rates for dyslexia as a reading disorder range from 5 to 10 percent of the entire population, although rates as high as 20 to 30 percent are also reported (Pennington, 1990). The *Diagnostic and Statistical Manual* (DSM-IV, APA, 1994) estimates the rate among school-aged children at 4 percent, with 60 to 80 percent of these being male.

Dyslexia and *learning disabilities* are not synonymous terms. Many children with reading problems are not categorically identified as learning disabled. And, while up to 80 percent of children who are learning disabled have reading difficulties, learning disabilities is best viewed as a syndrome of a number of behaviours.

Although the general public still clings to the descriptor, North American educators have long wished to dispense with the term *dyslexia* in favour of *reading disability*. As early as 1969, the National Advisory Committee on Dyslexia and Related Reading Disorders in the United States set out to examine its terminology. The next year, the Committee stated, "In view of . . . divergencies of opinion, the Committee believes that the use of the term dyslexia serves no useful purpose" (p. 38). Much later, Stanovich (1994) wrote, "Dyslexia carries with it . . . many empirically unverified connotations and assumptions" (p. 579) and suggested dispensing with the term. Writing in *Education Canada*, Elliott (2006) said that "there are so many different understandings and conceptualizations about what dyslexia is, and is not, that the term, as used in professional practice at least, has become almost meaningless" (p. 15).

In contemporary special education, we still classify and categorize learning disabilities in many ways, with some support for each classification scheme. The schemes are shown in Figure 5-1.

In Canada, the severity classifications of *mild*, *moderate*, and *severe* learning disabilities are the most widely employed. In Manitoba, as an example, very severely learning disabled refers to a student whose reading, language, and/or mathematics performance is significantly lower than expected on the basis of his or her intelligence or learning potential (Manitoba, 2001, p. E1). Severity classifications are founded on the belief that learning disabilities are less a question of kind than of degree and consequences and can occur on a continuum from severely learning disabled to subtle differences in attention and performance.

Learning disabilities are also classified as general or specific. With *general* learning disabilities, a student's academic progress lags behind that of normal peers in most areas. *Specific* learning disabilities, a classification used consistently in the United States, may imply that the student has difficulties in particular areas but performs adequately in others. The term is also used to refer to students who have very serious and deep-seated disabilities.

A final classification is that of *language* and *non-language* learning disabilities. Studies suggest that language is the primary deficit for up to 80 percent of school-aged students with learning disabilities. *Non-verbal* learning disabilities refers to the condition of the other 20 percent of students who demonstrate weak perceptual and processing difficulties in the auditory and visual modes, together with problems in coordination and motor skills, accompanied by social deficits.

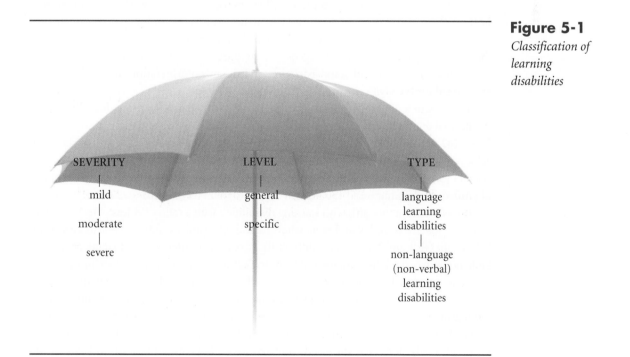

Figure 5-1

Classification of learning disabilities

PREVALENCE OF LEARNING DISABILITIES

Since 1963, the number of students identified and categorized as learning disabled has been astronomical. In Canada today, students with learning disabilities make up the largest single group of children with disabilities (see Table 1-2 on page 17). The Canadian Council on Social Development (1999) found that a learning disability affected approximately 17 in every 1000 children. In Ontario, for example, children with learning disabilities make up approximately half of the students identified as exceptional. It follows that the majority of teachers will, at some time in their careers, have a number of students with learning disabilities in their classrooms.

Increases in the percentages of students identified as learning disabled echoes the general trend that sees mounting numbers of children referred to special education. Still, the rates for this diagnostic category have been, and continue to be, huge. But rates are so unstable that some researchers are led to question whether learning disabilities is a disability at all (see Lyon, 1996). They see learning disabilities as increasingly unrecognizable as a discrete category and use terms such as "myth" or "questionable construct" or "imaginary disease" (Kavale, Holdnack, & Mostert, 2005).

A number of explanations for the increasing but unstable rates have been forwarded. First of all, definitional problems render statements about the population with learning disabilities problematic. Numbers have ballooned because so many behaviours are included that the term is often applied to students who could more accurately be described as slow learners, children who misbehave in class, or those who are absent often or move from school to school. Joined to this is the contention that increased rates are the result of the misdiagnosis of children with borderline intellectual disabilities as learning disabled (Gottlieb, Alter, Gottlieb, & Wishner, 1994).

In the United States, about 98 percent of states use a discrepancy criterion in their definitions (Gresham, 1997). So do most Canadian jurisdictions. In theory, the discrepancy conception should allow educators to distinguish children who are learning disabled from those who fail because of low intelligence, behavioural disorders, or other disabling conditions. However, the lack of standardization and the misinterpretation of the discrepancy are blamed for the high rates of learning disabled children.

The idea of a discrepancy initially arose in order to separate learning disabilities from intellectual ones. The criterion goes right back to 1975 when the regulations accompanying PL 94 142 stated that learning disabilities were present when "a severe discrepancy between achievement and intellectual ability" was demonstrated. In 1997, the IDEA reiterated discrepancy as the primary criterion in identifying learning disabilities. The population of identified children increased 150 percent (Kavale, Holdnack, & Mostert, 2005).

Boys far outnumber girls with learning disabilities, with a ratio of at least 4 to 1. The reasons for this are complex and somewhat unclear. Certainly, gender relates to classroom behaviour. Girls and boys behave differently at school, a difference that stems from both biologically-based predispositions and from socialization experiences. Boys are more aggressive, assertive, and dominant in school settings than girls. They call out more frequently and are more effective in obtaining and maintaining the teacher's attention. Because boys tend to indulge in more overt behaviour, they may be more likely to be referred for in-depth diagnosis. Or it may be that classrooms have increasingly become more girl-friendly and have unintentionally neglected the needs and nature of boys over the past 30 years. More important, perhaps, are the problems in language and reading that boys have more often than girls do, as we saw in the case of dyslexia and as we discuss again in the section on etiology.

ETIOLOGY OF LEARNING DISABILITIES

Experts do not agree on the causes of learning disabilities any more than they agree on definitions and classification. Some say that learning disabilities result primarily from physiological factors. Others stress that the school tasks we expect students to accomplish contribute to learning disabilities by making demands on their maturity levels or learning styles that they are unable to meet. Still others blame environmental factors such as inadequate nutrition, inappropriate diet, or allergies. Moreover, various suspected causes interact in subtle ways, rendering etiology even more difficult to determine. In most cases, the cause of a child's learning disability remains unknown.

Minimal Brain Dysfunction

Following the lead of Alfred Strauss and other pioneer neurologists, many of today's definitions of learning disabilities still include a presumption of some type of brain injury. The condition is described as neurological dysfunction or *minimal brain dysfunction*.

Researchers suggest that slight damage to the brain hinders its most efficient functioning, and focus on disruption of neural cell development during early fetal development. Findings from neurological studies remain inconclusive, although a small but increasing amount of data does indicate some neurological abnormalities as a cause of learning disabilities. Still, an easily identified pattern of neurological disturbance has not been found.

Genetic Factors

Genetic factors are prominent in studies directed specifically at dyslexia. Researchers know that reading disabilities tend to run in families, especially among male members. Their questions are "What is the rate of familial dyslexia?" and "Are familial reading problems due to hereditary factors or to similar learning environments?"

Investigations clearly identify the familial nature of some reading problems. One study (Scarborough, 1989, 1990) found that a family history of dyslexia accounted for 30 to 36 percent of the variance in reading. Another study that compared the families of 125 children with reading disorders to a control group of average readers found common reading problems in the families of the poor readers, especially among the male members (Decker & Defries, 1980, 1981).

The great majority of genetic studies have involved twins. These studies generally show that, if the twins are monozygotic rather than dizygotic, when one twin has a reading disability, the other twin is likely to have it too. Further on genetic traits, the neurobiological signature of dyslexic readers seems to emerge across cultures and across different languages That is, genetic transmission has no cultural or language bias (Paulesu et al., 2001).

Geneticists theorize that dyslexia is inherited, linked to a glitch in the brain's wiring. The influence of the genes operates at several levels but essentially manifests as interference with the ability to translate a written word into units of sound (phonemes)

(Wingert & Kantrowitz, 1997). This does not mean that a child is born reading disabled in the same way that a child is born redheaded or female. Reading, writing, and spelling problems per se are not biological features that can be inherited; nor are they amenable to medical treatment. What is implied is that manifested problems may stem from some underlying cognitive or neurological defect based on genetic transmission.

So far, research shows linkages between chromosome 6 and phonemic awareness and phonological decoding skills ("Reading difficulties . . ." 1997). It also appears that a genetic abnormality is found on chromosome 15, although the mechanism of transmission is still in question, as is the strength of the genetic influence (Wenar, 1994). The B2 microglobulin gene, which is thought to influence the immune system and male sexual development, is also found on chromosome 15, which may help explain the high prevalence of males among the reading-disabled population (Smith & Pennington, 1987).

Maturational Lags

maturational lag

Children with **maturational lags** are slower than average to reach some developmental milestones. A maturational (developmental) lag does not necessarily imply a major deficiency or limited potential. Some children may simply be progressing at a slower rate in language, motor, cognitive, or socio-emotional development. Most children overcome any problem as they grow older. For example, Badian (1988) found that developmentally young children who appeared to be reading disabled at grade 3 but responded by grade 5 developed into low to average readers by grade 8.

It may be that the effects of schooling on children with maturational lags itself creates the appearance of mild disabilities. Schools assign children to a grade level based on their age, assuming that children of the same age possess the same levels of ability. This is simply not true; children reach their developmental milestones at different times, and to expect all children to be ready to learn the same things on the same schedule is clearly not reasonable. When children are behind the expected schedule, they will manifest characteristics of a child with learning disabilities, such as behaviour, reading, and attention-span problems. These developmentally young children are penalized if they are drawn in by procedures intended to find potential problems and then labelled as learning disabled.

DEVELOPMENTAL CONSEQUENCES OF LEARNING DISABILITIES

Individuals who are learning disabled simply do not seem to learn in the same way as everyone else does—they sometimes do complicated things very well and then amaze and puzzle us with their lack of competence in areas that seem elementary. Sometimes these youngsters seem to remember incongruous items—they know all the words of TV jingles but forget simple spelling words from one day to the next. Their performance is inconsistent; they show great variability in areas of functioning and large differences between areas of skill.

Learning disabilities represent a constellation of widely varied behaviours and conditions. Some common characteristics and how they may manifest in the classroom are shown in Table 5-1. This list certainly does not cover all of the behaviours that have been attributed to students with learning disabilities, and it should be regarded with extreme caution. No child with learning disabilities will display all these behaviours, while the disparate characteristics of the population means that additional behaviours may exist in some children. Most importantly, one attribute or behaviour does not a learning disability make; we probably all have at least one or two of the listed behaviours.

Table 5-1 Some common characteristics seen in children who are learning disabled

Characteristic	What you might see in the classroom
Inflexible attitude and language	Is reluctant to try anything new. Gets upset when routine is different or the schedule changed. Has difficulty changing from one task to another.
Receptive language difficulties	Hears the dog barking or a truck honking, but barely hears mother calling or what the teacher says. Cannot understand a riddle or joke. Frequently confuses directions, both oral and written. Needs instructions explained for each assignment Asks the same thing over and over; asks constant questions but does not seem interested in the answers.
Expressive language problems	Shows many hesitations and repetitions in oral language. Has blurred pronunciations in speech. Uses poor syntax and semantics. Has trouble relating a story or incident. Stops and starts in the middle of a sentence or idea, talks about hospitals, animals, and enemies all at once. Has difficulty forming concepts. Calls breakfast lunch and is confused by yesterday, today, and tomorrow.
Academic problems	Is less task-oriented than peers. Has problems in all areas of the language hierarchy. Has problems reading. For example, skips words, omits them, or adds them when reading aloud. May be able to add and multiply but not subtract or divide; or can do math mentally but cannot write it down. Shows deficiencies in metacognitive skills; is weak in learning and problem-solving strategies. Doesn't complete lengthy assignments or homework.
Memory problems	Forgets assignments, homework, books, coats, and pencils. Forgets names of people, places, things, own address and telephone number (but does remember the ads on television). Cannot remember things seen or heard. Cannot remember the sequence of letters that make up a word.

Table 5-1 continued

Characteristic	What you might see in the classroom
Impulsive	Has attention problems; is easily distracted. Is disorganized, uncooperative. Says what first comes to mind. Calls out in class. Rushes headlong into work; is the first one finished, but does all the problems wrong.
Outward locus of control	Says "I don't care" or "I won't" but really means "I can't." Would rather be called bad than dumb. Is passive; lacks motivation.
Coordination	May hug the cat too tightly but can't hold a pencil. Has difficulty learning left and right. Has difficulty copying from the board Shows sloppy drawing and writing skills Reverses letters and numbers: may read *on* for *no*, write *41* for *14*, *p* for *d*, or *q* for *b*, May be a good swimmer but stumbles up the stairs. Does not look before walking, bumps into the door, swings lunch boxes into the nearest legs, and trips easily. Has trouble lining up, cannot help bothering the child ahead in the line.
Social	Relates poorly to peers, teachers, and other adults. Is less likely than others to be accepted; may be rejected or neglected by peers. May be socially inept and always on the fringe of a group. Shows poor self-esteem and self-concept. Does not seem to understand the affective status of others derived from facial expressions, body movements, and tone of voice.

Cognitive Development

Cognitive delays are associated with intellectual disabilities. A learning disability is not a cognitive delay. By definition, students with learning disabilities possess average or above-average intelligence. Also by definition, students with learning disabilities do not acquire academic skills at grade expectancy and at a normal rate, and will lag in some or all academic areas.

Thinking requires the ability to conceptualize and solve problems. Because children who are learning disabled are of normal intelligence, they are clearly able to think. Yet significant numbers of these students exhibit memory and thinking disorders; they have problems remembering information over long or short periods of time and demonstrate memory deficits for both auditory and visual stimuli. They have trouble recalling what things sounded like or looked like and forget math facts, spelling words learned only the day before, and directions. These children forget basic personal information, such as their telephone numbers and their addresses. They are more likely than their non-disabled peers to forget to take their homework home bring completed homework to school, lose their homework, not complete it, and make careless mistakes in it (Hallahan, Kauffman, & Lloyd, 1999).

Students with learning disabilities do not have deficits in the actual ability to learn. They seem to have performance deficits rather than ability deficits. Their problems relate to **metacognition**, an awareness of basic learning strategies and one's own awareness of how one learns. Their learning strategies—or lack of them—prevent them from using their basic abilities to the best advantage.

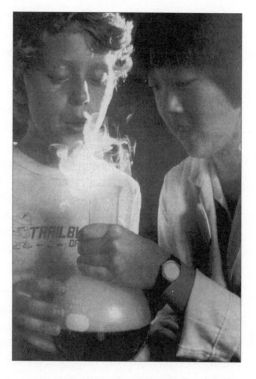

By definition, students with learning disabilities possess average or above-average intelligence.

metacognition

Communication

Language disabilities are closely connected with learning disabilities of all types. So much so that the term *language learning disabilities* is used to refer to the 60 to 80 percent of all students with learning disabilities whose base deficits are in language and reading. Students tend to reach a plateau of language abilities in the areas of semantics, syntax, memory, and pragmatics at levels expected of children between 8 and 10 years old (Wesanko, 1990). In the classroom, these may be the students who sit at the back and hope that the teacher won't call on them. They rarely volunteer answers and when they are asked to speak they may be hesitant, stumble over words, and use a sparse vocabulary.

For these students, problems are often apparent at every level of the **language hierarchy**—listening, speaking, reading, and writing. We describe the deficits for language and reading separately, but do remember that all the elements of language overlap and must develop in tandem if students are to be communicatively competent and adept readers. Deficits in one area spill over to affect the others.

language hierarchy

- *Listening.* The teaching-learning process proceeds on the assumption that articipants listen to each other. When instructing, teachers use an initiate-reply-evaluate mode. They ask questions, listen, and then evaluate whether or not children have mastered the task through their reply. Listening (and therefore responding accurately) may be problematic for children with learning disabilities. For example, they tend to misperceive phonemes requiring very fine discrimination such as /m/ and /n/ and confuse voiced and unvoiced consonants, such as /f/ and /v/ (Wiig & Semel, 1976).

- *Expressive language.* Although they have problems with both expressive and receptive language, students with learning disabilities seem to have greater difficulty using expressive language (Hessler & Kitchen, 1980), particularly semantics and pragmatics. For example, children may continue to overextend words into inappropriate contexts. A child may call all liquids that can be poured into a glass "juice," as opposed to milk, water, or soda. Or the child may learn to call all articles of clothing that have sleeves "sleeves," rather than shirts, sweaters, or coats, because something about the sleeve is meaningful to him or her.

Also apparent are difficulties with articulation, immature speech patterns, mild speech irregularities, general unintelligibility, and cluttered speech. Students may substitute inappropriate words, repeat the same phrase over and over, or use a monotonous voice (see Lue, 2001).

- *Semantics.* The vocabulary used by these students tends to be small, superficial, and reflective of reductions in the development of underlying concepts. Typical children eight or nine years of age recognize the multiple meanings of frequently used words; adolescents who are learning disabled may not perceive multiple meanings and misinterpret when they read or listen. They often take things very literally, missing the subtle nuances of the language. For example, one adolescent went to a laundromat for the first time with a small load of washing. On a towel, he read the instruction, "Wash colours separately." He proceeded to do exactly that, using a separate washing machine for each shade of colour. He spent nine dollars and infuriated the other patrons. Another student was handed a tape by a frazzled teacher and asked to "Put it on the video." The boy set it neatly on top of the machine.

Some children cannot remember the meanings of new words, whether these are identified by the teacher as necessary for general vocabulary acquisition or discovered by the students when attempting to read English literature, social studies, science, and so on. Research indicates that 43 percent of students with learning disabilities have word-finding problems (Wesanko, 1990). Because of limited vocabulary or the inability to absorb the full significance of words, these students then tend to be seriously affected in the areas of generalization, conceptualization, and abstraction.

- *Syntax.* Students with learning disabilities may have problems organizing phrases and words into sentences and are more likely to make syntactical and grammatical errors. They may talk about things out of order, produce rambling and repetitive utterances, and make unrelated statements. Children may also have difficulty in understanding negation, word order, and syntactic mood, which significantly reduces the complexity in their utterances (Kuder, 2003).

- *Pragmatics.* Students who have problems with the social use of language fail to communicate intent, show an inability in turn-taking in conversation, and fail to cue their listeners to the topic of discussion. Students with learning disabilities also seem to miss subtle clues in non-verbal communication. One study (Dimitrovsky, Spector, Levy-Shiff, & Vakil, 1998) that investigated students diagnosed as learning disabled in grades 3 to 6 found the children less accurate than a non-disabled group in identifying facial expressions of emotion. Gender-related differences among the students with learning disabilities were not found.

Academic Achievement

Academic underachievement is the hallmark of the learning disabled population. Some children show deficits in all subject areas; for others, only a few specific academic skills may be affected. Reading, writing, and mathematics are the three major areas of concern.

Students with learning disabilities appear to reach a plateau at about a grade 4 or 5 achievement level (matching their achievement in language). At this level, basic skill instruction generally ceases and students move on to apply their skills to reading comprehension, expository writing, greater use of textbooks in science and social studies, and math applications.

The gap between achievement scores and grade expectancy level widens as students with learning disabilities progress through high school. Even when placed in secondary school resource programs, students do not seem to recoup basic skills. Despite intensive instruction, many adolescents with learning disabilities do not master the higher-level skills involved in reading and written expression (see Chapter 17).

Homework, which accounts for about 20 percent of time spent on academic tasks, is an area of contention for students and teachers. These are the students with a myriad of excuses: "You didn't tell us," or "I lost it," or "I don't know." It is estimated that 56 percent of students with learning disabilities have difficulty completing homework (Bryan & Sullivan-Burstein, 1997).

Reading

Reading is the hallmark of success in school. It is also one of the most complex tasks that students are asked to perform. Reading represents the convergence of numerous cognitive skills and experiences with oral and written language. It involves numerous memory and attention skills as well as phonemic awareness, decoding, and comprehension skills. Little wonder that, among all children, reading problems are the major cause of poor school performance. Reading difficulties affect 15 to 20 percent or more children and adolescents (see Hallahan, Kauffman, & Lloyd, 1999). As well, 1 in every 5 children will experience reading difficulty sufficient to make learning and enjoyment of reading a major effort ("Reading Summit . . ." 1999).

Early problems translate into poor prospects for later learning. Research suggests that the grade 1 readers with the greatest reading difficulties are unlikely to catch up and 90 percent will remain poor readers later in their schooling (Torgesen, 1998). Children behind in reading in kindergarten and grade 1 are likely to be behind in grade 2 and 3 (Juel, 1988). And, if reading is still poor at the end of grade 3, then the prognosis for subsequent rapid gains is bleak (Badian, 1988). As well, most children whose reading disability is not diagnosed until grade 3 or later and receive standard intervention fail to show noticeable improvement (Lyon, 1996).

Children not only meet difficulties in the actual reading process, but also they lose motivation and interest. By the middle of elementary school, reading is so aversive to poor readers that they would rather clean their rooms than read (Juel, 1988).

Most children identified for special education are experiencing significant difficulties in learning to read (Bos & Vaughn, 1998), so reading disorders rank high on the list of academic problems of students who are learning disabled. Figures range between 65 and 80 percent. With the high numbers, it is not surprising that the "history of learning disabilities is full of attempts to identify factors that are key in reading problems" (Hallahan, Kauffman, & Lloyd, 1999, p. 332). Indeed, more is known about reading disabilities than about all the other aspects of learning disabilities put together.

Research findings indicate that students with hard-core reading difficulties manifest a variety of problems in every component and element. Below is an overview of some of the findings from the research literature.

- Phonological and phonemic awareness research first emerged in the 1970s but took 20 years to transit to the classroom. Today it is recognized that phonological weaknesses (clearly tied to the listening skills mentioned earlier) may underlie children's reading and spelling delays and are almost certainly related to problems in other areas, such as written expression (Lyon, 1995).

phonological awareness

- **Phonological awareness** is the ability to blend, segment, rhyme, or in other ways manipulate the sounds of spoken words. Blending and segmenting sounds appear to be the most closely related to reading achievement (Torgesen, Morgan, & Davis, 1992). Phonological awareness is developmental. First, young children recognize that sentences are made up of words; then they begin to understand that words are composed of syllables. Finally, they become sensitive to individual sounds within words and are able to manipulate those sounds. This final level is **phonemic awareness** (Abbott, Walton, & Greenwood, 2002).

phonemic awareness

There is a strong relationship between early literacy and phonological awareness. Good readers can rhyme at approximately four years of age and blend and segment orally presented words by the end of grade 1. The better a young child is at segmenting words into their individual sounds, the more likely he or she is to read and the faster the reading process. From the other side of the picture, we find that by the end of grade 2 most poor readers still cannot blend or segment words well. This deficit within the language system at the level of phonology impairs access to the higher linguistic processes and the ability to gain meaning from text.

- *Word recognition*, the rapid and automatic naming of visually presented material, is essential to the reading process. A problem with word recognition is an element of concern for students with learning disabilities, perhaps related to poor memory and visual processing skills.

- *Word-attack skills* are often deficient. Students may be unable to deal with symbols, synthesize parts of a word into a whole, or organize words into meaningful clusters.

- *Miscues.* When reading, students often miss or confuse details, such as small words—for example, *and* or *but*—resulting in confused interpretation of meanings. Some students do not understand morphological variations and how they change meanings.

- *Fluency.* Children with learning disabilities often have difficulties in fluency (Meyer & Felton, 1999). Oral reading may be stilted and full of substitutions, omissions, and additions. Children may be single-word readers. When they read this way, they clog their working memories so that their efforts at decoding single words prevent understanding at the content level.

- *Comprehension.* Comprehension is the main purpose of reading. It is a problem in all grades, but at the secondary level it becomes the primary reading disability of students who are learning disabled. Obviously, comprehension is not possible unless a reader can translate the printed words into the language they represent (decode). Since comprehension is profoundly influenced by decoding skills, reading is seriously inhibited in the student with decoding problems.

- *Main idea.* Many poor readers cannot identify the main idea of a piece of text and lack sensitivity to the relative importance of major and minor ideas.

- *Context clues.* Competent readers learn to use multiple sources of information—letters, phonemes, past learning, pictures, and context. Individuals with learning disabilities seem to miss context clues and to overlook various patterns of textual organization.

Written Expression

Many students with learning disabilities show marked impairments in all forms of written expression. Tasks that move from spelling and handwriting through syntactic and semantic skills to the complexities of creating sentences and paragraphing are all huge challenges.

Figure 5-2 shows the written work of an eleven-year-old student with many difficulties in his written expression and handwriting.

For students who are learning disabled, spelling has been described as a "seemingly impossible task" (Leuenberger & Morris, 1990), and their spelling achievement usually lags far behind their grade placement. Poor spelling correlates with reading difficulties; good readers can be deplorable spellers, but poor readers are always certain to be bad spellers.

Students with a handwriting disability show clearly deviant writing, with scrawling letter formations, reversals, transformations, uneven slant, and inability to keep to the lines on the paper. Uncoordinated motor movements and difficulty in judging the writing space are the most common causes of handwriting problems (Gerard & Junkula, 1980).

It follows that note-taking, so important in secondary-level programs, suffers. Students are often unable to identify important information, write fast enough to keep up, or make sense of the notes later. Rather than a record of pertinent information, the notes are often scribbles, single words, and drawings that have little relation to the content covered (Weishaar & Boyle, 1997).

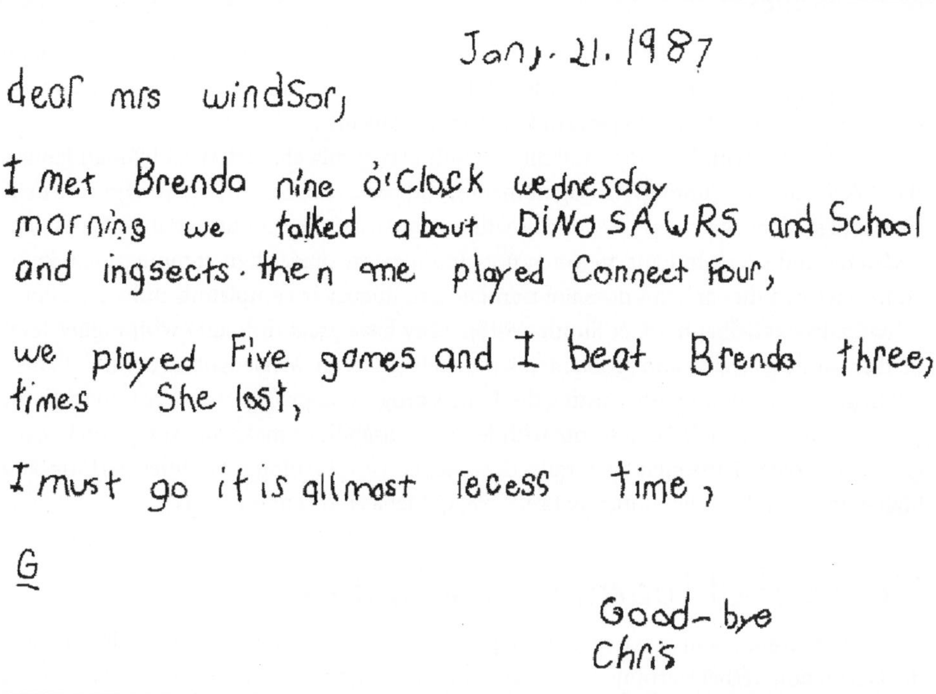
Jan, 21, 1987

dear mrs windsor,

I met Brenda nine o'clock wednesday morning we talked about DINOSAWRS and School and ingsects. then me played Connect Four,

we played Five games and I beat Brenda three, times She lost,

I must go it is allmost recess time,

G

Good-bye
Chris

Figure 5-2
Work of an eleven-year-old with difficulties in written expression

In order to express their thoughts correctly, students need to understand linguistic rules: they must know the rules of grammar, punctuation, and capitalization, and use correct syntax and paragraph construction. Students with a writing disability tend to write little or laboriously. They use incorrect grammar, syntax, and punctuation and show confused or truncated sentences, with an incorrect sequence of tenses, pronoun reference, and word order.

In a broad sense, text styles are described as *narrative* (stories written to entertain) and *expository* (material that communicates information). For many students, narrative style is easier than expository, which involves highly complex metacognitive skills and cognitive processes (Englert & Mariage, 2003). Indeed, expository writing represents one of the most daunting of all academic tasks demanded of students with learning disabilities (see Hallenbeck, 2002). The writing of these children is characterized by shorter and lower-quality work than that of normal students.

Good writers devote up to two-thirds of their writing time to planning, focusing on large issues such as the audience and how the final product holds together. They appreciate *story grammar*—the description of the typical elements frequently found in stories such as theme, characters, and setting.

Little is known about how students with learning disabilities plan their compositions. It does not appear that they begin with a plan that they consistently refine; instead, they have a less sophisticated approach to composing, one that minimizes the role of planning and operates largely without meta-cognitive control (De La Paz & Graham, 1997). When composing, they typically convert writing into question-and-answer tasks, quickly telling whatever comes to mind and producing papers with poorly developed ideas. In terms of generating content, these students produce written texts that are inordinately short.

Mathematics

The prevalence of arithmetic disabilities is estimated to be 5 to 8 percent of the general school-aged population (Miller, Butler, & Lee, 1998). It is higher among students with learning disabilities: about 25 percent have math problems.

For students with learning disabilities, math is typically characterized by high failure. Basic skills such as counting, writing numerals, and basic addition and subtraction are deficient and students have less developed math vocabularies: they confuse terms such as *plus*, *and*, *total*, and *sum*. Students are often not automatic in single-digit computational items and, even when they are, this does not translate into fluency in completing multi-digit items (Cawley, Parmar, Shephard, & Smith, 1997). They have great difficulty with higher-level math, including algebra and problem-solving skills (Maccini, McNaughton, & Ruhl, 1999).

In general, students with learning disabilities progress approximately 1 year in math for every 2 years in school. Adolescents with learning disabilities make an average of 1 year's growth in grades 7 through 12. Grade 12 students with learning disabilities perform at a high grade 5 level (Miller, Butler, & Lee, 1998; O'Melia & Rosenberg, 1994).

Non-verbal Learning Disabilities

Recently, educators and researchers have paid renewed attention to the difficulties of students with non-verbal learning disabilities. These children's major traits seem to be marked social problems. Non-verbal learning disabilities are also tied to weak psychomotor and perceptual motor skills that persist across time.

Perceptual Development

Perception involves the use of the senses to recognize, discriminate, and interpret stimuli. **Psychological processing** (more often called *learning styles* today) refers to how an individual processes sensory information and puts it to meaningful intellectual use.

psychological processing

Problems in visual perception were traditionally associated with learning disabilities. Many early studies (e.g., Calfee, 1977) indicated that, as a group, children with learning disabilities perform poorly on tasks designed to assess visual perceptual abilities. Other work (e.g., Harber, 1980) showed that auditory perception disorders occur with greater-than-normal frequency among children who are learning disabled. Auditory dysfunctions lead to difficulty in synthesizing sounds into words, analyzing words into word parts, and associating sounds with symbols. These deficits and their implications are shown in Table 5-2 on the next page.

Motor Problems

Laterality refers to an internal knowledge of the differences between left and right; **directionality** is an awareness of left and right in the environment outside the body. Out of an infinite number of motor experiments, children learn the differences between an activity on the right side of the body and the same activity on the left. The pattern thus becomes a skill, and the skill becomes a habit. At approximately five or six years of age, most children establish complete cerebral dominance and consistently prefer to use one side of their bodies in dealing with the world. Laterality is the motor basis for spatial concepts. When children have developed laterality, they can project this to directionality concepts in external space such as up and down, and in front and behind.

laterality

directionality

The laterality theory maintains that learning is adversely affected if the child does not establish a tendency to perform most functions with one side of the body. The failure to establish laterality, directionality, and dominance may account for many reversals and similar confusions in children's reading and writing. When mixed dominance is encountered along with other signs, such as *enuresis* (bed-wetting), preference for play with younger children, or infantile speech patterns, it may suggest a maturational lag that can interfere with a child's abilities to function in academic work.

In the past, many left-handed children were considered to be at high risk for learning disabilities. While it is true that among the learning disabled population (and indeed among nearly all populations of problem learners) there is a far higher proportion of left-handers than in the general population, the hand dominance in itself does not seem to be the problem. The difficulties arise with incomplete or *mixed dominance*, which translates into confusion in directionality or right and left discrimination.

Coordination

General uncoordination refers to a lack of muscular control. Uncoordinated children tend to be physically awkward and have particular difficulty in acquiring the gross motor skills

general uncoordination

Table 5-2 Examples of visual and auditory processes

Process	Ability	Implications and problems
Visual perception	The ability to make visual stimuli meaningful	The child may have problems attending to and interpreting visual stimuli.
Visual discrimination	The ability to perceive dominant features in different objects or symbols	The child may confuse letters and words that look alike.
		The child may not see the internal detail, as in *rid/red*, or may fail to see the general configuration, as in *ship/snip*.
Visual closure	The ability to identify a common object from an incomplete visual presentation	The child may have difficulty assembling puzzles and objects, identifying missing parts, or completing words by closing spaces between letters, as in rab-bit.
Visual figure–ground	The ability to focus on the foreground and ignore the background visual stimuli	The child may not be able to distinguish words; for example, the child may be unable to point to the first word of the second paragraph.
Visual memory	The ability to recall the dominant features of the stimulus item	The child may not be able to copy patterns or arrange blocks in a series.
Visual sequential memory	The ability to recollect the sequence of a number of items presented visually	The child fails to recognize visually familiar words and forgets the arrangement of letters in a word.
Auditory perception	The ability to recognize and interpret stimuli that are heard	The child may have problems attending to and interpreting auditory stimuli.
Auditory discrimination	The ability to recognize differences between sounds and to identify similarities and differences between words	The child may not hear the similarities in initial or final sounds in words or be able to discriminate short vowels such as pin, pan, pen.
Auditory closure	The ability to identify sounds and words from an incomplete auditory presentation	The child may have problems in sound–symbol association and especially in blending sounds.
Auditory figure–ground	The ability to focus on the foreground sound and ignore other sounds	The child may not focus on the dominant sound; the fan on the overhead projector may be more important than the teacher's voice.
Auditory memory	The ability to recognize and recall previously presented auditory stimuli	The child may have problems retaining and recalling auditory experiences.
Auditory sequential memory	The ability to reproduce from memory sequences presented auditorily	The child may forget or confuse oral directions, the sequence of events, the sequence of letters in a word, and the sequence of words in a sentence.

that are necessary for age-appropriate self-care and play tasks such as dressing, skipping, jumping rope, or riding a bicycle (Telzrow & Bonar, 2002). *Overflow movements*, which occur when the child wants to perform a movement with one hand and the other hand involuntarily follows in a shadow movement, may be present. In the fine motor domain, children with non-verbal learning disabilities perform significantly below average on standardized tests of visual and motor functioning and struggle with skills such as tracing, cutting, colouring, and handwriting.

Poor motor skills may correlate with adverse social interaction. Conte and colleagues (1995) found that the biggest problem for children with poor motor skills was being called names and being laughed at by other students when performing poorly at a game.

Haptic Problems

The term **haptic** concerns the information transmitted through touch, body movement, and position in space. Haptic problems are thought to be relatively uncommon. However, researchers do suggest a relationship between haptic abilities, body image, laterality, and tactile information. Tactile information is important in handwriting, as it dictates the grasp of the pen or pencil.

haptic

Body image refers to a person's awareness of the body, its capabilities, the interrelationship of body parts, and the relationship of bodies to the environment. Children with body image problems may not be able to organize themselves within their environment. They may be clumsy; slow in dressing and undressing and have difficulty in putting on a sweater; unable to walk across the classroom without knocking into chairs and desks; and unable to draw figures.

body image

Social and Emotional Development

Since the early 1970s, research has documented the social difficulties encountered by many students with learning disabilities. It suggests that social interaction and social acceptance for these students remains deficient in comparison with that of other children. The reported rates of manifested social deficits range from 33 to 75 percent of students with learning disabilities (Bryan, Burstein, & Ergel, 2004; Kavale & Forness, 1996; Lerner, 2000). The deficits in social skills may also be the defining difference between verbal and non-verbal learning disabilities, since children in the latter category appear to have significantly weaker interpersonal abilities and difficulties in expressing feelings and reading others.

Judith Wiener of York University in Toronto has studied the topic of social skills and social deficits in learning-disabled students extensively and sees the peer relationships of such children as pivotal to their behavioural adjustment (Wiener, 2004). One study (Wiener, Harris, & Shirer, 1990) found that approximately 50 percent of a sample of 90 children with learning disabilities in suburban schools had peer relationship problems, with about 35 percent being neglected and 15 percent rejected. Later, Kuhne and Wiener (2000) found that elementary children with learning disabilities were rated as having lower social preference and higher *liked least* scores on a sociometric scale, were less likely to be popular, and were more likely to be socially neglected and rejected. They were seen by peers as being less cooperative and less likely to be leaders than were children without learning disabilities. Moreover, peer status declines over the course of a school year (Wiener, 2004).

Children with body image problems often have difficulty with tasks such as dressing.

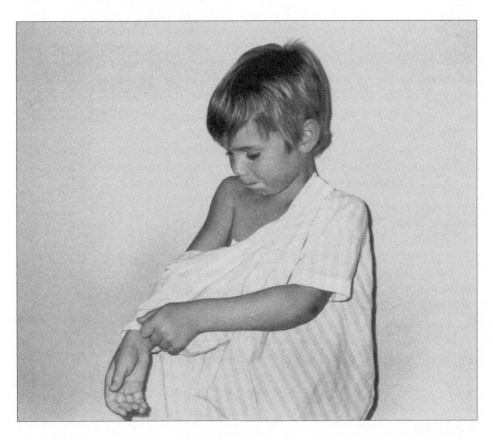

The reasons why individuals with learning disabilities inspire negative responses are not clear. They may stem from a mix of deficits in verbal and non-verbal communication, and social perception skills. Communication difficulties may make satisfying interactions less likely and communication breakdowns more frequent. Children with learning disabilities perform less well in role-taking in interpersonal tasks that require taking an alternative viewpoint: they demonstrate inadequate skills in social perception, specifically in skills employing empathy, role-taking, and making social inferences (Holder & Kirkpatrick, 1991). They tend to ignore interpersonal signals from their peers, have trouble perceiving the moods of others, and may have an inability to interpret facial expressions.

Some research indicates that social problems are more prevalent and serious in children with non-verbal learning disabilities than in other groups (Worling, Humphries, & Tannock, 1999). Confused and frustrated, and unsure of how to express their needs and have them met, these students often exhibit aggressive behaviour. As they grow older, they may internalize their problems and show pervasive anxiety and a high incidence of depression (Cleaver & Whitman, 1998).

The accumulated failure experiences of children with language disabilities and those with non-verbal learning disabilities lead to other negative characteristics. Students **self-concept** often develop secondary emotional problems that include lowered **self-concept**—a person's cognitive appraisal of attributes and characteristics, including physical, social, and academic competence—and self-esteem (self-worth)—an affective or emotional reaction to one's self. Compared to their peers, students who are learning disabled tend to hold lower self-concepts about academic performance, even in areas in which they have had little experience or instruction. They tend not to attribute their learning to their own ability, and develop an external locus of control. When this happens, students view themselves as controlled by outer rather than inner forces. They hold lower expectations for success, credit any successes to luck or the ease of the task rather than their own abilities or efforts, and view failure as further verification of their own persistent lack of ability.

These children have less optimism about improving their performance in the future, even when they receive special education services, and show reduced levels of effort and negative affect. They may become *resistant*, with a deliberate unwillingness to try to achieve. Unable to keep up with school work, but anxious to retain the goodwill of the teacher, they relieve the stress of trying and failing by no longer attempting to learn. A similar problem is *learned helplessness*. Children who display learned helplessness have no faith that their efforts will result in desired outcomes. Because they expect to fail, they lose their motivation.

With all of this, it seems little wonder that children with learning disabilities may also develop an **emotional overlay**, an adverse reaction to learning problems and academic failure. In many cases it is extremely difficult to determine whether the learning or the adjustment problem came first, and the exact interaction of these in a child's functioning.

emotional overlay

Co-occurring Disabilities

Between 24 and 52 percent of children with learning disabilities are reported to have significant social, emotional, and behavioural problems (Rock, Fessler, & Church, 1997). The most common co-occurring conditions are Attention Deficit Disorder (ADD), Attention Deficit Hyperactivity Disorder (ADHD), and behavioural disorders.

Compared to typical students, those with learning disabilities show externalizing behavioural disorders such as aggression, antisocial behaviour, and conduct problems, and internalizing problems such as anxiety and depression (Kavale & Forness, 1997). Students behave in a less appropriate fashion in both regular and special classes, and often display maladaptive styles of responses during instructional activities, possibly as a result of their poor cognitive performance (Bender & Smith, 1990).

Attention problems are endemic among youngsters with exceptional conditions, and those with learning disabilities are no exception. They are less task-oriented. One study found a learning-disabled sample to be on-task only 57 percent of the time, as compared to 70 percent for the non-disabled sample (McKinney, McLure, & Feagans, 1982). Another study (Roberts, Pratt, & Leach, 1991) reported that a group of students with mild disabilities were off-task twice as often as non-disabled students (see Figure 8-1 on page 261).

There is evidence of considerable overlap between the diagnostic categories of learning disabilities and ADD. But estimates of attention problems and hyperactivity in children identified as learning disabled cover a huge span—from 9 to 80 percent (McKinney, Montague, & Hocutt, 1993; Shaywitz & Shaywitz, 1987)—and are not very informative.

To compound the problems, adolescents with learning disabilities are at risk for emotional difficulties and more likely to experience depression (Heath, 1996; Heath & Ross, 2000). The prevalence of depression in students with learning disabilities may, in fact, be much higher than the 1 to 2 percent found in the general population (see Maag & Reid, 2006).

The interplay of learning disabilities and co-occurring conditions is shown in Figure 5-3. As you can see, when off-task behaviour, lowered motivation, and externalizing behaviour come together, they raise further barriers to successful learning. They limit a child's ability to profit from instruction and to have effective interactions with peers and teachers.

Family Variables

At first glance it may appear that parents of children with learning disabilities are much more fortunate than parents of children with more severe disabilities. In fact, when a child is identified as learning disabled, parents may feel relieved, hoping this identification will lead to solutions that will eliminate the child's learning or behaviour problem (Bos & Vaughn, 1998). It appears, rather, that learning disabilities create much confusion within a family. With a severe disability, the family's adjustment to the idea of future dependency can be made fairly easily. But with a milder disability, the family may find itself on a roller coaster of expectations, with hopes for the future alternately raised and dashed as the child progresses or falls back.

Figure 5-3

Interplay of characteristics

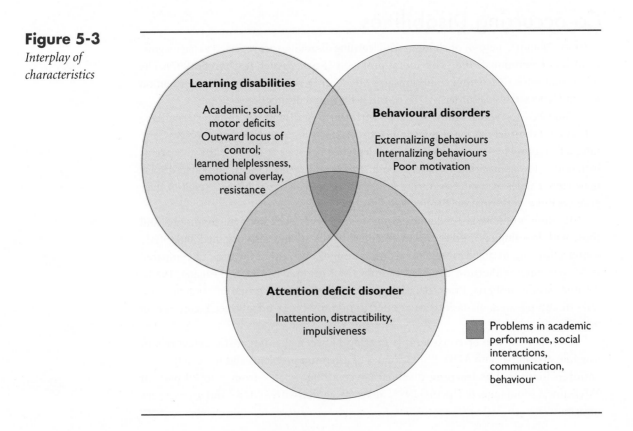

Lack of a clear diagnosis causes great concern and anxiety, resulting in high levels of stress for parents. Few learning disabilities are severely disabling to children younger than five, and therefore their detection before a child enters school is quite difficult (Vaughn, Bos, & Schumm, 1997). Parents, however, may detect subtle signs that lead them to suspect a difficulty. Even so, Faerstein (1986) found that a gap of 3.5 years elapsed between the time a learning disability was suspected and its diagnosis. This gap was not due to the mother's lack of responsibility, but more often to others who denied the child's problem and averred that he or she would outgrow it.

In the home, the receptive and expressive language problems of children who are learning disabled may cause them to appear slow, confused, impulsive, inattentive, even obstinate. Parents may react with guilt, overprotection, rejection, or concern. Thinking they are assisting the child, some parents may disrupt his or her activities by overusing responses and initiations. Or parents may react by giving the child too much responsibility, denying the gravity of the problem, or placing blame on themselves and accepting failure.

Cultural and Linguistic Differences

As we have already cautioned, too often cultural and linguistic differences, along with poor exposure to literacy or poor testing, are mistaken for disabilities in the areas of language, behaviour, and social skills. The misrepresentation is observable in the field of learning disabilities, where numbers of linguistic minority students are diagnosed as learning disabled. Limited English proficiency (LEP) is often confused with a learning disability because the characteristics of second-language learners, especially in the early stages of second-language acquisition, are similar to behaviours associated with certain categories of exceptionality, specifically learning disabilities and communication disorders (Winzer & Mazurek, 1998).

ASSESSMENT OF LEARNING DISABILITIES

While there is little agreement on definition, prevalence, or remedial procedures in the field of learning disabilities, there is almost universal agreement on the need for the efficient diagnosis of this population's members. Before setting up programs, it is incumbent on educators to conduct a thorough evaluation of a student in order to pinpoint the kind and degree of specific disabilities present as well as the strengths and weaknesses in each developmental domain.

The identification and assessment of children with possible learning disabilities is anything but easy. Assessment practices are fraught with problems: an acceptable assessment framework is lacking; appropriate instruments are not available; and many of the assumptions that have traditionally underlain assessment practices, such as the discrepancy criterion, are under attack. Early identification is critical but this requires the development of a costly, sophisticated system.

Often, the process suffers from lack of coordination. Many professionals within and outside the school system become involved, and each of these people may hold very different views regarding the nature of learning disabilities. A pediatrician may stress minimal brain dysfunction, a psychiatrist behavioural disorders, and a psychologist intellectual inadequacy. Even within the school system, identification and assessment is often a rather hit-and-miss process. There is currently no single procedure to identify learning disabilities. Clinicians rely heavily on personal diagnostic judgement and use a variety of tests that are often idiosyncratic—they conform to the preferences of local assessors. As well, there is little consensus regarding when children should be tested, by whom, and to what purpose.

Generally, identification involves two major processes: *screening* and a *psycho-educational diagnosis,* which depends upon a battery of psychological and educational tests. These should be supplemented by child observations, a physical examination, an evaluation of hearing and vision, and archival data—interviews with the child and the parents, school records, and the comments of earlier teachers.

We could not possibly detail, or even touch upon, the variety of information sources that are used as the basis for programming. Here we can only point out some single tools in a very large toolbox. Screening is discussed in Chapter 1.

As we observed earlier in this chapter, the discrepancy criterion—identification on the basis of a difference between potential and performance—is an area of debate and considerable controversy. But even though the area is filled with heated debate, it is still usual to investigate a discrepancy as part of identification procedures. Therefore, one of the first steps in the formal diagnosis is an assessment of intellectual potential to rule out the possibility of intellectual disability and simultaneously to establish the fact of normal mental ability. Broad-coverage tests such as versions of the Wechsler Intelligence Scale for Children (WISC-R, WISC-III, WISC-IV) are usually given first.

Once intelligence (potential) is judged to be normal, achievement tests are used to evaluate performance. Achievement tests examine a spectrum of tasks such as oral reading, reading comprehension, language, spelling, math, and general knowledge. Results are often presented as grade equivalents or percentile ranks. Further tools may assess auditory, visual, and motor processing; vocational skills; adaptive behaviour; or pinpoint specific areas of weakness. For language assessment, observations, language samples, and standardized tools are employed (see Chapter 4). Research on reading has validated a number of measures, such as the Woodcock-Johnson Psycho-educational Battery-Revised or 111 Test of Achievement.

Alternative systems are emerging to counter the problems with discrepancy. They are founded on the belief that discrepancy is neither necessary nor sufficient in learning disabilities and that diagnosis should have a basis in educational remediation rather than suspect neurology or psychometrics.

British Columbia researchers (Siegel, Lam, & Ladyman, 2000) suggest using a teacher-applied system that includes tests of word recognition, word decoding, reading comprehension, spelling, writing, arithmetic, and problem solving. A score of one standard deviation below the mean should be seen as a significant weakness; two standard deviations require specific remedial work.

The most widely employed model for assessing learning disabilities involves testing the child as a preliminary step to determining how to program. Many say that this should be turned around and assessment should begin with a controlled trial of intervention strategies to see how a child responds to both scientific-based instruction and a sound program of early intervention (Case & Taylor, 2005; Maloney, 2002). In pursuit of this, the

American IDEA of 2004 removed the discrepancy criterion and allowed responses to intervention as part of the learning disabilities assessment process.

Curriculum-Based Assessment

Programs for students with mild disabilities are centred in the general curriculum. It therefore makes sense to use curriculum-referenced testing or **curriculum-based assessment** (CBA), a procedure that directly assesses student performance within the course content for the purpose of determining his or her instructional needs.

curriculum-based assessment

The fundamental question of CBA is "How is the student progressing in the curriculum of his or her school?" The variety of models of CBA in use are all guided by the premise that curricula should serve as the basis for assessment, and all models emphasize measurement that is brief, frequent, and based on the student's classroom curriculum and that can be used to monitor instructional programs and effectiveness.

The core methods of CBA are frequent performance sampling, systematic recording and plotting of results, and the use of results to guide further teaching. To prepare CBA, teachers determine the annual curriculum goals for a student. They then devise and present short tests or **probes**—brief samples of academic behaviour. Two types of probes are commonly used—probes of basic skills in academic core areas and probes of content areas and the strategies needed, such as textbook reading and note taking. Teachers use the data generated to monitor student progress and adjust programs.

probes

The measurement of progress by using actual curriculum-based items and by direct daily measurement has a noticeable effect on academic achievement when the results are used to modify instructional planning. Apart from progress monitoring, CBA can be used for screening, individual education planning, and program evaluation. It has been found to be an accurate screening measure for referral to special education, less influenced than other measures by teacher variables (Overton, 2003).

Psychological Processing

As we pointed out in the section on non-verbal learning disabilities, theories in the field have long taken into account the possibility of processing deficiencies. Indeed, this was the major position for the first 40 years of intervention with learning disabilities.

The use of tests to diagnose underlying processing deficits was introduced at the same time that learning disabilities developed as a category of exceptionality. These measures have generated much concern and controversy. Opponents argue that because psychological processes are not directly observable and must be inferred from a child's performance, it is almost impossible to accurately assess underlying psychological processes. Nevertheless, a wide variety of measures that purport to assess such areas as auditory and visual processing, motor sub-skills, and kinesthetic functions is available.

Although processing is not considered as fundamental to learning disabilities as previously thought, and although the tests and special instruction based on their results are used far less frequently than in the past, we cannot totally discount these factors. Table 5-2 on page 148 shows the auditory and visual subskills upon which many of these tools focus.

INTERVENTION WITH CHILDREN WHO HAVE LEARNING DISABILITIES

Since a learning disability can be highly deleterious to a child's academic and social functioning as well as future success in life, treatment becomes a critical issue. Hope for a cure has been a compelling force in the field and has resulted, said Vaughn and colleagues (2000) in "a myriad of slippery interventions" (p. 100). Of course, as well as controversial and questionable interventions, the field has access to some well-validated methodologies. In fact, a hallmark of the past two decades has been the considerable progress made in designing, implementing, and evaluating effective interventions for students with learning disabilities.

Medical Intervention

Historically, medicine and learning disabilities have been closely linked, particularly in the area of diagnosis. Until quite recently, learning disabilities were conceptualized in relation to biophysical disorders—specifically some form of minimal brain dysfunction. Today, the field has moved away from a medical model to a diagnostic and educational model for remediation. However, the medical profession continues to have an active interest in learning disabilities. The current focus of medical interest is drug therapy, which is discussed in Chapter 8.

Technical Aids

A range of techniques is helping to improve the academic progress of students with learning and other mild disabilities. Computer programs can be particularly helpful for students with attention problems, those who are unmotivated or disinterested in reading, and those who lack organizational skills. One study (Higgins & Raskind, 2000) found that students with learning disabilities showed significant improvements after computer-assisted instruction in reading comprehension, spelling, and word recognition scores over a control group.

Educational Intervention

Educators must be deeply concerned about how and what to teach pupils who have demonstrated that they learn differently and not very readily the things with which education is charged with teaching them. The challenge for those involved with students who are learning disabled revolves around how to prevent learning failure, how to individualize education for a particular child, and how to provide programs for students who are not responding to traditional instructional approaches.

Service Delivery Models

How to provide the most effective services in the most appropriate setting is not an easy issue. Before the term *learning disabilities* emerged in 1963, some students were placed in special classes. The majority were in general classrooms, although their problems may have been unrecognized or ignored. During the mainstreaming period of the

1970s and 1980s, the general classroom/resource room combination was the most common method of program delivery. Today, a continuum of services is common. Most students with learning disabilities are educated in general classrooms; resource rooms remain popular in some school districts; and a number of very specialized schools exist in Canada, such as the Trillium Demonstration School in Milton, Ontario.

For placement and program, researchers today are investigating two interrelated questions: "What is the most effective model for students with learning disabilities?" and "What is the relationship of placement to outcomes?" Evidence remains inconclusive.

Many educators show great reluctance to segregate students labelled as learning disabled. They would prefer that such students be educated in the general classroom full time with some support. Some studies report that inclusion is beneficial, that students with learning disabilities achieve better academically in general classrooms, and that inclusion may be beneficial for certain subject areas or when specific strategies are employed (e.g., Marston, 1996; Rea, McLaughlin, & Walther-Thomas, 2002).

In contrast, some educators and parents feel that the move toward full inclusion is not warranted. Advocates for retention of a continuum of services contend that special classes and resource rooms contribute more to the academic achievement of some types of students with special needs, especially those who are learning disabled or emotionally disturbed, than general classrooms (Fuchs & Fuchs, 1995).

Despite the increasing frequency of inclusive placements, positive outcomes for students with disabilities have not been consistently associated with inclusive reforms. Outcomes appear to be most problematic for students with mild disabilities (Cook, Semmel, & Gerber, 1999). A study by Zigmond and colleagues (1995) of settings where students with learning disabilities were included failed to find academic benefits. Rather, they found that the achievement outcomes were "neither desirable nor acceptable" (p. 539). Another study (Klinger, Vaughn, Hughes, Schumm, & Elbaum, 1998) found that students with learning disabilities in inclusive classrooms made less-than-appropriate academic gains, even with atypically high levels of support. The students who were emergent readers made minimal progress in reading even when extensive professional development was provided for teachers.

You can see from the conflicting results presented above that full inclusion or some alternate model is not a decisive horse race for students with learning disabilities. There is no research evidence that any one service delivery model meets the needs of all students; indeed, empirical research in the field so far fails to support the efficacy of inclusion for students with learning disabilities (see Heflin & Bullock, 1999). The current consensus is for responsible and selective placement, which seems to translate as the retention of a full continuum of services.

Educational Approaches

There is a diverse range of generic and specific approaches in educational intervention for students with learning disabilities. *Generic approaches* refer to techniques such as adapting curriculum and grading requirements in the general classroom or providing resource room assistance in areas of academic lag. *Specific approaches* refer to a great deal more program adaptation and direction, such as teaching to sub-skill deficits or meta-cognitive training.

Table 5-3 outlines some generic strategies. Read these with two caveats. First, these approaches are suitable for all the students with mild disabilities to learning that we discuss in this section. Second, the heterogeneous nature of the learning-disabled population makes any menu of approaches tenuous at best. No single approach, method, or technique can be expected to offer a solution to every problem.

Table 5-3 Creating accessible classrooms

Accommodations

- Seat students near the front of the room so that distractions are behind them, or use carrels to cut down on distractions.

- Use many organizational devices to assist student learning such as dates for assignments written on the board or posted on a special bulletin board; reminders about homework; organizational folders; advance organizers; assignment notebooks; homework planners; and study guides to tell students what to study.

- Allow only about 10 seconds per student as you circulate to correct seatwork. If a student requires more assistance, then reteaching is probably necessary.

Adaptations, materials

- Have different coloured book coverings for each class.

- On worksheets, use a lot of spacing; provide ample space for writing or drawing; avoid crowding and extraneous print; limit the type of questions; provide clear and concise directions; provide examples; use typing or printing in place of handwriting.

- Write in complete sentences rather than phrases to help students apply the rules of grammar consistently.

Adaptations, instructional

- Teach test-taking skills. From 5 to 14 hours of instruction time spread over 5 to 7 weeks appears to be the effective range of instruction time needed to improve test-taking skills and "test wiseness" (Grossman, 1995; Samson, 1985). Students should be taught to focus on the types of questions that are likely to arise, read all the questions carefully, answer the easy questions first, allot time properly during a test, answer all the questions, develop an outline before writing an essay, and check their work.

- Use student self-evaluation. After students perform a task such as taking a test, give them a checklist of strategy tips and ask them which tips they used and which ones they didn't.

- Communicate expectations and grading guidelines clearly.

- Provide examples of finished products as models and guides.

- Preface all remarks with a title, or the main idea of the lesson.

- Stress important points in a lesson with "Watch now" or "Listen carefully."

- Define all requirements of a completed activity. For example, "Your math is complete when all five problems are complete and corrected."

Table 5-3 continued

- Provide multiple written prompts such as, "To answer this question, look on page 12" (Boyle & Yeager, 1997).

- Use cognitive frameworks (also called story maps, critical thinking maps, cognitive maps, semantic feature analyses, induction towers, flow charts, study guides, and structured outlines). These highlight the salient points of an academic activity and are anchors for knowledge around which students build new information (Boyle & Yeager, 1997).

- Use various models for reading, such as in-class text reading, semantic maps, pre-teaching new vocabulary, and silent reading.

- State a purpose for reading, such as looking for specifics.

- Use strategic note-taking. This procedure involves using special cued notepaper on which the student fills in the details during and after a lecture. The cues are as follows:

  1. Today's topic. Identify the topic and briefly summarize any knowledge you had of it before the class.
  2. Identify major points of the lecture, given in clusters.
  3. Identify new points included in the lecture.
  4. Later, write down five main points from the lecture and describe each one (Weishaar & Boyle, 1997).

- If homework is important to your program, keep in mind that too much can overwhelm the student who is learning disabled. Listen to what students say about their homework experiences.

- Put smiling, frowning, and neutral faces on the cover of homework assignments. Have students circle the one that describes their feelings about the assignment. Discuss

Focus on Underlying Subskills (processing)

Twenty years ago, educators stressed process-training approaches that sought to remediate processing deficits (see Table 5-2 on page 148). Such an emphasis is quite rare today, although some old wine is going into new bottles to accommodate students with non-verbal learning disabilities.

Behavioural (Skills) Approaches

Behavioural approaches, also referred to as *skill models* or *task-based perspectives*, assume that a child's problems are external and result from some gap in instruction. The major focus, therefore, is on the mismatch between school tasks and the unique ability patterns and learning styles of students with learning disabilities and their ability to perform academic tasks. Teachers provide direct instruction in weak academic areas and focus on the skills needed for academic success such as word decoding and basic number facts. Within each skill subject, a hierarchy of skills is defined.

Direct Instruction refers to activity-focused, highly scripted teacher instruction that incorporates numerous opportunities for students to respond. The components of Direct Instruction include explicit step-by-step teacher procedures that account for student mastery, immediate feedback, practice, and gradual fading from teacher direction. Learning

Direct Instruction

Figure 5-4

Steps in Direct Instruction

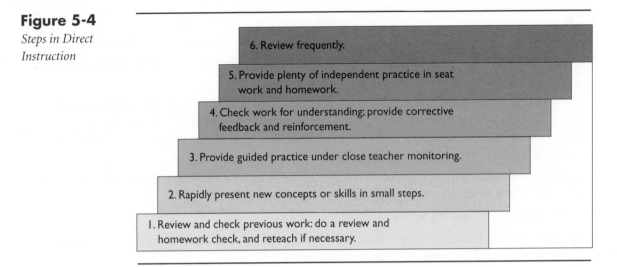

6. Review frequently.

5. Provide plenty of independent practice in seat work and homework.

4. Check work for understanding; provide corrective feedback and reinforcement.

3. Provide guided practice under close teacher monitoring.

2. Rapidly present new concepts or skills in small steps.

1. Review and check previous work: do a review and homework check, and reteach if necessary.

is achieved by identifying the specific objective to be attained, arranging appropriate stimuli to elicit the responses, programming learning sequences in small steps, and reinforcing desired behaviours. Procedures include prompting, shaping, or reinforcing, all implemented in a precise and consistent fashion. The steps in Direct Instruction are shown in Figure 5-4.

Direct Instruction is one of the more effective approaches validated through research. Intensive Direct Instruction can result in impressive learning for students who would otherwise fail to reach critical benchmarks. Walberg (1991) asserts that this direct didactic approach has the best track record for learners with special needs.

Cognitive Approaches

Advances in cognitive psychology have resulted in the development of programs that focus on learning and thinking skills, encompassed under the term *metacognition*. This term was first mentioned in publications by Flavell (1976) and Brown (1978), who defined **metacognition** as knowledge of one's own cognitive processes. Metacognition is the steering, regulating, and orchestration of cognitive processes, which in turn rely on cognitive objects such as language, attention, and memory.

metacognition

Metacognition is developmental, truly emerging (along with metalinguistics) in a child at around age five to seven, and improving throughout school. Metacognition plays a role in perception, such as "Am I really seeing that?" It helps regulate the flow of information through working memory, as in "I must remember that." It also affects long-term memory, as in "I know I know that," and self-evaluation, "I studied all the wrong stuff for the test."

Self-regulated learners have developed metacognitive competence. They own a combination of academic learning skills and self-control—they have both the skill and the will to learn. In contrast, poor learners fail to develop efficient metacognition; they simply do not understand the relationship between strategic learning and successful performance. Many students with learning disabilities fit into this group. They have metacognitive deficits; that is, they do not lack the processes entirely, but they seem to use them inefficiently and ineffectively. They fail to maintain and generalize learned strategies, do not understand the relationship between learning strategies and successful performance, and do not apply efficient strategies such as verbal rehearsal and chunking spontaneously (de Bettencourt, 1987).

What Are Metacognitive Processes? Before we discuss intervention, it makes sense to be clear about what metacognition is and the processes involved. Within the general concept of metacognition, there are two types of behaviour. These are *knowledge* (alternatively referred to as *cognitive strategies* or *control executive strategies*) and *skill* (*learning strategies*). Metacognitive processes are illustrated in Figure 5-5.

Knowledge is the overarching organizing process, the general strategies used in accomplishing a learning goal. It includes how a person thinks and acts when planning, executing, and evaluating performance on a task. The outcomes of knowledge are indicators of how well a person uses methods and strategies to control and promote his or her own learning. The ability is shown, for example, when competent readers reduce their reading speed when they reach a difficult passage.

Learning strategies (skills) refer to an individual's approach to tasks and are either generic or domain-specific. Generic strategies are problem-solving skills that apply across many areas of the curriculum such as planning, setting goals for studying, skimming information, locating information, generating questions, taking notes, and writing tests. Included are mechanisms such as tracking attention to task; asking questions such as, "Am I understanding this?"; monitoring speed; and assessing the amount of time it takes to learn and understand certain material. Specific strategies are those used in one situation, such as remembering a /sh/ combination in reading or a principle in geometry.

 **learning strategies**

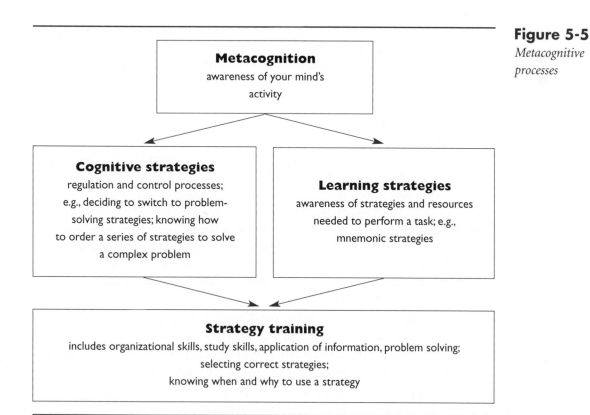

Figure 5-5

Metacognitive processes

Strategy Training Effective strategy users constantly monitor their progress to see whether the strategy they're using is as effective as it should be. They also use *conditional knowledge*—knowing when and where to use a strategy. An example of this is the matching of a strategy such as skimming to a goal such as getting an overview of the content.

Metacognition develops over time, but the process can be helped by effective instruction. Individuals with learning disabilities show significant improvement following strategy training, also known as learning-thinking instructional programs, cognitive training, cognitive behaviour modification, or strategic instruction. (Note that the differences in cognitive models are semantic. No matter what the terms used, each model stresses the importance of students learning systems of action that lead to the solution of problems.)

Strategy training incorporates elements of behavioural, cognitive, and social learning theories. It typically provides the learner with a set of self-instructional steps to increase effectiveness in the acquisition, organization, and expression of information. Training teaches the strategies needed for acquiring information from written material, techniques for remembering information, and methods for improving written expression. The ultimate aim is to provide students with tools that will enable them to become autonomous learners and devise their own strategies.

There are several important sequenced areas in strategy training.

- Teaching students to consider the many variables involved in problem solving. Students must analyze the task at hand; identify the steps necessary to complete the task; identify the effective strategies; delineate the necessary steps; and decide how to go about implementing the strategies.

- Teaching students to regulate the processes involved in problem solving, such as planning, checking, testing, revising, and evaluating. Here students reflect on what they already know, devise a plan for attacking the new problem, monitor their progress, and evaluate the outcome of the plan.

Increasing student effectiveness in the use of specific cognitive skills employed in problem solving. Simply telling students about effective strategies is not enough; practice is essential.

In math, for example, strategy training is the best intervention (Miller, Butler, & Lee, 1998). One way to teach the procedures is for an adult to first perform the specified task while verbalizing aloud, covering questions about the task, self-guiding instruction on how to do the task, and self-evaluating performance on the task. The student then performs the task while the adult instructs aloud. Following this, the pupil performs the task while verbalizing aloud. The student can now perform the task while using self-verbalization in a whisper and, finally, perform the task using merely subvocalizations. Throughout, the student should be provided with feedback about the utility of the self-instructions for performance.

- Keeping tasks within the learner's repertoire. Metacognitive ability is dependent on the interaction between person, task, and strategy variables. Students must be able to accomplish the tasks they are self-instructing themselves to do; self-instructional support for reading will be of little use if the passage is too difficult for a child.

- Learning appropriate strategy use and generalization. Teachers can explicitly point out other tasks and settings in which self-instruction can be used, and use a variety of trainers, settings, and tasks to increase the chances that the student will learn to use self-instruction successfully outside of training sessions.

- Knowing when to use certain strategies. For example, **mnemonic devices**—rhymes, jingles, or images that order information to aid memory—have emerged as some of the most powerful instructional techniques in special education for promoting the acquisition of academic content (Scruggs & Mastropieri, 1990). Mnemonics aid student recall of important information because they strengthen the relationship between what is known and what is to be learned. When Scruggs and Mastropieri (1989) taught adolescents with mild disabilities information about World War I using either a variety of mnemonic strategies or traditional methods, the students who learned through mnemonics recalled substantially more content than the group that was traditionally taught and retained the information for a longer period. Although mnemonics are powerful tools, students must know when they are suitable. They may help with science content but may not be as applicable to learning a passage of Shakespeare.

mnemonic devices

Strategy instruction is not a quick fix but it does work. In the largest study of its kind, Swanson and his colleagues (see Swanson, 1999; Swanson & Hosbyn, 1998) synthesized the findings of more than 260 studies of instructional interventions for students with learning disabilities. One of the most effective was strategy instruction.

For training in the use of learning strategies to have a significant impact on student success, the instruction must be intensive and extensive. Students should be trained in the techniques until reasonable criteria for performance have been reached, then offered follow up booster sessions in order to give them a better chance to maintain the trained skills. Extensive instruction may be necessary to foster the use and transfer of appropriate strategies.

There are a number of other techniques from the cognitive-behavioural school that match and supplement cognitive strategy training. These are discussed in Chapter 8.

CASE STUDY

Danny (continued)

At the team meeting, the psychologist talked about learning disabilities. The classroom teacher then suggested using a skills approach with much small-group direct teaching for Danny. As in any teaching approach, the skills model should be tailored to the child's individual needs. The teacher may need to adjust the materials, change the timing, alter the lesson format, or adjust evaluation techniques to help Danny.

Reports synthesizing the voluminous research base on reading instruction conclude that students who struggle with reading need explicit, intensive, and systematic instruction in the following critical elements: phonological awareness, word study, comprehension, opportunities to acquire fluency, and exposure to a variety of texts (see Levy, Coleman, & Alsman, 2002). Each of these elements will be part of Danny's daily routine. To provide initial success, the teacher will use a word-family approach to build on Danny's strong sight-word vocabulary while strengthening his weak phonic skills. Rather than focusing only on sound-symbol association, Danny may benefit from much work in structural analysis of such items as prefixes, suffixes, and compound words.

Danny also needs to return to intense instruction in phonological awareness, which will involve orally manipulating the individual sounds in words. Instruction will be oral (without print) but, at his age, integrated with instruction in the alphabetic principle (letter-sound correspondence).

Proficiency in writing relies on an expanded experiential and knowledge base and the development of adequate listening, speaking, and reading skills. To improve writing, the teacher must first build Danny's motivation to write and his confidence that his thoughts are worthy of communication. A writing program should include daily and sustained writing. As well, peer collaboration will allow Danny to use talk to elaborate writing and to become more familiar with words, ideas, and composing procedures.

Remediation of arithmetic problems requires an individual math program with step-by-step instruction, beginning at Danny's level of performance and advancing at his rate. Danny must learn the basic skills in which he is deficient. He must master the number facts to 19 and develop a concept of place value before he can learn the four arithmetic processes. For number facts, he needs daily oral and written drill as well as many opportunities to generalize these facts to other solutions. In learning math, he needs practical associations. Whenever possible, concrete materials should be used, although Danny will need much practice to translate concrete sums into numerical notation. Place value should be taught with many concrete materials, such as Popsicle sticks, Cuisenaire rods, and a calculator. Later, decimals should be taught as related to money, and integers can be taught using the temperature on a thermometer.

Danny's social problems appear to arise directly from his academic frustration. Learning tasks should be structured to allow him much success. He must demonstrate mastery of each step before progressing. To build Danny's self-esteem, praise should be realistic and consistent. Danny's progress should be charted with some type of graphic display.

EXTRACT FROM DANNY'S IEP

Name: Danny
Chronological age: 8–4
Grade: 3
Teacher: Mrs. Als
School: Warren Place

Assessment Results

Peabody Picture Vocabulary Test (PPVT):
46th percentile
Test of Early Reading Ability (TERA):
32nd percentile
Test of Early Mathematical Ability (TEMA):
12th percentile
Gates-MacGinitie Reading Test:
1.6 Grade equivalent

Present Levels of Functioning

In arithmetic, Danny exhibits a marked discrepancy between his potential and his performance. He functions more than two years below his grade level in this area. He is also delayed in his reading, though not as severely. By using his extensive sight-word vocabulary, he is able to partly camouflage his deficits in word-attack skills. Danny's academic problems seriously frustrate him, and he is increasingly resorting to overt acting-out behaviour.

Placement/Accommodations

- General classroom
- Individualized math program
- Although Danny should try to remain in the same reading program as the rest of his class, his success and attitudes to reading might improve with a special set of high-interest, low-language readers presented in small-group instruction.

Long-Range Goals

- Danny will develop competence in phonological and phonemic awareness.
- Danny will improve his decoding skills in reading.
- Danny's writing skills will be stimulated through daily and sustained writing with a peer.

- Danny will improve his math skills by learning basic facts.
- Basic facts will be applied to addition, subtraction, multiplication computation, and word problems.
- Danny will learn about days and months, time, and simple money exchange.
- Danny will demonstrate his motivation by making choices among assignments.

Short-Term Objectives

- Phonological awareness will be taught with a sequence that begins with rhyming and isolation of initial sounds (phonemes that stretch first such as /s/, /f/, rather than /b/ or /d/). Danny will then compare words or sounds such as "Does mat start with the same sound as man?"; isolate beginning, median, and final sounds; blend sounds, such as "What word do the sounds /m/ /a/ /t/ make?"; and segment sounds as in "What are the sounds in mat?"

- Using a listening station, Danny will decode 15 to 20 selected words.
- Danny will use the words in his own stories.
- Danny will read the decoded words in short paragraphs.
- In a paragraph, he will capitalize and use periods.
- Daily, Danny and a peer will write together for 10 minutes on a teacher-selected topic.
- Using a software program on calendar skills, Danny will recognize the days of the week and say them in order.
- Using concrete objects, he will say and write numbers to 100.
- With a peer tutor, Danny will practise number facts to 19 to 100-percent accuracy.
- When given short addition and subtraction problems, Danny will align them on the page correctly and solve them to 100 percent accuracy using concrete objects.

Interactive Models

To meet the instructional needs of a broader range of students, teachers may have to decentre some of their instruction and allow class members to function as instructors for themselves and others. Two popular approaches in this mode are co-operative learning and peer tutoring. Neither approach is new; both have been on the educational vista for more than a century. Nevertheless, they have new life in mixed ability classrooms.

Co-operative learning (also referred to as *shared learning, collaborative learning,* or *small-group learning*) is one of the most frequently recommended strategies for effecting the inclusion of students with disabilities in general classrooms. Co-operative learning is a multi-element academic and social intervention. It is an organizational arrangement where children are placed into small mixed-ability study groups in which participants co-operate with one another to achieve academic goals. Within their groups, peers pool their diverse knowledge and skills in completing assignments. Students accept responsibility for their individual achievements as well as those of peers included in their learning groups.

co-operative learning

The arrangement provides an accommodating learning environment, and the opportunity to develop and use social skills, quality learning activities, and peer assistance (Murphy, Grey, & Honan, 2005). Studies have found that inclusion in heterogeneous co-operative groups results in higher achievement, better self-esteem, and improved academic attitudes for students with learning disabilities.

Peer tutoring comes in many forms and goes by many names— peer-assisted learning, peer monitoring, peer facilitation, and peer-mediated instruction (Miller, 2005). Its common thread—the use of peers—is increasingly popular. Tutoring increases students' time on task, provides more opportunity for practice, and creates a positive learning atmosphere.

peer tutoring

Empirical evidence overwhelmingly shows the beneficial effects of peer tutoring (Tourkani & Criscietiello, 2003). Reading and math are the topics of most study. Research indicates that achievement in these subject areas is enhanced when students have opportunities to work in heterogeneous dyads during parts of a lesson and are provided with clear guidelines for peer interactions. Miller (2005) reported on studies that showed that peer tutoring increased student engagement from 15 to 35 percent with the teacher alone to 46 to 75 percent with the teacher and the peer tutor. Students with disabilities who use peer tutoring show higher academic achievement, improved relationships with peers, better personal and social development, and increased motivation.

SUMMARY

1. The term *learning disabilities* first appeared in 1963. As it implied an educational rather than a medical orientation and was relatively non-stigmatizing, it appealed greatly to parents and educators.

2. The reasons why students with learning disabilities do poorly in school are not easily discerned. In terms of etiology and clinical manifestations, the condition is generally regarded as a multi-faceted concept. Children and youth with learning disabilities do not fit into any of the traditional categories of disabled groups. Moreover, learning disabilities is not a unitary concept; it represents a group of students displaying disparate characteristics who fail to learn appropriately for diverse reasons. The problems take a different course in each individual. In some students, the effects are global; in others, they impinge on specific areas of functioning. Certain displayed behaviours may be more apparent in individuals with mild and moderate disabilities, while others are manifested in students with severe problems. Students with learning disabilities exhibit an entire syndrome or collection of symptoms. Their problems lie well outside the normal range for their age level and persist despite repeated efforts to correct them. They are hindered by their disabilities and prevented from realizing their full potential.

3. Some people see the current status of the field of learning disabilities as dismal. This is somewhat justified as there seem to be fewer lessons learned than there are gaps in knowledge. For one thing, even after a century of research and discussion, a universally acceptable definition of learning disabilities remains elusive. Current definitions fail to reflect any consistency, and this spills over to influence critical areas such as classification, identification, prevalence, and instructional approaches. There is also a blurring of mild disability categories so that today learning disabilities is a somewhat residual category that includes many students who would have been classified differently in the past, such as intellectually disabled and language-minority children.

4. Concerns about identification and the usefulness of the discrepancy criterion are consuming the field. The difference between potential and performance has traditionally driven assessment efforts. Tests of mental ability and academic achievement are used, supplemented with measures to identify the specific psychological processes in which a child is deficient, such as auditory discrimination or visual figure-ground processing. This method is increasingly suspect. Problems include the high number of students identified as learning disabled, the inconsistent results, and the overlap among categories.

The assumptions that underlie identification and classification are changing; active discussion focuses on the methods of identifying students with learning disabilities.

5. Whether inclusive schooling works to provide effective academic outcomes for students with learning disabilities is a matter of conflicting research findings. General classroom placements are appropriate for most students; however, concerns exist among parents, professionals, and advocacy groups regarding inclusion for students with serious learning disabilities.

6. Metacognition is defined simply as an individual's awareness of his or her own cognitive performance and the use of this awareness in altering one's own behaviour. Metacognitive strategies serve to support, guide, and extend the thinking processes of their users.

7. Recently, educators have begun to reconceptualize students who are learning disabled as those who have not developed effective learning strategies. They see a need for strategy training to teach students how to use metacognitive skills. Cognitive approaches are founded on the belief that learning is a mentally active and constructive process that involves the learner's use of strategies to acquire, store, retrieve, and apply knowledge. Programs stress information processing, organizational skills, study skills, application of information, and problem solving, which involve self-monitoring, practising, reality testing, and coordinating the processes of studying and learning. Essentially, the procedures are designed to improve learning effectiveness and social performance in school settings and to teach students to become independent learners.

8. One way to increase performance is to use classroom instruction that is highly interactive and socially mediated. A solid research base supports approaches such as co-operative learning and peer tutoring.

HISTORICAL NOTES

It is probably true to say that there have always been people with learning disabilities—if we are referring to persons of average intelligence who suffer some dysfunction that hinders their learning by traditional methods. By definition, however, learning disabilities are tied to academic achievement. Therefore, when pushing a plough was more important than pushing a pen, and when schooling was not a social norm for all children, the unique problems of individuals with learning disabilities would simply not have existed.

It was at the opening of the 20th century, when compulsory school laws propelled all children into some form of education, that the particular difficulties of students with learning disabilities came to the fore. As neurology and ophthalmology developed as medical specialties in the late 19th century, physicians began to describe problems in understanding and using spoken and written language that were associated with damage to specific areas of the brain. Many different disciplines contributed to the new field. Along with physicians, neurologists, and ophthalmologists, speech therapists, psychologists, and educators all brought their own professional orientation and focus.

Early research emphasized clinical investigation rather than practical application in the schools and focused primarily on three areas of disorders: spoken language, written language, and motor and perceptual problems. In 1877, for example, Kaussmaul first described "word blindness." In 1896 James Kerr, a British physician, and W. P. Morgan, an ophthalmologist, reported similar cases. Eye surgeon James Hinshelwood investigated cases of word blindness, word deafness, and mind blindness. He published *Congenital Word Blindness* (1917), the first true monograph on the unique problems of children we now refer to as *learning disabled*.

In the early 1920s, great emphasis was placed on brain theory and its relationship to aberrations in behaviour, and on traits such as mirror writing and mixed handedness. Samuel Orton, an American psychiatrist, noted that children with learning problems often displayed mixed laterality and suggested that the failure of one hemisphere of the brain to become dominant caused the disorder. Orton coined the term "strephosymbolia" for individuals who saw "mixed symbols" when they tried to read (Orton, 1927).

Although these early researchers made some provocative and relevant findings, it was the work of Alfred Strauss, a neurologist, and Heinz Werner, a developmental psychologist, that established the conceptual base and the research and theories in the field. Strauss and Werner investigated the impact of brain damage on children's behaviour and psychological development. When they began to study children of normal ability who were experiencing learning difficulties, Strauss and Werner were able to delineate a group of common behaviours that they believed characterized children suffering from minimal brain damage. From this work, five principal components were delineated—hyperactivity, hyper-emotionalism, impulsiveness, distractibility, and perseveration—which came to be known as the Strauss Syndrome. While these components have been expanded, subdivided, and made more specific over the years, they still describe the core behavioural characteristics of children with learning disabilities.

The actual term *learning disabilities* came into use in 1963 to describe students who experienced continual school failure yet did not fit into the traditional categories of exceptionality. It was first used as a standard description for children of normal intelligence with learning problems by Samuel Kirk, one of the pioneers in the field, at a Chicago parents' meeting in 1963. Kirk defined his term carefully:

> Recently, I have used the term "learning disabilities" to describe a group of children who have disorders in development in language, speech, reading, and associated communication skills needed for social interaction. In this group, I do not include children who have sensory handicaps, such as blindness and deafness, because we have methods of managing and training the deaf and the blind. I also exclude from this group children who have generalized mental retardation. (Kirk, 1963, p. 3)

Kirk's speech had four major effects. First, it isolated the general characteristics of the population to be subsumed under the label of *learning disabilities*. Second, it stimulated the growth of the Association for Children with Learning Disabilities (ACLD), renamed the Learning Disabilities Association (LDA) in 1989. Primarily a forum for parents of learning-disabled children, the ACLD expanded rapidly and became a powerful lobby group in both Canada (LDAC) and the United States. Third, the speech cemented Samuel Kirk's leading role in the new field of learning disabilities as it emerged from its roots in language disorders, reading, and brain injury.

Finally, the creation of a new term served as a catalyst to generate interest in the field. Kirk's conception created an entirely new area of special education and set it on the road to an astonishing expansion. The massive interest in the area, the number of students identified and served as learning disabled, the development of parent and professional organizations, and the contributions of allied disciplines has been little short of phenomenal. Today, learning disabilities is the largest single focus of special education in most Canadian school districts.

CHAPTER 6

CHILDREN WITH INTELLECTUAL DISABILITIES

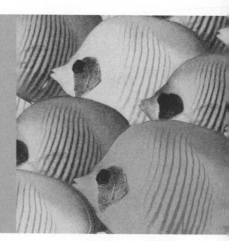

INTRODUCTION

Intellectual disability is neither an illness nor a disease. Essentially, the term refers to delayed intellectual growth that is manifested in immature reactions to environmental stimuli and below-average social and academic performance. However, individuals who are described as intellectually disabled vary widely in almost every aspect of human behaviour, personality, and temperament.

Students who are intellectually disabled have difficulties with complex academic material; they are markedly slower than their age-mates in reasoning, making judgements, using memory effectively, and associating and classifying information. Even so, it must be recognized that the development of children with intellectual disabilities, although on a slower timetable, parallels the developmental stages and sequence of other children. Despite their intellectual limitations, youngsters who are intellectually disabled show more similarities to typical children than differences. They feel, think, hope, play, have fun, and find mischief, just like everyone else.

In the first half of the 20th century, the field of intellectual disabilities held a primary position within special education. With the birth of the discrete field of learning disabilities in 1963, an about-face occurred. *Intellectual disability* as a category began to shrink. Fewer children were identified and labelled as intellectually disabled and the amount of research and funding available for this condition dwindled. Today there is a renewed excitement in the area of intellectual disabilities; it is characterized by change, evolution, and growth in attitudes research, expectations, and education and training.

In the social arena, attitudes toward individuals who are intellectually disabled are strikingly positive compared to even 30 years ago. Not only is public acceptance more established, but new research thrusts, such as the disability studies we mentioned in Chapter 1, are actively promoting the voices of persons with intellectual disabilities. Professionals in the educational fields entertain rising but realistic expectations for their students, whether they are mildly or significantly intellectually disabled. Reform efforts, such as inclusive education, have altered both perceptions and instructional settings.

On April 14, 2003, the Human Genome Project was pronounced complete. The field of medicine and the new discoveries in genetics are bringing the most massive changes to the field of intellectual disabilities. Over the past few decades monolithic and unidimensional conceptions of intellectual disability have crumbled as research on etiology-specific physical, cognitive, and behavioural features of child genetic syndromes has increased (Lee, Blasey, Dyer-Friedman, Glaser, Reiss, & Eleiz, 2005).

Today there are about 750 known genetic disorders associated with intellectual disability, and new syndromes are frequently being discovered. The new knowledge tells us that traditional comparisons between persons with different severity levels of retardation are often inadequate. Rather, different genetic syndromes show specific *behavioural phenotypes*—certain behaviours, psychopathology, cognition, language, and developmental sequelae (see Dykens, 2001; Fidler, Hodapp, & Dykens, 2002).

DEFINITIONS OF INTELLECTUAL DISABILITIES

Intellectual disability has long been recognized as an exceptional condition, and numerous attempts have been made within various disciplines, including medicine, psychology, social work, and education, to define the term. Still, definitions have never been standardized, and a universally accepted one does not exist.

Joined to this confusion is the always-controversial territory of terminology. As we discussed in Chapter 1, labelling is a complex, non-linear, and interactive process. In the field of intellectual disability, terminology has always been and still remains a particularly problematic minefield. You will notice that we use the terms *intellectual disability, cognitive disability,* occasionally *mental retardation,* in relation to historical antecedents, organizations, and persons with significant problems. Other people prefer the term *intellectually challenged,* which reflects the social aspects of the disability; that is, people have difficulties meeting the challenges of our highly industrialized, technologically oriented, and fast-paced society. Still others in the field prefer to use the more inclusive term *developmental disability.*

As a descriptor, *mental retardation* has been in use for more than 50 years. A major problem with this term is that it garners negative connotations because it is used for individuals with the most severe disabilities and evokes the impression of a permanent and comprehensive incapacity. Yet, especially in the case of mild conditions, intellectual disability does not fulfill the expectation of biologically based, permanent, and comprehensive incompetence. Mild intellectual disability is a condition that can improve as a result of changes in either the individual or the environment.

Therefore, the use of the term mental retardation is strongly discouraged today, particularly by educators and advocacy groups. However, as a classification, mental retardation is still used by the *Diagnostic and Statistical Manual* (DSM) of the American Psychiatric Association, major psychiatry journals, and the American Association on Mental Retardation (AAMR), the major North American body in the field. This does not mean that people are content with the term. For years, the AAMR has engaged in much soul-searching about it. The association knows that risks accrue to the traditional designations such as mental retardation and yet these terms remain, simply because there does not seem to be a better alternative.

The AAMR Definition

The American Association on Mental Retardation has revised its 1921 definition of mental retardation nine times (Scruggs & Mastroprieri, 2002). The primary definition used today was first adopted in 1959 and employs the term *mental retardation*. (The criterion for adaptive behaviour, which was not included in the 1959 version, was added later.) Under the AAMR definition,

> Mental retardation refers to substantial limitations in personal functioning. It is characterized by significant subaverage intellectual functioning, existing concurrently with related limitations in two or more of the following applicable adaptive skills: communication, self-care, home living, social skills, community use, self-direction, health and safety, functional academics, leisure, and work. Mental retardation manifests before age eighteen. (AAMR, 1992, p. 1)

There are other definitions that prescribe cut-off points to different IQ levels, or suggest that the developmental period ends at a later or earlier age. Despite the differences between various definitions, most of them share three critical points—subaverage intellectual functioning, deficits in adaptive behaviour, and manifestation during the developmental period. As researchers from the University of Quebec point out, regardless of definition, no doubt exists as to the requirement of including all three elements when diagnosing intellectual disabilities (Lecavalier, Tasse, & Levesque, 2001). Each element is discussed below.

Subaverage General Intellectual Functioning

Individuals are not considered intellectually disabled unless they score below 70 IQ on a standardized test of mental ability—that is, 2 or more standard deviations below the mean. This is a relatively recent cut-off point. Before 1962, the IQ level was variable; children who fell between 1 and 2 standard deviations below the norm (IQ 85 and below) were included in the category of intellectually disabled. The definition adopted by the American Association on Mental Deficiency in 1973 limited the category to those with an IQ of 70 or less. With this change, 80 percent of those previously defined as intellectually disabled were eliminated from the category (Zetlin & Murtaugh, 1990). Today, students whose IQ scores fall between 85 and 70 are considered at risk, borderline, or perhaps slow learners, but not intellectually disabled.

Adaptive Behaviour

Since the 1950s, changing definitions of intellectual disabilities have given increasing prominence to the concept of adaptive behaviour. This construct was first delineated as a component of mental retardation by Edgar A. Doll in the early 1930s. In 1973 Jane Mercer expanded the phenomenon of adaptive behaviour and described the "six-hour retarded child"; that is, the one who cannot cope with the methods, pace, and materials of the regular educational classroom but functions quite adequately in other environments. Adaptive behaviour was formally added as a criterion within the construct of mental retardation in 1961.

adaptive behaviour

Nearly all conceptions of adaptive behaviour use the basic definition formulated by the AAMR. In this definition, **adaptive behaviour** is seen as "the degree and efficiency with which an individual meets the standards of personal independence and social responsibility of his age or cultural group" (Grossman, 1977, p. 11). This means that adaptive behaviour is a dynamic construct influenced by cultural norms and age-related expectations. It refers to how well a person is able to adapt to environmental demands, and differs according to an individual's age group and particular situation. The preschooler, for example, needs sensorimotor skills, self-help skills, communication, and socialization to adapt to the environment. We do not expect the preschooler to be interested in vocational prospects and an expanded peer group; these are the adaptive concerns of the adolescent.

The dynamic nature of adaptive behaviour also implies that, over time and with experience, behaviour can change. Specific adaptive limitations often coexist with strengths and other personal capabilities; therefore, with appropriate supports over a sustained period, the life functioning of the person with intellectual disabilities will generally improve.

It is important to note that individuals must demonstrate poor adaptive behaviour as well as subaverage intellectual functioning before they can be classified as intellectually disabled. Students who manifest deficits in adaptive behaviour but score within the normal range on IQ tests are usually labelled *emotionally disturbed* or *learning disabled*.

Adaptive behaviour is crucial to current definitions. Competencies related to functional independence are perhaps the most widely accepted component of adaptive behaviour. Skills involved relate to toileting, dressing, feeding, avoiding danger, and maintaining a minimal level of health and safety.

Developmental Period

developmental period

Under the AAMR definition, the **developmental period** refers to the time between conception and the eighteenth birthday.

CLASSIFICATION OF INTELLECTUAL DISABILITIES

Many professionals still agree that the most useful classification system is that proposed by the AAMR, which considers the condition along a continuum, or scale, of severity. The AAMR's categories—mild, moderate, severe, and profound retardation—describe an individual's functioning clearly and carry no negative stereotyping and little stigma. As adjectives, the words *mild, moderate, severe,* and *profound* apply to many other things besides disability (Hallahan & Kauffman, 2003).

When severity classifications are employed, it is important to remember that there will probably be as much variability within any one group as there is among the groups and among or within groups of typical individuals. As well, the cut-off scores leave room

Table 6-1 Degrees of intellectual disability and expected developmental and academic characteristics

IQ level	Support needs	Degrees	Expectations
70–90	—	—	Not classified as intellectually disabled. Capable of competing in school in many areas.
55–70	Intermittent	Mild	Capable of basic academic subjects up to advanced elementary levels; will achieve about half to two-thirds of what normally developing peers do. General achievement ranges from grade 2 to grade 5. Gap widens in secondary school.
40–55	Limited	Moderate	Capable of attaining self-help skills, communication skills, and social adjustment. Limited academic achievement but can attain many functional skills and basic functional academics. Can achieve economic usefulness later in routine jobs under supervision.
25–40	Extensive	Severe	Can attain basic communication and self-help skills. May or may not be ambulatory. Additional disabilities hinder attainments.
Below 25	Pervasive	Profound	With intensive training, may learn basic self-help and communication skills. Often not ambulatory; may be medically fragile and/or technology-dependent.

for clinical judgement. An IQ of 54 may be judged as moderate or mild intellectual disability. Table 6-1 indicates, in broad terms, the educational expectations at each severity level.

Occasionally, we still hear the very traditional terms *educable* and *trainable*, which educators have used over the years to try to describe the educational needs of children who are intellectually disabled. This terminology reflects the ability of children labelled as *educable mentally retarded* (EMR) to benefit from academic instruction, whereas those called *trainable mentally retarded* (TMR) are presented with more non-academic programs that focus on training in life skills and skills for independent living.

Classification by Needs

Severity levels are still used by the AAMR and in the *Diagnostic and Statistical Manual* (DSM) (APA, 1994). In 1992, however, the AAMR introduced a new set of qualifiers that focus on needs and supports. Within the needs classification, the stress is on people's future potential rather than intellectual limitations; the focus changes from the impact of people's disabilities to the needs of "people who have a life and need support" (Butterworth, 2002, p. 85).

The new classification system changes dependency to support needs, keys terms to the level of services required, and describes them in ways that are prescriptive for programming needs. Specifically, it replaces the severity levels of *mild* to *profound* with *intermittent*, *limited*, *extensive*, and *pervasive*, terms that refer to how much and when support is needed. Within the broad supports, an individual's needs are further classified across several domains, such as communication.

Intermittent support translates to mean that the disability does not create an obvious and continual problem. A child needing intermittent supports, for example, may require only a little extra assistance in the classroom and at times of life transitions. Limited implies somewhat greater support needs. It means that the disability creates daily limitations on abilities, but that individuals can achieve a degree of self-sufficiency.

Extensive support carries on throughout a lifetime. It is for individuals whose disabilities prevent them from living independently. The pervasive support classification is used infrequently. It is reserved for those individuals whose disabilities hinder them in most self-help activities. Pervasive support is characterized by constancy and high intensity that are provided across environments and are often of a life-sustaining nature.

When the AAMR iterated its more skills-based system, many people thought the change was perhaps a harbinger of new directions for identification procedures (see Williamson, McLeskey, Hoppey, & Rentz, 2006). Despite the new system's efficiency, especially for those providing social and educational services, the system was at first largely ignored by the field (Vergason & Anderegg, 1997). It did not seem to provide the predictable sorting of the IQ-based system and most jurisdictions continued to use the AAMR definition. Today the needs classification is employed more widely, often by international bodies such as UNICEF. Nevertheless, you are likely to hear the severity and the needs classification used together rather than as alternate systems.

Figure 6-1

Classification of intellectual disabilities

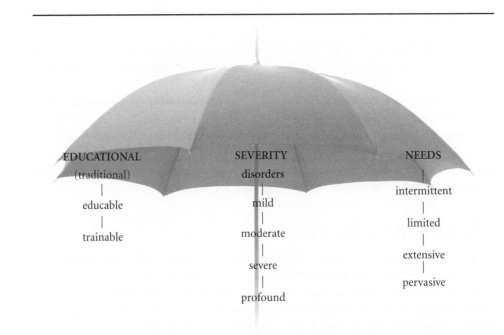

PREVALENCE OF INTELLECTUAL DISABILITIES

Any attempt to estimate the incidence rate of a relatively common disorder almost invariably fails to take into account some affected individuals. This occurs in the case of intellectual disabilities, where mild conditions prove elusive and difficult to accurately pinpoint. Many mild cases go unreported, although this is not true in the case of significant intellectual impairments.

A matrix of reasons contribute to the difficulty in obtaining true and accurate prevalence figures for intellectual disabilities. These include

- Different IQ cut-off points are used. Whereas the AAMR uses an IQ of 70 as the beginning of the designation of mild intellectual disability, a school system may use an IQ of 75.

- Different methods of gathering data for prevalence studies are used.

- Different definitions of adaptive behaviour are used.

- Different regions and social classes show different prevalence rates. The majority of children labelled as intellectually disabled come from a lower socio-economic bracket. As we discussed in Chapter 3, children from poorer strata have a greater risk of incurring brain damage because of factors such as malnutrition, poor prenatal and postnatal care, and environmental hazards during infancy. Hence, large urban areas with a poorer population show a greater proportion of intellectual disability.

- There are gender differences within prevalence estimates. Somewhere between 5 to 10 times as many boys as girls are considered to be mildly intellectually disabled. This may result from a higher probability of adverse biological factors affecting male children. It may also result from the fact that expectations tend to be higher for males, or it may be that the more aggressive behaviour usually found among males can lead to referrals for assessment and the label of intellectual disability (see Chapter 5).

- With reference to the above two points, the concept of mild intellectual disability is particularly controversial since children in this category are drawn almost exclusively from poor families, often of minority origin. Although gender and racial imbalance continue, there is also a greater hesitancy to label children as intellectually disabled. In the United States, there have been ongoing court challenges, such as Larry P. vs. Riles (see Winzer & Mazurek, 1998).

- Different age groups show different prevalence figures. Among the group classified as mildly intellectually disabled, prevalence is low in the preschool years (less than 1 percent in children below the age of five), increases dramatically during the school years, and declines later (Drew, Logan, & Hardman, 1992). Such high rates are no doubt a reflection of the environmental demands of school. As a social system, the school has a certain set of expectations that some children fail to meet. In fact, some researchers contend that high-functioning children with delays do not officially become disabled until they enter school and encounter reading, writing, and math. They pass through the school system labelled as intellectually disabled but then go on to occupy normal roles in society.

- There has been a redistribution among categories that is a direct result of the birth of the field of learning disabilities in 1963 and the redefinition of intellectual disability 10 years later. The overlap of categories is discussed in Chapter 1.

- When newly discovered genetic syndromes are taken into consideration, prevalence estimates are not well established and are being constantly revised. The trend is for greater identification of persons only mildly affected by syndromes that were previously believed to cause moderate and severe disabilities.

Given a normal curve, a theoretical 2.27 percent of the population might be expected to fall 2 or more standard deviations below the mean. In reality, this does not happen. Only about 1 to 1.5 percent of the population meets the AAMR definition of retarded in both intellectual functioning and adaptive behaviour.

More than 75 percent of those identified as intellectually disabled are in the mild range. For the moderate, severe, and profound levels (an IQ of 50 or below), a review of 20 studies found 3 or 4 persons per 1000 (McLaren & Bryson, 1987). Severe and profound intellectual disabilities are extremely low-incidence conditions. Note, however, that there is evidence of a recent increase in the number of children with severe and profound conditions, since children who may not have survived in the past are now being saved by medical advances (Alper, Schloss, & Schloss, 1994). Figure 6-2 shows the prevalence and severity of intellectual disability.

Figure 6-2

Prevalence and severity of intellectual disabilities

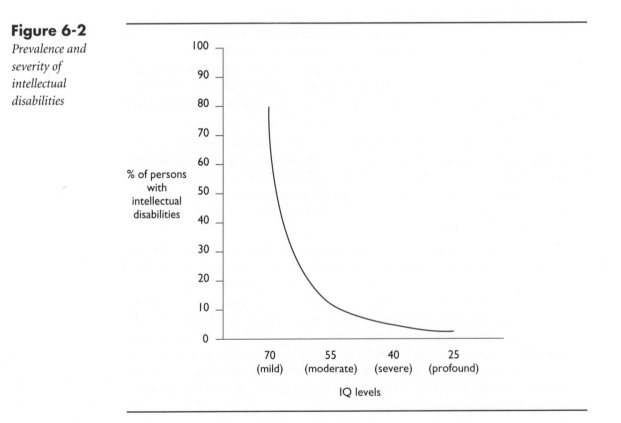

ETIOLOGY OF INTELLECTUAL DISABILITIES

As recently as the mid-1990s, experts estimated that only about 10 to 15 percent of cases of intellectual disabilities had a known cause. There have been rapid advances, but even now etiologic diagnoses are usually made in fewer than half the affected individuals (Hunter, 2000). In about half of all cases the etiology remains unknown.

The identified villians in intellectual disabilities are legion and include genetic and chromosomal differences; infections such as maternal rubella; intoxicants such as drugs; postnatal diseases; and childhood accidents. The following discussion on etiologies serves as a supplement to the information presented in Chapter 3. Table 6-2 on the next page presents a sample of etiologies, some common and some rare, that can lead to intellectual disabilities. Note that some conditions occur within more than one classification.

Chromosomal Problems

Chromosomal abnormalities include too many chromosomes, too few chromosomes, and chromosomes that are attached to one another. Abnormalities in the structure and number of chromosomes can be caused by natural mutation of genes, radiation, and a host of other factors that are only partly understood. Apart from those with Down syndrome, the number of children with intellectual disabilities due to chromosomal abnormality is quite small.

Down Syndrome

Worldwide, Down syndrome is the most common clinical cause of intellectual disability: it represents about 5 to 6 percent of all persons identified with mental retardation (see Goebe, Kassow, May, & Kundert, 2003). Intellectually, the child with Down syndrome can fall anywhere along the severity spectrum, but most tend to be classified in the moderate range.

Down syndrome occurs in approximately 1 in every 1000 live births (Wright & Bray, 2000). It is an equal-opportunity disability: it can occur in any family, regardless of the race, socioeconomic class, or education of the parents. It usually occurs only once in a family, and strikes most often when the mother is approaching the end of her child-bearing days.

The condition was first identified in 1866 by John Langton Down, a physician at the Earlswood Asylum in Surrey, England. The facial features of children with the condition prompted Down to refer to it as "Mongolian idiocy."

Down syndrome is a cause of intellectual disability, ranging from mild to profound.

Table 6-2 Some causes of intellectual disabilities

Infections and intoxicants	Infections: rubella, syphilis, toxoplasmosis, herpes simplex, bacterial infections, viral infections, parasitic infections
	Intoxicants: drugs, poisons, smoking, caffeine, alcohol, lead
Trauma or physical agents	Anoxia, irradiation, trauma
Metabolism or nutrition	Lipid storage diseases: Tay-Sachs disease, Hurler's, Hunter's
	Carbohydrate disorders: galactosemia, hypoglycemia
	Endocrine disorders: hypothyroidism
	Amino acid disorders: phenylketonuria
	Other: Prader-Willi syndrome, malnutrition
Gross brain disease	Neurofibromatosis (von Recklinghavsen's disease), Sturge-Weber syndrome, tuberous sclerosis (epiloia), Huntington's chorea
Unknown prenatal influence	Anencephaly, microcephaly, Apert's syndrome, meningomyocele, hydrocephalus
Chromosomal abnormality	Chromosomal aberrations: Down syndrome, Klinefelter's syndrome, cri du chat
	Autosomal dominant gene disorders: neurofibromatisis, tuberous sclerosis, Sturge-Weber syndrome
	Autosomal recessive gene disorders: phenylketonuria, congenital hypothyroidism, maple syrup urine disease, Tay-Sachs disease, Smith-Lemli-Optiz syndrome
	X-linked disorders: Lasch-Nyhan syndrome, fragile X syndrome
Gestational disorders	Prematurity, postmaturity, low birth weight
Psychiatric disorders	Psychoses
Environmental influences	Psychosocial disadvantage, sensory deprivation

He assumed that the condition represented a re-emergence of a more primitive evolutionary status, which he erroneously believed to be that of the Mongolian race. The Mongolian resemblance, however, is due simply to the development of a fold in the upper eyelid, which is caused not by inheritance but by the failure of the root of the nose to develop normally. Today we have discarded the term "mongoloid" as demeaning and developmentally inappropriate.

Down syndrome was one of the first conditions to be linked to a genetic abnormality. The major breakthrough came in 1959 when Swedish geneticists determined that the correct number of chromosomes in humans was 46. When they discovered the extra chromosome in patients with Down syndrome, the link between the condition and disjunction was confirmed.

There are 3 major types of Down syndrome—Trisomy 21, translocation, and mosaicism. In each type, the mental and physical problems of the child are caused by extra chromosomal material that somehow disturbs the orderly development of both body and brain. Chromosome 21 is the smallest human chromosome; it contains only about 1.5 percent of the total genetic material (Patterson, 1987). Yet cases of Down syndrome are somehow linked to this tiny chromosome. There are no individuals with the clinical symptoms of Down syndrome who do not have at least partial Trisomy 21.

Disjunction in the twenty-first pair of chromosomes (Trisomy 21) means that there are 3 chromosomes instead of 2. This may result from a mistake in chromosomal distribution in the egg or sperm, or may happen if the chromosomes are distributed unequally when the fertilized egg begins to divide. There are 14 different types of Trisomy 21, which account for the great majority of children with Down syndrome (about 93 percent).

Of the rest of the population with Down syndrome, 5 percent have *translocation*, in which only part of chromosome 21 is present in triplicate. In this condition, the extra chromosomal material most often attaches to chromosome 14, 15, 21, or 22 (Patterson, 1987). Although the actual chromosome count is 46, the affected child suffers from the same overdose of chromosome 21 as the child with standard trisomy. There may be hereditary components in translocation.

Mosaicism accounts for about 2 percent of Down syndrome cases. This condition results when there is a faulty distribution of chromosomes in later cell divisions. The child possesses some normal cells and some with a trisomy condition. Any resulting physical and mental anomalies depend on the number of affected cells.

More than 50 physical signs are listed as characteristic of Down syndrome. Some are apparent at birth, some appear much later, and some disappear with age. The number of physical features that a child displays bears no relationship to the degree of intellectual disability. Few children have all the characteristics typical of the syndrome. Table 6-3 on the next page outlines the most common.

The chances of having a child with Down syndrome increase dramatically with the age of the parents, particularly the mother. (Very young mothers are an exception to this rule: they are more likely to have a Down syndrome baby than women in their twenties or thirties.) The odds of having a child with Down increases from approximately 1 in 336 live births at thirty-five years of age to 1 in 97 live births at forty years (Bray, Wright, Davies, & Hook, 1998).

Many authorities believe that Down syndrome may result from a combination of two factors—chemical changes in the egg cells due to the mother's aging ovaries, and a reduction

Table 6-3 Some characteristics of Down syndrome

Head	Hair	Face
distinctive shape; skull rounded and small	sparse, fine, and soft	flat profile
Nose	**Eyes**	**Ears**
small and "pug"; flat bridge; undeveloped or absent nasal cartilage; mucous discharge common	epicanthic fold; speckling of iris (Brushfield's spots); strabismus or nystagmus common	small and low-set; overlapping upper letices
Mouth	**Teeth**	**Tongue**
high-arched; thick, fissured lips; narrow palate	small, irregularly aligned; late erupting	coarse, protruding
Hands	**Muscles**	**Feet**
broad, stumpy, with short fingers; palmar crease (simian line) on one or both hands; incurved little finger (clindactly)	general hypotonia; flexible joints	broad and short; excessive space between first and second toes
Skin	**Abdomen**	**Stature**
thick, dry, rough; mottled or flushed	prominent umbilical hernia common	short; average height: male – 152.4 cm female – 139.7 cm

in the secretion of various hormones in older women. The mother's age may not be the only factor. Researchers are discovering possible links between Down syndrome and the amount of the mother's exposure to radiation and certain viruses. They are also exploring the role of the aging father, who contributes the extra chromosome in 20 to 25 percent of the cases (Abroms & Bennett, 1983). For men aged 41 and up, there is an increased risk of fathering children with Trisomy 21, regardless of the age of the mother.

Fragile X Syndrome

The fragile X (Fra (X)) syndrome has attracted the interest of health, education, and human service professionals because it is common, its inheritance pattern is unique, and it presents a wide variety of disabilities. As the most common inherited cause of intellectual disability known, it is responsible for about 30 percent of X-linked retardation.

Fragile X is estimated to occur in 1 in 2500 to 1 in 4000 individuals, with males most often affected (see Saunders, 1999). The prevalence of carriers who may not display any of the characteristics of the syndrome and function normally in school and society is higher. Such high estimates indicate that fragile X may be second only to Down syndrome as an etiology of intellectual disability, particularly in males.

Fragile X is a single gene disorder, a marker on the X chromosome at position 927. The syndrome is caused by an abnormal gene or genes at the lower end of the long arm of the X chromosome. The defective gene creates an expansion of a trinucleotide DNA sequence. This results in too long a stretch of DNA, which disrupts the structure of the X chromosome and creates a fragile area which then makes too many copies or repeats of a particular gene. Fragile X can therefore be diagnosed through DNA analysis.

When a male is the carrier, he will not pass the condition to his sons, but will pass it to all his daughters. When a female carrier has children, she has a 50–50 chance of passing the faulty X chromosome to them. In other ways, the genetics involved in fragile X seem to be unlike those of most typical X-linked recessive conditions. Santos (1992) notes that fragile X runs through a family tree in a multi-step process, resulting two or three generations later in full activation of the mutation. During this time, many people can be affected to various degrees (physically, cognitively, and behaviourally) before the full syndrome appears. Males often show the full syndrome; girls are less affected, probably because they have a "good" X chromosome (Saunders, 1999).

Male fragile X patients undergo unusual changes in appearance from childhood through the adult years. During the growth period, the face grows in an elongated pattern, the forehead becomes more prominent, and the ears enlarge. The adult male patient typically has a long face, large ears, a prominent forehead, midface hypoplasia, and a prominent jaw. The most common feature seen in the postpubescent male is macro-orchidism (large testicles), although among prepubertal males macro-orchidism is reported in only approximately 50 percent of the population (Simen & Rogers, 1989). Table 6-4 on the next page outlines the common characteristics of fragile X males.

Some of the physical features typical of fragile X males can also be seen in female carriers, such as mildly prominent ears, a long face, and hyperextensible finger joints. However, facial features are exceedingly variable and do not serve as an aid in diagnosis.

Most males with the full mutation have intellectual disabilities. Approximately 30 percent will be severely or profoundly retarded; the majority are moderately or mildly retarded; 10 percent have borderline or low-normal IQs (Dykens, Leckman, Paul, & Watson, 1988; Hagerman & Sobesky, 1989). Preschool fragile X males show a rate of learning that is generally about half the rate we would see in typical children (Bailey, Hatton, & Skinner, 1998). Some studies suggest a developmental decline of IQ in males although the timing of the decline is not clear, nor is the reason.

Fragile X females are usually less cognitively affected than males, although one-third are cognitively impaired, usually in the mild range (Reiss & Freund, 1990). Females who are affected cognitively are more likely to show physical anomalies (Hagerman, 1988).

A significant number of fragile X children display specific behavioural and learning deficits. Significant learning difficulties are found in up to 80 percent of fragile X males.

Table 6-4 Features of fragile X syndrome

Physical	Non-physical
large head size	developmental delay
large flat ears	mental retardation
long narrow face	learning disabilities
prominent forehead	hyperactivity
broad nose	short attention span
high palate	autistic behaviours
large testicles	fearfulness, shyness
large hands; non-tapering fingers	rapid, repetitive speech
mitral valve prolapse (heart murmur)	talkativeness
increased birth-weight	difficulty adjusting to change
repeated ear infections	

These students tend to show global academic deficits and there is general consensus that the severity of the delay increases over time (Bailey, Hatton, & Skinner, 1998). Math appears to be an area of weakness for both boys and girls. There are also verbal and non-verbal problems; a lack of speech at three years of age is not uncommon.

Many affected children display characteristic behavioural problems such as hand flapping, hand biting, hyperactivity, aggression, challenging temperamental traits, and attention deficits. In addition, fragile X is associated with greater risk for a range of disorders involving social relations (Dykens, 1996). Children show gaze aversion and generally try to avoid eye contact by turning away the body during social interactions. Approximately 17 to 25 percent of individuals with fragile X have a diagnosis of autistic disorder. Boys with both autism and fragile X appear to have poorer developmental outcomes and more problem behaviours than others.

Genetic Defects

Advances in genetics have sparked renewed interest in the entire field of intellectual disability. Not only are geneticists discovering new disorders but they are finding that specific disorders are associated with distinctive behavioural features or behavioural phenotypes so that individuals display unique characteristics and learning styles (see Dykens & Kasari, 1997). However, the differential identification of children with many of these syndromes is of recent date and sample sizes are still small.

It is held today that genetic disorders may account for as many as one-third of all persons with intellectual disabilities, even a sizeable proportion of those with mild levels of delay (see Dykens, 2001; Hodapp & Fidler, 1999). Following this, it is estimated that almost one quarter of children in special education due to cognitive delay have known, identifiable syndromes that are characterized by specific patterns of deficits and abilities.

We could not possibly detail the hundreds of genetic disorders associated with intellectual disability. Here, we merely point out examples of disorders that are distinct in their manifestations and that bring different challenges to the classroom. Table 6-5 on the next two pages shows a further range of disorders and their unique sequelae.

Williams Syndrome

Williams syndrome is a genetic disorder that was identified in 1961 by New Zealand cardiologist J. C. P. Williams. It is a deletion syndrome on chromosome 7. Affected individuals lack one gene from each of about 15 pairs. Williams is estimated to occur in one in 20 000 to 25 000 live births (Healey, 1999; Reis, Schader, Milne, & Stephens, 2003). The condition is evident at birth, occurs in all ethnic groups and on all continents, and affects males and females equally (Pober & Dykens, 1993).

People with Williams syndrome show very specific behaviours and physical traits (see Table 6-5). Physically, there are cardiovascular abnormalities, short stature, and "elfin-like" facial features. Cognitively, there are developmental delays and a mean IQ of 60. Although those with this condition can be very fearful, children show social disinhibition; they have a strong interest in people and tend to be unusually friendly.

What is particularly interesting about people with Williams syndrome is their unique musical interests and talents. They have an affinity for music, if not increased musical talent and skill. These special asymmetric abilities differentiate them from others with disabilities (Reis, Schrader, Milne, & Stephens, 2003) and transcend traditional theories of intellectual and cognitive impairment. At the same time, relative strengths in music and language contrast with extremely poor math, visiospatial, and visiomotor skills (Don, Schellenberg, & Rourke, 1999; Dykens, Rosner, Ly, & Sagun, 2005).

Prader-Willi Syndrome

Prader-Willi syndrome, a genetic irregularity involving chromosome 15, was reported in 1956 by Prader, Labhart, and Willi in Switzerland. Why it occurs is unclear. However, it affects one in every 10 000 to 25 000 live births, which places it among the more frequently recognized genetic syndromes. There are about 3000 cases worldwide. Males and females are equally affected.

Prader-Willi is associated with unique physical development and behavioural characteristics. People with this symptom show obesity, small stature, and small hands and feet. Cognitively, the condition is associated with mild intellectual disability, learning disabilities, and language disorders.

Persons with Prader-Willi show high levels of maladaptive behaviour such as temper tantrums; hoarding; stereotyped skin picking; and obsessive-compulsive behaviour such as tying and untying shoes over and over. Two additional very serious behavioural disorders arise from two interactive conditions. First is an insatiable appetite that leads to incessant food seeking. Second is a type of obsessive-compulsive disorder in which children dislike changes from expected routines, especially with respect to access to food (Joseph, Egli, Koppekin, & Thompson, 2002). The extreme compulsion to eat not only leads to obesity

Table 6-5 Examples of genetic and chromosomal anomalies

Condition	Prevalence	Etiology	Sex	Anomalies	Social/Cognitive effects
Fragile X syndrome	1 in 2500 to 1 in 4000	X-linked, chromosomal	More obvious in males than females	Physical differences	Developmental delay a hallmark; severe mental retardation and other behavioural characteristics
Hunter's syndrome	Rare	Genetic lysosomal storage disorder; enzyme deficiency	Sex-linked: affects boys	Progressive cognitive, physical disabilities; IQ drops as the disease progresses; physical differences appear after age three with growth of body hair and musculoskeletal changes	Mental retardation and behavioural disorders, hydrocephalus, seizures. Results in early mortality, often by respiratory problems (Naggs, 1999)
Williams syndrome	1 in 20 000 to 25 000 live births	Genetic	Both sexes	Congenital heart and blood vessel defects, dental and kidney abnormalities, hernias, low muscle tone	Mild to serious mental retardation; mean IQ of 60. Unusual auditory hypersensitivity, good verbal but moderately low intellectual ability; visual/motor problems
Angleman syndrome	1 in 12 000 to 20 000 live births	Deletion on chromosome 15	Both sexes	Neurological and cranio-facial abnormalities, love of water	Severe delays in motor and intellectual development, episodic laughter, disparities in speech and language
Lesch-Nyhan syndrome	1 in 380 000	Chromosomal; X-linked; error of metabolism	Males	Physical handicaps, usually non-ambulatory	Mental retardation; often engage in self-biting

Table 6-5 continued

Condition	Prevalence	Etiology	Sex	Anomalies	Social/Cognitive effects
Prader-Willi syndrome	1 in 10 000 to 25 000 live births	Deletion syndrome, often paternal in origin; associated with a region on chromosome 15	Both sexes	Physical differences	Mental retardation; obsessive desire for food
Cornelia de Lange syndrome	1 in 45 000	Genetic mutation	Slightly more females	Hearing impairments, severe motor delays	Moderate mental retardation; severe speech delays
Rett syndrome	Affects one in 10 000 girls	Genetic	Predominantly females	Brain disorder	After normal development to six to eighteen months, severe regression appears and profound loss of skills in language, communication, hand use, and motor skills. Mental retardation results (Hill, 1997; Mount et al., 2003)
Cri du chat syndrome	1 in 50 000 live births	Chromosomal deletion syndrome	Significant female predominance	Abnormal face, microcephaly	Unusual catlike mewing sounds; mental effects retardation
Turner's syndrome	1 in every 2500 live births	Lack an X chromosome or a structural abnormality in one of the X chromosomes	Females	Short stature, growth failure, or gonadal dysgenesis (unformed that inhibits spontaneous pubertal onset and fertility	Characteristic pattern of cognitive abilities—normal verbal IQ and relatively lower performance IQ due to difficulty with space forms and number concepts.
Smith–Magenis syndrome	1 in 25 000 to 50 000 live births	Chromosomal deletion	Both sexes	Varied physical characteristics; subtle facial differences such as prominent jaw; short stature	Often mild mental retardation, but wide variability. Sleep disturbances and behavioural disorders

but is a potentially life- threatening eating disorder. Individuals can literally eat themselves to death (Joseph et al., 2002; Sigafoos, Pidden, & Curfs, 2000).

Angleman Syndrome

Angleman syndrome, a genetic deletion syndrome on chromosome 15, was first reported in 1965. Today the condition is estimated to affect one in 20 000 people, males and females equally (Walz, Beebe, & Byars, 2005). There are between 1000 and 5000 cases in the United States and Canada.

ataxia

Angleman syndrome is characterized by severe mental retardation, seizures, **ataxia** (problems with gait and ambulation), microcephaly, and a particular facial appearance, and often by a fascination with water. Perhaps the most salient and frequently cited behavioural characteristic is excessive laughter, reported in over 80 percent of cases.

It is the speech and language characteristics that make persons with Angleman syndrome so unique. Even in those with the highest level of functioning, conversational speech does not develop; however, there is much higher ability in understanding and responding to the language of others.

Infections and Intoxicants

Infections that lead to intellectual disabilities can occur in the pregnant mother, the infant, or the young child. Rubella and syphilis in the mother both cross the placental barrier and can damage the fetus. Pediatric AIDS is a fast-growing infectious cause of intellectual disability in children. Of infants born with HIV infection, 78 to 93 percent become developmentally disabled through central nervous system involvement (Gray, 1989).

Intoxicants and poisons in the mother or child can also cause intellectual disabilities. One of the most important in this category is Fetal Alcohol Spectrum Disorders (FASD), which joins Down syndrome, fragile X syndrome, and spina bifida as one of the most common currently known causes of intellectual disabilities. Of these conditions, FASD is the most directly preventable, at least in principle. FASD is discussed in Chapter 13.

In the developing child, meningitis and encephalitis can lead to cognitive impairments and other anomalies. More encephalitic children than meningitic children suffer adverse cognitive effects. Childhood accidents involving cerebral assault or prolonged loss of consciousness can also cause brain damage that leads to retardation. Child abuse is increasingly being cited as another cause of brain damage. (See Chapters 12 and 15).

Environmental Influences

The great majority of children with identified intellectual disabilities are categorized within the mild range. Because children often come from deprived backgrounds and many of their problems spring from psychosocial disadvantage, poverty, inadequate nutrition, family instability, lack of educational opportunity, or an unstimulating infant environment, the condition may be referred to as *cultural-familial mental retardation*.

Subtle genetic factors may interweave with socio-economic deprivation to further affect a child's development. Although it is recognized that environmental conditions modify biological processes, the relative influence of genetic factors on environmental ones is unknown.

DEVELOPMENTAL CONSEQUENCES OF INTELLECTUAL DISABILITIES

Intellectual disabilities cover a variety of physical, intellectual, academic, and behavioural characteristics. Viewing the condition on a continuum, we can place children who are mildly disabled and having trouble with academic subjects at one end and profoundly retarded youngsters who may be non-ambulatory and non-responsive to their surroundings at the other. However, when discussing the population of persons with intellectual disabilities, we must keep in mind that categories of severity often overlap and are subject to change.

These changes can occur because of outside perceptions. We mentioned, for example, that students with mild intellectual disabilities may only be labelled as such within the school system, where they encounter the complexities of reading, writing, and math. Change also results from very early intervention, which aims to reduce the impact of a disability on a child's development. For example, the psychological profile of babies with Down syndrome shows that they seem to develop normally in early infancy but their rate of development slows after six months of age. Early and sustained intervention halts the decline in cognitive development and also appears to prevent further decreases throughout the remaining early childhood years (see Guralnick & Bricker, 1987; also Chapter 16).

Physical Development

Individuals who are mildly intellectually disabled present few if any divergent physical symptoms that differentiate them from their peers. Minor differences may be seen in measures of health, physical and motor performance, and the age at which motor and language milestones are attained.

Physical impairments become more complex in the moderate range. Children in this range tend to be markedly less coordinated and physically able. Compared to typical children, these youngsters are much slower in reaching milestones such as learning to walk, talk, eat, and toilet themselves.

Traditionally, researchers and practitioners have tended to group together people who are severely and profoundly intellectually disabled, although these populations differ in several ways. Of course, the categories do overlap, as do severe and moderate disabilities. Individuals who are severely retarded may show poor speech, inadequate social skills, poor motor development or non-ambulation, incontinence, sensory impairments, seizures, and cerebral palsy.

The population of persons who are profoundly retarded can be divided functionally into two groups. "Relative" profoundly retarded persons have less organic damage and are capable of some degree of ambulation, communication, and self-help skills. "Absolute" profoundly retarded individuals are some of the most seriously impaired of all people with disabilities. The nature and degree of their disabilities are so great that, without various forms of intensive training and therapy, they exhibit virtually no adaptive behaviour. Many of these people are also extremely medically fragile.

Cognitive Development

cognition

Cognition is the process of recognizing, identifying, associating, and inferring meaning beyond the figural information provided by the environment that allows an understanding of a concept and application to new conditions (DeRuiter & Wansart, 1982). There is more to cognition than just conscious activity; it also includes the actions and activities that we do every day and don't even think about. We perform many of these tasks, such as reading a book or tying shoelaces, more or less automatically.

By definition, intellectual disability equates with deficiencies in cognitive development. But it is important to recognize that intellectual disability means slowing down, not stopping. Individuals with intellectual disabilities have impaired or incomplete mental development; their problems are specifically a retardation in the development of intellectual and adaptive behaviour. Their ability to learn and their capacity for putting learning to use is limited but certainly not non-existent.

Equally important is the realization that intellectual disability is quantitative rather than qualitative. Close parallels are found between normally developing children and those with intellectual disabilities. Children who are intellectually disabled pass through the same cognitive developmental stages in the same order and manner as do typical children; they simply pass through the stages more slowly and attain lower levels of achievement. For example, in the sensorimotor domains, some of the common developmental trajectories such as social smiling, laughter, visual self-recognition, attachment, affiliation, fear or wariness, and language and play develop in the same way but more slowly.

To continue with Piagetian stages, students who are mildly intellectually disabled function no higher than concrete operations. Those who are moderately disabled do not surpass pre-operational stages, and those who are severely and profoundly disabled are at the sensorimotor stage.

Learning and Memory

The most specific consequences of intellectual disability involve its effects on an individual's potential to learn and to progress academically. Individuals with intellectual disabilities basically learn in the same fashion as other people but they confront serious difficulties in all aspects of intellectual functioning including concept learning, attention, and language. Memory, a key aspect of learning, is particularly problematic. Memory efficiency decreases as the level of disability increases.

Memory is often explained through the constructs of information processing, which holds that we process information in different ways and at various levels of analysis. Essentially, information processing looks at the sensory register, where information is perceived and attended to; at short-term memory, where information that has been passed through the sensory register is held for about five seconds; and at long-term memory, where retained information is stored, probably permanently. We could use the example of a young child hearing a catchy jingle on TV. The child attends to the jingle (sensory register), takes it into short-term memory, and then sings along and repeats the jingle over and over (rehearsal and elaboration) and in this way passes it to long-term memory, where it is stored for retrieval later when the child, perhaps, wants to sing it for Daddy.

For information to move from short-term to long-term memory, we must do something to help retain the information. Memory strategies (which we discussed under strategy training in Chapter 5) include such things as rehearsal, sub-vocalization, and mnemonics. For individuals with disabilities, the greatest difficulty seems to be with short-term memory. In addition to using memory strategies inefficiently, students often do not understand why they are memorizing certain information, in what context the information is meaningful, or how to internalize the structure provided by teachers (Gerber, 1988).

Students can be taught to use strategies successfully and thereby improve their memory functioning (see Chapter 5). And, once individuals with intellectual disabilities have learned information thoroughly, their long-term memory is comparable to that of typical learners.

Difficulties with memory are compounded by problems with observational learning, *task demands*—sizing up a task—organization, selective attention, generalization, motivation, and studying for tests. Students with intellectual disabilities find it very hard to select learning tasks and attend to all of their relevant dimensions. They also have difficulty paying attention and keeping on task. In the classroom, they tend to be less attentive, spend less time on academic tasks, and spend more time out of their seats than their peers (McGee & Richgels, 1990). As well, they have problems in generalizing and transferring skills and are less able to apply the knowledge or skills they have learned to new tasks, problems, or stimulus situations. Concept development, especially at abstract levels, is weak. For example, children with mild disabilities have significant deficits in the understanding of basic concepts such as *above*, *always*, *other*, and *different*.

Motivation is defined as a force that energizes, sustains, and directs behaviour toward a goal. Motivated students appear to exhibit three main perceptions. They find value in their school experiences, enjoy what they are doing, or believe what they are doing will produce beneficial outcomes; they believe that they have the skills to be successful; and they trust their environment and expect that they can succeed in it (Siegle & McCoach, 2005). Children with intellectual disabilities are lower in motivation than their peers. Since there is a strong positive correlation between motivation and achievement, it is not surprising that academic performance suffers.

motivation

As the degree of disability increases, problems with learning and memory become more severe. However, learning is both possible and common for children with moderate to profound mental retardation. Using classical and operant conditioning procedures, educators have taught many skills in the domains of adaptive behaviour, simple academics, and vocational skill formation to severely retarded, and some profoundly retarded, individuals (see Chapter 15).

Communication Development

Youngsters with intellectual disabilities acquire language more slowly than others. Typically, their language levels remain below those of non-disabled children and are often below their general mental age. As well, it is estimated that speech disorders affect about 55 percent of the total population of persons with intellectual disabilities.

With language, children demonstrate delays in sentence length, sentence complexity, and speech-sound discrimination. Their expressive language tends to be less complex than that of their peers, and some children have difficulties in generalizing the rules of grammar.

They do not effectively gain information from verbal or non-verbal receptive language; both children and adults who are intellectually disabled do not decipher affective facial expressions as well as their peers (Adams & Markham, 1991; Maurer & Newbrough, 1987).

Speech and language problems are not related to the etiology of the condition but to its severity. Youngsters who are mildly intellectually disabled may be delayed in talking, but mutism is rare. Individuals in the moderate range use stereotypical language, rarely free of defects. Among persons who are profoundly retarded, expressive speech and language skills are extremely limited. Mutism is common among these individuals, as are primitive levels of speech such as babbling and jabbering.

When children with Down syndrome are examined as a discrete group, studies suggest that their language acquisition and development is essentially similar to the language development of other children. They follow the same general path in acquiring language, but their language lags behind their non-verbal cognitive abilities, may proceed at a slower rate, and is often significantly delayed. Babies with Down vocalize less frequently. Many of these children do not acquire two-word phrases until three or four years of age.

Throughout their development, many children with Down syndrome have difficulty with expressive language. Some do not acquire functional speech until eight years of age; others, not at all. Down syndrome often includes oral problems that affect articulation—an overly large tongue over which children have poor muscle control, or an inability to close the passage from the nose to the mouth, resulting in guttural and hypernasal speech.

Academic Achievement

Pupils labelled as mildly intellectually disabled form the largest group of learners in the intellectual disabilities category and possess the widest range of skills and needs. In general, these students are slower in developing motor and social skills. In the classroom, they tend

Figure 6-3

Differences in functioning of students with mild intellectual disabilities and typical children

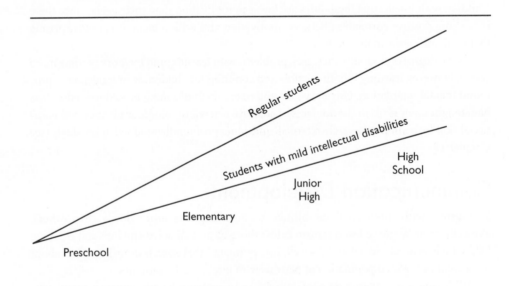

to underachieve in all academic areas and, as with language, they do not achieve in school at a level commensurate with their intellectual potentials.

The cognitive characteristics associated with intellectual disability that we pointed out in the previous section affect all learning. In elementary school, students who are mildly intellectually disabled accomplish about two-thirds of what other children will accomplish in an academic year (see Figure 6-3). This lag presents challenges to secondary level educators, as we discuss in the case study about Ben below and later in Chapter 17.

CASE STUDY

Ben

Ben is classified within the range of mild intellectual disabilities. He is now in his second year of high school. Ben is a nice young man, easy and amenable, always ready to help and to learn. He enjoys the same things that most adolescents do—among them, loud music and 'cool' clothes. He is just learning to drive although this is not yet a rewarding experience for either Ben or the instructor.

When he was only in his first year of formal schooling, Ben was identified as functioning at the level of mild intellectual disability. On the first assessment using the WISC 111, Ben showed a Full scale score of 66 with very little difference between the Verbal and the Performance scales and very little scatter among the subtests. He also tested with below-average language ability with syntactical lags and limited semantic use. Further assessments throughout his school career confirmed the initial results. Consistently, they show that although Ben is within the mildly disabled range, his language and academic performance is not commensurate with his intellectual ability.

Ben goes to school in St. John's, Newfoundland and Labrador. The province implements a categorical model of special education so that most programs for students with special needs are delivered in specialized classes, segregated placements, and/or pull out programs (Edmunds, 2003). Even though he showed lags as compared to his peers throughout elementary school, Ben was included in the general classroom with an adapted program based on an Individual Education Plan. For example, to assist Ben with his poor memory, low task commitment, passivity, and poor language, the IEP goals included structured direct teaching with much repetition, a focus on functional skills, and the use of materials from Ben's own interests and experiences.

Ben achieved about half of what the typical students in his class did. He learned to read, although comprehension was always a problem. In math, he became efficient at computations, money, time, and measurement; fractions and decimals defeated him. His achievement was somewhat better in the content areas of social studies and science, especially the latter in which he had a high interest.

Once in high school, it soon became apparent that the programs were too conceptually difficult with too much content and homework. Not only could Ben not be successful, but the general high school curriculum was not consistent with his future needs. He wanted to get a job and live independently.

Ben moved to a program that stressed life and occupational skills together with functional academics. In Ben's present classroom, for example, the teacher is working with him and his classmates on living and recreational skills in a thematic topic on communities. They are learning about shopping, restaurants, and independent living, including cooking and apartment upkeep. Under the shopping module, the students are learning how to make a shopping list; how to follow floor plans and aisle signs; the sequence of shopping and how to shop in aisle order; how to locate items and check prices and sizes; and how to unpack and store groceries. The restaurants segment includes topics such as standing in line, selecting a seat, ordering, and table manners.

In the section on transferring their skills to independent apartment living, the students are learning how to manage their own finances and prepare meals. For example, when learning how to manage household finances, Ben must correctly state the amount of bills and their due dates and learn when and how to pay each one. In the meal preparation module, Ben is learning to prepare meals and cook for himself. From pictorial recipes, he can prepare simple dinners without assistance, and use the stove appropriately (see Beakley & Yoder, 1998; Steere & Caviuolo, 2002.)

Ben's transition plan began to take shape in middle school. Now that he is in his second year of high school, the plan assumes critical proportions. Ben was invited to the IEP meeting at the beginning of this school year, and given opportunities for choice and decision-making through participating in setting his own goals. With the help of adult members of the transition team, Ben laid out his goals for the future. Because he hoped to be employed as a cook, they listed the things that Ben would have to do to qualify for this position. They included work experience, part-time work, completing application forms for summer jobs, and achieving the skills to access programs at the community college.

Reading and all the language arts suffer with problems and deficits similar to those we discussed for students with learning disabilities in Chapter 5. Math and arithmetic are equally problematic. Students with mild disabilities often have difficulty with such basic skills as counting, writing numerals, becoming automatic with the basic addition and subtraction facts, and learning basic associations. They encounter great difficulty in comprehending arithmetic concepts that involve abstract notions and symbols, and are unlikely to follow systematic strategies for solving word problems.

Individuals who are moderately intellectually disabled have limited intellectual ability, difficulties in working with abstract ideas, and problems in generalizing learning to new situations. Any academic work should be functional and relevant to daily living and needs.

Children and youth who are severely or profoundly disabled experience major challenges to successful adaptation. They have intensive instructional and technological needs that require a modified plan of instruction. Many individuals who are severely or profoundly disabled present such serious problems that they will likely require life care and supervision with extensive or pervasive supports. Nevertheless, learning is possible and individuals can acquire basic living and self-help skills; they may learn to regulate toilet habits, eat with a spoon or fork, throw a ball at a target, understand simple verbal directions, and participate in simple play and games. These groups of children are discussed more fully in Chapter 15.

Social and Emotional Development

To function successfully in school and society, all children need a range of social skills and must learn to cope with a large and diverse group of peers, a wide variety of social settings, and the fast-changing nature of everyday social interactions. But successful social adaptation is an elusive goal for many students with cognitive impairments.

In general, these students are not well accepted by their typical peers and often have trouble making friends. They are frequently the subject of teasing, which serves to diminish their self-concepts and further compounds the problems in self-esteem that accompany low achievement. Children may be rejected because they look different or show unusual behaviour, and they therefore give up trying because of low motivation.

A contributing factor seems to be difficulties with social perception—the ability to recognize and interpret social cues that include physical actions, facial expressions, tone of voice, and body language. Students who are intellectually disabled are poorer at interpreting social cues and generating strategies for solving social problems (see Leffert, Siperstein, & Millikan, 2000). It follows that they often have special personal and social problems and exhibit atypical development patterns in socialization. The more severe the disability, the lower the percentage of social interactions with non-disabled peers (Guralnick, 1981).

On the other side of the coin, studies (e.g., Wenz-Gross & Siperstein, 1997) of how children with disabilities feel about peers found that children with disabilities were less likely to view their peers as a source of support than normally developing children. This was particularly the case in the area of emotional support. Children with disabilities reported less intimacy, loyalty, self-esteem, and contact in their friendships than did typical peers. Perhaps we should not be surprised that when Field (1984) examined 16 children with intellectual disabilities in general education settings, she found that fewer than half had friends. Only 2 had friends who did not have disabilities.

Students who are moderately intellectually disabled have rather clear-cut deficits in adaptive behaviour; they have problems with interpersonal relationships, social concepts, emotional instability, and communication. As these children grow older, the progressive widening of their developmental lag tends to make their retardation more obvious. This is in contrast to persons who are mildly disabled whose condition becomes less obvious in adulthood.

The impairments of children with Down syndrome are relatively less pronounced in social development and in the mastery of adaptive skills associated with daily living. However, growth in these domains progresses at a slower rate than that of normally developing children.

Play Behaviour

Most delayed children, including those with cognitive delays, have difficulties engaging in group play. The problems are also far more extensive than would be expected (again matching academics and language) based on the children's levels of cognitive development.

Passivity, or disengagement from activity, is a distinguishing characteristic of intellectual disability, readily seen in children's play. In young children, the play is somewhat different, particularly noticeable when children participate in unstructured free play. The cognitively and behaviourally passive traits translate into periods of no play; substantial levels of solitary play; failure to respond readily to initial overtures from others; and less interactive play with peers and shorter sequences of reciprocal interaction (Beckman & Lieber, 1994; Guralnick & Hammond, 1999).

passivity

Behaviour

Children with intellectual disorders show a high rate of behavioural disorders compared to peers. Between 7 and 18 percent have co-occurring ADHD. In a study of the relationship between intellectual deficits and aggression (Huessman, Eron, & Yarmel, 1987), results indicated that childhood aggression was correlated with low intellectual and scholastic aptitude. Children with low intelligence abilities had difficulties learning needed skills for non-aggressive problem solving and probably experienced increased frustration and stress. They also had problems choosing strategies to resolve conflicts. One study (Leffert, Siperstein, & Millikan, 2000) found that the most common strategy was an appeal to authority—that is, the teacher.

As far as psychiatric disorders are concerned, it is well established that people with intellectual disabilities are vulnerable to experiencing the full range of mental disorders. The prevalence of mental illness has been estimated to occur in 14 to 64 percent of this population (see Galligan, 1990). One of the most serious problems is schizophrenia.

Studies also find a higher rate of depressive disorders in persons with intellectual disabilities. It is estimated that as many as 10 percent of people with intellectual problems suffer from depression, as compared to 1 to 5 percent of normally developing children (Stough & Baker, 1999). Many of those with cognitive impairments show symptoms of loneliness, sadness, and worry. Adults with Down syndrome seem to have more depression and dementia than other cognitively affected adults (Dykens, 1996).

Especially in children, it is extremely difficult, if not impossible, to determine whether the emotional disturbance caused the intellectual disability, or vice versa. Children who are emotionally disturbed in early childhood may be deprived of the normal sources of intellectual and social development. A low IQ (especially if below 50) increases the probability that an infant will have problems in perceiving, understanding, and responding to the environment and is therefore associated with the pathology of psychoses. Conversely, the child who is intellectually disabled may withdraw and display the behaviours characteristic of children who are emotionally disturbed.

Maladaptive behaviour is found across the spectrum of the population of intellectual disabilities but is more common in persons who are severely and profoundly retarded. As with skill development, the frequency of maladaptive behaviours is extremely variable. Serious maladaptive behaviour can be divided into three types—aggression toward other people and objects, self-stimulating behaviour, and self-injurious behaviour. The first type is fairly obvious; the latter deserve explanation, as they are found in many persons with significant disabilities and create major hindrances to an individual's learning.

Self-stimulating Behaviour

self-stimulating behaviour

Self-stimulating behaviour (often referred to as self-stimming) is a ubiquitous stereotyped behaviour that is seen in some form in people with different developmental disabilities. The behaviours are often stereotyped repetitive movements that do not seem to have any underlying reason. Commonly seen behaviours include meaningless repetitive movements, rocking, hand waving, and hand-mouthing (finger and hand sucking). Less prevalent are vomiting and rumination, disrobing, pica and coprophagy (eating inedible objects, including feces), stealing, and material hoarding.

Researchers do not yet understand the roots of these behaviours, although some are part of normal development and seem to provide sensory feedback. For example, studies show that approximately 10 percent of the general population of two-year-olds engages in head banging as part of a tantrum and 90 percent show body rocking as part of typical motor development (Berkson & Tupa, 2000). But research has not identified the variables that lead to self-stimulation and progress to become an aberrant behaviour.

Self-Injurious Behaviour

Self-injurious behaviour (SIB) is defined as any self-inflicted, repetitive action that leads to laceration, bruising, or abrasions of the client's own body. Individuals may engage in head banging, eye gouging, biting, scratching, self-pinching, self-hitting, hair pulling, hand mouthing or biting, scratching, hitting parts of the body, face slapping, body banging, self-choking, kicking, and rectal digging. Hitting the head with the hand is one of the most common behaviours.

self-injurious behaviour

Self-injurious behaviour is another topic of intense research interest. However, very little is known about the origin of these behaviours and the mechanisms that cause them to persist. It is recognized that SIB does not appear out of nowhere but rather is shaped over time by the child's exposure to the environment and social contingencies (Hastings & Noone, 2005). Various hypotheses suggest that individuals engage in SIB to avoid or escape a task orobtain attention from others, as a form of self-stimulation, or as a response to frustration. It does appear that SIB is associated with the degree of retardation. An estimated that 10 to 20 percent of individuals who are intellectually disabled engage in some form of self-injurious behaviour (Evans & Stough, 2002; Hastings & Noone, 2005).

Co-occurring Disabilities

A strong negative correlation exists between IQ level and the presence of brain pathology, central nervous system impairment, and other disabilities. Across the spectrum, persons with intellectual disabilities show more co-occurring conditions than the rest of the population. And, as one proceeds down the scale of disabilities, the incidence of co-occurring conditions increases, with blindness, deafness, cerebral palsy, epilepsy, and other medical and physical anomalies the rule rather than the exception.

People with Down syndrome are prone to a range of serious health problems. Only within recent years has their life span begun to approach that of the general population. In 1929, these individuals had a life expectancy of nine years; by 1980, it had advanced to more than thirty years; now 25 percent of individuals with Down syndrome live to the age of fifty (Patterson, 1987).

The mortality rate is still high, however, especially perinatally and in the first years of life, largely due to congenital heart conditions and increased susceptibility to infections. After age one, mortality is considerably reduced. Between ages five and ten, life expectancy is only 6 percent below normal.

About 40 percent of children with Down syndrome have congenital heart defects. Gastrointestinal malformations and reduced resistance to respiratory infections are common. As many as 75 percent of children with Down syndrome may have significant hearing losses due to otitis media. There are also biochemical differences. Research on chromosome 21 shows that its genes are linked not only to Down, but also to susceptibility among normal individuals to cancer, Alzheimer's disease, congenital heart defects, and vision problems (Kolata, 1988).

If individuals with Down syndrome survive to middle age, they are more likely to develop cataracts and leukemia. Adults with Down are predisposed to Alzheimer's disease, which is related to mutations on the 21st pair of chromosomes (Pinel, 2000). The prevalence rate of Alzheimer's is 54.5 percent in the sixth decade (see Prasher, Chowdhury, Rowe, & Bain, 1997).

Family Variables

The discovery that a child is intellectually disabled causes great stress for the parents and other family members. Across all socio-economic levels, mothers of children who are intellectually disabled report depression (Breslau & Davis, 1986). Parents must eventually confront three critical issues. They must decide how to train and educate the child, accept that the child may never be self-sufficient, and plan for the child's future.

Family functioning is a factor in outcomes. For example, research has discovered that highly functional families have children with Down syndrome who, over time, demonstrate significant benefits in communicating and socializing with others and engaging in independent self-care tasks (Hauser-Cram, Warfield, Shonkoff, Krauss, Lipshur, & Sayer, 1999). Chapter 16 discusses family issues fully.

Cultural and Linguistic Differences

In both historical and contemporary conditions, prejudice has caused individuals to be judged as deviant or disabled on the basis of characteristics that are typical for their minority group or from stereotyping. This is particularly true in the case of intellectual disability where the conjunction of disorder (or presumed disorder), ethnicity, IQ tests, and special education has a rather nasty history (see Winzer, 1993).

over-representation

The over-representation of certain groups in special education has been a recurring issue. **Over-representation** in special education occurs when a group's membership in a program is larger than its percentage in the educational system or within a given disability category. We have already mentioned that there is an over-representation of students from culturally and linguistically diverse groups in programs for speech and language disabilities and learning disabilities. This is also true in the field of intellectual disability, although there is far greater reluctance today than in the past to refer students to this category. This caution results from the growth of the field of learning disabilities, the inclusive movement, and the overlap among categories. Especially cognate are a number of court cases in the United States, such as Larry P. vs. Riles. These class actions have disputed the use of IQ tests and inappropriate placements for minority students.

ASSESSMENT OF INTELLECTUAL DISABILITIES

A complete assessment of a child suspected of intellectual disabilities fulfills several major needs. A full pediatric medical evaluation is needed to pinpoint secondary conditions, recognize and identify the child's strengths, and detail necessary medical treatment regimes.

An educational assessment covers two broad areas. First, it must be determined if a child's mental ability and adaptive behaviour fulfill the definitional criteria for mental retardation. Second, assessment data provide guidelines for the development of an appropriate program and/or treatment plan and the establishment of objectives and remedial strategies.

There are virtually thousands of tests, measures, inventories, and scales available for intellectual disability. Yet assessment remains problematic. Diagnosticians still encounter grave difficulties in arriving at an accurate assessment of the learning potential and adaptive behaviour of many children who are intellectually disabled.

Formal diagnosis is not one short affair. Assessment incorporates a range of medical, formal, and informal processes using a variety of instruments, procedures, and personnel. For example, in an extreme case, a child with a severe intellectual impairment and co-occurring disabilities may be seen by a physician for physiological assessment, an audiologist for hearing acuity, an ophthalmologist for visual efficiency, a physical therapist for gross motor functioning, an occupational therapist for fine motor skills, a speech/language therapist for augmentative communication, a psychologist for intellectual ability, and a teacher for educational achievement.

Educational procedures may include direct testing, ecological or functional behavioural assessment, assessment of adaptive behaviour, achievement tests, social skills assessment, or some other assessment procedure. The tools administered depend on the strengths and needs of an individual. A test or procedure that suits a child who is mildly disabled will almost surely be inappropriate for one with severe retardation.

Screening

As we saw in Chapter 2, educational screening precedes psycho-educational diagnosis. For children with moderate to profound intellectual disabilities, screening may not be necessary because these children display overt and obvious problems. Such clear-cut signs accompany severe disabilities that it is possible to identify affected children in infancy. In contrast, many cases of mild intellectual disability are not suspected until children enter school.

Teachers are often the first to recognize problems and are at the forefront in identifying needs and referring children for further assessment. Not only can teachers observe students over a period of time and note academic performance and social behaviour in and out of the classroom, but they also have access to pertinent school records and to the observations and comments of other teachers (archival data) who may have encountered the child in earlier grades.

Assessment of Intelligence

Founded on the AAMR definition, the formal assessment of intellectual disabilities has two major areas of concern—IQ and adaptive behaviour. IQ is the pivotal concept: an assessment of intelligence is necessary to meet the definitional criteria of an IQ level two or more standard deviations below the norm. IQ has been around for a long time and a range of measures to assess it are in use.

Children in the more severe ranges of intellectual disability are often untestable through the usual standardized IQ tests such as the WISC-IV. In cases where organic brain pathology and physical disabilities are present, IQ levels are estimated through the use of developmental scales, measures of adaptive behaviour, observations, and other tools. (See Chapters 14 and 15.)

Assessment of Adaptive Behaviour

The inclusion of adaptive behaviour in the definition of intellectual disabilities brought its own set of problems. Since there is no consensus on the exact nature of the adaptive behaviour, the question of how to effectively assess the construct is beset with difficulties. Since the original Vineland Scale of Adaptive Behavior appeared in the 1930s, numerous tools have appeared. Still, no single, quantifiable, and reliable assessment procedure exists.

Many adaptive skills are very visible, such as using the toilet, feeding and dressing oneself, and relating to peers. Adaptive behaviour scales, used with children in all severity ranges, generally consist of lists or inventories of these and other common behaviours, as well as maladaptive ones. The scales are completed by someone close to the child—a parent, teacher, or primary caregiver.

INTERVENTION WITH CHILDREN WHO HAVE INTELLECTUAL DISABILITIES

Many different types of intervention are used with individuals who have intellectual disabilities. Medical and pharmacological regimes are especially important for individuals with biological etiologies. Social and early intervention is critical for infants and preschoolers and their families (see Chapter 16). Various therapists may intervene to improve secondary motor, language, or speech disabilities.

The major focus of intervention occurs in the schools. Most students with mild disabilities are placed in general classrooms, and the crux of education for students with moderate to profound cognitive delays has altered in recent years to greatly expanded placements in neighbourhood schools.

Medical Intervention

No surgical procedures or miracle drugs are known to actually improve intellectual ability or adaptive behaviour. In general, medical intervention attempts to prevent or correct the organic causes of retardation rather than alleviate the condition itself. In Chapter 3, for example, we discuss the value of screening in cases such as phenylketonuria.

Surgical intervention has been used with children who have Down syndrome in an effort to alleviate speech and eating problems and to render their appearance more normal. One survey (Lewis, 2000) found that 70.9 percent of parent respondents felt that the facial features of Down would affect the social acceptance of their child.

Increasing numbers of families are seeking surgery to improve children's speech and looks. The surgery involves multiple procedures; tongue reduction is the most common, along with implants in the bridge of the nose, chin, cheeks, and jawbone (Goebe et al., 2003).

People with severe disabilities are more likely than most others in society to receive medication to change their behaviour. Some drugs offer great promise for selectively reducing challenging behaviour while improving other forms of adaptive functioning (Kennedy & Meyer, 1998). Nevertheless, there are serious reservations about the overuse of drug therapy.

Technical Aids

Technological advances have resulted in the development of devices designed specifically for persons with developmental disabilities. The range of instructional technology employed in classrooms primarily includes microcomputers and innovative software.

For people with severe disabilities, independent functioning is supplemented with aids for self-help skills and environmental control. Some examples include a device that produces a signal for a non-toilet-trained child to go to the bathroom, a self-feeding tray for persons who are multiply disabled, and special bathing devices. Adaptive equipment is discussed in Chapter 13.

Educational Intervention

Intellectual disabilities are related to delayed intellectual development in areas considered important for school success. Students achieve below grade level and usually experience difficulties throughout their school careers. The level of achievement is related to the degree of disorder. With such a heterogeneous population, there is a variety of settings and strategies. In Chapter 15 we return to intervention for persons with severe and profound disorders.

Service Delivery Models

Within the school system, the current trend is to include students with intellectual disabilities in the general classroom, especially those with mild disabilities but also an increasing number of children with moderate and severe intellectual disabilities. While this reflects a dramatic change away from segregated classrooms, students identified as intellectually disabled are still often educated in separate settings. Gordon Porter of the Canadian Association for Community Living (2004) reports that in Canada 40 percent of children with intellectual disabilities are still in special classes or segregated schools.

The majority of general classroom options are at the elementary level. A student's success depends on a number of factors that include his or her age, support services available, curriculum adaptations and modifications, acceptance by the other students, the classroom teacher's experience with and exposure to children who are exceptional, and the availability of community resources.

The provision of appropriate educational services remains problematic for many secondary-school-aged students with disabilities. Secondary education programs tend to be more explicitly vocationally oriented than those at elementary levels and are directed toward securing employment upon graduation. See Chapter 17 and the Case study about Ben earlier in this chapter.

Research has not yet provided a compelling body of data on the outcomes of inclusive placements for students with intellectual disabilities. For example, although academic considerations seem acceptable, there are still worries about social acceptance. Inclusion assumes that students with disabilities will be better accepted, have more friends, and feel better about themselves. There is little empirical data for this assumption. Mere physical presence in a class does not seem to enhance social competence and the social outcomes of placing students with intellectual disabiliies in regular classrooms have been disappointing. Often these children occupy a marginal position in the social network of the class (see Siperstein & Leffert, 1997).

Educational Approaches

There are three major goals in the education of students with intellectual disabilities: productivity, independence, and participation. To accomplish these goals, students are presented with instruction in the areas of academic, social, self-help, community living, and vocational skills. Depending on the extent and severity of the disability, the major goals may or may not always be fully achievable; success may be only fractional for children functioning at the low end of the continuum.

Table 6-6 presents some ideas for creating accessible classrooms for all students with problems in learning, including those with intellectual disabilities.

Table 6-6 Creating accessible classrooms

Accommodations

- Use small-group teaching to allow for more practice and feedback. Reduce group size; the ideal group is two to four students.
- Use Computer Assisted Instruction (CAI), proven to be particularly effective for children with intellectual disabilities.

Adaptations, materials

- Emphasize concrete, meaningful content with demonstrations, visual aids, or concrete models to watch and imitate.
- For added comprehension of content area texts, highlight textbooks.
- Provide supplementary content written to a lower level than the textbook.
- Provide outlines of textbook chapters and outlines of lecture presentations for older students.
- Teach textbook structure, such as headings, subheadings, differing print, introductory and summary paragraphs.

Adaptations, instructional

- Be honest but liberal with praise. Use consistent reinforcement and provide continuous and immediate feedback.
- Use evaluative feedback. For example, "I like the way you formed your letters," rather than "Good work."
- Use many *instructional scaffolds* (types of supports that help students take the step from their current learning to new skills or knowledge).
- Increase motivation by using thematic projects that allow children to pursue their interests and be active participants.

Table 6-6 continued

- Motivation increases as competitiveness decreases. Reward effort rather than ability as a motivator for all students.
- Promote transfer of learning by applying learning to other situations, objects, and problems in the learner's environment.
- Present tasks in an uncomplicated, brief, and sequential fashion moving from the simple to the more complex.
- Ensure mastery of new material through repetition and over-learning.
- Drill and over-learning is key to overcoming memory problems. Have students practise reading or math in a variety of ways and with a variety of materials.
- Teach specific learning strategies and strategies to improve memory, such as mnemonics.
- To improve memory, stop an activity for a few minutes and have the students write or tell you about what they've learned, any item that confuses them, and any questions they may have.
- To address low reading skills, read to the class in order to provide pacing and ensure better understanding.
- Use reciprocal teaching, which involves students and teacher, in a dialogue on written material to discover the meaning of a written passage. The steps are
    1. Summarizing: identifying and paraphrasing the main ideas of the text.
    2. Question generating: asking oneself questions about comprehension.
    3. Clarifying: discerning if and where there has been a lack of comprehension.
    4. Predicting: Guessing what will happen next (Palinscar & Brown, 1984).
- Use POSSE, a strategy to assist reading comprehension. Students follow these steps: predict ideas, organize the ideas, search for the structure, summarize the main ideas, evaluate (Englert & Mariage, 1991).
- For students with fragile X syndrome, stress rote learning.

Students Who Have Mild Intellectual Disabilities

The actual curricula objectives are the same for students with mild intellectual disabilities as for their peers. Students require instruction in basic academic skills, particularly basic literacy and numeracy. Teachers must also stress the cognitive, language, and social domains. Each program will be individualized based on a student's unique set of strengths and weaknesses. At the secondary level, the components of transition are critical.

Students Who Have Moderate Intellectual Disabilities

For students with moderate disabilities, the ultimate goal of education is functional independence to ready them to meet the demands of their community environments. The curriculum is less academically oriented than for children who are mildly disabled.

Functionality is the core of the curriculum, referred to as a *functional approach* or *life-skills instruction*. Adaptive behaviour, self-help skills, life skills, and social skills are the important

Training in life skills is essential for students with intellectual disabilities.

components of this approach. In general, children who are moderately disabled do not learn to read beyond the grade 1 level. The reading is functional—names, directions, and labels. Pupils are taught to write relevant names and words and introduced to numbers, time, and simple money exchange.

Students Who Are Severely and Profoundly Disabled

While almost all students with mild intellectual disabilities and many with moderate disabilities will be educated in general classrooms, the placement of students who are severely and profoundly disabled is more controversial. For these youngsters, there are conflicting ideologies that revolve around the issue of inclusive schooling.

There is no question that children who are severely and profoundly disabled force us to redefine the term *education* beyond its traditional academic limits. The goals of education for these children are different than those for typical students and those with milder disabilities. Many more personnel are involved: these children often require a range of other services from professionals such as doctors, speech therapists, social workers, and psychologists.

The major educational goals are to decrease dependence on others, increase awareness of environmental stimulation, teach basic communication and self-help skills, and push achievement levels higher. Training begins with basic survival and self-help skills, along with the elimination of undesirable behaviour. It involves imitation, language acquisition, self-feeding, ambulation, dressing skills, toilet training, and social and recreational behaviour. Applied behavioural approaches that employ repetition and simple conditioning are primary teaching strategies. Behavioural methods seem to succeed where others fail, and the behavioural emphasis on specific task analysis is particularly well suited to the problems of individuals who are severely disabled.

Social Intervention

Advocacy groups made up of parents and professionals exist for the sole purpose of improving life conditions for the population of persons who are intellectually disabled. The Canadian Association for Community Living (CACL) (formerly the CAMR) and its research arm, the Roeher Institute, are typical examples of advocacy groups.

SUMMARY

1. The criteria for intellectual disability have consistently emphasized the salience of cognitive and social competence deficits. Under the current AAMR definition, three factors must be present before an individual can be considered within the category of mental

retardation—subaverage general intellectual functioning, deficits in adaptive behaviour, and manifestation during the developmental period. Note that new systems to replace the traditional AAMR categories move from a dependent to a capability approach.

2. Adaptive behaviour is a difficult construct to operationalize, define, and measure. In the broadest sense, it refers to an individual's ability to cope or deal effectively with personal and social demands. The existence of limitations in adaptive skills occurs within the context of environments and an individual's age peers.

3. Current definitions of intellectual disability show considerable controversy about terminology, adaptive behaviour, and the use of IQ tests. Today's definitions, especially those concerning mild disability, do not see intellectual disability as a permanent condition but rather as one that improves with sustained intervention and is linked to the demands of formal schooling. There is a higher incidence of disability during the school years, with lower incidence figures during the preschool years and adulthood.

4. The agents that cause intellectual disabilities are legion. They include genetic and chromosomal differences, infections such as maternal rubella, intoxicants such as drugs, postnatal diseases such as meningitis, and childhood accidents. Recent genetic findings warn educators not to ignore distinctions among specific syndromes.

5. In trying to pinpoint the existence and severity of intellectual disabilities, clinicians are challenged to find a range of observations and measures that are appropriate for individual children. Data on a child's levels of cognitive functioning (IQ tests) are employed as one measure used to determine an individual educational program. Scales of adaptive behaviour supplement IQ data.

6. Students with mild intellectual disabilities learn in the same way as other pupils. Even if their rate of learning is slower and the level reached not as high, their learning curves approximate those of typical pupils. For those with moderate disabilities, learning is more restricted, often to functional skills. Individuals who are severely and profoundly retarded must often struggle to achieve ambulation and simple physical activities. For individuals in these last two categories, physical development is often impaired and co-occurring conditions are common.

7. Although there are parallel learning curves, some specific behaviours distinguish children with intellectual disabilities from typically developing children. Very young children are passive, which affects their play, cognition, and language. In school, the passivity continues, contributing to poor academic achievement. Children display slower learning rates; failure to identify relevant features of tasks; difficulty responding spontaneously to newly learned material; difficulty regularizing, generalizing and transferring learned skills to new situations; poor motivation; problems with short-term memory; and failure to use the strategies needed for successful learning.

8. Children labelled as mildly intellectually disabled form the greatest proportion of the retarded population. Today, the majority of these students are educated in general classrooms. Following graduation, many such individuals blend into the social fabric of their neighbourhoods, holding jobs, marrying, and having families. Once these adjustments have been made, they no longer fit the AAMR definition. Children with moderate levels of intellectual disability are presented modified programs and limited academic curricula with a stress on functional skills in all domains. The inclusion of

students who are severely or profoundly retarded is beset by controversy. Teaching targets a diverse array of skills—self-help, eating, toileting, dressing, socialization, and language acquisition together with the elimination of maladaptive behaviours.

HISTORICAL NOTES

Traditionally, intellectual disability received much less scholarly attention than mental illness. Yet, as a human condition, intellectual disability has been acknowledged in literature for 2500 years. In the eons prior to the French Enlightenment of the mid-18th century, little was done for those who appeared different or deviant. Often, they became the focus of society's accumulated fears and myths. Many were treated cruelly. Sometimes they were seen as buffoons, and sometimes as special conversants with higher powers.

Actual teaching of students with intellectual disabilities began in France in the early 1800s, and is often said to have begun with Jean Marc Itard and Victor, as we told in the story in Chapter 4. Philosophy and pedagogy rapidly translated to the New World, where special institutional facilities were established in Boston in 1848 and Ontario in 1873. Institutional placements remained important right into the early 1970s, although too often the intervention was repressive, heavy-handed, and coercive.

In the opening decades of the 20th century, the public school systems established special, segregated classes, euphemistically titled "opportunity classes," "auxiliary classes," or "classes for slow learners." Educational goals within the special classes focused on overcoming or compensating for the disability. Students were trained in manual arts, practical skills, handiwork, and personal and social adjustment skills.

It was not until the 1950s that the curriculum for students with mild intellectual disabilities changed and began to represent an extension of the general school curriculum. At the same time, interest developed in how to train and teach people with more significant disabilities; curricula for those with moderate and severe retardation emerged.

The 1960s represented a turning point for the field in terms of research, funding, teacher training, and more enlightened views of intellectual disability that reflected socio-political changes. One of the most significant events was the 1959 *Manual of Terminology and Classification in Mental Retardation* (AAMD, 1959), which departed from traditional definitions by no longer considering the condition as an incurable trait. Supporting the new professional constructs were such varied factors as parent pressure, legislation, litigation, a panel on mental retardation called by U.S. President John F. Kennedy, a series of efficacy studies about special classes, exposés of the deplorable conditions in institutions, and the normalization movement.

Within this climate for change, special education services for students identified as mildly disabled came to occupy a central role and take up a large share of fiscal and human resources in the schools. With the 1975 passage of Public Law 94–142 in the United States, the notion of educating all students in the least restrictive environment emerged. Soon, mainstreaming and then inclusion in the general classroom became a common option in the education of children and youth with intellectual disabilities.

SECTION 3

Children with Behavioural Disorders

Just about every parent has, at some time or another, been frustrated and annoyed by the behaviour of his or her child. In the classroom, on an almost daily basis, every teacher confronts minor misdemeanours and unacceptable behaviours from students.

The frequency and intensity of students' behavioural disorders has increased in the past several decades. The current research literature notes that today's teachers are facing far more challenging behaviours than their predecessors. Moreover, researchers such as Barbara Larrivee (2005) maintain that teachers will continue to face greater instructional, behavioural, and classroom management challenges as they strive to accommodate the increasing diversity of student learning styles and behavioural needs.

In contemporary classrooms, teachers more and more often face inappropriate behaviour, non-compliance, and conflict from students who show a litany of behavioural excesses that include interrupting conversations, refusing to complete work or follow directions, physical and verbal aggression, defiance, temper tantrums, lying, swearing, stealing, throwing chairs, spitting, and wearing attention-getting T-shirts.

At the same time, almost every classroom will contain one child with Attention Deficit Hyperactivity Disorder (ADHD). These children are, at the least, inattentive, distractible, and hyperactive.

The problems created by children and youth with behavioural disorders should not be underestimated. Nor should the challenges these students create for educational systems and teachers be seen as anything less than serious. Students who consistently break rules and cause disruption inevitably have a destabilizing influence on entire schools and can turn an individual classroom into a guarded and anxious environment.

Teachers frequently feel overwhelmed by misbehaviour in the classroom (Martin, Linfoot, & Stephenson, 1999); they report that challenging behaviours, ranging from physical violence to social withdrawal, are among the most difficult to manage in school settings. New teachers in particular consider classroom management an important, ongoing issue and want continued assistance with it.

In order to intervene effectively, educators need to understand the behavioural difficulties likely to be seen in children and youth so that they may better appreciate that these children are not in direct control of their deviant behaviours. In general, children do not go home and concoct plans to make the teacher angry or reduce the student teacher to tears. Rather, children with behavioural disorders are unable to understand and control their emotions. Among the diversity of symptoms seen in these children runs an undercurrent that includes such negative feelings as anger, rage, fear, sadness, grief, frustration, anxiety, inhibition, apprehension, depression, and over-control.

Once teachers and others clearly understand the complex and interconnecting issues and variables that underlie and affect behavioural disorders, they can identify early, formulate expectations, plan assessment strategies, and develop and implement strategic plans for intervening in the context of schooling (see Sprague & Walker, 2000).

Chapter 7 in this section addresses children with behavioural disorders and includes multiple approaches and strategies for prevention and intervention. Chapter 8 discusses the contentious, controversial, and issue-laden category of ADHD. The more profound disorders of behaviour, such as childhood schizophrenia, are discussed under the umbrella of pervasive developmental disorders in Chapter 14.

Learning Outcomes

After reading this section, you should be able to

People and Foundations

1. Understand the genesis and development of the field of behavioural disorders and the subfield of ADHD.

Issues

2. Recognize that the entire field of behavioural disorders is beset by unresolved issues that include problems with definitions, classification, terminology, prevalence, and effective intervention.
3. Understand the practical, academic, and ethical issues involved with psychopharmacology for children with exceptionalities, particularly those with Attention Deficit Hyperactivity Disorder.
4. Be aware of the controversies and discussions regarding the educational inclusion of students with behavioural disorders.

Knowledge

5. Be familiar with the different groups classified under the banner of behavioural disorders, their presumed etiologies, and developmental consequences.
6. Recognize the impact of different conceptual models used to explain behavioural disorders on etiological considerations and intervention modes.

7. Understand the juxtaposition of behavioural disorders with academic deficits and co-occurring disabilities.

Skills

8. Know the steps and the process of Functional Behavioural Assessment (FBA).
9. Be aware of some of the generic strategies that teachers can use to sustain appropriate behaviour, manage challenging behaviours, and eliminate poor behaviour in the classroom and school.
10. Understand the process and practice of school-wide programs and Positive Behaviour Supports (PBS).

CHAPTER 7

CHILDREN WITH BEHAVIOURAL DISORDERS

INTRODUCTION

Young people who show behavioural excesses and seem intent on satisfying impulses that are incompatible with the kinds of classroom control and academic activities that the teacher has in mind are likely to be referred to special education and may then be grouped under the categorical umbrella of *behaviourally disordered*. This extremely broad classification of exceptionality includes conduct disorders, anxiety and withdrawal, socialized aggression, Attention Deficit Hyperactivity Disorder (ADHD), and childhood psychoses.

Of all the deviant behaviours exhibited by these children, the two most common are aggressive acting-out behaviour and social withdrawal. In the classroom, overt acts, verbal and physical aggression, and coercive tactics by disruptive and defiant children are unlikely to escape attention. They are more likely to catch teacher attention than anxiety and withdrawal, although most teachers will soon respond to these unusual patterns of behaviour as well.

DEFINITIONS OF BEHAVIOURAL DISORDERS

After reading the case study about Andrew on pages 211 and 212, you may think that he is a typical child with a behavioural disorder and that these forms of behaviour are fairly simple to define and classify. Nothing could be further from the truth. There is no such thing as a typical child with a behavioural disorder—the only commonality is that the excesses are chronic and extend far beyond the norm. And, given the varied behaviours and uniqueness of every affected individual, definitions, terminology, and classifications are very confused.

The field of behavioural disorders has seen evolving terminology over the years. At the outset, a variety of descriptors, largely arising from a psychiatric base, were used: these included *neurotic*, *psychotic*, *obsessive*, and *emotionally disturbed*.

Current educators prefer to dispense with psychiatric terms, but still disagree over what constitutes a severe behaviour disorder, whether the use of the term is even justifiable, and whether to call these children *emotionally disturbed, behaviourally disordered, socially maladjusted, deviant, psychologically impaired, educationally handicapped, character disordered, children in conflict, delinquent,* or some other descriptor.

Given the varied terminology, it is not surprising that numerous ways to define behavioural disorders have emerged over the years, but a universally accepted definition remains extremely problematic. The many attempts to define disturbed child populations and aberrant behaviour have had varying degrees of success, and no single definition of behavioural disorders exists. In Canada in 1995, for example, 10 provincial or territorial jurisdictions had 8 different official definitions of behavioural disorders. (Robert, 1995).

Multiple interrelated factors feed into the definitional confusion. These include the following:

- Traditionally, the study and treatment of behavioural disorders has been the domain of clinical psychologists, researchers specializing in abnormal psychology, psychiatrists and, more recently, educators. It follows that deviant behaviour is defined and conceptualized in many ways, and the definitions proposed come from a variety of perspectives and disciplines.

- Abnormal behaviour has an obvious referent in normal behaviour. But there is a continuum that runs from mental health to mental illness, and human emotions and behaviour are so varied that a precise notion of normalcy is difficult to derive. Lack of an adequate definition of mental health or normalcy makes behavioural disorders an open-ended category of deviance rather than an entity. All behavioural disorders are abnormal in the sense that the word means "away from the norm," and behavioural disorders are deviations from average or standard behaviour. But problems in identification occur when we try to pinpoint just where on the continuum behaviour becomes aberrant; it is very hard to draw a line between serious behavioural disorders and problematic behaviour that is fairly common in childhood.

- All children exhibit varying behaviours, and deviant and unusual behaviours may exist in the repertoires of those who are developing normally. Such behavioural problems fluctuate and decline as children get older and are not necessarily signs of clinical deviance. Lying, for example, is reported for the majority (53 percent) of six-year-old boys; by the age of ten, lying decreases to 10 percent of boys. In girls, the pattern is more dramatic, with a high rate (about 48 percent) at age six and no lying reported as a problem at age eleven (see Kazdin, 1989).

- To confuse the issue further, children who are disturbed sometimes behave quite normally. Distinctions between normal and disturbed behaviour are generally in the amount or degree rather than kind. Children with behavioural disorders perform certain behaviours too often or intensely, or not often or intensely enough, but specifying this amount and degree is difficult.

- There is not a single symptom that is common to all pupils who are behaviourally disordered, or even to a subgroup of these children, because there is no such thing as a typical student who is behaviourally disordered.

- The patterns of behaviour exhibited by children with disorders are often unpredictable and subtle, rendering their conditions even harder to define. Some (but not all) children are versatile in their antisocial behaviour, and likely to display a wide variety of inappropriate behaviours or more than one type of problem or disorder. A child with a conduct disorder may also be depressed, and that child's behaviour may vacilate to such a degree as to show both internalizing and externalizing problems. Some children have only one anxiety or phobic disorder; most demonstrate comorbid anxiety and phobias (King, Heyne, & Ollendick, 2005). These children who show versatile antisocial behaviour are, by the way, generally likely to have the more severe problems, and their prognosis is usually poorer compared to those who exhibit only one type of antisocial behaviour (Kazdin, 1998).

- The behavioural problems change as children grow older. Four-year-olds may disobey their parents; as teenagers, they may engage in vandalism and delinquency.

- Behavioural disorders cannot be measured quantitatively. We have no instruments analogous to the IQ test to determine a mental health quotient.

- Legal and educational terms differ and, while the educational and legal systems are not at odds, their perspectives and their solutions may be different. *Delinquency* is a legal term applied by the criminal justice system to indicate that a youth has been adjudicated by the courts and found guilty of criminal behaviour. The educational term, *socialized aggressive*, is less restrictive than delinquency because it includes behaviours that are norm-violating but not necessarily delinquent.

- Social and cultural expectations differ. Behavioural disorders occur among the rich, the poor, the gifted, the intellectually disabled, and members of all racial and ethnic groups. There are, however, varying reactions to certain behaviours. Deviance is defined by social groups that recognize some behaviours as infractions of the rules and label as deviant persons who do not conform to these socially defined rules. This explains, at least in part, why a disproportionate number of students from culturally and linguistically different groups are labelled as behaviourally disordered.

- Children rarely decide for themselves that they are behaviourally disordered; that determination is made by teachers and parents. But any observer's interpretation of a situation is precariously subjective, and disruptive behaviour is often in the eye of the beholder. Teachers seem to carry their own private definitions of behavioural disorders (Kauffman, 2005) and students regarded as disruptive by one teacher may be ignored by another; rules might be enforced by one teacher but not by another.

- Following the above, it is true that, to some degree at least, behavioural disorders correlate with teacher tolerance levels. Teachers place different demands on students depending on their own behaviour standards and the degree to which they are accepting of specific maladaptive behaviours. Varying tolerance levels of deviant behaviours result in a high degree of variability in the teacher decision-making process about who has a problem and who should be referred to special education.

- There is often a relationship between behavioural disorders and other disabling conditions. This can be seen in each categorical chapter of this text when we list behaviour as a specific developmental consequence of other disabilities. As examples only, many students who are learning disabled develop an overlay of emotional problems that compound their learning difficulties and conceal their primary disorder. Students with intellectual disabilities are at risk for the same types of psychological disorders as students without cognitive defects (Stough & Baker, 1999).

Dozens of definitions of behavioural disorders are currently available. All of those that arise from an educational perspective include the following statements about behavioural disorders:

- The observed behaviours deviate in an extreme way from the norm.

- Children with behavioural disorders respond markedly to their environments in socially unacceptable and/or personally unsatisfying ways.

- The behaviours recur chronically. In children with behavioural disorders, they are not transient and episodic; rather, they last six months or longer, and interfere with expected age-appropriate functioning.

- The behaviours violate social or cultural expectations; they are inconsistent with current societal standards.

- Behavioural disorders affect a child's self-esteem, interpersonal relationships, and probably school achievement, and therefore require special education intervention.

CASE STUDY

Andrew

Persistent antisocial behaviour was seen in Andrew even before he entered formal schooling. In nursery school, he aggressively bit, fought, and scratched his way through the program. During the early school years, he became almost a legend at Maple Elementary. From the day he walked into the kindergarten, Andrew's overt, abusive, and aggressive behaviour was obvious. He would physically and verbally harass his peers on the smallest provocation and, when restrained or reprimanded by the teacher, revert to massive temper tantrums and language that was creative and explicit in its obscenity.

Andrew's excessive behaviours were chronic and far beyond the norm expected at his age. Few interventions seemed to work. The grade 1 teacher, for example, instigated a number of behaviour reduction plans that included daily report cards, time outs, a token economy, and high rates of teacher reinforcement for appropriate behaviour. But Andrew continued to strike out with hostility and aggression. His behaviour affected his own learning and social interactions as well as the equilibrium of those in his environment. He spent much of his time in early elementary school ejected from the classroom or in the principal's office.

It did not take long for the teachers to give Andrew the de facto label of *behaviourally disordered*, among other less kindly descriptors. But it was not until the close of his grade 2 year that Andrew's parents agreed to a formal assessment. The teacher's referral noted that in the classroom Andrew would attend to tasks for only a very short period and that he often failed to complete any work at all. He acted out his anger as well as verbalizing it. Not surprisingly, Andrew had trouble making and keeping friends and seldom participated in play, alone or with classmates. As well, Andrew seemed totally unresponsive to external pressure, whether in the form of a reward or punishment. In fact, it seemed the more he was rewarded, the worse he behaved and the less he learned. Likewise, the more he was punished, the worse he behaved and the less he learned.

An interview with Andrew's mother indicated that home reactions to his poor behaviour were not necessarily punitive but his parents often fell into the negative reinforcement trap. For example, Andrew's mother related how when she nags him to clean his room, he whines and complains so much that she eventually stops asking. This provides negative reinforcement to both players: the mother is negatively reinforced when Andrew stops whining; Andrew is negatively reinforced when his mother's nagging stops. The room remains uncleaned (see Patterson, 1980).

When a school-based team met to discuss Andrew's problems, the participants quickly decided that the first step should be a functional behavioural assessment (FBA). Prior to deciding on a placement and a behaviour reduction plan as part of an IEP, the team needed to pinpoint why Andrew behaved in such disruptive and aggressive ways. The FBA process and extracts from the behaviour plan and IEP are shown later in this chapter.

CLASSIFICATION OF BEHAVIOURAL DISORDERS

Over the centuries, children that we would today classify as behaviourally disordered have been larded with a plethora of labels. Nineteenth-century Canadians were wont to use descriptors such as *neglected, vagrant, waifs, strays, street urchins,* and *delinquents.* It was not until the first decades of the 20th century that more precise taxonomies emerged. The term *emotionally disturbed* appeared in the literature and gradually became widely accepted. The general category of *emotional disturbance* had two severity levels—*mildly emotionally disturbed,* and *seriously* or *profoundly emotionally disturbed* for those with conditions such as childhood schizophrenia. It was not until the 1960s that *behaviourally disordered* slowly crept into professional parlance.

Today, the terms *emotionally disturbed* and *behaviourally disordered* are both used. The American IDEA in 1990 specified *emotional or behavioural disorder.* The UK uses *emotional/behavioural disorder.* Canadian jurisdictions use both terms, but lean toward *behaviour disorders* as an omnibus term embracing a range of difficulties. We use the generic *behavioural disorders* in this text as this focuses on the most obvious problems in terms of classification, assessment, and treatment regimes.

With the confusion related to definitions and terminology, it is not surprising that a consensus does not exist about how to classify behavioural disorders into types and degrees of deviance. Researchers from many disciplines have tried to find meaningful classifications in various ways. The classifications most relevant to educational intervention are described below and shown in Figure 7-1.

Clinical Classification

The principal modern clinical classification scheme is the one provided by the American Psychiatric Association (APA) in its *Diagnostic and Statistical Manual of Mental Disorders* (DSM)(1994, 2000). **DSM** is a clinical manual primarily used by psychiatrists and

DSM

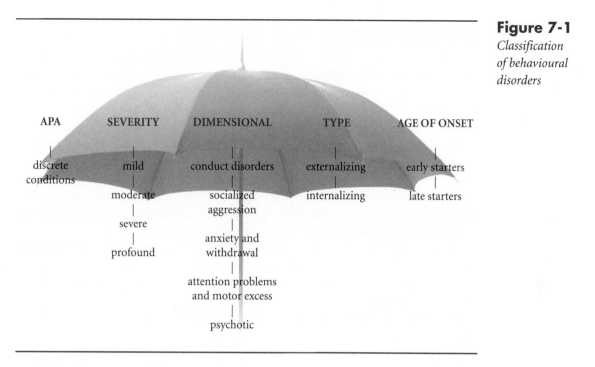

Figure 7-1
Classification of behavioural disorders

psychologists to diagnose mental health problems. It describes behavioural symptoms of all disorders currently recognized by the APA and defines the symptoms and signs required for the diagnosis of each disorder.

One problem with the DSM classification is that disorders are not defined as deviations from the norm and evaluated on a continuum but are simply judged as either present or absent. As well, although the DSM diagnostic criteria distinguish between child and adolescent onset, they were originally developed for adults and are not school-oriented (except for truancy). Further, there is some evidence that DSM criteria do not identify most preadolescent girls with early onset antisocial behaviour (Zoccolillio, Tremblay, & Vilano, 1996).

Classification by Severity

When severity levels are used, classification is not an either–or proposition as in the APA system; rather, it is based on how much behaviour differs from what is considered normal. Disorders are classified along the traditional severity lines as mild, moderate, severe, or profound.

Classification by Behavioural Type

Definitions of behavioural disorders can be based on excesses or deficits of social behaviour, referred to as *externalizing* or *internalizing behaviour*. This is not a formal classification, but it does provide a useful description. For example, students with conduct disorders and socialized aggression externalize their behaviour through such acts as disobedience, lying, stealing, fighting, sexual delinquency, and destructiveness. In contrast, anxious and withdrawn children internalize their behaviour. They may suffer from nausea, pains, headaches, phobias, fears, obsessions, shyness, nightmares, crying, depression, self-consciousness, and withdrawal.

Classification by Age of Onset

Age of onset is, again, not a formal classification. It gains credibility because of the differences in behavioural manifestations and particularly prognosis between *early starters* (onset before the age of ten) and *late starters* (characteristics not observed until after the age of ten).

Early starters are of greatest concern. While the onset of aggressive behaviour can be gradual—extending over many years—the long-term effects are more serious when antisocial behaviour begins early. Patterns of early poor behaviour are often highlighted at school entry, magnified in the classroom setting, and then show escalating conflict and an increasing cycle of severity and intensity. Once established, deviant patterns of behaviour are particularly resistant to change and the disorder becomes much like any other developmental disability—very unlikely to be reversed or eliminated.

Boys who begin their criminal careers in childhood or early adolescence have heightened risk for becoming chronic offenders (Farrington, 1983). There is some evidence that early onset is linked to more physical aggression and more violent crime (Moffitt, 1993), and boys who are first arrested between the ages of ten and twelve average twice as many convictions as later starters (Farrington, Gallagher, Morley, St. Ledger, & West, 1986).

Much less risk attaches to the late starter—someone committing his or her first offence in middle to late adolescence. Late starters are often not as extreme in their aggression as early-onset youth. Lacking the early training for antisocial behaviours, these individuals have not experienced the dual failure of rejection by normal peers and academic failure (Patterson, De Baryshe, & Ramsey, 1989).

Dimensional Classification

Dimensional classification systems use observer reports and the statistical procedure of factor analysis to determine clusters of discrete behaviours that contribute to a specific condition. Perhaps the most widely used dimensional system is the one formulated by Quay and his colleagues (1972, 1986). They found reliable empirical evidence of five different forms of behavioural disorders—conduct disorders, anxiety and withdrawal, socialized aggression, attention problems and motor excess, and psychotic behaviour.

The dimensional classification provides a relatively reliable basis for description. We discuss the major dimensions below. ADHD (motor excess) is addressed in Chapter 8; psychotic behaviour is addressed in Chapter 14.

CLASSIFICATION AND DIMENSIONS OF BEHAVIOURAL DISORDERS

Children and youth with behavioural disorders exhibit a spectrum of behaviours ranging from disruptive and cantankerous outbursts to severe withdrawal from social interaction. Dozens of different characteristics have been attributed to these children and youth. Most classroom teachers could add a few characteristics of their own.

Conduct Disorders

Students with conduct disorders form the largest portion of those identified in the schools as behaviourally disordered. The specific phrase **conduct disorders** describes hyper-aggressive and antisocial children and youth who display overt, aggressive, disruptive behaviour or covert antisocial acts that are repeated infractions of socially prescribed behavioural patterns and that violate social norms and the rights of others (Kauffman, 2005).

These troubled and troublesome students display a comparatively high number of problem behaviours and may be versatile in their repertoires. They tend to be volatile, unpredictable, confrontational, impulsive, distractible, hyperactive, and disruptive, and engage in attention-getting, limit testing, defiance, challenges, disrespect, verbal abuse, blatant rule violations, threats, and intimidation. Usually they show **non-compliance**— failure to follow adult delivered directions. And, because children with conduct disorders have failed to develop reliable internal controls, they often seem not to know right from wrong.

Sometimes, the behaviours are not age-appropriate. For example, temper tantrums are common among two-and three-year-olds as these young children strive toward independence. Among normally developing children, unfocused temper tantrums diminish during the preschool period and are uncommon after age four. In children who are behaviourally disordered, tantrums are more likely to continue; a twelve-year-old throwing a temper tantrum is demonstrating clearly inappropriate behaviour.

Aggression is a trademark of children with conduct disorders. **Aggressive behaviour** refers to "those behaviours—verbal, nonverbal, or physical—that injure another indirectly or directly and/or result in extraneous gains for the aggressor" (Zirpoli & Melloy, 1997, p. 332). DSM-IV, mentions two specific disorders involving aggression. Closely related to the conduct disorders we are discussing here are **oppositional defiant disorders** (ODD).

Children with ODD show persistent patterns of negativistic, hostile, or defiant behaviour directed primarily toward adults. They argue repeatedly with authority figures, show resentment, are touchy, angry, spiteful, and vindictive, and often throw temper tantrums. Because physical aggression is limited, ODD is seen as less serious than conduct disorders because students do not violate social norms and the rights of others. Do keep in mind, however, that ODD is often a precursor, merely a stop on the road toward full-blown conduct disorders.

Boys and girls show different types of conduct disorders. Robins (1986) found that the masculine antisocial behaviours included vandalism, fighting, and stealing; feminine behaviours included lying, running away, and substance abuse.

Aggression is an area of grave concern to teachers. One worrisome manifestation of child aggression is schoolyard bullying. (See the Research Notes box on pages 412 and 413 for more information on childhood aggression). The notes below address the precursors, development, and outcomes of bullying.

Socialized Aggression

Children and youth who display major discipline problems in school appear to substantially overlap with those who offend outside school. Youths are broadly characterized as *socialized aggressive*, which is often equated with socially maladjusted rather than emotionally disturbed

conduct disorders

non-compliance

aggressive behaviour

oppositional defiant disorders

RESEARCH NOTES

Schoolyard Bullying

Bullying has been around for a long time. It was traditionally viewed as some sort of perverse child's play and often elicited the comment, "Kids will be kids." Perceptions of the benign nature of bullying have changed; it is now recognized as an enduring problem in today's schools. For example, a 1996 nationwide poll revealed that 88 percent of adults believe school violence, including bullying, is a serious matter in Canadian schools (Hutchinson, 1997). In a survey of Edmonton-area junior high school students (MacDonald, 1995), over 50 percent considered bullying to be a "big" or "very big" problem. A Saskatchewan study (Bidwell, 1997) found that about one-third of teachers surveyed considered bullying a serious problem in their classrooms.

Worldwide, figures for bullying vary in interesting ways. For example, 24 percent of English six- to eight-year-olds report being victimized weekly but only 8 percent of German eight-year-olds (Wolke, Woods, Stanford, & Schultz, 2001). In Australia, 26 percent of children in grades 3 to 7 were victims (see Ma, Stewin, & Mack, 2001). Canadian researchers (Beran & Tutty, 2002) report that, across studies, the proportion of students in grades 4 to 6 who say they have been victimized ranges from 5 to 27 percent. A study in British Columbia schools by the McCreary Society revealed that 1 in 5 adolescents reported being physically or sexually abused (Cassidy, 2005). In Toronto, bullying and misconduct, persistent opposition to authority, and fighting are the most frequent causes of suspension; more than 75 percent of suspensions and expulsions are issued to boys, and 20 percent of student suspensions are sent home more than once.

Bullying is a form of aggression in which a more dominant individual, the bully, exhibits behaviour intended to cause distress to a less dominant individual, the victim (Smith & Thompson, 1991). There are different kinds of bullying, and bullying behaviour differs among individuals. However, most definitions show three things in common: bullying is a repeated action that occurs over a prolonged period of time; there is an imbalance of power; and the verbal, psychological, and/or physical negative actions of bullying are unprovoked (see Bentley & Li, 1995).

Name-calling and other types of verbal harassment represent some of the most prevalent forms of bullying. Then there is the situation where the perpetrator threatens to damage the victim's relationship with others, called relational bullying (Crick, Casas, & Nelson, 2002). Cyberspace represents new territory for peer mistreatment. Cyberbullying involves electronic mediums such as email, chat rooms, cell phones, instant messaging, and so on. Harmful messages intended to undermine the reputation of a victim can be far more damaging that face-to-face altercations (Stram & Stram, 2005).

Much of the bullying in school—coercion, intimidation, and threats that often start as mean-spirited teasing—progresses to extortion and physical attack. Direct bullying seems to increase through the elementary years, peak in the middle school years, and decline during high school. But while direct physical assault seems to decrease with age, verbal abuse appears to remain constant.

More boys than girls bully, and boys are victims of bullying more frequently than girls (Craig & Peplar, 1997; Marano, 1995; Olweus, 1993). But the acts of girls are underestimated because they take a different form. Girls display more subtle and complex forms of meanness than boys, and female bullying may be more difficult to detect. Some research sees gender differences not in numbers, but in reasons. Bullying for boys is more likely to be part of peer-based social relationships; for girls, affiliation activities are more frequently the source of bullying activities (Lane, 1989).

Alberta researcher Xin Ma (2001) finds that the occurrence of bullying is not linked with school size, class size, or the racial-ethnic structure of a school. Telling variables seem to be the school location (schools in large cities have higher rates of bullying than those in small towns) and the students' socio-economic status (schools serving students from a lower socio-economic background have higher rates of bullying).

The recent intense research interest in the bullying phenomenon has uncovered different types of bullying as well as different groups affected by the behaviour.

- First and foremost are the bullies themselves. For the bully, the actions may be part of a cluster of behavioural problems. Yet, in contrast to prevailing myths, it seems that bullies have little anxiety, possess adequate self-esteem, and do not tend to be socially isolated or victimize others because they feel bad about themselves (Olweus, 1993). However, bullies are likely to be impulsive, easily frustrated, have dominant personalities, have difficulty conforming to rules, and view violence in a positive light (AMA, 2002; Stevens, deBourdeuadhuji, & Van Oost, 2003). As well, bullies are more prone than others to dislike school, and poor school performers are more prone to bullying (Sweeting & West, 2001). Bullies are more likely to engage in behaviours that compromise their health, such as smoking (Evenson, 1999). The prognosis for chronically violent individuals is generally poor. They tend to become antisocial adults, have problems with

the law, and are more likely to have unstable relationships and abuse spouse and children (Ma, 2001; Marano, 1995).

- Bully victims are children who are both bullies and recipients of bullying. They may display the behavioural problems of bullies but also the passive behaviour of victims. These children tend to perform poorly in school.

- There may also be a profile of typical victims. These individuals tend to be vulnerable (Hoover & Stenhjem, 2003). Passive victims, the most commonly bullied group, tend to be cautious, insecure, sensitive, feel socially isolated and lonely, and have difficulty asserting themselves. Fox and Boulton (2005) reported on research that noted that victims are prone to cry easily and tend to hover rather than try to enter the peer group and tend to display an anxious vulnerability. For victims, the immediate consequences of bullying are fear, pain, and humiliation. They may suffer a loss of self-esteem, stress symptoms, difficulties with schoolwork, and long-term depression (Storch & Esposito, 2003). Calgary researchers (Beran & Tutty, 2002) report that the symptoms tend to increase in severity as the frequency of bullying increases.

- The majority of children and youth are neither bullies nor victims but may be present during incidents. Although not directly involved, children who witness bullying often report feelings of distress and discomfort. They seem to vicariously experience the trauma of bullying (Beran & Tutty, 2002).

or behaviourally disordered. The distinction is subtle and depends upon the effect of the condition on the student. It is felt that behavioural disorders are persistently distressing to the child, while social maladjustment may not be.

bullying

The students' lack of distress is related to their activity in delinquent groups and their loyalty to delinquent friends. Within their gangs, youths may enjoy considerable prestige as a result of their norm-violating behaviours. The antisocial behaviours are then rewarded by peer attention but at the same time attract some form of punishment from adult society. Thus a vicious circle is set in motion: more antisocial behaviour and more reward from the peer group, catalyzed by more punishment from the adult community and more anger on the part of the adolescent.

Quite a few of the behaviours seen in youth described as socialized aggressive match those of children characterized as conduct disordered; other behaviours develop with age and sophistication. Older students are chronic violators of broad cultural mores and social values. They view social problems in hostile terms, do not seek explanations, generate few solutions, anticipate few consequences for aggression, and see violence as a legitimate way to solve problems (Guerra & Slaby, 1990). These students take part in antisocial behaviour that includes aggression, non-compliance, bullying, intimidation, gang vandalism, stealing, fighting, truancy, and sexual harassment. Accompanying violent behaviour includes assault, rape, and property destruction.

The course of chronic antisocial behaviour follows an anticipated path—a progression from less serious incidents to more serious ones. Serious actions often fall under the rubric of *delinquent behaviour*—any illegal act by a juvenile. Once youths come to the attention of the courts, they gain a new label: *juvenile delinquents* or *young offenders* under the Young Offenders Act (Canada), now the Youth Criminal Justice Act.

Anxiety and Withdrawal

Anxiety appeared in DSM in 1980. Currently, DSM-IV lists 14 anxiety disorders, including obsessive-compulsive disorder, separation anxiety disorder, post-traumatic stress disorder, generalized anxiety disorder, and social phobia. The latter two are of most interest to teachers.

anxiety

Anxiety can be described as a fear with a future reference. It is vague, undifferentiated, and uncertain, relating to events that have not yet occurred. Feelings of anxiety include distress, tension, uneasiness, worries, and fearfulness. In some instances, anxiety may be an adaptive response to threats from the environment. Many people, for example, are anxious and apprehensive about entering a new situation and meeting new people. These anxieties are mild or short-lived, and most of us are able to deal with them after some initial worry.

phobias

Anxiety becomes abnormal when it occurs in situations that most people can handle with little difficulty. In *generalized anxiety*, symptoms are present most of the time and not directly related to a specific situation. Anxiety may also include **phobias**—persistent and irrational fears of a specific object, activity, or situation. Of the host of possible phobias, some of the most common are fear of the dark, animals, vehicles, and school.

School phobia (also referred to as social anxiety disorder) is one of the most common of childhood phobias. The condition seems to be more than simply an irrational fear of school; children also suffer nausea, abdominal pain, and other physical difficulties associated with tension and extreme agitation. Children with severe school phobia may simply refuse to attend school. If forced, they may spend most of the time either mute or crying. Sadness and deep depression are not uncommon. Symptoms subside on weekends and if the child is allowed to stay home on weekdays.

Although phobias in general are found more often in girls than boys (Erickson, 1992), school phobia affects about 2 percent of the school-aged population and appears equally among the sexes and in the 5 to 15 age group. This phobia is the same across all intelligence levels and is no more prevalent in children with learning problems.

obsessive-compulsive disorders

Very persistent and serious phobias many fall into the area of **obsessive-compulsive disorders**, which involve recurrent obsessions and/or compulsions that are severe enough to interfere with the child's daily life and cause significant distress. **Obsessions** are persistent ideas, thoughts, impulses, or images that are experienced as intrusive and inappropriate. Common obsessions include fear of contamination, fear of harm to self and others, aggressive or sexual themes, religiosity, forbidden thoughts, symmetry urges, and a need to tell or confess things. **Compulsions** are defined as repetitive behaviours or mental acts that serve to reduce anxiety or distress but do not serve to obtain pleasure or gratification. Common compulsions include washing, repeating, checking, touching, counting, ordering and arranging, hoarding, and praying (see APA, 1994).

Some anxious children become extremely withdrawn.

obsessions

compulsions

Most persons exhibit both obsessions and compulsions at some point in the course of the disorder, and the two are often related to one another. The disorders can result in high levels of anxiety or feelings of disgust, discomfort, and guilt (Adams, 2004).

The data on children who are anxious and withdrawn tend to be inconclusive in regard to later outcomes. Some researchers (e.g., Coie, 1985) conclude that withdrawn children are not at any greater risk for the development of maladjustment than other children. Other researchers see a pattern of adjustment that can hamper a child's educational career and future functioning. They note that, to cope with anxiety, children forgo assertive, independent behaviour; become excessively withdrawn, fearful, secretive, and apathetic; and often spend large amounts of time fantasizing and daydreaming instead of interacting with those around them.

School is the school environment in which anxious and withdrawn children in particular experience the most distress. In school, these children have acceptance problems. Some children who are withdrawn regress to earlier stages of development and show immature and even infantile behaviour. Some demand constant help and attention; others become depressed for no apparent reason (Klien & Last, 1989; Kovacs, 1989).

It was only in the late 1960s that the mental health community acknowledged depression could be found in children. Today there is overwhelming evidence that both children and adults experience depression severe enough to interfere with daily functioning.

Depression, along with dysthymia and bipolar manic depressive disorder, are categorized as mood disorders by DSM. Childhood depression, similar to that seen in adults, is more than just a feeling. It is accompanied by cognitive, motivational, and physical symptoms. The primary symptom is an overall depressed mood or loss of interest in daily activities (also called anhedonia) manifested over a two-week period. Four additional symptoms are increases or decreases in a child's appetite or weight, sleep, activity, or energy; feelings of worthlessness or guilt; difficulty thinking, concentrating, or making decisions; and recurrent thoughts of death or suicidal plans, ideation, or attempts.

The most extreme manifestation of depression is suicide. Severe behavioural disorders, in fact, are by far the most prevalent conditions associated with suicidal behaviour, and many studies have confirmed the link between suicidal behaviour and emotional instability (e.g., Pfeffer, 1984).

Suicides among young people are not new; the first symposium on adolescent suicide was held in Vienna in 1910 (McBride & Siegel, 1997). But numbers are on the rise and suicide has become the second leading cause of death for adolescents (Cole, 1992) (accidents are the first). Worse, for every successful suicide it is estimated that there are 50 to 100 attempts (Pagliaro, 1995).

There is a marked gender difference. Research indicates that adolescent boys are three times more likely to commit suicide than adolescent girls, although adolescent girls are one-and-a-half times more likely to attempt suicide than adolescent boys (Langlois & Morrison, 2002).

Suicide rates are higher in Canada than in the United States. Canada ranks third behind Norway and Australia for the 15 to 24-year-old group. The highest rates are in the Yukon and Northwest Territories (Cole, 1992; McBride & Seigel, 1997). Teachers should be aware that the death of a student by suicide increases tremendously the risk of further student suicides.

PREVALENCE OF BEHAVIOURAL DISORDERS

Based on media reports, official concerns, and educators' reactions, it would seem that the incidence of hyper-aggressive, undercontrolled behaviour and violence in our schools has increased dramatically during the past few decades. Worrisome reports indicate heightened rates of juvenile crime, with a decrease in the age of the children committing delinquent acts.

Prevalence rates, especially as reported by the media, should be treated with great caution and some scepticism. But we must also be cognizant of research such as that undertaken by Dolmage (1999), who reported on a Canadian study of the perceptions of 71 secondary school administrators in 2 large school districts. Of the sample, 62 percent felt that the prevalence of youth violence had increased significantly in Canadian society at large and 56.4 percent believed it had increased significantly in schools. However, only 28.1 percent believed that it had increased significantly in his or her own school. In Ontario, when Joony and Ridler (2005) investigated the state of violence prevention from the perspectives of teachers and students, they found that school violence was not increasing. But it was not decreasing, either.

It is true that mounting numbers of children are being identified as behaviourally disordered. However, accurate figures are not available, chiefly because of the lack of a clear and precise definitional construct. Estimates vary tremendously; indeed, they change in every revision of DSM. In Canada, a national study by the Canadian Institute of Child Health (2000) reported that the rates of behavioural and emotional problems for children aged 4 to 11 is "disturbingly high," with 1 in 10 children exhibiting behaviour consistent with hyperactivity problems, conduct disorder, or an emotional disorder.

Rates for disorders that are mild but require intervention range from 7 to 15 percent. Somewhere between 2 and 10 percent of the school-aged population exhibits serious and persistent behavioural problems (Gresham, 1998; Kauffman, 2005). Within these overarching estimates, the prevalence of conduct disorders ranges from 6 to 16 percent in boys and 2 to 9 percent in girls under age eighteen (see Kauffman, 2005). ODD is reported to occur in 4 percent of children and adolescents (Forness, Kavale, & Walker, 1999). Anxiety disorders (including phobias) occur in a range of 5.7 to 17.7 percent of the school-aged population, with rates slightly higher in adolescents (King, Heyne, & Ollendick, 2005).

Boys exhibit more overall behavioural deviance than girls, including learning difficulties, hyperactivity, bed-wetting, and antisocial behaviour. Sex ratios are especially marked in the preadolescent years, when rates of conduct disorders and Oppositional Defiant Disorder are three to four times higher in boys. First-born males are more likely than later-borns to exhibit behavioural disorders and to be rated by teachers as anxious and aggressive toward their peers (Lahey, Hammer, Crumrine, & Forehand, 1980). Note that anxiety disorders tend to be found more often in girls.

Many children with behavioural disorders come to the attention of professionals in the middle childhood and early teen years. The prevalence of behavioural disorders is low in the beginning grades, reaches a peak in the middle grades, and begins to fall off in high school. Socialized aggression peaks during adolescence.

There is a higher reported prevalence of aggressive behaviours among working-class children than among those from the middle and upper classes (Hallahan & Kauffman, 2003). And, as we have mentioned with cautions, a higher proportion of those identified as behaviourally disordered are from cultural and linguistic minority groups.

ETIOLOGY OF BEHAVIOURAL DISORDERS

Psychiatrists, psychologists, and educators have traditionally placed great emphasis on identifying the causes of behavioural disorders in children, hoping that an understanding of the origins of the dysfunctions would lead directly to their treatment and cure. Despite a vast amount of research, nobody yet fully understands the causes of any type of psychopathology, and there is no empirical evidence linking behavioural disorders to any specific causes.

What is apparent is that the trajectory of the disorders is determined by a variety of early genetic, biological, and/or environmental etiologies. Deviant behaviour usually involves the interaction of several factors rather than a single cause. Each additional variable increases the risk of disorder, and the risk is greater when several factors combine.

Most major developmental theories have been used to explain behavioural dysfunctions. These theories are founded on certain conceptual models that represent the different theoretical orientations of allied disciplines. As etiology is closely linked to conceptual models, there are considerable differences seen in both the presumed causes of the disturbance and in the importance that researchers attach to finding these causes. The psychodynamic model, for example, focuses almost exclusively on causation, while the behavioural model is concerned with the outward manifestations of deviancy.

These conceptual models are not just theoretical. The way in which childhood disorders and psychological disturbances are conceptualized by professionals influences the ways in which the problems are addressed and treated. As you can see in the overview of models and associated treatments in Table 7-1 on the next page, each model includes a set of assumptions about why children behave the way they do, different ideas about the role of individual characteristics and the influence of environmental conditions, a different emphasis on the elements that are considered essential, and different notions of what must be done to correct the disorders.

Table 7-1 Conceptual models and associated treatments in the area of behavioural disorders

Approach	Assumption	Treatment	Sample of methods
Biophysical	Behavioural difficulties represent a physiological flaw. They arise directly from constitutional, genetic, neurological, or biochemical problems. Disease, malnutrition, and substance abuse are included here.	Alter the child's physiology	Drug therapy; change in diet. (The only intervention that has a research base is drug therapy.)
Psychodynamic	Deviant behaviour is determined by past experiences; students with behavioural disorders are suffering inner turmoil; they can be helped by being made aware of their feelings and how to deal with them.	Discover the underlying conflicts that cause problem behaviour	Various therapies and counselling techniques: verbalization and clarification of previously repressed thoughts; corrective emotional experiences resulting from the child's relationship with understanding adults; presentation of alternate modes of behaviour.
Psycho-educational	An eclectic approach that sees behaviour as having various causes.	Create trust while helping the child to meet academic goals	Therapies, crisis intervention, success in academic pursuits. Preventative class room planning; permitting or sanctioning certain types of behaviour; tolerating behaviour that is beyond the child's control.
Behavioural	Emotional or behavioural deviance is the definable consequence of either mislearning or restricted learning. Normal, healthy,	Rearrange environmental events. Focus on the behaviour, not the underlying causes.	Reinforcers, punishments, time-outs, contracts, and so on. Selecting instructional programs on the basis of objectives to

Table 7-1 continued

Approach	Assumption	Treatment	Sample of methods
	and desirable behaviours may be acquired to supplement or replace undesirable behaviours by consistently applying established behavioural principles of learning.		be achieved through practice with reinforcement and measurement until criterion performance is reached.
Ecological	Behaviour disorders are a function of the reciprocity between a child and the environment; problems are the result of agitated transactions between the child and those in the environment.	Change the nature of the interaction between the child and the environment.	Counselling and a team approach. Crisis intervention; environmental modelling; curriculum planning. Identifying whatever norms happen to be used in the class setting; finding means for children to meet class room goals.
Psychosocial	Can be seen as part of an ecological model, although the focus is on a child's relationship to family, peers, and others in the environment.		
Holistic	Behavioural disorders have diverse etiologies that interact with each other.		

Biophysical Model

As the name suggests, a biophysical approach holds that behavioural disorders relate to biological causes—that certain biological factors such as genetic conditions, constitutional conditions, prenatal and birth factors, and environmental hazards increase the risk of behavioural disorders. But information about the relationship between biophysical factors and behavioural disorders is not yet persuasive. It is rarely possible to demonstrate a clear connection between a disorder and a specific biological factor, and to assume that disorders are only the result of biological insult is misleading.

Although geneticists maintain that genes do not directly determine behaviour, they do recognize biological intermediaries—the links between DNA and behaviour. That is, DNA does not control behaviour directly, but there are hormonal, psychopathological, and other links. Some genes determine enzymatic and biochemical functions, which, in turn, can have both major and subtle behavioural effects. At the same time, the central nervous system is undeniably involved in all behaviour, and all behaviour involves neurochemical activity. For example, the neurotransmitters serotonin, dopamine, and norepinephrine play important roles in regulating behaviour, and low serotonin levels especially have been linked to such aggressive behaviours as fighting, arson, and suicide (Sylvester, 1997).

From another line of genetic research, we know that *temperaments*—defined as biologically determined behavioural styles—are inherited. There is no one-to-one relationship between temperament and behavioural disorders, but difficult, irritable temperaments are more likely to lead children to become antisocial adolescents and adults (Baum, 1989). Boys and girls who are moody and ill tempered at age ten tend to be ill-tempered adults whose relations with their spouses and children are generally unpleasant and full of conflict (Caspi, Elder, & Bern, 1987). Anxiety disorders run in families; an overlap between parental and child anxiety disorders of up to 80 percent has been reported (Ginsburg & Schlossberg, 2002).

Along with genetic problems and neurological disturbances, disease, malnutrition, and substance abuse predispose children to develop emotional problems. Child abuse and other forms of severe trauma are known to contribute significantly to emotional and behavioural disorders in children (Saigh, 1997).

Psychodynamic Model

The psychodynamic model and approaches originated with the extremely complex theory first defined by Sigmund Freud in the early 1900s. Essentially, psychodynamic approaches are concerned with the development of and interaction among the intrapsychic (mental) processes believed to underlie human behaviour. In this model, behavioural disorders are observable symptoms reflecting inner turmoil created by abnormal intrapsychic processes.

Psycho-educational Model

Advocates of the psycho-educational model agree that children with behavioural disorders may have dealt unsuccessfully with developmental problems. As efforts are made to discover why children demonstrate deviant behaviour, there is a simultaneous stress on the acquisition of academic and daily living skills.

Behavioural Model

Early 20th century investigations of reflexive and voluntary behaviour, arising from the work of Ivan Pavlov and John B. Watson, laid the groundwork for modern behavioural psychology. Bolstered by B. F. Skinner's principles of operant conditioning, the behavioural model has exerted a profound influence on psychotherapy, counselling, education, and special education.

While the behavioural model includes a number of theories and perspectives about human behaviour, two points most clearly define it. First is the assumption that behaviour—including deviant behaviour—is acquired and is regulated by certain identifiable principles of learning. Second is a commitment to scientific methods of studying behaviour and behaviour change.

Behaviourists do not concern themselves with the deep-rooted probing of psychodynamic approaches. Nor do they categorize children's behaviour as abnormal, evil, mysterious, or deviant. Rather, they assume that the same principles that guide the development of normal behaviour are involved in the development of inappropriate behaviour. Since all behaviour is caused and controlled by environmental events outside the child, all behaviour is therefore observable, measurable, and subject to change through a change in the environment.

Three basic interrelated forms of treatment characterize the behavioural approach. The first uses teaching and training techniques to create behaviours that do not already exist. The second uses a number of techniques to maintain and generalize behaviours that are already established. The third uses other techniques to confine, reduce, or eliminate problem behaviour. Typically, all three modes of treatment are undertaken simultaneously. Examples of behaviours that can be modified include hyperactivity, aggressiveness, distractibility, bed-wetting, excessive fearfulness, and harmful anxiety.

Ecological Model

Ecology refers to the overall pattern of relationships involving an organism and its environment (ecosystem). From an ecological point of view, behaviour is the product of the interaction between an individual and all the variables in his or her environment.

Classrooms are ecological systems in which students and teachers are constantly interacting. Therefore, the etiology of a behaviour is not perceived as existing solely within the individual, but is viewed as an interaction between the environment and the child (Jackson & Panyan, 2002). Behaviour is formed and influenced by undesirable interactions and transactions between the student and others, and reflects disturbances in the "goodness-of-fit" between a child and the ecosystem. Some characteristics of a child (usually the behaviour) agitate the ecosystem, and the ecosystem responds in ways that lead the child to provoke further agitation. For example, a student's temper tantrums in school might be the problem, but from an ecological perspective, the behaviour of the student's teachers, peers, and parents—their expectations, demands, and reactions to the tantrums—must also be taken into consideration.

Psychosocial Model

The *psychosocial model* focuses both on the family and on **extra-familial influences**, those agencies outside the family that influence a child's cognitive, social, and emotional development. Extra-familial agents include schools, peer groups, and television. The family is by far the most critical source of child socialization.

extra-familial influences

Research and theory that focus on family patterns as possible sources of deviancy find that family conditions may predispose a child to develop behavioural disorders or precipitate maladaptive behaviours. Predisposing conditions include families characterized by harsh discipline, little parental involvement with the child, and poor monitoring and supervision of a child's activities. Precipitating factors are an immediate stress or incident such as divorce, separation, or the chronic illness of one or both parents.

Although parental attitudes and child-rearing techniques are often critical in the development of aggressive behaviour, it is not possible to obtain valid and consistent research findings that allow the blame for a child's problems to be placed primarily on the parents (Kauffman, 2005). Nevertheless, family adversity and life stress have been associated with future behaviour problems in young children. And as a predictor of an antisocial adult personality, having an antisocial parent places the child at significant risk for antisocial behaviour; having two antisocial parents puts the child at even greater risk (Robins & Earls, 1985). There also seems to be a high degree of intergenerational similarity for antisocial behaviour: children in aggressive families are more likely to be aggressive and, in turn, their children are more likely to be aggressive (Farrington, 1987; see also Chapter 12 on child abuse).

Holistic Model

The *holistic approach* attempts to encompass the other conceptual models. It therefore acknowledges that the etiology of inappropriate behaviours may be illness, childhood traumas, poor relations with others, inappropriate learning, problems in socialization, any combination of these, and many other factors.

DEVELOPMENTAL CONSEQUENCES OF BEHAVIOURAL DISORDERS

Children and adolescents with behavioural disorders deviate significantly from their peers in the quantity, quality, and modes of their emotional expression. As you have seen, apart from this overarching trait there is no symptom common to all pupils who are behaviourally disordered, or even common to a subgroup of these children. Behavioural disorders may take one or many specific forms, can be manifested in various ways, and the severity of disturbance may range from mild to serious and debilitating.

Cognitive Development

Studies show that intelligence and scholastic achievement are negatively correlated with aggression and delinquency for both boys and girls. Over the past 40 years, numerous studies have determined that children with behavioural disorders have IQs in the low average range with a mean of about 90 to 95 (Kauffman, 2005), with problems in specific types of cognitive processes. The slightly lower IQs of these students then work in predicting academic achievement and later adjustment.

Academic Achievement

Students with behavioural disorders are noted for their academic underachievement. Their levels of functioning are, on average, a year or more below grade level in all content areas (Reid, Gonzalez, Nordness, Trout, & Epstein, 2004). Research supports a relationship between underachievement and externalizing behaviour (Richards, Symons, Greene, & Szuskiewicz, 1995), as well as reading disabilities and aggression (Cornwell & Bawden, 1992), although the exact relationship and the direction of the phenomenon have not been identified.

What is evident is that reading problems are rampant. One study (Glassberg, Hooper, & Mattison, 1999) reported reading disability prevalence rates from 6 to 24 percent for students aged 6 to 16 who were newly identified with behavioural disorders. Another study (Benner, Nelson, & Epstein, 2002) found that 25 to 85 percent of children with social adjustment problems had beginning reading skills deficits.

Non-compliant and uncontrolled children create problems in classroom management, which alienates teachers and other students. Teachers react by instructing with fewer academic questions, less extended feedback, and fewer dyadic work interactions. With non-compliant behaviour and less instruction, students may rapidly enter a pattern of severe academic failure that becomes cyclical. First of all, at best, the academic deficits of children with behavioural disorders remain stable over time. However, evidence also suggests that academic deficits actually worsen (Mattison, Hooper, & Glassberg, 2002; Nelson, Benner, Lane, & Smith, 2004). Then as children do not learn the skills needed for coping with academic pressures, they react by withdrawing or lashing out in angry frustration. They soon learn to dislike the learning process, resent the school experience, and often resort to truancy.

At first glance, anxiety may not seem as academically and socially debilitating as aggression. But timid, passive behaviour, dependency, isolation, and withdrawal interfere with the development of potential. Children tend to acquire a defeatist attitude along with feelings of worthlessness and excessive self-criticism.

Different problem behaviours evoke different attitudes among teachers, and some writers contend that acting-out behaviours are viewed more negatively than withdrawn ones (Li, 1985). Others find that teachers consider socially withdrawn behaviours and non-communication (negative aggression and poor peer co-operation) to be the most difficult type of behaviour to manage (Safran & Safran, 1987).

Communication

Speech and language disorders cut across all areas of exceptionality. A higher prevalence of behavioural disorders are found among seriously language-delayed children; conversely, the most frequent secondary special education service provided for students with behavioural disorders is speech and language intervention.

The relationship between behaviour and language development is reciprocal: behaviour problems impair peer group social interactions, which, in turn, cause experiential deficits that can negatively affect language development. In Chapter 4 we discussed scenarios in which the communication problems come first. Children who are not successful in communicating often demonstrate negative, resistant, or attention-getting behaviour and are at risk for both psychiatric and learning disorders. Many times, the language and speech problems of these children are secondary conditions. For example, in a study of young children enrolled in Head Start programs (Kaiser, Cai, Hancock, & Foster, 2002), the investigators found that overall the children with behaviour disorders were more likely to have lower language skills than their average counterparts, although this was more true for boys than girls.

On the other hand, teachers sometimes feel that children who are behaviourally disordered communicate too well. They interrupt in class, swear, use aggressive language, speak defiantly to adults, and indiscriminately vent their emotions. They often use language to disrupt and control social situations. This excessive use of language may not be a communication disorder, but it is certainly a social problem.

Social and Emotional Development

The terms related to social development in both normal and deviant individuals are notoriously difficult to define. Researchers in the area use a plethora of related terms and concepts that arise from the general idea of socialization. These are shown in Table 7-2.

All of these concepts are relevant to students with behavioural disorders in the sense that such students exhibit deficits in socialization, social cognition, social competence, and social skills. Instead of being sociable, these children show excessive aggression and defiance and develop intense and far-ranging interpersonal problems with teachers, peers,

---

Table 7-2 Definitions and terms related to socialization

- *Socialization* is the means by which individuals become reasonably acceptable and competent members of their society. Through socialization, children acquire the discipline, skills, knowledge, ambitions, and empathy for those around them that allow them to participate in the life of the family and later the school and the community.

- *Social cognition* is the knowledge and cognitive activities employed by people in dealing with the social world (Pearl, 1987).

- *Social competence* is "the ability of children to successfully and appropriately select and carry out their interpersonal goals" (Guralnick, 1990, p. 4). It includes the development of meaningful and productive relationships with peers, social and communication development, degrees of independence, and other factors that may contribute to becoming socially acceptable.

- *Socially competent individuals* perform behaviours that they believe will effect rewarding outcomes and avoid acting in ways that might cause negative outcomes. Socially competent individuals possess certain groups of skills: interpersonal and self-related behaviour, academically related skills, communication skills, assertiveness skills, and skills related to peer acceptance.

- *Social skills assessment* is used to ascertain a child's social status and social/behavioural deficits, the behaviours that interfere with the acquisition or performance of social skills, the antecedents preceding and consequences following performance of a skill, and the target skills to teach.

- *Social skills,* though entwined with cognition, are a distinct area of learning and development. Social skills are "those responses which within a given situation prove effective or . . . maximize the probability of producing, maintaining, or enhancing the positive effects for the interactor" (Foster & Ritchey, 1979, p. 626).

- *Sociability* is a term that describes a child's willingness to engage others in social interaction and seek their attention or approval.

- *Prosocial behaviour* is voluntary behaviour intended to aid or benefit others (Holmgren, Eisenberg, & Fokes, 1998).

- *Social skills training* is in-class instruction and practice in a range of social skills. The type and progression of skills may be teacher generated or from a commercial package.

parents, and others in their environments. Compared to samples of typical children, those with conduct disorders are usually less responsive to social reinforcement, less empathetic, and less sophisticated in their understanding of and responses to their peers' behaviour (Baum, 1989). Aggressive children seem to perceive cues and make attributions differently than non-aggressive children (Lochman, White, & Wayland, 1990). They show a tendency to attribute hostile intent to others' actions, especially when the social cues are ambiguous. They generate more action solutions and fewer verbal assertion solutions (Lochman & Lampran, 1986). Those who are anxious and withdrawn fail to respond appropriately to others in their environments.

Accepted children display high frequencies of sociable behaviour, whereas rejected children show aggressive and disruptive behaviour (Siperstein & Leffert, 1997). At both elementary and secondary levels, students with behavioural disorders are seldom socially accepted; they are often actively rejected, not just neglected. This is especially true for highly aggressive children, who are the least likely to make friends and are disliked by most of their peers.

Aggressive children provoke a large number of fights and are also more likely to become the targets of aggression and be attacked by peers. Non-aggressive children who are harmed under ambiguous circumstances are much more likely to retaliate if the harmdoer has a reputation as an aggressive child (Sancilio, Plumment, & Hartup, 1989).

When aggressive children do make friends, they tend to gravitate toward peers with equal levels of aggressive, disruptive, antisocial behaviour. As early as middle childhood, antisocial children tend to associate with other antisocial and/or rejected peers either by choice or by default (Dishion, Andrews, & Crosby, 1995; Farmer & Hollowell, 1994).

Co-occurring Disabilities

Co-occurring problems that compound academic underachievement are common. We have already mentioned speech and language problems. Probably 25 percent of students with behaviour disorders have learning disabilities (Tyler & Colson, 1994). As well, many children with behavioural disorders carry specific psychiatric diagnoses, such as depression.

Family Variables

Of all caretaking demands, none seems to have more impact than the demands of coping with a child who has a behavioural problem. For one thing, daily hassles affect mothers' interactions with their children and lead to less parental support and involvement. And when parents cannot handle or control the child fully, the integrity of the family is threatened. Parents can become physically and emotionally exhausted if their preschooler is fussy and irritable and exhibits irregular patterns of eating and sleeping. Older children may display abusive, destructive, and cantankerous behaviour that causes disruption and disharmony in the home.

Cultural and Linguistic Differences

A potent factor that places children at risk for a range of adverse educational outcomes is minority/ethnic group identity with or without limited English proficiency due to residence, immigration, or community norms. Today, a high proportion of students who are served under the category of behavioural disorders are from culturally and linguistically diverse groups. Misdiagnosis is often a culprit here. When a student's linguistic and cultural background is perceived as a disability, he or she can then be diagnosed and treated as learning disabled or behaviourally disordered.

Equally important are the ideologies and expectations of school systems, which can have an immediate and profound effect on behaviour. Behaviour considered normal and adaptive in a subculture may be looked upon as deviant or inadequate by members of the dominant group. When minority group children bring to school different skills, expectations, and competencies than those valued by the dominant culture, they may be misconstrued as having problems that require special education. Or when classroom management procedures do not match cultural mores, students are less likely to change their behaviours, teachers become more frustrated, and a cycle is set in motion.

ASSESSMENT OF CHILDREN AND YOUTH WITH BEHAVIOURAL DISORDERS

Teachers refer children to special education for two main reasons—behavioural disorders and reading difficulties—that often occur in tandem. Teachers are fairly accurate in identifying behavioural disorders; both experienced and inexperienced teachers can accurately perceive difficulties among children on the basis of behavioural deviations (Schwartz, Wolfe, & Cassar, 1997). Even so, when it comes to referral for diagnosis and additional assistance, teachers tend to over-refer: childhood aggression accounts for a disproportionate number of referrals to special education programs and mental health and child guidance centres. On the other hand, teachers tend to under-refer children with internalizing problems such as anxiety and withdrawn behaviour (Epanchin & Paul, 1987; Hallahan & Kauffman, 2003).

Once students are referred, more formal assessment can proceed. Often, however, only those students who take teachers to the breaking point are provided a full assessment (Kauffman, 2005).

Given the varied components of behavioural disorders, it makes sense that a wide range of processes and tools exist. However, paradigms in the area of assessment of behavioural disorders have undergone a critical transformation in the past five years. The focus of assessment has expanded from defining and measuring problem behaviour to identifying and analysing the relationship between problem behaviours and their environmental events. The popular mode today is *functional behavioural assessment* (FBA) (also referred to as *functional analysis*, *experimental analysis*, *functional assessment*, *descriptive analysis*, and *structural analysis*).

Functional behavioural assessment came from the field of developmental disabilities, where it was successfully used to treat a variety of harmful behaviours such as aggression, self-injury, tantrums, and stereotypical behaviour. Now research has shown the FBA can be used efficiently across a wide range of student populations.

functional behavioural assessment

In brief, **functional behavioural assessment** examines the *function* of a child's behaviour—what purpose it serves—and plans how to reduce or eliminate the behaviour and replace it with a more acceptable alternate one. Arguments for employing FBA are persuasive. They can be summarized as follows:

- As part of the amendments to the Individuals with Disabilities Education Act in 1997, educational agencies in the United States are now required to conduct a functional assessment and develop a Behavioural Intervention Plan for students with disabilities when their behaviour is an issue and has resulted in a change in placement, in suspension, or in removal to an alternative placement.

- A high proportion of classroom management strategies are ineffective. They are arbitrary, inconsistent, spur of the moment, and do not fit the behaviour. FBA is closely related to treatment because it directly addresses the causes of a child's problematic behaviour. For example, if an assessment shows that misbehaviour repeatedly results in teacher attention, then a behaviour reduction plan will focus on behaviour that allows a child to access teacher attention in more appropriate ways.

- When teachers first encounter FBA, they often balk at what seems like a great deal of work observing, plotting, and counting and complain that they lack the time and expertise to perform long and complex assessment procedures. The argument for the counting and graphing is simple but compelling. All teachers have to devote some attention to classroom control—typically about 10 percent of their time (Crealock, 1983). Aggressive and non-compliant children can turn a temporary chore into a full-time occupation. Problem behaviours impose a tremendous demand on teachers, often consuming 80 percent of instructional time (Sugai & Horner, 1994). In a British Columbia study (Naylor, 2002), 34 percent of the respondents spent 30 percent or more of their time dealing with aggressive and disruptive students. Simply, FBA provides a plan to lessen disruptive time-consuming behaviour and bring serenity to a classroom.

Functional assessment should not be thought of as a single thing or procedure. Nor should it be viewed as a product but rather seen as a process that contains overlapping and complementary components with different procedures that make sense in different behavioural circumstances. That is, FBA relies on the systematic administration and interpretation of quite a range of indirect and direct measures of student behaviour.

The steps of FBA are shown in Figure 7-2 on page 232. The process is further illustrated in the continuation of the Case Study about Andrew, introduced at the beginning of this chapter and continued on pages 233 and 234.

Functional Behavioural Assessment

Functional behavioural assessment is predicated on three assumptions. First, behaviour is functional and serves a purpose for the child. The functions can be grouped into the specific areas of obtaining something—acceptance/affiliation (often translating as teacher attention); power/control; a tangible object; or escape from something (usually a school-related task). The functions are shown in Table 7-3. Second, behaviour is caused by the interactions of environmental factors and factors inherent in the student. Finally, the identification of these factors can lead to positive behaviour interventions.

Figure 7-2

Functional Behavioural Assessment (FBA)

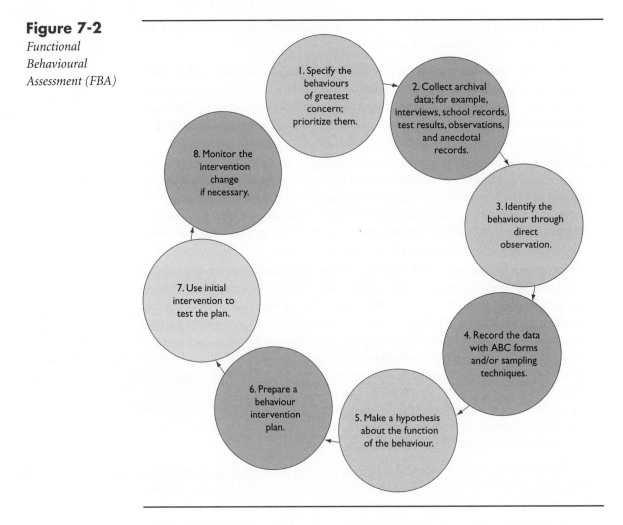

Table 7-3 Behaviour and its functions

Function of challenging behaviour	Example
To obtain attention	During group time, Mary continually leaves the area. The teacher stands up, guides Mary back, and sits her close to the teacher, providing teacher attention.
	James hits his peers, which brings a reprimand from the teacher, and serves as a reinforcer for James.
	Beth learns that when she pulls other girls' hair, she can consistently and independently obtain the teacher's attention every time.
To obtain power	Kim wisecracks all through math class; the other students laugh. Kim gains peer attention and the teacher loses some authority.

Table 7-3 continued

To obtain a tangible object	Abdul hits his peer and takes a toy. The teacher intervenes; sometimes Abdul keeps the toy.
	To be the first to obtain access to the computer, Peter pushes peers out of the way. Playing on the computer reinforces the pushing.
To escape a task	When Andrew is asked to read, he throws the book. The teacher removes the book—and the task.
	Martin is not participating during art class. When asked, he screams "No!" and throws his papers on the floor. The teacher walks away. Martin does not finish and does not clean up.
	When Mr. Smith tells Joe to get out his math book, Joe begins to make rude comments that don't stop until he has disrupted the class. At that point, the teacher asks Joe to take a time out away from the class. Joe escapes math.

CASE STUDY

Andrew (continued)

In the course of a school day Andrew slaps, punches, and generally annoys the other children in the room. He reads at a grade 1 level but is embarrassed to be seen with "baby" books and reacts by throwing his reading book across the room and using foul language. On any number of occasions, he has thrown other objects, including pencils and trashcans. When restrained, a tirade of cursing, often followed by a violent temper tantrum, ensues.

To get to the root of Andrew's behaviour, the school-based team decided to use FBA. First, the classroom teacher listed the behaviours of most concern to her—temper tantrums, lashing out violently when assigned work, using profanity, and refusal to follow directions—in that order. The second step involved a careful assessment of Andrew's archival information that included a meeting with the child, another interview with the mother, and an examination of past records on behaviour and school performance.

The school principal then played the part of observer and measured Andrew's behaviour (specifically tantrumming and ensuing acting out) over a period of five days. She entered a checkmark on a tally sheet each time Andrew tantrumed. She also noted the duration of each tantrum and used a separate ABC form to note the antecedents of the behaviours and the following consequences.

Andrew's interview provided little information; he was truculent and uncooperative. His mother indicated that the behaviour was poor (but certainly not worse) at home. Archival data showed the antisocial actions to be persistent and long-standing, interfering with school performance and socialization.

Direct observations in the classroom suggested that Andrew's problematic behaviour during academic work was being maintained and reinforced by the teacher's consequences. That is, the teacher often sent Andrew to the time out corner or asked him to lay his head on his desk. These consequences simply allowed Andrew to escape what was, for him, an aversive situation—performing academic work. The direct observation also revealed, however, that there were minimal disruptions throughout assigned math periods.

After long discussion, the team (which included Andrew's mother) decided that Andrew is a danger to himself and others. His disruptive behaviour, fighting, and irrational conduct require structured and consistent behavioural intervention in a supportive environment that offers much opportunity for success. A more restrictive setting may afford certain benefits not typically found in general classrooms. For Andrew, these are a smaller class size and a teacher who is trained in social skills, has strong classroom management skills, is able to modify the curriculum, and can offer more diverse, precise, and consistent instructional techniques. The team hopes that this is a temporary placement. The ultimate goal of segregation is rapid return to integration with peers once Andrew has learned to behave less aggressively and less disruptively.

A variety of models are used in FBA. Among the different models, fairly standard components are as follows:

1. *Specify the behaviours of greatest concern.* Here the teacher lists and then prioritizes the most disturbing behaviours a student is manifesting.

2. *Collect archival data.* This includes a variety of strategies designed to provide a broad overview of a child's behaviour over a time span, founded on the notion that past and present behaviour is the best predictor of future behaviour. Data are gathered through such procedures as structured interviews with the target student and his or her parents, general observations, direct observations of naturally occurring behaviour, review of anecdotal records, rating scales (teacher ratings, peer ratings, and self-ratings by the target child), checklists, personality tests, and formal and informal tools to assess the child's mental ability and academic achievement.

3. *Precisely identify the behaviour.* Direct observation is a cornerstone of behavioural functional assessment (Ollendick & King, 1999), particularly important for externalizing behaviour. To find out exactly what a child is doing, observers record instances of specific behaviours to establish their frequency, durability, and age-appropriateness in a variety of settings such as the classroom and playground, and in different circumstances such as time of day, subject area, and school activities. Observers look for form—the form or shape of a behaviour that involves a description of the behaviour itself, such as a temper tantrum. They also look for chronicity and frequency.

4. *Record the data.* Data recording may be as simple as a narrative system, or it may be more sophisticated, with codes to score behavioural deviations, language skills, motor behaviour, and so on. There are limits on the amount of behaviour that can be documented, and students are often versatile in the types of behavioural deviations they display. As we cannot observe all behaviour, various techniques and sampling methods are used to make observations more manageable.

A practical method is to record the ABC. This refers to A, the antecedents or events that were happening just before the incident. An example would be a teacher directing the class to finish its work. B speaks to the target child's behaviours. C is for the consequences or events that follow, such as a verbal reprimand from the teacher: "You are never going to finish this work!" When completed, the ABC describes the behaviour of interest, the situations in which the behaviour is likely or unlikely to occur, and the consequences that maintain or inhibit the behaviour.

As well, there are different sampling techniques; in each, systematic observations of a child are undertaken over a period of not less than a week, and preferably longer. Event sampling is used to determine the frequency or length of a specific behaviour. The procedure includes two types: frequency counts and duration recording. A frequency count is used for behaviour that is of relatively short duration, such as the number of times a child hits another. A duration measure (duration sampling) is an indication of how long something occurs and is used for behaviours that vary considerably in length, such as negative or positive peer interaction or self-stimulating behaviour.

5. *Make a hypothesis about the function of the behaviour.* This is a plausible explanation that draws from the information gathered. It attempts to define why a student behaves in a certain way and what function the behaviour serves, such as obtaining or avoiding an outcome.

6. *Write* a **behaviour intervention plan** *(BIP).* This is a written description of specific interventions to be used based on the presumed hypothesis that typically addresses behavioural issues, including programming needs, interventions, program supports, and outcomes. Because academic success is the first defence in combating poor behaviour, the BIP should be embedded within the IEP, joined to academic outcomes.

behaviour intervention plan

7. *Intervene based on the hypothesis and the plan.* The length of the intervention depends on the severity of the behaviour, the type of intervention, and how effective the teacher is in implementing the plan. Intervention includes teaching **replacement skills** or replacement behaviour—a different way for the child to accomplish the same purpose without deviant behaviour.

replacement skills

8. *Monitor the intervention.* This entails a second stage of data collection to determine if the hypothesis about the function of the behaviour was correct and the matching intervention effective.

INTERVENTION WITH CHILDREN AND YOUTH WHO HAVE BEHAVIOURAL DISORDERS

Successful behaviour change is related to the additive effects of multiple interventions based on diversified treatment modalities. Varied models and approaches are used both because of the myriad nature of the disorders and because no one method has proven effective for all of them. No single approach suits each child with a behavioural disorder, and the approach that works today may not work tomorrow.

Medical Intervention

If we return to the conceptual models used to explain and treat behavioural disorders, you can see that medical interventions nestle within the biophysical model. The main thrust concerns psychopharmacology (drug therapy).

Approximately 40 to 56 percent of youths with serious behavioural disorders receive psychotropic medications as part of their treatment (Wood, 2004). Anxiety disorders, for example, involve drug therapy. In medicating for depression, physicians usually begin with drugs known as selective serotonin reuptake inhibitors (SSRIs). Children who fail to respond may be placed on a regime of tricyclic antidepressants or atypical antidepressants. Medications used to treat obsessive compulsive disorders stress Anafranil, shown to be effective in young people (Adams, 2004). Table 8-3 in the next chapter lists common medications.

Therapy

The developmental histories of many students with serious emotional and behavioural disorders have often been characterized by turmoil, uncertainty, abuse, neglect, unclear family communication, abandonment, and ineffective modelling (Jones, 1996). Because many students suffer from a serious lack of self-esteem, depression, or anxiety impairment, the importance of interventions in the affective domain that help students understand themselves and their environment cannot be overestimated.

If we revisit the *psychotherapeutic and psycho-educational approaches,* we find that one essential element characterizes their numerous theoretical orientations and practices—the belief that traditional psychoanalytic concepts can be used to relieve a child's distress and encourage development.

Psychotherapy can best be seen as a continuum of interventions, characterized by distinctions in the intensity and type of intervention provided. At one end are techniques used by counsellors and psychologists such as social skills instruction and teaching self-monitoring. Children needing more intensive interventions are referred to other services, located further along the continuum, that are provided by clinical psychologists and psychiatrists (Etscheidt, 2002).

Individual psychotherapy relies heavily on discussion and the probing of feelings and attitudes. Because young children may not realize what they are experiencing, indirect methods such as music, art, play, and storytelling are used instead of traditional "talk" therapy. For example, since young children communicate more easily through play than words, play therapy involves a therapist creating an atmosphere in which they can freely express feelings, concerns, and conflicts. The therapist, who assumes the role of co-player, model, or observer, then interprets the child's play to find the source of fears and problems, or tries to reflect back the feelings expressed by the child.

bibliotherapy

A group of methods has moved from the clinic to the classroom. One is **bibliotherapy**: reading books with a therapeutic purpose. Bibliotherapy was first used for the remediation of emotional difficulties in adults. For children with disabilities, the procedures are based on the concept that books serve a therapeutic purpose (Pardeck, 1990). Not only are books relaxing, but reading stories with positive role models can affect an individual's attitudes and behavioural responses. It can also help children work through a crisis and help them see how others have confronted problems and gain insight into alternative solutions. For the process to be successful, you must match appropriate books with the student and his or her various problems (see Sridhar & Vaughn, 2000). See Table 7-5 on page 248 for the process of bibliotherapy.

Counselling

In addition to varied therapies, counselling is often employed with children and youth who have behavioural disorders and with their families. The major goal is to help a child eliminate unacceptable behaviours and learn more appropriate ways of responding to people and the environment.

Individual, group, family, guidance, and career and vocational counselling are used. Although individual counselling is popular, many counsellors suggest that *group therapy*—the simultaneous treatment of several clients, usually in the same age range—is a more natural way to work with children. By treating children in a group, the therapist can use group processes and face-to-face peer interactions as primary vehicles for change.

Group techniques make use of modelling, play, verbal interactions, peer influence, socialization, experience, and mutual support. Within the context of the group, children can unlearn inappropriate behaviours and learn new ways of relating more easily through interaction and feedback in a safe situation with peers. Groups show children how to help other people, accept help from others, talk openly about themselves and abandon facades, and accept responsibility for their growth and the growth of others.

Educational Intervention

As we have pointed out, conceptual models from various disciplines are used to explain and treat behavioural disorders. Yet no single method has proven adequate in the management of all children who are behaviourally disordered. Because a single cure-all strategy is not out there waiting to be discovered, educators tend to draw ideas from a number of approaches. Refer to Table 7-2 on page 228 for an outline of common interventions related to the various conceptual models. While recognizing that each model holds merit, in the next section we use a behavioural approach to discuss intervention. Behavioural models have demonstrated the most success in assessing and reducing challenging behaviours and increasing appropriate behaviours for a wide range of children with behavioural disorders and other disabilities.

Service Delivery Models

The inclusion of children and youth diagnosed with behavioural disorders has been a prominent and contentious issue for decades. Many experts (e.g., Kauffman, 2005) stress that for most school-aged children with mild behavioural disorders, the general classroom is the common milieu. With support, appropriate programming, and individualization, teachers can instruct and manage these students. On the other hand, some writers say that for students with serious and violent behaviour, inclusion is "fraught with peril" (Lago-Delello, 1998, p. 479). However, there is a surprising lack of empirical research concerning inclusion for students with behaviour disorders. Simpson (2004) points out, "In spite of the extraordinary attention given to this topic, there has been a general absence of empirically sound research to guide policy and practice" (p. 19). Added to this is the fact that "empirical research that directly spotlights outcomes of students with EBD as a function of their inclusion experience is generally unavailable" (p. 22).

We do know that such students are rated the least accepted and the most negatively stereotyped of all exceptionalities. This is often the last group considered when inclusive options are available (Eber, Nelson, & Miles, 1997) and those with serious behavioural disorders are often cited as exemplars of the times when inclusion is not appropriate. For example, in the United States, compared to the total of all students with disabilities, almost four times as many students with behavioural disorders are educated in segregated settings and only half as many in general classrooms (Cheney & Muscott, 1996). As another example, in Quebec, although there is increased recognition and encouragement of the inclusive model for children with behavioural disorders, the actual inclusion of such students remains a contentious issue (Finn, Heath, Petrakas, & McLean-Haywood, 2002).

The issues surrounding inclusion for students with behavioural disorders can be summarized within three major areas. That is, can students who are behaviourally disordered benefit from general classroom placement, can teachers effectively accommodate and instruct them, and will other students be fairly served? Some of the pros and cons drawn from the research literature about inclusion are shown in the Debate box and discussed below.

A MATTER OF DEBATE

The Educational Placement of Students with Serious Behavioural Disorders

INCLUSIONARY IDEALS

Pros	Cons
All students should be in general classroom settings.	Many general education teachers specifically disagree with the placement of students with intellectual disabilities and behavioural or emotional difficulties in the general classroom.
Efficacy studies suggest that special education classes are the most successful settings.	Surveys indicate that the overwhelming majority of teachers do not think that general classroom teachers have the skills to handle children with behavioural disorders.

TEACHER SKILLS

Pros	Cons
With collaboration and support, teachers can accommodate these students.	The needs of students may fall outside the limits of most effective general education teachers.

TEACHER SKILLS

Pros	Cons
	Many teachers are unwilling or inadequately prepared to meet the needs of disruptive students; they tend not to program differently for these children.
	Teachers tend to be very intolerant of challenging behaviour.
	Traditional approaches to managing problem behaviours are not sufficient. Teachers need a more extensive repertoire of instructional and management procedures.

STUDENT LEARNING

Pros	Cons
Included students have higher academic skills, better work habits, and higher grades.	Teachers provide little academic support or modifications Problems become increasingly resistant to intervention efforts as they proceed through the school system.

SOCIAL SKILLS

Pros	Cons
Contact and familiarity promote acceptance.	Children elicit dislike and rejection; they face acute difficulties in gaining acceptance.
Interactions improve children's self-image.	Children often reject prosocial models and gravitate toward a deviant peer group.
There is less aggression and extreme behaviour than in self-contained classes.	There may be too much disparity among children for effective modelling to take place.
Students benefit from social modelling of typical peers; they will naturally model appropriate behaviours.	Violent students are more likely to erupt in inclusive or crowded classes.

(Meadows, Neel, Scott, & Parker, 1994; Taylor, Richards, Goldstein, & Schilit, 1997).

CASE STUDY

Andrew (continued)

The school-based team found that Andrew's achievement and academic interests were minimal, hardly surprising given his behavioural problems and resentment of school and authority. Andrew had large gaps in reading skills, his spelling was poor, and creative writing exercises were beyond him. Only in math did he show any interest.

The team devised Andrew's IEP and behaviour reduction plan carefully based on the hypothesis that for Andrew the function of the behaviour was avoidance—to get out of work that was beyond him. The team listed a plan for dealing with behaviours and for the times when there was escalating behaviour, with interventions for each level of escalation. They tried to be realistic in their goals and took into account the presumed functions of Andrew's behaviour, his likes and interests, and positive as well as negative reinforcements. Initially, the teacher may need to accept behaviours that would ordinarily be deemed inappropriate. For example, when Andrew exhibits explosive anger, a realistic first step might be to accept screaming or cursing as long as he is not physically aggressive.

Within the special placement, the teacher focused on adapting the academic program to promote much initial success and, as an offshoot, reinforce specific new skills that Andrew needs to function successfully in the mainstream. The teacher also stressed Andrew's strengths in order to help his weaknesses. Reading, as a specific remedial subject area, was eliminated from his timetable. Math became the fulcrum of Andrew's education. During the math period, he was provided increasing opportunities to make choices. For example, he was given the chance to decide when to begin his math worksheet and prompted to select the type of manipulatives he preferred.

This proved a successful strategy. And, as Andrew tackled math word problems, his reading comprehension improved; he later enjoyed writing math problems for the class. Math concepts, such as

distance and scale, were extended to other areas— for example, social studies.

Andrew's classroom environment was changed so that students worked in cubicles on individual programs for the first half of the morning. At the same time, a token economy was established with the co-operation of all students in the class and a commercial social skills training package was used.

EXTRACT FROM ANDREW'S IEP

Name: Andrew S.
Age: 9–4
Grade: 3
School: Green Middle
Teacher: Mrs. Potts
IEP number: 1

Placement

At this time, Andrew is assigned to an alternate classroom. He can return to the general classroom when his aggressive and violent behaviour decreases.

Examples of responsible behaviour and/or strengths: Enjoys math; will take responsibility for classroom chores.

Examples of irresponsible behaviour: Tantrumming, swearing, physical aggression, verbal aggression, non-compliance.

Needs/Adaptations

No physical adaptations. Needs warm, supportive environment with structured program and much reinforcement. Work modified to ensure success, with math the fulcrum. Intervention by counsellor. Goals to be increased gradually.

Long-Range Goals

- To decrease/eliminate violent behaviour.
- To decrease aggressive behaviour and learn alternate responses to frustration.
- To follow reasonable adult requests.

- To decrease time required to begin assigned academic tasks.
- To participate in a class-wide token economy and a social skills program.

Short-Term Objectives

- Learn alternate responses to aggression, such as ignoring, through participating in role-playing that simulates real-life situations, such as interactions with peers and following adult requests.

- Participate in token economy with daily child and teacher evaluation.
- Undertake and practise skills from a commercial social training package for social skills.
- Conform to specific daily goals regarding behavioural and academic expectations.
- Use a timer for beginning work on time.
- Learn to set goals for himself for each set of tasks.

Students with Behavioural Disorders

A critical factor affecting the social and academic achievement of students with behaviour disorders is the interaction between students and their teachers (Nelson & Roberts, 2000; Sutherland, Wehby, & Yoder, 2002). But when students fall outside of teachers' tolerance boundaries, teachers are likely to form relatively negative attitudes toward them. Webber & Scheuermann (1997) describe a "growing attitude of vengeance" toward children who disrupt the classroom (p. 168) and reduce the effectiveness of a teacher's instruction. Teachers respond to accepting students with behavioural disorders with varying degrees of fear and scepticism (Heflin & Bullock, 1999) and show considerable resistance to including them.

There seem to be seven attributes needed by the teacher in order to establish teacher-student relationships—teacher attention, nurturing, acceptance, constant encouragement, recognition, warmth, and reassurance (Franklin, 1992). Yet teacher instruction for students with behaviour disorders is less frequent than for normal students. Studies find that behaviourally disordered students received extremely low rates of teacher praise, ranging from 1.2 to 4.5 per hour per student. There are infrequent rates of positive reinforcement, and high rates of reprimands (Sutherland, 2000). Thus, an unhappy cycle is established. For the behaviour of students with behavioural disorders to improve, teachers need to be involved and to have the attributes mentioned above, but they are wary of these students and less involved than with typical children.

Arguments about how to effectively educate students with behavioural disorders should be more compelling than those that focus simply on general classroom placement options. Persistent and non-responsive antisocial behaviour suggests the need for comprehensive and intensive intervention. Some students may require situations that provide a structured environment, individualized attention, consistent behaviour management practices, and reward systems that allow them to learn more socially acceptable and personally gratifying behaviour.

The decision to place a child in a general classroom or in a different program involves multiple factors that often interact and may change over time. Educators must first examine the extent to which a student's behaviour deviates from that typical for his or her age and grade. A second consideration revolves around responses to interventions. In some students, commonly used sanctions such as verbal reprimands fail to produce the desired outcomes. The failure of conventional strategies is one measure of the magnitude and persistence of problem behaviour. Another question is, is the general classroom the safest haven? When children are disruptive and defiant, deficient in social skills, and do not fit either the teacher's or the peers' expectations for classroom behaviour, they are likely to be disliked and rejected and the usual positive aspects of life in school and community are not present. A student who does not have much fun and does not learn much is not well matched to a setting (Kauffman, Lundrum, Mock, Sayiski, & Sayiski, 2005).

Teachers

One of the major tasks of teaching is to establish and maintain order, and discipline is usually the number one issue facing individuals who are responsible for any classroom. Controlling behaviour and teaching discipline and self-control are aspects of the broader construct referred to as classroom management. In general terms, **classroom management** refers to "the way in which teachers manipulate the classroom environment to minimize disruptions and give all children the optimum opportunity to engage in appropriate behaviour and reach learning and social goals" (Winzer, 1995, p. 627).

classroom management

The word *discipline* derives from *disciple*, a follower of the master's teaching. **Discipline** means helping children to learn to guide their own behaviour in a way that shows respect and caring for themselves, other people, and the physical environment. **Self-discipline** involves being able to consider an outcome and select the behaviour that will achieve it. The best way to handle inappropriate behaviours is to prevent them from happening in the first place. **Preventative discipline** refers to strategies and procedures that militate against any discipline problems arising.

discipline

self-discipline

preventative discipline

For both beginning and veteran teachers, issues related to the behaviour or discipline of students are a major worry and cause of stress. In surveys, teachers consistently reveal that disruptive student behaviour and classroom discipline are their primary educational concerns (see Otis-Wilborn, Winn, Griffin, & Kilgore, 2005).

Novice teachers are absorbed by their immediate concerns; they tend to worry about survival. Many young teachers find that the job is much more difficult than they envisioned. Some have learned a variety of techniques but usually know more than they can do. They may establish clear rules, for example, but fail to enforce them. Others feel ill-prepared to deal with issues related to classroom management and discipline and may be caught unaware by serious behavioural deviations. Lacking specific skills and experience, they draw from their own school careers, ask other teachers, believe that all students will respond to a warm teacher demeanour, or just hope that good intentions will control behaviour. Children with challenging behaviours also pose significant challenges to many veteran teachers who do not have adequate training in the prevention and remediation of this behaviour.

Teachers' belief systems determine the standards they maintain for students, what behaviour they will tolerate, and how they expect individual students to behave. Kauffman and colleagues (2002) list the behaviours that the majority of teachers find intolerable. These are inappropriate sexual behaviour; stealing; physical aggression; destruction of property; responding inappropriately to correction; refusing to obey classroom rules;

disturbing or disrupting the activities of others; self-injury; lewd or obscene gestures; ignoring teacher warnings or reprimands; creating disturbances during classroom activities; cheating; and being verbally aggressive toward others.

Class Members

It seems important that intervention plans address not only the social deficiencies of the child with a behavioural disorder but also the needs of others in the environment. Placement decisions must also address the consequences for other class members. When teachers take excessive time to respond to behavioural problems, valuable classroom instructional time is lost. Dupre (1997) argued that students should not have to endure hindrances to their learning "merely to elevate the concept of inclusion" (p. 847).

Positive Behaviour Supports

The current research tells us that the real key to generally improved student behaviour is a clear, consistent plan for school-wide discipline. Interventions at the school-wide level generally eliminate a substantial number of the problems a typical school encounters (Sadler, 2000; Taylor-Greene & Kartub, 2000).

School-wide programs, grouped under the rubric of **Positive Behaviour Support(s)** (PBS), are proactive and systematic programs defined by multilevel layers of prevention and support (Scott, 2003). In general, PBS is a framework for considering the predictability of common school problems and then using that information to prevent or ameliorate them. The overarching aim is to create simple and effective prevention strategies in school-wide, classroom, and non-classroom settings, or at individual student levels (Sugai & Horner, 1999).

Positive Behaviour Support(s)

There is nothing novel or magical about school-wide programs; different versions have been available for a long time. What is different about the current agenda is that the interventions under the PBS umbrella are built on the foundations of applied behaviour analysis and repackaged in a more positive, collaborative, and holistic framework (Safran & Oswald, 2003). The current procedures are hailed as exciting, sophisticated, and capable of changing the fundamental character of behavioural intervention (Neilsen & McEvoy, 2004).

Planning a coherent and structured school-wide program is complex and challenging. It requires a total staff commitment to managing behaviour and a strong adult presence in every aspect of the school environment. Common features of school-wide behavioural management systems include the following interconnected systematic features:

- Form a school-based team. A within-school team enables each school to individualize the PBS process according to its particular characteristics and needs.
- Identify predictable problems. The team assesses trouble areas, such as lockers and the cafeteria.
- Develop staff consensus. Stakeholders discuss and agree upon logical and realistic strategies that include expectations, routines, and physical arrangements to prevent predictable problems.

- Formulate clearly defined expectations and rules. These are communicated to all students together with consequences and clearly stated procedures for correcting rule-breaking behaviours.

- Implement rules consistently and correctly to depersonalize conflict. Students learn that what happens when they misbehave is procedural, not personal.

- Put in place a consistent method for reporting behaviour infractions.

- For persistent and chronic problems, implement other components such as teaching students self-control and/or social skill strategies.

- See each classroom in the school as its own unique system and devise your own set of rules that supplement the broader school rules.

All the various approaches to FBA emerge from a framework that promotes a positive and proactive set of strategies. It is recognized that although no single environmental strategy will be sufficient for deterring all misbehaviour, using preventative strategies in a consistent manner is a more efficient approach than always responding after the fact. But no matter how well schools are managed or how conscientious, consistent, and fair they are, there will inevitably be some children who fail to respond as positively as others and who consistently test authority. Therefore, the best way to look at PBS is to envision it as an approach based on three levels of care—primary, secondary, and tertiary. These levels are shown in Figure 7-3.

Primary Prevention

Primary prevention is the most ethical, effective, and cost-effective approach. The primary level of prevention is aimed at all students in a school; it is estimated that about 80 percent will respond favourably. A myriad of procedures fit within the primary prevention frame. We explain reinforcement below; a potpourri of techniques and ideas are found in Table 7-4 on page 246.

Reinforcement

Within behavioural approaches, reinforcers (rewards) are used to increase desirable behaviour, and aversion techniques to decrease or extinguish undesirable behaviour. Reinforcement can be provided by anything that a child finds pleasurable. Reinforcers are usually divided into two types: primary reinforcers are things like candy and food; secondary reinforcers include objects that have no intrinsic value of their own, such as tokens and stars. Whether a child receives a primary or a secondary reinforcer, it should always be accompanied by a social reinforcer such as a smile, hug, or pat on the back.

Selecting and using reinforcers is not as simple as it seems. As Mossish (1997) points out, the Achilles heel of the reward and consequences system is that it works only if children care about the rewards and the consequences. If children develop an immunity, they can defeat the system—as in, "Send me to the office. I don't care."

Typically, teachers use neutral or negative commands in classrooms with children with behavioural disorders (Kyger, 1999; Shores & Wehby, 1999). Often, children hear over and over how bad they are instead of how well they are doing. Teachers should reduce the number of verbal reprimands and negative attention. Instead, they would be wise to incorporate components of strong and systematic reinforcement—five positive reinforcements to every negative instance is a good rule of thumb.

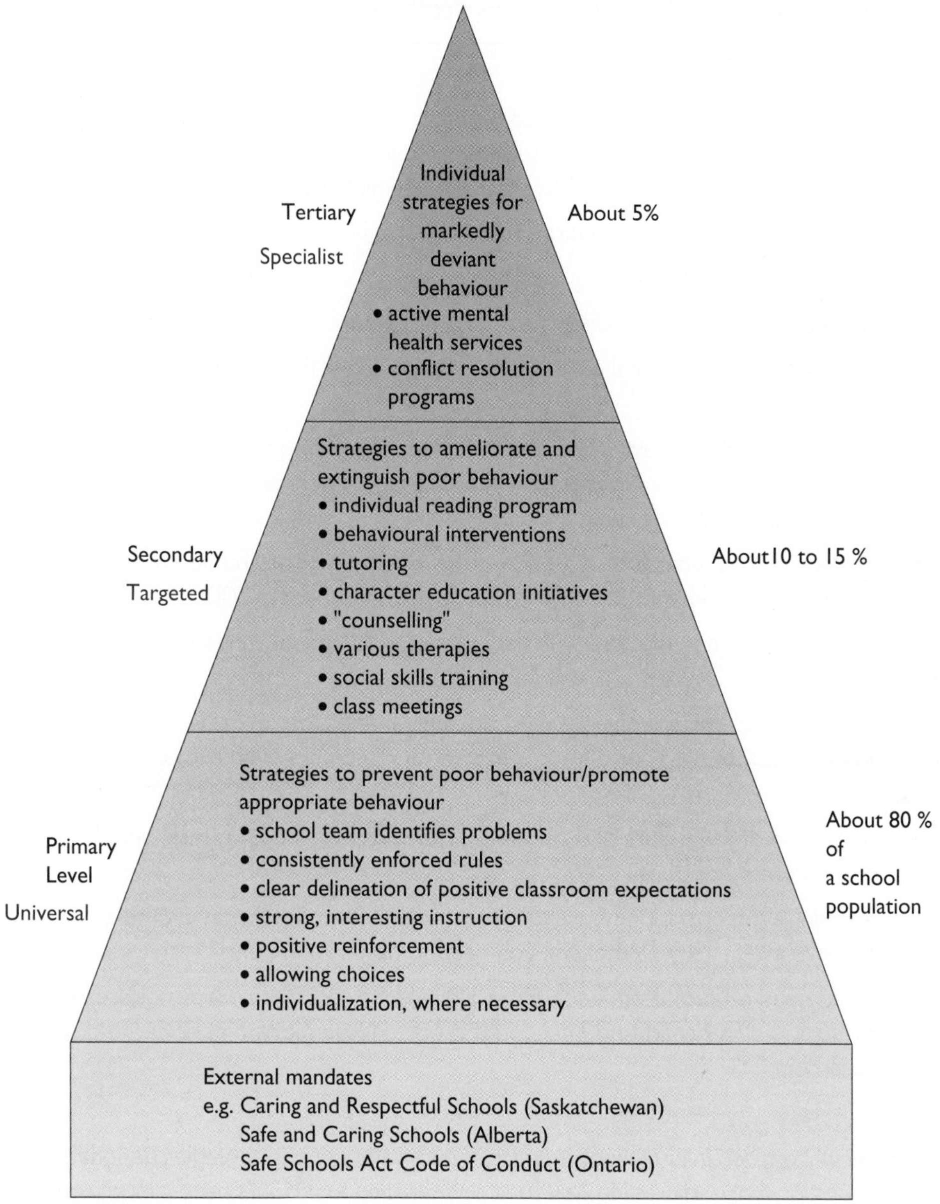
Tertiary
Specialist
Individual strategies for markedly deviant behaviour
• active mental health services
• conflict resolution programs
About 5%
Secondary
Targeted
Strategies to ameliorate and extinguish poor behaviour
• individual reading program
• behavioural interventions
• tutoring
• character education initiatives
• "counselling"
• various therapies
• social skills training
• class meetings
About10 to 15 %
Primary Level
Universal
Strategies to prevent poor behaviour/promote appropriate behaviour
• school team identifies problems
• consistently enforced rules
• clear delineation of positive classroom expectations
• strong, interesting instruction
• positive reinforcement
• allowing choices
• individualization, where necessary
About 80 % of a school population
External mandates
e.g. Caring and Respectful Schools (Saskatchewan)
Safe and Caring Schools (Alberta)
Safe Schools Act Code of Conduct (Ontario)

Figure 7-3
Levels of positive behaviour supports

Secondary/Tertiary Intervention

Secondary level intervention focuses on the 15 to 20 percent of students who do not respond to preventative measures and are at risk for adverse outcomes. Interventions are designed to reverse the effects of risk exposure and stop the acceleration of maladaptive behaviour toward more extreme forms. The tertiary level of supports includes plans to address the needs of the roughly 5 percent of students with chronic, challenging behaviours. We discuss one selected intervention designed to be used with specific at-risk groups or individuals and its response below. Further ideas are found in Table 7-5 on pages 247 and 248.

Table 7-4 Creating accessible classrooms: Proactive strategies

Accommodations

- Create a welcoming and responsive school setting. Classroom climate contributes significantly to the number and seriousness of behaviour problems: positive levels of school environment have been linked to elevated levels of student classroom participation and academic achievement (Bennett & Smilanich, 1994).

- Establish a signal to silence students and gain attention, such as clapping or dimming lights.

- Personalize by using student names frequently.

- Devise a simple overarching daily routine that students can learn by heart.

- Make class rules sparingly. Remind students of the rules often. The younger the students, the more often the rules should be reviewed.

- Be specific, consistent, and systematic in expectations, actions, and responding to behaviour. Provide clear expectations so that students know what to expect of the teacher, what is expected of them, and what the consequences are for success and failure.

- Students respond to consistent and genuine praise. But consider whether praise should be public or private recognition and do not praise when it is not warranted (Lewis & Bullock, 2004).

- Ignore negative behaviours if they do not interfere with the learning of others or influence others' behaviour.

- Give people choices. Choice-making opportunities occur frequently in the classroom. They can be as simple as allowing a student to choose a colour of magic marker or deciding which explorer he or she will write about.

- Use precorrection—the artful use of reminders and prompts before students begin a task; simply, jumping in on a behaviour before it happens.

- Ask rather than tell; give students the opportunity to state what they need to do. As an example, instead of "In 10 minutes you will have to . . ." say "What will you need to do in 10 minutes?"

- Sometimes you and the child need a break from each other. Have some sealed envelopes addressed to other teachers with a note saying, "This child and I needed a break. Please thank him or her and send him or her back to the classroom."

Adaptations, instructional

- The use of multiple, consistently applied interventions is critical. Four major generic strategies designed to improve behaviour are instruction that is interesting, relevant, and directed to a child's needs; much use of positive reinforcement and feedback; consistent rules and routines; and allowing choices in the classroom.

- What and how a teacher teaches contributes directly to student behaviour, so good instruction is a first line of defence in behaviour management. Provide a curriculum that is meaningful, well presented, and matched to children's needs.

- Promote participation and many opportunities to respond. Increasing a student's correct academic responses is often effective in reducing classroom behaviour problems (Gunter, Hummel, & Conroy, 1998), more so than modifying behaviours such as task attention.

- When circulating around the classroom, do so randomly. When your movements are unpredictable, students are less likely to misbehave.

Table 7-5 Creating accessible classrooms: Reactive strategies

---

Accommodations

- Use FBA to determine why the student is acting in a certain way before you consider creating a behaviour intervention plan. If you can discover what a child is trying to get with a behaviour, then you can find an alternative behaviour that meets his or her needs.

- Seat disruptive children among ones who are well behaved.

- Consider the timetable: if a certain time or subject seems to cause disruption, alter the scheduling.

- Levy mild penalties following inappropriate behaviour to promote consistent behaviour change.

- Immediately remove the results of poor behaviour, particularly vandalism.

- Use proximity control; that is, use your presence to discourage inappropriate behaviour.

- Provide reinforcement for non-aggressive behaviour; do not allow positive reinforcement for aggressive behaviour. For example, reward students when they are doing something well, even in the middle of misbehaving. For example, you might say "You're very angry but I appreciate that none of those books are going in the direction of people."

- If you step into an aggressive act, devote as much attention as possible to the victim and ignore the perpetrator as much as possible.

- Send for help; get the names of participants and witnesses.

- Make the office aware of the incident.

- If a student is confrontational or threatens violence, give him or her a chance to save face and cool down. For example, "It's your call. Take a minute to think about it." But if you are in doubt about the confrontation, do nothing and take a minute to think over the options.

- In the presence of serious threatening behaviour, you should disengage and break the cycle of successive interactions by delaying your response. Delay—briefly look at the student, look at the floor, look detached, pause. Disengage—for example, say "Excuse me," and move to your desk and pick something up. Return to the student, redirect, and withdraw.

- Because bullying differs from other kinds of violence, it does not lend itself to the kinds of interventions that may work with other behaviours. Trying to make a bully behave differently rarely leads to permanent change. You need group pro-victim attitudes; that is, other students who will intervene. To do this, first discuss and raise awareness with the class. Then encourage self-reflection through strategies such as role-playing and rereading class rules.

- Involve the child's parents: make daily communication with the home or issue daily report cards (home note programs).

- Use a travelling notebook—a sort of diary that goes from school to home and back again.

- Use contingency contracts that zero in on one behaviour for students in grade 5 and above.

- Allow older students to be involved in setting up reinforcement systems, such as a token economy.

- Provide social skills instruction to promote the acquisition, performance, and generalization of prosocial behaviours (Forgan & Gonzalez-DeHass, 2004).

- Use role-playing in which participants assume a specific role in a demonstration or simulation. Involve students in specifying the details of each role-playing sequence, such as a fight at school, to increase

Table 7-5 continued

the similarity between the role play in the instructional session and what the student has experienced outside the classroom.

- Use social scripts that structure the role-playing. In the scripts, show the roles played by the members, the sequence of activities, and the reward structure.

- Use discussion-oriented social autopsies to analyze behaviour by dissecting and discussing social mistakes, discussing who was harmed, and planning for the future.

- Keep rigorous documentation of behavioural interventions.

Adaptations, instruction

- Students with behavioural disorders may significantly improve their behaviour as away to increase their access to computers. Incorporate technology and use the Premack principle: "You can use the computer after you finish your math."

- Implement a unit on bibliotherapy, the process of reading books with a therapeutic intent. There are three sequential and essential elements in bibliotherapy. These are as follows:

  1. A book is either read aloud by the teacher or by the students individually. Students then reflect about the story. This leads to *identification,* which occurs when the student recognizes the thoughts and behaviours of others and identifies with the main characters and events of the story.

  2. *Catharsis* occurs when the student finds familiarity with the feelings of others and develops emotional ties with the characters.

  3. *Insight* targets an individual's specific problems and brings issues to the surface. It occurs as students come to realize how the characters deal with situations and how these relate to the individual reader (Sullivan & Strang, 2002–2003).

- In light of the reading limitations of so many students with disabilities, videotherapy offers an alternative to print media. It provides endless possibilities for learning and growth. Videotherapy incorporates the use of videos, videotaping, and role-playing to develop understanding and growth in students with disabilities (Wilson, 2004).

Promoting Social Skills

social skills

Social skills are specific behaviours that people perform when interacting with others. Knowing and using these skills has important implications for children's academic and vocational success as well as their long-term mental health adjustment. By definition, children with behavioural disorders do not spontaneously acquire the skills necessary for adequate social functioning.

Training in social skills was popularized in the 1980s and has since become an important academic feature for children with behavioural disorders. Instruction is intended to develop and increase prosocial and positive behaviour. Training typically focuses on two areas. These are skill acquisition deficits—the absence of a particular skills or behaviour—and/or performance deficits—a skill or behaviour that is present but not used (Gresham, 1995). The skills may be taught to an entire class, a small group, or be directed solely at a child who show deficits. Socially competent peers should serve as models.

The list of social skills is huge. It includes greeting behaviours; ways to extend and receive invitations; positive listening skills, such as listening attentively, sharing and encouraging, and engaging in verbal and non-verbal interaction with others; conversational skills, such as asking about other people's interests, responding to others' questions, and maintaining an extended conversation by taking turns to comment on a topic; giving verbal and non-verbal compliments and positive feedback; using positive methods of gaining teacher attention (for example, when asking about a work assignment); acceptable habits of cleanliness, grooming, and health; and the ability to inhibit reactions to stimuli to stem inappropriate outbursts.

Punishment

We are not suggesting punishment as a strategy. But it must be mentioned if only because teachers embrace punishment as an easy response to administer, it is highly reinforcing to them, and it works for many students who have occasional minor misdemeanours (Maag, 2001).

Aversive responses such as punishment should be used sparingly. Using punishment to proscribe transgression can generate students' anger, bringing greater conflict. Punishment does not answer the "why" of poor behaviour, teach appropriate behaviour, or suppress behaviour, and it often fails to create attentive, quiet, compliant students.

With the current stress on zero-tolerance policies, suspension and expulsion are frequent. Despite their significance and wide use, however, there is little research to support the effectiveness of such policies in improving student behaviour (Skiba, 2002). In fact, these exclusionary practices are often counter-productive because they are likely to result in grade retentions, dropping out of school, academic failure, delinquency, and recidivism.

Social Intervention

It is futile to treat the child in only one context; equally futile to ignore the complex needs of the interrelated systems in which the child functions. Intervention must consider the range of dysfunctions, the diversity of behaviours, and any associated family and parent dysfunction.

The coordination of multiple service programs to help children with behavioural disorders and their families is referred to as *wraparound*. The process emerged from the concept known as system of care, which is a community-based approach to providing comprehensive, integrated services through multiple professionals and agencies and in collaboration with families (Eber, Sugai, Smith, & Scott, 2002).

Wraparound is not a program but an approach with an integrated plan that addresses the needs of a child or youth during and beyond the school day. The process is used to build consensus within a team of professionals, family members, and natural support providers to improve the effectiveness, efficiency, and relevance of supports and services developed for children and their families (Eber et al., 2002).

wraparound

Mental health and child welfare agencies have traditionally been the primary points of entry for the wraparound approach. New ways of looking at the process see more commitment and collaboration from schools.

SUMMARY

1. The omnibus term *behaviourally disordered* describes children and youth who are meeting difficulties in adjusting to normal behavioural expectations. Classroom behavioural problems are one of the most common reasons children are referred to special education.

2. In the field of behavioural disorders, the most fundamental and pressing question involves how to find precise definitions. Lack of a clear and widely accepted definition of just what a behavioural disorder is then creates problems in estimating prevalence, identifying characteristics, assessment, etiology, devising treatments, and educational approaches.

3. A secure classification system is as problematic as a general definition. Children and youth present such a heterogeneous population with disorders so multidimensional and ambiguous that there is frequent disagreement about how particular behavioural characteristics should be named and classified. Classification systems may use the severity system, the psychiatric classification of DSM-IV, or a system founded on clusters or dimensions of behaviours. Behaviours are also seen as internalizing or externalizing and in terms of time of onset.

4. The characteristics of children and youth with behavioural disorders are varied. Children with conduct disorders perform noxious behaviour and attract attention with their overt disruptions and aggressive outbursts. Those who are anxious and withdrawn internalize their behaviour; they worry excessively about events and activities, tend to have low self-concept, and are self-conscious, hypersensitive, and sad much of the time. Phobias—specific, out-of-proportion anxiety—are common.

5. Of the many variables contributing to human experience, none has been conclusively shown to underlie emotional problems. It is extremely unusual to find a single cause that leads directly to a behavioural disorder. Many factors can lead young people to act out in ways that are unacceptable and reprehensible. Causes may be genetic, biophysical, disturbed family climate, deleterious environment, academic difficulties, faulty learning, and other school factors, to mention only a few. A combination of risks has far more negative effects on children than any single source of risk.

6. Many youngsters with behavioural disorders are underachievers at school; their academic performance is reported to be significantly below that of students without disabilities They are usually behind in reading, written language, arithmetic, and spelling.

7. Bullying is the most prevalent form of low-level violence in schools today. It is a form of aggression, a particular kind of violence to which children are exposed. In general, bullying is a school problem that starts early and thrives in the middle school years. Whether the bullying is direct or indirect, the key component is that the physical or psychological intimidation occurs repeatedly over time to create an ongoing pattern of harassment and abuse.

8. Behaviour intervention is a complex, scientific process. Functional behavioural assessment (FBA) and Positive Behavioural Supports (PBS) are two management approaches that are extensions of applied behaviour analysis. FBA is recognized as a critical component of effective behaviour intervention programs. A basic assumption is that behaviour has a purpose and does not occur randomly. Therefore, the focus is on the function— what purpose that behaviour serves for a student. Assessment identifies specific relationships between behaviour and the circumstances that trigger it, provides leads on how to reduce or eliminate the behaviour, and suggests how to replace it with more acceptable

alternate forms. PBS is a school-wide process founded on the notion that the best way to control poor behaviour is to prevent it from happening in the first place.

9. Significant debate continues to surround the issue of recommending students with behavioural disorders for placement in general classrooms. Considerations include the individual child and the types of behaviours manifested, the learning and comfort of other class members, the teacher and his or her effectiveness in handling deviant behaviours, the supports available to teacher and child, and the assistance provided to teachers regarding how to manage misbehaviour. However, when a child raises classroom management from a chore to an obsession, disrupts the learning of other students, demands too much teacher time, or displays violent and dangerous behaviours, serious consideration of what is actually the least restrictive environment must be undertaken.

10. Discipline is one of the most universal and troubling problems facing teachers. Teachers use a variety of individual methods learned from diverse sources. Good teachers know that management plans for the entire classroom group should be proactive and multidimensional with multiple strategies aimed at preventing problem behaviour before it becomes severe. There must also be reactive strategies for students who display serious deviations.

11. Psychotherapeutic approaches search for a child's inner conflicts and motivations. Various therapies and counselling techniques provide students with an understanding of their own dysfunctional perceptions, clarify their own reality, and lay the basis for healthy self-esteem and productive self-talk. Behavioural approaches are more concerned with producing desirable behaviour. Ecological approaches acknowledge that each environment has multiple dimensions and climates and that people in the environment influence the child just as surely as the child influences peers, teachers, parents, and siblings. They emphasize the need to look at the total interaction of a child with the social environment and the fit between child and ecosystem.

12. The most effective schools are those that have proactive school wide programs for facilitating a positive climate and maintaining discipline. Programs, referred to as called Positive Behaviour Support, are simply frameworks for identifying predictable problems and developing strategies for intervention. PBS looks beyond the behaviour itself and emphasizes positive incentives and strategies to encourage and teach new behaviours rather than simply reacting to poor behaviour.

13. Education alone is often too late to address the problems adequately. Young children require early and sustained intervention; older children and youth need a complete emotional tune-up, subsumed under the term wraparound.

HISTORICAL NOTES

Children and youth who were neglected, vagrant, and delinquent (mild behavioural disorders) gained the attention of reformers and educators in the middle decades of the 19th century, becoming a part of what was referred to as the *child rescue movement*. Child rescue advanced in tandem with the stress on free and compulsory education for all students that began in Canada in the late 1840s and became law in the 1870s. At the same time, legislation was gradually passed in the areas of child labour, family courts, juvenile courts, and children's aid societies. The first Juvenile Delinquency Act was passed in 1905.

The how and where for educating students with behavioural disorders is a long-standing dilemma in special education. From the outset, educational placements and services for such students relied heavily on a range of restrictive and segregated settings such as reformatories, Houses of Industry, industrial schools, training schools, special schools, and special classes (Winzer, 1993). The first segregated classes in the public schools, called unruly or ungraded classes, opened in 1879.

Special classes, together with more restrictive placements, remained the most important vehicle for providing services right into the early 1970s. In that decade, strong attacks on the legitimacy of a medical paradigm in the treatment of childhood behavioural disorders were heard. Attempts to remediate disruptive behaviours as an illness with a heavy reliance on indirect intervention approaches such as counselling and improving self-esteem were not powerful enough to solve the intractable problems of deviant behaviour. Instead, behavioural psychology was systematically incorporated into work with students with behavioural disorders.

There was also marked discontent with settings and educational intervention. In Canada, a number of provincial and national reports on education stressed the need for expanded and more effective educational services. They urged the federal and provincial governments to assume educational responsibility, and asked local education authorities to provide educational services for all children within their jurisdictions (Csapo, 1981). After that, services developed rapidly.

Nevertheless, despite more than 150 years of various solutions that have emerged and decayed, the prognosis for children and youth with behavioural disorders is anything but hopeful. Writers observe that educating these troublesome people will continue to be one of the most stressful, complex, and difficult challenges facing public education today. Programs have not been associated with generally positive outcomes (Eber, Nelson, & Miles, 1997) and this area is "perhaps one of our greatest failures" (Osher, Osher, & Smith, 1994, p. 7).

To date, no instruction has been devised that permanently alters the conditions and that successfully diverts children and youth from a trajectory leading to a host of long-term negative developmental outcomes. Students continue to be expelled, suspended, or shunted into a variety of alternative placements. Many are underserved. In 1999, James Kauffman noted that in the United States, "Far less than half of the population of students with behavioural disorders have been identified for special education and are typically identified only after several years of serious difficulties" (Kauffman, 1999). Others are served only after their problems have become serious. As well these students continue to be in more restrictive settings than other students with disabilities. The only students less likely to be included in general settings are those with severe and multiple disabilities.

CHAPTER 8

CHILDREN WITH ATTENTION DEFICIT HYPERACTIVITY DISORDER (ADHD)

INTRODUCTION

In the past few decades, Attention Deficit Hyperactivity Disorder (ADHD) has become one of the most popular disabilities. Writers observe that "not since the establishment of learning disabilities as a special education category has a condition so captivated both the professional community and general public as has attention deficit hyperactivity disorder" (Reid, Maag, & Vasa, 1993, p. 198).

The terminology and interest may be fresh, but the condition is not new to the fields of education, psychology, and pediatrics. There have always been children who couldn't sit still, who wriggled and fidgeted and seemed not to concentrate on anything for longer than a few seconds. In the past, teachers and parents might have called them Fidgety Phils. Psychologists and other health professionals used terms such as *neurological dysfunction*, *anatomical dysfunction of the right cerebral hemisphere*, *cognitive memory deficit*, *soft neurological signs*, and *minimum brain dysfunction syndrome* (Campbell, 1997; Meents, 1989).

There is little doubt that the diagnosis is popular among educators and parents, more so in North America than anywhere else. But even as ADHD has become one of the most common diagnosed disorders of childhood, it has also become one of the most controversial. Many people look askance at the high number of children being diagnosed with ADHD and have concerns that arise from quite different viewpoints.

Typically, ADHD has been the domain of active prepubescent males. This had led some people to declare that the label ADHD is a hoax designed only to make boys more compliant, more like girls. Other critics say that the explosion of ADHD really implies that child misbehaviour is being recast as child pathology. As one psychologist chided, "The diagnosis has become a wastebasket into which any misbehaving child can be tossed" (in Campbell, 1997, p. 30). Other skeptics view the diagnosis of ADHD as an attempt to legitimize teachers' or parents' inadequacies. They argue that good teaching and discipline at home and at school would resolve the problems in all but a small percentage of cases (e.g., Armstrong, 1995).

Within the special education community, some educators view the diagnosis as more a function of political pressure and professional fad than student reality. Critics note that a clinical diagnosis of ADHD does not lead to special placement or predict responses to instruction. Further, ADHD is not included among the 13 categories in the American IDEA (1997). Many critics hold that adding ADHD as a disability category is unnecessary because students who manifest symptoms severe enough to impair educational performance are currently eligible for educational services under existing categories such as learning disabilities or behavioural disorders (e.g., Ysseldyke, Algozzine, & Thurlow, 2000). Other educators object to the label of ADHD because the disorder is difficult to define and identify and may divert resources away from children with serious disabilities (Aleman, 1991).

Drugs were first used in the treatment of hyperactive children in 1937. Since this seminal work, psychopharmacological approaches to treatment have increased dramatically. Drug companies have come to the fore, marketing a variety of high-powered central nervous system stimulants and other medications that are used extensively with children who demonstrate ADHD.

The United States and Canada lead the world in the use of methylphenidate, more commonly known as Ritalin. European countries make minimal use of the stimulant. By 1996, American youngsters were consuming 90 percent of the world's Ritalin (Will, 1999). By 2002, data from the U.S. Drug Enforcement Agency showed an increase in the production of methylphenidate, 90 percent of which was consumed for treatment of ADHD (Snider, Busch, & Arrowood, 2003). Across Canada, prescriptions for Ritalin jumped 500 percent throughout the 1990s (Van Rijn, 2000). Health Canada estimates that the amount of Ritalin consumed in Canada in 1996 was 4.6 times more than the amount consumed in 1990 (Campbell, 1997). A report on Alberta from the Federal Therapeutic Products

Ritalin is often prescribed to treat ADHD.

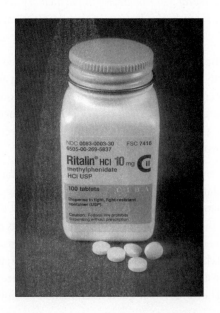

Program found a 37 percent increase in usage in that province in 1999 over 1995 (Ecklund, 2000).

Some critics conclude that we are simply drugging healthy children into submission. Others deplore psychopharmacology "employed to relieve burdensome aspects of temperament" (Will, 1999, p. C6). Still others see drug therapy as a ready remedy for teachers who blur the distinction between education and therapy. Some experts paint a concrete and sobering picture that juxtaposes the mounting number of drug prescriptions with the high value placed on mental performance in contemporary education. There are concerns that increased pressures for school performance are associated with an increased diagnosis of ADHD (Schneider & Eisenberg, 2006). Other experts posit the following chain of events: first comes greater awareness of ADHD by teachers, parents, and physicians. For the drug manufacturers, ADHD is good business. More drugs are invented and produced to fill the need, along with more advertising by the drug companies. This produces even more awareness among stakeholders … and so on and so on.

In the entire arena of ADHD there are certainly more questions than there are answers. However, despite complaints and deep concerns about diagnosis and inflated numbers, even a cursory examination of the literature shows that ADHD is real. Teachers agree. Daily they observe children in class talking, wriggling, and squirming, getting out of their seats, chatting with their friends, sharpening pencils down to tiny stubs, or not engaging in active listening. In fact, most practitioners and researchers agree that some children do indeed face problems of inattention, distractibility, and motor excess that can seriously impair their learning, social interactions, and adult roles.

Although exact prevalence rates are difficult to arrive at, the number of children diagnosed with ADHD is high. Some Canadian estimates are that almost 1 in 20 children is diagnosed with ADHD (Sanghavi, 2005). Since this is the equivalent of approximately 1 child in every classroom, the impact upon teachers is inevitable and makes the issue of how best to assist children with ADHD one of the leading educational challenges today. At the same time, it is teachers who make the initial referrals for children suspected of ADHD in 40 to 77 percent of cases (Frankenberger, Farmer, Parker, & Cermak, 2001; Snider, Frankenberger, & Aspensen, 2000). What teachers know and understand about the condition is likely to influence the selection and implementation of interventions for these children.

DEFINITIONS OF ADHD

The terminology and classification of ADHD is a perplexing issue. Definitions, diagnoses, and evaluation procedures remain rather unclear, leading to confusion among practitioners, researchers, and parents. Over the past few decades, Attention Deficit Hyperactivity Disorder has been defined in several ways that are discussed fully in the Historical Notes box at the close of this chapter. A general definition from the DSM revision (DSM-IV-TR, 2000) defines ADHD as

> a persistent pattern of inattention and/or hyperactivity/impulsivity that is more frequent and severe than is typically observed in individuals at a comparable level of development (APA, 2000, p. 78).

Classification of ADHD

ADHD is characterized by three primary features: inattention, impulsivity, and hyperactivity. It is important to first understand the behaviours that make up each component and the accompanying criteria. In brief:

attention disorders
- **Attention disorders** are characterized by difficulty in concentrating, tuning in to sensory information, and engagement or active participation. DSM provides nine symptoms of inattention, as shown in Table 8-1.

  Attention and engagement are developmental; the younger the child, the lower the rates of engagement. Very young children cannot discriminate between what is and what is not important. They flit from activity to activity, show high rates of movement, and are easily distracted by visual and auditory stimuli. The parts of the brain that allow the child to sustain attention and screen out distractions become increasingly myelinated between the ages of about four and seven.

Table 8-1 Some general characteristics of ADHD

Inattention	Often fails to give close attention to details; makes careless mistakes in schoolwork, work, or other activities.
	Often has difficulty in sustaining attention to tasks or play activities.
	Often does not seem to listen when spoken to directly.
	Does not follow through on instructions; fails to finish schoolwork, chores, or duties in the workplace.
	Has difficulty organizing tasks or activities.
	Avoids, dislikes, or is reluctant to undertake tasks that require sustained effort.
	Loses belongings—things necessary for tasks or activities, such as toys, school assignments, pencils, books, or tools.
	Is easily distracted.
	Is often forgetful in daily activities.
Hyperactivity/ Impulsivity	Fidgets with hands, squirms in seat.
	Is unable to stay in seat when required.
	Exhibits inappropriate behaviours in certain situations, such as running or climbing excessively.
	Has difficulty playing or engaging in leisure activities quietly.
	Is often "on the go" or acts as if "driven by a motor."
	Talks excessively
	Blurts out answers at inappropriate times or before questions have been completed.
	Has difficulty awaiting his or her turn.
	Interrupts or intrudes on others in conversation or games.

The construct of attention is complex and includes a number of subtypes—initial focus, sustained attention, selective attention, and avoidance of distractions. The facets work in tandem and together are prerequisites for engagement and on-task behaviour. **Engagement** refers to the amount of time that children spend involved with the environment, including peers, teachers, and classroom materials, in a way that is appropriate for their age, ability, and surroundings. **On-task behaviour** is important for academic functioning. It describes the amount of time that a child is engaged with the instruction or materials needed for learning.

engagement

on-task behaviour

Impulsivity represents a child's difficulty in withholding active responses, such as blurting out statements or grabbing materials (Zentall, 1993). Impulsive students do things without thinking and do not learn from experience. They have difficulty organizing themselves, need much supervision, speak out of turn, and don't wait their turn in games or groups. They may be social isolates, exhibit angry outbursts, blame others for their problems, or be quick to pick a fight, and are very sensitive to criticism (Alderson, 1993). They are poorer at tasks requiring sustained attention and face challenges with problem solving and planning. Students may **perseverate**: they purposelessly and sometimes disadvantageously repeat an activity. For example, a child may finish addition problems on page one and continue to add on page two, even though the instructions clearly indicate a switch to subtraction.

impulsivity

perseverate

Hyperactivity is described as "a child's frequent failure to comply in age-appropriate fashion with situational demands for restrained activity, sustained attention, resistance to distracting influences, and inhibition of impulsive response" (Whalen & Henker, 1980, p. 56). DSM, along with professionals and parents, often describes hyperactive children as behaving as if they are being driven by a motor, incessantly in motion. Hyperactive children display rates of motor behaviour that are too high for their age group. They seem unable to restrain their activity, to sustain attention, to resist distracting influences, and to inhibit impulsive responses. Boys are three times more prone than girls (Wicks-Nelson & Israel, 1991).

hyperactivity

In the classroom, hyperactive children are unable to sit still. When confined to a seat, they translate their need to be active into finger and foot tapping, as well as other disruptive activities. These children tend to lose interest quickly when someone is reading to them; they will play with their toys for a moment, then move on to the next thing, and often annoy or bother their classmates (Wender, 2000). Hyperactive teenagers may drum their fingers, shuffle their feet, open and close their desks, or continually visit the pencil sharpener, other desks, and other areas of distraction.

Using the markers of inattention, impulsivity, and hyperactivity, DSM (2000) describes subtypes of ADHD. These are

- *ADHD, predominantly inattentive* type. For this diagnosis, a child must show six or more inattentive symptoms, but fewer than six hyperactive/impulsive symptoms.

- *ADHD, predominantly hyperactive/impulsive* type. Within this classification, a child will display six or more hyperactive/impulsive symptoms that are inconsistent with his or her developmental level but fewer than six inattentive symptoms.

- *ADHD, combined* type. In this group, a child will display six or more inattentive symptoms and six or more hyperactive/inattentive symptoms.

- *ADHD, not otherwise specified,* is detailed in DSM (1994). It covers disorders that include prominent symptoms of attention deficit or hyperactivity-impulsivity but that do not meet the criteria for ADHD.

The condition of predominantly inattentive is referred to as ADD; with impulsivity and hyperactivity, it is ADHD. For ease of discussion, we use the encompassing term ADHD throughout this chapter except when ADD is specified.

There is general agreement that the subtypes differ in terms of developmental course as well as cognitive, intellectual, academic, and behavioural correlates. For example, inattention remains relatively constant. In contrast, hyperactivity/impulsivity declines substantially with the child's increasing age. Probably about half of adolescents show a decline, of unknown origin, of hyperactive symptoms. In behavioural terms, hyperactivity/impulsivity is more strongly correlated with oppositional and antisocial behaviours. Inattention is linked with affective disorders. While hyperactive and impulsive children move and fidget, often those who are categorized as predominantly inattentive seem to be sometimes in a dream—they move and think slowly and have difficulty with the rapid and efficient performance of tasks.

PREVALENCE

According to the National Institute of Mental Health (2003), ADHD is now the most commonly diagnosed psychiatric disorder among school-aged children in the United States. The American IDEA does not pinpoint ADHD as a specific category but allows it to be included within the grouping of "other health impairments." From 1990 to 2000, this group increased 351 percent, more than any other classification eligible for funding under the IDEA (DePaepe, Garrison-Kane, & Doelling, 2002). Currently, approximately 3 to 7 percent of children in the United States are diagnosed with ADHD (Forness & Kavale, 2002; Pastor & Reuben, 2002). In Canada, the diagnosis rate increase of ADHD has similarly been staggering, perhaps as high as 1 in every 20 children (Sanghavi, 2005).

ADHD is far more frequent among males than females (Wender, 2000). General prevalence rates are approximately 2 to 3 percent in girls but 6 to 9 percent in boys during the six to twelve age period (Barkley, 1998).

It is important to be aware of caveats that attach to these reported rates. It may be that females are simply not identified or are under-identified as exhibiting ADHD. For one thing, about 99 percent of research into ADHD concerns boys (Elias, 2005); only very recently have researchers begun to study girls with ADHD. For another, although girls and boys with ADHD show similar rates of fidgeting and inattentiveness, boys are far more likely to show overt behaviours such as disruptiveness and rule breaking. Girls express the disorder through talking or being busier, which is more socially acceptable than the gross motor activity often seen in boys. This means that girls are less likely to be hyperactive and also less likely to receive special education services for the condition (Hinshaw, 2002).

As well, prevalence rates fluctuate depending on the nature of the population. Variables such as ethnicity, urban or rural status, the age range of the individuals, and the criteria that are utilized to define ADHD all influence these rates. For example, a U.S. study of 9278 eight-year-old children (Schneider & Eisenberg, 2006) found, among other things, that 5.44 percent of the children were reported to have a diagnosis of ADHD. The research revealed that girls, Black children, and Hispanic children were less likely to have the diagnosis even after controlling for other characteristics. There were also regional variations in diagnosis, with the western region of the United States having significantly lower instances of ADHD cases than the rest of the nation.

ETIOLOGY

Despite being one of the most studied disorders of childhood, Attention Deficit Hyperactivity Disorder is still not well understood. The research literature does not identify a single cause for ADHD, and efforts expended to find a biological etiology have been generally inconclusive and often contradictory. There is yet no persuasive evidence that children diagnosed with ADHD differ from other children in any identifiable neurological or biochemical manner (Snider, Busch, & Arrowood, 2003). Today it is widely held that the varied symptomatology of the disorder may result from various causal mechanisms.

The biological underpinnings of ADHD often focus on brain scanning and neurochemical evidence of neurological dysfunction (Kooistra, Crawford, Dewey, Cantell, & Kaplan, 2005). For example, there is some agreement that the neurochemical imbalances in the fronto-striatal networks of the brain play a major part in causing ADHD. This suggests that the brain is underactive in specific areas that are involved in inhibitory responses, attentional processes, and sensitivity (Brown, 2000).

Other studies use Magnetic Resonance Imaging (MRI) on the frontal lobes of the cerebrum, temporal gray matter, caudate nucleus, and cerebellum of children with ADHD. They indicate 3 to 4 percent smaller brain volumes in all regions (National Institute of Mental Health, 2003). However, researchers caution that MRI is a research tool that cannot be used to diagnose ADHD.

There is considerable evidence that ADHD has a powerful genetic component. The familial basis has been convincingly demonstrated over the past three decades by adoption, family, and twin studies.

ADHD is a highly heritable disorder among first-degree biological relatives (DuPaul & Stoner, 2003). According to Wender (2000), fathers and close relatives of ADHD children have indicated that they themselves have ADHD characteristics. In addition, the siblings of ADHD children are more than likely to have ADHD problems. Among biological siblings, there is a greater likelihood of this—20 to 50 percent of siblings of ADHD children are likely to suffer from the disorder as well (Murphy & Barkley, 1996).

Other studies have validated the heredity argument when they compared the prevalence of ADHD among children and parents who are biologically related with that of children who are adopted. Further evidence arises from twin studies. Gilger and colleagues (1992) indicated that if one twin was diagnosed with ADHD, the probability that the other twin would have ADHD was 81 percent for monozygotic twins and 29 percent for dizygotic twins.

The case is also building for a significant role of environmental toxicants (Koger, Scheltler, & Weiss, 2005). Theories suggest that ADHD symptoms are attributable to environmental factors such as lead poisoning, nutrition, and prenatal exposure to smoking or alcohol (Barkley, 1998; National Institute of Mental Health, 2003) (See Chapter 3). The theory that ADHD is caused by nutritional factors proposes that some children may be behaviourally sensitive to certain foods or food components, and consequently, that decreasing their exposure to these foods will improve their behavioural symptoms (Rojas & Chan, 2005). Some pediatric sleep experts believe that as many as 30 percent of children diagnosed with ADHD may actually suffer from sleep disorders that can cause virtually the same daytime symptoms.

Poor parenting and family stress have not received much research support in the field of ADHD. However, one recent study (Ford, Goodman, & Meltzer, 2004) found no independent association between ADHD diagnosis and socioeconomic and family characteristics.

DEVELOPMENTAL CONSEQUENCES

ADHD is most likely to be diagnosed during a student's elementary school years (APA, 2000). However, children do not "catch" a disability when they enter school and ADHD does not just suddenly appear. Rather, it is a developmental disorder that usually begins in children's early years (Teeter, 1998). As infants, children may be more restless and colicky than others. As they move through preschool, kindergarten, or first grade, cognitive, behavioural, linguistic, and affective characteristics that have developed over time will interact with the academic and social ecology of the classroom and the manifestations of ADHD will be more noticeable.

Academic

Many children with ADHD are of average or above average intelligence. However, the general characteristics of ADHD—inattention, impulsivity, and hyperactivity—are magnified in a school setting where there are constant demands to perform, demonstrate knowledge, sit still, and engage in tasks of the teacher's, not the child's, choosing. Performance is compromised by inattention, distractibility, disorganization, memory problems, and difficulty with completing work.

Up to 80 percent of students with ADHD have been found to exhibit performance problems (Harris, Friedlander, Scaller, Frizzele, & Graham, 2005). Specific academic deficiencies among these children are reported in overall academic achievement, reading, math, and written expression. ADHD students also show difficulties in problem-solving skills, expressive language abilities, and fine and gross motor skills. They often have low motivation for schoolwork, show avoidance of tasks requiring sustained self-application, and lack persistence in the face of failure.

Obviously, children who are easily distracted learn less than those who pay attention—and, by definition, children diagnosed as ADHD are easily distracted and have short attention spans. They have lower rates of on-task behaviour during independent work than their peers, and as a result, they complete less work. Figure 8.1 shows graphically what can happen in a typical elementary classroom. After lunch and recess are taken into account, children may experience as many as 15 to 20 transitions between activities each day, which can collectively consume up to 70 minutes of instructional time (Fisher, Berliner, Filby, Marliave, Chen, & Dishaw, 1980). Typical learners are on task about 75 percent of the time. Those with ADHD (and other learning and behavioural disorders) may be on task only 20 to 30 percent of the time, which seriously impairs learning.

Students with ADHD are three to seven times more likely than their peers to be retained, suspended, or expelled, or to require special education (LeFever, Villers, Morrow, & Vaughn, 2002). Over half of children with ADHD who are taught in general education classrooms fail at least one grade by adolescence (Barkley, Fischer, Edelbrook, & Smallish, 1990) and one-third fail to finish high school (Pfiffner & Barkley, 1990; Weiss & Hechtman, 1986).

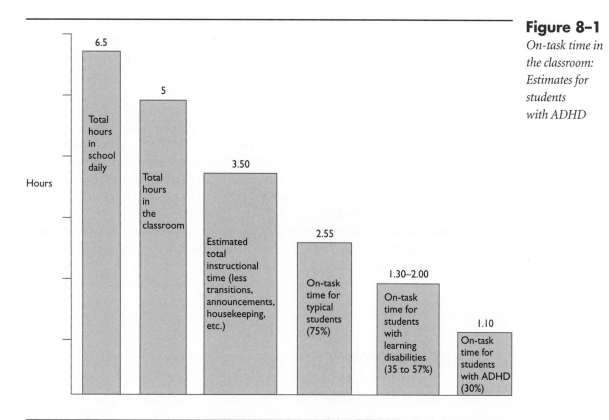

Figure 8–1

On-task time in the classroom: Estimates for students with ADHD

Behaviour

Problems of hyperactivity, inattention, and impulsiveness play a key role in the development of antisocial behaviour, at least for boys (Loeber & Stouthamer-Loeber, 1998). Children with ADHD exhibit a low tolerance level for or violent reactions to frustrations, as well as noncompliance with teachers and parents and argumentativeness (DuPaul & Stoner, 2003; Wender, 2000). To deal with difficult situations with their peers, they are likely to use aggression (Stormant, 2001). Students who evince a persistent pattern of behaviour and learning problems that interfere with their ability to succeed in school, as well as the social problems we discuss below, may be headed toward a lifetime of poor outcomes. As Walker and colleagues (2004) observe, "It is well established that children who are poorly accepted or rejected by peers, who have few friendships, and who adjust poorly to schooling are at much greater risk for lifelong maladaptive outcomes" (p. 181).

As mentioned, there is so far much less research data on girls as compared to boys. The largest, most thorough study so far comparing girls with ADHD to their peers without the condition tracked 140 girls with ADHD aged twelve to sixteen and compared them with 122 girls without the disorder. By seventeen years of age, the ADHD girls were far more likely to be clinically depressed, have anxiety disorders, and have a conduct disorder (see Elias, 2005).

Co-occurring Conditions

Approximately 50 percent of children with ADD (see Chapter 5) or ADHD qualify for an additional diagnosis. Given the behavioural issues above, it is clear that specific forms of learning and behavioural disorders are rife.

Among children with the diagnosis, the most common comorbid condition is oppositional defiant disorder (ODD), found in 30 to 45 percent of these children (Volk, Neuman, & Todd, 2005). ODD is associated with increased severity of ADHD and a poorer prognosis. An estimated 20 percent of ADHD children also exhibit conduct disorders. About 10 to 20 percent exhibit mood disorders (Volk, Neuman, & Todd, 2005). There is also more anxiety, depression, and Tourette syndrome than seen in children who do not have ADHD (Powell, Welch, Ezell, Klein, & Smith, 2003).

DuPaul and Stoner (2003) report that, academically, approximately 20 to 30 percent of students with ADHD are classified as having a learning disability because of their deficits in specific academic skills. One study of 37 children identified with ADHD (Bin, 2001) found evidence of expressive language deficits that were secondarily associated with social competency.

Social Behaviour

Children with ADHD exhibit such substantial social competence deficits and difficulties in interpersonal relationships that some authorities argue that the social problems experienced by these students are so common that they should be considered the defining characteristic of the condition (Landau, Milich, & Deiner, 1998). Many affected children have problems understanding how to approach social situations. Common social performance difficulties include inappropriate attempts to join peer group activities (for example, barging in on games), poor interaction behaviours (such as interrupting, not listening to peers), and losing tempers when conflict arises (Guevremont, 1990).

It is hardly surprising that, as a group, children with ADHD are strikingly unpopular with peers. They are more likely to be rejected, have few friends, and be unable to maintain friendships. Children with ADHD are perceived by peers and teachers as annoying, boisterous, intractable, and irritating and are often described as intrusive, bossy show-offs (DuPaul & Stoner, 2003; Turnbull, Turnbull, Shank, & Leal, 1999).

The time periods required for peers to notice and disapprove of children with ADHD are distressingly brief—measurable in hours or minutes (Bickett & Milich, 1990). Not only do peers and teachers perceive these students as having negative characteristics, but they also tend to respond to the children with aversion, criticism, rejection, and sometimes (in the case of peers) even counter-aggressive behaviour after only a few contacts (Olmeda, Thomas, & Davis, 2005).

On a somewhat different note, Toronto researchers Barbara Shea and Judith Wiener (2003) studied four boys with an average age of twelve years, their parents, and their teachers. They concluded that, among other things, there were parallels between the social, behavioural, and psychological attributes of victims of bullying and children with ADHD, suggesting that children with ADHD may be at risk for chronic peer victimization.

Family Variables

ADHD in a child can relentlessly affect family relationships. The accelerated rates of activity and the excessive, non-purposeful movement disturbs everyone and causes families discomfort and even despair. A young hyperactive child is constantly on the move, pushing, poking, and asking questions, but never waiting for answers. Even when asleep, the child shows excessive activity and sleep problems (Alderson, 1993).

ASSESSMENT

The diagnosis of ADHD is among the most difficult in all of childhood psychopathology. ADHD is a medical diagnosis but it is not a condition like measles, strep throat, or a sore toe, which a doctor can confirm with a blood test, a stethoscope, or an X-ray. Nor is there a valid neurological or physiological test that can be used to diagnose ADHD or differentiate children with ADHD from children and adults without the condition.

There is no scientific proof to validate ADHD as a neurological disorder. There are, however, patterns of behaviour that are attributed to ADHD that may lead a physician to diagnose a child as such. ADHD is diagnosed by establishing the developmental deviance and occurrence of symptoms (DuPaul & Stoner, 2003). To fit within the predominantly inattentive group (ADD), for example, children must exhibit six or more of the nine inattention symptoms that are inconsistent with their developmental level and have persisted for at least six months.

Still, problems abound. While the behavioural manifestations seem to be specific and rather clear-cut, the DSM criteria themselves are problematic. They are both inherently subjective and lack standardization. Attention, impulsivity, and hyperactivity are not simply present or absent. Rather, each occurs on a continuum. DSM items such as "often has difficulty organizing tasks or activities" or "fails to give close attention to details" can be interpreted in a number of ways. Because these descriptions may mean different things to parents, teachers, administrators, and, especially, medical personnel, one person's criteria for thinking a child has ADHD can be substantially different from another's.

As well, other conditions can mask as ADHD. Numbers of young children arrive at school unready for the structure and routine of kindergarten or grade 1. They don't follow instructions, fidget and squirm, don't finish tasks, move about the room, intrude on the space of others, and seem unwilling to engage in activities not of their own choosing. These may be children with maturational lags or children who lack experiences. At the same time, as you read through this text you will notice how many of the traits described for conditions such as nonverbal learning disabilities, mild behavioural disorders, and even Asperger's syndrome seem to match those seen in children with ADHD. Only a thorough and clear diagnosis can rule out alternate causes for a child's inattention, impulsivity, and hyperactivity.

A proper diagnosis of ADHD must be comprehensive and multimodal in nature. It should include information from parents, teachers, and other school personnel about the core symptoms, including settings, age of onset, duration, and degree of functional impairment. Educational tools cannot be used to diagnose ADHD, but they can support the diagnosis. Tools include interviews, questionnaires, observations, and standardized measurements such as child behaviour rating scales, parent self-report measures, and direct behavioural observations of students.

ADHD can often be confused with other mild disabling conditions due to similarities in behavioural traits.

Medical personnel employ DSM-IV criteria. It is estimated that an effective diagnosis requires more than six hours of interviews with the child, the family, and teachers. But today, with many family doctors making the diagnosis, a child may be labelled as ADHD after a 20-minute examination (see Campbell, 1997), which means that the child may be superficially evaluated and prematurely placed on a medication trial.

A diagnosis of ADHD is subject to other influences, particularly because it is often first suggested by schoolteachers and parents rather than by health professionals. In about 66 to 75 percent of cases, teachers are responsible for recommending that a student be assessed for ADHD (Lloyd, Kauffman, Lundrum, & Roe, 1991; Snider, Busch, & Arrowood, 2003). One recent study (Sax & Kautz, 2003) reported that in most cases, an ADHD diagnosis was first suggested by a child's teacher or other school personnel (52.4 percent), followed by parents (30.2 percent), and by a physician or psychiatrist in only 14.4 percent of cases.

If teachers are in a position where they are initiating referrals and then providing other professionals with information about students' behaviour and learning, it seems reasonable to expect that teachers possess wide knowledge about ADHD. The research literature, however, indicates that teachers have less knowledge about the condition than one would expect (Snider, Busch, & Arrowood, 2003; Stormant & Stebbins, 2005; Wilde, 2006). For example, a large number of teachers appear to hold some misconceptions about the cause of the disorder, such as the influence of diet and poor parenting. Many believe that stimulant medication is beneficial for treating ADHD and also hold the (unfounded) belief that medication improves students' academic performance. One study (Kasten, Coury, & Heron, 1992) found that teachers frequently offered advice to parents regarding stimulants for their children although the same teachers felt that they received too little training on the use of stimulants to control ADHD. In a more recent study (Bussing, Gary, Leon, Garvan, & Reid, 2002), teachers reported the need for training in areas such as managing the stress caused by ADHD students, modifying lesson plans, and developing behavioural contracts.

As an aside, note that some American states (Connecticut, Illinois, Virginia, and Maryland) have enacted legislation concerning the diagnosis of ADHD. The legislation prohibits teachers in public schools from recommending that students be evaluated by appropriate medical practitioners or be given psychotropic drugs (Schneider & Eisenberg, 2006).

INTERVENTION

There is an unwarranted assumption that ADHD can be cured. ADHD is a chronic developmental disorder, probably present from birth, and one that continues to impair functioning at some level throughout a person's lifetime. There is no cure for ADHD, although there may be changes in the symptoms, particularly in hyperactivity in adolescents. All interventions have as their major aim helping an individual to improve and to cope with the multiple domains affected by ADHD. Interventions are complex and multimodal, accounting for learning, behavioural, and social deficits. You can see an example of how a child may be accommodated in the Case Study below.

CASE STUDY

Geoffrey

Sunnydean Public School is a large, multi-grade elementary school on the outskirts of Winnipeg. It is both policy and practice at the school to integrate students with exceptionalities into general classrooms.

In his grade 2 classroom, Geoffrey is far behind his peers in reading and math. He has a short attention span, poor on-task behaviour, low motivation, negative peer interactions, and generally seems to find school very trying and difficult. He can stay in his seat for only about three minutes. He misses instructions, wanders around the classroom, gets a drink, chats to his friend, and generally disrupts proceedings. His behaviour grows worse almost daily and his academic levels seem to have plateaued.

Geoffrey's teacher, Mr. Allen, has attempted a number of adaptations, such as peer tutoring in reading and a token economy to improve on-task behaviour, but to little avail. He eventually referred Geoffrey to the school principal, asking for an assessment and some assistance in developing an appropriate program for him. When making the referral, Mr. Allen detailed some of the academic and behavioural problems he saw every day in the classroom. "Geoffrey," he said, "acts as if he is driven by a motor. He seems to have a lot of muscles

to move but none at all to sit down and work. He fidgets in his seat and leaves it constantly." He went on to explain that Geoffrey seemed capable of handling the grade 2 work, but his inattention, off-task behaviour, and constant movement meant that he rarely paid attention and almost never completed work.

A first step was to have a school psychologist administer a number of measures to Geoffrey to try to obtain an accurate description of his academic and behavioural profile. She began with the WISC-IV. The Kaufman Test of Educational Achievement was used as a measure of academic ability. To round out the assessment, the psychologist used the Social Skills Rating System-Teacher Version and a scale of adaptive behaviour, a series of statements answered by Geoffrey's mother. Throughout, the psychologist also carefully noted Geoffrey's *presenting behaviour*—the way he approached the situation and the measures, the way he interacted with her, and any indications of distractibility, inattention, and hyperactive behaviour.

Although the WISC Full scale score confirmed Mr. Allen's thoughts and indicated a child of average ability, the Kaufman measure showed that Geoffrey was significantly below the level expected for his age. He answered about as many items correctly as a child entering grade 1. The social skills and adaptive behaviour scales indicated that Geoffrey had many social deficits, chiefly in the school environment.

A physician then assessed Geoffrey. He added Geoffrey's teacher's observations to his own as the most direct and objective indicators of the boy's behaviour and the most direct evidence of the presence or absence of ADHD. With the psychologist's report also in hand, and after talking to the parents, the physician gave a diagnosis of ADHD combined type. He suggested that Geoffrey be placed on a trial regimen of Ritalin. At this time, the parents are resistant to drug therapy.

The psychologist, the school principal, the classroom teacher, and the parents met to discuss Geoffrey's program. The teacher reiterated his concerns about behaviour and school achievement, stressing that Geoffrey was lagging further and further behind his classmates. The psychologist concurred. She spoke about the assessment, during which Geoffrey was constantly off task and distractible. She noted that data from standard psycho-educational instruments can support a diagnosis of ADHD but that there is no clear evidence to warrant using these results as the primary or sole indicators of the condition. However, she concluded by pointing out that Geoffrey fit within the commonly accepted definition of ADHD, combined type, the same finding as the physician.

A school program should focus on reducing the effects of distractibility and inattention while stressing the acquisition of basic academic skills. In the behavioural realm, the psychologist urged Mr. Allen to "pick his battles." She explained that it is simply not possible to make Geoffrey behave the same as everyone else. Unless the teacher wants to indulge in constant nagging (which is more than likely to increase Geoffrey' behaviour problems) he should be willing to tolerate a higher level of activity and shorter attention span than he would normally expect from children of this age. At the same time, he should use high levels of positive reinforcement and adopt behavioural principles, such as a token economy. An IEP would support academic functioning.

An extract from Geoffrey's IEP is shown below.

EXTRACT FROM GEOFFREY'S IEP

Name: *Geoffrey*
Teacher: Mr. Allen
Chronological age: *8–2*
Grade: *2*
School: *Sunnydean*

Reason for Referral

Geoffrey was referred by his classroom teacher for psycho-educational assessment because he is falling further and further behind his classmates, especially in the core areas of reading and math. Behaviour control is poor and worsening, showing large amounts of inattention and hyperactivity.

Results/Present Levels of Functioning Cognitive

On the WISC-IV, Geoffrey scored within the normal range.

Kaufman Test of Educational Achievement

	Grade equivalent	Percentile
Reading composite	1.0	1
Math composite	1.0	1
Battery composite	1.0	1

Social skills

Geoffrey appears to have performance deficits in social skills that impair his interactions with peers and teachers.

Core areas

Geoffrey has barely made a start in formal reading. He is at a beginning grade 1 level. He is also functioning at a beginning grade 1 level in math. All the basic math concepts seem to be deficient. He does not know number facts to 19, simple computation, or understand place value or any applications to word problems. He does know the names of coins and seems further advanced when questioned about money, such as the names of coins and making change.

Placement

- *General classroom*

Adaptations

- IEP
- Direct instruction in reading and math
- Peer tutoring
- Promotion of social interactions

Long-Range Goals

- Increase Geoffrey's attention by showing the teacher his work after completing a designated assignment. The teacher will provide social praise and feedback.
- Improve Geoffrey's task behaviour by having the teacher implement a token economy system with him.
- Improve phonemic awareness, beginning with sound identification and moving to segmenting and blending.
- Develop a sight-word vocabulary.

- Read very short paragraphs and books.
- Participate in small-group math activities and complete all related tasks.
- Use coins as the major manipulative to teach rational counting, place value, addition and subtraction facts, and basic computation.

Short-Term Objectives

- Learn 10 sight words with the teacher, in a small group, or with a peer tutor.
- Read and discuss short paragraphs in a small group.
- Use written exercises (fill-in-the-blank, draw, underline the word) to stress sight words and to teach reading directions.
- Use pennies for rational counting to 99, forward and backward.
- Use coins for simple equations.

Medical

Children diagnosed with ADHD are considered to have a medical disorder that must be treated by a physician (Snider, Busch, & Arrowood, 2003). Very often, psychopharmacological treatment is the first recommended method of management.

Earlier in this text, we touched upon drug therapy directed toward students with serious and pervasive behavioural disorders. It is estimated than only 2 to 3 percent of all children and adolescents in general education are prescribed medications. Among those in special education, 15 to 20 percent are medicated. About 40 to 60 percent of persons in residential facilities are on drug regimes (Forness, Kavale, Sweeney, & Gresham, 1999). However, medication rates among students with a clinical diagnosis of ADHD range from 52 to 71 percent (Safer & Zito, 2000).

Table 8-2 presents a listing of the common drug types, trade names, and targeted users. Do be aware that this is only a partial listing—new drugs appear almost monthly. As well, the drugs may be prescribed for a variety of problems. For example, stimulants are the drugs of choice among physicians in the treatment of ADHD but tranquilizers and antidepressants may be administered to a smaller group of patients who do not respond to stimulants or who have adverse responses.

North American children diagnosed with ADHD consume 90 percent of the stimulants produced worldwide. Data from the U.S. Drug Enforcement Agency are telling. They show that there was a 900 percent increase in methylphenidate production from 1990 to 2001. Production of other drugs also increased. From 1993 to 2001, the production of amphetamines (Dexedrine and later Adderall) increased by 5767 percent (Snider, Busch, & Arrowood, 2003).

Table 8-2 Sample of psychopharmacological treatments

Type	Trade name	Targeted at
PSYCHOSTIMULANTS		
methylphenidate	Ritalin, Concerta, Metadate, Focalin	ADHD
dextroamphetamine	Dexedrine, Deanol, Adderall, Dextrosat	
NONSTIMULANTS		
	Strattera Atomoxetine	ADHD
ANTIPSYCHOTICS		
Tranquilizers		
thioridazine	Mellaril	serious behavioural
chloropromazine	Thorazine	disorders; schizophrenia;
haloperidol	Haldol, Serenace	other psychotic disorders;
fluphenazine	Prolexin	occasionally resistant
thiothixine	Navane	depression or anxiety
risperidone	Risperdal, Zyprexa, Seroquel, Clozapine	disorders
Antidepressants		
SSRI (selective serotonin receptive inhibitors)	Paxil, Luvox, Zoloft, Prozac	depression, bed wetting, obsessive-compulsive disorders, Tourette syndrome
tricyclics	Tofranil, Elavil, Anafranil	
atypicals	Wellbutrin, Effexor, Serzone	
stabilizers	Lithium, Depakote, Divalproex	
anxiolytic (anxiety breaking)	Klonopin, Ativan, Buspar	
amitriptyline	Taroxyle, Tryptant, Elevil	
imipramine	Tofranil	
Antihypersensitives		
SNRI (selective norepinephrine reuptake inhibitors)	Clonadine	

Table 8-2 continued

Type	Trade name	Targeted at
ANTICONVULSANTS		
AEDs (antiepileptic drugs)		epilepsy
lorazepans	Ativan	
phenobarbital	Phenobarbital	
clonezepan	Klonopin	
phenytoin	Dilantin	
ASTHMA		
	Flovent, Albuteral Prelone, Predinisone	asthma

In general, three major categories of drugs are used with individuals diagnosed as ADHD: stimulants, major tranquilizers, and antidepressants. Selecting the appropriate medication involves a process known as *titration*. The goal of titration is to use the lowest effective dose of medication while avoiding unwanted side effects. Forness and colleagues (2003) point out that titration is somewhat easier with stimulants because these drugs usually act within an hour or so and wash out of the body within a few hours or by the end of the day. The process of finding the right dose or changing to another medication may be accomplished within a few days or weeks.

In terms of pharmacological action, stimulant medication seems to be the least complicated of the possible drugs and seems to produce the fewest side effects. Psychotropic drugs mimic brain neurotransmitters. They affect the neuron cells of the central nervous system either by increasing or decreasing their excitability. They essentially stimulate the cells to work better in inhibiting inappropriate behaviour. Ritalin is the first choice of doctors, who prescribe it about 10 times more often than antidepressants and tranquillizers combined (Gadow, 1986).

An enormous scientific literature exists on the use of stimulant medications to treat children with ADHD. Connors (2002) reported that there have been several thousand studies investigating the use of stimulants on the symptoms of ADHD, of which over 1500 studies involved methylphenidate.

Children often like their "magic pills" (Conrad, 2004). Most respond positively to the medication—about 70 to 80 percent in various studies. Researchers at McMaster University, for example, systematically compiled 92 studies and showed that more than 70 percent of patients taking Ritalin and Adderall responded positively to the drugs (Sanghavi, 2005).

The effects of the stimulants are apparent after 30 minutes. Depending on the type of medication, the effect of the stimulant can last from 3 to 10 hours (Hall & Gushee, 2002). General duration rates are: Ritalin, 3 to 4 hours; Dexedrine, 6 to 8 hours; and Adderall, 7 to 10 hours. Concerta, a single-dosage extended-release drug, lasts from 10 to 12 hours and can be taken by the child before leaving for school.

But because any beneficial effects dissipate rapidly upon discontinuation of the medication, researchers are concerned about what they refer to as "short-term efficacy." About one-third of children suffer a rebound effect from the medication; as the pill wears off, they show behaviour that may be worse than what was present before the medication was taken. Children on stimulants often have a whiny period in the evening as the medication wears off. Meltdowns can occur over trivial matters.

About 1 in 10 patients stop using stimulants for ADHD because of the side effects (Szabo, 2006). Adderall (a combination of various amphetamines) is used for the 30 percent of children who do not have a favourable response to Ritalin. Non-stimulant ADHD drugs, such as Strattera or Atomoxetine, are an option, although they are not as potent as stimulant drugs. As mentioned, antidepressants and antipsychotic medication are also used for treating ADHD.

Child psychopharmacology is a controversial field. It is often sensationalized in the popular media and the increased use of stimulant medication for ADHD has caused concern among many professionals. Such worries are not new. As early as 1971, the Office of Child Development and the Office of the Assistant Secretary for Health and Scientific Affairs held a conference to discuss the use of drugs in children with hyperkinetic disorders (Lerner, 1981). Current discussions revolve around not only dramatically increased drug use but also the targeted populations, the ethics of drugs because of their illegal use in our society, the advisability of long-term drug use with children, potential physical and psychological side effects of drugs, and academic criteria.

Stimulant drugs for school-aged children have been approved by the FDA since the early 1960s (see the Historical Notes at the close of this chapter). What is not yet approved is the use of stimulant drugs by children younger than six years of age. Still, even without approval, and despite a dearth of studies, the positive benefits shown in the studies available has resulted in an escalating rate of prescriptions for younger children (Zito, Safer, dosReis, Gardner, Boles, & Lynch, 2000). In this vein, Stormont and Stebbins (2005) reported that 68 percent of preschool teachers believe that too many preschoolers with ADHD are put on stimulant medication.

Concerns remain that stimulant drugs can have negative side effects. Many children show an appetite loss that gradually decreases after a few weeks of drug use. Some children may initially have headaches and stomach aches. Long-term effects may include growth inhibition, sleep and diet disturbances, and persistent tics. Reports of serious heart and stroke reactions in 2005 reverberated across Canada among doctors, parents of children who had been diagnosed with ADHD, and educators. In February 2005, Canadian health authorities removed Adderall from the market over concerns about sudden deaths, but the drug was allowed back on sale six months later.

There is evidence that children build up a tolerance to stimulant medication with prolonged use, causing it to lose its effectiveness over time and possibly leading the side effects to increase (Doherty, Frankenberger, Fuhrer, & Snider, 2000; Moline & Frankenberger, 2001). There is no evidence, however, that taking stimulant medication causes addiction or an increase in taking medication as an adult.

Another concern in the ethical realm is that a move from therapeutic to recreational use of stimulant medication is common. Sweden banned Ritalin in 1968 because of heavy abuse (Diller, 1998). Some students' Ritalin ends up on the street, used in combination with other pharmaceuticals that have an abuse potential similar to that of Demeral and cocaine. When Ritalin enters the bloodstream at a rapid rate, the drug can give a sense of euphoria. Abuse of Ritalin can include dissolving it in water, cooking it, or grinding the pills to inhale the powder (see Diller, 1998).

For students with ADHD, drugs are prescribed to help them become calmer and easier to manage; improve their attention span and task completion; allow them to better follow classroom rules and directions; and decrease their hyperactivity, distractibility, and impulsiveness and the number of times maladaptive behaviour occurs in the classroom (Ryan, Reid, Epstein, & Evans, 2005; Wender, 2000). It is hoped that the effect will spill over to produce better peer relationships, improved self-image, and pleasure in acquiring competencies.

No one doubts that the drugs work. Between 70 and 80 percent of the time, Ritalin makes a child more tractable and better focused in school. Two conditions that respond particularly well are poor selective attention and concentration, and impulsivity. But there is no clear evidence that medication improves academic achievement in general. Alto and Frankenberger's (1994) longitudinal study, for example, revealed that students from grade 1 and 2 who were taking stimulant medication showed no improvement in academic achievement. In a follow-up study, Frankenberger and Cannon (1999) found that even after four years, children treated with stimulant medication did not demonstrate improvement in specific or broad areas of academic achievement. In fact, they seemed to fall further behind academically.

Medication will not "make up" for skills that a student does not have, nor will it address learning problems (Waldron, 1999). Because medication alone will not improve essential skills, some educators recommend *combination therapy*, which involves using a combination of psychosocial interventions and stimulant medication, for children with ADHD (Forness, Kavale, & Crenshaw, 1999). Although the jury is still out on the long-term efficacy of combination methods, in one study (Glass & Wegar, 2001) 213 teachers out of 235 chose the combination of medication and behaviour modification as the best intervention.

Research regarding the benefits of stimulant medication on improving peer relationships is conflicting. Mrug and colleagues (2001) reported that combination treatments with medication and behavioural therapy did not result in improvement of peer acceptance with students with ADHD. In contrast, other reports from teachers of students with ADHD reported that, after taking stimulant medication, the students behaved more appropriately in social situations (see Doherty, Frankenberger, Fuhrer, & Snider, 2000).

Educational

Students with ADHD present considerable problems for their teachers. ADHD (with hyperactivity and combined) is considered within the classification of behavioural disorders and takes up teachers' time and energy. The question is how to handle and effectively instruct children who regularly squirm in their seats, stare at walls, misplace and lose their belongings, sit at desks that are avalanches of crumpled papers and pencil stubs, do not finish assignments, and cannot refrain from disrupting the classroom.

Teachers need to provide environmental accommodations as well as materials and instructional adaptations to teach basic skills. Samplings of ideas are shown in Tables 7.4 and 7.5 in Chapter 7. Also see Table 8-3 on the next page.

Service Delivery Models

Approximately 12 to 34 percent of children diagnosed with ADHD require special educational services (DuPaul & Stoner, 2003). The general classroom is the common and appropriate milieu for almost all of these students.

Table 8-3 Creating accessible classrooms

Accommodations

- Reduce unnecessary clutter in the classroom.
- Arrange the seating in the classroom in a traditional row seating pattern since this is the most structured and predictable option.
- Placement in the classroom is crucial. The desk should be positioned in the front row, where the child is less likely to be disturbed by other students.
- Do not seat the student near a high-stimuli area such as the door, windows, pencil sharpeners, or bulletin boards.
- Cover the desk with brightly coloured paper to draw attention to work.
- Define the student's work space.
- Allow stand-up desks and table.
- Allow the child to get up and move when it will not distract others.
- Use study carrels.
- Be organized and consistent. Disorganized and chaotic classrooms can elevate hyperactivity in children, as can unpredictable classroom schedules.
- Have a daily schedule laminated and placed in the student's desk.
- Establish a routine and procedure for recording and handing in homework or completed assignments.
- Provide checklists for long, detailed assignments.

Adaptations, materials

- Allow the child to move, doodle, or squeeze a small ball while in class. This can actually increase concentration.
- Students selectively attend to novelty, such as colour, changes in size, and movement. Provide many opportunities.

Adaptations, instructional

- Allow some degree of freedom in selecting tasks or assignments. Provide the student with two or more options and allow him or her to independently select an option.
- Continually reinforce students' strengths in order to minimize the negative impact of ADHD (Brook, Watemberg, & Geva, 2000).
- Move from documentation of deviance to demonstration of competence. "Catch them being good." That is, stress positive reinforcement.
- Set clear limits to behaviour and ensure that children know the consequences for misdemeanours.
- Implement token economies that involve students earning points or tokens based on their appropriate behaviour. Tokens can then be exchanged for various privileges, such as free time, computer time, or tangible reinforcers. Clearly display the token accumulation of a token economy system.
- Students persist longer if they are given attribution feedback on effort ("You've been working hard,") or ability ("You're good at this,") or some blend of the two.

Table 8-3 continued

- Make precise requests but give only one specific task at a time.

- Provide much drill and practice. When properly conducted, drill and practice is a consistently effective teaching method. A recent meta-analysis of intervention with learning disabled students (Swanson & Sanche-Lee, 2001) found successful learning arising from instruction that included systematic drill, repetition, practice, and review.

- Break assignments into small pieces and provide extra time to complete tasks.

- Provide many concrete examples and use concrete objects.

- Use many diagrams, charts, and other graphic cues.

- Hold students' attention for longer periods by facing them and establishing eye contact.

- Incorporate movement into classroom life in the form of role play, drama, and so on.

- Use peer tutoring since positive peer attention can directly influence the behaviour of students with ADHD (Carbone, 2000).

Educational Approaches

Children with ADHD often face their greatest challenges in school. The core characteristics—inattention, impulsivity, and hyperactivity—cause the most difficulties in three areas of the school setting: academic underachievement, noncompliance and aggression, and poor peer relationships.

Prescription of stimulant medication for students with ADHD is the most widely used management procedure. As we pointed out, medication does not make up for skills that students have never mastered, nor does it deal with learning problems. To be successful academically, students with ADHD must focus their attention on the teacher and lesson instead of on the abundant other stimulating items in and around the classroom.

Many methods arising from behavioural psychology are beneficial in controlling the difficulties of ADHD children in the classroom. Included are positive reinforcement, token economies, and time out for misbehaviour. Do remember that students with ADHD live in a world of reprimands. It is important that teachers reinforce the positive. You should give reinforcers frequently and change the rewards often, because students with ADHD habituate quickly to reinforcers. Time outs should be used cautiously because some students may already have low self-esteem or feel rejected by their peers. Time outs may add to the child's sense of being isolated and serve to alienate him or her (Teeter, 1998).

Cognitive-Behavioural Approaches

Together with behavioural difficulties, children with ADHD show a host of academic deficits. Cognitive-behavioural interventions are part of metacognitive strategies that emphasize a child's involvement in cognitively planning the completion of an educational task. We described learning strategies in Chapter 5.

cognitive-behavioural processes

Cognitive-behavioural processes are a conceptually related set of educational or therapeutic treatments. The varying regimes under the umbrella have in common the conviction that students can and do learn to direct their own behaviour and, in so doing, ultimately can direct at least part of their own social development (Gerber & Solari, 2005). Over the years, these interventions have been employed successfully with students with learning disabilities, behaviour disorders, and intellectual disabilities (Reid, Trout, & Schartz, 2005).

self management

The overarching concept is **self management**, defined as a set of procedures designed to develop the self regulation of behaviour (Meichenbaum, 1979). *Self-management skills* help children to work responsibly and independently, enabling them to select appropriate choices based on probable consequences.

Self management broadly encompasses four types of programs that are not mutually exclusive—self monitoring or self recording, self assessment or self evaluation, self reinforcement, and self instruction, as explained below.

- *Self monitoring* (self recording) is a multi-stage procedure by which an individual is taught to discriminate and record his or her own behaviour with some type of data collection system such as graphing or colouring a square on a chart. Students may self monitor attention or performance.

- *Self assessment* (self evaluation) is a process where the individual assesses his or her own behaviour by determining the adequacy of the responses and recording whether they have occurred.

- *Self reinforcement* is the process whereby students are taught to evaluate their own behaviours and then deliver self-selected rewards if appropriate. The individual chooses the reinforcer and determines the schedule for reinforcement.

- *Self instruction* is the process where students verbalize to themselves the questions and responses necessary to identify problems ("What am I being asked to do?"); generate potential answers ("What are the ways to do this?"); evaluate solutions ("What is the best way to do this?"); and determine the effective solution ("Does this work?"). See also Chapter 5.

attributions

An offshoot of self management is attribution training, relevant to students who have developed an outward locus of control. **Attributions** are the reasons that people give for what happens to them, so attribution training attempts to show students the relationship between hard work and success (Hallahan, Kauffman, & Lloyd, 1999). Students are guided to think of their success or failure in terms of the use or non-use of a strategy. For example, "I wrote a good paper because I used a writing strategy" (Stevens & Englert, 1993).

SUMMARY

1. Following its introduction as a diagnostic category in 1982, research and interest in ADHD increased dramatically. Nevertheless, there are numerous definitional and diagnostic problems, not the least being a lack of consensus about an exact name for the condition, the characteristics that accompany it, and its prevalence rates. There is also controversy over interpretations of the DSM criteria, and recurring concerns about teachers' wholesale adoption of the category.

2. In terms of manifested behaviours, students with ADHD are at higher risk for academic difficulties, increased rates of non-compliance, and problems with peer relationships. When serious and persistent antisocial behaviour accompanies school failure, then predictions for adult adjustment are poor.

3. The procedures for identification, assessment, and especially treatment remain embroiled in controversy. No proven diagnostic criteria exist for ADHD; there are no neurological or physiological indicators; and no physical tests exist to confirm its presence (or absence).

4. Faced with rambunctious, contrary, or unfocused children, some people leap to the conclusion that drugs can solve the problem. While drugs have become the standard treatment regimen, and an increasing number of children are being prescribed drugs for use at school, the use of psychotropic drugs to control behaviour and increase academic functioning remains a matter of concern and considerable controversy.

5. Many experts contend that by understanding and exploiting psychopharmacology, we can multiply the effects of intervention approaches for students with ADHD. A number of different medications have been used. The aim is to reduce hyperactive behaviour and increase attention skills with a spill over to improved academic functioning.

6. A set of intervention strategies has proved to be successful in helping students with ADHD to succeed in school. Strategies such as stimulant medication, behaviour therapy, or a combination of both are the most popular choices amongst professionals working with students with ADHD.

7. Cognitive behaviour management is a generic term that refers to the way in which students' beliefs impact their behaviour and perception of that behaviour. Strategies focus on teaching students self-control with emphasis on self management, self reinforcement, self instruction, and self monitoring. In total, the processes require students to stop, think about what they are doing, compare their work to a criterion, record the results of the comparison, and receive reinforcement for their behaviour if it meets the criterion.

HISTORICAL NOTES

The terms used to classify ADHD have gone through several changes over the years, although the symptoms of the disorder have not changed much over time. *Hyperactivity* was first described in 1845 by German physician Henrich Hoffman; the term Fidgety Phil is attributed to him. In the following years, hyperactivity became one of the most deeply investigated and controversial disorders within the fields of pediatric medicine, clinical psychology, and education.

In 1902, Dr. Richard Still presented a series of lectures to the Royal College of Physicians in England. Still described 20 children he had seen in his practice and characterized them as excessively emotional, defiant, aggressive, resistant to discipline, overtly active, and inattentive. On the other side of the Atlantic, an outbreak of encephalitis in North America from 1917 to 1918 left many children with "post-encephalitic disorder," characterized by impairments in attention, impulse control, and activity level, and with memory and social problems. An acknowledgement that brain pathology produced these behavioural outcomes was important in turning medical and psychological interest toward the brain as the likely site of such problems.

In the 1930s, in fact, children with the characteristics of ADHD were referred to as *brain injured* or *brain damaged*. Some teachers described *restlessness*, which was shown through squirming in the chair, playing with the pencil, tapping with the feet, and the like (Challman, 1939). In the 1950s, the term used was *minimal brain damage*, as professionals realized that many children who showed these behaviours had no history of brain trauma. In 1957, researchers described *hyperkinetic impulse disorder*. Further labels included *hyperactive child syndrome* and *learning* disability (see Winzer, 1997).

The first categorization of the ADD syndrome in DSM was called *hyperkinetic reaction of childhood* in DSM-II (APA, 1968). It was not until 1979 that a psychologist named Robert Spitzer gave us the phrase *attention deficit disorder* and created a list of specific symptoms to make the diagnosis in children (Sanghavi, 2005). The APA adopted the term *attention deficit disorder* in DSM-III in 1980. As well, DSM-III listed the behavioural symptoms of each feature separately and specified two primary subtypes based on the presence or absence of hyperactivity. With the new term, DSM-III changed the conceptualization of the disorder from one that was defined primarily as the presence of hyperactive-impulsive behaviours to one that reflected developmentally inappropriate levels of inattention, impulsivity, and hyperactivity.

Since 1980, every new version of DSM has presented a revision of the ADD/ADHD criteria. The term *Attention Deficit Disorder* appeared in DSM-III in 1982. In 1987, DSM-III-R used the term *Attention Deficit Hyperactivity Disorder.* The revised APA edition (APA, 1987) maintained the three features of inattention, impulsivity, and hyperactivity but listed three types of symptoms together in a composite syndrome called Attention Deficit Hyperactivity Disorder. Between 1987 and 1994, the research data necessary to document the existence of a subtype of attention deficit without hyperactivity emerged.

Many of the drugs used to treat ADHD have been around for decades; the treatment was available long before the disorder was clearly conceptualized (Conrad, 2004). The story begins with Charles Bradley, a Rhode Island psychiatrist, who in 1937 gave a stimulant drug, Benzedrine, to 30 children who were having various problems in school. Bradley noticed an overall improvement in the children's mood, activity level, and educational achievement. He noted that 14 of the children had a great increase in interest in school material (Bradley, 1937).

Ritalin was originally patented in 1950 by the CIBA Pharmaceutical Company and promoted as an amphetamine without the more undesirable side effects. Ritalin was approved by the FDA in 1955; in 1961 it was approved by the FDA for use with children. Since then, drug use has increased dramatically and synthetic compounds have rendered the effects of drugs more predictable. As examples, Samuels (2006) reported that 2.5 million children in the United States aged four to seventeen were receiving medication for ADHD in 2003. In 1998, an estimated 710 000 prescriptions were issued in Canada for stimulants (Chernos, 1999).

SECTION 4

Children Who Are Gifted, Creative, and Talented

After reading about the children and youth with disabilities in this text, you may think that educating students with gifts and talents is a facile process, easy for teachers, well-accepted in the educational community, and underlaid by enabling legislation and appropriate funding. Nothing could be further from the truth. It is a given that students who are gifted learn more, faster, and more thoroughly than their peers. It is not as well accepted that children with gifts and talents should be considered exceptional and provided special education services to develop their full potential.

In Chapter 2, we talked about the reform movement in general education in the early 1980s and its two major threads—equity and excellence. One impetus for reform was the U.S. publication of *A Nation at Risk* (National Commission,1983), which, among other things, gave the startling estimate that 50 percent of gifted students were failing and/or failing to achieve their potential.

It would be logical to assume that such a devastating appraisal would give a kick-start to gifted education. This did not happen. Among the myriad of reform initiatives, the one field that did not ultimately benefit was gifted education. Indeed, the years following 1983 witnessed a lessening of concern. "[T]he gifted field has been under virulent attack for almost two decades since its ascendancy in the 1960s and 1970s," wrote Pfeiffer in 2003 (p. 161). Gallagher (1998) described current gifted education as being in a state of "quiet crisis." This is the result of directing our special education programs, and the taxes that support them, largely into programs for students who are disabled. General education programs are designed to serve the needs of average children. But the gifted we leave to fend for themselves, even when this involves a waste of their potential.

Educators must recognize that gifted, creative, and talented students have special educational needs—they may learn in ways different from other students, they are more curious, and they think more abstractly. At the same time, students who are gifted are vulnerable to the same forces that affect other children and youth and can become frustrated and bored in unstimulating learning environments. Special education is necessary to enable these students to reach their full potential.

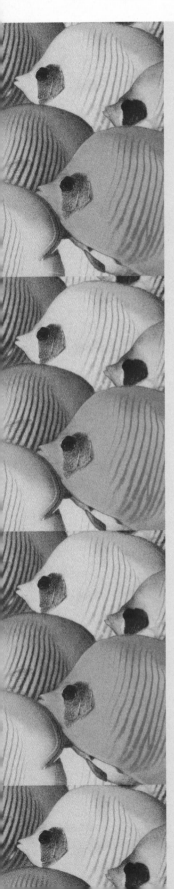

Learning Outcomes

After reading this section, you should be able to

People and Foundations

1. Understand the development of the field of education for gifted students and the contributions of Francis Galton and Lewis Terman.
2. Appreciate how Terman's longitudinal study defined the field for more than 50 years.

Issues

3. Be aware of the dichotomies that affect gifted education, particularly egalitarian schools versus individual programming, and inclusion versus specialization.
4. Understand the major placement options and how they impact on gifted learners.

Knowledge

5. Know the classifications within the field and the developmental consequences of giftedness.
6. Recognize the difficulties in identifying specific groups of gifted learners such as females and children who are both gifted and disabled.

Skills

7. Know the process of independent studies.

CHAPTER 9

CHILDREN WHO ARE GIFTED, CREATIVE, AND TALENTED

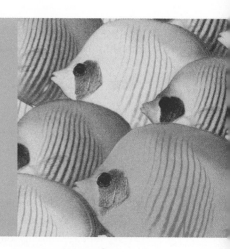

INTRODUCTION

Gifted is a somewhat abstract term applied to people who, by virtue of outstanding abilities, are capable of high performance (Clark, 1988). Gifted individuals have greater ability in some areas than most of us. Generally, we admire such people, but occasionally we are a little envious of their talents and achievements. We seem to have to work much harder than they do to achieve only mediocre results.

The variables that figure in the scenario of giftedness are complex and abstract in themselves and include talent, aptitude, creativity, personality, and motivation. Some individuals soar to great heights in the talent domain, others in intellectual ability, and still others in creative endeavours. A few individuals achieve remarkably high levels across several domains.

DEFINITIONS OF GIFTEDNESS

To be gifted is to be superior in some way to the average. But beyond this benign statement, no universally accepted definition of giftedness exists, and no set of traits adequately defines any gifted child. The uniqueness of each student with gifts and talents is shown in the Case Study box on page 280. William is compliant and helpful, Troy is resentful and outspoken, and Richard's other problems mask his potential.

This does not mean that the field of gifted education has not been on a constant search for a universally accepted definition of giftedness. It has. But the quest has been frustrating and has led to the "conceptual fuzziness in the field" (Gagné, 2005, p. 12).

Defining *giftedness* is a complicated and often controversial task and the definitions are continually debated and modified. The only definition with any consensus is that of Sidney Marland, proposed as far back as

CASE STUDY

William, Troy, and Richard

The Jones School is a kindergarten to grade 6 elementary school in a pleasant neighbourhood in Edmonton, Alberta. Alberta has policies and funding dealing with gifted students and the province's review of special education in 2000 identified the need for increasing attention to those who are gifted and talented.

In the three grade 5 classes at Jones School, there are three students considered to have gifts and talents. Each of these children is unique and each is posing different challenges to the school and the teachers.

William's giftedness was identified early and, as a result, he was accelerated and skipped grade 4. In the classroom, William reveals outstanding abilities in verbal tasks and abstract thinking, particularly shown in written classroom assignments. He is an "easy" child, good at games, and well accepted by his peers. He works far above the classroom norm but does not seem to resent the drill and practice that is part of the day.

In his first years in school, Troy was seen by most of the teachers as an almost perfect student. He always finished his work, performed at a high level, and was well behaved, compliant, polite, and helpful. Troy was identified during grade 2 as a gifted child. After that, each teacher attempted to put in place different types of enrichment activities for him. The fact that Troy was sometimes bored and a little frustrated was masked by his good behaviour and happy nature.

This situation changed once Troy entered grade 5. Mr. Jane, Troy's teacher, did "not believe in giftedness" and insisted that Troy do exactly the same work as everyone else. The teacher was surprised to then see mounting behavioural problems, acting-out behaviour, and poor peer relations, chiefly attributable to Troy's bossy and directive attitude. There was a concomitant significant drop in Troy's achievement, all compounded by his inability or unwillingness to comply with expected school behaviour in matters of dress and personal hygiene.

Troy frustrated and angered the teacher, especially when he contested the information being presented.

This happened so often that Mr. Jane finally referred Troy for special assistance as a student with a behavioural disorder. When Troy was reassessed, he was found to be well above the norm (Full Scale IQ 144). During the testing sessions, however, Troy was resentful and manipulative, and stated that he "did not appreciate having his brain examined." He eventually complied with the examiner's requests and finally confided that, "When I was five I was an optimist; at seven a pessimist. Now I'm a cynicist."

When another grade 5 teacher used a nomination scale, the results did not indicate gifted potential in Richard. However, the teacher was puzzled by the peaks and valleys in performance that emerged as she filled out the scale. Richard has excellent reasoning ability but difficulties in memorizing, paying attention, and following several directions at once. Solving oral math story problems is often easier for him than remembering multiplication facts. He frequently talks about complex ideas but writes slowly and illegibly. He seems to have difficulty in managing time and is slow in processing information.

Similar ups and downs in Richard's performance were pointed out by his parents. They agreed, for example, that Richard suffered serious lags in reading but judged him highly in his oral language abilities, his commitment to projects once started, and his interest in a range of hobbies and collections. Richard did not rate himself highly, but his peers did. In the peer nominations, they agreed overwhelmingly that Richard was the student who could think up unusual and interesting stories and games.

With such contradictory evidence, the teacher asked if the school psychologist could present Richard with an assessment. On the WISC-III he scored 142 on the Verbal Scale and 138 on the Performance Scale, for a Full Scale of 140. Achievement testing showed his reading to be at a grade 2 level, although his math was at about a grade 5 level.

1972, adopted by the United States Office of Education in 1977 and revised in 1981. It states that

> Gifted and talented children are those identified by professionally qualified persons who, by virtue of outstanding abilities, are capable of high performance. These are children who require differentiated education programs and/or services beyond those normally provided by the regular school program in order to realize their contribution to self and society (p. 2).

This definition manages to be inclusive, specific, and practical. It encompasses a wide range of gifts, talents, and creative aptitudes; stresses the necessity for special education provisions for students identified as gifted; and ties identification to the necessity for appropriate programming.

Nevertheless, the definition is not universally accepted and dozens of others exist. Many factors underlie the continuing definitional problems found in the field. First of all, there is no such thing as a typical child who is gifted; particular talents and social environments give rise to varying personality patterns. Some students who are gifted in language arts may have only an average aptitude in math; others who are mathematically gifted may not do well on tests of verbal abilities.

Although many different gifts and talents have been identified, and creativity can be, at least partly, explained and measured, gifted, talented, and creative individuals are typically lumped together as a single category. As well, the identification of signs of giftedness and of the potential for high-quality creative achievement remains a relatively inexact science. There is no consensus on how to measure superiority or how to recognize potential giftedness.

To add to the confusion, concepts and definitions of giftedness have changed over the past 100 years. When the roots of the field of gifted education were laid down by pioneers such as Francis Galton and Lewis Terman, high IQ was viewed as the critical dimension of giftedness. Children above the norm were the most deeply investigated, and early definitions tended to be narrow and restricted, relying on psychometric measures that limited giftedness to specific performance on an intelligence test. The focus was on "school-house giftedness," connoted by high test scores and good grades. This is discussed in the Historical Notes at the end of this chapter and in the Research Notes on Terman's studies on the next two pages.

Today, IQ-based definitions may be used but are generally joined with other concepts. Essentially, two quite different views about giftedness now exist. One looks at giftedness as potential; the other looks at it as the actual production of outstanding work.

The giftedness-as-potential view follows the traditional model. It often uses an IQ cutoff between 120 and 140 or restricts giftedness to a percentage of the population, ranging from the top 1 percent to the top 20 percent. Some school districts (for example, in Pennsylvania and the East York Board of Education in Ontario) make an IQ score of 130 the cut-off for a child to be identified as gifted (Mark, Beal, & Dumont, 1998).

The giftedness-as-product view dismisses the idea that IQ alone determines giftedness. Rather, the focus is on the attributes of identified individuals who are gifted and their potential value to society. In this view, giftedness becomes an individual's consistently outstanding achievements and remarkable performance and products in some socially useful area. Products, often tangible things such as art or literature, are the public face of giftedness (Cropley, 2006). They must be deemed socially acceptable and useful—some products can be unacceptable, eccentric, deviant, or downright criminal.

The notion of giftedness as a univariate construct, basically consisting of those traits that were measured by IQ tests, was established by a U.S. educator, Lewis Terman. In the early 1920s, Terman initiated the first full-scale longitudinal study of the nature of giftedness, which both legitimized the field and led to the serious inception of a gifted movement (see the Research Notes for more on the Terman studies).

RESEARCH NOTES

The Terman Studies

Lewis Terman, an American educator and psychologist, expanded the concepts and procedures related to IQ developed by Alfred Binet in France at the beginning of the 20th century. Terman believed the Binet scale assessed a wide range of performance and could be adapted for use with high-functioning children. In 1916, he published the Stanford-Binet Individual Intelligence Test in conjunction with Stanford University.

Terman held that intelligence was manifested essentially in the ability to acquire and manipulate concepts. He defined the gifted as those who scored in the top 1 percent of general intellectual ability as measured by the Stanford-Binet Scale or a comparable instrument (Terman, 1926). Terman carefully distinguished giftedness from talent and creativity. He viewed talent as the potential for unusual achievement, but only when combined with high IQ scores. Creativity, he believed, was a personality factor, and thus differed from both giftedness and talent.

In 1922, armed with the Stanford-Binet test and a single-measure concept of intelligence, Terman embarked on a massive study of giftedness among California schoolchildren. The study, which included 1528 children (856 males and 672 females) "was designed to discover what physical, mental, and personality traits are characteristic of gifted children as a class, and what sort of adult the typical gifted child becomes" (Terman & Oden, 1951, p. 21). To determine his population, Terman relied on teacher nominations and group intelligence tests. He then identified the gifted children from those scoring at or above 140 points on the Stanford-Binet Individual Intelligence Test.

Although Terman died in 1956, the study continued. Few "Terman kids" are alive today. Terman's findings shed light on giftedness across the age span. The longitudinal research found the following:

- Most students in the sample came from a middle or higher socio-economic group, with a low incidence of broken homes.
- Nearly half of the children could read before entering kindergarten.
- One in five children skipped part or all of grade 1.
- The children averaged 40 percent higher than their age-mates on achievement tests.
- They preferred abstract subjects, such as literary debate and ancient history, and were less interested in such practical concerns as penmanship and manual training.
- They read more and better books, made numerous collections, and had many hobbies.
- On average, the children finished school 14 percent faster than normal students.
- When retested as adults, they were found to have retained their intellectual superiority.
- As adults, they were ahead in terms of occupational status, income, publications, and patents. They earned more money, had more managerial jobs, and made more literary and scientific contributions than the average adult. When checked in 1959, Terman's group had published over

2000 scientific papers and 33 novels and taken out 230 patents (Sprinthall & Sprinthall, 1990).

- Middle-aged people in Terman's sample maintained their superior physical characteristics. They were far above their age-mates in general health, physique, mental health, and emotional adjustment. Fewer than 5 percent of Terman's population were rated as seriously maladjusted, and the incidence of problems such as ill health, psychiatric disturbance, alcoholism, and delinquent behaviour was but a fraction of that normally observed in the general population.

- Although reaching college age just before the Great Depression, when college attendance was not common for women, over 67 percent of the Terman women earned at least a bachelor's degree. One-quarter of the 672 women attended graduate school.

- The female sample contained more childless women than normative samples of similar ages and as a group had relatively higher incomes and levels of employment than women of comparable ages (Holahan, 1991).

Giftedness as product is epitomized in the work of Joseph Renzulli, who holds that, in the end, giftedness is determined by the contributions an individual makes to humanity. Children who are gifted and talented, said Renzulli (1978), "are those possessing or capable of developing this composite of traits and applying them to any potentially valuable area of human performance" (p. 261). Renzulli reached these conclusions after studying adults known to be gifted. He found that the mechanics of success were much more baffling than a simple linear relationship between intelligence and achievement.

Renzulli deduced that three characteristics were required for remarkable achievement: high intellectual ability, high creativity, and the ability to carry tasks through to completion. The interaction is shown in Figure 9-1 on the next page. It is not enough to possess only one of these traits; as the figure shows, it is only where the circles intersect and the three traits come together that, according to Renzulli, true giftedness is found (Renzulli & Reis, 1991).

CLASSIFICATION OF GIFTEDNESS

The classification systems found in the field of giftedness are quite different from those in areas such as intellectual ability. Severity levels would not make much sense. We could perhaps call a person *mildly* or *moderately* gifted, but not *severely* or *profoundly* gifted. Any classification, therefore, revolves around the varied components that contribute to giftedness.

The correct terms to use in the field are actually *gifted*, *creative*, and *talented*. Other terms crop up, the most common being *precocious* and *genius*. The word *precocious* comes from the Latin *preacox*, meaning to precook or to boil beforehand. Because **precocity** refers to remarkable early development, the term is applied to young gifted children. Many children who are highly gifted show precocity in particular areas of development such as language, music, or mathematical ability. The fields that have produced the most prodigies are music and chess (Feldman, 1993). *Genius* was the original term used to indicate a particular aptitude or capacity. Today, we reserve the word for those persons who demonstrate extremely rare (superior) intellectual powers.

precocity

Figure 9-1
Interaction of Renzulli's characteristics

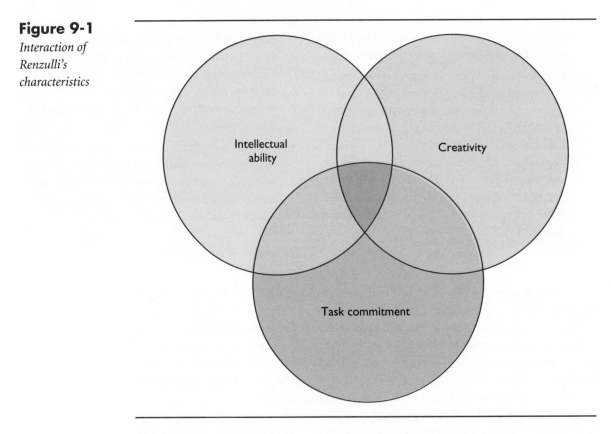

The terms *gifted*, *talented*, and *creative* are frequently used together; just as often, they are used interchangeably. Leadership, although sometimes critical in outstanding performance, is a neglected area. We discuss these terms below.

Giftedness

As a term, *gifted* is most often used to refer to students with above-average academic endowment, sometimes called "school-house giftedness." This happens because, educationally speaking, the most important components of giftedness are those defined relative to the school in which an individual finds himself or herself.

academic ability

academically endowed students

Academic ability refers to intellectual ability measured by performance on IQ tests and other standardized tests of academic achievement. **Academically endowed students** are generally considered to be those scoring at the 95th percentile or higher on these measures. Note that many researchers are critical of the concept of school-house giftedness because it is only weakly associated with adult eminence or creative contributions (Siegler & Kotovsky, 1985; Sternberg, 1987).

Creativity

During the 1960s, definitions of *giftedness* began to include components of creativity. Today, *creativity* is a popular but heterogeneous word in educational parlance. The problem lies in actually defining *creativity*. As Barbara Clark (1988) observed, "creativity is a very special condition, attitude, or state of being that nearly defies description" (p. 46).

Paul Torrance (1966), a pioneer in the study of creativity, defines it as the process of sensing problems or gaps in information, forming ideas or hypotheses about such gaps, and communicating the results. Others note that creativity may be seen as the "activities and products invented in the interest of solving a problem" (Cole & Sarnoff, 1980, p. 6). Howard Gardner (1983) pursues a similar route and sees a creative person as one "who regularly solves problems, fashions products, or defines new questions in a domain in a way that is initially considered novel but that ultimately becomes accepted" (p. 35). Or creativity can be seen as the ability to produce work that is novel, high in quality, and appropriate (Sternberg & Lubart, 1999).

The components of creativity are perhaps less elusive than an exact definition. Torrance elaborated on four characteristics: fluency of ideas, or producing a number of responses to a given stimulus; flexibility, or shifts in thinking from one category to another; originality, or unusual and clever responses; and elaboration, or the addition of details to basic ideas or thoughts (Torrance, 1969).

Later researchers have followed Torrance's lead and see several dispositions working together to foster creativity: curiosity, flexibility, insightfulness, optimism, and the ability to blend divergent and convergent thinking. Divergent thinking is the type of thinking in which considerable searching is done and a number of answers are produced. It seems to be only a component of creativity, however, as divergent thinking in childhood is not highly correlated with creative abilities in adulthood (Feldhusen & Clinkenbeard, 1987). Divergent thinking is in some ways the opposite of convergent thinking, which focuses on one right answer, or toward a relatively determined answer. This relationship is diagrammed in Figure 9-2.

The link between intelligence and creativity is difficult to pinpoint. Above a threshold score of about 120 IQ, the correlation between giftedness and creativity disappears. Nevertheless, June Maker (1993) postulated that creativity and intelligence are two components of the same construct because the key element in giftedness is the ability to solve complex problems in the "most efficient, effective, or economical ways" (p. 71).

Other research (Sternberg & Lubart, 1995) suggests that creativity uses three kinds of intelligence. *Synthetic intelligence* allows a creative person to see a problem in a new way.

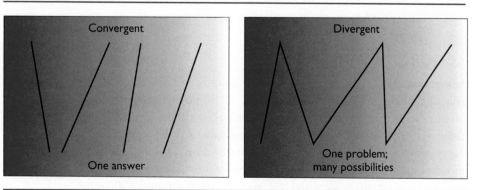

Convergent — One answer

Divergent — One problem; many possibilities

Figure 9-2

Convergent and divergent thinking

Analytic intelligence helps an individual to recognize which new ideas are productive and allocate resources to solve the problem. In using *practical intelligence*, a creative person promotes an idea by using feedback from others.

Creativity may very well be an innate trait that can be stimulated or quashed. Creativity tends to occur in spurts and seems to generally decrease as children get older. Early research (Bernard, 1973) noted that during the first three years of school, most children's creativity increases, perhaps because teachers in these grades allow much freedom of expression. After grade 3, a sharp drop in creativity occurs, followed by a gradual decrease during the remaining elementary and middle-school years

Talent

talent

If giftedness is above-average competence, then **talent** is above-average performance. Talent refers to a specific dimension of a skill in areas such as music, visual arts, drama, athletics, and particular academic domains. Canadian psychologist Francoys Gagné calls talent "the developmental product of an interaction between aptitudes and intrapersonal and environmental catalysts" (1991, p. 66).

Some children have unusual talents in one field and limited abilities in other areas. However, talented children begin to nurture their special traits early, and are often encouraged by their parents and extensively tutored or coached by experts. But there seems to be more to talent than that. Some of us may practise our pitches and putts forever but will never play with Tiger Woods. Why? It seems that certain aptitudes make it easier to learn certain skills, and genetic factors may influence one's abilities in a particular area (Gagné, 1991). As well, the direction of an individual's talent depends on many factors such as experience, motivation, interest, emotional stability, hero worship, parental urging, and even chance (see Gagne & Schader, 2006).

Three phases occur in talent development. First, there is playful exploration, which entices the learner into further involvement. Then there is acquisition of skills and attention to detail, with rigorous practice. Finally, a commitment to excellence is made (Bloom, 1985).

Just as the link between creativity and giftedness is complex and confusing, so research has also not yet shown the relationship of talent to giftedness. When Gagné (1985) presented one of the first major attempts to delineate talent as distinct from giftedness, he suggested that talent is an ability focus that emerges out of general ability. Therefore, giftedness is a prerequisite for talent, but an individual who is gifted is not necessarily talented.

Leadership

leadership

Leadership is defined as the ability to effect positive and productive changes that are self-enhancing or group-enhancing. Sternberg (2005) points out that leaders have wisdom, intelligence, creativity, and synthesis, which allows them to make judgments that are creative, intelligent, and wise. Children who display early leadership qualities will interact easily with a variety of people; be sought out by others; possess confidence; establish the mood of the group; be sensitive to the feelings of others; show others how to improve on a task; and generate many ideas and solutions (Karnes & Strong, 1978).

PREVALENCE OF GIFTEDNESS

The lack of a universally accepted definition of giftedness makes it very difficult to estimate its prevalence in the population at large and in children and youth. However, we can reasonably assume that only a small percentage of the population will show the traits of giftedness, creativity, and talent. Overall, giftedness is estimated to occur in 2 to 5 percent of school-aged children.

To differentiate the heterogeneous population of persons who are gifted, new terms have emerged. Writers speak of *modestly gifted*, *highly gifted*, and *superior*, with arbitrary thresholds of IQ of 130, 150, and 180. Most of the individuals in this heterogenous population are modestly gifted. Highly gifted persons are "those whose advancement is significantly beyond the norm of the gifted" (Silverman, 1989, p. 71); their numbers are probably 1 in 10 000 of the entire gifted population. Only a few rare individuals are superior, with IQs beyond 180; they are perhaps less than 1 percent of the gifted population (1 in 50 000 or fewer).

FACTORS CONTRIBUTING TO GIFTEDNESS

Just as levels of severity as used in concepts of disability are not relevant to giftedness, neither is the notion of etiology. However, we can discuss the factors that appear to contribute to giftedness. But keep in mind that we do not yet understand what contributes most, or why some gifted people achieve eminence and others fade into obscurity. The multiplicity of factors that bring a Tiger Woods or a Margaret Atwood to prominence have not yet been untangled and identified.

The effects of heredity and environment are both important in the development of children who are gifted and talented, but the relative contribution of the various factors is not clearly understood. Genes carry potential for various characteristics from parent to child down through the generations, but the genes alone cannot produce a human being.

The relative contribution of genetic and environmental factors with respect to giftedness is not clearly understood

Each of us is born into a unique environment in which conditions act and react with one another. The individual human being is the total expression of all these complex and constantly interacting forces.

Ever since the time of Plato and Aristotle, the pendulum has swung between nature and nurture conceptions of human growth and learning. In today's egalitarian society, the proposition that intelligence and abilities are inherited is not popular. Yet behavioural genetics makes it abundantly clear that there is a significant role played by genetic transmission in the development of intelligence. There is also no doubt that some of us have more inborn capabilities in music or visual perception or linguistic ability than others (Plomin, 1989).

This, of course, does not in any way deny the great influence of environment on cognitive development. Genetic factors are undoubtedly influential, but the unique development of gifted traits can occur only through specific interactions within family units and later with appropriate training and education.

The importance of nurturing is clearly evidenced by the many deprivation studies that have demonstrated the negative effects of malnutrition and lack of stimulation on infant functioning. The high proportion of first-borns among the gifted population further suggests the importance of environment to the full development of intellectual potential. Unlike younger siblings, first-borns receive much attention and stimulation from their parents, even if only for a short time.

No race, ethnic group, or culture holds a monopoly on giftedness. Yet the statistical probability of giftedness increases when a child's parents have higher than average intelligence and provide a better-than-average home environment. Other factors in the environment that seem most clearly to affect the development of giftedness are the values and expectations of the culture; the socio-economic level of the family with accompanying nutritional and other health variables, attitudes, and values; the number of children in the family; and the presence of environmental stimulation.

Using the family as a starting point, many investigators have attempted to unravel the specific family variables associated with gifted-level abilities in children. What they find are many favourable qualities in these families, particularly parental interest in child-rearing and a strong commitment to the development of the child's talents and abilities. When Benjamin Bloom and his colleagues (Bloom, 1985; Bloom & Sosniak, 1981) examined the home environments and the early training of exceptional people in the arts, in athletics, and in cognitive skill areas, they found that the home environment and the person's parents were almost entirely responsible for nurturing the child's early interests and the development of his or her skills.

Highly educated parents are more likely to produce children who are gifted and to provide them with enriching environments. On the Stanford-Binet Individual Intelligence Test, the average score for children of college graduates is more than 10 points above the mean, whereas for children of parents with less than high school education it is about 6 points below (Kaplan & Saccuzzo, 1993). In a Canadian study of gifted kindergarten children, Barbara Perks (1984) found that 59.5 percent of their fathers and 50 percent of their mothers had post-secondary education. This compared to 30.9 percent of fathers and 27 percent of mothers for non-gifted children. Perks compared the reading material available in the children's homes and found that 61.9 percent of the families of children who were gifted had more than 300 books, as compared to 18.4 percent of families of non-gifted children.

Certainly, bright children can also come from lower socio-economic homes, but not as often as we would expect. Intervening factors may include lack of motivation, family expectations, neighbourhood aspirations, and financial pressures.

DEVELOPMENTAL CONSEQUENCES OF GIFTEDNESS

Like every population, individuals who are gifted form a heterogeneous group. Differences run the gamut of possibilities; among persons who are gifted will be found the active, the lethargic, the healthy, the infirm, the high achievers, the low achievers, the painstakingly patient, and the lightning quick. The single thing that children who are gifted have in common is "the ability to absorb abstract concepts, to organize them more effectively, and to apply them more appropriately than the average youngster" (Gallagher, 1975, p. 19).

Table 9-1 outlines some of the common characteristics of students who are gifted, talented, and creative and joins them to possible classroom implications. View this list with caution; probably no child displays all of these traits. Rather, each child possesses a unique subset of descriptors that come from, but do not include, all the behaviours of the larger set. As well, classroom behaviour is as individual as the child and these are only broad possibilities.

Table 9-1 Some common characteristics of children who are gifted, creative, and talented

Characteristics	What you might see in the classroom
Wide range of ability	Learn easily and quickly
	Ability to synthesize large amounts of diverse information
	High academic achievement
	Rapid movement through basic skills and concepts in traditional areas
	Use learning strategies efficiently
	Superior reading ability
Verbal fluency	Convey ideas effectively
	Large vocabulary; use metaphors and abstract ideas
	Enjoy debating issues
	Boredom with recitation and memorization of facts
	Ask many questions which may be controversial, embarrassing, or advanced
	Challenge the teacher and the textbook

Table 9-1 continued

Work independently	Little or no need for adult monitoring
	Pleasure in working alone
High motivation	Stick to a topic to completion
	Become absorbed in self-selected tasks
	Refusal to change tasks when requested by a teacher
Creative	Good problem-solving ability
	Unexpected answers
	Unusual ways of solving problems; work that is off the beaten track.
	Willing to redefine problems and able to do so
Insatiable curiosity	Inquisitive about the world; committed to finding out what happens if something is done, as in a science experiment
Organizational and planning skills	Assume and discharge responsibility
	Decision-making capabilities and leadership qualities
Strong belief in personal abilities	May have too high expectations that are not always realistic
Multiple interests	Avid collectors and hobbyists
	Join many clubs
Appreciate social values	Advanced ethical thinking
	Interested in political and social issues
	Attempt to organize people and things; young children may invent complex games and organize their playmates
Often a keen sense of humour	Reputation for wild and silly ideas

Physical Development

Throughout history, there has been a persistent stereotype of the individual who is gifted as an "egghead"—physically weak, homely, socially inept, narrow in interests, and prone to emotional instability. Such stereotypes were shattered by Lewis Terman, who found that, as a group, individuals who are gifted exhibit superior physical traits. The children in Terman's study were larger at birth, walked sooner, went through puberty earlier, had fewer diseases and operations, and reported less nervousness than average persons (Terman & Oden, 1959).

Although children who are gifted may physically outstrip their age-mates later on, their superiority is seldom detectable at birth or even during their first year. Nor do children who are gifted show advanced motor skills as a general trait. Teachers are very likely to find young children who can read far above level yet are unable to write their own names legibly. This gap in development is referred to as *dyssynchrony*.

Academic Development

Three general characteristics seem typical of the learning behaviour of students who are gifted: an internal locus of control, independence, and self-motivation. In regard to the latter, one of the most ubiquitous traits of both productive students and eminent adults is high motivation and persistence.

Students who are gifted like learning, enjoy difficult subjects, and are willing to spend extra time on projects that stimulate their interest. They learn more, faster, and more easily than their age-mates. They also learn to read sooner and continue to read at a consistently more advanced level. Children at this level of functioning are also more adept at critically evaluating facts and arguments. Because they more readily recognize relationships and comprehend meanings, they can reason out problems more effectively.

All these factors place children who are gifted far ahead in academic achievement. They can master the curriculum content of a grade two or three times faster than the average child. One study of curriculum compacting (Reis & Purcell, 1992) found that gifted students had already mastered from 25 to 75 percent of the math and language arts curriculum before it was taught. Put another way, in September, many of these youngsters could take the provincial assessments that students take toward the end of the year and still score above the 95th percentile (Winebrenner, 2000). In elementary mathematics, a good general rule for students who are gifted is that two years of standard content can be covered in one year (Van Tassel-Baska, Landau, & Olszewski, 1985). All of this places gifted students so far ahead that many of them spend 25 to 50 percent of class time waiting for other students to catch up (Smith, 2003).

Social and Emotional Development

One common and persistent myth regarding individuals with gifts, especially those in the arts, is that they are prone to mental disease. The question of whether individuals who are gifted are more emotionally stable, self-sufficient, and less prone to neurotic and psychotic disorders than average people has been the subject of research. However, little is yet available that addresses the characteristics, identification, and needs of gifted students with emotional or behavioural disorders (Bianco, 2005).

The consensus seems to be that persons who are gifted are at least as well, if not better, adjusted than their peers (see Neihart, 1999). Good adjustment relates more to students who are modestly gifted; those who are extremely precocious may be at greater risk for social problems. Students with very high IQs are less popular and have more difficulty with peer relations than their age-mates. Possibly, their unusually high intelligence makes it difficult for their peers to relate to them intellectually or socially. Dauber and Benbow (1990) discovered that extremely gifted students viewed themselves as more introverted, less socially adept, and more inhibited. These adolescents also reported that their peers saw them as much less popular, less socially active, less athletic, and less active in the crowd.

Modestly gifted children tend to be well liked by their peers, although popularity may taper off in secondary school settings. Sometimes adolescents alienate peers simply by the discrepancy between them or by their eagerness to demonstrate their unusual talents. Tannenbaum (1962) reported that bright students most favoured by peers were intelligent, athletic, and non-studious. The least-favoured gifted students were intelligent, studious, and non-athletic. In the Tannenbaum studies, boys rated more highly than girls. A later study (Cramond & Martin, 1987) of teachers and preservice teachers found much the same. Respondents valued not academic brilliance but athleticism as a critical determinant in a person's likeability. Again, males were rated more highly than females.

Behaviour

Like other children, students who are gifted are not always well behaved. They may interrupt others; fail to listen; be argumentative; refuse to comply with requests they view as trivial; be excessively critical, teasing, or bossy; or display a high energy level that results in perpetual motion and disorganized work habits. Perfectionism is a common trait (Parker, 1997). Students are often too critical of others and of themselves and need help in accepting failure.

Nevertheless, it is a bit of a myth that gifted children become behavioural problems when they are not challenged. Some may, but in general the research has not found significant differences in the attitudes of gifted and non-gifted students toward school. Indeed, it has found gifted achievers to be notably lacking in rebelliousness.

Even though they may not rebel, students who are gifted are often impatient with the routines in a regular classroom. Chalk and talk, endless drill and practice, and repetition, along with a concomitant lack of stimulation and challenge, can bore and frustrate advanced learners. In fact, children who are gifted and talented complain a great deal about the boredom of their classroom experiences. They say they are forced to spend a lot of time being taught things they already know, doing repetitive drill sheets and activities, and receiving instruction on new material at too slow a pace (Feldhusen, 1989).

Creativity leads to a set of personality traits characterized by a strong self-concept that gives little credence to outside academic and social sanctions. Creative children tend to have high independence and be less conforming than their peers. This is especially true of boys. In junior high school classrooms, creative boys are eight times as likely to quarrel with the opinions of peers and teachers as creative girls.

Ethical Development

Students who are gifted develop steadfast values quite early, with strong concerns for right and wrong. Students have issue awareness—they wrestle with problems that we often associate with adults. When Derevensky and Coleman (1989) asked 70 children aged seven to thirteen in a Toronto school for the gifted, "What are the things to be afraid of?" the students mentioned fears generally expressed by chronologically older students, such as death and nuclear war. Nicholas Colangelo (1989) asked 125 gifted children to define problems that were important to them. More than 50 percent chose typical teenage dilemmas of friendships and love relationships. However, they also identified 36 issues dealing with more adult themes, such as public welfare and life and death scenarios. Ontario researchers (Edmunds & Edmunds, 2005) also note that the existence of a sensitivity factor among gifted individuals is widely accepted, although this does not necessarily translate to people skills.

Family Variables

Gifted children are advantaged in many ways, but they may cause disruption within the family. For one thing, the advent of a child who is gifted can alter normal parental roles. Ross (1979) hypothesized that the degree of a gifted child's impact on traditional family roles is directly related to the degree of discrepancy between the child's intellectual capacity and that of other family members. Parents sometimes have difficulty clarifying the differences between parent and child roles: they wonder whether they should treat their offspring as a child or as an adult.

For another, parents may treat the child differently. The family of a gifted child may wish to make special adaptations that can include costly and time-consuming measures, such as special schools and extra equipment. When special adaptations are made for one child, siblings may resent the extra money and attention spent by their parents, leading to sibling competition and jealousy.

Cultural and Linguistic Differences

Two of the most troubling issues in special education are the persistent over-representation of minority and economically disadvantaged populations in special education and their under-representation in programming for gifted students. Many students who are non-white, non–middle class, or from language minority groups are not identified and taught as gifted learners.

A major reason accounting for under-representation is an implicit demand that children always manifest giftedness in the same way—equating with the majority culture's definitions of giftedness. The demand is not reasonable; children from other cultures are shaped by different value systems. Certain traits that define giftedness in the dominant culture may not even have the chance to appear because culturally different children show different interests and attitudes.

For example, definitions of giftedness in a First Nations context are quite different from those commonly used by psychologists and educators who primarily function in the institutions of dominant society (Friesen, 1997). What is clever and creative for the child on a reserve, where different value systems are in operation, will not be the same as for the child growing up in a suburb. White, middle-class gifted children tend to display a high level of verbal ability; in contrast, Native children raised on reserves are normally very quiet, and verbal precocity would not be an indicator for Native gifted children. But knowing about spirituality—the sacred traditional ways—is a manifestation of giftedness (Friesen, 1997).

ASSESSMENT OF GIFTEDNESS, CREATIVITY, AND TALENT

At first glance, the identification of gifted and talented children and youth may seem to be a relatively simple task. Nothing could be further from the truth. From the outset, one of the major concerns in gifted education has been the problem of identification and its measurement correlates. Even today there is much confusion, and the issue of identification and assessment remains highly problematic. So much so that Borland (1989) suggested that the process of selecting students and placing them in appropriate programs is the most difficult, controversial, and thankless of all the tasks involved in developing and implementing programs for the gifted.

It makes sense that much of the success of programs for students who are gifted is contingent upon sound identification procedures. But an ideal identification system has not been developed: identification of signs of giftedness and of potential for high-quality creative achievement "remains a relatively inexact science" (Feldhusen, 1989, p. 8). Multiple reasons account for the difficulties. For example,

- There is a wide range of areas that need to be assessed. Outstanding ability comes in a number of different forms and requires a variety of ongoing identification procedures. Yet no single adequate identification procedure or combination of procedures exists that addresses all important areas and therefore effectively taps a high proportion of students who are gifted.

- All forms of identification systems are less than perfect. The younger the child, the less confidence can be placed in the reliability and validity of the measures. So when the term *gifted* is used to describe young children, it essentially applies to potential rather than accomplishment and is making guesses about the future with limited information.

- The selection of students for gifted programs should be a recurring activity, not a one-shot affair. Both IQ and interests can change and specific abilities can emerge. The correlation of the IQ of a child at age six or seven with the same person's IQ at age seventeen is approximately +0.7 (Bloom, 1964).

Earlier in this chapter, we discussed how Lewis Terman conducted an important longitudinal study into giftedness. Many of Terman's findings remain remarkably relevant; so far, his study is unsurpassed in the field of giftedness. The one area that has been disputed and altered is Terman's establishment of IQ tests as the sole measure of giftedness. Contemporary researchers are finding evidence of multiple intelligences rather than a single general intelligence. J. P. Guilford (1988) and Howard Gardner (1983) are the modern proponents of the concept of multiple cognitive abilities.

MULTIPLE INTELLIGENCES

Psychologist J. P. Guilford of the University of Southern California was one of the first to propose a multidimensional theory of intelligence. Guilford's Structure of Intellect analyzes intelligence in terms of its specific skills and divides intellectual performance into three dimensions: operations, contents, and products. Each of these dimensions encompasses several abilities. *Operations* stresses the methods people use to process information; *contents* has to do with what people are thinking about and how a learner classifies processed information; and *products* refers to the forms and structures used to organize information.

Guilford's novel and distinctive approach was widely influential within the psychological field. It prompted researchers to reconsider intelligence as a diverse range of intellectual and creative abilities. Within gifted education, Guilford was the impetus behind creativity research. He inspired interest in the characteristics of creative thought processes, in tests of creativity, and in other psychometric measures based on the 120 factors of the Structure of Intellect.

Howard Gardner (1983) proposed an alternate theory of multiple intelligence that departed from Guilford's more traditional psychometric approach. In essence, Gardner holds that many forms of thinking are prominent both inside and outside of school. He sees intelligence as involving the use of problem-solving skills that enable people to resolve genuine problems, create effective products, and find or create new problems. Both the problems and the products must be relevant to the particular cultural context. That is, individuals develop competence in different domains that are independent of each other, and society plays a role in shaping and defining the competencies through its value system.

Gardner originally postulated that the capabilities that people develop fall into seven areas: linguistic, logical-mathematical, spatial, bodily, kinesthetic, musical, and interpersonal-intrapersonal. Gardner later (1997) added one-and-a-half intelligences to the seven previously identified. He called the eighth *naturalistic intelligence* (sensitivity to the ecological environment), and the half intelligence (which he was not certain consisted of a full-blown intelligence by itself) he labelled the *moralistic-existential* (sensitivity to ethical concerns) (Sarouphen, 1999). These are shown in Figure 9-3 on the next page. Gardner holds that each is a separate intelligence, not just another separate ability. They use different symbols (such as words or numbers) and originate from distinctive portions of the brain.

Most people are not gifted or even highly competent in all areas. However, Gardner holds that children evidence strengths in many domains of development that have not been traditionally identified with intelligence, such as art, music, and movement. In his view, humans do not have a single fixed intelligence and, if a child's intellectual profile is identified at an early age, it should be possible to channel specific talents in ways that enhance his or her educational opportunities. Gardner believes that the development of high-level competence requires innate capacity, motivation, and opportunity. Environment, cultural context, and language may also influence all of these important factors.

Research on multiple intelligences is not without its critics. Some sceptics, for example, hold that to claim music is a type of intelligence implies that other skills should be added, such as chess intelligence, political intelligence, and so on. Others believe that Gardner's ideas offer much for the classroom. Hence, like Guilford before him, Gardner has had an impact on the education of students who are gifted. Today, those involved in the identification and assessment of children who are gifted are strongly persuaded to look not only for children with high IQs but also for those who are gifted in other dimensions as well.

Assessment Measures

Recently, the process of identifying learners with gifts and talents has become very diversified. When educators define giftedness in terms of potential, they use identification procedures that emphasize IQ tests and other predictive measures such as academic achievement, creative products, and critical thinking. When giftedness is seen as current achievements, identification procedures stress observations and nominations, performance in academic subjects, performance assessment, or a review of a portfolio.

There is little evidence to indicate that any one identification procedure is better than another. For example, when researchers (Shore & Tsiamis, 1986) compared two groups of children either on the basis of traditional measures of achievement or on that of parent and

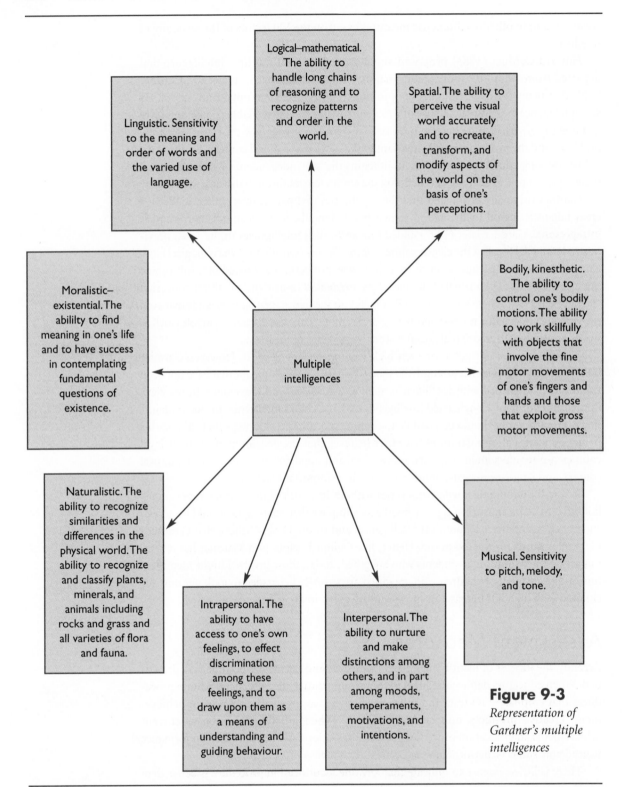

Figure 9-3

Representation of Gardner's multiple intelligences

Sources: Gardner, 1983; Gardner & Hatch, 1989.

teacher identification, they found that the groups were not distinguishable and concluded that formal selection by testing was not necessary for a substantial number of students who are gifted.

We discuss some of the most commonly used measures below.

Tests of Mental Ability

In many ways, individual IQ tests appear to be the best single method for identifying children who have superior cognitive abilities. The tests possess high validity as predictors of success in academic settings, and their scores are relatively stable over time. Assuming that motivation remains constant, these tests can reveal not only a child's present abilities, but also those that will develop in the future. IQ tests can also identify those children who are gifted but still underachieving. Finally, IQ tests for identification are a legal requirement in some areas. The Stanford-Binet Individual Intelligence Test and the Wechsler Intelligence Scale for Children (WISC-R, WISC-III, or WISC-IV) are the most commonly used measures.

Often, a shortened measure of an IQ test is highly desirable. There are two types of shortened intelligence tests—those created independently and marketed as short tests and those that exist as short forms of already well-established, more involved IQ scales such as the Wechsler Abbreviated Scale of Intelligence (WASI) (Wechsler, 1999). Mark, Beal, and Dumont (1988) recommend a short form of the WISC-III because an "unusually high performance on a number of subtests would indicate, with a high degree of predictability, that a score well within the gifted range could be expected" (p. 2).

Keep in mind that the tests are not a panacea; a number of problems exist. Intelligence quotient measures may reflect a racial or socio-economic bias and reinforce existing inequalities in selection of children for special programs. As well, giftedness seems to be characterized by qualitative differences in thinking and insightfulness, which may not be clearly reflected by performance or intelligence tests (Reis, 1989). The tests may fail to measure some traits, behaviours, and potentials that are significant indicators of giftedness and thereby fail to identify some of our most promising and potentially capable students.

Also, be aware that some schools begin by screening students with standardized group intelligence tests. However, all currently available group intelligence tests have a high prevalence of under-identification and over-identification of exceptional children, particularly with reference to creative divergent thinkers, very young children, and lower socio-economic and minority groups.

Achievement Tests

Achievement tests can be employed systematically to identify children with gifts and talents who are already achieving at a high level academically. These tests have been used very successfully to identify school children who are performing extremely well in specific fields, such as mathematics.

Portfolios

A **portfolio** is a type of performance test made up of continual collections of a student's   **portfolio**
work. As joint projects between teacher and child, portfolios include information selected

by the student under the guidance of the teacher, as well as a series of statements that reflect a student's thoughts about the contents. The portfolio will include work samples and projects, and may include the results of tests.

Used as authentic assessment measures in both general and special education, portfolios are highly popular—and becoming more so. Portfolios serve to examine the learning process as well as the outcomes of learning; they stress products rather than tests and test scores; and their use is appealing because of their instructional relevance. As such, portfolios may be a better predictor of future student achievement than most instruments (Johnsen, Ryser, & Dougherty, 1993). Although suitable for all learners, portfolio assessment is emerging as a promising measure in the assessment of learners who are gifted.

rubric

Portfolios are messy and labour intensive. Teachers have to struggle to make sense of patterns of growth shown in a collection of work. To assist in evaluation, the teacher may prepare a **rubric**—a generic scoring tool used to evaluate the quality of products and performance in a given area. Rubrics consist of a fixed measuring scale (such as a four-point scale) and a list of criteria that describe the characteristics for each score point.

Observation

Especially for young children, observation is a potent method to identify those who are potentially gifted. A three-year-old may be observed to tackle mathematical problems that are taught in grade 3; a four-year-old may be able to read at a high-school level. High verbal ability with early and extensive vocabulary development is a good indicator of IQ. A child may say first words at seven months; an eighteen-month-old may use language like most children at thirty months; older children ask many questions and have good memories.

Many children with advanced vocabularies have an intense interest in books. They learn to read relatively early and easily and carry out the task fluently. One-half to three-quarters of verbally talented children are reading by the age of five (Piirto, 1994). (Parenthetically, very advanced reading in the early grades does not guarantee that students will still be outstanding years later [Mills & Jackson, 1990].)

Parents and teachers should not expect very young children to be gifted in everything. Especially in preschool children who are potentially gifted, we see the dyssynchrony mentioned earlier. The uneven development applies particularly to motor skills. Certain children learn their letters from some combination of teaching by parents, older siblings, and preschool teachers and try to write early. But even if children know the letters, they probably do not possess the fine motor skills to form them well.

Teacher Nomination

A body of research suggests that teachers are highly accurate "tests," meaning that they are accurate when they select students who are of low achievement, low intelligence, at risk, or will need special education support services (Gresham, Lane, & Lambros, 2000; Lane, 2003). The paradox is that, accurate as teachers are in identifying students with potential problems, they are not very good at all in pinpointing gifted learners. One early study (Renzulli, 1979) found that teachers were only 50 percent successful when requested to identify those students whom they considered to be gifted and talented. Others (Haywood Gear, 1976; Perks, 1984) discovered effectiveness rates of between 10 and 57 percent, with effectiveness measured as the number of pupils correctly identified as gifted.

Yet teacher nomination has traditionally been, and remains today, a major method in the identification of students who may be gifted, talented, and creative. Even though teacher nominations are suspect, they are still used as an inexpensive screening method.

Why are teachers, who know their students well, so poor at identification procedures? Teachers may look for the wrong things. Some tend to choose one sex over the other; others pick conformist high achievers and overlook creative or divergent thinkers. Or teachers may simply not understand giftedness. One study found that 61 percent of public school teachers and 54 percent of private school elementary teachers reported that they had never had any training in teaching students who are gifted (see Reis & Westberg, 1994).

Teacher accuracy is increased by up to 40 percent with the implementation of training programs, questionnaires, and rating scales. (Perks, 1984; Reis & Westberg, 1994). Rating scales are particularly helpful in objectifying teacher judgement because they identify children on the basis of clearly defined characteristics such as learning, motivation, creativity, leadership, communication, and the arts.

Parent Nomination

Parent nomination questionnaires are another economical means of identifying children who are gifted and talented. Parents see their children make up games and stories, invent and build things, solve problems, and create all sorts of products. From these observations, parents may identify high performance. One study (Louis & Lewis, 1992) found that parents' implicit beliefs about their children's ability levels closely related to the children's actual tested IQ. Parents were especially accurate in their assessment of creative thinking, abstract thinking, and memory abilities. In another survey in the United States of 1039 parents of gifted children, 70 percent of the children were identified accurately by age three. Of all the characteristics that caused parents to suspect giftedness, "early verbal expression" was mentioned most frequently (Gogel, McCumsey, & Hewitt, 1985).

Parent accuracy varies from 11 to 76 percent (Khoury & Appel, 1979), which still tends to be better than teacher nomination. Nonetheless, problems do exist. Parents from lower socio-economic neighbourhoods are more likely to report their child as gifted than parents from higher socio-economic locales, partly because well-educated parents tend to set higher intellectual standards for their children. Other parents may be unaware of their child's outstanding abilities, especially if they have little chance to compare his or her accomplishments with those of other children of a similar age.

Peer Nomination

Peer nominations have been judged very favourably by experts in the field and are growing in popularity as a screening technique for giftedness (Gagné, 1989). Davis and Rimm (1985) wrote that "peers are extraordinarily good at nominating gifted and talented students" (p. 78).

Self-nomination

Self-nomination forms have been used with students who have strong artistic, creative, scientific, or other interests and talents. They are especially recommended at the junior and senior high-school levels, where peer pressure may cause youths to mask special talents (Davis & Rimm, 1994).

Measuring Creativity

Children who are gifted—especially academically gifted—may be identified by their high levels of achievement and motivation. Omitted from the equation here is creativity, which is difficult, if not impossible, to measure accurately. An instrument that yields a single score or index of creativity simply does not exist. This is hardly surprising. First, creativity is so varied and shown in so many ways that it is not reasonable to try to use a standard measure to assess what is in reality such a non-standard trait. Second, there is still no unifying theory of creativity embraced by all researchers and practitioners, and it seems unlikely that a general theory will ever emerge. Despite these difficulties, more than 60 instruments for measuring or assessing creativity exist (Treffinger, 1986).

Leadership

Leadership does not describe inborn characteristics but cumulative capabilities that result from an intermixing of the child's innate abilities and experience. To assess leadership, observation of performance together with some rating checklist is most appropriate.

Visual and Performing Arts

There has been a paucity of research about artistically talented students and programming for them (see Clarke & Zimmerman, 2001) and also about identification procedures. Experts in the arts are not enthusiastic about the use of tests to determine artistic ability and prefer exhibitions, performances, auditions, and interviews. Nevertheless, a range of measures is available to assess potential and aptitude, especially in the areas of music and visual art (Khatena, 1982).

Many young children display their gifts at an early age.

Problems in Identification

Identification problems abound in the field of gifted education. Not only are there questions about how and what to identify, but also, in any procedure some special populations tend to be overlooked—and then these children pass through school unidentified, their gifts and talents uncultivated. Because of this, one of the major initiatives in current gifted education is attempts to locate and nurture hidden talent (Gallagher, 2000).

Gifted Underachievers

Gifted students are one group of exceptional learners who are not normally considered at risk for academic failure or problems. Given this, the phrase *gifted underachiever* is seen by some people as an oxymoron. On the other hand, there are few students who vex teachers more than gifted children who won't do their schoolwork.

These students are referred to as *academic underachievers*—those about whom we can make a reasonable prediction of academic potential that is not fulfilled. These are children who are gifted on IQ tests but whose academic achievement is grade level or less (Yewchuk, 1984). Their performance does not necessarily equate with failure or underproduction; children may indeed work at an average level but not at one commensurate with their ability. Some others, of course, do not attain even average levels.

A complex of factors contributes to the high proportion of underachievers among the population of persons who are gifted. These include

- *Impossible expectations.* Pervasive misunderstandings of the nature of giftedness may result in inappropriate expectations and consequent adult responses that place students at risk (Whitmore, 1988). For example, when parents and teachers believe that learning and school achievement are easy for all students who are gifted, they tend to demand more effort and tolerate little error or imperfection. Or, when adults believe that such children are so much more mature than their peers developmentally, they tend to expect more mature behaviour than is reasonable and forget the childishness that is necessarily present in all children.

- *Conflict between giftedness and creativity and the typically rigid classroom.* Children who are gifted are turned off by conformity to precise directions, excessive repetition, memorization and drill, uniformity of assignments, and the lack of opportunity to pursue interests and work independently. In a classroom that requires a high degree of conformity and achievement on schedule with a restricted and often dull curriculum, these children may feel stifled and frustrated. They can't or don't conform to classroom mores, feel that there is nothing to learn that is interesting and challenging, and gradually sink into underachievement.

- *Learning not to learn.* In the early years, a child who is gifted may need to make little, if any, effort to make good grades. Consequently, when academic demands become greater, the student does not know how to apply effort. Such children may then lack confidence, have poor study habits, and do inconsistent work.

- *Social and emotional factors.* Some students may underachieve because it is socially safe. If they feel that peer relationships are jeopardized by expectations of superior performance, they may not want to be singled out as different. Other students may have unfavourable self-concepts that distort their perceptions of the world and undermine their motivation and goal orientation. One father described his underachieving son as "an emperor and a Renaissance man at age four, dethroned by age six, and a behaviour problem and underachiever thereafter" (in Rimm & Lowe, 1988, p. 358).

- *The perfectionism that is common among gifted students.* Perceived academic competence is an important factor in the global self-worth of children, especially girls, who are gifted. By the age of thirteen or fourteen, some of these youngsters have a motivation to avoid failure at any cost rather than a motivation to succeed.

Females Who Are Gifted

Both in school and in the working world, a disproportionate number of males are recognized as gifted, and men achieve high status and recognition more frequently than women of the same age. The reasons for the discrepancy have been examined and debated for decades but, since they affect girls who are gifted in contemporary schools, they are worth reiterating.

First of all, there are no hard data that biological differences cause the disparity. Available research points far more clearly to social and cultural expectations as an explanation. Society still encourages narrow role definitions and behaviour options for women and broader ones for men. Females have not been encouraged to enter academic disciplines and careers historically dominated by males. Girls who insist on their giftedness are encouraged to become musicians or artists, rather than physicists or engineers. Certainly, more women are entering such non-traditional professions as chemistry, engineering, dentistry, and physics, but the numbers are still small. Also, relative gains in non-traditional disciplines may be partly the result of declining interest among men (see Lee, 2002).

A second issue revolves around acceptance. It is considered neither proper nor advantageous for girls to be too superior. Some writers contend that girls who are gifted find it difficult to reconcile their academic interests with the areas of excellence traditionally seen by society as sex-role-appropriate for women (Schwartz, 1980). As high achievers, girls who are gifted are expected to be active, assertive, and exploratory; as females, they are encouraged to be nurturing, passive, and dependent (Handel, 1983). At the same time, girls tend to be more conformist than boys in school and social contexts. Therefore, if giftedness is aberrant, and girls strive to conform, then giftedness does not become role enhancing. For example, when Kerr and her colleagues (1988) studied the attitudes of 184 adolescents toward their giftedness, they found that 90 percent (significantly more girls than boys) viewed giftedness as a potential handicap in social relations with peers.

It is during early adolescence, the age when sex roles are heavily reinforced by parents and peers, that girls generally begin to encounter problems that obscure their giftedness. Often, parents of girls who are gifted are more concerned about their daughters' social adjustment than their academic boredom. In the classroom, too, girls and boys may be experiencing different socialization pressures; teachers are more likely to praise girls for conforming behaviour—that which is quiet, non-aggressive, and non-competitive (see Rimm-Kaufman & Kagan 2005).

There are also educational variables. Elementary school gifted and talented programs identify girls in equal or greater numbers than boys. Later, boys are more likely to take math and science gifted programs, whereas girls populate gifted programs that focus on language arts (Sadker, 1999). And by grade 10, girls begin to drop out of these programs at a greater rate than boys.

For girls in particular, math and science are tied to ambition—girls who like these subjects seem to be more likely to aspire to careers as professionals (Orenstein, 2000). However, Lee (2002) quips that "In secondary schools, science education forms a talent pipeline that quickly develops leaks" (p. 350). Girls are far less likely than boys to retain their affection for math and science, and they often evaluate their skills as lower (Orenstein, 2000). Talented girls are then less likely than talented boys to pursue a career in the sciences.

Gifted Students Who Are Disabled

A child who is both gifted and disabled may be described as one who demonstrates giftedness and at least one attribute of educational, emotional, or physical/sensory impairment.

Gifted females should be encouraged to participate in traditionally male-dominated activities.

Most disabling conditions do not preclude the possibility of giftedness (Bianco, 2005). Yet many children with disabilities are overlooked in identification procedures. The reasons are entwined with common perceptions, the traits of disability, and the identification procedures themselves.

A gifted child who is also disabled fails to meet stereotyped expectations of giftedness. Many teachers, administrators, students, and parents have trouble accepting that a child with a disability may also have outstanding abilities: they focus entirely on the child's disability to the exclusion of his or her individual potential and capabilities.

Individual students probably exhibit many contradictions by deviating substantially both above and below the norm, showing both strengths and weaknesses that are very pronounced. This means that a major portion of their classroom time is spent in remediation of learning to circumvent the effects of the disability, which in turn may preclude the recognition and development of cognitive abilities (Willard-Holt, 1998).

Not only may children lack the opportunity to reveal superior mental or creative ability, but the identification of students who are disabled as well as gifted is particularly problematic. No single instrument or checklist is capable of identifying the range of characteristics and conditions that may be present. Critical in identification are teacher observations of a child's behaviour that must be made over time rather than in isolation. Teachers should look for attributes such as the ability to solve complex problems mentally; aptitude in specific subject area;, persistence, independence, and determination; the development of skills to compensate for the disability; and an early ability to read (Willard-Holt, 1998).

Gifted Students Who Have Learning Disabilities

Intense research interest in children who are both gifted and have learning disabilities has spawned a new term—*twice exceptional* (Nielson & Higgins, 2005). These students are a puzzle and a paradox; they have talents and strengths in some areas and disabling weaknesses in others (see Coleman, 2005).

Twice exceptional students form the majority of the gifted disabled population. They face numerous challenges in the classroom and in life. They often wonder, for example, "Why am I so good at math but need special help with reading? Where do I fit in?" (King, 2005, p. 16).

In general, twice exceptional children fall into three groups. One group consists of mild underachievers—students who are identified as gifted and have subtle learning disabilities. The next group are those who are severely learning disabled with no giftedness recognized. In these students, giftedness and learning disabilities tend to mask one another. These students' disabilities may depress their IQ and achievement scores so that they are not eligible for gifted programs. Yet their giftedness allows them to compensate well enough for their weaknesses to maintain grade-level expectations, which prevents detection of their learning difficulty. The result is that they frequently do not qualify for special education services. At other times, a child may be receiving special education services, and the giftedness is completely overlooked. The final group is made up of children who are identified as both learning disabled and gifted.

Gifted Students Who Are Culturally Different

When the issue of identifying gifted students from culturally diverse groups is approached, the general tenor of the research is that standardized tests are inappropriate. Instead, teachers should use a collection of instruments and procedures that include observations, nomination forms, and rating scales. Assessment and identification procedures should measure how a child meaningfully manipulates a symbol system held valuable in the culture; thinks logically when given appropriate data; uses stored knowledge to solve problems; reasons by analogy; and extends or extrapolates knowledge to new situations or unique applications (Clark, 1988).

INTERVENTION WITH STUDENTS WHO ARE GIFTED, CREATIVE, AND TALENTED

The basic educational goals for children with gifts and talents are the same as for all other students: to develop their abilities in ways that are consistent with their personal needs and the best interests of society. To accomplish this broad aim, a variety of practices and programs have been devised over the years to cater to gifted students. Still, the research literature is quite unhelpful about the best approach. Nobody is sure of the best way to educate students with gifts, and it is true to say that there is a lack of systematically developed models and systematic experimental evaluation of programs and program models that have explicit goals, objectives, and specified outcomes. Focused educational models and approaches are a function of policy and definitions, be they implicit or explicit. Across

Canada we find somewhat different definitional constructs and varied ways of addressing the education of students with gifts and talents, all based on different provincial and territorial policy. Most jurisdictions include gifted students in some definition of exceptional pupil, either at the legislative, regulatory, or administrative policy level. Related funding tends to be different in each area; only Alberta provides a funding formula that specifically includes programs to meet the needs of these students (McFadden & Ellis, 2000).

Of the numerous models and programs that have been attempted, all are intended to come to grips with three major problems: the balance between the quest for excellence and a zeal for equality; the wide range of abilities among the gifted population; and teachers' lack of special instructional methods. The four most common types of educational provisions used in Canada are acceleration, ability grouping, mentoring programs, and enrichment. These are discussed on pages 306 to 313.

Service Delivery Models

As in every area of contemporary special education, debates about placement rage in the field of giftedness. Many educators argue that special programs for the gifted run counter to the spirit of the inclusive movement and therefore promote general class placements with additional accommodations. Others detail countervailing forces that grew in strength in the late 1980s and 1990s, and that may prove disadvantageous for students with gifts and talents. These are the promotion of detracking; heterogeneous groupings by age and grade level; and particularly the inclusion movement, which means serving precocious youngsters in general classrooms. Because they feel that the goals and practices of existing programs are often ineffectual for gifted students, people on this side of the fence promote specialized instruction in separate placements, at least part of the time.

Teachers' voices are important in this debate, as are their attitudes about and perceptions of students who are gifted. In fact, so critical are teachers' attitudes that some researchers argue that children who are gifted should be placed in general classrooms only if the teacher is prepared to assist them (see McCarthy, 1994).

A review of the literature (Cramond & Martin, 1987) found that teachers hold conflicting attitudes toward students with gifts. Some studies saw teachers viewing such students positively and giving them preferential treatment; others found teacher discomfort and resentment that could lead to apathy toward gifted education. Other research has found "disturbing evidence of neglect" in general classrooms (Culross, 1997, p. 24). Finally, in a sample of 98 parents of gifted children, Kaufman and Sexton (1983) found that 45 percent had encountered a teacher who the parents felt was unsympathetic to the special needs of the child who was gifted.

Some teachers disagree with special programming on both philosophical and pragmatic grounds. Bransky (1987) found negative attitudes among classroom teachers, which she attributed to a poor foundation of knowledge about the pull-out programs for students who are gifted. Some teachers argue that the classroom that loses children who are gifted is robbed of leadership. Others express concern about the fragmentation of their programs or about the need to reschedule lessons (Meyers, 1984). Occasionally, teachers are averse to designing programs for learners who are gifted. Others realize that teachers of students who are gifted need special traits, but are unaware of what these are or have little confidence in their ability to develop them. Archambault and Hallmark (1992) found that 42 to 62 percent of the 7000 teachers in their studies had absolutely no exposure to methods for teaching gifted students.

Educational Approaches

As we said, the education of students who are gifted is replete with different models offered in varied settings. Typically, more program options are available in urban and suburban areas and in the elementary schools. Of the models below, only enrichment is always offered in the general classroom. Mentoring and ability grouping have traditionally been mainly pull-out models; settings for acceleration vary.

Acceleration

acceleration

Acceleration means moving faster through academic content. Students speed up their progress through the existing curriculum to complete a prescribed program in a shorter time period. Included within acceleration models are early school beginning, grade skipping, ungraded classes, continuous progress, self-paced instruction, telescoping the curriculum, extracurricular programs, concurrent or dual enrolment, credit by examination, correspondence courses, high-school courses for credit, extra load, seminars for college credit, early admittance to post-secondary programs, and honours programs.

Two general characteristics define acceleration models. First, acceleration is one of the most time-honoured options in gifted education and has been practised throughout the history of providing educational provisions for this population. Second, there is probably no other area in the education of students who are gifted that is more controversial. Essentially, we have a situation where the literature on the academic acceleration of students who are gifted consistently demonstrates a lack of harmful effects, but many educators and administrators resist the implementation of the model in their schools (Feldhusen, 1989; Southern, Jones, & Fiscus, 1989). The major arguments from both sides are presented in the Debate feature.

Supporting acceleration practices is a body of data that "are unanimous in their support of the benefit of accelerative alternatives, both academically and socio-emotionally"

A MATTER OF DEBATE

Acceleration for Students Who Are Gifted

EQUITY, EXCELLENCE

Pros	Cautions
Students are entitled to challenging and appropriate instruction.	Violates the concepts and principles of the inclusionary movement.
Students can enter high school, post-secondary, and graduate studies earlier, and get a faster start on their careers.	
A paucity of evidence exists for approaches that are non-accelerative in orientation.	

Pros	Cautions
The one-size-fits-all mentality of the inclusion movement reflects a mistaken view of human development. Violates the concetps and principles of the inclusionary movement.	

ACADEMIC FACTORS

Pros	Cautions
Positive changes in academic achievement.	May lead to gaps in knowledge or poor retention of material learned at an accelerated pace.
Provides academic settings well suited to the needs of high-ability students.	Inappropriate for students with uneven talent profiles.
Students perform as well as older students	
Enhanced motivation, improved study habits and productivity	

SOCIAL/EMOTIONAL CONSIDERATIONS

Pros	Cautions
Lack of negative effects on social and emotional growth.	Deficient or retarded psychosocial development.
	Jeopardizes social acceptance.
	Students lose the ability to function in the larger world of average people.
	Will not fit in with more mature classmates.

SELF-CONCEPT, ESTEEM

Pros	Cautions
Suffer boredom and negative peer pressure in self-esteem heterogeneous classrooms.	Hurts self-concepts to be set apart from average counterparts.
	May become conceited and self-centred; contemptuous of age peers.

Sources: Benbow, 1991; Davis & Rimm, 1994; Southern, Jones, & Fiscus, 1989; Swiatek & Benbow, 1991; Van Tassel Baska, 1989; Van Tassel-Baska & Brown, 2000

(Keating, 1980, p. 56). From the point of view of its proponents, even the word *acceleration* is a misnomer; the process is really one of bringing youth who are gifted and talented up to a suitable level of instruction commensurate with their achievement levels and readiness so that they are properly challenged to learn new material (Feldhusen, 1989).

Advocates cite 80 years of positive research findings. They further contend that highly talented young people suffer boredom and negative peer pressure in heterogeneous classrooms. With acceleration, boredom, restlessness, frustration, underachievement, and disruptiveness can be replaced by enhanced motivation, improved self-concepts, and improved study habits and productivity (Davis & Rimm, 1994).

Opponents of acceleration marshal an impressive array of arguments that focus on psychosocial rather than academic reasons. They view the practice of allowing students who are gifted to progress through the educational system at their own rate as potentially hazardous to social and emotional adjustment. Children, they argue, cannot escape the physical and emotional limits imposed by chronology. Accelerated pupils will not socialize with older children, will have fewer friends, will not be happy, and will miss important social interactions.

Ability Grouping

ability groupings

As the name suggests, **ability groupings** refer to changing the environment to bring students who are gifted into contact with each other. The assumption is that students who are gifted need interaction with those who share their interests and concerns; that is, social and emotional support from a group of *true peers*—simultaneously a student's intellectual and chronological equals—to maintain a positive self-concept and intellectual interaction and to transform abilities into productive reality.

Ability grouping most often translates into pull-out programs. While in some cases independent groups of students progress at different rates within the same classroom, often students are removed from heterogeneous settings and placed in special groups in special classrooms. Special groups may meet full-time or only part-time. They may be made up of students from a single school or from several schools within a district. Groups may meet during regular school hours or on an extracurricular basis.

Certain criteria ensure the success of pull-out programs. These include integration with the regular curriculum, daily program experience, placement with intellectual peers, pace of program matched with the students' learning rate, a complex and higher level curriculum, and excellent teachers (Belcostas, 1987).

As with acceleration, pull-out programs are far from universally accepted. Opponents claim that the practice is undemocratic because it fosters intellectual elitism and limits contacts between gifted and normal children. Pragmatically, they contend that pull-out programs are often frivolous. Programs often diverge from the regular school curriculum, do not give grades, do not have instruction in traditional subject matter, focus on the affective rather than the academic, and do not have written curricula (Van Tassel-Baska, 1987).

In contrast, advocates argue that only when children who are gifted are grouped together can they be provided with truly effective instruction. As far as curriculum is concerned, they believe that since separate gifted programs provide for students who differ from the norm, the programs also should differ in their adherence to the conventional structures associated with education. On this theme, it may be that gifted programs are most justifiable when the content of the special program is truly an accelerated curriculum, not just add-ons. The

RESEARCH NOTES

Classroom Grouping

A primary method to accommodate students who are not at grade level is through the use of various modes of grouping. Maheady (1997) describes grouping as one of the instructional variables that is alterable and that "can powerfully influence positively or negatively the levels of individual student engagement and hence academic progress" (p. 325).

Grouping has both its advocates and its detractors. Critics note that grouping creates logistical problems because different lessons and assignments are required. Mentoring students in different groups on different tasks is difficult, and improper group placements tend to become permanent. The major argument centres on labelling. Many contend that low groups are stigmatized, the self-esteem and motivation of low groups suffer, friendship choices are restricted, and the gap between high and low achievers often widens.

The pro side contends that grouping enhances instruction by allowing the teacher to adjust the rate, methods, and materials to better suit student needs. Because pace and assessment are similar for a particular group, instruction is easier for the teacher.

Often, the planning frame of general classroom teachers is the whole class. Yet, when compared to one-to-one and small-group teaching arrangements, whole-class arrangements are consistently associated with the lowest levels of engaged behaviour (see Logan, Bakeman, & Keefe, 1997). It is small-group instruction that equates with improved academic achievement (Elbaum, Vaughn, Hughes, Moody, & Schumm, 2000).

For students with learning disabilities, for example, three variables explain achievement outcomes and produce the strongest impact on student learning across domains. These are control of task difficulty, teaching students in small groups of six or fewer, and direct response questioning (direct instruction) (Swanson, 1999; Swanson & Hosbyn, 1998). Similarly, a meta-analysis of reading outcomes for students with disabilities revealed that positive outcomes in reading achievement correlated with small-group instruction and student pairing (Elbaum, Vaughn, Hughes, Moody, & Schumm, 2000).

In the discrete field of giftedness, promoters of special placements contend that "gifted education and gifted students are in deep trouble without grouping practices" (Davis & Rimm, 1994, p. 10). For high-ability students, achievement is positively affected by ability grouping that includes curriculum modifications directed to their learning characteristics (Kulik, 1992; Kulik & Kulik, 1991, 1992).

Evidence on whether grouping affects children's self-esteem is contradictory. It has been shown that children of medium and low ability are either not affected or are negatively affected by ability grouping (Kulik, 1992; Kulik & Kulik, 1991, 1992). Gifted youth may have self-concepts that clearly relate to and recognize giftedness, and their self-concepts may be influenced positively by participation in a gifted program (Feldhusen & Hoover, 1986).

---

most popular subject for acceleration is math. (Language arts or social studies are usually the focus of enrichment programs.)

The research literature fails to provide clear evidence for or against ability grouping in terms of academic achievement. When Goldring (1990) analyzed 23 studies on delivery methods, he found that students who were gifted in special classes achieved more than students of high ability in regular classrooms, but the benefits of the special classes depended on the subject. The largest effects were in science and social studies, with smaller effects in math, reading, and writing. The higher the grade level, the stronger the advantage of special classes. Similarly, Vaughn and colleagues (1991) analyzed the research and found small to medium positive effects on academic achievement and critical and creative thinking. Kulik and Kulik (1997) state that, on average, gifted students who experience ability groupings for enrichment activities outperform equally gifted students in mixed-ability classes by four or five months in a year. Bourque and Li (1987) found that what students liked most about being in a special program was freedom of choice and self-directedness.

The issue of grouping—whether small heterogeneous or homogeneous classroom groups or pull-out groups—is germane to all students with special needs, not only those who are gifted. The Research Notes discuss some of the research on grouping in general terms.

Mentor Programs

Mentorship has been recognized as one of the most effective organizational configurations to help students who are gifted to realize their potential. There are three common but inter-related types of mentorship programs (McFadden & Ellis, 2000).

Career exploration, guidance, and development programs are cost-effective and serve as a liaison between the school and the community. Students work in the community with adults with whom they share a special interest. Usually the teacher, the mentor, and the student set up a project with the final results to be presented to the class in some form. This type of mentoring can play a catalytic role in helping students negotiate the major transitions of academic life. Benefits include career and interest advancement; an increase in knowledge and skills; the development of talent; enhancement of self-esteem and self-confidence; development of a personal ethic or set of standards; establishment of long-term friendships; and enhancement of creativity (Edlind & Heansly, 1985).

Personal growth mentor programs stress self-awareness in any area; many programs lead to higher student aspirations. *Content-based programs* focus on enrichment in an area of interest to a student. Both of these programs involve self-directed learning. Although there are almost as many conceptualizations of self-directed learning as there are researchers and theorists, **self-directed learning** means essentially that students are given autonomous control of their own instruction. Included are library research projects; scientific research projects; independent study in art, music, and drama; learning centres; and field trips.

self-directed learning

SAMPLE ENRICHMENT UNIT

Plants and Seeds

Knowledge

- List all the parts of a seed plant you can find.
- Define the following terms (related to seed plants): bulb germination, dormancy, dicotyledon, dissemule, root hair.
- List the many methods of seed dispersal.
- Name the conditions necessary for germination and development in a plant.

- List the enemies of plants (as many as you can find).
- Look at several beauty magazines to see how plants are used in make-up and other beauty aids.

Comprehension

- Why do leaves change colour in the fall?
- Explain how a plant takes water from the earth and uses it in its living processes.

- Explain the difference between coniferous and deciduous.

- Describe how a plant grows, from fertilization through to maturity. If you like, you can use an example to help you.

- Describe the role of chlorophyll in photosynthesis, explaining why green plants turn yellow and die if they do not get enough sunlight.

- Describe the role of a seed plant in the ability of life to exist on earth.

Application

- Using a microscope, diagram the cell structure of a leaf.

- Diagram the different parts of a seed plant.

- Show how you can tell how old, and how tall, a tree is.

- Make your own perfume, using the leaves of flowers.

- Show how a seed plant takes root and begins to grow.

Analysis

- Conduct an experiment to see how far seeds can travel.

- Compare and contrast coniferous and deciduous trees, and the way they grow.

- Conduct an experiment to see what happens when seeds are crowded too close together.

- Compare past and present uses of plants in the field of medicine. Are there any similarities?

- Conduct an experiment to see what will happen to a leaf when it is coated with Vaseline. Why does this happen?

- Conduct an experiment to determine the lengths to which plants will go to get sunlight.

Synthesis

- Design an environment possessing ideal conditions for the growth of seed plants.

- Choose two plants and, using your knowledge about genetics and plant breeding, predict the outcome of a cross between them. Describe the new creation. What are its strength and weaknesses, if any?

- Grow several bean seeds, controlling different environmental conditions in each instance. Predict the outcome in each case, and compare it with the actual results.

Evaluation

- Decide whether or not the commercial use of greenhouses can be beneficial to people in the long run.

- Acid rain has a great effect on plants. What exactly is that effect, and what can we do about it? Are we doing all we can right now?

- Assess the value of gardens in space. Are they worth the trouble?

Source: Hicks, 1987.

CASE STUDY

William, Troy, and Richard (continued)

In the education of students who are gifted, a deeper examination of the regular curriculum cannot be achieved by adding a few tasks. Rather, it needs a consistent and structured curriculum expansion founded on broad goals directed at their specific needs. Curricula should be designed to allow children of high ability such as Troy, William, and Richard to master important conceptual systems that are at the level of their abilities in various content fields.

Richard's needs are the most special. It appears that a learning disability is masking his giftedness, and an IEP must account for both additional assistance to improve reading and activities to stimulate his giftedness. In the other class, Troy's behaviour has begun to hinder his academic achievement and his acceptance in the classroom. A first step is to bring Mr. Jane on side. Then Troy needs enrichment activities in the general classroom and time with the resource room teacher with a special program. An extract from Troy's IEP is found below.

EXTRACT FROM TROY'S IEP

Name: Troy
Teacher: Mr. Jane
Date: November 12, 2005
Grade: 5
School: Jones

Results from Formal Assessment Administered October 21, 2005

Test

- WISC-III: Full Scale IQ 144
- Key Math Diagnostic Arithmetic Test: 91st percentile
- Test of Language Development (Primary): 98th percentile

Strengths

- Works well alone
- Is a high achiever when motivated
- Has strong oral language
- Is very inquisitive
- Seeks to organize (but can be bossy)
- Enjoys problem solving
- Exhibits intense concentration
- Shows high energy, alertness, and eagerness in preferred tasks
- Has diverse interests and abilities
- Is independent

Weaknesses

- Is a perfectionist
- Gets bored with classroom work
- Constantly argues with teacher on any topic
- Refuses to conform to school rules

Major Needs

- Opportunities to make use of high-level thinking skills
- Activities that build on logical and thinking skills
- Research skills
- Self-selected projects

Setting

- Regular classroom/resource room

Long-Range Goals in Pull-Out Program

- Learn basic research skills
- Explore a topic of own choosing in depth
- Communicate findings to grade 5 class

In-Class Goals

- Complete general classroom work before moving to own projects
- Adhere to a contract for an independent project prepared with the teacher

Special Program

- Take part in debating club

Enrichment

enrichment

In many situations it is not possible to take children who are gifted from their assigned classrooms. **Enrichment** programs, which provide special activities in the general classroom setting, are the solution.

Enriched experiences focus on adjusting the breadth and depth of the curriculum, the tempo and pace at which the curriculum is introduced, and the kind and content of material that is presented. Activities involve a broader range of skills and deeper understanding than the regular curriculum, and are designed to challenge and interest children while focusing on their unique patterns of strengths and weaknesses. Of course, enrichment activities are good for all students, but it must be kept in mind that for students who are gifted there must be higher-order objectives outlined within enrichment. We can see this in the sample enrichment unit presented here. This example examines seeds and plants and is loosely based on Benjamin Bloom's taxonomy of educational objectives (1956). This type of unit can be used effectively with students who are gifted—as a group assignment or as independent study.

Advocates of enrichment maintain that the programs allow a child to remain in the general classroom with age-level peers. Detractors point out the difficulty of meeting individual needs with a few extra activities in a generally inadequate learning environment. They contend that enrichment often promotes the false impression that something substantial is being done for the gifted when it is really "busywork and irrelevant" (Stanley & Benbow, 1986).

Research does not yield clear evidence that enrichment adequately stimulates children who are gifted. In fact, it generally does not find achievement benefits. Inclusive schooling is likely to accommodate the needs of only the mildly gifted students who are strong in specific domains (see McFadden & Ellis, 2000).

Curriculum

The difference between the regular program and the program for students who are gifted is one of degree. Some classroom practices currently being studied include independent projects, creative writing on self-selected topics, teaching thinking skills, encouraging discovery, and using classroom questioning that encourages reasoning and logical thinking (Gubbins, 1991). Some generic ideas are presented in Table 9-2.

Table 9-2 Creating accessible classrooms

Accommodations

- The degree of conformity in the classroom should be reasonable and flexible. Mary, for example, may not listen intently when you read to the class, but neither should she be permitted to divert the attention of others.
- Provide opportunities for choices in assignments.
- Let students teach each other through small-group work and cluster groups.
- Provide time for students to do their own work at school.
- Have students regularly share with the class what they are doing.

Adaptations, instructional

- Do not work in a qualitatively different way than for other children; just present more advanced material. First teach the basic structure of a discipline, but then try to have the students approach it as a specialist would.
- Pace is one of the most important variables in teaching. Present material more rapidly and with less practice than for average learners.
- Teach methods by which students can discover knowledge for themselves (research skills).
- Stress technical writing. For example, teach how to phrase research questions.
- Teach how to write proposals and how to present primary research data in graph, table, diagram, and statistical form.

Table 9-2 continued

- Stress the processes of problem solving as well as the products of work.
- To stimulate creative students, allow learning by exploring, testing the limits, searching, manipulating, and playing.
- Use written expression for a variety of purposes—informative and persuasive as well as narrative.
- Use individual reading assignments with self-selection of materials.
- Design a curriculum that facilitates the movement from teacher-directed to self-directed learning styles.

Use individual studies. The steps are as follows:

1. Select and delimit a subject or topic.
2. Formulate key questions to pursue and answer.
3. Develop a plan and time sequence.
4. Locate and use multiple resources.
5. Create a product.
6. Share the findings of the study.

Use a specific validated model. For example,

1. The Revolving Door Model (Renzulli & Smith, 1984) is designed to identify giftedness, provide enrichment activities, and overcome many of the problems related to student selection, motivation, and interests.
2. Tannenbaum's (1986) Enrichment Matrix Model includes techniques for differentiating the curriculum, supplementary content areas (anthropology, leadership, psychology), and interdisciplinary content areas (aesthetics, humanities).
3. The Integrated Curriculum Model (Van Tassel-Baska, 1994, 1995) incorporates interdisciplinary themes in advanced content areas as well as higher-order thinking and processing skills.
4. The Schoolwide Enrichment Model (Renzulli & Reis, 2000; Reis & O'Shea, 1984) delineates three types of enrichment activities: general exploratory activities, group training activities, and small group investigations.
5. The Autonomous Learner Model (ALM) (Betts, 1985) is designed for secondary-level special classrooms but can also be used at elementary levels. In a three-year sequence, students move through five major dimensions. These are orientation—understanding giftedness and group building activities; individual development—learning skills and career involvement; enrichment activities—exploration and investigation; seminars—general interest and advanced knowledge; and in-depth study—independent projects and mentorships.

Various processes that encompass content and skills are used to provide enrichment in the regular classroom. These include the following:

curriculum compacting

- **Curriculum compacting** (telescoping) is used to bring the content up to the level of the child and to move students through the curriculum far more rapidly. It is designed to adapt the regular curriculum to meet the needs of above-average students by either eliminating work that has been mastered previously or streamlining work that may be mastered at a pace commensurate with the student's ability. A major goal of curriculum compacting is that students' time is used more efficiently on appropriate topics or activities rather than completing tasks they already know.

- **Horizontal enrichment** involves examining a certain curriculum area in greater depth. Students who are gifted don't need more work, but rather different work that is challenging and interesting. They should do the regular curriculum, but may delve into it in deeper ways. For example, a child in grade 3 may do all the addition problems set for the other students but then go on to do another set in Roman numerals.

  horizontal enrichment

- **Vertical enrichment** refers to students doing additional independent work of their own choosing in the classroom such as the individual studies discussed earlier.

  vertical enrichment

- Research skills. For students who are gifted, we need to add a fourth *R*—research skills—to the curriculum. Students must be assisted in developing skills and strategies that enable them to become more independent, creative, and self-sufficient seekers after knowledge. Lacking research skills, students cannot undertake *self-directed learning* (also called *autonomous learning, self-teaching, individualized education, independent learning*, and *personalized teaching*).

There are quite a number of recognized and validated instructional models and enrichment activities that apply to the whole class, groups, or individuals. These are listed in Table 9-2.

For individual students, teachers can use **independent studies**, which are individualized learning experiences that allow students to select a topic, define problems or questions, gather and analyze information, apply skills, and create a product to show what has been learned. Individual studies individualize and extend classroom learning experiences in ways that incorporate interdisciplinary and higher-level thinking skills. Students can go beyond the confines of the classroom, pursue personal interests, develop self-directness, explore the world of work, and develop research and other skills. Students do not necessarily work alone. Committee studies allow collaboration based on shared interests and abilities (see Table 9-2).

independent studies

SUMMARY

1. Giftedness is considered an integral component of special education because students who are gifted require appropriate educational opportunities and challenges if they are to develop to their full potential. However, there is not another category in special education so fraught with political, emotional, and educational issues. Difficulties revolve around just who is gifted, how to identify gifts and talents, how to offer special programming, and how to balance the needs of students who are gifted within the parameters of an egalitarian school system.

2. Definitional problems plague the field of gifted education. The literature abounds with definitions of giftedness and theories of intelligence but a definition that encompasses all children and youth who are gifted, talented, and creative does not exist. Part of the definitional dilemma relates to the broad array of characteristics and behaviours seen in these students.

3. Since Terman's day, perceptions of giftedness and beliefs about what abilities should be recognized and developed in Canadian schools have changed dramatically. Newer definitions of *gifted* and *talented* give a broader view of the concept. They have become much more liberal in terms of both the types of behaviours attributed to individuals who are gifted and the degree of behaviour that must be elicited before the label *gifted* is applied. Current perceptions overthrow the notion that giftedness is merely manifested through outstanding academic performance.

4. Opinions abound as to how to explain the unique quality of giftedness. Although we no longer claim that giftedness springs entirely from the genes, it is only reasonable to assume that heredity has some effect. Environment is important, but, beyond the obvious general advantages, it is not known what specific factors in upper- and middle-class homes encourage giftedness.

5. As a field, gifted education has spent inordinate time and effort in determining who qualifies for programs for gifted students. For a long time, identification was dominated by a single variable—a child's tested IQ. Today, the most widely used identification models call for multiple tools and procedures. The heterogeneity of the population, the plethora of available definitions, and the administrative problems make identification particularly difficult and uncertain. Problems can and do occur at various points in the process. Many children with gifts go undiscovered, particularly those who are culturally, ethnically, linguistically, socially, or economically different from the norm, gifted females, and gifted children with disabilities.

6. Children with disabilities can also be gifted. The highest incidence of giftedness is most likely to be found among disabilities that are most frequently occurring, such as learning disabilities.

7. The provision of programs for students who are gifted is one of the most controversial issues in special education. With the exception of classroom enrichment, all of the practices recommended for academic achievement of students with gifts and talents focus on separate programs or different curricula—the opposite of inclusionary practices.

8. To educate students who are gifted, a school can make changes in the learning environment, in the content of lessons, and in the skills taught. Environmental changes include acceleration and ability grouping. Content includes what students study and the rate at which they study it. Skills relate both to process—how the students work with information—and to products—how they represent what they know.

9. Various modes of acceleration exist. All entail progress through an educational program at rates faster or ages younger than considered the norm. Acceleration appears to have a strong edge in promoting academic achievement, but practitioners seem to regard acceleration in general, and early entrance in particular, as risky approaches in serving the needs of children who are gifted. Enrichment in the classroom implies more than tacking on a few activities to the existing curriculum. Many strategies and well-validated models are available for raising the level of challenge for students who are gifted.

HISTORICAL NOTES

Cultural values have always determined the attitudes of society toward its outstanding members. Different eras have valued achievement in different fields of endeavour. Ancient Greece admired the philosopher; Rome, the soldier and orator; and Renaissance Italy, the artist. In the modern age, remarkable early development, or precocity, was seen in many major historical figures. Beethoven performed in public at age seven, Thomas Jefferson began serious study at five, and Pablo Picasso drew before he could walk. Others who contributed significantly to our cultures bloomed late and only after surviving hardships or overcoming disabilities. Winston Churchill was a sickly child with a speech impediment; Edison's teachers described him as "addled"; and Auguste Rodin had a learning disability. Vincent van Gogh suffered crippling bouts of depression that eventually led to his suicide.

Before the mid-19th century, giftedness was a visible, yet poorly defined and understood, phenomenon. Although much honour was paid to individuals who made significant contributions to their own or succeeding cultures, genius was often misunderstood and popularly viewed as directly related to insanity.

Francis Galton, an English scientist, was one of the first to research and write about giftedness. Sickly himself, he went a long way toward cementing the genius-insanity link. As well, Galton proposed that motivation to achieve was innate and inborn, and claimed that genius would actualize itself despite external circumstances—a position that led to the enduring and dangerous myth that "the cream will rise to the top" regardless of difficulties or lack of environmental support.

As a descriptive term for a specific group of individuals who are highly intelligent and strong academic achievers, *gifted* was first used in the literature by Guy M. Henry in 1920. It was not until the 1960s that the constructs of *talented* and *creative* came into being. At the same time, additions and deletions to the terminology occurred as educators tried to shed the elitist attitudes and stereotypes associated with the terms gifted and giftedness.

Special day classes for gifted pupils emerged in the United States during the 1890s, but the movement was small and the classes scattered. In Canada too, the movement, compared to that for children with disabilities, was small. Community-based gifted education was founded in London, Ontario, in the late 1920s, manifested in an enrichment program for the elementary grades (Bain, 1980). On the Prairies,

the Enterprise Method developed and trained students in learning and community-oriented group activities. The Major Work Program, first adopted in Alberta, flourished briefly across the country. It offered selected children greater intellectual stimulation, along with training in advanced creativity and problem solving (Bain, 1980).

Other programs developed in Canada, based largely on the philosophy of Samuel Laycock of Saskatchewan. From the 1930s to the late 1960s, Laycock championed the cause of those exceptional children who were capable of creativity and leadership but were too often ignored by society. Saskatchewan, in fact, has had a continuous program since the 1930s for very gifted learners (Lipp, 1988).

The 1970s saw huge interest in children who were gifted. One spur came when North American educators saw their school outcomes drop far below those of the Japanese and the Europeans. Another was an offshoot of the women's movement that began to open avenues for females to enter less traditional roles. As well, evidence accumulated that many gifted students were bored with the lockstep of mass education and were turning into chronic underachievers and dropouts.

After the 1970s, interest in gifted education seemed to drop in proportion to the mounting number of students identified with disabilities. In the equity-excellence equation, equity held sway as far as funding and resources went. The restrictions placed on programs for students who are gifted were, and are, both academic and attitudinal.

Attitudes reflect popularly held stereotypes such as Galton's myth that "the cream will rise to the top." This view sees giftedness as an already developed capacity and not as one that requires nurturing and support. As students typically do well in school, easily meet age and grade levels for achievement, and tend to be well behaved, it is rationalized that pupils who are gifted are smart enough to make it on their own and will develop their abilities even if not provided with special education. If students don't do well, then they're not gifted, anyway.

A closely related notion holds that giftedness is highly desirable and a boon to social status. Children with gifts and talents are not perceived as suffering from social stigma or unhappiness. They rarely arouse the same level of concern as youngsters who are disabled, and they demonstrate no immediate problems that can serve as a basis for an emotional appeal for special services. These children are already advantaged, so while many feel that we are morally obliged to help children with disabilities, they view programs for the gifted as making as much sense as welfare payments for the rich.

Both of the above ideas feed into the argument that special programs for individuals who are already well endowed violates the ethics of a democratic school system. The underlying concern of opponents of such programs is that special education for the gifted might subvert our commitment to egalitarianism and jeopardize the principle of democratic education by creating an over-advantaged elite or meritocracy within the school population.

SECTION 5

Children with Sensory Impairments

Hearing and vision are known as the distant senses because they are so important in connecting us with our environment. Even when we are not aware of them, and even when we are asleep, these two senses, especially hearing, keep us connected and in touch with the world. With this in mind, it is easy to realize how the loss of hearing or vision isolates an individual from family, friends, the community, and the physical environment. It is also not surprising that such isolation has the potential to damage a person psychologically, socially, emotionally, and educationally. The greater the loss of hearing or vision, the greater the potential isolation for the affected individual.

Blindness and deafness are low-incidence conditions. Although general classroom teachers may encounter some children with significant disabilities, it is far more likely they will meet students who see poorly or who are hard of hearing. Because these hearing and vision problems are mild, many go undetected until children reach school age. Some children's problems are never identified, which places them at risk for being mislabelled as learning disabled or dismissed as dull, stupid, or lazy.

In educational settings, the techniques and approaches to include hearing impaired or visually impaired students are, of course, quite different. The main difference is in language and communication: children with visual impairments use language to keep in contact with their environments; those with hearing impairments use visual means that usually include speech reading and sign language.

This section explores hearing loss (Chapter 10) and visual impairment (Chapter 11), from mild to profound, their developmental consequences, and educational services and practices. Because hearing loss and visual impairment are, at root, physiological conditions, the discussion begins with an examination of the anatomy and physiology of the ear and the eye. A general concept of how the impairments are caused will help to make more sense of the developmental consequences. Note that the complex problems of children who are deaf-blind are addressed in Chapter 15, where we address multiple disabilities.

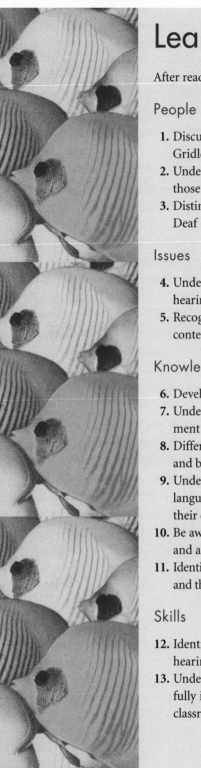

Learning Outcomes

After reading this section, you should be able to

People and Foundations

1. Discuss the contributions of pioneers such as Louis Braille, Michel de l'Épée, Samuel Gridley Howe, and John Barrett McGann.
2. Understand the development of Braille for those who are blind and sign language for those who are hearing impaired.
3. Distinguish the characteristic of being deaf (loss of hearing) from having an identity as Deaf (Deaf culture).

Issues

4. Understand why integrating students with sensory disabilities, especially those with hearing impairments, is challenging to teachers.
5. Recognize the nature of Deaf culture and the Deaf community and how they influence contemporary education for students who are deaf.

Knowledge

6. Develop a working knowledge of the anatomy of the ear and the eye.
7. Understand the various classification systems used for hearing loss and visual impairment as well as the varied etiologies involved.
8. Differentiate between the categories of deaf and hard of hearing, low vision and blind, and between legal and educational blindness.
9. Understand the developmental consequences of hearing loss, especially in relation to language and speech acquisition, as well as the various types of visual impairments and their causes and developmental consequences.
10. Be aware of the range of techniques used in the medical and educational identification and assessment of visual impairments and hearing disorders.
11. Identify the various devices used for reading and mobility in the field of visual impairment and the assistive technologies and medical therapies used with persons who are deaf.

Skills

12. Identify the variety of communication modes used in the education of students with hearing impairments and how these affect integration into a general classroom.
13. Understand the types of adaptations, modifications, and supports necessary to successfully include children with severe visual impairments or hearing disabilities in general classrooms.

CHAPTER 10

CHILDREN WITH HEARING IMPAIRMENTS

INTRODUCTION

If you were to take a casual survey of 100 people and ask who had had a medical checkup, dental checkup, eye examination, or hearing assessment in the past 12 months, only a very few would mention a hearing test. Why? Because in North America we pay less attention to hearing loss than to almost any other medical condition.

Hearing loss is silent, painless, subtle, and invisible. It is one of the least recognized and most misunderstood disabilities. Loss of hearing, noted Arthur and colleagues (1990), "is America's biggest and least admitted ailment" (p. 5). In fact, hearing loss is considered the fastest growing disability in the world (Canadian Hard of Hearing Association, 2000). More people suffer from it than heart disease, cancer, blindness, tuberculosis, venereal disease, multiple sclerosis, and kidney disease put together (Arthur, Gardner, & Murphy, 1990).

Most people think of severe hearing impairment as simply a lack of sound, but this is one of the least of the problems. The greatest single result of a serious hearing loss is the concomitant impact on communication skills. Hearing impairment, a physical ailment, spills over to affect the development of speech and language, the most important components of interpersonal communication. As Helen Keller (1933) pointed out, deafness also means "the loss of the most vital stimulus—the sound of the voice that brings language, sets thoughts astir, and keeps us in the intellectual company of men" (p. 68). When Beethoven lost his hearing, he wrote that he was "soon obliged to seclude myself and live in solitude" (Freeland, 1989, p. 1).

For children, hearing impairment poses a serious threat because hearing is so critical for learning. In normal child development, speech and language are acquired spontaneously and almost effortlessly. Normally hearing infants have intact auditory processes on which to build an early mastery of the sound, shape, and sense of language. From their earliest days, babies take in, process, and organize the language they hear, preparing to become competent communicators. For babies who are deaf, life is devoid of sound effects and spoken script. Children who are hearing impaired do not hear the sounds made by themselves and others. They are isolated from the human voice, and this inevitably hinders or halts their acquisition of speech and language.

In the past, few children with serious hearing impairments were admitted to general classrooms. However, the vigorous advocacy of the past 20 years on behalf of all children who are exceptional has wrought profound and fundamental changes in the particular area of the education of students with hearing impairments. Although provincially funded residential/day schools remain important instructional and cultural vehicles, the current emphasis on appropriate integration with support services has meant shifts in program locations, student placements, and general class participation for youngsters who are hearing impaired.

Nevertheless, educational integration is an issue (only one of many) that remains beset with controversy. Many deaf people, advocacy groups, and some professionals working with students who are deaf see little benefit within the present inclusive practices. The issue is intertwined with the continuing viability of Deaf culture and the Deaf community, as well as with the mode of communication and bilingual education for children and youth who are deaf.

Students with hearing impairments have special needs in the classroom.

THE HUMAN EAR

The human ear is a truly marvellous instrument designed to collect sound, process it, and transmit it to be decoded in the brain. The ear is one of the most complex organs in the body, a triumph of miniaturization, fitting into a space not much larger than a hazelnut. It can detect sounds much softer than the dropping of a pin but still filter sounds a million times louder.

Hearing impairments are caused by interference with any part of the ear's transmission system. Impairment may take the form of restriction in the range of frequencies received, distortions along the frequency spectrum, or a failure to perceive sounds.

The ear's anatomy is usually discussed in terms of the external, the middle, and the inner ear. Figure 10-1 illustrates the major parts of the human hearing mechanism.

The External Ear

The outer ear is the visible cartilage structure on the side of the head, referred to as the pinna. This is the least complex part of the hearing mechanism and the least important for hearing. An external canal, or meatus, runs obliquely from the pinna to the eardrum. The eardrum, or **tympanic membrane**, is a tough, tightly stretched tissue that separates the outer from the middle ear. It is at the eardrum that hearing really begins.

The pinna serves to collect sound waves and filter them into the meatus. The external canal is lined with coarse hairs and 4000 wax glands that secrete cerumen. The wax traps insects, dust, and other irritants, guards against infection, and lubricates the canal and the eardrum.

The eardrum is a concave mechanism that vibrates freely when struck by sound waves. Even the faint vibrations of a whisper cause it to vibrate, but perhaps only a millionth of a centimetre.

tympanic membrane

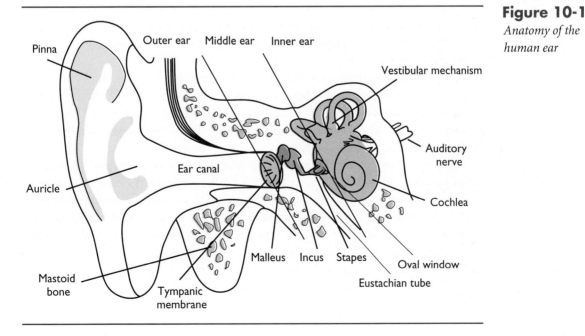

Figure 10-1
Anatomy of the human ear

Pinna

Outer ear   Middle ear   Inner ear

Vestibular mechanism

Auditory nerve

Ear canal

Auricle

Cochlea

Mastoid bone

Malleus   Incus   Stapes

Oval window

Tympanic membrane

Eustachian tube

The Middle Ear

The inner surface of the eardrum is located in the air-filled cavity of the middle ear. The middle eardrum surface holds three small bones, the malleus, the incus, and the stapes, also called the hammer, the anvil, and the stirrup. These tiny bones, the smallest in the human body, form a bridge, the *ossicular chain*, between the eardrum and the inner ear entrance at another drum called the *oval window*. There are two muscles in the middle ear, one joined to the stapes and the other to the eardrum. The Eustachian tube connects the middle ear to the nasopharynx.

In the middle ear, the transmission of sound becomes more sophisticated. When sound waves strike the eardrum, it vibrates and moves the three small bones. These bones transmit the vibrations across the middle ear cavity to the inner ear through the oval window. The middle ear amplifies the sound about 22 times, and also protects the inner ear from very loud noise.

The Eustachian tube serves to equalize the pressure on both sides of the eardrum. You may have experienced the discomfort of unequal pressure in an airplane descent. To clear the Eustachian tube, and to make the ears "pop," passengers yawn deeply, suck on hard candy, blow their noses, or swallow.

The Inner Ear

The inner ear, the real organ of hearing, is located in a cavern of the skull. It is about the size of a pea, an intricate mechanism with thousands of moving parts. Because it looks like a complex maze of passages, the inner ear is called the *labyrinth*. It contains the cochlea and the vestibular mechanism, which are independent in their functioning.

cochlea

The **cochlea** is a tiny, snail-shaped structure filled with a liquid similar to cerebrospinal fluid. Its twisting interior is studded with thousands of microscopic hair cells, each one tuned to a particular vibration that responds to a particular fragment of sound. Within the cochlea are highly specialized structures, such as the organ of Corti and Reissner's membrane. The auditory nerve, which is about the diameter of a pencil lead and consists of more than 31 000 nerve fibres, relays messages to the brain.

Behind the cochlea lies the vestibular mechanism, composed of three fluid-filled semicircular canals. These loops of tubing are the organs of balance. Information regarding movement and balance is fed to the brain through the vestibular mechanism. Other nerve endings in the body also contribute to the sense of balance—those in the eyes, feet, muscles, and joints.

The intricacy of the inner ear structure is matched by the complexity of its function. When air-carried (conducted) sound pushes on the eardrum, it causes the stapes to vibrate on the oval window leading to the inner ear, which makes the fluid in the cochlea begin to move. A low-pitched sound pushes at the top of the cochlea and a high-pitched sound pushes at the base. For example, if middle C is sounded, then the cochlea's middle C hair cells vibrate, waving in the fluid. The waving produces a wisp of electricity that feeds into the auditory nerve and is transmitted to the brain. There the signal is unscrambled and converted into meaningful sound. An overview of the sequence is provided in Table 10-1.

Table 10-1 The sequence of hearing

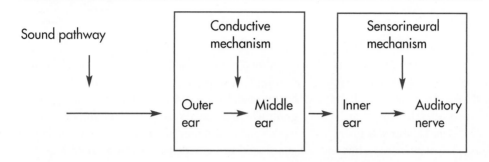

1. Sound waves enter the ear, travel through the external canal, and vibrate the eardrum.

2. The vibrations of the eardrum move the bones of the middle ear.

3. The footplate of the stapes moves the oval window and sets the cochlear fluid in motion.

4. The movement causes the hairs immersed in the cochlear fluid to move. This stimulates the attached cells to send a tiny electrical impulse along the fibres of the auditory nerve to the brain.

5. In the brain, impulses are translated into meaningful sound.

Most sound travels on air (air conduction). With bone conduction of sound, sound travels directly through the jawbone and the mastoid bone to the inner ear fluid. Because we hear our own voices by bone conduction, we hear ourselves quite differently from how our listeners hear us, and we often have trouble recognizing our own voices on a tape recorder.

DEFINITIONS OF HEARING IMPAIRMENT

The broad category of *hearing impairment* stretches from marginal hearing losses that may be a real concern only in noisy situations to profound deafness, where individuals cannot hear voiced sounds, even with amplification (hearing aids), and must resort to speech reading and, often, sign language. Steven, the child in the Case Study on the next page, has a severe to profound hearing loss. He cannot hear speech and has resorted to his own idiosyncratic home signs for basic communication.

More specifically, **hearing impairment** is a generic term indicating a hearing disability that may range in severity from mild to profound. It includes the subsets of *deaf* and *hard of hearing*.

hearing impairment

Deaf persons are those whose hearing disability precludes successful processing of linguistic information through audition, with or without a hearing aid. A **hard-of-hearing person** is one who, generally with the use of a hearing aid, has residual hearing sufficient to enable successful processing of linguistic information through audition.

deaf person

hard-of-hearing person

CASE STUDY

Steven

There did not seem to be any identifiable reason for Steven's severe hearing loss. Mrs. J. was healthy throughout her third pregnancy. She was slightly, but not overly, concerned when her infant arrived nearly a month before term. Labour was normal, lasting about 14 hours. The infant cried lustily, and Mrs. J. readily accepted the explanation that he was in neonatal intensive care only because he was of slightly low birth weight. Steven spent only a month in the neonatal unit. Once at home, he proved an easy baby who smiled and cooed at everyone. He began to babble early, but at about ten or eleven months of age stopped making any sounds at all.

Steven's mother was aware quite early that something was amiss with him. She suspected a hearing impairment when, by about eight months, Steven seemed impervious to cleaning, vacuuming, or telephone sounds. At this time, his mother took him to a pediatrician, who simply told her that the child would grow out of whatever she thought was ailing him—or alternatively, she was simply an overprotective parent. When Steven was a year old, another doctor suggested that perhaps he was developmentally delayed.

As Steven grew, he reached all the physical developmental milestones and became a sociable, gregarious child. His mother knew that a diagnosis of a significant cognitive disability did not suit her outgoing little toddler. But it was not until Steven and his mother saw two other physicians when Steven was almost a year-and-a-half old that a diagnosis of profound hearing impairment was made.

Almost immediately, Steven was fitted with hearing aids, which, to everyone's surprise, he readily accepted. He was placed on a home-visiting program where a teacher came to the family's home weekly and taught him language, including sign language, and promoted speech. She showed Mrs. J. how to stimulate vocalizations, and gave her some tips on receptive language development.

Mrs. J. behaved toward Steven and disciplined him just as she did the older children. She accepted his disability but held appropriate expectations for his development. He became an integral part of the family circle. Sibling resentment was not directed at any special treatment Steven received; it surfaced only when he got into the same type of mischief that any preschooler does.

By age two-and-a-half, Steven's expressive language was restricted to two words—*ma* for all his wants, and *moo* for a special toy car. Receptively, he responded consistently to his own name and "No." Steven also began to develop his own unique set of gestures and actions to convey meaning to his listeners.

When he was three, Steven's mother enrolled him in a preschool program that used American Sign Language (ASL). This decision had more to do with geography than a preference for any one mode of communication. Although his parents would have desperately liked Steven to speak and not sign, the program was in the area. As well, they realized that language acquisition was the important goal, whatever the mode.

CLASSIFICATION OF HEARING IMPAIRMENTS

Although very specific definitions for *deaf* and *hard of hearing* exist, the distinctions are not as clear-cut as the definitions imply. Both groups are heterogeneous, and subcategories of each are often used to further specify classification parameters.

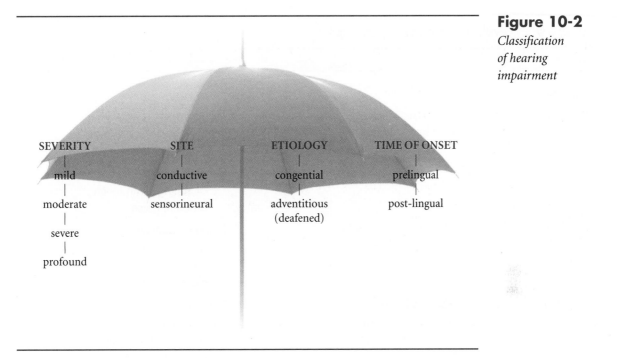

Figure 10-2
Classification of hearing impairment

The classifier's orientation often determines the system of classification. Those with a strictly physiological perspective are interested primarily in the measurable degree of hearing loss. On the other hand, educators want to know how hearing impairment will affect a child's functioning. Because hearing loss is closely linked to language delay, educators tend to categorize chiefly on the basis of language ability.

Four major, though closely interrelated, classification systems for hearing impairment are in use. These are founded on the degree of hearing impairment, the cause, the site of the deficit, and the age at which the impairment developed. Figure 10-2 shows the main classification of systems.

Classification by Severity Levels

Severity levels classify hearing loss according to the amount of hearing (acuity) in a person's better ear. Acuity is measured by the subject's response to loudness across a range of frequencies. *Decibels* and *hertz* are used to measure loudness and frequency, respectively. Individuals are classed as deaf or hard of hearing depending on whether they hear sounds at certain intensities of loudness across a range of frequencies. This classification is further structured by designation as mild, moderate, severe, or profound hearing loss. Table 10-2 illustrates the levels of hearing impairment.

A *bel*, named after Alexander Graham Bell, is the unit of loudness intensity. Each bel is broken down into 10 parts, known as *decibels* (dB). A **decibel** represents the smallest difference in loudness intensity that can be perceived. Hearing loss is measured on a decibel scale, beginning with 0 dB, a figure that designates the point at which people with normal

decibel

Table 10-2 Levels of hearing impairment

Range	Severity	Implications
0–25 dB	Insignificant	
25–40 dB	Mild hearing loss; hard of hearing	May have difficulty with faint or distant sounds.
		May have problems in conversations, groups, or settings with much ambient noise.
40–60 dB	Moderate hearing loss; hard of hearing	Frequent difficulty with normal speech, especially in conversations, groups, and class discussions.
60–90 dB	Severe hearing loss; hard of hearing	Great difficulty with even loud or amplified speech, which seems faint and distorted. Requires amplification and intense speech and language training.
90 dB+	Profound hearing loss; deaf	May be aware of loud sounds and vibrations, but generally cannot understand even amplified speech.

hearing can detect the faintest sound. Inability to hear sounds of 25 to 30 dB or more is considered to be a hearing loss. However, a loss of 60 dB is not merely six times greater than a loss of 10 dB. The figures are logarithmic, not arithmetic, so that 60 dB is 10^6 times louder than 10 dB. Figure 10-3 shows the decibel (dB) level of some common sounds on an **audiogram**, a chart on which hearing is recorded.

audiogram

Sound waves are produced by the to-and-fro waving movement of molecules. One complete to-and-fro movement makes a cycle; the number of cycles per second determines the frequency of a sound. Cycles per second are measured in **hertz** (Hz)—a frequency of 1000 Hz indicates 1000 cycles per second. As the frequency increases, the pitch of the sound becomes higher.

hertz

Although the human ear is sensitive to frequencies between 50 and 20 000 Hz, most human speech falls between 500 and 2000 Hz. This range of pitch is known as the **speech range**. Middle C on a piano is about 500 Hz.

speech range

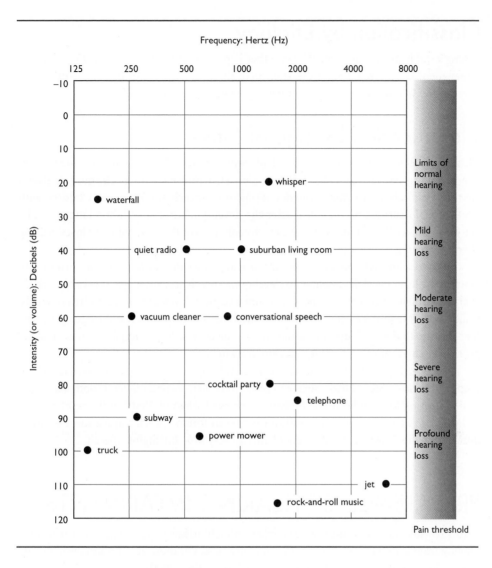

Figure 10-3
Chart showing the hearing level of some common sounds

Classification by Site of Loss

Hearing impairment is also classified according to the part of the hearing mechanism that is affected. Problems in the mechanical transmission of sound waves through the outer and middle ear are called **conductive hearing losses** because something stops the air conduction of sound. Conductive losses generally affect the intensity of sound reception but do not distort the sound. Conductive losses, affecting the outer and middle ear only, usually respond favourably to medical or surgical intervention.

conductive hearing losses

Impairment in the inner ear is caused by abnormal sense organs (sensory) or defective auditory nerves (neural). These **sensorineural hearing impairments** interfere with the conversion of sound waves into neural impulses for the brain. Not only is sound intensity hampered, but any sound received may also be distorted. Sensorineural hearing loss is the common type among children with serious losses.

sensorineural hearing impairments

Classification by Etiology

A *congenital* hearing impairment is one that is present at birth; an *adventitious* hearing impairment is acquired some time after birth through accident or disease. People with adventitious hearing losses are sometimes described as *deafened*.

Classification by Age of Onset

prelingual deafness

post-lingual deafness

Closely connected to the classification of adventitious and congenital hearing impairment is a grouping concerned with the age of onset. Children with **prelingual deafness** are those who are deaf prior to the development of speech and language. Children with **post-lingual deafness** become deaf after the development of speech and language. The cut-off point is often set at 2 years of age. Note that fewer than 1 child in 10 loses hearing after the age of 2.

Children with prelingual (congenital) hearing losses do not have the opportunity to practise the listening skills essential to developing speech and language. Inevitably, prelingual impairment affects every aspect of communication development from birth onwards. Children who acquire hearing impairments after they develop speech and language usually find it easier to develop communication skills. The later in life an impairment occurs, the greater the child's linguistic capabilities are likely to be.

The case study of Steven is illustrative here. Although the medical profession could not pinpoint a reason, Steven had a severe to profound sensironeural bilateral (both ears) congenital hearing loss. Audiometric assessment showed a loss of 95 dB in the right ear and 100 dB in the left. Even with amplification, Steven found speech acquisition extremely difficult. By the time he arrived at school, he had very little intelligible speech.

PREVALENCE OF HEARING IMPAIRMENTS

Across North America, about 1 in 10 people is thought to have some degree of hearing loss, ranging from a mild impairment to profound deafness. For those aged 65 and over, the rate rises to 50 percent (Canadian Hard of Hearing Association, 2000).

Hearing loss is most tragic when it strikes the very young. Its incidence at birth is quite low, however. About 1 infant in every 1000 is born profoundly deaf, or is deaf before the age of 3. But about 1 percent of all children have minimal hearing loss (Berg, 1987), so when infants with mild losses are included, the numbers are as high as 1 in 750 (Ruppert & Buhrer, 1992). Put together, this means that approximately 5 percent of school-aged children have hearing outside the normal limits. Of this number, 10 to 20 percent require some type of special education ("Children with communication …" 1995).

The figures are only estimates. It is difficult to arrive at an exact determination of the prevalence of hearing impairment, and reported rates vary considerably. Of the many factors that hinder researchers from arriving at accurate prevalence figures for hearing loss, the most important are

• Inconsistent definitional data

• Confusion regarding identification and reporting

- Methodological problems in surveys. For example, after comparing surveys in Canada and the United States, Jerome Schein (1994) found that hearing impairment in the United States has a prevalence rate of 86 per 1000, as compared to 41 per 1000 in Canada, which reflects the younger overall age of the Canadian population. Schein also found that rates vary considerably across the Canadian provinces, from a low of 34 per 1000 in the Northwest Territories to 61 per 1000 in Prince Edward Island and Manitoba.

- Difficulties in accurate early identification of hearing loss. The average age of identifying childhood hearing loss is quite late—between 17.5 and 25 months (Mayne, Yoshinaga-Itano, Seday, & Carey, 2000).

- Increasing prevalence of hearing impairment with age. Hearing loss among elderly persons is especially common.

- Difficulties in estimating hearing impairments among individuals with multiple disabilities, who are often reported according to their primary disability

- A shortage of research in some areas. An extensive body of research deals with deafness; much less exists in relation to hard-of-hearing individuals. While hard-of-hearing children are much more common, their true numbers are unknown, since many cases are misdiagnosed or simply overlooked.

ETIOLOGY OF HEARING IMPAIRMENTS

Etiological and diagnostic considerations in hearing impairment are the responsibility of medical and paramedical personnel. *Audiologists* are chiefly involved in the assessment of hearing and recommending and fitting amplification equipment. *Otolaryngologists* are medical personnel concerned with the problems of the ear, nose, and throat that affect hearing and speech. They also handle voice disorders through medication and surgery.

Impairments of the Outer Ear

External otitis, or swimmer's ear, is an infection of the skin of the external auditory canal. Also in the canal, an excessive buildup of wax can result in decreased hearing acuity. Infrequently, a child is born with missing or undeveloped auditory canals. This condition, known as *auditory atresia*, interferes with the air conduction of sound and requires medical or surgical intervention before it impedes a child's education. *Microtia* refers to a misshapen or extremely small pinna. Perforation of the eardrum, resulting from any number of causes, can also produce hearing impairment.

The problem of foreign objects in the ear has always existed and probably always will. Nature designed the ear to clean itself. An old saying claims that if a finger were intended to go in the ear, it would have been made small enough to fit. Unfortunately, many other things do fit—the ends of pencils, beads, carrots, peanuts, and bobby pins. Even cotton swabs can do enormous damage, either by puncturing the paper-thin eardrum or pushing accumulations of wax further into the ear.

Impairments of the Middle Ear

Middle ear hearing impairments are more serious than those affecting the outer ear, but most are surgically correctable. The great majority of middle ear conditions are conductive hearing losses, meaning that the conduction of sound by air is hindered. The result is a loss of intensity of sound, though not usually a distorted pattern. Conductive losses do not exceed 65 dB.

otitis media

The most common form of ear infection in children is **otitis media**, a condition in which the mucosal lining of the middle ear becomes inflamed and the cavity filled with fluid. Infections use the Eustachian tube to reach the middle ear from the nose or throat.

Otitis media is most extreme in infancy, when the Eustachian tube is shorter, wider, and in a more horizontal position. It is estimated that 50 to 75 percent of children have one episode of otitis media in the first year of life (Roberts, 1997). The peak prevalence for otitis media is between 6 and 36 months (Bluestone, 1982). After six years of age, the incidence steadily decreases. However, in the normal school environment, 20 to 30 percent of children between the ages of five and twelve will have at least one bout of middle ear effusion.

Otitis media affects males more often than females. The prevalence is higher among lower socio-economic groups, in children with cleft palates, and in those with other cranio-facial anomalies. Children with Down syndrome are especially susceptible to otitis media and its resulting conductive hearing loss. Researchers have also found a higher prevalence among Native children, but a lower prevalence among Blacks (Robinson, Allen, & Root, 1988). The reason for the higher prevalence among Natives is unclear, but it may be a combination of genetic, sociocultural, environmental, and economic factors.

otosclerosis

Otosclerosis is a hereditary condition characterized by the destruction of the capsular bone in the middle ear and the growth of a web-like bone that attaches to and restricts the stapes. Otosclerosis, which is twice as common in females as in males, affects 2 percent of the population and is clinically active in more than 0.5 percent ("Hearing loss …" 1982). The condition is rare in children and is not usually noticed until adolescence or the early 20s. Resultant hearing losses can be at the 50 or 60 dB level, necessitating the use of a hearing aid or corrective surgery.

Other middle ear problems can be caused by a blow to the head or a fall. They can also result from congenital defects.

Impairments of the Inner Ear

The most devastating hearing impairments are caused by sensorineural problems of the inner ear. A great many of these childhood sensorineural impairments are attributed to "causes unknown." Identifiable causes include the traditional villains, with the most profound losses stemming from meningitis, maternal rubella, and hereditary factors.

Today, rubella and Rh factor are well controlled, if they have not been eliminated, and there are inoculations against forms of meningitis. Genetic factors remain prominent; estimates range from 30 to 60 percent (Moores, 1982). There are about 65 types of hereditary deafness. Hearing problems may be inherited on a dominant trait (14 percent), a recessive trait (44 percent), or as a sex-linked disorder (2 percent) (Lowenbraun & Thompson, 1982).

Prematurity itself does not cause deafness. However, premature and low-birthweight babies are at higher risk for hearing disorders. Deafness can also result from birth complications such as prolonged labour, abrupt birth, or the use of obstetrical instruments. Failure to breathe immediately after birth—*apnea*—is another commonly reported cause of hearing problems.

Among adults, progressive nerve deterioration, known as **presbycusis** (deafness of age), is the most common cause of auditory defect. The older one gets, the more one is prone to presbycusis. As well, intracranial tumours, cerebral hemorrhages, inner ear fistula (a build-up of inner ear fluid), acoustic neuroma (tumour on the auditory nerve), and viral infections and vascular spasms in the inner ear can cause permanent or temporary Sudden Hearing Loss Syndrome.

presbycusis

Noise assaults on ears from bars, dance clubs, subway trains, motorcycles, farm and factory equipment, power tools, guns, and stereo earphones cause damage. For example, a power lawnmower emits 100 dB, a subway train 90, a riveting gun 130, and a jet take-off 105 or more. Modern music also causes hearing impairments: rock bands often reach 115 dB. Muscles in the middle ear protect the inner ear from excessively loud low-pitched sounds, but no such action protects the ear from these high-pitched sounds. Prolonged exposure to tones of high intensity causes the tiny hair cells in the inner ear to eventually break and die.

Ménière's disease, a condition characterized by nausea, vertigo—a spinning sensation—and tinnitus, is a particularly devastating problem. Ménière's is caused by a buildup of endolymphatic (inner ear) fluid that creates increased pressure on the inner ear. The pressure increases ruptures in the inner ear compartments, which causes the vertigo.

The tinnitus that accompanies Ménière's disease can also occur as a sole condition in both deaf and hearing individuals. The word *tinnitus* derives from Latin, meaning to "tinkle or ring like a bell." For some sufferers it may be hearing a ringing or a hiss, but for others it is living constantly with the noise of a squeaking door hinge, the squealing of an unoiled metal bearing, or the sound of fingernails being dragged across a blackboard (Agnew, 1986). The chronic nature of the condition causes great distress and becomes the central issue in the lives of some affected people.

Tinnitus is not an audiological phenomenon but a medical condition. The actual mechanism is not known. Tinnitus does not have a specific site of origin; it can be produced anywhere along the auditory mechanism, or it may not be generated by the auditory system at all. Anything that can go wrong with the ear may have tinnitus associated with it as a symptom—wax against the drum, tumours on the nerve, otosclerosis, Ménière's disease, and exposure to excessively loud sounds (Agnew, 1986). Tinnitis affects about 17 percent of the population (Canadian Hard of Hearing Association, 2000).

Syndromes

Hearing loss can be inherited alone or in combination with other abnormalities in a syndrome. Impairments of hearing accompany skeletal deformities in Treacher-Collins syndrome and abnormal skin pigmentation in Waardenburg's syndrome, and are sometimes part of the multiple disabilities of Down syndrome. Approximately 4 to 5 percent of congenitally hearing-impaired individuals suffer from Usher's syndrome, which results in hearing impairment and a progressive deterioration in the visual field through retinitis pigmentosa (see Chapter 15). Pendred's syndrome, Alpert's syndrome, and Jervell and Lang-Neilson syndrome are also associated with hearing impairment.

DEVELOPMENTAL CONSEQUENCES OF HEARING IMPAIRMENTS

The major disability associated with hearing impairment is the impact on the development of speech and language. This can, and often does, spill over to adversely affect other developmental domains.

Cognitive Development

The relationship between cognitive development and how it is affected by auditory and linguistic deficits is a long-standing, provocative, and challenging area of research. Studies show that in general the hearing-impaired group fits on the same curve for intelligence as the rest of the population (Quinsland & Vanginkel, 1990). In addition, children who are deaf consistently demonstrate the same thinking processes as hearing children, with language as the mediating factor. That is, students who are deaf but who have acquired some language consistently outperform those with less language ability.

Communication

If you look back to the Case Study on page 326, you will see that Steven is a normal, outgoing, sometimes mischievous little boy. The way in which he differs from his siblings and peers is in his acquisition and development of speech and language. For Steven and all other children with hearing impairments, speech and language are the areas of development most severely affected. Deficits vary considerably as a result of many factors, including the degree of hearing loss, the training and use of residual hearing, the child's age at the impairment's onset, the etiology of the impairment, the family climate, the early mode of communication, and the educational setting.

For children with mild or moderate hearing losses, the effect on speech and language may be minimal. In fact, communication for the child who is hard of hearing has more in common with that of the normally hearing child than with that of the child who is deaf. This happens because both hearing and hard-of-hearing individuals use audition rather than vision as the primary mode for speech and language development. In other words, children who are hard of hearing use their residual hearing to develop speech and language, and they use spoken language adequately to transmit and receive information, although they may speech read as a supplement to auditory skills.

Even so, a number of related variables may place children who are hard of hearing at risk for educational failure. For one thing, the general environment of most classrooms presents serious problems. Berg (1987) estimated that typical levels of noise in schools range from 45 to 60 dB within classrooms, and up to 70 to 90 dB in the gymnasium, cafeteria, and computer rooms. A teacher generally speaks at 55 to 70 dB, the same level as the background noise. In such settings, children with any hearing loss are challenged to hear spoken language at a distance in the presence of background noise. Hence, mild to moderate hearing loss (10 to 40 dB) can impair the listening performance of a young child to the extent of becoming an auditory handicap.

Otitis media, a medical problem, has significant social and educational implications. It leads to temporary to chronic mild fluctuating hearing loss, causing children to receive variable input rather than a consistent model of language (Walker & Wrigglesworth, 2001). This can affect the development of auditory discrimination and processing skills, phonological awareness, short-term auditory memory skills, and auditory sequential memory skills, and may be implicated in later speech disorders. It is also known that children with minimal hearing loss have higher levels of language delay, and there is a strong correlation between early incidence of minimal loss and later problems in academic learning, particularly reading development (Luotomen, Uhari, & Aitola, 1996). The accumulated effects are usually felt in about grade 3 or 4.

For children who are deaf, the impact on communication is far more devastating. Speech is inaudible to the child, even with the most sophisticated hearing aids. This means that children face major difficulties in learning language, as well as significant articulation, voice quality, and tone discrimination problems.

Because children who are deaf cannot hear the words of people around them, they have no language models. Even with optimal intervention, their language levels are seriously retarded. Every element of language is affected—semantics, syntax, morphology, pragmatics, and phonology.

One study of 132 deaf and hard-of-hearing children who used a variety of communication modes found an average of 300 signed or spoken words at three to four years of age, and 514 words at five to six years of age (Yoshingata-Itano, 1994). This must be compared to the 10 000 to 14 000 or so words we would expect to find in a hearing child of six (see Chapter 4). Not only is vocabulary in any mode restricted, but students who are deaf plateau in vocabulary development when they are about twelve or thirteen (Mayne et al., 2000).

Constructions such as phrasal verbs (*turn off, run in*) pose great difficulties. Similarly, figurative language (idioms, similes, metaphors, proverbs, and so on) involves every area of comprehension and semantics and is beyond most students who are deaf (see Arnold & Hornett, 1990). An idiom such as "hit the road" transgresses the laws of logic and is almost impossible to justify for a literal-thinking deaf person. One teacher tells how a young child looked bewildered when she signed to him, "Your nose is running." To the deaf child, running was something done on the playground and not something that noses did.

Individuals who are hearing impaired have specific voice and speech characteristics and vary in their speech intelligibility. In general, however, speech is dismayingly difficult for deaf students to acquire. Reports place the average speech intelligibility of children with severe to profound losses who wear aids at about 20 percent, although there is wide variability in estimates (Carney, 1986).

Academic Achievement

The educational outcomes for students with hearing impairments has not improved significantly over the decades (Holden-Pitt & Diaz, 1998). Because academic achievement is so closely aligned to the acquisition of language, the academic performance of students with hearing disabilities compares poorly with their documented potential. Students who are deaf uniformly appear to lag educationally by three to five years.

Reading is a primarily a linguistic skill. Pupils who are hard of hearing and rely primarily on residual hearing and speech for communication sometimes have language deficiencies that limit their reading comprehension as well as their oral communication skills.

The majority of students who are deaf find acquiring reading and writing skills to be the most difficult academic hurdle that they face. Numerous studies of reading achievement show the mean reading scores of children who are deaf are well below those of hearing children; there is a lag of two to eight years. According to data published by Gallaudet University (Center for Assessment, 1991; Traxler, 2000), the average eighteen-year-old with a severe to profound hearing loss reads with the comprehension of a normally hearing child in grade 3 or 4. This is below or barely at literacy level. Only 3 percent of deaf eighteen-year-olds read at the same level as the average hearing reader of the same age.

Children who are deaf are less educationally behind in more mechanical skills such as arithmetic and spelling. But while they seem to achieve well in mathematical computation, they are less successful at mathematical problem solving, which is predicated on a language base.

Social and Emotional Development

Because severe hearing loss so dramatically affects language and communication, it may produce barriers to normal social interaction that appear impossible to overcome. The severity of social maladjustment patterns often depends on the depth of the hearing loss and the type of impairment. Severe and profound hearing losses are more likely to result in social isolation.

Students who are hard of hearing represent an unaddressed population that is often misunderstood and underserved (David, 1990). Sometimes the hearing impairment may be misdiagnosed and a child's inappropriate responses may be erroneously seen as behaviour problems or learning disorders. When this happens, the child's self-sufficiency, social maturity, and personality development are placed at risk.

Children with hearing impairments consistently experience difficulties in maintaining social interactions with their peers (Lederberg, 1991; Remine, 1996). There is also a higher degree of emotional instability, neurosis, and maladjustment than what is seen in hearing children. Estimates of the rates of emotional disturbance among students who are hearing impaired range from 8 to 22 percent. Although this range is broad, there is also sufficient evidence to conclude that the frequency of behavioural disorders is higher than for the general population of school-aged children (Adams & Tidwell, 1989).

Abnormal social development in children who are hearing impaired is often manifested by impulsive, irresponsible, and dependent behaviour. Frequently, children seem to disregard the feelings and misunderstand the actions of others. They typically exhibit a high degree of egocentricity and a low frustration threshold. These traits cause them to make inordinate demands and act out their frustrations if these demands are not met.

Play Behaviours

In young hearing children, close parallels exist between the development of pretend (dramatic, symbolic) play and the development of language. Australian researchers (Roberts, Brown, & Rickards, 1996) summarized the research on the play of deaf children.

They note that, compared to typical children, those who are deaf initiate interactions less frequently. They experience greater rejection, engage in less complex and less dramatic play, and have less interaction with partners during play. Deaf children prefer solitary constructive play, whereas hearing children of the same age prefer co-operative dramatic play.

Co-occurring Disabilities

An estimated 25 to 33 percent of students who are deaf or hard of hearing have secondary learning problems (Schildroth & Hotto, 1996). Emotional disorders, intellectual disabilities, and learning disabilities are the most common (see Holden-Pitt & Diaz, 1998). As well, all studies on vision screening indicate a higher incidence of visual deficits than among normally hearing children (Silberman, 1981).

Family Variables

The way in which the parents and the family react to and accept a child's disabling condition profoundly influences his or her development. This is even more true in the area of hearing impairment, where the hearing status of the parents is a significant variable and where parental child-rearing attitudes appear to be the best predictors of the self-concept of children who are severely to profoundly hearing impaired (Warren & Hasenstab, 1986).

Approximately 10 percent of babies who are hearing impaired are born to deaf parents. These children form a distinct subgroup within the hearing-impaired population. Children deafened by genetic factors tend to have far more positive outcomes than children who are deaf and born to hearing parents. Emotional and behavioural disturbance is about half as prevalent among deaf children with deaf parents as among children who are deaf with hearing parents (Stokoe & Battiston, 1975). Children who have deaf parents outperform children with hearing parents on measures of language skills. In school, these same children consistently perform at a higher level on tests of academic achievement than deaf children of hearing parents. Several studies demonstrate that deaf children of deaf parents have higher reading achievement and better language skills than deaf children of hearing parents (Bornstein, Selmi, Haynes, Painter, & Marx, 1999).

The reasons that underlie the differences between children who are deaf who have hearing parents and those who have deaf parents are not difficult to pinpoint, but they are important to understand in light of our upcoming discussions on bilingual–bicultural education and the Deaf community. The prominent factors that emerge are

* *Early identification.* It is during infancy that children who are born deaf most closely resemble their hearing peers. Deaf infants follow the normal patterns of visual exploration and motor development. They also cry and coo and vocalize like other children during the first few months of life. Not until they reach the babbling stage at about six months do their sound patterns become differentiated from those of hearing infants. By the age of ten months, infants who are deaf show a significant decrease in babbling behaviour. This happens because they cannot hear their own babbling and do not receive reinforcement from the speech of adults.

  For a child of parents who are deaf, early vocal behaviours will not outweigh the anticipation of hearing loss and parents will naturally sign to the baby. In constrast, hearing parents are not expecting a loss and, unknowingly, will provide language input that is unsuited to the child. As well, it is typical of children of hearing parents to be identified much later—between seventeen-and-a-half and twenty-five months—and much prime intervention time is lost.

- *Acceptance of the diagnosis.* Deaf children who have deaf parents are born into families that already have experience with deafness. Parents who are deaf understand the child's condition and seem better able to cope with any negative feelings that accompany diagnosis. Hearing parents are much more likely than deaf parents to view their child's diagnosis as a tragic crisis; they often express feelings of incompetence, self-doubt, and sorrow.

- *Language use.* Parents who are deaf are fluent in sign language, so their children usually experience language acquisition and family interaction earlier and at a greater rate than other children who are deaf. Mothers who are deaf help their infants acquire language in the same way that hearing mothers do with hearing babies. Deaf mothers of infants who are deaf seem to sign more slowly and modify the location of the sign so that the child can see it more easily, and use more repetitions (Erting, Prezioso, & Hynes, 1990).

- *The Deaf community.* Children who are deaf with parents who are also deaf have closer exposure to other deaf people and to the discrete culture of the Deaf community. Such cultural awareness and identity enhances self-concept (Innes, 1994). Identity with deafness seems important because anecdotal reports suggest that some students do not realize that they will be deaf adults when they grow up because they have never seen a deaf adult. One study found that one-third of young deaf people had, as children, thought they would grow up to be hearing (Gregory, Bishop, & Sheldon, 1995).

- *Co-occurring disabilities.* Deafness in families is genetic and children rarely suffer additional injuries to the nervous system before birth. As a result, their incidence of secondary disabilities is no greater than for the population at large.

Hearing Children of Deaf Parents

We must also give a passing glance at another subgroup with potential language, speech, and social and emotional difficulties. Although not hearing impaired, the communication and emotional prognosis for hearing children of deaf parents can be problematic.

Research in this area is fairly scattered. One early study (Schiff & Ventry, 1976) of 52 hearing children of parents who were deaf found that only 23 had developed normal language. The other 29 showed speech and language problems, including defective articulation, deviant stress and intonational patterns, and fluency disorders, problems which did not disappear after the children entered school. In another study of 6 preschool hearing children of deaf parents (Murphy & Slorach, 1983), 3 of the children showed delayed and deviant language development and 3 had other language problems. Finally, a British study (Flaxbeard & Toomey, 1987) of 10 hearing children of parents who were deaf found that the children exhibited conversational difficulties, memory problems, reasoning difficulties, and poor language comprehension.

Socially, young children may take on unexpected burdens simply because of their parents' deafness. Hearing children feel a strong responsibility to help parents make decisions, explain deafness to hearing people, and be an advocate for the Deaf community.

Cultural Differences

Cultural and linguistic differences take on a somewhat different meaning and must also be expanded when applied to persons who are deaf. On the one hand, there are many students who are recent immigrants or refugees and are also hearing impaired. These children have their own unique set of problems (see Akamatsu & Cole, 2000). On the other hand, we must look to deafness as culture, manifest in the Deaf community.

The Deaf community has been studied from a variety of disciplines—including psychology, sociology, history, anthropology, and linguistics—and various definitions have evolved. In general, the term **Deaf community** refers to those hearing-impaired people who share common attitudes, experiences, and language, and participate in social institutions run for and by the Deaf. (Note that in this context *Deaf community* and *the Deaf* are acceptable descriptors. An uppercase *D* in Deaf indicates a community with its own language and culture, analogous to, say, French or Greek culture).

Deaf community

Like any other group, the deaf population is extremely heterogeneous, comprising people of varying levels of auditory capabilities, linguistic skills, cognitive abilities, social skills, and emotional development, as well as varying in ethnicity, socio-economic status, geographic location, and so on. This disparate and heterogeneous population has one defining commonality—people in this group use sign language and therefore find that their lives are defined by unique experiences and communication modalities that differ from those of an oral-language-based hearing society.

As a discrete group with a common language binding it, the Deaf community in Canada can be traced back to the formation of the first residential schools in the mid-19th century. Today, the Deaf community is growing both in numbers and in political and social activism.

In the past few decades, the fertility of deaf adults has rapidly approached that of the general population. Moreover, a deaf person typically marries someone else with a hearing loss. Currently, in-group marriages are estimated at between 86 and 90 percent of all marriages involving deaf people (see Reagan, 1988).

Socially and politically, deafness is not on the defensive as it once was. Quite the contrary. Deaf people today lay claim to make decisions about their own lives, their own mode of communication, their own schools, and the curriculum presented therein. From this you can see that the Deaf community in the cultural sense is not a claim about hearing status but rather a claim about the self-recognition that defines all minority or ethnic groups, and that the term *Deaf* designates cultural group membership.

Deafness as culture is also an overarching concern in educational placement and curriculum. The Deaf community promotes segregated schooling, preferably in residential settings. As the child who is deaf is a member of a unique linguistic and cultural group, "Forcing deaf children to be part of the hearing world denies them the right to themselves" (Elliott, 1993, p. 11). When we discuss cochlear implants later in this chapter, you will see that this also forms a contentious issue for the Deaf community.

ASSESSMENT OF HEARING IMPAIRMENTS

Measuring a hearing impairment and its effects is quite complicated because measurement must incorporate the physical, psychological, and educational aspects as well as the impact on speech and language acquisition and development. To assess the various domains, a number of professionals and related disciplines are involved—physicians, audiologists, psychologists, educators, and speech and language therapists.

Measurement of Hearing Loss

audiology

Audiology is the science of detecting and correcting hearing impairment. The major purposes of audiology are to assist in medical diagnosis; to provide an overall assessment of hearing in order to ascertain the need for supportive services; and to detect changes in hearing that may have resulted from exposure to hazards. Audiologists use many sophisticated methods to assess hearing. In general, three major categories of hearing tests are used—pure tone audiometry, speech audiometry, and specialized tests for very young and difficult-to-assess children.

Pure Tone Audiometry

Almost all children with severe or profound hearing losses will be identified well before the school years. Detection of those with milder losses is far more problematic.

It is estimated that 80 percent of children with hearing impairments are identified through informal means, usually observations by parents or teachers (Barringer, Strong, Blair, Clark, & Watkins, 1993). Table 10-3 outlines some of the behaviours that suggest mild hearing loss. Teachers and parents should be alert to these behaviours and send children with suspected problems for audiological evaluation.

School systems provide screening at set intervals. The most common screening procedure is the *sweep test*. In this procedure, an audiometer is used to present tones at

Table 10-3 Possible signs of mild hearing loss in children

- There appears to be a physical problem associated with the ears, such as buzzing, earaches, discharge, or frequent colds and sore throats.
- The child has poor articulation, particularly missing some of the consonant sounds.
- The child cocks the head or turns the body toward the speaker in an obvious effort to hear more accurately.
- The child has more than usual trouble following directions.
- The child frequently asks for information to be repeated.
- The child appears to be inattentive when spoken to in a normal voice.
- The child speaks or sings too loudly or too softly.
- The child talks too much and appears not to want to relinquish control of the conversation.
- The child is withdrawn and unwilling to mingle with classmates or neighbours.
- The child gives incorrect answers to simple questions.
- The child is functioning below potential ability in school.
- The child is becoming a behaviour problem at school or at home.

20 to 25 dB across a range of frequencies. The sweep test establishes an individual's *threshold of hearing*—the level at which a person first detects a sound—at different frequencies. Problems at the screening level indicate the need for in-depth audiological testing.

Pure tone testing is a relatively simple procedure. The audiologist presents a variety of tones at levels from 0 to 110 dB across a range of frequencies, usually 125 to 8000 Hz, testing each ear individually. The person being tested responds by raising a hand when a sound is detected, and the data for each ear are plotted on a chart of hearing called an *audiogram*.

Figure 10-4 shows an audiogram on which the average loss (both ears) of three individuals is plotted. Person A has a flat loss of about 70 dB. This person begins to detect sounds only at the level of 70 dB and would be regarded as moderately hearing impaired. Because of the amount of residual hearing, especially across the speech range (500 to 2000 Hz), a hearing aid would help this individual. Person B suffers a hearing loss described as a "ski slope loss" because of its shape. This person, with little usable hearing above 90 dB and none across the speech range, would be categorized as profoundly deaf. Person C displays a saucer-shaped audiological pattern and is also profoundly deaf but with some hearing at the very low and very high frequencies.

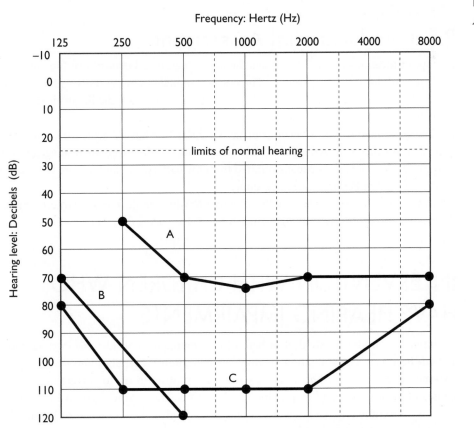

Figure 10-4

Audiogram

Speech Audiometry

speech reception
threshold

Speech audiometry is designed to assess an individual's ability to detect and understand speech. The speech detection threshold refers to the intensity level at which a person can hear, but not necessarily understand, speech. Much more important is the **speech reception threshold** (SRT), the level at which an individual actually understands speech.

To ascertain the speech reception threshold, the tester presents the person with a list of two-syllable words (called *spondees*) that have equal stress on each syllable—*baseball* or *ice cream* are examples. Each ear is tested separately, and the level at which half of the words are understood is the speech reception threshold.

Tests for Young Children

Pure tone audiometry can be used only with people who understand what is expected of them; that is, people who can discriminate among sounds of different intensity and tone and then communicate their discriminations. For a child under the age of about four, the process is too complicated. A number of special tests have been devised for very young children and for those whose disabilities do not suit standard pure tone audiometric testing. The two most common forms of specialized hearing tests are *electrophysiological* and *behavioural*. We discuss these in Chapter 14.

Psycho-educational Assessment

A range of measures is needed to assess the psychological and educational functioning of students with hearing impairments. The one commonality among tools and procedures is that they circumvent the effects of the hearing loss and match the linguistic deficits of the child.

To assess mental ability, versions of the Wechsler Intelligence Scale for Children are used. This is believed to yield fairly valid IQ scores for children who are deaf aged nine to sixteen. The Verbal Scale is usually omitted from the battery, and an IQ score is calculated on the basis of the Performance Scale alone.

Assessment of the English skills of students who are deaf has a large literature. Assessment tools for American Sign Language (ASL) are being developed.

INTERVENTION WITH CHILDREN WHO HAVE HEARING IMPAIRMENTS

Children and youth who are deaf or hard of hearing require considerable intervention to provide health care, rehabilitation, therapy, and education. Generally, intervention involves two major components. The first is medical intervention to try to correct the physical causes of hearing loss and to provide amplification. The second form of intervention focuses on minimizing the educational and psychological consequences of hearing loss through counselling, special education, and support services.

Medical Intervention

Most conductive hearing losses can be medically corrected. Chronic otitis media is alleviated by antibiotics in the early stages or by a **myringotomy**, a procedure in which ventilating tubes are placed in the eardrums to provide proper ventilation between the middle ear cavity and the outside environment via the external ear canal.

myringotomy

Otological surgeons can free the stapes in the case of otosclerosis; surgically reconstruct the middle ear (tympanoplasty); rebuild the three tiny bones of the ossicular chain; repair, shift, or rebuild an eardrum; and construct new membranous windows into the inner ear. When infants are born with an atresia, surgeons make a bony canal into the middle ear.

Ménière's disease is treated with diet and varying surgical approaches. Surgery exposes or decompresses the endolymphatic sac from its surrounding bony structures behind the mastoid bone and a shunt then drains excess fluid.

Cochlear Implants

There are no prosthetic devices capable of restoring normal hearing. However, some lost function of the cochlea may be replaced through the use of a prosthesis called a cochlear implant. Cochlear implants were developed in Australia in the late 1970s. In 1985, the U.S. Food and Drug Administration approved the use of cochlear implants for adults; in 1990, approval was given for children (Harrington & Powers, 2004). Since the clinical introduction of the device, more than 20 000 people around the world, half of them children, have received cochlear implants (Bonn, 1998).

Implantation is far more suited to children. According to the U.S. Food and Drug Administration, a child must be at least twelve months of age, show limited or no benefit from amplification, and limited development of auditory skills to qualify for a cochlear implant procedure (Zwolen, 2000). Older persons who are deaf are not always suitable recipients for implants; those with tinnitus, for example, may actually suffer an increase of head noises with the devices.

The term *cochlear implant* is somewhat misleading, as it implies surgical reconstruction of the cochlea by repair or transplant. In fact, a **cochlear implant** is an electronic device that provides auditory information to individuals who have severe to profound sensironeural hearing losses in both ears and who receive limited or no benefit from conventional hearing aids (McKinley & Warren, 2000).

cochlear implant

In persons with profound deafness, the specialized hair cells in the cochlea that stimulate the nerve endings no longer work. In essence, the implant replaces the function of these hair cells: they bypass the absent or damaged hair cells of the inner ear and directly stimulate the surviving hearing nerve fibres with electrical current (Nelson & Johnston, 2003).

Cochlear implants consist of surgically implanted internal components as well as externally worn components. The components vary depending upon the manufacturer of the implant and the ever-changing technology. The internal device picks up sound, creates the sensation of sound in the inner ear, then sends it to the brain for interpretation. Externally, there is a microphone that looks like a behind-the-ear hearing aid and is connected to the speech processor and transmitter.

For a person who is profoundly deaf, a cochlear implant will produce hearing at the severe level (71 to 90 dB) (Spencer, 2002). However, the competencies a person may attain with an implant depend on a group of variables. These include the age of the person, the age of onset of the loss, the duration of deafness, the length and regularity of implant use, and the engineering process of the actual device.

Once a person has a device, speech production with cochlear implants is slower than speech perception. Post-lingually deaf children and adults attain better results during the first year after implantation than congenitally and prelingually deaf children who show slow progress in the first two years. Even so, it is suggested that production will improve as long as the child is trained and challenged in the oral modality (Nevins & Chute, 1996).

Of course, there are downsides to implantation. It is invasive surgery that destroys any residual hearing in the implanted ear. Nor are implants universally accepted. McKinley and Warren (2000) wrote that "Cochlear implant professionals have met tremendous opposition from the Deaf community" (p. 252). Many Deaf advocates consider the devices as genocidal to Deaf culture (Lane & Bahan, 1998). They argue that implantation of children conflicts with the right of the Deaf cultural minority to exist and flourish.

Technical Aids

In the classroom, it is seldom necessary to find special materials or equipment for children with hearing impairments other than their particular prosthetic equipment. Such equipment involves amplification or tactile methods to improve auditory comprehension, computers, and information technology.

Amplification

Conventional hearing aids are primarily sound amplifiers—they make sounds louder. Amplification helps children to develop residual hearing, improve the audition of their own voices, use speech in a purposeful way, and expand their vocabulary and language abilities. Even for those who are profoundly deaf, the few distorted fragments of amplified sound that reach them may assist in the development of speech and language.

gain

Aids differ in size, cost, and efficiency. While the various types can provide equivalent amounts of amplification (technically called **gain**), certain aids are designed to provide more amplification than others. This means that there can be a close match between the type of aid and the user's unique needs.

Massive research has brought new digital hearing aids that operate in a fundamentally different way from the previous generation of analog hearing aids. Digital aids operate in ways similar to a mini-computer. The sound waves that strike the microphone are digitally encoded, processed, and manipulated with each manipulation capable of producing a different acoustical output—for example, different amounts of amplification and different degrees at different speech frequencies.

An individual hearing aid has a restricted range of about two metres. One of the biggest difficulties facing all hearing aid users is background noise. When the signal-to-noise ratio is poor, an auditory signal may be audible to the child who is hearing impaired but may not be intelligible.

In classroom situations, group amplification systems can be adapted for a wide variety of difficult listening situations and can cut out at least some extraneous classroom noise. The FM (frequency modulation) system is the most popular. There are three types of FM system configurations. With personal FM units, the carrier wave is transmitted through the air via frequency modulation from a teacher-worn microphone to a student-worn FM receiver. There is not a connecting cord between the units, so teacher and pupil can move freely. A classroom Soundfield system consists of a teacher-worn microphone and speakers in fixed areas around the classroom. A Personal Soundfield Amplification system is similar, except that the speakers sit right next to the target student (Nelson & Johnston, 2003).

Telephone and Other Devices

The telecommunication device (TTD), sometimes called the TTY (tele-typewriter), offers persons who are deaf direct telephone access to each other and to community services. Instead of listening to a message and responding orally, the person with a TTD communicates by reading and typing. Typed messages are changed to electrical signals and then translated back to print on a TTD at the other end of the telephone connection.

Hearing aid compatible (HAC) telephones are used by hard-of-hearing aid wearers. Without the HAC, the user may only hear a loud, high-pitched squeal.

To aid deaf adults in the home, a number of tools have been developed. These devices visually signal through flashing lights when, for example, the baby is crying, the telephone or doorbell is ringing, or a wake-up alarm, smoke alarm, or fire alarm has sounded. As well, captioned television shows have been a boon to the hearing-impaired population.

Educational Intervention

There is a plethora of opinions regarding appropriate philosophies for instructing students with hearing impairments. The one commonality is that all educational approaches attempt to improve a child's linguistic competence. Students who are seriously hearing impaired require extensive curricular modifications to compensate for the educational lags that accompany severe and profound hearing impairments. Modification of educational objectives may also be necessary to address the child's actual functional level rather than chronological age or grade placement.

Service Delivery Models

There is much more to placement decisions for students with severe and profound hearing impairment than simply consideration of the inherent classroom communication difficulties. Both practical and political problems abound.

Political overtones arise because many deaf people and professionals working with students who are deaf do not accept today's educational integration. They describe inclusive schooling as "forced assimilation"—an "unnatural attempt to make deaf persons hearing" (Elliott, 1993, p. 11) and support a strong separate special education system. Supporters of segregated settings marshal arguments that centre on deafness defined as culture. They argue that deaf persons "constitute a legitimate cultural and linguistic group and that they are entitled to educational programs which take this into account" (Reagan, 1988, p. 1). Viewing themselves in this fashion, deaf people tend to see the residential schools as a cultural component vital in creating group solidarity. Furthermore, in specialized settings, multiple social supports are in place.

At the more practical level, experts contend that "Deafness is arguably ... the most difficult [impairment] for teachers to deal with, since in its severe form it is not so much the deprivation of sound but the deprivation of language which creates a barrier to learning" (Palmer & Sellars, 1993, p. 37). Many general classroom teachers are not very knowledgeable about hearing impairment and it is not unusual for teachers to express anxiety about working with a student with a hearing impairment in a general setting, especially if adequate communication and social supports are lacking (see Jones, Clark, & Soltz, 1997). In Nova Scotia and New Brunswick, for example, surveys revealed that the primary areas of concern for teachers are information on hearing loss in general, techniques for attaining comprehension, expectation levels for students with hearing impairment, effective techniques for teaching and managing behaviour, and the effective use of amplification (French & MacDonnell, 1985).

Taking note of the above, it is not surprising that a clear picture of inclusion for students with severe hearing losses has not yet emerged. It seems reasonable to argue that there should be various educational settings available. In general, the educational setting for a specific child is determined by linguistic needs; the severity of the loss and the potential for using residual hearing with or without amplification; academic level; social, emotional, and cultural needs, including appropriate interaction and communication with peers; and communication needs, including the child and the family's preferred mode of communication (Marschark, 1993).

In 1995, approximately one-third of students who were deaf attended residential schools, the most traditional setting. The other two-thirds attended programs in residential/day schools or day classes located in regular schools ("Children with communication ..." 1995). However, mounting numbers of students are attending their neighbourhood school.

When students are included in regular classrooms, they should be supported by interpreters, resource rooms, or itinerant teachers. Resource rooms offer hearing-impaired students from general classes a chance to obtain tutorial assistance in a special class from a trained teacher of deaf students. Itinerant programs provide specialist teachers who offer tutorial assistance to include hearing-impaired students. The itinerant teacher assists the child and the general classroom teacher, and also acts as a facilitator or liaison with other support personnel, parents, and school administrators.

CASE STUDY

Steven (continued)

Steven's preschool teachers set him several long-range goals. These included the introduction of simple nouns, verbs, and colour signs; some awareness of gross sounds through play activities and listening exercises; and increased vocalizations. They also structured many activities to expose Steven to language, such as storytelling, "dress up," and arts and crafts activities. Steven's teachers showed his parents how to stimulate home communication and how to use home-making activities such as cooking to present language. The parents were encouraged to learn more sign language.

When Steven reached age five, his mother went to enrol him in the local kindergarten. The principal listened to her explanation of Steven's problem and agreed to place the child in a general classroom for kindergarten, although no special aide or interpreter would be available. The principal did not seem to think this would be a problem, as she said, "Socialization is far more important than learning at this age, especially for a disabled child." How surprised she was when Steven's mother explained carefully that she was placing Steven in the general classroom not for socialization but for learning. She expected him to learn everything that other children did, and she also expected the school to provide assistance to ensure that he could.

What finally happened was that Steven remained in nursery school for the kindergarten year and then went to the local school for grade 1, where he was provided with an interpreter. The home visiting teacher, and later an itinerant teacher, collaborated with the classroom teacher on his IEP, although the teacher was somewhat initially reluctant to make special adaptations. She felt that having an interpreter in the classroom was the only change that would be needed for Steven.

Once Steven's needs were explained to the classroom teacher, she met with the school's special education consultant, the interpreter, and Steven's mother to plan an IEP (an extract is shown below). While the curriculum would parallel that taught to the other children, there would be a greater stress on speech and language using a natural approach. For example, Steven would receive extra classroom assistance in learning new vocabulary, and would be provided with many opportunities to interact in small groups with other children. Reading would be taught through a whole-word method rather than a phonics approach, although Steven would participate in all of the many literacy activities offered, with an emphasis on storytelling and language experience approaches. A speech therapist would work with Steven weekly and, as new sounds or words were acquired, the teacher would stress these in classroom activities and reinforce correct usage. As well, the ongoing assessment of communication development would be a feature of Steven's program.

During the IEP planning process, the special education consultant provided the teacher with many teaching tips and techniques. Throughout the school year, the two teachers collaborated closely. The teacher also used a few signs, such as "Good morning," and "Nice work, Steven."

EXTRACT FROM STEVEN'S IEP

Child: Steven
Teacher: Ms. Smith
School: Sunny Heights
Grade: 1
Birthdate: June 12, 2000

Medical Information

Audiological assessment shows Steven to have a bilateral hearing loss in the severe to profound range.

Adaptive Equipment

- Individual hearing aid
- Special seating—middle row, front
- Interpreter

Areas of Need

Speech training, auditory training, language, and communication (both oral and sign mode)

Areas of Strength

Normal cognitive functioning, good motivation, strong social skills

Assessment/Performance Information

Date   October 2006
Test   Informal observations
Result Restricted receptive and expressive language; limited vocabulary; little speech use with many deviations. Uses sign for most communication; also speech reads to some extent.
Date   October 2006
Test   Test of Early Reading Ability—Revised (TERA-R)
Result Very basic literacy skills; understands the use of print and conventions of language such as reading from left to

right. Barely started on formal reading. Only a small sight vocabulary—logos, own name, McDonald's, and so on.

Date   October 2006
Test   WISC-IV, Performance Scale only
Result   Normal cognitive functioning.

Persons Responsible

Teacher, Ms. Smith: Stress oral skills; include in all activities; work with interpreter. Reinforce therapy sessions.

Interpreter, peer tutors, speech therapist (weekly): Auditory training, speech acquisition, language, sign vocabulary.

Long-Range Goals

- Steven's program will target speech and language development within the regular curriculum and with specialized assistance from an interpreter to assist classroom interactions. In the classroom, the teacher will stimulate language and communication skills through promoting interaction with other children; incidental teaching that includes expansions, paraphrasing, and open-ended questions (see Chapter 4); specific language intervention such as stressing therapy goals and correction where appropriate; and group learning.

- A second long-term goal is to begin to teach literacy skills. The teacher will use a word-recognition approach to circumvent the problems caused by the hearing loss, joined to the more holistic, experience-based method that is in place for other class members.

Short-Term Objectives

- When presented with words on flashcards, Steven will say the word, say it in a sentence, and write it.
- Steven will read short sentences containing new words.
- Steven will write/draw in his journal daily with encouragement to use new reading words.
- Steven will be placed in small learning groups as much as possible for socialization and language development.
- To further promote peer interaction, peer tutoring (20 minutes daily) will be arranged for oral reading. Cross-age tutoring will also be arranged.
- Steven will independently read one self-selected book and be able to retell (in sign) the general storyline to a peer and/or the interpreter.

Educational Interpreters The great majority of classroom teachers do not have proficiency in sign language and finger spelling. Enabling students to attend general classes requires special assistance, and teachers may have to work with an interpreter in the classroom. The **interpreter**, sometimes called a *transliterator*, is a normally hearing person who facilitates the transmission of information between individuals who do not communicate with a common language or code. Educational interpreters translate directions, content, and assignments presented orally by teachers, relay the comments of peers, and share the student's responses and questions with teachers and peers (Salend & Longo, 1994).

interpreter

There are different types of interpreters. A *signed system interpreter* makes speech visible and, in turn, converts manual communication to speech. The interpreter translates spoken language directed toward a student with a hearing impairment into a signed system such as ASL or a school-based system. An *oral interpreter* facilitates the student's understanding of verbal messages by subtly mouthing the complete verbal message or its paraphrased equivalent.

In general, the interpreter should be seated in a glare-free, well-lit location with a solid-coloured background free of visual and auditory distractions. Interpreters should sit in front of the student without blocking the view of the chalkboard, overhead projector, or

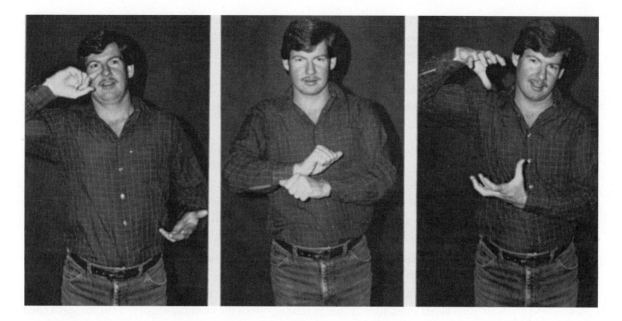

the teacher. However, the positioning of the interpreter depends on the nature of the instructional activity. When the teacher is using a lecture format, it may be better for the interpreter to stand or sit to the side and slightly in front of the teacher, with the student's desk located three to five feet away. In a one-to-one instruction setting, the interpreter should be placed facing the student from a distance of about four to six feet. During group activities, the group should be seated in a circular fashion with the interpreter located across from the student (Salend & Longo, 1994).

There is little extant research on educational interpreting in kindergarten to grade 12 classrooms. We do know three things. First, interpreters can function most effectively as an instructional resource in the classroom only when they carefully coordinate their efforts with teachers (Salend & Longo, 1994). Second, the tasks undertaken by interpreters are complex. For example, the interpreter must not be controlling, must know when to talk and when to pause, must sustain the child's attention, explain and clarify concepts, and prompt on-task behaviour (see Monkman & Baskind, 1998). Finally, there is consensus that educational interpreting often falls short of deaf students' needs, especially at the secondary and postsecondary levels because the content knowledge in upper level classes is often beyond the educational background of the interpreter (Harrington, 2000; Kluwin & Stewart, 2000). When interpreting is of questionable quality, there is impoverished communication in the classroom and students struggle.

ASL has its own semantic and syntactic structure. This deaf sign-language user is talking about his work. Literally, the signs translate as (a) boring, (b) work, (c) a lot.

Educational Approaches

Authenticated evidence of the education of students with deafness can be traced back to the late 16th century. Shortly after that, teachers divided themselves into two irreconcilable camps. The *oralists* viewed deafness as a human handicap to be overcome through the development of speech and speech reading. The *manualists* argued that deafness is a human difference that requires its own language, the language of signs.

Rampant conflicts in expert opinion about the use of manual modes in the education of hearing-impaired children still exist. The stances are not as irreconcilable as they once were, but educators still hold quite different philosophies about the most effective means to impart language, promote academic development, and about whether or not to stress speech teaching.

Communication mode is the fulcrum. Many modes developed over the centuries and are still possible. The most important ones still used today are described below, moving from unisensory to multi-sensory approaches.

acoupedic (unisensory) approach

- *Acoupedic methods.* The **acoupedic (unisensory) approach** is an oral method that aims to develop intelligible speech through the maximum development of listening skills. It is founded on the belief that children in the first year of life have hearing abilities that, if activated sufficiently, play a functional role in determining speech development. On the other hand, auditory deprivation during this time irreversibly diminishes these abilities and obstructs speech development.

  The acoupedic approach requires early intervention, early amplification, a normal listening environment, the use of auditory feedback mechanisms, and the preparation of parents to act as first models of communication (Pollack, 1980). This method excludes all visual clues, such as speech reading—thus the term unisensory. It encourages a child to use residual hearing to the greatest extent possible.

- *The oral/aural method.* Like other processes in special education, the oral/aural method used with children who are deaf today evolved through a number of stages. Beginning in about 1867, teachers employed a pure oral method that placed stress on speech reading and writing but forbade the natural gestures that we all use as part of our communication. The pure oral method evolved into the oral method of speech and speech reading along with amplification through hearing aids, which were invented in the 1920s. This method downplayed the importance of writing and permitted natural gestures.

  From this grew the current oral method, more correctly called the oral/aural approach. It places stress on speech and speech reading and uses amplification and auditory training as integral components of speech and language development.

speech reading

Lip reading or **speech reading** is the skill of understanding speech through watching the lips and face. The latter term is more accurate because facial expressions impart to spoken words a whole spectrum of feelings, attitudes, and visual clues.

Speech reading is a difficult skill to acquire because only about 30 percent of English sounds are visible on the lips (Stewart, 1984). For example, the colour words *red, white,* and *green* all look pretty much the same on the lips, as do *bat* and *mat, manic* and *panic,* and *measure* and *pleasure.* The difficulties with such look-alike words are almost insurmountable. Imagine a child trying to distinguish between "a red bat" and "a green mat."

When words look the same, speech readers must anticipate them and fill them in, but this takes sophisticated language knowledge—an area of deficit for most people who are deaf. To add to the problems, the average speaker makes about 13 articulatory movements a second during normal conversation. The average observer, however, can only visually record 8 or 9 movements a second (Sanders, 1971).

- *Total Communication.* In the early 1970s, penetrating appraisals of Deaf education castigated school programs across North America for their ineffectiveness. The benefits of using some manual components in the education of children with hearing impairments were apparent, and many educators turned from an oral emphasis to one that stressed a combination of methods.

Total Communication uses speech, speech reading, and amplification, along with a school-based manual system. The school-based manual systems of Total Communication are a marriage of necessity between American Sign Language and English. In systems such as Signing Essential English and Manual English, signs are presented in the order of English and with correct morphological structures.

* *American Sign Language.* Until quite recently, ASL was viewed as an "invented language" and classed with systems such as that of the Klingons in *Star Trek* (Davis, 1997). However, a veritable explosion of research into ASL from the fields of linguistics, psycholinguistics, and socio-linguistics led to recognition that ASL is a true language. It is not related to or in any way derived from spoken English but is more accurately viewed as a distinct and genetically unrelated language (Reagan, 1988).

Unlike school-based manual systems, American Sign Language (ASL or Ameslan) does not follow the semantic and syntactic structure of spoken language. ASL has its own rule-governed syntactic system, a rich system of morphological processes, and a large lexicon of vocabulary.

ASL is founded on a combination of symbolic gestures produced by the shape, the location, and the movement of the hands. Many of the signs symbolize concepts rather than individual words. Most have an arbitrary tie to the referent. Some are iconic in that they represent an object or action for which they stand; some are metonymic—they take a relatively small aspect or feature of the referent and use that as the basis of the sign. For example, the sign for *dog* is snapping the fingers. ASL has no signs for the grammatical markers, such as -ed or -ing endings, that express verb tense and condition. Rather, users depend on facial expressions and body language to replace voice intonation and enhance meaning (Meadow, 1980).

Deaf people see ASL as their natural mode of expression and show great attachment to their "beloved language" (Schein, 1989, p. 29). In 1988, Manitoba recognized ASL as a heritage language of the deaf; Alberta followed in 1990.

Although sign language is typically associated with people who are deaf, some of it has crept into everyday usage. For example, the football huddle was invented by a deaf player in the 1890s. Similarly, a deaf athlete was responsible for the ball and strike hand signals used in baseball. These were devised in 1888 by a deaf baseball player in Washington, D.C. (Pirro, 1993).

Sign systems around the world essentially evolved from the sign language systemized by de l'Épée in France in the mid-1700s. These systems are not universal. They were quickly adapted to local needs and, like spoken language, each country has its own unique version. In North America, ASL is used as an almost generic term. There is also CSL (Canadian Sign Language) and LSQ (Langue de Signes Québécoise).

Bilingual-Bicultural Programs

Among deaf adults, the common mode of communication is American Sign Language. Because they hold that ASL is the natural language of the Deaf community throughout anglophone North America, deaf adults favour bilingualism for all children who are deaf.

In schools for the Deaf, this translates into the phrase *bilingual-bicultural* (bi-bi), which refers to the classroom use of two languages—ASL and English—and to two cultures—Deaf culture and hearing culture.

Bilingual-bicultural education was first explored at Gallaudet University in the 1970s (Swanwick, 1998). Today, an increasing number of schools for the Deaf are utilizing the practices of bi-bi education. From the United States, Miller and Moores (2000) present data to indicate that bi-bi education is already a reality in 75 percent of the largest programs for deaf students. As this occurs, the pedagogy for language instruction is emerging based on ASL, with English as a second language (Easterbrooks, 1999).

In 1993, Ontario became one of the first places to authorize the use of ASL as the language of instruction for students who are deaf. Ontario schools for the Deaf now use ASL and written English and allow students opportunities to develop their auditory and speech potential. There are five key principles to Ontario's bilingual-bicultural policy: child-centred education, development of literacy skills in ASL and English, understanding and appreciation of Deaf culture, appreciation of cultural diversity, and the development of a positive self-image ("Statement ..." 1993, p. 1).

One of the prominent ideas underlying bi-bi programs is that the developmental delays typically experienced by deaf children are entirely preventable. What they need for normal social and linguistic development is to mingle daily within a sign environment. Bilingual education uses ASL and English. The bi-bi approach also stresses immersion in a program where all of the child's experiences are couched within Deaf culture, and the interaction with deaf peers and role models both in and outside the classroom provide "for the self-esteem and emotional well-being of [the] deaf child" (Gallimore & Woodruff, 1996, p. 93). Advocates see the world of deafness as distinctive, rewarding, and worth preserving, and focus on the rich heritage of folklore, literature, customs, and values therein.

ASL is the major medium of instruction in preschool through the primary grades, with a major focus on sign production and comprehension. The natural first language—ASL—then provides deaf children with a base to support the transition to reading and writing English (Marschark, 2001; Wilbur, 2000).

Development of English literacy begins in grade 3 and from then on ASL and English are used fairly equally for instructional purposes (MacAnally, Rose, & Quigley, 1987).

Compelling arguments underlie the use of bi-bi educational approaches, the two most important centring around Deaf culture and language acquisition. Equally persuasive points arise from opponents, usually founded on social interactions and academics, specifically reading.

From the bi-bi side arises the contention that language is commonly taken as central to group identity and is its most important marker. The Deaf community stresses the role of deaf persons in determining their own destiny and denotes sign language as essential to their identity. Another strand argues that deaf children are "preprogrammed" to learn sign. Proponents point to the tendency of young childen to develop their own idiosyncratic systems without instruction. Without any contact with sign language, deaf children invent their own "home sign," a kind of communication through pantomime. Home signs progress from simple single signs to real "sentences" (see Mayberry, Woodlinger, Cohen, & Goldwin-Meadow, 1987). Further, language studies point to an array of meaningful research that clearly shows ASL to be a viable, rich language. When young children are exposed to the more formal language of ASL, they acquire language at the same rate and with the same milestones as hearing children do with spoken language. Such a strong base in one language facilitates learning another one. Children arrive at school with a firm linguistic base, which proves of enormous benefit in problem solving and academic performance. Indeed, the use of signing has led to a general improvement in the academic achievement of deaf students (see Miller & Moores, 2000).

Finally, intelligible speech is a mark of success for oralists, not for deaf persons who have other criteria for success. Deaf children rarely develop functional oral communication skills, so little is lost by the absence of spoken language in their environments. Only about 17 percent of students taught by oral methods ever become orally fluent, but nearly 75 percent become fluent manually.

The major arguments of those who hold reservations about bilingual education for students who are deaf centre on the critical nature of English and speech for functioning in our society. They argue that 90 percent of deaf children are born to hearing parents who are not part of the Deaf community and who use spoken language as their primary mode of communication. For these parents to learn ASL is equivalent in difficulty to the learning of any spoken language (Kemp, 1998). They further contend that audiological differences need attention if individuals are to function effectively in the wider hearing society. The language of the majority culture is English, not ASL. Access to the patterns and rules that govern the mainstream discourse is critical if a deaf person is to navigate the world successfully. Speech is important, but whatever aptitude a child may have to develop speech may be jeopardized by a practice that fosters ASL to the exclusion of it.

As well, there is some minimum threshold level of English proficiency needed before a deaf student can productively read and write (Mayer, 1999). Children who are deaf are often learning to read at the same time they are learning English. ASL may impact on reading because it is structurally different from English and deaf readers must recode print into their own language.

Curriculum

In the education of students with hearing impairments, the content is similar to that presented to hearing children. Differences are chiefly a matter of degree. For hearing students, teachers build a mastery of reading and written language upon a child's intact linguistic base of listening and speaking. In contrast, students who are hearing impaired must learn an entire language system. For example, to learn the single word mother, a child who is deaf must

- Learn the concept.
- Learn to say the word.
- Learn to speech read the word.
- Learn the sound of the word through the hearing aid.
- Learn to recognize the printed word.
- Learn to recognize the written word.
- Learn to spell the word.
- Learn to print or write the word.
- Learn to sign the word.
- Learn to read the sign.
- Learn to finger-spell the word.

- Learn to read the finger-spelled word.
- Learn to use the word in context.
- Learn to use the word in different contexts. (Levine, 1981, p. 100)

As you can see, the process of developing language skills is long, arduous, and often tedious. Some generic accommodations and adaptations for students who are hearing impaired are shown in Table 10-4.

Two major strategies for the teaching of language have evolved—the formal or grammatical approach and the informal or natural approach. Experienced learners respond better to the grammatical approach, younger children to the natural.

The grammatical approach pinpoints specific language objectives, focuses students' attention on the structural aspects of language, and incorporates massed practice to encourage the establishment of new skills. Armed with structural information, students learn to generate language deductively.

Table 10-4 Creating accessible classrooms

Accommodations

- The environment should be as quiet as possible so that a child can obtain the best auditory message. Minimize background noise to the greatest extent possible and keep auditory and visual distractions in the classroom to a minimum.
- If you use an overhead projector, try to find one without a fan.
- Check daily that hearing aids are working.
- Keep a supply of extra batteries.
- Always face the child and the light source. Natural light is better than fluorescent lighting.
- Be aware of seating; the middle of the second row is the best place for speech reading and amplification usage.
- Be in close proximity when speaking. Speech reading is best at about two metres; hearing aids function best within the same distance.
- To promote speech reading, try to stand still while talking.
- Remember that children cannot speech read if the teacher talks to the chalkboard or speaks in the dark during a movie or filmstrip.
- When providing individual assistance, do not kneel beside the student but position yourself in front of him or her. Squat to the student's level.

Adaptations, materials

- Use many visual aids. These are helpful for hearing children as well.
- Write key information such as instructions and homework assignments on the chalkboard.
- Provide the student with an outline of a lecture.
- Because it is difficult for students to take notes and watch, devise a means (such as photocopying another student's notes) for classroom notes.

Table 10-4 continued

Adaptations, instructional

- Use gestures to reference information.

- Repeat and rephrase information and directions and encourage children to ask questions if they are not sure.

- Point or move your head to cue children in to the person who is talking or the object under discussion. Allow a child to turn in his or her seat when other students are talking or to move seats when a better view is needed.

- Even with an interpreter, always address the student directly.

- Speak naturally. Do not over-enunciate; this makes speech reading more difficult.

- Try not to smile or whisper while speaking; this distorts the shape of the lips.

- Meet regularly with the interpreter to assess the delivery of communication services. Provide the interpreter with previews of lessons to be taught and with class routines, projects, and long-term assignments to help students understand and prepare for them.

- Learn a few signs for vocabulary frequently used in your classroom.

- When reading aloud, keep the book low to allow children a good view of your face.

We discussed naturalistic strategies for teaching language in Chapter 4. These models attempt to parallel the ways in which hearing children acquire language. The focus is on what the adult can do to encourage more spontaneous conversational use with a child. Teaching is incidental, with the content and sequence of instruction determined by the needs of individual children.

Social Intervention

The Deaf community provides a huge variety of organizations at the local, regional, national, and global levels. Choices include such general categories as religion and sports as well as more specialized groups such as deaf rock climbers, deaf leadership camps for adolescents, and the International World Games for the Deaf.

The Canadian Hearing society was founded in 1940. Its mission is to provide services that enhance the independence of deaf and hard-of-hearing people and encourage the prevention of hearing loss.

SUMMARY

1. *Hearing loss* (or *hearing impairment*) is a generic term that encompasses two major groups—those who are deaf and those who are hard of hearing. The difference lies in the intensity of the hearing loss and the amount of auditory input that an individual can use. People who are deaf cannot, even with the use of a hearing aid, hear speech;

those who are hard of hearing can hear speech with or without amplification (hearing aids).

2. A hearing impairment is not only the deprivation of sound; it is the deprivation of language. Because hearing loss interferes with both the reception and production of language, the greatest single handicap of defective hearing is its effect on the development of communication skills. Children who are hearing impaired are isolated from the human voice and therefore isolated from language. Since teaching is essentially a linguistic activity, hearing impairment poses a serious threat to children's learning.

3. Children who are deaf are likely to be identified during the preschool years. In contrast, the auditory problems of hard-of-hearing children may not be detected until they undergo a routine school screening, and perhaps not even then. Apart from the immediate problems for children, non-identification means that incidence and prevalence rates are extremely difficult to determine.

4. As long as the sounds of conversational speech remain audible, effective communication skills are possible. However, even mild losses can be educationally devastating. Individuals who are deaf are usually deficient in the language of the majority culture even when expert in the language of signs. Although they possess the same intellectual potential as the rest of the population, their deprivation in language can create problems in every aspect of functioning.

5. Many of the etiologies responsible for hearing losses affect many domains of development. It is estimated that up to 33 percent of children with hearing impairments suffer co-occurring disabilities.

6. Once a child's medical and audiological data have been gathered, he or she should receive and wear a personal hearing aid as soon as possible. All infants, children, and adults who are hearing impaired can benefit from an aid. As technology continues to improve, many parents have a choice between hearing aids or a cochlear implant for their young child with prelingual deafness. Unlike aids, which merely amplify sound, cochlear implants bypass damaged hair cells and stimulate the auditory nerve directly with electrical current. They bring some speech into a world that was previously silent.

7. Socially, many deaf persons turn to the Deaf community, where sign language is the accepted mode of communication and where deafness is seen as a distinct culture.

8. Discussions of effective teaching practice in the education of students who are deaf and hard of hearing are dominated by considerations of language, literacy, and communication mode.

9. Inclusive schooling for students who are severely hearing impaired remains controversial. The setting for instruction makes a difference in the communication mode used, the type and amount of support services, the stress of the curriculum, and the possibility of identification with the Deaf community and Deaf culture.

10. One essential service for many students with hearing impairments attending general classes is an educational interpreter. This allows a student access to the same curriculum that is afforded hearing peers. FM systems and classroom amplification systems help to improve the speech signal received by the child by countering the effects of distance and background noise.

11. Although the Deaf community wants children to use what they see as their natural language and wants educators to accept bilingual education that includes ASL, bi-bi education for students who are deaf is founded as much on political arguments as it is on educational considerations, and the idea is not yet universally accepted.

HISTORICAL NOTES

It is to the Abbé Michel Charles de l'Épée (1712–1789), a French cleric, that people who are deaf owe their education and their sign language. In 1760, de l'Épée opened a school for deaf students in his own home in Paris. At the outset, the Abbé knew little about deaf people, their education, their language, or the impact of deafness. But as he studied his pupils closely, de l'Épée noticed that without any teaching or guidance, they evolved a language of simple signs by which to communicate.

Building on these basic signs, de l'Épée developed a system of what he called "natural signs." Then, to teach his students metaphysical and abstract concepts, as well as the grammar of French, the Abbé also created a system of "methodological signs." With this structure, de l'Épée systemized a language of signs for persons who were deaf.

The first American teacher of the deaf, Thomas Hopkins Gallaudet (1787–1851), trained at de l'Épée's school and then established the American Asylum for the Education and Instruction of Deaf and Dumb Persons in Hartford, Connecticut, in 1819. In 1857, Gallaudet's youngest son, Edward, became president of the National Deaf Mute College in Washington, D.C. In 1864, the college, with Abraham Lincoln as patron, became a degree-granting institution. In 1893, its name was changed to Gallaudet College in memory of Thomas Hopkins Gallaudet. Now Gallaudet University, the facility remains the world's foremost degree-granting institution for students who are hearing impaired.

The education of students who were deaf was the first form of special education to be undertaken in Canada. In 1829, one Ronald McDonald, a reporter with the *Montreal Gazette*, was sent by the government of Lower Canada to train with Gallaudet in Hartford. McDonald opened a school for deaf children in Champlain, Quebec, in 1831, which operated for five years. Later, the Catholic Church in Quebec opened schools for deaf boys in 1848 and deaf girls in 1851. Halifax also established a school in 1848.

The most prominent pioneer in the early history of Canadian special education was John Barrett McGann (1810–1880), who arrived in Toronto from Ireland in 1855. With assistance from Egerton Ryerson, McGann's work culminated with the Ontario Institution for the Education and Instruction of the Deaf and Dumb, established at Belleville in 1870, and the Ontario Institution for the Education and Instruction of the Blind, at Brantford in 1872.

Residential schools to serve the needs of students with serious hearing impairments were eventually established in all provinces; most remain today. At the outset, the mode of instruction was sign. Then from 1905 to 1975, oralism (speech and speech reading) took precedence and sign language was virtually outlawed. Schools did not allow sign language in classrooms and deaf teachers were not generally employed.

By the 1970s, the failure of the oral system was glaringly apparent. At the same time, the Deaf community began to regain some of its political and social power. For example, the Deaf Pride organization, which began in 1972, fuelled the Deaf Power movement, which led many deaf persons to re-evaluate their characteristics, status, and self-image. Then in 1989, in 14 cities and towns across every region of Canada, deaf people took to the streets in the first-ever mass protest against the system of deaf education in Canada. They called for the use of their language and a greater voice in decisions directly affecting their future (MacDougall, 1989).

A shift in communication modes that began in the 1970s led to ASL as an accepted mode of instruction, especially in residential schools. Deaf adults regard sign language as a defining characteristic of a recognizable minority group and often prefer to send their children to residential schools, as these facilities foster the concept of a Deaf community and a Deaf culture.

CHAPTER 11

CHILDREN WITH VISUAL IMPAIRMENTS

INTRODUCTION

It is difficult for most of us to imagine life without sight. Vision and hearing are the senses that most connect us with our world. Well over half of the information our brains receive about the world comes through our eyes (Immen, 1995). In fact, the visual system is so dominant that many of us close our eyes to think more clearly and concentrate. To many people, a world without images would seem bleak, frightening, and virtually impossible to navigate. It would seem socially cold; through expression and eye contact, our eyes play a crucial role in social interaction. Sight also affects our other senses; seeing something good to eat, for example, can trigger hunger pangs.

Vision is intimately involved with 70 to 80 percent of all tasks that occur in educational programs (Li, 2004). In a classroom, teachers use demonstration, modelling, pictures, photographs, and a variety of colour-coded materials in their instruction. For students, quite a bit of every day is spent on close-up or near tasks such as reading and writing. Then there are distance tasks such as watching the teacher at the front of the classroom. Other common activities are near to distance to near, such as copying notes from the board. Still other activities involve motor skills as well as vision, such as handwriting or playing sports.

Any vision problem may hinder a student's learning ability. Visual impairments also interfere with play, social growth, adjustment, and mobility, and cause complex developmental problems that make special education a necessity. Unique education needs include, but are not restricted to, early intervention; concept development; listening, study, and research skills; alternative methods for reading, writing, and mathematical computation; sensory training; daily living, socialization, and recreational skills; sexuality, career, and vocational training; utilization of low vision; accessibility to technology; orientation and mobility training; and meaningful transition programs (Huebner, 1985).

visual system

Many individuals overcome visual impairments

Children with visual disabilities that cannot be corrected are the smallest group that qualifies for special education services. The great majority of these children will be included in general classrooms. Teachers must be aware of the adaptations and accommodations that assist and enhance the performance of students with visual disabilities. Since understanding the visual loss underlies at least some teacher attitudes, we open this chapter with overviews of the anatomy and physiology of the visual system and then discuss the complex of etiologies that contribute to visual impairments.

The Visual System

The **visual system** consists of the eye, which receives the light image; the nerve pathways, which transmit the image to the optical centres of the brain; and the brain itself, which interprets the image. Visual impairments can result from any interference with the passage of light as it travels from the outer surface of the eye along the nerve pathways to the brain.

The Eye

The eye is probably the most precious square inch in the human body. It is only 2.5 centimetres in diameter, but its functions are extraordinarily complex and precise. It is composed of

Figure 11-1
Anatomy of the eye

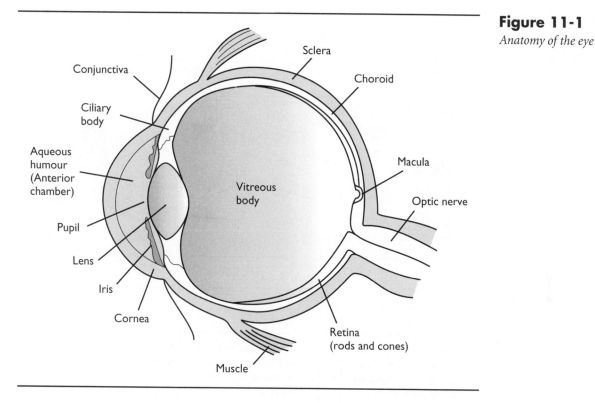

the eyeball and its accessory structures, such as the eyelids and muscles that protect and move it. The eyeball is held in place by connective tissue in the orbit and is protected in front by the upper and lower eyelids. Figure 11-1 shows the structure of the eyeball.

The eyeball is a sphere wrapped in three layers of tissue. The outermost layer consists of the *sclera*—a tough, flexible, white outer covering, part of which is commonly recognized as the white of the eye—and the **cornea**—a transparent window covering the front of the eye, continuous with the sclera. The middle layer contains the **iris**, which gives the eye its colour and adapts the size of the pupil aperture in response to light intensity, and the **lens**, a crystalline structure held in suspension by the iris. The middle layer also contains the six ocular muscles connected to the outside of the eyeball that allow the eye to focus on an object, follow a moving target, and rotate; the lacrimal glands that provide the tear film essential to the health of the cornea; and the fluids that fill the eye's two chambers. The inner layer that lines the back of the eye is the **retina**. This tissue-thin, intricate, and sensitive layer is the actual seeing part of the eye. It consists of up to a quarter of a billion photoreceptors and other nerve cells.

Light is essential for sight. The clear lens serves to focus light gathered from the environment onto the retina. On reaching the cornea, the rays of light are refracted to pass through the anterior chamber of the eye. As the rays pass through the crystalline lens, they are further refracted. The lens is capable of changing its shape to accommodate light from objects at various distances. From the lens, the light makes its way through the *vitreous humour* and comes to focus on the **fovea**, the most sensitive spot of the retina. Images received by the fovea are here inverted, making the bottom appear like the top and vice versa. The refraction and inversion of an object are illustrated in Figure 11-2 on the next page.

cornea

iris

lens

retina

fovea

Figure 11-2

Refraction and inversion of an object

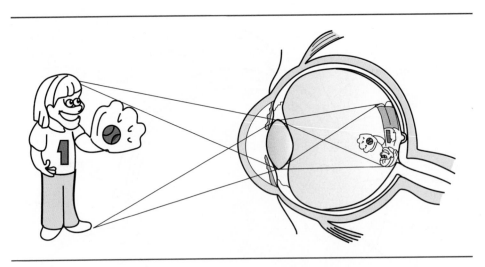

Figure 11-3

Sequence of vision

Visual Pathway

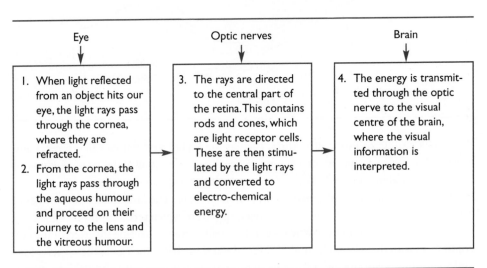

The fovea possesses a rich supply of light-sensitive nerve cells, the rods and cones, which convert the light into electrochemical impulses. These impulses are transmitted to the brain from the back of the eye through the bundles of nerve fibres that form the optic nerve. Immen (1995) describes the nerves that connect the eye to the brain as "the original information highway." The data are sent digitally in a steady stream of electrical impulses along a chain of nerve endings. Images are received and interpreted in the occipital lobe of the brain. Hence, vision is a function of the brain, not the eye. The sequence of vision is shown in Figure 11-3.

DEFINITIONS OF VISUAL IMPAIRMENT

Quite a number of terms are used to refer to visual losses. The varied terminology stems from the history of the field, the agencies intervening, the breadth and complexity of the conditions, and the degrees and severity of visual impairment.

visual impairment   **Visual impairment** is the generic term; it ranges from people reading this text who have very mild visual impairments to those with low vision, and includes those who are totally blind. In this chapter, we are interested in serious visual losses that affect living and learning. These problems are divided into two general categories: low vision and blindness. **Low vision** means that a person's corrected vision is lower than normal. **Blindness** means that individuals have no sight, or so little that learning takes place through the other senses.

low vision

blindness

Together with generic definitions of visual impairment, two other types are used—medical/legal definitions and functional/educational definitions.

Legal Definitions

Legal definitions are founded on **visual acuity**, the measure of the smallest image distinguishable by the eye, and **visual field**, the entire area that can be seen when staring straight ahead, reported in degrees. The normal horizontal field is approximately 160 to 180 degrees and the vertical is 120 degrees.

visual acuity
visual field

Acuity measures begin with the 20/20 normal vision with which we are all familiar. This derives from the **Snellen chart**, developed in 1862 by Herman Snellen, a Dutch ophthalmologist. It consists of a series of letters, numbers, or symbols that must be read from a distance of 20 feet (6 m). Each line is a different size, corresponding to a standard distance at which it can be distinguished by a person with normal vision. This gives the measure 20/20 normal vision, which should not be read as a fraction. Snellen's equation was $V = d/D$, where V is visual acuity, d is distance, and D is the distance at which letters are clearly read.

Snellen chart

In Canada, legal blindness is defined as an acuity measure of 20/200 (6/600) or less in the better eye with the best correction; or visual acuity of more than 20/200 if the widest diameter of the field of vision subtends an angle of no greater than 20 degrees (tunnel vision)(CNIB, 1980). Visual acuity of 20/200 means that a normally sighted person can see at 200 feet (approximately 60 m) what the visually impaired person can see at 20 feet (6 m).

There is also a legal definition of low vision (partial sight). A partially sighted individual has a visual acuity greater than 20/200 but not greater than 20/70 in the better eye after correction (CNIB, 1980).

Educational Definitions

Visual functioning (visual efficiency) refers to what a visually impaired person does with his or her residual vision; it is the way in which an individual uses vision for purposeful behaviour in the various activities of daily life. There is no correlation between the amount of residual vision a person has and the way in which vision is used. Two people with the same etiology and visual acuity may be very different in the way they use their residual vision.

visual functioning

Some people may be able to discern light, colours, or shapes. Some may be able to read by seeing clearly through one small area but have trouble getting around. Others may be able to see the whole work area but have difficulty reading. In others, fatigue, lighting, and emotions may affect the manner in which residual vision is utilized.

For these reasons, functional/educational definitions that indicate how well the child can use vision for learning are more useful than legal ones for educational purposes. Under a functional educational definition, a *child with a visual impairment* is one whose visual impairment interferes with his or her learning and achievement and requires adaptations in the presentation of learning experiences and/or the nature of the materials used in the learning environment.

CLASSIFICATION OF VISUAL IMPAIRMENTS

There are many kinds of visual disabilities attributable to diverse causes and defined slightly differently. As a result, there are a number of ways to classify the conditions. One classification system is not necessarily better than another; the various systems just describe different things and are used for different purposes. Classifications and definitions are shown in Figure 11-4.

Classification by Degree

Following the generic definitions discussed earlier, individuals with visual impairments may be classified in terms of the type and degree of disability—as *mild*, *moderate*, or *severe*. General severity classifications are as follows:

- *Near-normal vision.* Many people reading this text will have mild impairments that are correctable through prescription glasses. These individuals are able to function without special training regardless of the strength of corrective lenses or reading aids they may need.

- *Moderate visual disability (moderate functional impairment).* People in this group have a moderate reduction of acuity, but no significant visual field loss. Specialized aids and lighting are needed, but sight is comparable to normal vision with correction.

- *Low vision.* As a term, low vision was introduced after World War II, when a distinction from *totally blind* was necessary to tailor specific rehabilitation services for veterans returning to the workforce (Goodrich & Bailey, 2000). Even today, the term *low vision* is not easily defined; it generally describes people who are neither totally blind nor fully sighted (Griffin, Williams, Davis, & Engleman, 2002). More specifically, low

Figure 11-4

Classifications of visual impairment

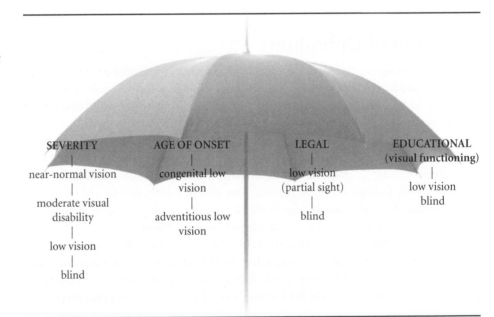

SEVERITY	AGE OF ONSET	LEGAL	EDUCATIONAL (visual functioning)
near-normal vision	congenital low vision	low vision (partial sight)	low vision
moderate visual disability	adventitious low vision	blind	blind
low vision			
blind			

vision refers to a person "who is still severely visually impaired after correction, but who may increase visual functioning through the use of optical aids, non-optical aids, environmental modifications and/or techniques" (Corn, 1980, p. 3). A person with low vision can read with special aids such as magnifying glasses or large-print books. Low vision is defined as between 20 70 and 20 180 if the visual field extends from 20 to 180 degrees.

- *Blindness (profound visual disability)*. Individuals in this group are the most visually impaired; they require education, habilitation, or rehabilitation to function at an independent level.

Classification by Age of Onset

Children with visual impairments are often classified by age of onset of the problems. *Congenital low vision* refers to conditions that are diagnosable at birth or shortly thereafter. *Adventitious low vision* refers to conditions caused by accident or disease some time after birth.

Because many eye conditions change over time, age of onset can be critical in adjustment and learning, particularly in the development of concepts such as colour. Teresa Abang (1980) tells of a congenitally blind man who, when asked what he saw, said, "I see nothing." An adventitiously blind man responded to the same question with "I see darkness all around me." While the first man did not realize that he was experiencing darkness, the other had a memory of light and darkness.

PREVALENCE OF VISUAL IMPAIRMENTS

Severe visual impairment, including total blindness, is a low-incidence condition. In children, blindness is the least prevalent of all disabilities. Only about 1 in 1000 children under the age of eighteen have severe visual impairments (Hatton, Bailey, Burchinal, & Ferrell, 1997); only 1 in 10 000 Canadian babies is diagnosed with legal blindness of some kind.

Impairment of vision is primarily an adult disability, probably one-tenth as prevalent in children as in adults. In the general population, rates are 2.6 percent. When visual impairment is examined as a problem secondary to other established disabilities, the prevalence rises to 15.9 percent (Naeyaert & Grace, 1990).

People with low vision far outnumber totally or functionally blind people; only 10 to 15 percent of the entire population of persons with visual impairments are totally blind. Among the school-aged population, students with low vision comprise between 75 and 80 percent of those visually impaired (Bryan & Jeffrey, 1982).

It should be noted that although severe visual impairment is a low-incidence condition in the Western world, it is of particularly high prevalence in many countries of the Third World, where blindness affects millions of children and adults. In Asia, Africa, and South America, conditions such as water-borne blindness and vitamin A deficiency join poverty and lack of sanitation to allow severe visual impairments to thrive. There are probably 10 million blind people living in the world today (Mazurek & Winzer, 1994).

ETIOLOGY OF VISUAL IMPAIRMENTS

Visual problems arise from any interference with the formation of images on the retina or the transmission of retinal images to the brain. Optical errors, defects of the eyes, diseases, syndromes, and associated conditions all affect vision to a greater or lesser extent. An outline of some conditions, their consequences, and their etiologies is shown in Table 11-1.

Table 11-1 Examples of types of visual impairment and their etiologies

Category	Example	Manifestation	Etiology
Refractive errors	Myopia	Nearsightedness	Aging, heredity, disease, and infection
	Hyperopia	Farsightedness	
	Astigmatism	Distorted or blurred vision	
	Cataracts	Growth over lens	
Eye pathologies	Glaucoma	Impaired outflow of vitreous fluid causes pressure on eyeball	Congenital, hereditary
	Retinopathy of prematurity	Fibrous mass that destroys the retina	Prematurity; oxygen in incubator
	Retinoblastoma	Malignant tumour on the retina	Genetic
	Albinism	Lack of skin pigmentation	Genetic, error of metabolism
	Optic nerve atrophy	Nerve degeneration	Damage to the optic nerve
	Retinitis pigmentosa	Narrowing of field	Hereditary of vision
Oculomotor problems	Strabismus	Seeing double	
	Nystagmus	Rapidly moving eyeballs	
	Amblyopia	Lazy-eye blindness; lack of depth perception	Arises from strabismus
Other problems	Colour blindness	Deficient in colour vision	
	Photophobia	Extreme sensitivity to light	Genetic
Syndromes	Usher's syndrome	Retinitis pigmentosa and progressive hearing loss	Genetic
	Joubert syndrome	Ataxia, slow motor activity, nystagmus	Neurological disorder

In the 19th century, the major causes of visual impairment included ophthalmia neonatorum (inflammation of the eyes of the newborn); syphilis and smallpox; and massive epidemics of meningitis and scarlet fever. Measures such as washing the eyes of the newborn, vaccinations, and vastly improved sanitary conditions have eliminated most of these causes. In the following section, we outline the current common etiologies and consequent conditions in visual impairments.

Refractive Errors

Many people reading this book probably have minor visual losses caused by one of the four common types of refractive errors—*myopia*, *hyperopia*, *astigmatism*, and *presbyopia*. Refractive errors are caused by irregularities in the shape or size of the eyeball, the cornea, or the lens. Errors of refraction may also occur in association with diseases of the eye or with oculomotor disturbances.

Myopia (nearsightedness) is the greatest single cause of defective vision in children and young adults. The myopic eye is unable to focus the image precisely on the retina; the length of the eye or the shape of the cornea cause light rays to focus in front of the retina. In most cases, myopia can be corrected with concave optical lenses.

myopia

Hyperopia (farsightedness) is caused by too short an eye or too flat a corneal surface. The image is focused behind the retina. Corrective lenses aid hyperopic people. **Astigmatism** is the result of an irregularity in the curvature of the cornea or lens of the eye. The rays of light are refracted unevenly so that horizontal and vertical rays are focused at different points on the retina. In most cases, astigmatism is correctable.

hyperopia

astigmatism

With advancing age, numerous body changes occur. Some of these natural developments relate to aging in the eye's muscle tone, the lens, and other tissues. With normal vision, the lens changes shape and lets us concentrate on a particular spot. To focus on distant objects, it flattens somewhat; when moving in close, it gets rounder. As we get older, the lens loses some of its adaptability and up-close focus becomes more difficult.

Presbyopia, from the Greek word meaning "sight of age," is the condition in which the lens of the eye loses its ability to accommodate to near objects. In addition to blurring and difficulty with reading at normal distances, persons with presbyopia will usually experience "tired eyes" or headaches while doing close work. Most people at the age of 40 or thereabouts develop some degree of presbyopia and need glasses for reading and other close work.

presbyopia

Disturbances of Ocular Motility

Normal vision requires the coordinated use of two eyes. Images from each eye are fused in the vision centres of the brain so that only one image is perceived. To achieve a synchronized image, the ocular muscles (which are among the most rapidly responding muscles in the body) in both eyes must work in perfect harmony. *Ocular motility* (eye movements) deal with the extra-ocular muscles and their effects on eye movements such as localizing, tracking (the ability to follow a moving target), tracing (the ability to follow a stationary target), gaze-shifting, and scanning (Li, 2004). *Oculomotor disturbances* occur when the eyes cannot control their direction of focus.

strabismus

Strabismus, one of the most common oculomotor problems, results from inefficient ocular motor mobility. It can affect one or both eyes. Strabismus may be evident at birth or may not appear until the child begins to look at objects close up. Divergent strabismus causes what is called a "wall eye." Amblyopia, sometimes called "lazy-eye blindness," results from strabismus. The brain will not tolerate double vision and eventually suppresses the image coming from the weaker eye.

nystagmus

Diplopia, or double vision, is another result of lack of coordination between the two eyes. **Nystagmus**, a rhythmic involuntary movement of the eyes, is often found in conjunction with other disabilities, such as Down syndrome. Ocular motility problems are also common in children with cerebral palsy and other neurological disorders.

Eye Pathologies

Eye pathologies result from damage or disease to one or more of the structures of the eye. They are most common in adults. In children, the most common pathologies of the eye cause clouding of the cornea and lens and dysfunctions of the retina and optic nerves. Conditions may be congenital or adventitious.

cataract

A **cataract** is an opacity of the lens or its capsule that restricts the eye's ability to receive light and therefore interferes with central and peripheral visual acuity. If the lens becomes cloudy, the light rays are blocked or distorted when they reach the retina, making things look hazy or dull, or dazzlingly bright.

Cataracts are caused by a chemical change in the lens itself. The exact reasons for the change are not understood, although there may be a hereditary tendency to develop cataracts. For the most part, cataracts are associated with aging, and almost half the population over the age of 65 will suffer some degree of cataract formation ("Cataracts … " 1990). Younger people may be affected in association with conditions such as diabetes. Some babies are born with cataracts, often the result of maternal rubella. In rare cases, cataracts result from a blow to the eye or from exposure to radiation, toxic chemicals, or intense heat ("Cataracts … " 1990).

glaucoma

Glaucoma, a condition responsible for 12 percent of the blindness in Canada and the United States, has been called "the sneak-thief of sight" because its onset is slow and insidious. Glaucoma is caused by the increased intra-ocular pressure that occurs when the eye fluid that should be continually drained backs up along the outflow route. The increased pressure destroys intricate, sensitive structures in the retina, which then loses its ability to transmit pictures to the brain. *Congenital glaucoma* is a baffling and mysterious hereditary condition that is a major cause of severe visual defects in children. Untreated glaucoma can cause total blindness in both children and adults.

retinopathy of prematurity

Retinopathy of prematurity (ROP), until recently called retrolental fibroplasia (RLF), describes a condition affecting the retina and the vitreous humour. ROP, first described in 1942, is seen in low-birth-weight babies (under 1.5 kg), and was first attributed to high levels of oxygen in incubators. After its cause was discovered, there was a drop in the incidence of ROP. Since the mid-1960s, however, the incidence of milder ROP has been rising, and the 1980s saw a further resurgence as babies with even lower birth weights survived (Trief, Duckman, Morse, & Silberman, 1989).

Current research indicates that oxygen alone does not account for all cases of ROP, and the condition is not always restricted to premature infants (Teplin, 1995). Birth weight, gestation age, and duration of administration of oxygen together are the most important factors. Today,

ROP primarily affects babies with a birth weight of less than 1000 grams. About 20 percent of infants born weighing less than 1500 grams also show evidence of ROP (Trief et al., 1989).

The problems of ROP begin as a distortion and outgrowth of the blood vessels of the retina. This is followed by the separation of the retina and the formation of an opaque mass behind the lens composed of detached retina, blood vessels, and fibrous tissue. There is bleeding, scarring, and detachment of the retina. The extent of visual impairment depends on the amount of scarring.

Retinitis pigmentosa (RP) is a hereditary condition that is actually a collection of diseases caused by as many as 150 different genes. An estimated 1 person in 80 carries the gene for recessive RP, and the condition affects about 1 in 4000 people worldwide. Retinitis pigmentosa causes degeneration of retinal tissues and loss of peripheral vision. Age of onset varies from childhood to early adulthood. Other abnormalities, such as cataracts and glaucoma, may also be present. RP is associated with deafness in Usher's syndrome, a major cause of deaf-blindness (see Chapter 15). **retinitis pigmentosa**

Damage to the blood vessels that supply the retina can cause macular retinal degeneration. The macula is the small area in the central portion of the retina that is responsible for fine or distinct vision, such as is required for reading. Macular degeneration may be inherited, but it is also associated with injuries such as contusions and concussions. The condition results in extremely poor central vision and may be undetected in young children.

Another type of retinal degeneration is associated with a high degree of myopia. Abnormal growth in the length of the eye causes a thinning of the retina and destruction of the retinal cells.

Diabetes is a major cause of retinal disease. Diabetic retinopathy is a disease of the retina's blood vessels. Not all diabetics develop retinopathy; generally, however, the longer the diabetes is present, the more likely that changes in the retina will occur. People who have had diabetes for more than 15 years are at greatest risk, and as medical technology and synthetic insulin prolong the life expectancies of people with diabetes, retinopathy is becoming more common. The type of diabetes affecting a person does not seem to be the critical factor; some people with mild diabetes that is completely controlled by diet lose their sight, while others with severe forms of the disease do not experience any visual loss ("Diabetic … " 1990).

In the early stages of diabetic retinopathy, the blood vessels in the retina start to weaken and break. The leaked fluid distorts the light rays entering the eyes, and the person's vision blurs and fluctuates, or the person may see floating spots and a reddish haze. In the later stages, the blood vessels may shut down completely, which causes the retinal nerves that transmit sight images to the brain to die from loss of nourishment.

This kind of vision loss is gradual but permanent. New abnormal blood vessels may replace the old ones, but they are unable to nourish the retina properly. They may start to grow into the normally transparent inner chamber of the eye, further interfering with the person's vision. If scar tissue forms, it can pull on the retina, tearing or detaching it completely. The result is total blindness ("Diabetic … " 1990).

Retinal detachment occurs when a hole or rip in the retina allows the inner retina layer to separate from the back portion. Eye fluid can then enter through the break, seep between the layers, and further pressure the inner layer to peel or detach. Total blindness may result if the detached retina is not promptly reattached. **retinal detachment**

Optic nerve atrophy results from damage to the fibres of the optic nerve. Degeneration of the nerve may be partial or complete; onset may be gradual or abrupt. Optic nerve atrophy may result from inadequate blood supply to the nerve or from optical diseases such as glaucoma or retinal degeneration.

Optic nerve hypoplasia (ONH) occurs when the optic nerve fails to form fully during fetal development. Vision can range from normal to total blindness. ONH is associated with other neurological and endocrine abnormalities and is among the most prevalent types of eye disorders in young children (Hatton, et al., 1997; Teplin, 1995).

retinoblastoma

Retinoblastoma is a rare form of childhood eye cancer that occurs in 1 in 15 000 live births and may involve one or both eyes (Ulster & Antle, 2005). It results from a malignant tumour on the retina that may spread to the optic nerve and other areas. The condition can be inherited as a Mendelian dominant trait with incomplete penetrance, which means that the person carrying the trait may not manifest the lesion but can still pass it on to offspring. In the past, surgical removal of the eyes was necessary. Today, the malignancy can be arrested without removal of the eyes.

Other Defects

colour blindness

Colour blindness is a rare, sex-linked, hereditary disorder found almost exclusively in males. Defects of colour vision arise from the absence or malfunctioning of the cone cells—photoreceptors that collect bright light—of the retina. Cones come in three varieties, sensitive to the wavelengths of either blue, green, or red light. In some people, one of the three types of cones is missing, making them colour blind for that range of the spectrum (Immen, 1995). Persons with colour defects are likely to confuse colours, most commonly red and green. True colour blindness (seeing everything in shades of grey) is very rare. Note that colour blindness may or may not be associated with visual impairments.

albinism

Albinism is a condition carried as an inherited autosomal recessive trait. It is not sex-linked and the gene must be inherited from both parents, each of whom either has albinism or is a carrier of the trait. Albinism affects the production of melanin, the pigment contained in hair and skin. A pigment deficiency in the retina, iris, and choroid causes the pupil to take on a deep reddish colour and the iris to appear greyish, light blue, or pink. For the visual system, albinism is characterized by decreased acuity, astigmatism, nystagmus, and **photophobia**, a condition in which very bright light blinds the individual and thus decreases acuity (Abang, 1980).

photophobia

Some central nervous system disorders may manifest as a lack of response to light stimulus in the cortex. *Cortical blindness* sometimes refers to blindness caused by swelling in the brain tissue due to trauma or congenital malformations (Hammer, 1984). At other times, the term describes blindness that cannot be medically explained. Most often, children who are congenitally cortically blind have other problems that are serious enough to affect several body systems.

Syndromes

Usher's syndrome

A number of syndromes are associated with visual impairment. As mentioned, deafness associated with retinitis pigmentosa causes a condition known as **Usher's syndrome**, named after the British ophthalmologist who in 1918 stressed the link between visual and auditory impairments. Usher's syndrome is a leading cause of deaf-blindness (see Chapter 15). Joubert syndrome is a rare neurological disorder. Individuals show ataxia, slow motor activity, and often abnormal eye movements, including nystagmus. Leger Congenital Amaurosis is an inherited retinal degenerative disease.

DEVELOPMENTAL CONSEQUENCES OF VISUAL IMPAIRMENTS

Obviously, the developmental consequences of total blindness differ from those related to low vision. The correlation is certainly not clear-cut but, as a broad generalization, we can say that the greater the degree of visual impairment, the more sharply reduced will be the range and variety of a child's experiences and the greater will be the restrictions placed on the child's ability to move freely within an environment.

We can also say that visual impairment, including the type of eye condition, is linked to altered developmental pathways in children. The global development of young children who are visually impaired tends to be delayed when compared to the development of sighted children.

Motor Development

Social, exploratory, and manipulative experiences lay the foundation for competence in communication, concept development, motor development, and self-reliance. Vision plays a leading role in an infant's first efforts to independently explore the environment. As the new world comes into sharper visual focus, the developing neuromuscular system sparks a push toward motor exploration and the infant reaches out to touch, feel, taste, and probe. Without vision, infants find it more difficult to explore their environment, to reach out into space, and to become aware of their bodies in space.

Very young children who are blind have no natural motivation to lift their heads or roll, and they are less able to orient themselves to the external environment through such skills as reaching, crawling, and walking. Although infants who are blind acquire early motor skills such as sitting and standing at about the same time as other children, restricted experiences mean that they may be slower in crawling and walking. Delays in walking until sixteen to nineteen months are common, and even children with sufficient vision for orientation and mobility purposes may show a lack of confidence and a delay in ambulation.

Older children with visual impairment have significantly lower levels of habitual physical activity, consider themselves less fit relative to peers, and report more limitations for physical activity participation that may be explained by mobility and orientation issues (Lieberman & McHugh, 2001; Longmuir & Bar-Or, 2000). Moreover, these children show delays in motor development, such as poor balance and inefficient gait, which may be by-products of the sedentary behaviour during the developmental years (Bouchard & Tetrault, 2000).

Cognitive Development

The intelligence levels of persons who are visually impaired parallel those of the general population. How children learn, and which lags in learning are attributable to visual impairment are, however, subjects of intense debate.

Researchers ask whether or not children who are blind do more poorly on tasks involving abstract thinking and whether they are much more likely to deal with their environment in concrete terms. Because these children rely far more on non-visual perceptions, the notions they form may differ from the notions of sighted children. However, many current researchers argue that the assumption that children who are blind experience problems of sensory reference has little basis in truth (Landau, 1983).

Another area of contention revolves around whether or not children with severe visual impairments lag significantly behind their sighted peers in the development of Piagetian tasks such as classification and conservation. Research is equivocal because much traditional testing of classification and conservation is based on visual information and, even when traditional visual tasks are adapted into a tactual mode, they cannot be considered comparable.

Perceptual Development

For children who are blind, the world is one of smells, sounds, and textures uninformed by the visual information that offers such a rich variety of colour, shape, and size detail to sighted persons. Hearing is the only distance sense available, and individuals who are blind must build their knowledge from auditory experiences joined to those that are olfactory, tactile, and kinesthetic.

It takes effort and concentration to learn to use the other senses to compensate for lack of sight. There is no magical sensory compensation of the remaining senses; blind persons must learn to pay more attention to auditory and tactual clues that sighted people can afford to ignore.

For the person who is blind, texture, weight, temperature, shape, and size merge into a sequence of touch sensations to permit identification of an object. An individual uses *synthetic touch*—the tactual exploration of objects small enough to be enclosed by one or both hands. For larger objects, the person employs *analytic touch*, exploring the various parts of an object and then mentally reconstructing the parts (Hallahan & Kauffman, 2003).

Communication

Verbal language is critical in information-gathering functions for children who are blind. Even before they develop speech, infants with visual impairments use vocalizations to achieve and maintain social contact. They learn a great deal about people in their environment from voices, learn to measure personal attention by the nearness of the speaker and the touch gestures that accompany speech, and become adept at interpreting meaning from nuances or variations in voice tone.

Studies of the speech and language development of children who are visually impaired have provoked as much controversy as those on abstract thinking and Piagetian tasks. Whether language development parallels that of sighted children or whether it is delayed or different is not clear. There seem to be language differences in the types of words acquired and in reciprocity and pragmatics (see Hatton et al., 1997). Bigelow (1987) found that very young children who were blind acquire vocabulary in the same way as sighted children, although some differences emerged in the percentage of words in each classification. Others have studied *verbalisms*—the tendency to use words whose concrete referent is unknown to the speaker.

A different line of research has looked at the increased numbers of questions that children who are visually impaired tend to ask as part of their information gathering. As sight decreases, so questioning increases, although children who are blind tend to ask fewer open-ended questions than sighted children (Fichten, Judd, Tagalikis, Amsel, & Robillard, 1991).

Academic Achievement

The educational achievement of children who are visually impaired is as variable as the population itself. One general trait is performance peaks and valleys. That is, students who are visually impaired tend to achieve more highly in some academic areas than others. For example, arithmetic is problematic; students who are blind do not perform well and tend to be from 8 to 27 percent below average-sighted children in basic arithmetic performance (Weiss & Weiss, 1981).

Even though visual impairment directly interferes with the observation of symbols and events that are key to the development of early literacy skills, generally, students' performance in literary subjects is about the same as that of their sighted peers. When reading is a problem, the primary cause is the slower rate of reading large print or braille. Spelling needs are greater—students who use braille often have problems with spelling because the contractions in braille do not conform to English spelling usage. Braille is discussed later in this chapter.

Social and Emotional Development

Vision has a neuron growth spurt at the age of two to four months that corresponds with the time that babies really begin to notice the world, and peaks at eight months (Begley, 1996). During this period, sighted infants typically respond to attentive social initiations from their parents by visually focusing on their parents' eyes, smiling, and occasionally shifting their gaze to scan their parents' faces and the environment. In contrast, infants who are visually impaired demonstrate a flat, solemn affect characterized by bland facial expressions and the absence of expressive behaviour. Smiling is difficult to elicit (Baird, Mayfield, & Baker, 1997). All this can adversely affect parent–child relationships, as we further discuss below.

As they grow, children who are visually impaired often demonstrate special needs in relation to self-awareness, self-esteem, and social skills. This happens because severe visual impairments tend to interfere with spontaneous social activity and with social interaction and communication. The visual impairment affects a child's ability to utilize visual clues, which are needed for the modelling and feedback that underlie social skill acquisition. For example, children do not possess built-in feedback for appropriate head and facial movements once they are engaged in conversation.

Children who are visually impaired miss many important non-verbal cues given by their teachers and peers through facial expressions, gestures, and body language. Since these children fail to make expected eye contact with peers and typically will not smile, communication with sighted people may be harmed by lack of eye contact (Fichten et al., 1991). The failure to look at people may be interpreted as disinterest rather than as a manifestation of the disability itself.

Not only do they miss visual clues, but children with severe visual impairments often behave in ways that decrease their effective interaction with peers. Research indicates that children with severe visual impairments initiate interactions less frequently than their peers, have difficulty extending appropriate conversation with them, and are more likely to be rejected (Mar & Sall, 1995).

Children with visual impairments seem to be aware of their lacks in social interaction. For example, when MacCuspie, a Canadian researcher, interviewed five children with visual impairments—one of whom was blind—about friendships (1996), she found that these children thought that their friends were the children who did not make fun of their eyesight or who supported them. Similarly, when Rosenblum (2000) interviewed ten adolescents who were visually impaired, the students reported that they were not part of a popular group in school and felt left out because they were non-drivers. Ontario researchers (George & Duquette, 2006) found that many students with visual impairments are lonely and isolated from their sighted peers. They have fewer friends, fewer opportunities to socialize, and fewer occasions to develop their interpersonal skills than sighted students.

Play Behaviours

Of all disabilities, autism and blindness seem to be the ones that affect the development of sensorimotor and symbolic play the most significantly. Children with severe visual impairments do not display a full range of play behaviours; the delays seem to be related to the limitations imposed by the visual impairments. Children with severe losses may be substantially delayed in sensorimotor play and exhibit delays or deficiencies in symbolic and social play, being at least two years behind sighted children (Hughes, Dote-Kwan, & Dolendo, 1998). At the same time, those with visual impairments are rarely sought out by their peers, infrequently serve as role models, and are the least preferred play partners of typical children (Celeste, 2006).

Co-occurring Disabilities

Between 33 and 70 percent of children with visual impairments have co-occurring disabilities, the most frequent being intellectual disabilities (Hatton et al., 1997), followed by emotional disorders and learning disabilities. Data also point to a relatively high incidence of autism among children who are congenitally blind.

The literature on the dual occurrence of learning disabilities and visual impairment is scarce. Existing studies suggest that between 14 and 65 percent of students who are visually impaired also have learning disabilities. This is much higher than expected with a typical cross-section of school-aged students, probably because of the original etiology, such as neurological problems or prematurity (Erin & Koenig, 1997).

In the behavioural domain, young children who are blind often engage in self-stimulating behaviours such as body rocking, side to side head rolling, and eye poking or eye pressing. This is somewhat different from the self-stimulation often seen in students with developmental disabilities (see Chapter 6) and should not be taken as a necessary signal of problem stereotypical behaviour.

Family Variables

Maternal interaction behaviour has been an important focus of research in the field of visual impairments. General findings indicate that many parents of infants with severe visual impairments feel anxious and apprehensive, even grief-stricken, when they learn of their child's disability. Parents may be worried and frustrated by the infant's responses, or seeming lack of responses. From infancy, parent-child relationships may be harmed (Dote-Kwan, 1995).

Attachment behaviours between infants and parents are facilitated by the infant's ability to elicit parental responses, but very young visually impaired children do not always react to their parents in the same way that sighted children do. For example, babies who are blind do not reach out in the "Pick me up" gesture seen in typical babies at about five months. The facial expressions of babies who are blind are less varied and less frequently seen; they smile significantly less frequently than sighted ones, and the mother's voice does not automatically and consistently evoke smiling. Babies who are blind vocalize much less frequently than sighted ones, and their vocalizations to initiate contact with parents appear much later, even when families encourage such interaction and reward it.

Parents of older children with severe visual impairments tend to expect less of their children. This may lead to a child's lesser accomplishments and slower development (see McConnell, 1999). For example, Heinze and Leyser (1998) studied 130 parents of children with visual impairment and 78 parents of non-disabled children to examine stressors and coping strategies. They found that the parents of the children who were visually impaired felt uncertainty about the future, doubts about being able to meet their child's needs, financial strains, concerns about the availability of adequate services, and an increased need for planning ahead. Parents felt that for themselves there was less time for intellectual, cultural, and recreational activities.

ASSESSMENT OF CHILDREN WHO HAVE VISUAL IMPAIRMENTS

Most children with severe visual impairments either are born with the disability or acquire it at an early age. Therefore, they are usually assessed early so that intervention can begin. In this way, at least some of the consequences of severe visual loss can be aided through the use of lenses, medication, and surgery.

On the other hand, many children with mild visual problems are not identified until after they are enrolled in school and expected to read. In the identification of milder visual disorders, teachers are often on the front line when they observe children who have no outward appearance of anything wrong but exhibit abnormal behaviour. This includes frequent rubbing of the eyes, excessive blinking, crossing one eye when reading, or holding a book abnormally close or far away. Children who are suspected to have a visual problem should be referred for comprehensive eye examinations. Signs of visual problems that teachers can observe are presented in Table 11-2 on the next page.

A comprehensive assessment of a child with a visual impairment takes into account two areas. These are medical diagnosis and treatment of the problem, and psycho-educational assessment that leads to efficient educational planning.

Screening

Screening procedures assess large numbers of children in order to identify those needing additional diagnosis. The most common screening procedure used in the measurement of

Table 11-2 Some signs of visual problems

One eye turns in or out.

In near work, the child squints, closes, or covers one eye.

The child rubs the eyes, squints, or shakes the head while looking at near or far objects.

The child shows excessive head movement; the child tilts the head or closes one eye.

The child is fearful of walking down stairs or running freely.

The child frequently falls or bumps into objects, trips over things, and
    may side-swipe people, objects, and furniture.

The child holds objects very close to—or far away from—the eyes.

The child appears to have abnormal eye movements.

The child complains of fuzzy vision.

The child has frequent eye infections, reddened eyes or lids, swollen or encrusted eyelids or frequent sties
    on the lids, or watery eyes that tear excessively.

The child is poor or slow in reading, shows a lack of interest in reading
    and writing, or is inattentive during reading class.

The child often loses the place when reading or persistently skips lines and confuses letters.

The child often stops to rest after brief periods of reading.

Pages in notebooks are poorly organized.

The child misaligns both horizontal and vertical series of numbers.

The child shows slow copying or difficulty in focusing on the chalkboard.

The child shows poor results with colouring or drawing.

central vision acuity is the Snellen chart. This standard letter chart, familiar to most adults, may not suit young children and those who cannot read. Children are screened with the symbol E chart, which has E's pointing in different directions. Or the chart may have an outline of common objects rather than letters.

Diagnosis

As in the field of hearing impairment, both electrophysiological and behavioural measures are available for intensive diagnosis, used depending on both the needs and the condition (ability to respond) of the child.

In infants, diagnosis relies on observations of the child's responses to visual stimuli, such as a light or a moving object. Clinicians look for reactions of the pupils of the eyes to light, blinking in response to light presentation, eye movements in response to objects moving in the visual field, and eye fixation on stationary objects. In one test, the child is held over a parent's shoulder facing the examiner while a toy or other familiar object is moved into the temporal field. The child is tested for each eye separately and for both eyes together, and his or her reaction is observed.

Eye examinations, used with older children, consider physical aspects—visual acuity, visual field, and oculomotor control; the effects of specific diseases or injuries and prenatal factors; functional aspects such as the extent to which residual vision is being utilized; whether the child has opportunity, incentive, or optical aids to enable him or her to use residual vision; the child's maximum potential for achieving acuity; and the type of optical aids the child needs to reach the maximum acuity level (Abang, 1980). As well, there are clinical charts for testing reading acuity which use sets of unrelated words or sentences.

Psycho-educational Assessment

When a child is deficient in a sense modality, assessment is fraught with problems. For students with visual impairments, many interlocking factors contribute to the difficulties met in the assessment process.

First of all, assessors must be aware that the intelligence levels of blind and sighted children cannot easily be compared and that intelligence tests that are equally meaningful for both sighted and visually impaired children do not exist. Simply using the non-visual verbal portions of common IQ tests may still disadvantage pupils. At the same time, tools especially designed for visually impaired populations such as the Interim Hayes Stanford-Binet, which eliminates items requiring sight, may not evaluate them in a way comparable to the evaluation of sighted children. Finally, there is a lack of viable effective or standardized procedures for testing both the totally and partially blind populations (Johnson, 1989).

The most appropriate tools for children who are blind completely circumvent the visual disabilities and use tactile or auditory modes. For those partially sighted, tests employ aural modes, large type, or magnified materials.

INTERVENTION WITH CHILDREN WHO HAVE VISUAL IMPAIRMENTS

Intervention with students who are visually impaired serves different purposes, depending on the nature and degree of the visual loss as well as the unique goals of differing professional disciplines. Generally, the major areas of intervention are habilitation (therapy) and education, which includes reading and optical enhancement, learning to use alternate modalities, and orientation and mobility training.

Medical Intervention

Preventative medical intervention begins immediately after birth, when the eyes of newborns are routinely washed with a 1 percent silver nitrate solution to prevent infection. Later, children are inoculated to prevent diseases that may result in visual impairments.

To identify and treat serious visual impairments, medical intervention is provided by an *ophthalmologist* (a medical doctor); an *optometrist* (a specialist in vision problems); and an *optician* (a technician who makes lenses). Protocols include medication, surgery, technical aids, and prescriptive lenses to control and maximize visual function. Surgery, eye exercises, patches, or prescription lenses are used for strabismus. Treatment becomes less effective the longer it is postponed, and the longer suppression goes untreated, the more difficult it becomes to restore normal visual functioning.

In the surgical area, laser-beam techniques are used to reattach damaged retinas, and there are sophisticated techniques for corneal transplants, artificial lens transplants, and the removal of cataracts. Various types of drug therapies and medications reduce the risk of blindness from glaucoma and diabetes.

Therapy

For children with severe visual impairments, special attention must be directed toward the efficient use of residual vision, gross motor skills for mobility, and fine motor skills for independent functioning, including compensatory hand skills. Occupational therapists evaluate the effect of a child's visual impairment on daily living, play, and motor skills, and then design programs to improve these. For example, young children with visual impairments tend to use their hands in broad sweeping motions, fail to acquire precise search and grasp skills, and may have weak hands and fingers and need hand skills. Their program may incorporate manipulation of clay and Plasticine, squeeze toys, pegboards, and puzzles.

Technical Aids

There is not another field that has benefited as much from technological advances as that of visual impairment. More than 2000 technical aids, accessories, and devices exist for reading, mobility and orientation, and magnification. In the classroom, a student may use adaptive computer peripherals such as a voice output system, a specialized keyboard, or a screen-enlarging device. There is also a four-track tape recorder/player, a Perkins brailler, a laptop Braille computer, a print enlarger machine, a talking calculator, and different types of reading aids.

For everyday living, an example of an exciting innovation is Voiceprint, a 24-hour reading service telecast specifically for persons who are blind, which is broadcast on television to an estimated 5 million Canadian households that have cable systems. Supported mainly by Communications Canada and Rogers Communications, Voiceprint is a non-profit organization providing time-sensitive news, current affairs, and topical information from all major English daily newspapers, plus over 100 Canadian and international newspapers, magazines, and periodicals (Hysert, 1993).

We address technology again later in this chapter, under the heading, "Special Aids and Equipment."

Educational Intervention

We point out in the Historical Notes that end this chapter that many different options have traditionally been available for the education of students with visual impairments. Integration into general classrooms is a long-standing tradition, and so are residential schools and special classes. The needs of an individual student at a particular point in his or her educational career have been, and are, the deciding factors.

A variety of technical aids have been developed to assist children with visual impairments.

Service Delivery Models

In recent years, the emphasis on inclusion has meant a shift from segregated residential school education for students with severe visual disabilities to education in neighbourhood schools. Nevertheless, residential schools still play a role in Canada. Some educators contend that short-term placement in residential schools may be a feasible solution to the difficulties experienced by some children with visual impairments (MacCuspie, 1993).

Many school districts make available a continuum of placement options, which can include *self-contained programs* designed mainly for younger children or students with special learning difficulties. *The resource room* functions as a part-time classroom staffed by a specialist teacher. *Itinerant teacher assistance* makes it possible for most children with visual disabilities to be integrated into general classes. A specialist teacher travels from school to school within a district to offer special instruction to children at all school levels, including those in special programs. Specialist teachers design and provide instructional programs in Braille reading, Braille math, and other academic subjects; teach the use of visual aids and electronic reading devices; may assess Braille-reading readiness, visual perception, mobility, and social development; and design and provide instruction in self-help skills.

Today, many students who are totally blind or severely visually impaired are enrolled in general classrooms in all grades from kindergarten to secondary school. Successful integration depends on five components—the availability of specialist teachers; access to special equipment and optical aids; a Braille transcription service; co-operation among principals, teachers, and special education personnel; and access to alternative programs for students who need them. Classroom needs include a flexible teacher and peer acceptance and interaction. Personal student characteristics include social skills, a positive self-image, independence, family acceptance, and inner motivation (Bishop, 1986).

There are cautions about inclusion for all students with visual impairments but, possibly because of a history of successful integration, these do not approach the clamour of, say, hearing impairments or behavioural disorders. Most arguments centre on balancing the needs of students.

Those with cautions point out that as children are given opportunities to learn more skills associated with general educational expectations they are likewise restricted in the attainment of special skills such as braille and orientation and mobility. Social interaction, the activities of daily living, and incidental learning are difficult in inclusive settings. Other critics worry about social isolation. We have already noted that, especially during the adolescent period, many students who are visually impaired encounter difficulties in establishing relationships with peers. Even in integrated settings, they often do not interact. Competition with sighted peers can also cause difficulty, even with training and education.

Educational Approaches

Education for students who are visually impaired can be clustered into seven major areas to form a curriculum that combines the general curriculum goals of the child's grade level with specialized instruction. Areas of focus are the general curriculum; use of special aids and equipment; communication skills; visual stimulation; orientation and mobility; personal competence, such as self-help skills and daily living skills; and vocational guidance and career education. These are discussed below; considerations for adolescent students are found in Chapter 17.

Some generic accommodations and adaptations for students who are visually impaired are shown in Table 11-3.

Table 11-3 Creating accessible classrooms

Accommodations

Orientation and mobility

- Walk with the child through the classroom, pointing out landmarks such as the chalkboard, file cabinet, teacher's desk, and the door. Go around the perimeter of the room and then diagonally.
- Assign the student a buddy at first if necessary, but do not allow the student to grow too dependent.
- Don't move furniture in the classroom without informing the student.

Lighting

- Cut down glare on glass, desks, and chalkboards in the classroom. Cover with paper, if necessary.
- Check the lighting needs of the child. In children who are sensitive to light, acuity increases with decreasing illumination. For others, more light is needed.
- Use adjustable lighting, such as a table lamp. Put 60-watt bulbs in lights for illumination and contrast.

Visual stimulation

- Know how, when, and under what circumstances students can use their vision most effectively. Students with central field defects may benefit from eccentric viewing techniques. Those who have nystagmus need to discover the best posture for reading. Those with poor peripheral vision can turn their heads rather than move their eyes for scanning.

Table 11-3 continued

- If the child wears glasses, be sure that they are clean.
- Provide adequate storage space for materials while still keeping the student physically integrated.
- Provide an easel to hold reading materials.

Adaptations, materials

- Visually impaired students require tactual information that is accessible to their hands or other parts of the body. Charts, models, maps, and graphs will have greater value for students if they can be "read" using touch. For example, outline map boundaries with string.
- Each child will have a *critical print size*—the smallest print that allows for maximum reading speed. Adapt all materials to the critical print size.
- When preparing worksheets, be aware of spacing such as the width of rows of print and the number of rows per page.
- Format factors are equally important. For example, limit the use of capital letters to important titles or phrases; capital letters used for long sentences are harder to read because the letters are almost the same size and students cannot use the shape of the letters to aid in word recognition. Bold letters placed close together are more difficult to read than smaller letters placed further apart. Do not use underlines; underlining makes words harder to read.
- Choosing colour is important. Avoid white and grey with other light colours; don't use pastels with each other, or dark colours with each other.
- On application worksheets, blacken the print.
- Use buff rather than white paper.

Adaptations, instructional

- Determine the modality (touch or hearing) through which the child learns best.
- Provide direct learning experiences through a distance sense. Use a multisensory approach.
- Low-vision students write in a size compatible with their own visual capacity. Stress legibility, not size.
- Every student, even one who is blind, needs a personal signature. Teach and practise this.
- When using the chalkboard, give much verbal information.
- Explain, using concrete terms. Use words such as look and see, but avoid this, that, and other intangibles. Take care with statements that require visualization, such as "Pick up the papers."
- Don't raise your voice.
- When students have a slower reading rate with Braille or large print, allow longer time for tasks that require reading.
- To develop reading concepts, use story boxes. Add raised pictures, models and artifacts.
- Tapes or records are helpful teaching devices, giving the student a break from visual fatigue.
- Students work under extra pressure and will be tired at the end of the day. Do not assign large amounts of homework.

Curriculum   Students who are visually impaired can participate in practically all aspects of school activities. Reading is one potential area of difficulty, often because of slower reading speeds. For students who use Braille, extra attention must be paid to English spelling forms. Mathematics may be problematic. To master mathematical concepts, students need to explore the dimensions of shape and build up a vocabulary of meaningful mathematical terms. Students with visual impairments meet difficulties in learning about parts of a whole. Sighted children can, for example, see a drawer and everything in it, but children with visual impairments do not have the same spontaneous understanding (see Lewis & Tolla, 2003). Concept formation, then, is an area requiring special attention.

Special Aids and Equipment   The greatest challenge facing people with visual impairments is the overwhelming mass of printed material in our world. Students are usually unable to use standard printed materials such as textbooks, classroom handouts, reference materials, and schedules, cannot access material written on the board or on an overhead projector, and cannot participate when media such as slides are used.

Students with low vision often require magnification in some form to read print material. Magnification is provided through decreased working distance, enlarged print, optical magnification devices, and electronic magnification devices. *Large-print materials* form the major reading medium for the majority of students classified as severely visually impaired. In large print, 18 point is the most popular type size.

Closed-circuit-television reading aids resemble regular television sets. They have a camera that scans reading material and conveys it to a monitor for enlargement. Users can regulate the size of the image to their own needs.

Low-vision aids augment residual vision by increasing the size of the retinal image (Zammitt, Hare, Mason, Elliott, 1999). Optical aids may be as simple as a magnifying glass or a Visolette—a low-vision magnification aid. Personal reading devices such as Visual Scan and telescopes enlarge regular print such as that found in newspapers and magazines. Other types of magnification include hand-held magnifiers; stand magnifiers, fixed focus or focusable; and headband aids—spectacles, clip-on loupes, and telescopes.

Braille is the traditional medium of literacy for persons who are blind. After its acceptance in North America in the 1890s, Braille was widely used (see the Research Notes). Then, during the 1960s and much of the 1970s, a strong emphasis on the use of residual vision meant that the number of Braille users declined dramatically. Some people even felt that high-tech advances would eliminate the need for Braille completely.

RESEARCH NOTES

Braille

Braille arose originally from the work of Charles Barbier, engineer, inventor, philanthropist, and officer in Napoleon's army, who devised a code that he called *criture nocturne*—night writing. These were not tracings of the ordinary alphabet but a secret code based on a 12-dot unit, or cell, 2 dots wide and 6 high. Each dot or combination of dots stood for a letter or a phonetic sound.

When Barbier's system was presented to the French Academy of Sciences in 1808 it was hailed as a brilliant invention. Various adaptations of the code were undertaken by Barbier and duly submitted to the Academy. One report found its way to the school for the blind in Paris. The 12-dot system was tried but rejected in 1820 as impractical: the cells were simply too large to be read by a single fingertip.

Louis Braille (1809–1852), the son of a harness maker, was born in Coupvray, a French town about 45 kilometres from Paris. He slit an eye at age three while playing with a sharp knife in his father's workshop, and the resulting infection destroyed the vision in his other eye. Louis first attended the village school, where he did very well even without the advantage of schoolbooks. Then in 1819 his father sent him to the Paris Institute for the Blind. Louis proved an outstanding student and eventually became a teacher at the school.

Frustrated with the methods of teaching reading to blind pupils, usually raised print or embossed regular print, Braille embarked on a search for a more efficient means and soon discovered Barbier's military code. When Braille undertook the adaptation of the Barbier system, he first solved the problem of the size of the cell by cutting the number of dots in half. He then devised a new code, alphabetic rather than phonetic, employing combinations of six dots. Because the new code was arbitrary, the symbols could stand for anything the users wanted. With his new system, Braille taught his students to read with more efficiency than was possible with embossed letters.

Braille's alphabetic code was published in 1834, his music notations in 1839. The Braille system for reading and writing was officially adopted at the Paris School for the Blind in 1854. Dr. Simon Pollak, one of the founders of the Missouri School for the Blind, brought Braille from Europe in the 1850s, but the Braille code failed for many decades to find a niche in North America. Educators preferred systems closer to regular written language. Schools for the blind used typefaces such as Moon print, New York print, and raised print. It was not until 1892 that resistance to Braille was finally overcome. Once accepted as a means to assist blind persons with reading and writing, Braille evolved into a well-established system with a variety of levels and codes applicable to any language. Braille has been adapted to many written languages, including those that do not use Roman letters.

The percentages of Braille users are telling. In 1955, more than 50 percent of all persons with severe visual impairments used braille. In 1963, it was about 55 percent of legally blind children. By 1978, the rate dropped to 18 percent, and in 1989 only 12 percent used Braille. By 1994, only 9.45 percent were Braille users; in 1995, the number was 9.62 percent (De Witt, 1991; Schroeder, 1996).

Today we see an increased emphasis on Braille that rests on a number of factors. First, both educators and adult blind persons recognize that it is important to have more than one literacy medium. Second, the ability to read and write Braille maximizes students' chances of educational and vocational success and lays the foundation they need to benefit from many new technological advances (Stephens, 1989). Data also suggest that Braille is not only a tool of literacy but an identity mechanism for adults who are blind, a symbol of independence and competence, even group identity (Schroeder, 1996).

The Braille alphabet uses 6 dots arranged in 2 rows of 3 dots each. Each dot is numbered. (Figure 11-5 on the next page shows the Braille alphabet.) Numbers and punctuation signs are also represented in Braille; numbers use dots 3 to 6, and the use of dot 6 just before a letter indicates a capital.

For literacy, there are two Braille alphabets. Grade 1, or alphabetic Braille, is referred to as the simplified Braille code. Alphabetic Braille matches the print exactly. Grade 2, or abbreviated Braille, is more common and much faster although there are complex rules

Learning Braille is complex and time consuming.

underlying its structure and its many abbreviations. Grade 2 Braille is used in commercially published materials. There is also a Grade 3 Braille. The Nemeth code is the Braille code for math and scientific symbols.

North American students in the course of their school careers may actually have to learn four Braille codes—English Braille, American edition for literacy; the Nemeth code of

Figure 11-5
Braille alphabet

```
1 •        • 4
2 •        • 5
3 •        • 6
```

A	B	C	D	E	F	G	H	I	J

"A–J" use Dots 1, 2, 4, 5 only.

K	L	M	N	O	P	Q	R	S	T

"K–T" add Dot 3 to A–J Dots.

U	V	W	X	Y	Z

"U–Z" add Dot 6 to K–O.

"W" was not in original Braille developed by Louis Braille because "W" was not a letter in the French alphabet. It has its own combinaton of dots.

Braille mathematics and science notation; computer Braille code; and the Braille code for chemical notation. It is not surprising that today there is a strong surge toward a Unified Braille Code that is a literacy code but has scientific symbols embedded in it.

Teaching students braille reading is more complex and time-consuming than teaching print reading. Once acquired, the process of reading Braille is slower than print reading because the range of the fingers is much narrower than that of the eye. Reading and writing Braille is a skill that needs maintenance; the less often a student uses the skill, the more likely it will diminish or disappear.

Reading efficiency is also more difficult to achieve: readers must develop tactile tracking skills, a light touch, good reading posture, and smooth coordination of both hands. A skilled two-handed reader begins by placing both hands at the beginning of a line. When the middle of the line is reached, the right hand continues across the line while the left hand locates the beginning of the next line. The left hand begins to read the first several words of the new line while the right hand moves to its new reading position.

The Optacon (Optic to Tactile Converter) is an optical scan of a printed page that generates a tactile representation of letters. Reading with the Optacon is not the same as reading with Braille. With the Optacon, the user holds a small camera (the scanning device) in one hand. The scanner converts the printed material into impulses. With the index finger of the other hand, the user can feel the letters and numbers through a tactile array of 144 small vibrating rods. If the camera moves across the letter H, for example, the user of the Optacon feels 2 vertical lines and 1 horizontal line moving beneath his or her fingers and tries to recognize the letter shape (Abang, 1980). Recognition of letter shapes requires a great deal of skill and practice.

Variable-speech tape recorders are the most commonly used speech compressors. Raymond Kurzweil's reading machine, first introduced in 1976, is also designed to convert printed materials to an audio output. Kurzweil readers are compatible with computers and use synthesized speech to read the text aloud at varying speeds.

For writing, students who are large-print readers will generally use normal handwriting in their work; the size of the writing is likely to conform to their type-size preference. For braille users, the slate and stylus are the braille version of pen and paper. The user presses the stylus through openings in the slate that holds the paper. Since the material must be read from the underside of the paper, it must be written in reverse by starting at the right margin and moving toward the left.

In the first decade of the 20th century, Frank Hall invented the *Perkins brailler*—a machine that looks like a small old-fashioned typewriter—that allows a person to type Braille using six keys with the Braille dots. Although less portable than a slate and stylus, the brailler is easier to use. Paperless braillers, such as the Cranmer Modified Perkins Brailler, allow students to feed information into a computer and receive a Braille printout. The user can also write in Braille, store material, and correct or amend material as on a standard computer.

Visual Stimulation   Until the 1960s, it was believed that children with visual impairments should conserve their vision so as not to "wear it out." Today's educators believe that residual sight should be used rather than saved: the more children use their vision, particularly at close range, the more they stimulate the pathways to the brain. The brain accumulates a variety of visual images and stores them as memories, which enables children to function more as visual learners and can actually improve their visual functioning. Vision is further stimulated with the use of prescription devices and low-vision aids, which can considerably increase a child's ability to maximize near-vision potential.

Orientation and Mobility   To move freely and confidently, individuals who are visually impaired must know where they want to go, how, and in what direction. They must be able to move at a reasonable rate and with grace, comfort, and safety along existing routes between an origin and a destination. Teaching independent travel is referred to as *orientation and mobility* (O and M) training. **Orientation** refers to an individual's knowledge of his or her position in space; **mobility** refers to negotiating that space. Training means learning to use a travel aid, such as a cane or a dog. Also stressed is the use of auditory, tactual, and kinesthetic senses, together with any residual vision.

An orientation and mobility instructor (pripatologist) teaches mobility skills. Traditional O and M follows a sequence of skill building beginning in an uncomplicated controlled setting and extending slowly to functional tasks. O and M has usually been reserved for persons who are blind. Today some experts recommend it also for individuals with low vision (Smith, Del'aunne, & Geruschat, 1992).

Orientation (cognitive mapping) involves knowing the spatial relations among objects or landmarks and one's own position in relation to the relevant objects or landmarks. Sighted persons who use their visual system for orientation are well aware of where a seen object is in relation to the body, whether or not the object is moving, and its relative direction. These orientation tasks involve the retina, eye movements, visual direction, kinesthetic judgements, the vestibular apparatus, and auditory location.

Persons who are blind have little or no access to the visual information needed to construct the cognitive maps that underlie orientation in space. They use the tactile, proprioceptive, or auditory modes to recognize spatial relations. Often, persons who are blind must rely on sound distance to judge their relationship to an object. They learn to detect subtle changes in the pitch of high-frequency echoes as they move toward objects. This is the *Doppler effect*, a physical principle that says the pitch of a sound rises as a person moves toward the source (Hallahan & Kauffman, 2003).

When guides are used, human guides are probably the most efficient (called the *sighted guide technique*). But human guides are not always available, and a constant human guide would inevitably lead to a decrease in independence.

Teaming a properly trained dog with a person who is blind helps in the achievement of independent mobility. Only a small proportion of the blind population actually uses a dog guide. To qualify, the individual must be over sixteen, emotionally mature, responsible, and selected by an O and M specialist for dog training. Children do not use guide dogs. The most usual breeds used for guiding are German shepherds, Labrador retrievers, golden retrievers, and sometimes setters, and these dogs are too big for young children to handle. As well, the dogs are not pets and need constant grooming and care, and children are not mature enough to keep from playing with the animal or competently care for its needs.

Ideally, all guide dogs are placid, steady, precise animals of constant concentration, oblivious to people around them as they work with their blind owner to whom their responses are exclusively directed. But such dogs are rare, and all have idiosyncrasies that must be taken into account when matching a dog with a master. Some dogs are too fast for the owner; others are too slow. The accompanying Case Study, about Pete and his dog, illustrates what can happen when there is a mismatch between dog and owner.

orientation

mobility

CASE STUDY

Pete

Pete is now twenty-seven years old. He lost his vision as the result of an accident when he was only three years of age. Pete was sent to a residential school for the elementary years but attended the local high school near his home. He is now taking his Master's degree at university.

At school, Pete was taught to use the Hoover cane and developed excellent mobility and orientation skills. But he wanted a guide dog, and as soon as he was old enough, he applied to a centre for one.

When Pete's application was accepted, he went to the centre and worked for nearly a month with the dog selected for him, under the guidance of a highly qualified trainer. Not only did Pete learn about how the dog could assist his own mobility, but he learned how to care for the dog—to feed it properly, to groom it regularly, and to provide it with lots of exercise.

After Pete brought his dog home, workers checked on both his progress and the dog's care and health.

Pete's first dog eventually grew too old to work and Pete keeps him as a beloved pet. He now has a second dog, a young Irish setter. He is, however, finding this experience a little different. The dog is young and more skittish than the first one. When people, not realizing that the dog is working, play with and pet it, the dog responds. The dog loves the snow and, as they live in St. John's, has plenty of opportunity to go bounding over snowbanks and icy sidewalks. When this happens, the dog seems to be in control of Pete, rather than Pete being in control of the dog. Pete is not sure he can overcome these problems and is thinking that the white cane may be more suitable for him at the moment.

The *prescription cane*, also called the *long cane*, the *white cane*, and the *Hoover cane*, is the most common travel aid used by children and adults. It essentially came from the long staff that has been the symbol of blindness at least since Roman times. The cane is made of aluminium or fibreglass; its length is determined by the user's height and comfort level. The traveller holds the cane in front, swinging it in small arcs to detect obstacles.

A wide variety of other travel aids exist. Some are as simple as *tactile maps*—raised maps that portray immediate indoor and outdoor environments and that become a supplemental aid for travel, navigation, and mobility. More sophisticated devices work on a radar principle, sending out beams of ultrasound that cannot be heard by the human ear. If the beam hits an object, some of the ultrasound is reflected back to the device and converted into audible tones. For example, the Sonicguide supplies three kinds of information about an object—direction, distance, and general characteristics. The Sonicguide may be used with a long cane or a dog guide, and can be fitted into eyeglass frames. The laser cane transmits invisible infrared light. When it detects an obstacle, some of the light beam is reflected back to the cane, vibrating a pin beneath the user's index finger. The Mowat Sensor is a small hand-held device, light enough to be carried in a pocket or purse. It can be used to locate fallen objects, doorways, or even mailboxes.

The age of onset of a visual impairment does not predict an individual's ability with mobility skills. Canes are used with young children who are blind to increase mobility, early exploration of the environment, and self-confidence, and to decrease dependence on others. Children as young as one year can also be taught to use specially adapted sensing devices to assist with locomotion and mobility.

Personal Competence Young children who are visually impaired often need assistance in acquiring self-help skills such as dressing, feeding, and toileting. In older children, personal competence revolves around social skills. Adolescents often need assistance to balance their interests, tackle new areas of learning, take risks, and overcome a fear of failure. This is discussed further in Chapter 17.

Social Intervention

The care and training of persons who were blind made rapid advances with the return of blinded soldiers from Europe after the World War I. In 1917, a representative group of blinded soldiers and civilians met with women's organizations and businessmen and set about forming the Canadian National Institute for the Blind (CNIB). Since that time, the CNIB has developed as a national voluntary service that serves more than 39 000 blind and visually impaired Canadians. The CNIB has two major objectives: to foster the integration of visually impaired Canadians into the mainstream of society and to prevent visual disabilities.

The Canadian Council of the Blind is a national organization made up of and run entirely by blind people. It is concerned with the welfare of individuals who are blind and maintains active committees on legislation, recreation, employment, and other matters of concern to blind Canadians. The Council works in close liaison with the CNIB.

SUMMARY

1. Visual impairments vary widely in both degree and type. At one end of the spectrum are people who are totally blind; at the other are those with near-normal vision. Mild visual impairments are a high-incidence condition; the incidence of severe visual impairment and blindness is very low. Severe visual impairment accounts for only about 1 percent of all children who are disabled.

2. At the simplest level, the human eye can be seen as consisting of three parts—the eye itself, which picks up visual messages; the optic nerve, which transfers the messages; and the brain, which interprets the messages. Images are passed through the eye and along the optic nerve to the brain by light. If anything stops or hinders the correct passage of the light, visual problems occur.

3. Because people categorized as visually impaired have vision problems that range from mild disability to total blindness, a number of terms and educational and legal definitions are used to cover this wide spectrum. Definitions also reflect the different agencies interested in visual impairment.

4. All children should be screened and observed in the classroom for behavioural and physical symptoms of visual impairment. Complete eye examinations are necessary to diagnose visual acuity and functioning and to determine optical needs. In psycho-educational assessment, children with severe visual impairments are particularly difficult to assess using standard measures and procedures.

5. A severe impairment in one of the most important of the human senses affects many other areas of a child's functioning. Although they may be at expected developmental

levels in domains such as receptive language and cognition, children with severe visual impairments are lagging in play skills, motor and mobility skills, and imitation and social reciprocity. They face obstacles in obtaining the full benefits of peer interaction and may have trouble in acquiring an adequate repertoire of interpersonal skills.

6. Surgery and correction are the most common forms of medical intervention.

7. Students with low vision have been one of the groups that have profited most from the movement to use assistive technology to enhance the learning environment. Vastly improved optical aids have been developed to enable children with severe sight impairments to read print materials. Advanced computer technology has brought many sophisticated devices that compensate for lack of vision.

8. Provided there are appropriate supports for both the student and the classroom teacher, most students with severe visual impairments are included in general classrooms. Ideally, specialists in the area of visual impairment collaborate with classroom teachers in assessing and developing instructional programs for children who are visually impaired and those with co-occurring disabilities.

9. Training in orientation and mobility enables children who are blind to move with confidence and independence within their environment.

HISTORICAL NOTES

Most of us have a special fear of blindness. A 1988 survey found that blindness was the most feared disability for 42 percent of the 1072 adults surveyed. In the same survey, blindness was listed the fourth most feared disease, after AIDS, cancer, and Alzheimer's disease (Augusto & McGraw, 1990).

Sighted people tend to react to blindness on an emotional level and to see persons who are blind as either dependent or heroic. These two contradictory themes are long-standing and pervasive. Over the centuries, one notion of blindness has been surrounded by fear, myth, and superstition, associated with darkness, despair, loneliness, and punishment. The opposing theme held that blind persons were compensated for their lack of sight by both psychological and physical factors. Superhuman and spiritual powers, uncanny memory ability, and musicality were all traits attributed to blind persons.

Perhaps because blindness is such an obvious disability and one that is so feared by many people, blind persons were early granted special privileges, albeit ones that confirmed their deviant and different status in society. In ancient Rome, only those who were blind were allowed to beg on the steps of the temples, and throughout the centuries this privilege extended to the steps of churches in many places. Beginning in the 4th century, hospices for the blind were established. In the 13th century, one of the first hospitals was founded in Paris for blinded soldiers returning from the Crusades.

Formal schooling for persons who were blind began in Paris in 1784, in Boston in 1832, and in Halifax in 1870. Many positive changes were wrought by dedicated educators such as Samuel Gridley Howe, by slowly evolving legislation, and by advocacy groups such as American Printing House for the Blind and the Canadian National Institute for the Blind (CNIB), which was formed by blinded veterans after the World War I.

John Barrett McGann, the teacher of the deaf whom we met in Chapter 10, undertook the education of students who were blind beginning in 1861.

He admitted blind children to his Toronto school, where they were taught by his fifteen-year-old daughter, Effie. In 1866, the Grey Nuns founded the Nazareth Institution in Montreal. Publicly supported institutions opened in Halifax in 1870 and in Ontario in 1872. These schools gathered pupils from all across the Dominion. For example, as late as the 1970s, it was common practice for Alberta students with visual disabilities to be sent to the Ontario institution (Conn-Blowers & McLeod, 1989).

Chicago in 1900 witnessed the establishment of the first special class for blind students. After that, classes for children who were blind and sight-saving classes for those with visual impairments who were able to read print opened in most urban school districts. In sight-saving classes, children with poor sight were encouraged to "save" or reduce demands on their vision.

Educational integration came rather easily for students with severe visual impairments based on arguments by early educators that children with visual impairments were easily assimilated and taught in general classrooms. By 1956, 25 percent of children with visual impairments attended regular schools; by 1980, the numbers had risen to 95 percent. Today, the great majority of students with visual impairments are educated in general classrooms.

SECTION 6

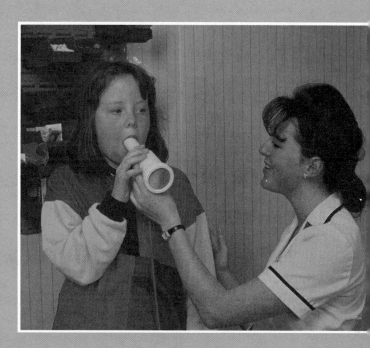

Children with Low-Incidence Disabilities

Nowhere in the study of exceptionality or special education is the spectrum of possible disorders more apparent than in the area of children with special health care needs, neurological disabilities, and orthopedic and physical disabilities. Of youngsters with these disabilities, almost half have cerebral palsy. Children with asthma and allergies make up almost all the remainder of the population. Other conditions, such as cystic fibrosis or spina bifida, form only a tiny percentage of those with physical and health disabilities.

Given such a diverse population, the medical, social, technical, and educational needs of these children vary dramatically. Some students require intense intervention; others need only minor adjustments to classroom physical layout or scheduling. Some children use adaptive equipment, including orthotic and prosthetic devices, to assist their functioning. Much adaptive equipment is used for support, mobility, and positioning.

Physical, neurological, and health disorders are low-incidence conditions. Pervasive developmental disorders (PDD) such as childhood schizophrenia and multiple disabilities are conditions of even lower incidence. Autism Spectrum Disorders, covered under the PDD umbrella, are presently showing disturbing increases in rates.

Pervasive developmental disorders have devastating effects on children's development and potential. These children present such a tremendous challenge to the school system and so test the ingenuity of teachers and diagnosticians that they have been the subject of intense research activity that has spawned a variety of treatment approaches.

Definitions are particularly untidy in the fields of health disorders and physical disabilities and there are many ways of categorizing the conditions for purposes of discussion. In this section, we arbitrarily discuss children with specific health care needs in Chapter 12 and then look at children with neurological difficulties in Chapter 13.

We reserve Chapter 14 for pervasive developmental disorders, specifically children with childhood schizophrenia and those with Autism Spectrum Disorders. In Chapter 15 we address children with severe and multiple disabilities. The reader must remain aware that much overlap exists in all the conditions mentioned in this section. Many children with autism, for example, are actually multiply disabled, and many children with multiple disabilities exhibit autistic behaviours.

Learning Outcomes

The range and types of disabilities covered in this section is enormous. Little commonality exists among the categories save that most are low-incidence conditions.
After reading this section, you should be able to

People and Foundations

1. Discuss the development of residential schools, special schools, and special classes, as well as educational integration for students with pervasive developmental disabilities.
2. Detail the development and growth of the areas of childhood psychoses and Autism Spectrum Disorders and recognize the work of pioneers such as Eugen Blueler, Hans Asperger, and Leo Kanner.

Issues

3. Understand the huge variety of disabilities subsumed within the broad category of pervasive developmental disorders.
4. Appreciate the many types of classroom environments, interventions, and assistive technologies that are needed to accommodate this population.

Knowledge

5. Be familiar with the terminology of pervasive developmental disorders, multiple disabilities, health disorders, orthopedic disabilities, musculoskeletal impairments, and neurological disabilities.
6. Demonstrate a working knowledge of the human nervous system and its functions.
7. Identify the major types of disabilities discussed in this section, their etiology, and their developmental consequences.
8. Understand the types of child abuse, the family variables involved, and the developmental consequences.
9. Be aware of assessment in terms of the tools and procedures used, the challenges to assessors, and the adaptations that can be employed.

Skills

10. Be familiar with the range of devices used for mobility by children with neurological and other motor disorders and be able to identify types of assistive technology and augmentative communication.

11. Understand the principles and practices of educational intervention for students with health disorders, neurological disabilities, pervasive developmental disorders, and multiple disabilities and identify tactics that will support these children in inclusive classrooms.

12. Prepare an emergency protocol.

CHAPTER 12

CHILDREN WHO HAVE SPECIAL HEALTH CARE NEEDS

INTRODUCTION

Special health care needs are diseases and conditions that affect the lives and functioning of children and adults. The category includes a huge range of diseases and conditions, such as cancer, diabetes, asthma, allergies, cystic fibrosis, and muscular dystrophy.

Many health problems result from a variety of genetic and environmental causes; others are associated with prenatal problems, prematurity, and problems of gestation. There are also critical distinctions among illnesses. An illness may be *acute:* it may be serious or severe but can be resolved so that an individual recovers. An illness can also be *chronic:* it is ongoing and cannot be resolved. Other illnesses are *episodic:* an individual may function normally in periods between attacks. Some illnesses are *progressive*: they become more serious over time (Hallahan & Kauffman, 2003). Some conditions occur more frequently in children than in adults. When found in children, the majority of chronic illnesses manifest themselves during the first three years of life.

Special health care needs is a category at an educational and medical crossroad. Essentially, special health care needs are medical problems that are handled within medical parameters. Nevertheless, with the advances in life-saving and life-extending technology, teachers are encountering more children with life-threatening conditions (Munson & Hunt, 2005). In fact, it is predicted that most classroom teachers will meet a child with special health needs at least once in their careers ("Growing challenge … " 1998). Mild medical problems are more common. On average, for example, there are two children in every classroom with asthma at any given time (Getch & Newharth-Pritchett, 1999).

Heller (1997) warned that students with health and physical impairments are at significant risk when educators are not adequately prepared to meet their specialized health care needs. This makes it imperative that contemporary teachers possess at least some knowledge of *health maintenance*—they must be familiar with the appropriate medical procedures and interventions that are part of the regular care of students with special health care needs as well as those required in emergency situations. Teachers should recognize too that children with special health needs are often on a roller coaster of changing needs that is unlike any other disability. These students are subject to unpredictable ups and downs due to the changing course of some illnesses. Other conditions result in a different sort of roller coaster of changing needs as children are in remission or in acute periods or are recovering from surgery or serious bouts of illness. Teachers must be aware of changing treatments, new medications and treatment regimens, and accompanying side effects.

Regardless of the diagnostic category, children with special health care needs have the same wants as other youngsters, and the basic goals of their education are the same as they are for all students. But while the challenges presented by children with health care needs are more environmental and attitudinal than educational, educators must be aware of the factors that put students at risk for learning difficulties. These include fatigue, limited vitality, short attention span, and limited mobility.

While children with special health care needs require additional monitoring by school personnel, most will be in general classrooms and will not require special education services. Special services for remedial education may be warranted only because the condition or illness results in loss of school time and the child is consequently falling behind in schoolwork.

The number of health problems is staggering. In this chapter we restrict discussion to a few specific and sometimes life-threatening conditions most often seen in our classrooms. We also discuss child abuse and neglect; musculoskeletal impairments; and abnormalities of the bony structures, which include limb deficiencies and a number of congenital conditions such as muscular dystrophy, spinal curvature, and osteogenesis imperfecta.

DEFINITIONS OF SPECIAL HEALTH CARE NEEDS

One of the major difficulties in discussing health care needs (and neurological disorders) is the diversity of conditions and their sequelae, which leads inevitably to a range of overlapping descriptors. For example, although orthopedic and neurological impairments are two distinct types of disabilities, they may cause similar limitations in movement. This means that a single child can be described in a number of ways. A child with muscular dystrophy, for example, can be said to have a health disorder, a musculoskeletal impairment, a physical disability, an orthopedic problem, or a motor impairment. Similarly, cerebral palsy can be categorized as a neurological impairment, a significant motor disability, a physical disability, and an orthopedic disability. The conditions discussed in this chapter and in Chapter 13 (excluding child abuse) are shown on the next page in Table 12-1 along with their possible descriptors. We discuss broad groupings below.

- **Health impairments** refer to "having limited strength, vitality, or alertness, due to chronic or acute health problems such as heart condition, tuberculosis, rheumatic fever, nephritis, asthma, sickle cell anemia, hemophilia, epilepsy, lead poisoning, leukemia, or disabilities that adversely affects a child's educational performance" (see Heller, Frederick, Dykes, Best, & Cohen, 1999, p. 220).

health impairments

Table 12-1 Conditions and descriptors

Chronic health problems	Neurological dysfunction	Musculoskeletal impairment	Orthopedic impairment	Physical/motor disability	Technology dependent/ medically fragile
Allergies	x				
Arthritis	x		x		x
Asthma	x				
Cancer	x				
Cerebral palsy		x	x	x	x
Clubfoot			x	x	x
Cystic fibrosis	x				
Diabetes	x				
Epilepsy	x	x			
Hydrocephalus					x
Limb deficiencies			x	x	x
Multiple sclerosis	x	x		x	x
Muscular dystrophy			x	x	x
Pediatric AIDS	x	x			
Scoliosis		x	x	x	x
Sickle cell anemia	x				
Spina bifida with myelomening-ocele		x	x	x	x
Traumatic Brain Injury		x			

physical disabilities

- **Physical disabilities** are those that affect body systems; they include health disorders and problems related to mobility and motor skills. Physical disabilities that have associated motor disabilities and deviations include cerebral palsy, muscular dystrophy, and spina bifida.

- *Orthopedic conditions* are those that arise from any cause; they affect mobility and adversely affect a child's educational performance. The term includes impairments caused by congenital anomalies, such as club foot, or absence of some member; impairments caused by disease, such as poliomyelytis or bone tuberculosis; and impairments from other causes, such as cerebral palsy, amputations, and fractures or burns that cause contactures (see Heller et al., 1999).

- **Musculoskeletal impairments** are specific disorders involving bones or muscles that impede bodily movements in the absence of damage to the central nervous system. Causes range from inherited diseases and congenital malformations to infections and accidents.

musculoskeletal impairments

- **Neuromuscular diseases** are acquired or inherited conditions that affect cells in the spinal cord, the peripheral motor nerves, the myoneural functions between the nerves and muscles, and the muscles themselves (Sandoval, 1998). Neurological dysfunctions occur before, during, or after birth and include cerebral palsy and head traumas.

neuromuscular diseases

- *Technology dependent* refers to conditions that require technological intervention. Children need "a medical device to compensate for the loss of vital bodily function and substantial ongoing nursing care to avert death or further disability" (OTA, 1987, p. 3). For example, a child may be ventilator dependent, oxygen dependent, or nutritional supplement dependent. Or a child may need heart monitoring, apnea monitoring, or kidney dialysis.

- *Medically fragile* is a term that overlaps the above category. Medically fragile children require specialized technological health care procedures for life support during the school day.

In this chapter we restrict our discussion to health problems and musculoskeletal impairments that do not have neurological involvement. Impairments directly related to damage of the central nervous system are discussed in Chapter 13.

PREVALENCE OF SPECIAL HEALTH CARE NEEDS

The number of students with physical and health disabilities is increasing (Heller et al., 1999). Beyond this general statement, the prevalence of chronic health problems is very to determine. This is primarily because:

- There is such a variety of conditions, and there are inconsistencies in defining various disabilities;

- Different provinces use different methods for gathering data, producing very different results;

- Nationwide health statistics tend to rely on a limited number of categories, which means that many health problems go uncounted;

- In both provincial and national surveys, individuals with multiple disabilities may be counted twice;

- Reported increases in certain physical disabilities over the past three decades, especially allergies and asthma, skew numbers;

- Physical disabilities are often found co-occurring with other disabling conditions.

Although it is difficult to obtain exact prevalence and incidence figures for specific conditions, we can say that most are very low-incidence problems. The major exceptions are asthma and allergies, with asthma both a high-incidence and an increasing condition in most developed nations. In fact, asthma severe enough to restrict childhood activities rose approximately 65 percent between 1970 and 1990 (Newacheck & Taylor, 1992). The increased prevalence of asthma now makes it the most common chronic disease in children.

Within Canada, the prevalence of asthma in children is slightly higher than in the United States (Pfeuti, 1997). Asthma affects about 7 to 10 percent of the Canadian pediatric population, as opposed to 5 to 10 percent of children in most industrialized countries (Canadian Lung Association, 1997).

CLASSIFICATION OF SPECIAL HEALTH CARE NEEDS

Health disorders are essentially medical conditions requiring a complex and sophisticated range of interventions that include surgical procedures, prosthetic devices, drug therapy, diet management, and ongoing medical treatment. There is no necessary correlation between health disorders and impairments in other domains of functioning.

Cystic Fibrosis

cystic fibrosis

Cystic fibrosis (CF) is a genetically determined inborn error of metabolism characterized by pervasive dysfunction of the exocrine glands (glands in which secretions are passed through ducts). The condition seems to be both ethnically and geographically variable—it is very rare among Swedes and African Americans and virtually non-existent among Asians. Among Caucasians, cystic fibrosis is the most frequently occurring genetic disorder in North America and many European countries. One out of every 20 Caucasians is a carrier of the gene for cystic fibrosis. Affected children inherit 2 copies of the defective gene, 1 from each parent. Approximately 1 birth in every 1600 to 2000 among North American Caucasians is affected (Brinthaupt, 1991). In a family with an affected child, two out of three siblings are likely to be carriers, and one out of five is likely to have the disease.

Cystic fibrosis is transmitted through an autosomal recessive gene, although it appears that more than one genetic defect causes the disease. The main malformation in the CF gene's twisted double chain of DNA is the absence of a few chemicals. However, some 15 000 DNA samples taken from patients around the world with cystic fibrosis indicate that there are at least 60, and probably a good many more, additional malformations that produce the symptoms that are classically lumped together as cystic fibrosis. Cystic fibrosis is therefore an extremely complex and involved disorder, quite variable in its manifestation.

The condition primarily affects the respiratory and digestive systems, with varied degrees of system involvement. Fully manifested cases present a triad of chronic pulmonary disease, pancreatic enzyme deficiency, and inordinately high sweat electrolytes. Symptoms include high salt concentration in the sweat glands and the production of thick sticky mucus that clogs breathing and digestion. The mucus obstruction disrupts the

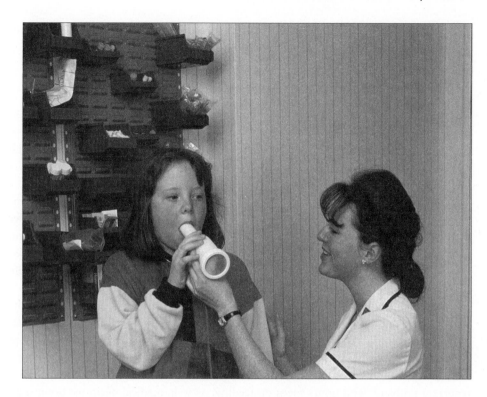

Treatment for cystic fibrosis is extensive. It involves diet management, respiratory disease management, and drug therapy.

functions of the lungs and other vital organs. In the lungs, it creates pockets of infection and pulmonary dysfunction, which frequently results in chronic episodes of pneumonia and bronchitis. With repeated infection, the lungs are gradually destroyed. As lung deterioration occurs, the heart is also burdened, and heart failure is a common by-product of cystic fibrosis.

Because people with cystic fibrosis have insufficient amounts of digestive enzymes for normal digestion, virtually every part of the digestive system is affected. The pancreas, gall bladder, liver, and intestines often function abnormally and show changes in the tissues. Children often fail to gain weight despite increased appetite. They grow very slowly and never appear to thrive.

Although the gene responsible for cystic fibrosis was identified in 1989, there is no cure, and intervention is as varied and complex as the disease, requiring diet management, therapy and management of respiratory disorders, and various regimes of drug therapy. Before antibiotics were available, approximately 75 percent of children with cystic fibrosis died before age ten. Life expectancy has been greatly extended and many older patients are being treated. Recently, surgical transplants have become an option.

Today's primary treatment procedures are medication and therapy. Antibiotics are prescribed when lung infections are present. Children need oral and/or inhaled medications during the school day to improve lung function and to fight infections (DePaepe, Garrison-Kane, & Doelling, 2002).

In percussion therapy, the chest is vigorously clapped and vibrated to elicit coughing, which encourages the elimination of mucus. The changes in posture also aid in the draining process. Special diet high in protein, high in calories, and low in fat can be quite effective in the management of disorders of the digestive system. This is combined with dosages of an enzyme needed to compensate for the insufficiency of the pancreas.

Developmental Consequences of Cystic Fibrosis

Children with cystic fibrosis do not suffer any form of intellectual impairment and should be educated in general classrooms. However, they will probably miss many days of school because of respiratory infections or intestinal disorders. They may have a chronic cough and may need extra snacks during the day. As adults, some men and most women with cystic fibrosis are unable to have children.

The greatest impact that a child with cystic fibrosis (or any serious health disorder) seems to have is on the family. In general, parents of children with special health care needs suffer many traumas and stresses. Family reactions include depression, denial, anxiety, resentment, and anger (see Chapter 16). A chronic illness such as cystic fibrosis is an affront to an assumed developmental order for the family life cycle. Parents must confront the abbreviated life expectancy of the child; some must handle the additional stress of a dying child.

In the short term, everyday activities are dependent on the current health status of the ill child. Regimens of treatment, medication, feeding, positioning, and medical care can take up most of the day. Parents must learn the therapeutic techniques required to assist in their child's treatment. This usually consists of twice daily half-hour sessions involving chest percussion and postural draining. When the child is young, meal times can be a recurrent problem, with hours spent on feeding. As well, medical decisions become an ongoing part of family life. Parents spend much time searching out information and becoming fluent in the medical terms related to their child's illness.

Diabetes Mellitus

diabetes mellitus

Diabetes mellitus is an autoimmune illness similar to rheumatoid arthritis or multiple sclerosis. The disorder involves sugar metabolism and is caused by a pancreatic disorder in the production of insulin, a hormone needed to metabolize glucose. In diabetes, the white blood cells target the cells that produce insulin.

Unlike many chronic health disorders, diabetes is a high-incidence condition. In Canada, diabetes is a growing health problem. In 2000–2001, there were 6.7 cases per 1000, up from 4 per 1000 in 1999 (Robbins, Ugnat, & Waters, 2005). Diabetes affects 1 in every 600 children under the age of ten.

Diabetes is divided into two major types. Type I, or insulin-dependent diabetes, is usually associated with early onset (under twenty-five years of age and as early as six months) and includes juvenile diabetes. Type II, non-insulin-dependent diabetes, ordinarily occurs after age forty. Type II diabetics produce quantities of insulin, but they do not use it efficiently.

Type I diabetes brews silently for several years. The onset of the disease is signalled by thirst, hunger, weight loss, fatigue or weakness, excessive urination, and sometimes, blurred vision. Onset may occur several months after the outbreak of specific viruses (Rodger & Hunt, 1980).

Young people stricken with insulin-dependent (Type I) diabetes once faced certain death within a year of diagnosis. As the pancreas lost its ability to make the insulin required for normal metabolism, glucose accumulated in the blood stream and urine. The body then drew on other sources of energy until it literally starved, and death ensued. In 1921, isolation of the insulin hormone from animals made it possible to control diabetes with daily insulin injections and has since meant survival for millions of diabetics. Note that neither animal insulin nor the more modern human form offers a cure. Injections must be taken once or more a day for life. Also, many diabetics eventually suffer from devastating complications. As the disease persists, blood vessels can be damaged, leading to heart disease, stroke, blindness, or kidney failure. Nerve damage is also common (Atkinson & MacLaren, 1990).

The treatment of Type I diabetes involves a diet low in carbohydrates and fats accompanied by regular injections of insulin. Food intake, insulin, and exercise must be carefully balanced and monitored throughout the diabetic's life to prevent immediate and long-term complications associated with hyperglycemia (high blood sugar) or hypoglycemia (low blood sugar).

Hyperglycemia develops slowly over a period of hours or days. Unchecked, it leads to ketoacidosis, a chemical imbalance that produces acute and serious illness, unconsciousness, coma, and ultimately death. Although moderate but chronic hyperglycemia is thought to cause the long-term complications associated with diabetes in adulthood (such as retinopathy and microvascular disease), the specific effects of a moderate elevation of blood glucose on children's brain functioning is not known.

Severe hypoglycemia has a rapid onset. It is caused by an excess of insulin intake and produces unconsciousness and seizures. Hypoglycemic convulsions have been associated with abnormalities in brain functioning (Rovet, Erlich, & Hoppe, 1988).

The symptoms of non-insulin-dependent diabetes, a disease caused by an entirely different mechanism that is not fully understood, are more subtle than those of Type I diabetes. Type II diabetics are usually older than forty and overweight; susceptibility may be genetically transmitted. These patients produce various quantities of insulin, but they typically use it inefficiently. Some are treated with insulin to control blood glucose levels, but they do not require the drug for day-to-day survival (Atkinson & MacLaren, 1990).

Developmental Consequences of Diabetes Mellitus

Children who are diabetic can participate in all school activities unless otherwise advised by a physician. In addition to regular education, children are taught to manage their condition. They learn to inject their own insulin, monitor their blood sugar and urine sugar levels, and maintain a balance among nutrition, exercise, and insulin levels.

In young children, this critical balance is often difficult to maintain, particularly in the presence of illness or infection. It is therefore imperative that teachers understand a child's condition and recognize signs of imbalance. Health personnel should provide appropriate guidelines regarding the timing of school meals and school exercise.

Children with diabetes have an average range of intelligence, although those who develop the condition early in life are at risk for subsequent neuro-cognitive impairments and often show specific skill deficits. The earlier the onset, the more difficulties are experienced. Researchers who explored the effects on children's cognitive development of insulin-dependent diabetes mellitus concluded that those who develop diabetes before the age of four are at greatest risk for subsequent intellectual impairment (Rovet, Erlich, & Hoppe, 1988). Particularly affected are skills in the visio-spatial area of cognitive functioning and mathematical ability. These findings correlate with a poorer academic history and a greater need for special education. Girls appear to be somewhat more affected than boys.

Diabetes is more than simply a matter of diet, insulin, and urine testing. It also involves an individual's emotional and physical development, which largely depend upon the reaction of others to the condition. The environment affects diabetic control, and diabetic control, in turn, affects the environment. This is particularly true of the school environment, since children spend so much time in school. Students who are diabetic may experience embarrassment over their unusual diets, the urine testing, and any symptoms of diabetic shock that may be displayed. Peers may ridicule them and treat them differently.

Bob's story in the Case Study is illustrative. Here is a boy who was struck suddenly with a chronic and somewhat mysterious disease. It changed his entire life, bringing in its wake medical interventions, constant physical monitoring, and daily injections. Bob is now different from his peers and his life is more restricted.

Cancer

cancer

Cancer is a general term used to describe about 100 conditions characterized by abnormal and uncontrolled cell growth. Although more children recover from cancer than adults, Shaw and colleagues (2004) report that childhood cancer is the leading cause of death from disease in Canadians less than twenty years of age. Each year, approximately 1300 children and adolescents are diagnosed with cancer in Canada.

CASE STUDY

Bob

Bob is entering his first year of high school this year. While many students worry about the move to a large, somewhat impersonal school plant with many teachers and different responsibilities, Bob's reactions are far beyond the usual. He has told his parents over and over that he does not wish to attend high school and that if they force him, he'll run away from home. His parents, deeply concerned, nevertheless understand Bob's reluctance.

Two years ago Bob was stricken with juvenile diabetes. For a healthy, active, and outgoing child, the effects were devastating. Bob was old enough to understand the chronic nature of the disease and to realize the restraints it would place on his life in terms of insulin injections and diet. He abandoned many of his usual pursuits, ignored his friends, and began to fall seriously behind in schoolwork. Type I diabetes can result in wide daily swings in blood sugar levels, which means a constant rebalancing of insulin with food and exercise. But although Bob was old enough to administer his own insulin, monitor his urine, and adapt his diet, he tacitly refused to do any of these things. It took a psychologist many months to help Bob to realize the necessity of attending to his own health care needs.

Even though he now looks after his own needs, Bob is resentful of the disease and embarrassed about it in front of his friends. His reluctance to attend high school centres on his fear of acute embarrassment in the case of an insulin coma (of which he has suffered a few) as well as his dislike of anyone knowing about his condition. To help Bob, his parents have again contacted the psychologist and hope that counselling will help overcome some of his deep-seated resentment about the diabetes.

In adults, the most common cancers are those of the lung, colon, and skin. The most common cancers in children are of the blood, bone, brain, nervous system, and kidney. Acute lymphocytic leukemia (ALL) is the most prominent of the childhood cancers: approximately one-third of all cancers diagnosed in children are leukemias (Peckham, 1993), and leukemia is responsible for two-thirds of the deaths of children with cancer.

Survival rates have increased dramatically in the past three decades. Today, over 75 percent of children diagnosed with cancer will survive five or more years past diagnosis. More specifically, a child diagnosed in 1960 with acute lymphocytic leukemia had only a 1 percent chance of survival. Today 70 percent of children treated for ALL can expect long-term survival and cure (Bearison & Muhern, 1994). Wilms' tumour (a kidney cancer) has a survival rate of more than 90 percent. Long-term survival rates for children with brain tumours are approaching 50 percent.

Major treatments for cancer are surgery, chemotherapy, and/or radiation. More than 60 percent of children are today effectively cured by surgery, chemotherapy, radiation, or a combination of these treatments (Bessell, 2000). After diagnosis, a four-week treatment period begins with intensive therapy. When remission is confirmed, oral drugs are introduced. Children respond to treatment in a variety of ways, which may result in short- and long-term effects.

Developmental Consequences of Cancer

The effects of childhood cancer extend beyond the physical domain and linger after treatment. One of the major outcomes is the physical and emotional problems arising from treatment. Each child will have a unique experience at the hospital and in the diagnosis and treatment of a particular kind of childhood cancer.

For many children, chemotherapy drugs cause plumpness and hair loss. Other physical results include amputation, disturbances in normal growth patterns, mood swings, difficulties in concentration, muscle weakness, fatigue, nausea, and dramatic weight gain or weight loss.

School is a major part of each child's life, and children with cancer gain special benefits from education at all stages of their illness. They need the satisfaction of being normal, productive learners and should attend school even in the terminal stages of the illness, if possible. School attendance provides peer contact, helps to distract children from their physical concerns, and assists in their long-term emotional and physical rehabilitation.

Children with cancer are told of their problem to enlist their help in treatment. Teachers too must understand the illness and how it affects the child at each maturational stage. They should be aware, for example, that after a period of hospitalization a youngster may be less energetic and very likely to hold deep concerns about the nature of the illness. A child's anger about forced dependency on parents and frustration at having to submit to the disruptions of therapy can cause withdrawal and regression. All this can result in decreased educational motivation, poor self-concept, social isolation, and an abnormally close relationship with one parent.

While the teacher is a valuable link in the total care of the child, research has not shown promising outcomes. In a survey of 11 parents of children with cancer (Goreau, Kennedy, & Sawalzty, 1996) researchers found that parents felt that schools, on the whole, are not prepared to deal with children who are cancer survivors. Most parents were disappointed with the schools' responses; teachers were not informed about childhood cancer and its effects.

When a teacher is knowledgeable, he or she can help by communicating with and supporting parents, being a liaison between them and other professionals, and helping the child to interact with others. Teachers can prepare other class members for their classmate's physical changes—loss of hair, weight gain, and the like.

Sadly, it is not unusual for a teacher to have a student in the classroom who has a terminal illness. When this occurs, the inevitability of death has to be faced by the teacher and the other children on some level. Teachers may need special training in managing their own and their other students' attitudes toward death and dying. When a child with cancer is in the classroom, for example, students fare best when honest discussions about terminal illness occur right from the beginning (Weiner & Septimus, 1991). Children with cancer need to know they had no part in causing the illness and that it is not catching.

Sickle Cell Anemia

The most common forms of this disease are *sickle cell anemia* and *sickle-hemoglobin C disease*. Two defective genes cause the far more serious sickle cell anemia. Sickle-hemoglobin C disease refers to the trait borne by carriers.

The defective recessive gene involved in sickle cell causes the production of defective hemoglobin, which leads to distortions in blood cells—under certain conditions, the red blood cells "sickle" (change shape). Sickle-shaped cells tend to clot together; the shape causes the cells to pile up and block small blood vessels, causing pain and tissue destruction (Pierce, 1990). The intensity of the effects varies widely.

Because the sickle cell trait protects against death from malaria, it is common in populations from malaria-prone parts of the world, which include areas of Africa and the Mediterranean countries. Among Hispanic Americans, about 1 in 20 is a carrier. Of the 10 percent of African Americans with sickle cell, most are heterozygous (that is, sickle-hemoglobin C disease with one normal and one abnormal gene). Only about 0.25 percent are homozygous (sickle cell anemia with two defective genes).

Individuals with full-blown sickle cell anemia often have long bouts of illness and die in childhood. Because sickle cell impairs circulation, it causes inadequate oxygen delivery to miscellaneous organs, including the brain. Sufferers experience severe pains in the abdomen, back, head, and limbs. The disease also causes the heart to enlarge and deprives the brain cells of blood, so people are prone to strokes. Ten percent of children with sickle cell anemia will have a stroke before they reach adulthood (DePaepe, Garrison-Kane, & Doelling, 2002). People with severe cases may also suffer heart and kidney problems and pneumonia, which can be fatal.

Those who are heterozygous (carriers) suffer fewer effects and their intensity varies widely. Sickling occurs under certain conditions, such as exposure to low oxygen levels. In carriers, 40 percent of the red blood cells may assume a sickle shape when the supply of oxygen to the blood is reduced. Treatment of a crisis usually involves rest, medication for pain, blood transfusions, and oxygen inhalation therapy.

In older children and adults, it appears that the sickle cell trait is generally benign and does not shorten life. The situation seems to be more serious for infants. In the United

States, investigators have reported a mortality rate of 13 to 14 percent among sickle cell children under the age of two (Grover, Shahidi, Fisher, Goldberg, & Wethers, 1983). The spleen, the most efficient blood filter in the body, is vulnerable.

Pediatric AIDS

Acquired Immunodeficiency Syndrome (AIDS) was first reported in 1981. Around the world today, more than 40 million people are living with HIV; 2.5 million of them are children younger than fifteen years of age (UNICEF, 2005). In Canada from 1991 to 1998, there were 243 children diagnosed with AIDS and another 1193 with HIV (Roberts, 2000).

Twenty years ago, AIDS research was in its infancy: becoming HIV positive meant almost certain death. There has been significant progress in understanding the mechanism of HIV transmission and prevention and in the development of more sophisticated classification systems for AIDS and its associated syndromes. Today's researchers have begun to discuss HIV as a serious but manageable disease.

AIDS is caused by the human immunodeficiency virus (HIV), which attacks and seriously disrupts the body's immune system, its defence against disease. Without the protection of the immune system, AIDS sufferers are prone to infections and cancers.

There are really only two major populations of children with HIV infection. The first is children with congenital or birth-acquired infection. This group forms the vast majority of children with pediatric AIDS; they have obtained the infection during birth from their mother, who used intravenous drugs or was sexually active with infected partners (Baumeister, Kupstas, & Klindworth, 1990). The second group of HIV-infected students is adolescents who acquire the virus sexually or through intravenous drug use. A very small third group is those infected by transfusions.

Developmental Consequences of AIDS

Affected children show typical symptoms that can include attention difficulties; cardiac disease; cognitive deficits; cold sores; coughing; diarrhea that can be acute and chronic; emotional problems; fine and gross motor difficulties; hearing problems; infections that include frequent bacterial and viral infections and middle ear, eye, and joint infections; seizures; shortness of breath; speech and language delays; visual problems; weakness; and weight loss (Le Roy, Powell, & Kelber, 1994). Some studies show that language deterioration often occurs and is frequently seen before other cognitive and central nervous system abnormalities are detected (Roberts, 2000).

School transmission of HIV is unlikely. The major health risk is to the child who has the virus, because that child will be more susceptible to and seriously affected by common childhood illnesses or may develop life-threatening complications.

While children with pediatric AIDS are not necessarily special education candidates, many qualify because of limited strength and vitality and acute health problems. When provided with special education services, the most successful programs for them parallel those for other special learners. Instruction should be designed for success, based on concrete experiences, and broken down into small, manageable steps.

Allergies

allergy

The term **allergy** means "altered reaction." It is used interchangeably with *hypersensitivity* and refers to an abnormal and varied reaction that occurs following a contact with substances or agents that normally do not cause symptoms in other individuals.

Allergies (which include asthma) are the most common chronic disease in pediatrics. Allergic conditions are estimated to occur in 6.6 to 33 percent of children and adolescents (Crawford, 1982). In Canada, studies show that one in every five school children has a major allergy (Alberta Response, 1989).

There are two major categories of allergies. *Atopic* allergies are associated with hereditary and/or familial factors. The risk to children when both parents have a positive history of allergy is 30 to 40 percent, while the risk to children when one parent has a positive history is 20 to 30 percent (Kuzemko, 1978). *Non-atopic* allergies do not have a hereditary component but result from antibodies produced in response to allergens in the environment.

A huge range of substances create allergic reactions in humans. Generally, substances are divided into four categories: inhalants, contactants, injectants, and ingestants. *Inhalants* include dust, pollen, mould, aerosol sprays, and strong odours. *Contactants* are substances that come into contact with the skin, including fabrics, metals, cosmetics, and chemicals.

Injectants are agents or substances that enter the body through the skin, including insect bites, bee stings, and some drugs. *Ingestants* are foods and drugs. True food allergies occur in 3 to 8 percent of children. Ninety percent of allergic reactions are caused by wheat (gluten products), eggs and egg products, milk and milk products, tree nuts and nut products, shellfish, fish and fish products, peanuts and peanut products, and soybeans and soy products (Taylor & Hefle, 2001).

True food allergies should not be confused with food intolerance and secondary food sensitivities. Food intolerance is an abnormal reaction to certain foods; food sensitivity may be an effect of another health situation. However, a true allergy affects the immune system. As such, it can cause severe, life-threatening reactions. The most common allergies are to peanuts, tree nuts, shellfish, fish, and eggs.

There are a number of types of allergic reaction. One of the most common is *allergic rhinitis*, which may be either seasonal or perennial. The seasonal type—hay fever—is induced by windborne pollens; the perennial form is present throughout the year. Both forms involve nasal congestion, itching of the nose, or repetitive sneezing. *Urticaria* and *eczema* are skin reactions resulting in rashes, itching, swelling, and seeping of body fluids through the skin. *Physical allergy* is a response to cold, heat, or sunlight. *Allergic conjunctivitis* involves itching of the eyes and excessive tears. *Gastro-intestinal allergy* is a response to specific foods or drugs. *Allergic pulmonary disease* is usually referred to as bronchial asthma.

Asthma

asthma

The word **asthma** derives from the Greek, meaning "panting" or "difficulty in breathing." It refers to a chronic lung condition characterized by inflammation, obstruction, and increased sensitivity in the airways.

Asthma is the most common chronic disease of childhood (Hamm, 2004). About two-thirds of affected children have mild conditions; for the remaining one-third, the conditions are moderate to severe (Getch & Neuharth-Pritchett, 1999). About 20 children and 500 adults die as a result of asthma each year in Canada. Of all provinces, Alberta has the highest asthma mortality rate; compared to Saskatchewan and Manitoba, for example, Alberta's death rate is three times higher (Canadian Lung Association, 1997).

An individual's asthma can be a continuous state of frequent attacks ranging in severity, or an intermittent state consisting of occasional attacks ranging from mild to severe (Howse, 1988). Episodes may be brief or can last for a few hours or weeks at a time. In young children, boys are twice as likely as girls to exhibit the condition. Many children improve or go into remission in adolescence. At the same time, a levelling occurs so that the male-female ratio is 1 to 1 after the age of fifteen.

When a person with asthma is exposed to a trigger, additional mucus is produced, subsequently clogging air tubes that then tighten and constrict. The most common signs of an asthmatic episode are wheezing, difficulty breathing, persistent coughing, chest tightness, sneezing, dark circles under the eyes, and clipped speech (Hamm, 2004). While a wide variety of stimuli are associated with bronchospasms, there may also be an inherited susceptibility. Many modern researchers believe that asthma is caused by the interactions of heredity and environment (Isabell & Barber, 1993).

Different triggers account for asthmatic attacks. The first group, *known factors*, include allergens, drugs, exercise, industrial exposure, infections, and reflexes. The second category, *probable causes*, includes things such as air pollutants, chemical irritants, sinusitis, and vasculitis. The final group, classed as *possible triggers*, includes emotions, hormonal imbalance, and weather. Nevertheless, it is extremely difficult to pinpoint exactly which factor or factors trigger an individual asthma attack because the same factors are not always responsible for subsequent attacks (Howse, 1988).

Children with severe attacks need attention in a matter of minutes or seconds. Indicators include such things as the lips or fingernails turning blue; difficulty in talking or crying; unresponsiveness to stimuli; inability to drink liquids; and looking limp and extremely lethargic (Getch & Neuharth-Pritchett, 1999).

Various long-term medications and quick relief medications, of which drugs are the most common, are employed in asthma treatment. Since adrenalin, the first drug treatment of asthma, was introduced, a wide number of other drugs has emerged. These include drugs that act on the airways directly, drugs that halt the production of antigens, and corticosteroids that also hinder antigen production (Howse, 1988). Bronchodilators are used to relieve obstruction of airflow. In severe cases, corticosteroids are useful. Both have side effects, although the changes are often temporary. Medications may affect an individual's ability to concentrate, increase feelings of depression and anxiety, and interfere with short-term memory (Bender, 1995).

Common-sense factors in treatment, other than medications, include rest, sufficient fluids, play and work to tolerance, avoidance of the allergens that cause attacks, and regular exercise to improve postural drainage, strengthen the diaphragm muscles, and expand lung capacity (Pilecka, 1995).

Developmental Consequences of Asthma

The disease process of asthma does not negatively affect school performance; however, school absenteeism is the major problem, especially in the first three years of school.

A child with asthma has three times the number of school absences as compared to a nonasthmatic child (Hamm, 2004).

This means that children with asthma are likely to be under-achievers and behind in school work, especially as adolescents. Children with asthma also have more emotional difficulties, but the nature of the relationship between psychological problems and asthmatic episodes is poorly understood (Pilecka, 1995).

CHILDREN WHO ARE ABUSED AND NEGLECTED

The history of humanity is rife with examples of cruelty to children, ranging from infanticide in early societies to child factory labour in the 19th and 20th centuries. (This is discussed in the Research Notes on child abuse.) So although some researchers feel that child abuse is on the increase, it is more likely that abuse, under modern definitional constructs, is simply more open to identification and reporting.

Child mistreatment is a major problem in our society. For example, in 1996 there were 3500 cases of physical or sexual maltreatment investigated by the Metro Toronto Police (Gadd, 1997). In that same year, children under eighteen represented 22 percent of victims of assaults reported to a sample of 154 police agencies; children represented 60 percent of all victims of sexual assault and 18 percent of all victims of physical assault (Fitzgerald, 1999). An earlier report of sexual assaults by family members reported to police found that girls represented 79 percent of cases while boys were victims in 21 percent of cases (Fitzgerald, 1996).

It is not possible to assess the exact dimensions of child abuse and neglect, and there is a general consensus that the actual rate is underestimated by official reports. Various reasons contribute, as outlined below.

- There are no national statistics for child abuse in Canada.
- Although child abuse is a heavily researched area, scientific studies of the actual prevalence of sexual abuse are rare.
- There is social stigma attached to child beating.
- There are cultural variations in expectations concerning the roles of parents and children.
- Only a portion of abused children are taken for medical intervention.
- Abusive parents make up believable stories, and children are too young or too frightened to disclose what actually happened.
- Some physicians would rather attribute the symptoms of abuse to an accident than confront the awful truth.
- With sexual abuse there are severe consequences of disclosure—public retribution, family disruption, unemployment and subsequent economic disaster, loss of friends, and incarceration (Csapo, 1988).

Child abuse exists in all forms of relationships regardless of occupation, educational attainment, religion, marital status, and family configuration. Abuse occurs at every socio-economic level, although it is more frequently reported among poorer families. The frequency of child abuse appears to vary across cultures (Korbin, 1987).

Definitions of Abuse and Neglect

There have been many thoughtful discussions about appropriate definitions of child abuse and neglect, psychological maltreatment of children, child sexual abuse, and spouse abuse. No consensus has been reached, and one of the most critical issues in research remains the lack of clear and reliable definitions of maltreatment.

In a general sense, *child abuse* is defined as "any interaction or lack of interaction … which results in non-accidental harm to the individual's physical and/or emotional state" (Helfer, 1987, p. 61). Within the broad definition, subcategories have developed to describe specific aspects of abuse and neglect.

Physical abuse is a non-accidental physical injury to a child. Overt and consistent signs indicate physical abuse. For example, children acquire many strange bruises in the course of normal activities; it is the frequency of such bruising that arouses the suspicion of abuse. Further indications of physical abuse include bald spots, burns from cigarettes or hot water, and marks from a strap or rope. Behavioural indicators include intolerance of physical contact and wearing inappropriate clothing that covers the body. Abused children may arrive at school early and stay late, suggesting a fear of going home.

Sexual abuse is one of the most studied areas. Sexual abuse is defined as "the sexual exploitation of a child who is not developmentally capable of understanding or resisting the contact, and a child or adolescent who may be psychologically and socially dependent upon the perpetrator" (Csapo, 1988, p. 121). Sexual involvement imposed upon a child by an adult includes pedophilia, rape, and all forms of incest. Incest, the most common type of sexual abuse, refers to any kind of sexual activity between a child and relatives, either blood or legal, including fathers, mothers, step-parents, siblings, and so on.

Victims of sexual abuse display a number of manifestations. Children may have difficulty walking or sitting, or may cry without provocation. They may show sudden drops in school performance or sudden non-participation in school activities accompanied by unusually infantile or withdrawn behaviour.

Neglect is the failure to provide adequate supervision, hygiene, nutrition, medical care, or the basic love and nurturing that children need to grow and develop. Neglect has been cited as the most common form of abuse as well as the most destructive, causing more deaths, injuries, and long-term problems than other types. Neglected children tend to be ill-clothed and poorly fed. They may have untreated physical or medical problems and appear to be tired and listless. Possible behavioural responses include stealing food, falling asleep in class, frequent school absences, and pugnacious and destructive activity.

Emotional neglect refers to the failure of caretakers to provide the loving positive emotional atmosphere necessary to the development of self-esteem in a child. *Emotional abuse* consists primarily of verbal attacks on a child's sense of self, such as persistent humiliation, belittling, or rejection. Indicators of emotional maltreatment are varied. Many children develop emotional or behavioural disorders for no apparent reason, which could be the result of the caregiver failing to meet the child's basic emotional needs. Observers may note delayed development, neurotic traits, or antisocial behaviour.

RESEARCH NOTES

Child Abuse

Child abuse is not new in Western society. As Lloyd de Mause points out, "The human track record of child raising is bloody, dirty and mean" (1975, p. 85). For many centuries, maltreatment was justified in the belief that severe physical punishment was necessary to maintain discipline, transmit educational ideas, please certain gods, or expel evil spirits.

In tracing the history of child abuse, de Mause placed common societal reactions to children within six major, though overlapping and intertwined, stages: infanticidal, abandoning, ambivalent, intrusive, socializing, and helping. Infanticide existed in very early societies. It was not until the 4th century that the church halted the practice. After that, many children were abandoned to wander, beg, or die by the wayside. The ambivalent mode appeared first in the late Middle Ages. Parents still displayed aggressive tendencies toward their children but generally kept them at home. Intrusive parenting, characterized by draconian authoritarianism, arose in the early 18th century.

The need for children to be socialized and helped paralleled the full blossoming of the notion of childhood as a discrete stage of development and children as separate beings, not miniature adults. By the mid-19th century, children were provided with special environments such as schools, and child labour laws began to bring them out of the mines and the factories.

Overt forms of child abuse prominent in earlier periods may have disappeared. Nevertheless, child abuse remains an endemic problem in modern society. In its modern garb, the problem of child abuse was first brought to the forefront by Caffey (1946), who suggested that ill-treatment of children might be an intentional act on the part of parents. This caused a wave of concern, and throughout the 1950s research increased. In the early 1960s, a seminar on child abuse led to the identification of what became known as the Battered Child Syndrome (Kempe, Silverman, Steele, Droegemueller, & Silver, 1962). Following this, there was a flurry of articles, books, and research papers reflecting a heightened interest on the part of educators, social workers, welfare agencies, and politicians. By the 1970s, policies were established and laws enacted that recognized and protected abused children.

In Canada, a plethora of child protection laws have led to the development of policies and programs for intervention, education, and prevention. The law requires the reporting of possible instances of abuse to the authorities. Teachers, neighbours, physicians, and anyone else who suspects child abuse is required to seek assistance for the child.

The Family and Child Abuse

Essentially, abuse is not a fixed single incident but an ongoing interaction between parents and children that is associated with dysfunctional parent–child relations. When looked at in this way, abuse becomes a complex combination of parent variables and child behaviours. Studies attempting to define the typical abusive family or parent are confounded by the fuzzy line between ineffective child management and abuse. They draw only one definite conclusion—there is no real prototype of an abusive parent.

Many descriptions have emerged. Abusive parents have been described as immature, impulsive, self-centred, hypersensitive, quick to react with poorly controlled aggression, and tending to show extremely inconsistent patterns of interaction with the child (Steele, 1986).

Abusive parents have little knowledge of good parenting and tend to hold unrealistic expectations; they ascribe adult functions to children and cannot understand that children possess limited control, capabilities, and comprehension. They expect children to be good, loving, and obedient at all times, and when their child's disobedience or inattention threatens their perceptions of themselves as good parents, they use excessive discipline because they see it as their duty to make children behave.

Many abusing parents are unable to cope with the complex problems of life. They tend to be isolated, or their lifestyle may be chaotic. There seems to be a significant over-representation of alcoholism in severe cases of child maltreatment (Famularo, Stone, Barnum, & Wharton, 1986).

Although unable to pinpoint the exact characteristics of abusive parents, much of the literature points to a *cycle of abuse* theory. That is, abusive parents were abused children themselves, and patterns of maltreatment can often be traced back three or four generations (Steele, 1986). Spousal violence also intrudes. Violent men are almost three times as likely as non-violent men to have witnessed spousal violence in childhood, and women who were raised in similar circumstances are twice as likely to be victims of spousal violence (Fitzgerald, 1999). Not only do parents who were abused mistreat their own children, but they tend to repeat the same types of abuse to which they were subjected, be it physical, sexual, or neglect (Steele, 1986).

The *cyclic* theory posits that children learn parenting techniques from their own experiences in the family. A loving, cared-for child learns to become a good parent. A child who is unloved, neglected, and abused learns poor parenting behaviours. If a parent who was abused has a healthy, docile child, abusive tendencies may be held in check. However, if the child is ill or difficult to manage or if other stresses occur, the parent may well harm the child. Abuse and neglect may occur from conception (for example, alcoholic mothers) to adolescence.

Other researchers feel that the assumptions underlying a cyclical theory are not supported by available data and that the majority of abused parents do not abuse their own children (e.g., Widom, 1989). However, many studies show that anywhere between 25 and 33 percent of all children who are abused grow up and abuse their own children (Kaufman & Zigler, 1989; Widom, 1989), and whether parents continue the cycle of abuse is influenced by many aspects of their developmental history, not just the abuse.

In some families, only one of several children is abused. This child may be different by virtue of sex, resemblance to a disliked family member, or failure to meet the parents' expectations. There is a correlation between excessive crying and child abuse, although which is the cause and which is the effect is a matter of debate.

When children with exceptionalities are considered, research has looked in two directions—abuse of children with disabilities, and abuse as an antecedent of disability. Children with disabilities, sick children, and premature and low-birth-weight children who require special attention or costly treatment and who fail to respond to the caregivers' efforts in ways the parents can appreciate appear to be at greater risk for abuse (Augoustinos, 1987; Frodi, 1981). Abuse seems very common among children with behavioural disorders (Zirpoli, 1990).

When abuse is examined as an antecedent of behavioural and learning problems, there is sufficient empirical evidence to support the widely held assumption that child abuse and neglect have detrimental developmental effects. The data strongly suggest that systematic abuse causes significant dysfunction in intellectual, neurological, emotional, and motoric ability. Intellectual development has been found to be delayed among some abused and neglected children who have no evidence of neurological impairment (Augoustinos, 1987).

With regard to academic performance, child abuse directly affects the amount of time children are in the classroom and their ability and interest in learning while in school. Social and emotional difficulties are endemic. Abused toddlers often respond to agemates' distress with fear, anger, or physical attacks (Main & George, 1985). Abused elementary-aged children tend to be highly aggressive and are often rejected by their peers (Downey & Walker, 1989). The Research Notes below speak to the genesis, development, and consequences of childhood aggression. Among adolescents, systematic abuse creates substantial at-risk conditions for psychological, interpersonal, academic, medical, and legal problems. Self-image, motivation, personal satisfaction, and success in the workplace are negatively affected (Fink & Janssen, 1992). Adolescents frequently respond to abuse through depression, suicide attempts, explosive anger, alcohol, drug abuse, self-mutilation, running away, or prostitution (see Destad, 1987).

RESEARCH NOTES

Childhood Aggression

Among all human emotions, aggression is probably the most studied; it was a favourite topic for psychologists throughout the 20th century. Explanations for aggression have come from evolution (no group in the animal kingdom is free of aggression), social learning (aggressive behaviour is learned and often rewarded), and modelling (children do what they see). All theories agree that although aggression in moderation is a useful survival tool, it becomes a problem when it is prolonged, frequent, and severe.

Aggression seems to be one of the true differences between the sexes. It is found more strongly in males and is also more tolerated in boys. Normally developing children learn to use aggressive behaviour to overcome resistance and tend to become more aggressive as they develop. Older children (grade 8 students) judge aggression to be less reprehensible than younger children.

The major influences on aggression are temperament, family, peers, and television. In relation to temperament, the temperamental traits that make infants difficult may be related to behaviour problems of aggression and anxiety (Bates, 1987), but infancy is at best a modest predictor of later problems. Parents' attitudes and child-rearing strategies play a more important role. Cold and rejecting parents and those who are hostile and punitive often apply physical punishment erratically and permit their children to express frequent aggressive impulses. In early life, stress and constant threats seem to rewire emotional circuits, as in the mother who screams at a child who falls down, "It's your own fault," as opposed to the soothing parent (Begley, 1996).

Aversive behaviour and physical punishment provide models and a partial sanctioning of aggressive responses. This may reinforce a child's aggressive behaviour toward others and teach patterns of attack and counter-attack so well that children become blind to alternative ways of solving conflicts.

Eventually, children who live in highly coercive family settings may become resistant to punishment.

The use of arbitrary, high-intensity tactics elicits defiance from young children, rather than the compliance that parents want (Crockenberg & Litman, 1990). Children learn to fight coercion with coercion, often defying their parents by repeating the same acts for which they are punished. If they are spanked, for example, the spanking serves as a model of the very aggressive behaviour that the parents are trying to suppress.

To be aggressive, children must know that they can get others to do what they want by causing them distress. The early part of life is a particularly critical time, when techniques for controlling others by aggressive means are rapidly acquired. Patterns of aggressive behaviour frequently seem to be well established before age nine (Patterson, 1982).

Once established, antisocial behaviours show relatively high continuity, and there is substantial stability of aggression over time. Childhood aggression is highly predictive of later substance abuse, criminal behaviour, and psychopathology. One study (Herronkohl, Egolf, Ellen, & Herrenkohl, 1997) found the severity of physical discipline in the preschool years to be related to assaultive behaviour in late adolescence. Males were more assaultive than females; people with higher intelligence and women were more likely to break the violence cycle (Kaplan, 1996).

The more extreme the antisocial behaviour in young children, the more stable it tends to be throughout childhood and adolescence. Antisocial or non-compliant behaviour is particularly likely to be stable over time when the first instance appears at a young age, is frequent, appears in more than one setting, and consists of several distinct forms of antisocial behaviour (Loeber, 1990).

Child maltreatment is destructive to the child who experiences it, to the caregiver who commits it, and to the society that allows it. Teachers hold both a moral and a legal responsibility for reporting suspected cases of abuse. They must know how to recognize the signs of abuse, how and where to report it, and what the school can do to offer support. When considering the significance of symptoms or behaviours, consultation with a public health nurse will prove to be very helpful.

MUSCULOSKELETAL IMPAIRMENTS

Musculoskeletal impairments are those that affect body movement and functioning but are not caused by neurological damage. These include a wide range of conditions, a few of which are discussed in more detail below. Depending on the type and severity of the impairment, physical and motor development may be affected.

Note that when discussing physical and motor development we are referring to the acquisition of postural control and the necessary movement patterns to produce functional motor acts. **Motor** is a term used to denote muscular movement; **motor development** is the process through which a child acquires movement patterns and skills.

motor

motor development

Limb Deficiencies

Limb deficiencies include the loss or absence of entire limbs or parts of limbs. A child born with such a condition is said to have a *congenital amputation*. Congenital amputations of unusually large proportions occurred in the late1950s and early 1960s due to Thalidomide, an anti-nausea drug prescribed to pregnant women for morning sickness. In Canada, the United States, and Europe, thousands of children were born with missing or deformed limbs. This specific condition is called *phocomelia*, a congenital deformity in which parts of limbs or entire limbs are very short or missing.

Congenital amputations are much less prevalent than acquired amputations. Many children lose limbs in mishaps involving vehicles, contact with high-voltage power lines, burns, and other accidents. In some instances, surgical amputations may be performed to prevent the spread of bone cancer or massive infections. Defective limbs or parts of limbs may also be amputated to permit the use of *prostheses*, functional devices that substitute for missing body parts.

Spinal Problems

There are three types of curvature of the spine: lordosis, kyphosis, and scoliosis. *Lordosis* is an anterior (forward) curvature when viewed from the side. *Kyphosis* is a posterior (backward) curvature when viewed from the side. *Scoliosis*, which refers to a lateral (side to side) curve that is absent in normal spines, is the most common form of curvature. It is associated with prominent shoulder blades, poor posture, uneven shoulders, and a flattening of the back (Bauer & Shea, 1989). Scoliosis can impair motor functions.

Muscular Dystrophy

A number of conditions are characterized by a weakening and wasting away of muscular tissue. If there has been neurological damage or if the muscles are weakened due to nerve degeneration, the condition is known as *atrophy*. *Myopathy* occurs when there is no evidence of neurological disease or impairment. When the myopathy is progressive and hereditary, the condition is referred to as *dystrophy* (Hallahan & Kauffman, 2003). The conditions are rare and most have adult onset. Some are related neuromuscular disorders, such as *Friedreich's ataxia*. All result in weakness and fatigue, but the predicted lifespan varies from one type to another.

muscular dystrophy   The most common types of conditions in children are forms of **muscular dystrophy**, which refers to a group of inherited conditions characterized by degeneration of muscle fibres without neurological deficit. The condition occurs in different forms, all characterized by progressive muscle weakness. The types differ with regard to age of onset, the site of initial muscle involvement, and the kinds of hereditary transmission. The exact biological mechanisms responsible for muscular dystrophy, are unknown.

The major types of disorder are Duchenne's muscular dystrophy, Becker's muscular dystrophy, myotonic muscular dystrophy, and Charot Marie Tooth Syndrome (Strong & Sandoval, 1999). The most common form of the disorder is Duchenne's muscular dystrophy, often called *pseudohypertonic muscular dystrophy*. The term *pseudohypertonic*, meaning "false growth," describes an enlargement of the calves and sometimes other muscles. This enlargement occurs as a result of fatty deposits in the muscle along with degeneration of the muscle fibres. As Duchenne's muscular dystrophy is inherited through a sex-linked recessive gene, this form typically occurs in boys.

At birth, the child appears normal. In the early stages, the condition is painless and the symptoms unnoticeable. But onset is early and may be evident when the child is learning to walk. Gradually, muscle fibres waste away, to be replaced by fatty tissue. The child's pelvic area is affected first and then the shoulder girdle.

In the second stage of the condition, the child suffers difficulty in muscle movement. By the age of four to seven, he exhibits a waddling gait and frequent falls, and has difficulty climbing stairs and standing up from a sitting position (Berkow, 1982). By the age of five, many affected children require ambulation aids. The condition worsens so that by the third stage, at somewhere about eight years of age, the child is confined to a wheelchair. Finally, the individual is bedridden and totally dependent.

For children with Duchenne's muscular dystrophy, the progressive muscle weakness equates with an abbreviated lifespan. Before the advent of antibiotics, life expectancy was even shorter than today's twenty to thirty years. Death usually occurred in adolescence as a result of exhaustion, respiratory infection, heart failure or, most often, pneumonia. Although life expectancy has been extended and recent investigations have located the gene for muscular dystrophy, no treatment has yet been found to halt muscle decline.

Another form of the condition is *Landouzy-Dejerine muscular dystrophy*, also known as *facioscapulohumeral muscular dystrophy*, reflecting the fact that the facial and shoulder-girdle muscles are the areas first affected. The shoulder girdle is weakened but the forearms are spared. As well, the facial features of affected children show drooping of the eyelids and thickening of the lips. Landouzy-Dejerine muscular dystrophy is inherited through dominant genes but is not sex-linked (Berkow, 1982), and is therefore found in both sexes. The condition commonly manifests itself in adolescence, although onset may occur any time between childhood and late adulthood. The progression of the condition alternates with prolonged periods of apparent arrest. Landouzy-Dejerine muscular dystrophy is not life threatening; life expectancy for affected individuals is normal.

Arthritis

Arthritis is a common term for a variety of chronic systemic conditions involving inflammation of the joints. Many people assume that arthritis is a condition exclusive to adults, especially the aged. In reality, it occurs frequently in children and is then called *juvenile arthritis* or *Still's disease*. Juvenile arthritis is similar in some respects to the adult type. It affects the large joints, sometimes to the extent of interfering with growth in the bony structures. Joint pain is a common feature, and destruction of the joints may ensue. Other complications of juvenile arthritis include eye and respiratory infections, enlarged spleen, and inflammation of the tissue covering the heart. The most severe form is *juvenile rheumatoid arthritis*, which affects the heart muscles and can be fatal. More girls than boys suffer from this condition (see Bigge, Best, & Heller, 2001).

arthritis

Among children with other disabilities, *osteoarthritis* is the most common form of arthritis. The cartilage around the joint is damaged, the space between the bones becomes smaller and loses its lubrication, and movement becomes painful or impossible. Osteoarthritis is especially likely to occur when the child has a condition in which a joint has been dislocated. Children with cerebral palsy, for example, may have recurring dislocation and suffer from painful arthritis (Hallahan & Kauffman, 2003).

The causes of both adult and juvenile arthritis are unknown and there is no cure. Aspirin seems to be the most effective medication. For children the prognosis is more favourable than it is for adults; about 75 percent of children with arthritis experience remission of the disease (Berkow, 1982).

ASSESSMENT OF CHILDREN WHO HAVE SPECIAL HEALTH CARE NEEDS

Given the enormous range of conditions, malformations, and diseases encompassed in this category, it is well nigh impossible to make definitive statements regarding assessment. Nor is it necessary. Generally, health disorders and skeletal malformations do not impinge on cognitive and intellectual development, and assessment employs the same range of tools and tests as would be used with typical children. However, adaptations in test materials and procedures may be necessary to circumvent a physical disability that impedes movement or mobility, such as muscular dystrophy (see Chapters 13 and 15).

INTERVENTION WITH CHILDREN WHO HAVE SPECIAL HEALTH CARE NEEDS

Health disorders and physical disabilities affect children's learning and progress in a number of ways. Learning will be hindered when a child has experienced a great many medical procedures that lead to long periods of recuperation as well as missed time in the classroom. Once in school, children may tire easily, have limited vitality, short attention spans, and limited mobility. A physical impairment can affect a child's range of motion, physical strength, communication, interaction with materials, independence, and daily living skills.

The children discussed in this chapter require a variety of medical, psychological, and educational interventions. Social service agencies frequently become involved with them and their families. As they grow older, students may require counselling and other supports for independent living (see also Chapter 17).

Medical Intervention

As essentially medical conditions, health disabilities require a complex and sophisticated range of interventions, which include surgical procedures, prosthetic devices, drug therapy, diet management, and ongoing medical treatment. The medical management of these children is intensive—far beyond the scope of this text.

In classrooms, health-related procedures could, however, include gastrostomy tube feeding, administration of oxygen, nebulizer treatments, and suctioning (Lowman, 1998). Children with AIDS need medications several times a day (Roberts, 2000).

One of the issues in this field relates to who should provide medical aid to children. Just as we provide a quality education for students with disabilities, we must also ensure that they receive quality medical services that enhance their school experience ("Growing challenge …" 1998). It is therefore incumbent on school districts to develop policies that protect both students and teachers. When a child with a health impairment is in a school, two related documents are necessary. First is a *health services plan*—a document that outlines the child's specific needs, the strategies needed to support the child, the responsibility of staff, and training and resources needed (see Lowman, 1998). Second, teachers should keep an *emergency protocol* that contains information on emergency practices and strategies

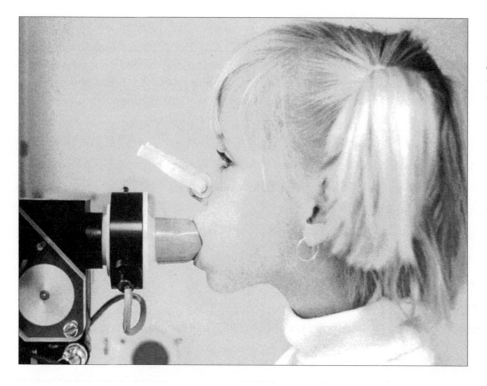

Medical management for health problems can be a significant part of a child's life.

developed by parents, school personnel, and medical personnel. The protocol includes names, addresses, and telephone numbers of parents or guardians, emergency contacts, and family physicians. An example procedure for planning for a child with complex health care needs is shown in Table 12-2.

Table 12-2 Planning for a child with complex health care needs

1. Form a planning team to gather all necessary information, for example, information on the condition or understanding the intervention procedures.

2. Plan strategies to support a child's needs. Note the responsibilities of staff, and the training and resources needed.

3. Prepare the environment. This could include special seating or accommodations for medical equipment such as a ventilator.

4. Prepare other children.

5. Develop a *health services plan* that outlines a child's specific needs. For example, note a child's schedule for drug dosages and special diet considerations, or how to monitor the status of a diabetic child, the symptoms of insulin reaction, and the immediate remedies. Note the warning signs and symptoms of an asthma attack—the child may wheeze, show retractions where the tissue of the chest wall is sucked in as he or she breathes, prolonged exhalation, rapid breathing, or cold symptoms. Or if a child is wearing braces, teachers must be alert to circulation problems that may show up as swelling, coldness, change of colour, evidence of infection, or other skin problems. In a child with hydrocephalus, a shunt malfunction

Table 12-2 continued

can be seen in a child's behaviour and physical functioning; for example, the child has a headache or pain in the neck area. Drug-exposed children are often stressed and distressed. Some of the most common stressors are transitions, classroom interruptions, and school disruptions such as field trips and fire drills.

6. Prepare an *emergency protocol*. This should contain
   - Parents' or guardians' names, addresses, telephone numbers
   - Any other relevant parties' names, addresses, telephone numbers
   - School assistants' names, telephone numbers
   - Family physician's name, address, telephone numbers
   - Emergency contacts' names, addresses, telephone numbers
   - Local hospital's telephone numbers
   - Ambulance services' telephone numbers
   - Emergency practices based on the needs of a particular child. For example, what to do during an asthma attack or an epileptic seizure.

7. Prepare a medication log, if necessary.

Therapy

Students may need rehabilitation training and therapy from a range of therapists—physical, occupational, and speech and language. Counselling assumes importance to help students understand and deal with the stresses of the disability and the treatment. Serious psychological and emotional correlates of physical and health problems are the rightful concern of professionals within the discipline of pediatric psychology.

The level of knowledge children have about their own orthopedic disabilities is related to age. Generally, children move from a broad understanding of the disability at age six to a more acute realization of the implications by age eight (Dunn, McCartan, & Fugura, 1988). By adolescence, most students will have gained a realistic appreciation of their health condition and the manner in which it affects their lives.

Technical Aids

Many technical devices are designed to increase personal independence. Compensatory (assistive, adaptive, prosthetic, and orthotic) devices and equipment allow individuals to compensate for or minimize the effects of a disability. These devices are fully addressed in Chapter 13.

Educational Intervention

Education is a social norm in the lives of children, and the presence of a physical or health problem should not be seen as a reason to halt schooling. Educational intervention for children with special health care needs represents a critical aspect of the child's total health planning. Lacking school experiences, the child's psychosocial development will be seriously jeopardized. Special education assistance may be necessary simply because students are likely to be absent from school often.

Some generic accommodations and adaptations for students with special health care needs are shown in Table 12-3.

Table 12-3 Creating accessible classrooms

Accommodations

- Establish a building team, a kind of SWAT team of medical conditions to address complex health needs.

- Learn as much as you can about the condition, including the etiology, developmental consequences, and prognosis.

- Be aware of the treatment procedures being used, the potential side effects of certain medical treatments on appearance and behaviour, and the approximate schedule of upcoming treatments.

- Check your school district's procedures for drug administration.

- Keep an emergency protocol.

- List and display special needs for substitute teachers.

- Adjust classroom schedules for students with limited vitality to create maximum on-task learning time.

- Make children feel a part of the class even if illness keeps them absent for long periods.

For children with diabetes

- Be aware of the child's food regimen and insulin schedule.

- Always allow bathroom or water breaks.

- Observe carefully. Anxiety, stress, and physical illness influence blood sugar levels and it is almost impossible to keep these constant.

- The child who is diabetic often experiences feelings of being punished (injections and no sweets) and of being different and inadequate. He or she is likely to lack self-confidence and self-esteem and may avoid activities for fear of failure. Additional praise and encouragement for accomplishments may be necessary.

For children with asthma

- Be diligent in guarding against common asthma triggers. These include cold air; chalk dust; dust in the classroom or gymnasium; photocopy toner fumes; science class chemicals; perfumes, cosmetics, and hairspray; cleaning fluids; paint fumes; and viral infections such as colds.

- If a child has an asthma attack, remove him or her from the trigger area if it is known.

- Try to relax the child by sitting with him or her while you model deep breathing exercises. Then have the child use the inhaler. If he or she is not responding to medication, seek medical advice immediately.

For children with cancer

- Answer accurately any questions asked by other children about the differences in appearance and behaviour of the special child. This should be done at the time questions are asked, whether or not the special child is present. The questions children ask most often are, What is cancer? Can our friend die from it? What does it feel like to have cancer? (Peckham, 1993, p. 28).

Table 12-3 continued

- Provide time for a child to talk about the disease and its treatment; be sympathetic to the child's feelings about hospital and separation.
- Remain as natural as possible, particularly with young children.
- Have open lines of communication with the parents.
- Answer the child's questions truthfully.
- Listen to the child's fears.

Hygiene in the classroom

- Provide a hygienically safe learning environment to help prevent the spread of all infections, including hepatitis B, hepatitis C, and HIV.
- Immediately clean up blood and bodily fluids.
- Wear disposable latex gloves. Household gloves may be used but need cleaning with a 1:10 bleach–water solution.
- Use paper towels to clean up and rinse spill areas. Disinfect spill areas with bleach solution (150 millilitres of regular household bleach to 10 litres of water).
- Wash hands well and carefully.

Service Delivery Models

Historically, educational services for children with chronic illnesses were developed to address specific diseases such as polio and tuberculosis. These services typically followed a medical model and were offered in special schools or centres that segregated students from their peers (see the Historical Notes at the end of this chapter). While the great majority of children now attend general public schools, the needs of children who are technology dependent and/or medically fragile present great challenges to the school system. These youngsters may be placed in a variety of educational settings, depending upon the type and severity of the condition, the related services available, and the prognosis of the disability (see also Chapter 15).

Students themselves seem to prefer general environments. In a study of 106 graduates of a school for students with severe physical disabilities, investigators (Liebert, Lutsky, & Gottlieb, 1990) found that many graduates felt they would have benefited from a less sheltered environment and more exposure to peers without disabilities. However, when researchers from Ottawa (Pivik, McComas, & Laflamme, 2002) studied students with physical disabilities in eight schools, they found that students themselves identified attitudinal barriers as the most deleterious to their school experiences. All of the participants had experienced negative comments, teasing, staring, and isolation.

Some chronically ill students are in hospital schools found in facilities that specialize in providing long-term care for children. In these, the classroom setting is designed to provide the children with familiar surroundings and continued interaction with other students. Academic involvement helps the child to keep abreast of schoolwork and aids in self-development. Special education teachers provide regular organized instruction in a classroom setting where possible, or on a tutorial basis.

For the child who is no longer hospitalized but still unready for school attendance, homebound instruction is a valuable option. A home-visiting or itinerant teacher provides individual tutorials on a regular basis, following the curriculum of the child's classroom.

SUMMARY

1. *Special health care needs* and *physical impairments* encompass an enormous variety of conditions and diseases. Some, such as cancer, are life-threatening; others, such as muscular dystrophy, bring an abbreviated life span; still others require that the child carefully monitor activities, diet, or drugs.

2. *Health impairments* (chronic health problems) refer to the presence of a disease or medical condition that interferes with school attendance and learning and hinders the ability to lead a normal life. Musculoskeletal impairments are disabilities that relate primarily to disorders of the skeleton, joints, and muscles, including clubfoot, the absence of some members, or other congenital anomalies; impairments caused by diseases such as poliomyelytis or bone tuberculosis; impairments caused by cerebral palsy; amputations; and contractures caused by fractures or burns.

3. Health disorders are so heterogeneous that no commonality can be found in students' behavioural, intellectual, and psychological functioning. Even with the same conditions, no two youngsters are affected in exactly the same way. The impact of a health or physical disorder depends upon a number of variables: the age of onset of the condition, the degree of disability, the visibility of the condition, family and social support, the attitudes toward the individual, and the individual's social status with peers.

4. With current medical intervention, many illnesses that were fatal in the past are no longer life-threatening. But as affected children enter the school system, they bring with them a range of challenges that extend from simply monitoring drug usage, to watching for fatigue, to classroom adaptations that accommodate neurological dysfunctions, to adaptive equipment for mobility and communication. Many students need pharmacological management; others may require supplemental assistance from support personnel such as physical and occupational therapists, nurses, and paraeducators.

5. Medical management can be a significant part of a child's daily life. In order to adequately assist children with exceptionalities in the classroom, teachers must be aware of physical conditions that may require special equipment or prosthetic devices; alterations that may be needed in work, play, and rest schedules; special positioning or handling techniques or special feeding techniques; and special arrangements that may be needed to accommodate seizure activity, medications, allergies, susceptibility to illness, poor muscle strength, and special feeding problems. They must also be willing to provide necessary assistance beyond that of an educational nature.

6. Children with health problems generally show normal development in cognitive, communication, and socio-emotional skills. However, there may be disruptions attributable to the condition, such as long periods of illness, hospitalization, and missed school. These mean that special accommodations and programs are sometimes required.

7. With child abuse, many questions remain about the prevalence, type and severity, duration of harm, and mediators of damage for causing disabilities. Child abuse actually consists of

two problems—the abused child and the abusive parents. Among parents, child abuse and neglect cannot be attributed to any single cause or to any particular class of people. Parents often feel overwhelmed by stress, isolated, incapable of coping, and lacking in resources.

8. Child abuse and neglect have developmental effects on the physical, neurological, intellectual, and emotional development of children. Sexually abused children often carry emotional scars for life, while the experiential deprivation that is part of neglect affects every aspect of a child's development. Children can be more open to abuse because of the mental, physical, and behavioural anomalies that increase their vulnerability to abuse, or because they have developed characteristics that increase the likelihood of abuse. Preschoolers, boys, children with disabilities, sick children, and premature and low-birth-weight children appear to be at greater risk for abuse.

HISTORICAL NOTES

It is reasonable to assume that health disorders have plagued humanity from its beginnings. For example, archeology provides evidence that the ancient Egyptians were aware of asthma and its effects. They treated it by "administering camel or crocodile dung, or by burning herbs on hot bricks and having the asthma patient inhale the fumes" (Isabell & Barber, 1993, p. 247). In ancient Greece, Hippocrates (ca. 460–377 B.C.) intervened with a variety of conditions. Ancient Rome saw physicians such as Aulus Cornelius Celsus (25 B.C.–A.D. 50) and Galen (A.D. 130–200), an anatomist, physiologist, and neurologist, produce a body of writing that influenced medical progress until the Renaissance.

With the Renaissance came the development of more sophisticated surgery and medical practices. An age-old fear of dissecting the human body dissolved, and a huge spurt in anatomy and physiology was witnessed. In the following centuries, medical advances continued apace. Franz Gall's discovery of the hemispheres of the brain, the discovery of vaccination and anesthesia, and the first glimmerings of the hereditary aspects of certain conditions lent light to medical diagnosis and prognosis. Amputation became feasible and safe in the 19th century with the use of anesthetic (Lowey, 1993).

However, the conditions we discuss in this chapter were often lethal—and indeed, still are. Before the very recent advent of sophisticated medical intervention and technical assistance and devices, affected individuals could anticipate only an abbreviated lifespan. Causes, prevention, and cures are still, to a greater or lesser extent, baffling. While, for example, cystic fibrosis and muscular dystrophy are known to result from identifiable defective genes, cures are not yet available. Since the discovery of insulin in the early 1920s, diabetes has been controlled, but it has not yet been prevented or cured. Intense medical research has not yet established precise causes and cures for cancer and AIDS.

CHAPTER 13

CHILDREN WITH NEUROLOGICAL DISABILITIES

INTRODUCTION

Normal development of the central nervous system is the outcome of a carefully timed and precisely regulated combination of structural and chemical events. Something amiss in these events can lead to damage to, or deterioration of, the central nervous system, which in turn is one of the most common causes of physical and neurological disabilities in children.

As in the case of health and musculoskeletal impairments, a huge range of neurological disorders exists. Some are associated with impairments of the nervous system; others result from diseases and accidents. For many children, the decreased range of motion, the reduced strength of movement, or the addition of unwanted or uncontrolled movement can dramatically affect the way they perform.

Many youngsters in this category also suffer co-occurring disabilities such as seizures or diabetes, and can therefore be viewed as multiply disabled. As the Historical Notes at the end of this chapter show, school placements have altered dramatically in recent years. Depending on the severity of the condition, the related services available, and the prognosis, students with neurological disabilities are served in general classrooms, general classroom and resource room combinations, or very occasionally, in special classes. But as their conditions are not in themselves inherently intellectually disabling, we should soon see almost all children with physical and neurological impairments integrated into general classrooms.

Table 13-1 presents some causes and effects of damage to the central nervous system. In a short chapter like this one we cannot possibly catalogue and describe the range of neurological disorders that can affect individuals. Therefore, we focus on the disabilities that teachers are most likely to encounter. The discussion begins with an overview of the human central nervous system.

Human Central Nervous System

Structurally, the **human central nervous system** consists of the brain, the spinal cord, and all the associated nerves and sense organs. Half of the genes—50 000—are involved in the central nervous system in some way (Begley, 1996).

Structures in the central nervous system are the fixed anatomical and physiological features, which are similar across the healthy brains of most individuals. But how these structures respond to, organize, analyze, and synthesize incoming information varies with individuals and with the task involved. The way information is processed represents the problem-solving strategies of each person.

The spinal cord and the brain, the two major components of the central nervous system, are each composed of neurons and *glial cells* (derived from the Greek *glia*, meaning "glue"). The number of glial cells is probably 10 times the number of neurons (Groves & Rebec, 1988). Glial cells serve in a supportive role for the neurons—they transmit food (glucose and amino acids) from the blood supply to the neurons; contribute to the blood/brain barrier that limits the passage of chemicals into the brain; help to facilitate communication between neurons; form biological scaffolding that helps hold the brain together; and manufacture a substance called *myelin*. The glial cells develop later than the neurons. They start to

**human central
nervous system**

Table 13-1 Some causes of damage to the central nervous system, with examples

Causes	Examples
Neoplasms	Brain tumour
Oxygen deprivation	Carbon monoxide poisoning, anoxia
Maternal infection	Rubella, syphilis
Maternal intoxication	Fetal Alcohol Spectrum Disorders
Child intoxication	Lead poisoning
Child infection	Encephalitis
Malnutrition	Inadequate protein to fetus or young child
Vascular accidents	Brain hemorrhage
Radiation	Excessive X-rays
Genetic defects	Errors of metabolism
Developmental errors	Absence of brain substance
Trauma	Automobile accidents resulting in direct head injury
Chromosomal abnormalities	Down syndrome
Gestational problems	Prematurity

form at about 13 weeks after conception, reach their peak of cell division from 18 weeks after conception to 4 months after birth, and cease to form new cells by 15 to 24 months after birth.

Neurons (nerve cells) are the basic units of neurological function; they undoubtedly hold the secrets of how the brain works. Researchers know their role in the transmission of nerve impulses and how the neural circuits work, but they are just beginning to unravel their more complex functioning in memory, emotion, and thought.

Neurons differ markedly in size and appearance, but they do possess some common characteristics. Similar to nearly all cells, neurons have a cell body, a cell membrane, a nucleus, and a cytoplasm. Each neuron consists of three parts: the *cell body*, a simple long *axon* that transmits impulses away from the cell body, and several branching *dendrites* that receive impulses from other cells and transmit them toward the cell body. Neurons do not actually touch each other but are close enough to enable chemical electrical impulses to jump the minuscule space (synapse) between the axon of one neuron and the dendrites of the next. In short, the electrical charge of the neuron is changed by the release of *neurotransmitters* at its axon, which in turn affects the release of other neurotransmitters at the dendrite end of the second neuron. In the adult brain there are at least 1 million billion connections between neurons—that's 1 quadrillion.

During the 9 months of fetal development, there is a massive proliferation of neurons: they develop at the average rate of 250 000 per minute. At birth, the brain has approximately 100 billion neurons in the cerebral cortex. Neurons are generated in germinal sites and then migrate to terminal locations where they are differentiated into appropriate neuron types. They are myelinated, form synapses with other neurons, and undergo some selective attrition.

What makes the nervous system work is a process in which the nerve fibres become sheathed with myelin—an insulating fatty covering—in a process called *myelination*. The myelin sheaths around individual nerves insulate them from one another and make it easier for messages to pass along the nerve pathways; they help speed up neural transmission and make the brain more efficient. Brain architecture is refined right into adolescence; myelination continues until about age twenty, although the time and sequence is highly variable for individuals.

The Brain

New research from the neurosciences is having an enormous impact on our knowledge of the human brain and, more specifically, how the brain functions. Most of what we know about the human brain has been discovered in the past 10 years. See Figure 13-1 for an illustration of the human brain.

The *cerebrum* of the human brain—the grey matter that controls higher-level intellectual functioning—is subdivided into two hemispheres. Joining the two cerebral hemispheres is the *corpus callosum*, a thick, boomerang-shaped band of fibres. The corpus callosum contains millions of neurons and is the massive midline conduit for processing and relaying information between the left and right hemispheres.

Each hemisphere is divided into four lobes—occipital, parietal, frontal, and temporal. The brain also contains four ventricles. At these sites, cerebrospinal fluid—the fluid that circulates around the brain and the spinal cord—is manufactured.

On casual examination, the two halves of the human brain look like mirror images of each other. However, there are both structural and functional differences. Structurally, for example, the left half is almost always larger. Functionally, the right hemisphere is specialized for holistic processing through the simultaneous integration of information. It primarily

Figure 13-1

The human brain

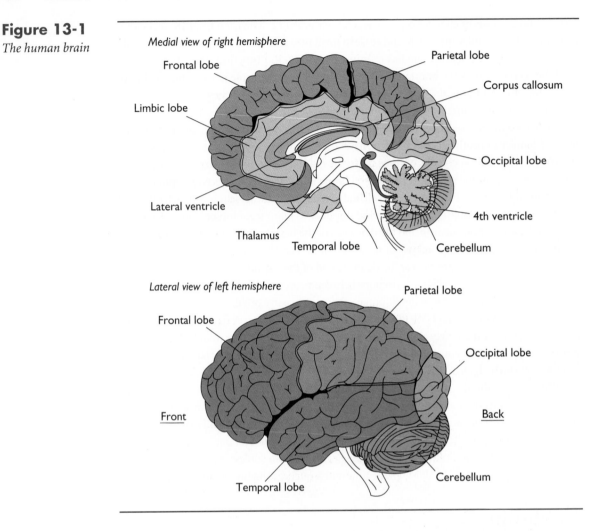

Medial view of right hemisphere

Frontal lobe
Parietal lobe
Corpus callosum
Limbic lobe
Occipital lobe
Lateral ventricle
4th ventricle
Thalamus
Temporal lobe
Cerebellum

Lateral view of left hemisphere

Frontal lobe
Parietal lobe
Occipital lobe
Front
Back
Cerebellum
Temporal lobe

houses areas such as visio-spatial organization; orientation in space; perception; and recognition of faces, pictures, and photographs. The left hemisphere controls verbal function and the linear logical thinking associated with verbalization.

There are differences in the structure of the male and female brains. Female brains, for example, have a larger corpus callosum. Female brains also tend to develop in a more uniform manner than those of males. Some researchers say that neurological differences such as these explain why girls are more verbal than boys, and why boys squirm and fidget in class, or fail to turn in their homework on time.

The Spinal Cord

Hemispheres rest on the brain stem, which serves as the connection to the *spinal cord*, a pencil-thin, segmented collection of neurons that are related to specific parts of the body. Each segment contains both sensory and motor neurons. As damage to a particular portion of the brain will result in disability in the area of the body controlled by that part of the brain, so damage to the sensory cells in the spinal cord results in loss of sensation to the parts of the body affected by those cells.

DEFINITIONS OF NEUROLOGICAL DISABILITIES

Neurological impairments is one of the subcategories of physical disabilities that we describe in Chapter 12. Essentially, we can say that **neurological impairments** result from damage or dysfunction of the brain and/or the spinal cord. Such damage may occur before, during, or after birth. Potential risks include severe deprivation of oxygen before birth, especially during the first trimester, when various important neural structures and inter-connections between the brain cells are developing. Other risks are damage incurred during the birth process and damage directly caused by diseases, especially those that attack the central nervous system.

neurological impairments

The effects of the damage vary greatly, and wide differences are seen in the onset of symptoms, the parts of the body involved, the nature of the symptoms, the degree of severity, and the possible multiplicity of impairments. Injury to the brain may result in a relatively limited specific disorder. For example, one of the traditional etiologies of learning disabilities is minimal brain dysfunction. On the other hand, generalized and diffuse brain damage may cause very wide-ranging effects, including motor disturbances, sensory loss, speech and language disorders, and emotional and behavioural disorders. Diffuse damage will result in intellectual disabilities; damage to the motor areas will cause cerebral palsy.

Injury to the spinal cord alone tends to result in motor and sensory disabilities without affecting intellectual function and special sensory functions (vision, hearing, and speech). Damage to the motor cells of the spinal cord results in *flaccid paralysis*, an inability to move the muscles because the neural impulses needed for muscle contractions are lacking.

Children who are physically disabled can participate in many activities with their non-disabled classmates.

How physical and neurological disabilities affect an individual's development and lifestyle also varies dramatically. Some people are devastated by the condition and never achieve their optimal development. On the other hand, Canadians remember with special pride young people like Rick Hansen and Terry Fox who worked through their physical disabilities in efforts to help others.

PREVALENCE OF NEUROLOGICAL DISABILITIES

While neurological conditions are extremely varied, they are low-incidence disabilities. The prevalence is only about 0.2 to 1.5 percent, or about 2 per 1000 of the school-aged population (Jones, 1983), although rates vary from locale to locale and from decade to decade.

CEREBRAL PALSY

Cerebral palsy is a condition characterized by damage to the brain before, during, or after birth. It is sometimes referred to as Little's disease, after the 19th-century surgeon who first described it. An alternative label is *significant developmental motor disability*.

Depending on its location and severity, the brain injury that causes a child's movement disorders may also cause other problems (Lin, 2000). We see this in Kent, the child described in the Case Study. The damage has left Kent with a range of disabilities. Not only does he have *hypertonia* (spasticity), but there are further co-occurring conditions that place him in the category of multiple disabilities. This is not always the case, but cerebral palsy is a complex condition.

CASE STUDY

Kent

Kent is a seven-and-a-half-year-old boy who has just entered grade 2. He has spastic cerebral palsy that restricts his movement and has led to a number of secondary disabilities. The motor impairment has affected Kent's speech and he has developed very little oral communication. He has a constant drool. Kent also has a moderate-to-severe bilateral hearing loss and the audiologist has fitted him with two hearing aids. The loss seems to fluctuate, as Kent is prone to otitis media in the winter months.

Kent uses leg braces and a walker. With the braces, he can walk for short distances with a little help. To go from class to class, he needs his wheelchair, which he can handle by himself. He uses the wheelchair for seating in the classroom, but consistently needs repositioning. A paraeducator provides special help with the braces and walker, the wheelchair, with toileting, and with dressing.

The teacher presents a modified curriculum based on Kent's unique strengths and weaknesses. The focus is on communication development and functional skills. In her daily planning for Kent, the teacher considers many factors such as stamina levels; present levels of academic achievement; intellectual ability; independence in mobility and ambulation; and personal motivation.

Despite the presence of additional conditions, cerebral palsy is classed chiefly as a motor disorder. It is one of the most common crippling conditions in children. Most incidence rates for cerebral palsy put it at 1.5 to 2 cases per 1000 live births (Pope & Tarlov, 1991). About 50 000 Canadians have cerebral palsy. More boys than girls are affected. In more than two-thirds of cases, cerebral palsy is present at birth (Verhaaren & Connor, 1981).

About 25 percent of cases have no definable cause (Tyler & Colson, 1994). However, an extensive study of children with cerebral palsy (Nelson & Ellenberg, 1986) found that the most likely associated factors were cognitive disability of the mother, premature birth, low birth weight, and a delay of 5 minutes or more before the baby's first cry. A more recent study undertaken in Central Europe by UNICEF (2005) found that half of babies with cerebral palsy had low birth weights, although the relationship between the two issues is complex.

Classification of Cerebral Palsy

Cerebral palsy may be classified by topography or by type. The topographical classification system, as shown in Table 13-2, refers to parts of the body and is not limited to cerebral palsy. In the topographical system, the suffix *plegia* refers to paralysis. When classified by the type of brain damage and consequent motor disability, cerebral palsy can be differentiated according to specific motor patterns, as outlined in Table 13-3.

Spastic or *pyramidal* cerebral palsy (more correctly referred to as *hypertonia*) affects approximately 50 percent of children with cerebral palsy. Individuals have suffered damage (lesions) to the motor cortex or to the pyramidal tracts of the brain (Batshaw & Perrett, 1986). Pyramidal cerebral palsy results in problems with voluntary movements. Spasticity therefore refers to slow, laborious, poorly coordinated voluntary movements related to the continued presence of a number of primitive reflexes. *Reflexes* are automatic, involuntary motor patterns that are triggered by specific stimuli. *Simple* reflexes (stretch or spinal reflexes) involve the spinal cord. Above the spinal cord is the brain stem, the seat of tonic reflexes. *Spinal* and *tonic* reflexes contribute to muscle tone, posture, and allow a child to prepare for movement.

Table 13-2 Topographical classification of cerebral palsy

Monoplegia	One limb impaired
Diplegia	Four limbs involved, with legs most impaired
Hemiplegia	One side of the body impaired
Paraplegia	Lower limbs of the body impaired
Triplegia	Three limbs impaired
Double hemiplegia	Both sides of the body impaired, with each side affected differently
Quadriplegia	All four limbs impaired

Table 13-3 Classifications of cerebral palsy

	Pyramidal cerebral palsy (spasticity)	Extrapyramidal cerebral palsy (dyskinesia)				
		Athetosis	Rigidity	Hypotonia	Tremor	Ataxia
Movement	Slow and difficult	Consistent, involuntary, writhing	More severe than spasticity	May develop into spastic or athetoid type	Involuntary, rhythmic	Clumsy
Coordination	Poor	Poor	Poor	Varied	Depends upon affected limbs	Poor
Muscle tone	Weak, hypertonic	Fluctuating	Continuous tension	Low	Varied	Varied

Most of the primitive reflexes present in all newborns disappear by about six months of age. If these reflexes persist, as they do in spastic cerebral palsy, they act as impediments to the development of smooth, coordinated movement.

Types of abnormal reflex movements seen in children with cerebral palsy include the rooting reflex, startle reaction, stretch reflex, asymmetrical and symmetrical tonic neck reflex, protective extensive reactions, and righting reactions. In the presence of the stretch reflex, for example, a muscle contracts involuntarily when suddenly stretched. Thus, when the arm is bent suddenly, the biceps contract but the reflex causes contractions in the opposing triceps as well. A mini-war results, rendering movements impossible to control. This means that children with spastic cerebral palsy cannot move when and how they choose.

Extrapyramidal cerebral palsy differs from spasticity in that the damage is outside the pyramidal tracts. The conditions include athetosis, tremor, rigidity, and ataxia. *Athetoid* cerebral palsy, found in approximately 25 percent of affected individuals, is caused by lesions of the basal ganglia. The condition is characterized by constant, involuntary writhing movements, especially in the hands and wrists. Contractions occur in successive groups of muscles, creating extraneous movement that interferes with purposive action. Children show abrupt involuntary movements, difficulty in maintaining posture, and are unable to stop moving when they want to. Athetosis stops during sleep.

Rigidity occurs when there is a low level of motor stiffness that never relaxes. The condition is rare, as is *tremor*, an involuntary movement in one extremity, usually one hand or arm. In constant tremor, the movement is continuous; in intention tremor, the involuntary movement happens only when the child undertakes to do something.

Ataxic cerebral palsy occurs in approximately 15 percent of affected individuals. Ataxia is characterized by poor coordination of the movements associated with balance, posture, and spatial orientation. Children tend to walk with a wide gait, their legs well apart to compensate for poor equilibrium. They also exhibit a generalized lack of coordination of both fine and gross motor movements. The eyes are often uncoordinated (Jones, 1987).

When there is damage to both the pyramidal and the extrapyramidal regions of the brain, the child may show mixed effects, such as spasticity of the legs and rigidity of the arms. About 25 percent of cases are classified as *mixed cerebral palsy* (Batshaw & Perrett, 1986).

Developmental Consequences of Cerebral Palsy

The consequences of cerebral palsy vary in relation to many factors that relate chiefly to the type and severity of the condition, and the presence or absence of co-occurring conditions. While no two children with cerebral palsy develop in exactly the same way, the presence of extensive motor disorders alone is sufficient to interfere with normal development.

In typical children, each stage of motor development causes a shift in the child's interaction with the environment. Within twelve to fourteen weeks of birth, for example, normally developing infants achieve control of head movements. Within six months, they pull to a sitting position. At about twelve months, they begin to walk unaided. These milestones offer children increased opportunities to make better use of sensory experience, to gain greater perceptual awareness, and to learn to manipulate objects and their own bodies. Damage to the motor system impedes this normal developmental course. Children with cerebral palsy have little control of the musculature necessary to reach developmental milestones.

Early diagnosis is difficult; cerebral palsy is generally not diagnosed right at birth because there are few abnormal neurological signs at this time. In fact, a brain-damaged neonate may appear to be perfectly normal for the first several weeks of life. Clues to neuromotor disturbance in infants include irritability, excessive listlessness, pallor, stiffening, arching, excessive startle, nystagmus, and jaundice. Infants with cerebral palsy tend to sleep excessively, have a weak cry, a poor suck, and show little interest in their surroundings. They rest differently, lying in a floppy extended position instead of a semi-flexed one (Batshaw & Perrett, 1986). Note that not all of these signs are found in all infants with cerebral palsy, and not all infants who manifest these signs have cerebral palsy.

As the child develops, predictions can be made on overall progress. If the child can sit by two years of age, for example, he or she will probably walk. About 80 percent of children with cerebral palsy are capable of learning to walk, although many need to use braces and other assistive devices. If the child is able to utter recognizable sounds by age two, that child will probably learn to speak (Bleck & Nagel, 1982).

The brain damage that results in cerebral palsy is not always limited to motor areas. Indeed, as the case of Kent indicates, cerebral palsy can often be seen as a multi-disabling condition. A high percentage of children exhibit one or more additional impairments.

These include intellectual disabilities, learning disabilities, sensory loss, epilepsy, and emotional and behavioural disorders. Impaired vision can result from loss of control of ocular muscles.

Many people assume that all children with cerebral palsy are intellectually disabled. As a blanket assumption, this is incorrect. However, it is true that the incidence of intellectual disability is significantly higher than average. Estimates of the number of children with some degree of intellectual impairment range from 25 to 75 percent (Gersh, 1991b; Nelson & Ellenberg, 1986). Little evidence exists to link the severity of intellectual impairment with any particular type of cerebral palsy, although hemiplegia seems to be associated with the best mental development (Batshaw & Perrett, 1986).

In some cases, damage—usually to certain areas of the left cerebral hemisphere—results in language delays and disorders. Estimates of co-occurring speech and language problems range from 50 to 83 percent. Language problems are less common than speech disorders. Motor dysfunctions that affect the organs of speech may make intelligible speech impossible (see Jones, 1987). The errors of articulation that accompany cerebral palsy are known as *dysarthria*, a condition discussed in Chapter 4. The speech characteristics of children with spastic forms of cerebral palsy may include articulatory defects, laboured speech with distortions of sound, uncontrolled pitch changes, and husky voice quality.

Visual and auditory problems are the most prevalent and serious of the associated sensory difficulties. It is estimated that more than 50 percent of children with cerebral palsy have visual defects of some type (Lefebrue, 1983). There is a high incidence of middle ear problems; approximately 25 to 30 percent of individuals have hearing defects (Jones, 1983). Other sensory problems include deficits in tactile sensation and the determination of pain, pressure, and temperature.

Children with cerebral palsy may also show learning disorders such as short attention span and distractibility. It is estimated that from 15 to 20 percent are likely to have some type of specific learning disability (Telford & Sawrey, 1981). An additional problem is some form of convulsive disorder. It is estimated that 25 to 50 percent of children with cerebral palsy suffer epileptic seizures (Gersh, 1991a; Jones, 1987). These are most common in hemiplegics and quadriplegics.

As the number of accompanying disorders indicates, cerebral palsy is a very complex multi-disabling condition. However, not every affected child faces all or even most of these disorders. Usually children with limited and localized brain injuries face fewer limitations than children with diffuse, extensive brain damage.

For children with orthopedic and motor disabilities such as cerebral palsy, a key factor is the extent to which the disability affects movement potential. Motor skills are integral to almost everything that a child does or wants to do in the environment, and physical and motor problems affect educational and social progress in other ways than mobility. Deficient motor skills can affect cognitive development because they hinder a child's manipulation and exploration. Children with motor impairments have different first-hand knowledge and experiences than their peers because they cannot explore the environment as other children can. At the sensorimotor stage, for example, children with cerebral palsy have been found to include more visual exploration and less tactile exploration of toys than is seen among children developing normally (see Rogers, 1988).

Social skills may suffer because efficient motor skills are necessary for many forms of play with peers. Play depends on experience and opportunity, and this by itself places restraints on children with severe physical disabilities. Children with cerebral palsy cannot manipulate toys and other objects, join in dramatic, pretend, or rough and tumble play, or engage in games in which children run and jump and skip.

SPINA BIFIDA

Midline defects, often referred to as *clefts*, result from the failure of parts of the embryo to fuse completely. Such defects may occur in many parts of the body, including the lip, the palate, the eye, and the spine. **Spina bifida** is a congenital midline defect of the spinal column.

spina bifida

Technically, the term *spina bifida* refers to a defect in the bony arch of the vertebrae protecting the spinal cord. In the early weeks of pregnancy, the neural tube of the embryo fails to develop normally. The bony arches of one or more spinal vertebrae do not fuse to protect the spinal cord, which leaves part of the nerve fibres of the cord exposed. The spinal defect may be found anywhere between the skull and the lowest segments of the vertebrae. Generally, spina bifida is evident by the end of the fourth week of gestation, and the severity of the problem is apparent at birth.

Although the process is fairly well understood, the actual cause of spina bifida is unknown. Etiologically, it is believed that both heredity and environment are interweaving factors. Spina bifida can be detected prenatally by a test that looks at the level of alpha-fetoprotein in the mother's blood. Higher concentrations than usual indicate the necessity for ultrasound or fetoscopy.

The prevalence of spina bifida varies widely from country to country, area to area, and even within the limits of a particular city. Worldwide, spina bifida occurs in from 0.1 to 4.13 live births per 1000 (Bleck & Nagel, 1982). The incidence in Ireland is about 4 or 5 children per 1000 live births, while in parts of Nigeria it is 0.2 per 1000 live births. In Canada, the highest rate of spina bifida is found in Newfoundland and Labrador. There is a slight tendency for the condition to run in families. If one baby is born with spina bifida, there is a 4 to 5 percent chance of siblings having the same defect (Myers, Cerone, & Olson, 1981).

Classification of Spina Bifida

The problems associated with spina bifida range from few or no adverse effects to severely disabling, depending on the form—*spina bifida occulta* or *spina bifida cystica*. Of the affected population, about 40 percent have spina bifida occulta; the remainder, cystica. This latter form is divided into two types: *spina bifida with meningocele* and *spina bifida with myelomeningocele*. The former accounts for 4 percent of individuals suffering from spina bifida cystica; the latter for 96 percent (see Figure 13-2).

Spina bifida occulta is the mildest form of the condition and has few or no negative effects. The only visible sign of the condition, if any, is a clump of hair on the skin covering the area of the cleft. In fact, this variety of spina bifida may affect up to 20 percent of North Americans; because overt symptoms are rare, affected people may not even know they have the condition (Moore & Persaud, 1993).

Figure 13-2

Types of spina bifida

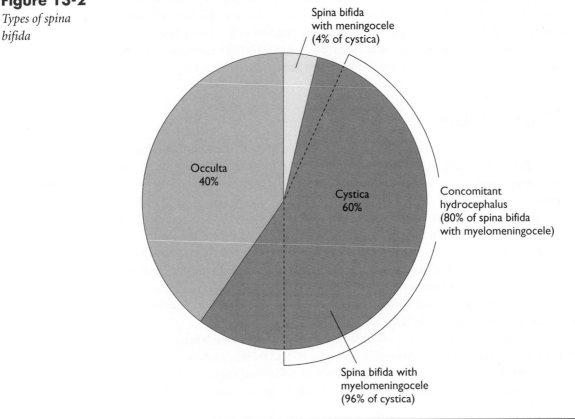

The two forms of spina bifida cystica—with meningocele and with myelomeningocele— have different results. In spina bifida with meningocele, the *meninges*, the membranes surrounding the spinal cord, protrude from the plane of the spine and form a sac containing cerebrospinal fluid. Surgery is usually performed in the first days of life to restore the sac within the spinal column. Following treatment, this condition does not usually create any major difficulties, although children must be wary of being hit directly on the area.

Spina bifida with myelomeningocele, the most severe type, results in a protruding sac that contains parts of the spinal cord as well as cerebrospinal fluid. The spinal cord not only enters the sac but is itself abnormal. Surgical treatment is necessary to deal with the sac, but the neurological damage is irreversible.

The effects of myelomeningocele vary considerably depending on the location of the cleft. The higher the cleft, the greater the damage. Clefts in the lower part of the spine may result in incontinence without paralysis. Clefts in the higher spinal regions produce paralysis and loss of sensation in the lower limbs, incontinence, and kidney problems. In addition to the cleft of the vertebral arches associated with spina bifida, other vertebrae unusual in slope or connection can occur, resulting in an uneven growth of the spine.

Twenty-five years ago, more than 90 percent of children with spina bifida died within a few years of birth from urinary infection or infection of the sac. Today, 90 percent live an average-length lifespan (Kaplan, 1996).

Developmental Consequences of Spina Bifida

In the absence of co-occurring conditions, spina bifida does not preclude adequate learning ability. Children with spina bifida occulta exhibit a normal range of intelligence; those with meningocele are also likely to have normal intelligence. Children with spina bifida with myelomenigocele may show intellectual disabilities, however. Perceptual and cognitive dysfunction is prevalent, especially in children with accompanying hydrocephalus. Often, cognitive development is uneven. While children show poorer general performance in reading, spelling, and arithmetic, most have good verbal ability, which may tend to mask the cognitive defects. Children are at elevated risk for problems with math; about 25 percent of school-aged children with spina bifida have a math disability (Fletcher, Dennis, Northrup, Barnes, Hannay, Landry, et al., 2004).

Children with myelomeningocele suffer neurological damage that interferes with growth and development. The most obvious neurological damage is the flaccid paralysis of the lower part of the body, which makes braces, crutches, walkers, or wheelchairs necessary. Children may also lack sensation and control of their bladders and bowel sphincters. Incontinence in itself does not create learning difficulties, but it may create social and psychological barriers for children in school. Typical children usually view incontinence as a sign of immaturity or infantile behaviour and react accordingly. As incontinent children mature, they learn to cope with their condition. Using a procedure called *clean intermittent catheterization,* they catheterize themselves every three or four hours (Myers, Cerone, & Olson, 1981).

Although spina bifida may occur as a solitary condition, nearly 80 percent of children who have spina bifida with myelomeningocele have accompanying hydrocephalus. The combination of the two conditions dramatically increases the number of disabilities. The damage to the brain from hydrocephalus and to the spinal cord from spina bifida is likely to render a child multiply disabled.

HYDROCEPHALUS

Hydrocephalus is a condition characterized by an excessive accumulation in the brain of cerebrospinal fluid due to an obstruction of its flow. Normally, cerebrospinal fluid is constantly manufactured in the ventricles of the brain, circulates through the ventricles and the space between the two layers of meninges, and is absorbed into the circulatory system. Since fluids are largely non-compressible, a blockage of the flow results in the accumulation of cerebrospinal fluid in an enclosed area, placing pressure on the brain and the skull. The pressure against the skull creates thinning of the bone and separation of the *sutures* (the seams between the plates of the skull). The fluid also presses on the brain tissue, causing distortion of brain substance and damage and death to the neurons.

hydrocephalus

In some instances, hydrocephalus arrests itself spontaneously. In other cases, the condition progresses and creates increasing pressure on the skull. The progressive accumulation of cerebrospinal fluid results in a range of disorders. Because mental retardation is a primary result, hydrocephalus is included among the clinical forms of mental retardation. Other sequelae include motor disorders, seizures, and even death.

Before the 1950s, no effective treatment existed for hydrocephalus. Children developed marked symptoms; by the age of three months, their heads became too large and heavy for them to lift, and the condition often ended in death. In 1952 an engineer named Holter developed an effective shunt (tube) to drain off cerebrospinal fluid away from the brain and into a vein behind the ear or in the neck and thus reduce the pressure on the brain. Since Holter's invention, many children with hydrocephalus have been spared extensive impairments.

EPILEPSY

epilepsy

The word *epilepsy* is derived from the Greek, meaning "to be seized," and we still describe epilepsy in terms of seizures. During the 1800s Hughlings Jackson, a pioneer neurologist, defined epilepsy as a condition produced by a sudden violent electrical discharge of brain cells. Echoing Jackson's definition, **epilepsy** is still defined as

> a convulsive disorder [that] is the expression of a sudden, excessive, disorderly discharge of neurons in either a structurally normal or diseased cortex. The discharge results in an almost instantaneous disturbance of sensation, loss of consciousness, convulsive movement, or some combination thereof. (Harrison, 1980, p. 131)

Implicit in this definition is the idea that epilepsy is not a disease but a symptom of a brain disorder that may be caused by any condition that results in damage to the brain. This does not imply that brain damage necessarily results in epileptic seizures, although it may. The definition further stresses the chronic and recurring nature of epilepsy.

Chronicity is important because many people will have some form of epileptic seizure in their lifetime. A single event such as this is not epilepsy, but rather may reflect some transient event, such as a high fever, heat exhaustion, ingestion of certain chemicals, or interference with the normal supply of oxygen to the brain.

The causes of epilepsy are varied and often unclear. Perinatal conditions, early childhood infection, and head trauma are identified as known causative factors. Heredity rarely plays a role; unless both parents have a strong family history of epilepsy, the chances that their children will inherit a tendency to have seizures is very slight. The most common causes are brain tumour and stroke; head trauma of any type; injury, infection, or systemic illness of the mother during pregnancy that affects fetal brain growth; brain injury to the infant during delivery; the aftermath of an infection such as meningitis; and poisoning from substance abuse or alcoholism (Epilepsy Canada, 1994).

For about 75 percent of persons with epilepsy, a specific cause cannot be found. In these cases, the condition is referred to as *idiopathic epilepsy*, or *epilepsy of unknown origin*. If an individual shows strong evidence of brain damage, the condition is known as *symptomatic epilepsy*.

Epilepsy affects more than 1 percent of the population—more than 280 000 Canadians. No one is immune; epilepsy can strike anyone at any age. However, from 70 to 80 percent of patients develop epilepsy before the age of eighteen. About 55 percent develop epilepsy before the age of ten, and 44 percent before the age of five. One of every 2000 people is diagnosed with epilepsy each year; about 14 000 new cases are reported annually (Epilepsy Canada, 1994). Also, the recognized incidence of epilepsy is greater today than in the past due to a higher survival rate among infants and persons with brain injuries.

Classification of Epilepsy

As a term, *epilepsy* describes two things: the conditions of seizure and the convulsions accompanying some types of seizures. Seizures occur as a result of a temporary breakdown in the brain's communication system caused by disorderly cell activity. There are many types of seizures, some fairly well understood and some still confusing to researchers. The type of seizure depends on the region of the brain where the discharge of energy originates and, to some extent, on the brain's maturation and its ability to spread the electrical discharge to other parts of the body.

The three main classifications of epilepsy are generalized seizures, partial seizures, and unclassified seizures. Seizure types and their progress are described in the accompanying Research Notes.

RESEARCH NOTES

Types of Seizures

Generalized seizures are bilateral and symmetrical without local onset in the brain. They are often accompanied by loss of consciousness and most have motor components. Generalized seizures include absence seizures (traditionally known as *petit mal*), *myoclonic seizures*, tonic-clonic seizures (the traditional *grand mal*), and *atonic seizures*, which include infantile spasm convulsions. The most common forms of generalized seizures are tonic-clonic and absence. Many individuals experience both these forms, which may be either idiopathic or symptomatic.

The most frightening seizure for the observer is the generalized tonic-clonic seizure, in which a child loses consciousness. Children may also suffer from absence seizures—an extremely brief loss of consciousness. Other seizure types include Jacksonian and psychomotor. The developmental consequences of epilepsy are extremely varied; children have more learning and behavioural problems than their peers, and have higher rates of psychiatric disorders.

The tonic-clonic seizure proceeds through relatively distinct stages. Some epileptics consistently experience an aura just before the seizure's onset. This aura may be a subjective sensory or memory experience, such as an odour that is not present in

reality. It may take the form of an odd internal sensation, or even a memory phenomenon in which the person actually experiences a scene from the past (Krupp & Chatton, 1983).

Shortly after the aura appears, the individual loses consciousness, falls, and develops generalized stiffness of the body. During this *tonic* phase, the arms are flexed (bent) and the legs extended. The trunk muscles are also in spasm, so that breathing ceases. After a short but varying period of tonic activity, the *clonic* stage follows. In this phase, the person exhibits alternate relaxations and contractions of the skeletal musculature, which produce what is often referred to as *thrashing movements*. In the throes of the clonic state, the person may lose bladder and bowel control, bite the tongue, and froth at the mouth. After two to five minutes, convulsive movements diminish and finally stop. This is followed by a gradual regaining of consciousness. During this time, the person may experience confusion, headache, or other symptoms. A period of deep sleep marks the end of the seizure.

If a child suffers a major seizure and then immediately passes into another seizure, the condition is known as *status epileptus*. This is potentially life-threatening and medical aid should be sought immediately.

Major generalized seizures can occur at any time and in a school setting can be frightening for the beholders and distressing for the victim. Teachers can ease the situation by trying to provide privacy during and after a seizure. If a child begins to have a seizure, the teacher should allow or help the child to lie down, move away furniture, loosen restrictive clothing, and tilt the head to one side to drain saliva. Teachers should never try to hold the child, stop the seizure, or force anything into the child's mouth.

Absence seizures are most frequently seen in children. Some children suffer up to 200 absence seizures a day. These often occur when the child is sedentary, and infrequently, during exercise (Berkow, 1982). The classic absence seizure lasts only 15 to 30 seconds and is so brief that it is often overlooked or misinterpreted. The child ceases all activity and appears to stare vacantly, as though daydreaming. During this period, there is a loss or clouding of consciousness. The return of consciousness is abrupt and the child immediately resumes interrupted activities. In more than 70 percent of all cases, absence seizures cease altogether by age eighteen (Nealis, 1983).

There are other forms of absence seizures. During these, the child's eyes may blink or shift and the hands may move aimlessly. On some occasions, the seizure may be prolonged, lasting for minutes or hours. During these long seizures, the child may simply appear confused and dazed.

Minor motor seizures, often called Lennox-Gastaug seizures, are similar to absence seizures. They can be characterized by momentary loss of muscle tone. *Myoclonic seizures* are so called because they are characterized by a single repetitive contracture of a muscle or group of muscles.

Partial seizures begin locally (in a specific area of the brain) and may or may not cause loss of consciousness. They occur in many forms, but the common feature in all is the localized origin of brain irritability. Because they affect very local motor or sensory areas, partial seizures are sometimes referred to as *focal seizures*.

One form of partial seizure is the Jacksonian seizure, which occurs only in cases of symptomatic epilepsy. It is characterized by motor symptoms without impaired consciousness. Spasmodic (clonic) movements might start in the peripheral portion of a limb, such as the left thumb. These movements might then progress in an orderly fashion toward the central portion of the body and down into the left leg. Sometimes the violent electrical discharge that begins in one hemisphere of the brain spreads to the other. If this happens, the individual loses consciousness and undergoes a major convulsion.

Another type of partial seizure is the *psychomotor seizure*, sometimes called the *psychomotor equivalent* or *temporal lobe seizure*. It is most characteristically associated with lesions of the temporal lobe of the brain. Psychomotor seizures are poorly understood. They often include a clouding of consciousness and amnesia (loss of memory of the event). Along with altered consciousness, other manifestations include a change of body position or limbs, confused activity, a dazed expression, nausea, vomiting, drooling, muttering, mumbling, wandering, pallor or flushing, incoherent or irrelevant speech, and inappropriate emotional disturbances. Sometimes these symptoms are accompanied by relatively complex, well-organized movements, such as plucking clothing or any other patterned activity.

The category of *unclassified seizures* includes all other types.

Developmental Consequences of Epilepsy

The effects on learning resulting from epilepsy can be chronic, with permanent impairment in the ability to process information. In other cases, the influence on learning is relatively short-lived, and includes brief transient disturbances in attention and short-term deficits in cognitive functioning. Effects chiefly depend on factors such as the nature of the seizure disorders and the medications used. Even so, one study found that retention in grade and placement in special education was twice as frequent for children with epilepsy as for typical children (see Williams, Sharp, Bates, Griebel, Lange, Spence, & Thomas, 1996).

Children with idiopathic epilepsy are more likely to develop normally than those with symptomatic epilepsy. Most children with idiopathic epilepsy function normally between attacks. Symptomatic epilepsy is often seen in children who experience seizures before age two. The early onset of seizures that are unremitting or persistent for several years are more likely to be related to learning problems than later onset or lower seizure frequency (Rodin, 1989). These children are usually suffering the effects of developmental defects, birth injuries, or a metabolic disease affecting the brain, and are more likely to exhibit multiple disorders that can include intellectual disabilities, sensory loss, or motor disability. As well, generalized seizures are more likely than partial epilepsy to be associated with learning problems. Individuals with more generalized seizures are usually expected to suffer greater disability than those whose seizures are more focused and partial.

Together with possible learning problems, a range of psychological and social adjustment difficulties have been associated with epilepsy. Included are increased psychiatric and behavioural disturbances, poor self-esteem, and excessive dependency. Boys consistently show problem outcomes with greater frequency than girls (Williams et al., 1996).

Adjustment difficulties may be a function of the fact that epilepsy is unique among chronic illnesses. For the individual child, the chronic nature of the disorder and the unpredictability of seizures are disturbing. Although the majority of children with epilepsy are well controlled with medication, and although some may outgrow seizures, none can look forward to a cure and all must learn to live with the possibility of lifelong seizures. In addition, no one can predict when a seizure will occur; for this reason, there is little chance to adjust to epilepsy. Children may feel powerless at the prospect of losing control: the ambiguous nature of epilepsy can increase a child's apprehension at not knowing when and under what circumstances his or her behaviour will become visible to others.

Society's reaction to epilepsy remains problematic. Despite the success of modern treatment, confusion and misunderstanding still surround the condition. Some people continue to equate epilepsy with intellectual disabilities or mental illness. This is not correct. Some persons with symptomatic epilepsy may exhibit mental retardation, but they are a minority in the epileptic population. Among persons with idiopathic epilepsy, mental illness or intellectual disability do not occur more frequently than in the general population.

TOURETTE SYNDROME

Tourette syndrome is a condition characterized by multiple involuntary muscular, cerebral, and sometimes vocal tics that occur many times a day, usually in bouts. The onset is between the ages of two and fifteen, with six to seven years of age the most common time of onset. Tourette results from a chemical imbalance in the brain, but exactly what neurological glitch causes the disorder is unknown.

Probably 1.6 percent of the entire population is affected with Tourette syndrome. Three times as many males as females have the condition. About 50 percent of those affected show hyperactivity, short attention spans, restlessness, and poor impulse control. Only about 30 to 50 percent of persons with Tourette syndrome have *caprolia*, the verbal tic that results in uncontrollable uttering of obscenities (Lemon & Barber, 1991).

Comings and Comings (1987) found that persons with all grades of Tourette syndrome were significantly more likely to be placed in special education classes, to have reading problems, and to have difficulties with the retention of material read. The condition is often treated with a combination of medication and cognitive behavioural approaches that involve changes in the social environment. Children need highly structured individual programs.

HEAD TRAUMA

In the past, head injuries occurred most often in the fifteen- to twenty-four-year-old range. Among adolescents today, vehicle accidents—involving either pedestrian or passenger vehicles including automobiles, motorcycles, and bicycles—are the most common cause of head injuries. However, Traumatic Brain Injury (TBI) is almost as frequent in children under age fifteen. Among young children, head injuries result from falls (the most frequent cause), bicycle accidents, other recreational activities, assaults, and child abuse.

In the United States, more than 1 million children a year are identified with TBI (Keyser-Marcus, Brid, Sherron-Targett, Yasada, Johnson, & Wehman, 2002). Injuries, usually accidents, are the leading cause of death among children aged one to fourteen; almost half of these deaths occur among children aged one to four. Boys are involved in twice as often as girls. The same is true in Canada, where injuries are the leading cause of death for children and youth after the age of one. More than 300 children die and more than 20 500 are hospitalized with serious injuries each year, although the rates of death and hospitalization have actually dropped by one-third in the last decade (Picard, 2006).

Rates vary greatly across Canada and among groups. The preschool rates of injury in the territories are generally much higher than the national average. Injuries are more likely to occur among poor children, boys, and Aboriginal children and youth ("Injuries . . . " 1994).

Traumatic Brain Injury

Traumatic Brain Injury (TBI) is defined as an insult to the brain, not of a degenerative or congenital nature but caused by an external physical force, that may produce a diminished or altered state of consciousness, which results in impairment of cognitive abilities or physical functioning. It can also result in the disturbance of behaviour or emotional functioning. These impairments may be either temporary or cause potential or total functional disability or psychosocial maladjustment (Savage, 1988, p. 13).

TBI is unique in several ways, which are explained below.

- TBI is characterized by sudden onset (usually from motor vehicle accidents and falls).

- In some individuals, the effects are not always immediately seen; they may not become apparent for months or even years.

- Advances in acute medical treatment technology have increased survival rates for individuals with TBI. However, about 20 percent are left with some degree of disability.

- TBI is not selective in its damage. It can cause diffuse cerebral swelling due to increased cerebral blood volume, and several areas of the brain can therefore be affected. Because of this, children and adolescents who suffer head injuries can be expected to present concomitant physical and perceptual motor defects and organically based behaviour and emotional disorders (De Pompei & Blosser, 1987).

- Each child with a Traumatic Brain Injury has survived a catastrophic event and progresses through the recovery process in a unique way. Recovery is influenced by the site and extent of the injuries to the brain, the child's age, and other injuries or complications. Children are often in a coma and may at first show a state of confusion, as well as memory, attention, or speech and language impairments.

- The age at which the injury is sustained has a significant impact on the ultimate extent of recovery. Damage to the neural system of young children may be very different from damage to the system of the older elementary-aged child. The older the child is when the trauma occurs, the closer the resemblance to adult-like injury and behavioural outcomes.

- TBI in children disrupts normal developmental processes and results in a loss of previous levels of personal, academic, and social functioning. The trauma often shatters an individual's sense of self. Recovering identity may require a long period of habilitation and multidisciplinary efforts (see Kauffman, 2005). Personal changes spill over to changes in behaviour and self-management that can affect a student's performance, self-esteem, and social relationships (Berglund & Hoffbauer, 1996).

- Behaviour may be different than before the accident; many children manifest long-term behavioural problems, despite apparent recovery. In one study (Scaringi, 1994), parents reported that, in general, their children's behaviour tended to be more volatile; they were more short-tempered and their tolerance level with frustrating tasks was lower. In addition, they had become quite stubborn. These children would often adamantly refuse to perform chores at home, complete homework assignments, and so on. During therapy sessions, they were highly distractible. They played with pencils, erasers, and tried to engage the reporting clinician in conversation that had nothing to do with the task at hand.

- Frontal lobe damage is the most common form of injury and ensures diminished cognitive capacity. Other insults to the brain also compromise cognitive functioning. Associated cognitive or information-processing deficits, particularly memory losses, impair a student's ability to learn new information and, consequently, harm academic performance. But although TBI can result in learning disabilities of varying degrees, students with this condition show more variability in performance than those with other learning disabilities.

- Language difficulties, the aphasia we discussed in Chapter 4, are common. In acquired aphasia, the age of onset of the injury is a critical factor. In children as young as four, evidence exists that the hemispheres of the brain process symbolic communication differently, with left-hemisphere dominance in speech and language. With age, the brain becomes fixed, and its various functions cannot be easily assumed by its other related segments. By about school age, the brain has lost much of the organic plasticity found in the brains of younger children. In adults, this is even more pronounced, and they are less able to recover functions lost through brain injury than children.

- Following on the above, children who sustain injuries before the age of three may become temporarily mute and show a general inability to respond to the speech of others. However, very young children often make rapid improvement. They seem to relearn language in the same sequence as children acquiring language for the first time. In children more than three years old, the symptoms of aphasia are usually different.

These children may find it hard to retrieve words they used only moments earlier. Recovery is slower and residual problems are likely to remain.

- Assessments should occur very frequently, at least annually. Children recently injured need even more frequent testing because in even three to six months a child may perform at a completely different level than when he or she left the hospital.

- Severe TBI is a significant family burden and source of stress during acute hospitalization and in the early weeks following discharge. Stress is multidimensional and affects siblings and the nuclear family. The long-term impact is the greatest concern.

Developmental Consequences of Head Trauma

If you return to the above section on the outcomes of TBI, it is easy to understand why teachers familiar with affected students often report classroom difficulties. As examples, children who have suffered a head injury may show chronic fatigue for up to a year. Some may experience problems with the physical layout of the school such as long hallways and stairs. These obvious motor problems may be resolved relatively quickly, but problems with the execution of refined and complex psychomotor movements, particularly when speed is involved, may remain.

Persistent language problems are common. When deficits such as lack of speech, restricted expressive output, and problems of breath control are present right after a trauma, they may subside rapidly, but as part of a global disorganization process, more subtle and long-standing difficulties with language comprehension and expression may be observed. These include problems of word finding, organization of sequenced utterances, and comprehension breakdown as instructional complexity increases (Mira & Tyler, 1991; Ylvisaker, 1986). Attention, retention, and auditory and recent memory difficulties are also common. Students may demonstrate problems in planning, organizing, and initiating activities and in attending to and focusing on a task. These difficulties influence, at the very least, the degree to which the child can keep up with class procedures such as copying, organizing material, producing significant amounts of work, and comprehending the language of instruction.

Given the range and intensity of the possible deficits, it is estimated that between 9 and 38 percent of students with TBI will be referred to special education (Keyser-Marcus et al. 2002). For either special or general programs, there are no particular tested techniques or educational modifications in place. Effective education and treatment often requires a combination of classroom behaviour management, family therapy, medication, cognitive training, and communication training (Iverson & Osman, 1998).

DRUG-EXPOSED CHILDREN

In Chapter 3 we pointed to the range of possible physical and behavioural difficulties that can affect a child exposed prenatally to drugs. It is important to keep in mind that there is a continuum of casualty risk. That is, the popular notion that all drug-exposed babies are severely affected is a myth; the effects vary dramatically and are moderated or exacerbated by social factors such as poverty, neglect, or drug use by others in the home.

For children who do suffer effects, there are problems in classroom participation. Such children may perceive as stressful some events that teachers view as normal or routine

(Evans, Tickle, Toppel, & Nichols, 1997). They are often overwhelmed by the ordinary experiences of school—the classroom and environmental noises, the instructions, questions, interactions, and general business. Some children may withdraw; others may become wild and difficult to control (Rest, 1990).

FETAL ALCOHOL SPECTRUM DISORDERS

It has long been recognized that alcohol during pregnancy endangers the developing fetus. In the mid-1900s there was a retreat from knowledge on the dangers of alcohol. The link between drinking and birth outcomes was not only denied but alcohol was thought to offer therapeutic benefits during pregnancy. Then in 1968 French researchers re-established that women who drank during pregnancy gave birth to underweight infants with distinct facial features, cognitive delays, and challenging behaviours (Armstrong, 2003; Golden, 2005).

Today the conditions caused by maternal consumption of alcohol during gestation are an area of intense medical and educational research interest. New terminology and classifications have emerged that use the general term *alcohol related birth disorder* or, more often, the collective Fetal Alcohol Spectrum Disorders (FASD) (Astley & Clarren, 2000).

FASD describes an entire spectrum of disorders that include such diagnostic categories as neurobehavioural disorders, statis encephalopathy, and Fetal Alcohol Syndrome (Miller, 2006). As one disorder within the syndrome, *Fetal Alcohol Syndrome* (FAS) is a clinical diagnosis (Astley & Clarren, 2000). (Note that the term *Fetal Alcohol Effect* (FAE) is no longer considered a useful diagnostic label, as it is too vague to be of much use to educators or clinicians) (Miller, 2006).

A clinical diagnostic code for FAS has now been established (Astley & Clarren, 2000). Diagnosis of FAS is based on four primary criteria—growth deficiencies that stunt prenatal and/or postnatal growth; permanent brain damage resulting in neurological abnormalities, delay in development, intellectual impairments, and learning or behavioural disabilities; facial anomalies, including short eye opening and thin upper lip; and maternal use of alcohol during pregnancy (Astley & Clarren, 2000).

The level of impairment or severity across these areas can range from mild to severe. Diagnosticians now use a 4-digit code to rate FAS in the above areas in terms of the level of impairment, beginning with 1 (no evidence of impairment) and going to 4 (definite/severe evidence of impairment). The 4-digit code can result in 256 possible combinations in each category, defined by severity and impact on the student.

Because prevalence rates of FAS in the past have depended on different criteria, they have tended to be quite scattered. With a more settled process, we can expect clearer prevalence figures to emerge. At the moment, the incidence in the general population is estimated to be 1.9 per 1000 live births (Murphy-Brennan & Oei, 1999). About 1 of every 750 infants is born with FAS (Feldman, 2000).

Much is still unknown about FAS. The exact connection between the amount of alcohol consumption and reproductive risk is not clear. The medical profession has not yet determined a safe level of alcohol for a pregnant woman. One would assume that infants of mothers who drink heavily are at greater risk. Alcoholics and binge drinkers are certainly at high risk (Phelp, 2000) but even normal social drinking may be harmful to the fetus. It is suggested that as little as one ounce of alcohol a day can create a drop of six or seven points in IQ

(Kanter & Streissguth, 1997). Other research finds that even in mothers who drink moderately, infants are less attentive and alert, with the effects still present at four years of age (Santrock, 1999).

Fetal damage occurs because the body uses large quantities of oxygen to metabolize alcohol, oxygen that the developing fetus needs for cell growth. Also, the ethanol in the alcohol takes fluid from the developing brain, causing the death of brain cells. Keep in mind, however, that given the metabolic variations between individuals, there is no correlation between the quantity and frequency of the ingestion of alcohol and the number of defects in a child.

Developmental Consequences of FAS

FAS can affect the whole body system (see Table 13-4). According to Berk (1998), autopsies of FAS babies show a reduced number of brain cells and major structural abnormalities. Facial anomalies include microcephaly (small head circumference); short eye openings, flat midface, indistinct ridges between nose and face, thin upper lip, small chin, short upturned nose, cleft palate, minor ear anomalies, low nasal bridge, epicanthic folds (skin covering the inner corner of the eye), and narrow forehead (Murphy-Brennan & Oie, 1999). Features are present at birth and may or may not disappear into childhood. Children show a high rate of epilepsy, which may persist through the early school years (Williams, Howard, & McLaughlin, 1994).

The notion that FAS and intellectual disability are inevitably tied has now been discarded. However, intellectual functioning is often compromised, and many researchers believe that FAS is a leading cause of intellectual disability in the Western world

Table 13-4 Specific sequelae associated with FAS

Neurological	Craniofacial
mental retardation	low-set ears
microcephalus	short low-bridged nose
seizures	epicanthic folds
tremors	short lower jaw
irritability	long upper lip
poor fine coordination	droopy eyelids
hyperactivity	high-arched palate

Skeletal	Other
clubfoot	cardiac defects
spinal fusion	kidney defects
growth deficiency	genital problems
abnormal palmar creases	poor weight gain

(Murphy-Brennan & Oei, 1999). Cognitive disabilities are found in about 44 percent of people with FAS. As the condition varies in intensity, there are also differences in the degree of delay involved. Severity is related to the severity of the physical anomalies, in particular microcephaly.

Although many of the characteristics of FAS, such as slow academic progress, processing difficulties, and attention problems, are shared by many students with disabilities, particular facets of FAS are unique. Students frequently demonstrate challenging behaviours that are long lasting and varied. These include verbal and physical aggression, temper tantrums, impulsivity, non-compliance, hyperactivity, lying, and stealing. As students grow older, we find mental health problems, disrupted school experiences, trouble with the law, confinement, and drug or alcohol problems. Kanter and Streissguth (1997) reported that 50 percent of the FAS population demonstrate inappropriate sexual behaviour; that is, any compulsive or problematic sexual behaviour that results in sentencing of an individual for sexual offender treatment.

ASSESSMENT OF CHILDREN WHO HAVE NEUROLOGICAL DISABILITIES

Many of the conditions characterized as neurological disabilities require intensive medical diagnosis and management. Vision and hearing assessment are crucial; specific measures are discussed in Chapters 10, 11, and 15.

Some children may meet with a *neuropsychologist*—a specialist in understanding and treating the problems that occur following damage to the brain. Following the child's neuropsychological assessment, teachers may gather information on interactions with peers; problem-solving skills; frustration tolerance; reading and writing skills; and attending behaviour (Keyser-Marcus et al., 2002).

There is general agreement that psycho-educational assessment for many children who are neurologically impaired is beset with difficulties that relate to the depth of physical and mental disabilities. Educators also agree that the standard diagnostic and evaluation tools currently used with children who are mildly disabled will often be of little use to those involved with individuals with physical and neurological disabilities, but no consensus exists as to the types of alternate measures to use.

The problems associated with the use of standardized tests with this population are well nigh insurmountable. For one thing, norm-referenced tests are largely standardized on the physically normal population; in general, measures have not been specifically developed for children with physical and neurological disabilities. Just as importantly, using standardized tests as the sole measure with these children places serious limitations on them and may result in depressed scores that simply confirm the impairment without providing any functional information regarding potential for achievement.

Assessors are challenged to find ways to circumvent the disabilities in order to provide accurate assessment results as well as to find tools and procedures that reflect a child's knowledge and skills, not disabilities. The aim is to gather information that takes into account all the relevant factors, so that intelligent decisions can be made regarding academic planning. Faced with this task, assessors usually incorporate a battery of measures, use different test procedures, and allow various adaptations to tests and responses.

There are a number of ways to modify administrative procedures. For example, eliminate verbal tests from a battery; adapt the way a test is presented, such as holding a picture closer to the child's eyes; alter the test stimuli by providing larger pictures or speaking more slowly; or allow more time for timed tasks.

Administration procedures are germane to the tester, as are response requirements to the child being tested. When altering the latter, there are three general techniques. First, a *support adaptation* is used when the child must be placed in a certain position or provided some general form of support before being able to pass an item. A *prosthetic adaptation* is provided for the child who needs a specific piece of equipment, such as braces or a hearing aid, to demonstrate a skill. A *general adaptation* is one that does not require support or a piece of equipment but still represents a change in the basic requirements of the task or that changes the utility of the skill. For example, a child who is hearing impaired may need to perform communication tasks with sign language. A child with a physical disability may be allowed to look toward the response rather than pointing manually or a therapist may be on hand to assist in handling and positioning techniques.

For children with physical or neurological disabilities, regular and periodic assessment of development in communication and motor movement provides data about how many skills a child has developed, what type of skills they are, and how they are used. Communication assessment is discussed in Chapters 4 and 15. Motor assessments are usually conducted by physical or occupational therapists, who have in-depth knowledge of the neurobiological system and can recognize the impact of specific impairments on movement and stability. A **motor assessment** considers physical status, mobility, and functional aspects (how the child uses motor skills).

motor assessment

INTERVENTION WITH STUDENTS WHO HAVE NEUROLOGICAL DISABILITIES

Physical and neurological disabilities are primarily medical and therapeutic conditions, so intervention stretches far beyond the academic and educational. No single professional can effectively fill the multiple needs of all these children; they receive help from educators, physicians and medical specialists, occupational and physical therapists, speech and language pathologists, counsellors, and others. It is the secondary difficulties in areas such as academics, communication, and mobility that are of most concern to educators.

Medical Intervention

Medical interventions cover a broad spectrum of treatments. As examples only, children with cerebral palsy (and spina bifida) often suffer from *contractures*—a permanent shortening of the muscles, tendons, and ligaments that results in postural distortion and decreased joint mobility. Surgery can ease contractures and correct dislocations, and may also involve repair of the joints to reduce the risk of arthritis (Batshaw & Perrett, 1986).

The primary goal of anticonvulsant therapy for epilepsy is to achieve maximum control with the fewest possible drugs and side effects. The choice of drugs is related to the type of seizure pattern and the presence of side effects from other drugs. Currently, using one drug is the treatment of choice as it reduces the probability of numerous side effects (see Table 8-2 on pages 268 and 269).

In the case of head trauma injuries (TBI), immediate medical attention may help to reduce the extent of damage. Trauma medicine has made a great deal of progress in recent years; new brain scan techniques can pinpoint sites of injury.

Children with Tourette syndrome may be treated with SSRIs or antihypersensitive medications such as Clonidine.

Therapy

Physical, occupational, and speech and language therapies are indicated for many children with neurological and orthopedic disabilities. Therapies are most commonly associated with sensorimotor development, postural control, activities for daily living, environmental adaptations, and augmentative communication.

The need for occupational or physical therapy is determined by deficits such as an absence of robust righting (coming back to a sitting position), inefficient sitting and standing posture; limited ability to perform sensorimotor tasks; and inadequate physical fitness for daily living activities. Speech and language therapy is used with children who have difficult or unintelligible speech. These students require augmentative communication devices that act as substitutes for speech (see Chapters 4 and 15).

Teachers must recognize that promoting optimal postures and movement patterns for functional activities is an important objective for children with physical and motor disabilities. Areas of special concern are positioning and carrying. **Carrying** refers to the way that a child with a physical or motor disability is moved; **positioning** refers to how the child is seated or otherwise positioned. Individual positioning is prescribed for each child in order to facilitate normal muscle tone and symmetry, provide stable and aligned posture, inhibit primitive reflexes, facilitate normal movement patterns, stabilize head and trunk control, and compensate for the lack of sitting balance (Copeland & Kimmel, 1989).

carrying

positioning

Technical Aids

The huge range of equipment now available for individuals with disabilities is making a significant difference in the quality of their lives by affording them more control of events in their environment. Devices and equipment range from the very simple, such as adapted spoons and switch-adapted, battery-operated toys, to the very complex, such as computerized environmental control systems.

Adaptive (assistive) equipment, an umbrella term, refers to any device designed or modified to lead individuals with disabilities to independence. The IDEA (2004) defines an assistive device as "any item, piece of equipment, or product system, whether acquired commercially off the shelf, modified, or customized, that is used to increase, maintain, or improve functional capabilities of a child with a disability" (IDEA, 2004, Sec. 602, 1). Within the broad category of adaptive equipment are prosthetic, orthotic, and adaptive devices, chiefly used to assist children with physical and motor disabilities and those with sensory impairments. There is quite a lot of overlap in these categories.

adaptive (assistive) equipment

Prosthetic devices are used to replace lost functions and/or provide support. They duplicate normal body movements as nearly as possible while restraining normal

prosthetic devices

Teachers should know how to position children in wheelchairs.

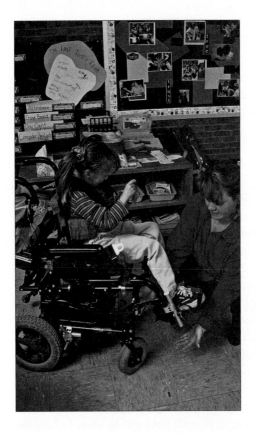

functions as little as possible. For example, an artificial leg is a prosthesis for a child missing a leg.

Much special equipment is used for support in mobility and standing. Included are leg casts and braces, ankle/foot equipment, crutches, walkers, and wheelchairs. The most common mobility devices are braces, crutches, and wheelchairs.

Wheelchairs are designed for people who are unable to ambulate, people whose ambulation is unsafe and unsteady, or those for whom ambulation is too strenuous. Wheelchairs are almost as varied as the people who use them. The main types are self-propelled wheelchairs, attendant-operated chairs, transit chairs, and electric or battery-powered chairs. An electronically controlled wheelchair can provide movement through voice-activated commands for a person who is severely disabled; it is programmed to respond to the owner's voice and requires no muscle control.

Orthopedic braces are for the lower extremities. Braces do not prevent contractures or develop walking skills but serve to control and support. There are three main types: short leg braces, long leg braces, and hip braces. A short brace would be used on the ankle joint; a long leg brace from the knee to the ankle. For children with cerebral palsy, braces are used chiefly for control. They help in ambulation, control involuntary movements, and serve to prevent or correct deformities. In spina bifida and muscular dystrophy, the braces are used chiefly for support. Support braces weigh less than control braces.

Crutches are used during periods of temporary disability to help with balance and locomotion, and to reduce weight on the lower extremities. When the disability is of long duration or permanent, crutches have to be designed to reduce the weight the legs must bear and to provide stability and support. The surface on which the crutch may operate is important. If the surface is slippery, rubber-tipped ends, spiked ends, or tripod legs should be provided.

Walkers are upright devices used to provide support and movement. There are various types of walkers that can be modified in various ways to assist the individual, but all provide standing support with forward inclined standing. Supported standing forces weight bearing, which is necessary for the normal formation of the hip joints.

Prosthetic equipment may assist in the therapeutic techniques of positioning and carrying. Positioning equipment and strategies allow children with motor problems to achieve postures and movement that might otherwise be impossible or non-functional. Some children need support in a lying position and use adaptive boards, wedges, and bolsters. Positioning equipment is typically designed to place the child in one or more basic postures in as normal a body alignment as possible.

Sitting may be difficult for children with motor disorders. Because children spend a lot of time sitting, it is important that they sit in the most beneficial position. They need to find positions that allow the best hand use, that are easiest for eye-hand coordination, and that present the least difficulties for balance. *Modified chairs* are for children who have difficulty sitting well or for those who have abnormal hip and leg patterns. A *special chair* aligns the body, limbs, and head; flexes the hips, knees, and ankles; and brings the head and shoulders slightly forward. Adapted chairs include corner chairs and bolster chairs. Both usually have removable trays.

Dangling feet are harmful to children with motor problems, so an *abduction block*—a chunk of something that the child's legs can straddle—is often used to prevent the child from sliding to the floor, while a footstool ensures that the child's feet reach a flat solid surface. Straps and other props are sometimes used to improve posture.

Standing frame

Boston jackets, AFOs, and hand splints

Pommel walker

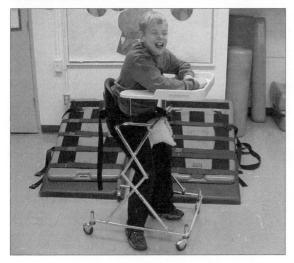

Tilt table

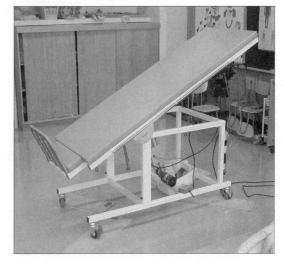

orthotic devices

Orthotic devices assist a limb's action. For example, special utensils (spoons, forks, and dishes) facilitate eating and drinking for a child with a movement dysfunction. Some eating implements have Velcro straps to make them easier for the child to handle and control. Adapted spoons have a built-up handle, or swivel so that gravity can right the spoon and prevent spillage. A hand splint to support wrist extension can also be used to allow greater finger movements for manipulative tasks.

In the classroom, children may require specialized equipment. Page turners and book stands assist in reading. Magnetized pencils and equipment are helpful for writing and drawing; there are specially adapted scissors for cutting.

Adaptive Devices

Much of the current technology requires pre-academic readiness skills, and most of today's technological devices operate through one dominant modality (for example, touch for keyboards, vision for monitors). However, devices are increasingly allowing for alternative modalities, such as voice-activated computers and television captioning. The availability of instrumentation that permits persons with disabilities whose cognitive level is less than two years of age to control devices in their environment is also increasing. As well, many technologies are becoming more transparent (less noticeable and obtrusive) because of miniaturization, the use of lighter materials, and higher capacities for information processing.

Microswitches are adaptations of particular use to people with motor impairments. Switches—including push switches, pull switches, grasp switches, wobble switches (activated by bending in any direction), pneumatic switches (activated by puffing or sucking on a straw), and sensor switches (activated by very small movements) can be set to operate under the control of almost any muscle in the body. They can be set to operate lights, appliances, or a computer.

Students with physical disabilities can use voice commands to enter information into a computer verbally. Some students may need peripherals to increase accessibility. Peripherals include a mouse, alternative keyboard, touch screen, touch tablets, optical pointers, alternative keyboards, single switches, trackball, key guard, head or mouth typing stick, voice-controlled devices, or a hand splint for physical disabilities. Or there may be special modifications to the software. For example, a word processor for individuals with limited fine-motor ability may present a grid of all the letters and other characters in the upper corner of the screen. Each character may be highlighted briefly, and the user strikes the spacebar or uses another input aid when the desired character is highlighted (Maddux, 2000).

Educational Intervention

In the past, non-educational considerations would have taken priority when considering placements for students with physical and neurological disabilities, and many students would have been taught in separate classrooms or special schools. Progress in medical science, improved technology, and changing attitudes have dramatically altered service delivery for these students, and today most are found in general classrooms.

Service Delivery Models

Inclusion in the general classroom is appropriate for almost the full range of students with neurological disabilities. Special class placement may still be provided for students who have additional severe problems with perception, cognition, or language. Children with recent TBI may require a more structured and quiet environment (Rempel, 1992). Other children may miss numerous days in school for surgery, medical appointments, and therapy. If lost schooltime is extensive, students may be provided hospital or home instruction.

Some generic accommodations and adaptations for students with neurological disabilities are shown in Table 13-5.

Table 13-5 Creating accessible classrooms

For students with physical and motor disabilities:

- Become familiar with any special equipment that a student uses in the classroom, such as wheelchairs and other mobility devices, visual and travel aids, amplification systems, catheterization equipment, ventilators, and so on.
- Try to have classroom displays at the student's eye level.
- Provide tilt-top desks.
- To adapt books for easier page turning, put paperclips on pages to make them easier to flip, or make slides of pages so that a child can hit a button on a slide projector to turn the pages.
- Use pencil holders to assist children who have motor problems with grip. Use a pencil grip made of a piece of clay or foam material wrapped around the pencil or pen.
- Use large chunks of sponge for painting.
- Use marking pens for free flow.
- Use magnetized rulers and instruments on the equipment chair table.
- Anchor paper by taping it to the table or easel.

For students with cerebral palsy:

- Do not pull the child by the arms; lift the child under the arms.
- When helping a child dress, put clothes on the more affected side first. Don't try to pull a hand or foot through a sleeve or pant leg—the limb will only bend tighter.
- To straighten a limb, push it out at shoulder and elbow or hip and knee first.
- When moving the child in a wheelchair, always ensure that the child's feet are on the footrest.
- Wear rubber-soled shoes.
- Do not place the wheelchair too close to heaters.

Table 13-5 continued

- Be constantly aware of positioning. Individual positioning is designed for each child and proper positioning for one may not be appropriate for another.
- Know how to position children in wheelchairs. This refers to providing support for the child's body, changing the child's sitting position in the chair, and arranging instructional or play materials in certain ways.
- Constantly check on sitting position; reposition the child at least every half-hour.
- Learn about handling—how the child is picked up, carried, held, and assisted.
- Tell the child what you are going to do at all times, whether in positioning or moving.
- At a desk, make sure that the child's heels touch the floor, knees are bent, and back is supported.
- Use an abduction block; don't let feet dangle.

For children with Traumatic Brain Injury and other neurological problems:

- Allow mini-breaks during class.
- Use ear plugs when completing assignments.
- Keep a notebook for homework and other relevant information.
- Tape-record lectures.
- Always begin a lesson with a review and then overview (Keyser-Marcus et al., 2002).
- Use tape recorders and computers to overcome writing difficulties.
- Provide an extra set of textbooks for home.
- Let a buddy help the child move efficiently from class to class.
- Early dismissal will allow the child to move from room to room.

For students with Fetal Alcohol Syndrome:

- The classroom should have soft, low-key colours; low lighting, not fluorescent; a comfortable temperature; and space for movement.
- Provide flexible scheduling.
- Have few transitions.
- Have a clear schedule and a structured day.
- Adapt the schedule to take advantage of students' attentive times.
- Set up carrels or quiet spaces in the classroom.
- Delineate student workspaces with coloured tape or a furniture arrangement.
- Provide plastic trays, boxes, and so on to assist children in organizing their materials.

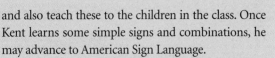

CASE STUDY

Kent (continued)

A revised IEP was prepared for Kent at the opening of his grade 2 year. Psycho-educational assessment shows Kent to be functioning in the low area of the intellectually disabled range. With limited ability joined to other deficits, Kent's academic achievement is low. He can recognize his own name, a few sight words, and perform simple counting to 10. Socially, he waves to friends, smiles appropriately, and seems to enjoy stories, singing, and other oral activities in the classroom.

The IEP team consisted of the school principal, classroom teacher, special education consultant, physical therapist, speech/language therapist, and the parent. Areas of particular need were prioritized and personnel assigned. Since Kent lives in Digby, Nova Scotia, the general classroom is considered the primary setting.

Since Kent has only minimal linguistic skills, the development of a system by which to communicate at some level with those in the environment is a first priority. Kent's individual program must include a mode of communication and ways to teach it. The language taught using the system and other related activities will build on what have been identified as Kent's interests. He is, for example, very interested in his classmates, so his language will stress names and simple actions such as "See Joe," or "Peter draws." Kent also enjoys books—both being read to and turning the pages himself—so much exposure to highly coloured print materials will be important. He also seems to enjoy music, so he will learn to listen to simple songs on a tape recorder that he will operate himself.

The language therapist decided to introduce Kent to a new language system. In the past, both Blissymbolics and American Sign Language were tried, but these seemed to be too conceptually difficult for Kent. Because Kent's hand use is quite good, the therapist suggested that the teacher introduce some basic signs from the Amerind system (see Chapter 15)

and also teach these to the children in the class. Once Kent learns some simple signs and combinations, he may advance to American Sign Language.

To assist with mobility, the physical therapist will work with Kent and provide advice for the teacher and the paraeducator. With the child, she will try to develop stronger skills with his walker so that he will rely on the wheelchair less during his time in school. As well, the therapist will work proactively with the teacher and aide to provide ideas and strategies for Kent's participation is particular parts of the school day, such as moving to art class and going to the gymnasium.

EXTRACT FROM KENT'S IEP

Name: Kent
Age: 8–6

Present Levels of Functioning

Kent has cerebral palsy. There may be some language, but so far there is no speech development.

Placement

Kent is in a general classroom setting. The object is to expose him to language and social models.

Adaptive Equipment

Wheelchair; behind-the-ear aids in both ears; magnetized equipment for writing; large implements.

Additional Assistance

Physical therapy, speech therapy, paraeducator in general classroom.

Long-Range Goals

- During therapy, Kent will learn a simple manual communication system, Amerind. Signs will be used in the regular classroom by the paraeducator.

- Kent will be provided many opportunities to read books either alone or with a peer.
- Kent will operate a tape recorder to listen to simple songs.
  - Kent will independently walk for up to 15 metres using a walker.
  - Kent will improve social skills—greeting and interacting with peers.

Short-Term Objectives

- With assistance, Kent will use the walker to negotiate classroom transitions.

- Within classroom activities, the paraeducator will sign to Kent and prompt him to use known signs.
- Kent will join in small groups with assigned tasks to improve language and social skills.
- Kent will use greeting behaviour—waving—when requested.
- Kent will maintain a supported sitting position in the carpeted reading area.
- Kent will use page turners, with support.
- Kent will look at the book as a peer reads a story.
- When given a tape recorder, Kent will depress the special switch to turn the recorder on and off.

SUMMARY

1. Of the many physical disabilities, the conditions described in this chapter all stem from some form of neurological damage. In this sense, the conditions are not curable, although they can be ameliorated by medical intervention, therapy, drugs, and education.

2. Neurological impairments can occur before, during, or after birth. Any factor that leads to hormonal, chemical, or blood-flow imbalances can cause central nervous system problems. Along with prenatal and perinatal causes, the incidence of preschool and childhood brain injury is increasing.

3. The human brain is a unique creation composed of a hundred billion neurons connected by trillions of synapses. *Neurons,* the basic functional units of the nervous system, send messages by releasing chemicals that jump across the synapses—the tiny spaces between the neuron fibres. *Glial cells* provide support and nutrients for the neurons. In one sense, the nervous system is complete at birth. The central nervous system of newborn children contains the full complement of neurons, but comparatively few of the axons are covered with myelin. Hence, all the structures are present and the number of nerve cells does not increase, but the size of these cells does.

4. *Physical and neurological disabilities* include a huge range of conditions. Because of the diverse nature of physical and neurological disabilities, their varied severity, and co-occurring conditions, it is impossible to draw a profile of a typical affected child. In general, physical problems may limit mobility, socialization, play behaviours, independence, learning, and educational opportunities. Children may be further hindered by their lack of ability to explore the environment adequately.

5. *Cerebral palsy* is the most common neurological difficulty seen in children. Over half the children with cerebral palsy have spasticity, in which the muscles don't work in harmony—some muscles are too tight, some too loose. Children with athetosis show jerky, uncontrolled, and writhing movements; those with ataxia show uncoordinated movement and difficulties with positions in space. Together with motor problems, cerebral palsy can include any number of intellectual, sensory, and behavioural disorders.

6. *Spina bifida* arises from a complex pattern of genetic-environmental interactions that produce a neural tube defect assessed at birth with distinctive physical, neural, and cognitive consequences. Spina bifida comes in a number of forms. Damage to the developing nervous system will leave varying degrees of paralysis, sensory loss, bowel and bladder incontinence, and hydrocephalus.

7. *Epilepsy* is a condition in which the smooth functioning of the brain's electrical system is briefly disturbed, causing a seizure—an electrical storm in the brain. Manifestations depend upon the location, severity, and type of short-circuit coming from the brain.

8. A group of conditions subsumed under Fetal Alcohol Spectrum Disorders includes *Fetal Alcohol Syndrome* (FAS), a condition caused by maternal consumption of alcohol during gestation. The past few years have witnessed progress in determining the diagnosis, sequelae, and epidemiology of FAS.

9. *Traumatic Brain Injury* (TBI) is an insult to the brain caused by an external physical force. Associated problems include cognitive, behavioural/psychological, sensory/motor, and language disorders. Students may experience problems with physical, cognitive, or psychosocial functioning well past their initial physical recovery and rehabilitation.

10. An assessor can use adaptation for assessing students with neurological and physical disabilities. Adaptations tend to cluster into four categories—*presentation*, *response*, *setting*, and *timing*.

11. Depending on the extent and nature of a condition, a child may require the services of many disciplines, including psychology, physiotherapy, occupational therapy, speech pathology, audiology, and medicine. Occupational and physical therapists work in close collaboration with teachers and parents to assist the child in different functions.

12. *Adaptive (assistive) technical devices* are pieces of equipment used to increase, maintain, or improve the fundamental capabilities of students with disabilities. Adaptive devices serve to make living easier, aiding mobility and ambulation, seating, classroom interaction, and daily living.

13. A physical or neurological disability, of itself, is not a reason for special education services. Students with these disabilities benefit from the same instructional practices and curriculum as others.

HISTORICAL NOTES

When institutional settings for students with special needs were first established in the 19th century, they served discrete categories, specifically those who were deaf, blind, and mentally retarded. Significant disabilities were seen as potential hindrances to programs because of the individual care they needed, so children who were seriously crippled, not toilet-trained, or considered to be uneducable were not provided with schooling in the institutions or in the public system.

The one major exception was epilepsy. Probably no other 19th-century exceptional group was as misunderstood and inappropriately handled. In that period, no drugs to control the condition or technical devices to assess its etiology existed, and seizures engendered such fear in beholders that they held that epilepsy and insanity were inextricably joined. Institutionalization was imperative, either with those who were mentally retarded or those mentally ill.

There are reports of a class in Boston in 1866 for crippled children. But compared to schooling for deaf or blind children, intervention for children described as crippled was a very late development. In Montreal, the world's first organized movement on behalf of crippled children was started in 1906 by a group of educators at the Children's Memorial Hospital.

From the outset, as mentioned, segregation was the mode. Despite the fact that students presented a wide range of abilities, potential, and educational need, and that there was little or no difference between their classroom performance and that of typical students, the majority of pupils who were physically disabled were restricted to special schools or special classes. Among other reasons, teachers felt that these youngsters would be too difficult to handle and take a disproportionate amount of time. There was also the traditional predisposition that stereotyped these children and focused on their disabilities while ignoring their strengths. As well, many school plants were not equipped with the physical structures, modifications, technical equipment, and support personnel to handle and teach such students. It was seen as more economical to construct one barrier-free building than to alter all the plants in a school district and transport children to one central location and then bring the therapists, teachers, and other intervenors to the students.

The history of another entire field feeds into the development of education for students with physical disabilities. *Prosthetics* is the field of science concerned with the artificial replacement of body parts, and includes designing, manufacturing, and fitting artificial limbs (Tiessen, 1996). Prostheses have been used probably since the beginning of humankind. Artificial limbs and braces appear in ancient frescoes, mosaics, and pottery. The first written account is 2200 years old and concerns one Marcus Sergius, a Roman general who lost his right hand in battle and had it replaced with a metal one.

Ambroise Pare, the surgeon general from the French army in the 16th century, is considered to be the modern father of prosthetics and orthotics. He made advances in surgical techniques and had many devices made for wounded soldiers. Many people, from pirates to panhandlers, were leg amputees who used crude peg legs to replace limbs severed by sword or saw. These were fashioned out of forked sticks or tree branches, and fit was forsaken for function (Tiessen, 1996).

Artificial limbs have come a long way. With miniaturized power sources such as motors with sophisticated sensory control and hydraulic and pneumatic components, artificial limbs and braces are extremely functional today. Child amputees, whose residual limbs continue to grow, are the most susceptible to poor fit (Lowey, 1993).

CHAPTER 14

CHILDREN WITH PERVASIVE DEVELOPMENTAL DISORDERS

INTRODUCTION

Pervasive developmental disorders (PDD) is a broad category that in general encompasses children with significant disabilities. The very terms are telling. The adjective *pervasive* implies that the conditions will probably be extremely long lasting, if not lifelong. The word *developmental* implies that the conditions represent a significant delay in the process of development and affect many or all developmental domains. Note that since the process of development is significantly affected, the term pervasive developmental disorders does not refer to a maturational lag or an at-risk child. With such a broad swath of conditions included, there is considerable debate about how to subdivide severe disorders in a reliable and helpful way. Following DSM IV (APA, 1994), we examine PDD under the following groupings: Autism Spectrum Disorders, autism, and Asperger's syndrome; childhood disintegrative disorders, including Rett's syndrome; childhood psychoses, specifically childhood schizophrenia; pervasive developmental disorders, not otherwise specified; and dual and multiple disabilities.

In this chapter, the focus is on Autism Spectrum Disorders and childhood schizophrenia. The serious types of psychoses and Autism Spectrum Disorders represent the most extreme forms of pervasive developmental disorders. Probably no other conditions are so hard to understand and so far removed from the range of normal experience. They strike at the very essence of human relatedness and human communication, and must therefore be considered the most devastating disorders that affect a child's learning and behaviour. Every aspect of functioning is affected.

Children who are autistic frequently exhibit strange and inappropriate behaviour. They may display bizarre body movements; suffer inordinate fears; or indulge in repetitive motor activity, self-stimulation, and self-mutilation. Many children are completely withdrawn; they never speak at all but pirouette in a silent internal dance, impervious to all around them. Their world may consist of touch sensations, familiar routines, and rigidly obsessive behaviour. Still, such children may fly into tantrums at the smallest change in their surroundings, from a parent's new hairstyle to a door left slightly ajar.

Some symptoms of Asperger's syndrome seem to overlap with classic autism; others are differentiating. In general, Asperger's is seen as a developmental disability marked by impairments in verbal and non-verbal communication, socialization, and behaviour.

Subsumed within the broad category of pervasive developmental disorders are *childhood psychoses* that affect many basic areas of psychological development at the same time and to a severe degree. Children with psychoses display severe abnormalities and disturbances that are seen as distortions of development. Our focus is on childhood schizophrenia, a mental illness with physiological causes that are poorly understood. The condition is characterized by serious loss of contact with reality and a marked deterioration in the ability to function. Children show delusions and hallucinations, emotional disturbance, apathy, and withdrawal.

Historically, childhood schizophrenia and autism were discussed in one breath. Late 19th-century authorities viewed autism as a psychosis and lumped the "juvenile insane" into one category. In the first half of the 20th century, the term *schizophrenia* was used to classify all presumed childhood psychoses. The research done at this time actually explored autism and other psychiatric disorders as well as schizophrenia. A disproportionate number of studies focused on autism, but research into the area of childhood and early adolescent schizophrenia was limited. However, the same researchers worked on both topics and often simply generalized the research, although there was far more on

Bizarre behaviour is characteristic of children with childhood psychoses and infantile autism.

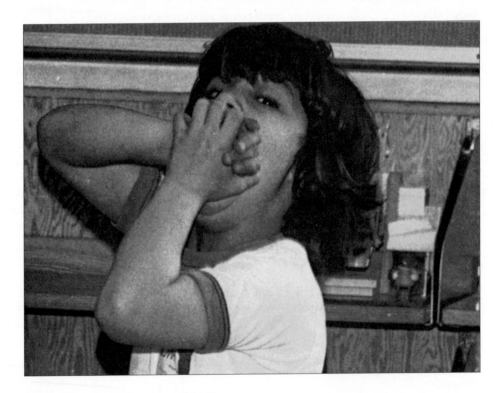

autism than schizophrenia and the generalization of data had little direct relevance to the schizophrenic group (Winzer, 1997).

The research bent toward autism Spectrum Disorders is still prominent. However, today there is sufficient evidence to clearly demarcate psychotic and autistic behaviour. This chapter therefore takes a somewhat different organizational stance than previous chapters in this text. After introducing the general category of pervasive developmental disorders, we delve into the topic of Autism Spectrum Disorders and then into childhood schizophrenia in the latter part of the chapter. The two conditions then merge again when we discuss classroom interventions. Do note also that many of the interventions already mentioned in Section 3 are germane to students in this group, and vice versa. That is, many of the strategies pinpointed here are relevant to students with milder disabilities.

DEFINITIONS OF PERVASIVE DEVELOPMENTAL DISORDERS

Quite a number of terms and definitions appear as researchers and practitioners try to describe the complex needs of children with pervasive developmental disorders. These terms overarch and meld with the terms used in the field of severe and multiple disabilities that we lay out in Chapter 15.

The overriding term is **pervasive developmental disorders** (sometimes referred to as simply *developmental delay* or *developmentally disabled*). The term describes individuals who suffer from chronic disabilities, attributable to mental or physical impairments, or a combination of these, that are manifested before age twenty-two and that result in functional limitations in major life activities, requiring special services and treatment that are lifelong or of extended duration.

pervasive developmental disorders

CLASSIFICATION OF PERVASIVE DEVELOPMENTAL DISORDERS

Dissension and controversy surround the classification of pervasive developmental disorders and the subcategories of psychoses and Autism Spectrum Disorders. Many of these problems stem from the historical antecedents of the field (see the Historical Notes at the end of this chapter) as well as the rapid alterations brought to the area by new genetic, psychological, and educational research.

For clarity and focus, we are following the classification shown in the introduction to this chapter. The classifications are shown in Figure 14–1.

Autism Spectrum Disorders

Today the general terminology speaks to *Autism Spectrum Disorders*—spectrum implying that the conditions range from mild to severe. The major categories are autism and Asperger's syndrome.

Figure 14–1

Classification of pervasive developmental disorders

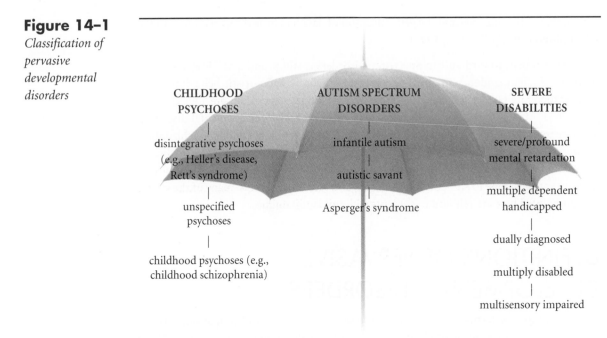

CHILDHOOD PSYCHOSES	AUTISM SPECTRUM DISORDERS	SEVERE DISABILITIES
disintegrative psychoses (e.g., Heller's disease, Rett's syndrome)	infantile autism	severe/profound mental retardation
	autistic savant	multiple dependent handicapped
unspecified psychoses	Asperger's syndrome	dually diagnosed
childhood psychoses (e.g., childhood schizophrenia)		multiply disabled
		multisensory impaired

Autism

The word *autism* comes from the Greek *autos*, meaning "self." It is fitting, because the most prominent feature of children with autism is their apparent self-absorption and socially withdrawn behaviour. Despite being the subject of massive research efforts, autism remains difficult to understand. A precise definition does not exist and the boundaries of autism remain vague and undifferentiated. The enigmatic nature of the condition perhaps explains why so many advocacy groups and societies have on their logos some depiction of a puzzle with a piece missing (Smulker, 2005).

As we pointed out, autism was considered for a long time to be a severe emotional disturbance, a childhood psychosis. Ongoing etiological research in the 1970s showed that autism is a developmental disability, not an emotional disturbance. In light of this, American guidelines first moved autism into the category of "other health impaired." With the IDEA (1990) autism moved again to become a separate category. According to the American legislation (IDEA, 1990),

> Autism means a developmental disability significantly affecting verbal and non-verbal communication and social interaction, generally evident before age three, that adversely affects educational performance. Characteristics of autism include irregularities and impairments in communication, engagement in repetitive activities and stereotyped movements, resistance to environmental change or change in daily routines, and unusual responses to sensory experiences. The term does not include children with characteristics of the disability *serious emotional disturbance*. (National Association, 1991, p. 2)

This definition manages to be both inclusive and specific. It stresses the age of onset (manifestation is generally before thirty six months of age). It also focuses on the characteristics, the behaviours that affect educational performance, and the groups excluded.

Asperger's Syndrome

Asperger's syndrome was first discussed by a Viennese pediatrician, Hans Asperger, in 1944. He published a paper that described a pattern of behaviours in several young boys who had normal intelligence but also exhibited autistic-like behaviour and marked deficiencies in social and communication skills.

The disorder was formally recognized in the United States in 1994 but much remains unclear. It appears that the profiles of individuals with Asperger's syndrome differ from those with classic autism. The same domains of communication, socialization, behaviour, and activities are affected, although there is relatively normal development in cognition and language.

Disintegrative Psychoses

A number of forms of psychoses—due to multiple etiologies—affect children. Heller's disease, for example, is due to disintegrative brain disease. The condition is rare, affects more males than females, and is typically diagnosed in children below the age of ten. Heller's disease was considered a purely medical condition until 1994, when it was included in DSM.

Subacute sclerising panencephalitis (SSPE) is an organic psychosis—a serious viral encephalitis of children that seems to develop after contracting measles. More males than females are affected. Symptoms include progressive deterioration and mental changes that eventually end in dementia.

Rett syndrome was first described by Andreas Rett in 1966 but not generally recognized as a medical disorder until 1983. The syndrome is found almost exclusively in girls, about 1 in every 10 000 to 15 000. After normal development in infancy and early childhood, there is a gradual regression characterized by abnormal growth patterns, often epilepsy, deterioration of hand use, and language loss. Some girls may retain a few single words or simple phrases but typically they communicate with gestures, vocalizations, and body positioning (Skotko, Koppenhaver, & Erickson, 2004).

Psychiatric disorders subsequent to brain injuries in older children have also been reported (see pages 440 to 442 in Chapter 13 for more about TBI). Steinhert muscular dystrophy is accompanied by a primary brain dysfunction in which generalized deterioration of learning is one of the first signs of disorder.

Childhood Psychoses, Schizophrenia

Individuals with schizophrenia exhibit a wide variety of symptoms and send very mixed messages to the outside world. They show extremes of activity, sudden mood changes, and verbal disturbances. They also develop delusions and experience hallucinations.

Pervasive Developmental Disorder, Not Otherwise Specified

When children exhibit some autistic characteristics but do not meet all the criteria for autism, they may be classified as having pervasive developmental disorders, not otherwise specified (PDD-NOS).

PREVALENCE OF AUTISM SPECTRUM DISORDERS

Not long ago, Autism Spectrum Disorders were assumed to be comparatively rare. Today, autism "has moved from being a relatively unrecognized disability to having a position of notoriety" (Simpson, 2004, p. 137).

Initial surveys in 1966 estimated that Autism Spectrum Disorders were found in about 4 to 5 persons per 10 000. But worldwide, troubling increases have been seen recently in the number of children with the condition. As examples, studies in Europe and Asia since 1985 have found that as many as 6 of every 1000 children have at least one autistic type disorder (Center for Disease Control, 2004). In the United States, estimates vary, but experts say that 4 to 5 percent of children have Autism Spectrum Disorders (Vedantam, 2006).

It is estimated that more than 100 000 individuals in Canada are currently diagnosed with Autism Spectrum Disorders (ASD) with about 3000 new cases identified each year (Autism Society Canada, 2004). Collected data from three provincial departments of education (Quebec, Saskatchewan, and British Columbia) showed that there has been a 150 percent increase of cases in 6 years. Based on figures such as these, the Autism Society Canada (2004) estimates that 1 in every 200 children in Canada has an Autism Spectrum Disorder.

All in all, studies suggest that as many as 1 in 150 children aged ten and younger may be affected by autism or a related disorder. Nash (2002) observes that this makes the problem five times as common as Down syndrome and three times as common as juvenile diabetes. Autism is four times more common in males (Vedantam, 2006); when girls are affected, the conditions tend to be most severe. There are no known racial, social, economic, or cultural distinctions.

In terms of the prevalence of autism, do be aware of three points. First, there appear to be worrisome increases in the rates of children with severe autism. Second, the category of ASD has also expanded to include everything from severe to mild. Third, research and epidemiology cannot truly provide explanations for the surge in autistic disorders.

The United States National Research Council (2001) feels that concern for the apparent increases in autism and related disorders can probably be accounted for by better diagnoses and a broader definition, not by dramatic changes in the occurrence of the disorders. For example, when Eric Fombonne evaluated published surveys, he concluded that "there is good evidence to support that higher prevalence rates reflect changes in diagnostic practices, improved identification and availability of services, and other similar factors" (Fombonne, 2003, p.88). On the other hand, some epidemiologists see a real surge in absolute numbers. A study in California found that the number of children with profound autism had increased from 1987 to 1998 by 273 percent, a number that continues to grow (Gross, 2003). In the California study, the increasing numbers could not be attributed to loosening diagnostic criteria, a rise in the number of children with cognitive impairments misdiagnosed as autistic, or an in-migration of children with autism to the state (Bird, 2002).

Although Hans Asperger described the condition in 1944, DSM did not include the diagnosis of Asperger's syndrome until 1994. Today, Asperger's syndrome is known as a relatively common developmental disorder (Myles & Simpson, 2001). It is estimated that as many as 48 to 70 out of 10 000 children could have Asperger's (Kadesjo, Gillberg, & Nagberg, 1999; Safran, 2002). But as the condition is at present only minimally recognized and diagnosed, others note that any numbers are really "guesstimates" (e.g., APA, 1994).

ETIOLOGY OF AUTISM SPECTRUM DISORDERS

Linked to mounting prevalence rates are massive research agendas searching for the etiology and prognoses of Autism Spectrum Disorders. So far, etiological data are best described as inconclusive. The best approach may be multifactorial, viewing these disorders not as a single entity but rather as the final common pathway of multiple etiologies; that is, attributing developmental disorders to a combination of biological and environmental factors. Autism is probably a final expression of multiple determinants and may be the result of metabolic, infectious, developmental, environmental, and genetic insults.

Many of the theories concerning the causes of developmental disorders can be categorized as either nature or nurture. Nature theories stress biological dysfunction; in contrast, the nurture approach views the environment as the vital developmental factor. Until the late 1960s, theoretical constructs of Autism Spectrum Disorders focused on psychosocial (nurture) origins, as detailed in the Historical Notes at the close of this chapter. Compelling recent research increasingly leans toward biological interpretations.

Advances in neurobiology, brain imaging, and neuropsychology are allowing new insights into the possible brain basis of autism. Neurobiological investigations indicate that factors critical to the normal development of the central nervous system seem to have gone awry in autism. The condition almost certainly involves dysfunction of brain circuits that support the functioning of a variety of brain regions. Investigations have looked at brain lesions or pathological enlargement of the left temporal horn; attempted to account for autism on the basis of dysfunction in the vestibular area of the brain, the area thought to modulate the interaction of sensory and motor functions; and strongly implicated the medial temporal lobe. (See Dawson, Metzoff, Osterling, & Rinaldi, 1998, for a full discussion.)

In the 1940s, both Hans Asperger and Leo Kanner noted that genes might be central to autism. Today, genetic loading is clearly identified; the importance of genetic factors or a genetic predisposition in the etiology of autism well established. However, the genes that actually contribute to the condition have been hard to track down. Unlike, say, Down syndrome, where an entire chromosome is affected, many gene mutations are probably involved in autism.

Support for genetic factors has a number of prongs. For one thing, classic autism is often accompanied by minor physical anomalies, such as fine hair, large head circumference, and malformed ears (Links, Stockwell, Abichandani, & Simeon, 1980). More compelling are twin studies and an increasing number of reports on multiple incidence in siblings and second-degree relatives.

Infantile Autism

The prevalence of infantile autism is far higher in siblings of children with the disorder than in the general population. In family studies (e.g., Folstein & Rutter, 1988), only about 2 percent of the siblings of children who were autistic displayed the condition, but this is 50 times greater than the expectation for the general population. The incidence of autism in the identical twin of a child who is autistic is also high. If one identical twin has autism, there is a 60 percent chance that the other will too and a better than 75 percent chance that the twin without autism will exhibit one or more autistic traits (Nash, 2002).

Autism has also been associated with various X-linked chromosomal abnormalities, and in particular with the genetic subtype fragile X, which has the highest incidence of autism of any documented syndrome or chromosomal abnormality. Of the entire population diagnosed with autism, it is estimated that 10 to 14 percent have fragile X syndrome, which makes this syndrome the most commonly known organic cause of autism (Hagerman, 1988).

Asperger's Syndrome

Etiological investigations into Asperger's syndrome indicate that there are differences between Asperger's and high functioning autism. Among other things, Asperger's appears to be even more strongly genetic than classic autism (Nash, 2002).

DEVELOPMENTAL CONSEQUENCES OF AUTISM SPECTRUM DISORDERS

Autism Spectrum Disorders can affect almost every domain of a child's development and seriously hinder all aspects of progress. Some affected individuals exhibit a range of disordered behaviour and may appear to be severely retarded; others show only social deficits. This means that the group is extremely heterogeneous; individuals show wide variability in the type, number, and severity of observed deficits in cognitive functioning, communication, social interaction, and overt behaviour.

Autism

DSM-IV lists the primary characteristics of autism as communication deficits or delays, stereotypical behaviour, and limited social relatedness. These traits together present children who demonstrate severe self-isolation, lack of appropriate use of language, stereotypical and inappropriate use of objects, a preoccupation with music, and abnormal motility patterns such as toe walking, body rocking, and bizarre choreoathetotic posturings. The most common behavioural problems are tantrums and non-compliance. These and other behaviours that may appear as the child develops are presented in Table 14-1. Keep in mind that this is only a partial list. Also be aware that while we have pinpointed a core group of symptoms, a further cluster of traits may be present in any given child.

Severely affected children never begin to establish normal human attachments. They are extremely alone from early childhood and are unresponsive to other people. As infants, some children who are autistic show far less mutual gaze and facial responsiveness than other children. They may be indifferent to physical contact, or may even show aversion to it. Parents report that their children do not respond in normal ways to being held. Infants do not make the usual anticipatory movements prior to being picked up and fail to make the usual body adjustment to adapt to the person carrying or holding them.

In other children, the condition may be seen in the toddler stage. Children may display behaviours such as prolonged rocking and head banging in the crib, apathy and

Table 14-1 Some characteristics of children with ASD

Trait/characteristic	What you may see in the classroom
Extreme variability in intellectual functioning	Many children function at pre-academic levels
	Requires modified programming
	Tantrums, non-compliance
	Tendency to be easily frustrated
	Difficulty with classroom routines
	Inability to transition easily; becomes stressed
	Much resistance to change
	Easily confused by assignments that have multiple components
Language comprehension difficulties	Gaze aversion
	Difficulty processing high amounts of auditory input
	Difficulty with the questions *who, what, when, where,* and *why*
	Cannot easily read the facial expressions and body language of others
Expressive language problems	Lack of speech or unusual speech
	Echolalia or vocal perseveration
	Parroting, meaningless jargon, incessant repetition of questions and statements
	Unusual pronoun use
	Low repertoire of social interaction behaviours
	Can't stay on a topic in conversation
	Limited or inappropriate facial expressions
	Awkward body language
	Proximity difficulties
Restricted interests	Repetitive, ritualistic, and solitary activities
	Preoccupation with, or attachment to, inanimate objects
	Narrow topics of conversation
Withdrawal and isolation	Self-injurious behaviour
	Repetitive actions and stereotyped movements
	Aloofness and indifference
Motor difficulties	Difficulties with toilet training
	Abnormal motility patterns
	Awkward and clumsy with fine and gross motor skills
Sensory differences	Odd eating habits and food preferences
	Feeding problems, such as poor sucking (unable to use a straw) refusal to hold food in mouth, refusal to chew or swallow, gagging
	May mouth objects
	Body image problems
	Bizarre reactions to sensory input

disinterest in the surroundings, unusual fear of strangers, obsessive interest in certain toys or mechanical appliances, highly repetitive and ritualistic play, insistence on being left alone, demands that the physical environment remain unchanged, and very unusual language behaviour.

In older children, autism reveals itself in fleeting eye contact, the failure to develop any relationships, and insistence on rituals and routines. Children fail to form attachments to other people. They seldom initiate contact; sometimes seem to look or walk through others; appear distant, aloof, or in a shell; and are extremely alone. They have severely impaired communication skills and show an obsessive insistence on sameness. Objects are preferred to people so that a child's only strong attachment is toward inanimate things. A child may be fascinated by things that spin, and sit for hours with a toy car upside down, endlessly spinning its wheels. It is virtually impossible to distract the child from this behaviour.

Physical and Motor Development

Children with autism tend to be healthier than other children with pervasive disorders (Schreibman & Charlop, 1989). Motorically, they may show grace and normal motor skill development; however, it is not unusual to find ten-year-olds who are not yet toilet trained or capable of dressing themselves.

Cognitive Development

Although there is no common theoretical base, conceptions of autism share the assumption that it stems from some deficient cognitive structure. Poor cognitive development affects children's ability to learn, while behaviour problems interfere with attention and motivation.

Accumulating data show that the IQs of most children with autism can be reliably determined and that the majority score in the moderate to severe range of intellectual disability. It is estimated that 50 to 75 percent of individuals with autism are intellectually disabled (Goodman, 1987; Sigelman & Shaffer, 1991). Kauffman (2005) notes that the vast majority of autistic children have an IQ of between 35 and about 70. Only 20 to 25 percent of children with autism are in the normal range of intelligence; a few are in the gifted range.

Cognitive development appears to differ from that observed in typical retardation. In youngsters with autism, IQ scores become stable over time, predictive of later functioning, and fail to rise with age-related improvements in clinical symptoms. Evidence suggests that females with autism tend to be more seriously affected, with lower intelligence scores and greater problems in cognition and language.

A fairly common myth is that autism is accompanied by compensatory intellectual gifts. However, researchers recognize that this is not always so; autism is, in fact, far likelier to be characterized by heartbreaking deficits and mental retardation. The myths probably arose from tales of *autistic savants*, a rare, fascinating, and barely understood subgroup considered a subset of Autism Spectrum Disorders.

Michael Howe (1999a, b) studied these children and found that, although they led basically bleak lives, in each case some special event had occurred that rewarded them in some way. For example, if a relative visited and the child remembered the date of the previous visit, the family may have praised the child and showered him or her with attention. From this point on, the child developed an internal obsessive desire to memorize calendars or pursue whatever the particular fixation was.

Perceptual Development and Sensory Response

Children with Autism Spectrum Disorders may display abnormal responses to visual stimuli. They seem to suffer from constraints in attending to relevant cues and may exhibit a generalized over- or under-responsiveness to incoming stimuli. While fixating on an object or lights, they may flutter their hands, cross their eyes, glance to the side, or unfocus their eyes. They may try to smell new objects, or run their hands and tongues over rough and smooth surfaces. Sound may elicit indifference, distress, or intense fascination.

This faulty modulation of sensory input is intrinsic in the pattern of autistic behaviour. To try to explain the disturbances of sensory input, a number of models have emerged. Some investigators believe that the child is overwhelmed by sensory input and unable to attend to pertinent environmental stimulation. Others see the child as showing overselectivity: he or she seems to select a part of a stimulus and maintain attention to that part. Once fixated on relatively few stimuli, the child becomes incapable of scanning the environment.

Self-stimulation, a persistent, stereotypic, repetitive mannerism, is one of the defining characteristics of autism. It involves activities such as prolonged and repetitive body rocking, toe walking, spinning, jumping, pacing, gazing at lights, twirling objects, excessive and repetitive vocalization, finger playing, swishing saliva, flapping the hands, patting the cheeks, and humming for hours on end. These behaviours are socially stigmatizing and decrease a child's responsiveness to educational instruction.

Language Development

Professionals have long been intrigued by the language patterns observed in children who are autistic. It is the deviance in the quality and pattern of language usage, rather than its delay, that makes the language so unusual and that differentiates autism from other developmental disorders.

Many children with autism seem to lack the awareness, intentionality, or competence to use language as a tool to convey messages to others. As infants, they show little or no ability to analyze or make sense of sounds. Later, language and communication skills remain seriously impaired.

Many children fail to speak at all. In those who do speak, attempts to communicate are characterized by immaturity, abnormalities in grammatical constructions, delayed echolalia, metaphorical language, pronoun reversals, and stereotypic utterances. Children with autism often use unusual words, with curious metaphors and odd expressions. They use **neologisms**, defined as non-words or words that are obviously peculiar. **neologisms** There are frequent pragmatic oddities, with language used in ways that are socially or contextually inappropriate. Children typically perseverate on topics and fail to recognize turn-taking rules. Pronoun usage is unusual. Children frequently use their given names, as in "David wants cookies," rather than "I want cookies," or "You want ride," when they mean "I want to ride."

Facial and gestural expression of emotions can also be abnormal. Children with autism are thought to have a visual motor imitation deficiency akin to dyspraxia, which interferes with the learning of normal body language and the understanding of non-verbal communication, so important during the pre-verbal stage of development. Affected children fail to use gestures appropriately, and do not interpret such gestural clues as eye contact, body posture, tone of voice, and facial expression (Hobson, 1988).

If language is impaired, speech problems almost inevitably ensue. In fact, speech is almost always delayed. Almost half of the children who have autism fail to develop functional oral language (Kauffman, 2005), especially those who are also intellectually disabled. In the other 50 percent, speech is severely delayed and, if present, frequently consists of meaningless repetitive and stereotypical utterances.

When learning speech, the process in autistic children is abnormal and different from that seen in, say, children who are intellectually disabled. Acquisition of first words is often delayed, and after that vocabulary often doesn't grow the way it does in other children. New words may appear but old ones are forgotten, resulting in a plateau. Some children with autism begin to speak and then lose all speech. Some then regain speech; others do not.

In autistic children with speech, prosody is often peculiar; for instance, everything may be said staccato or in a monotonous drone. In spontaneous speech usage, these children display a lack of expressive intonational features, such as stress and pitch, although echolalic children can repeat sentences and phrases with uncanny accuracy of intonation.

echolalia

Echolalia is the most frequently cited language characteristic of individuals with autism who are verbal, present in 75 percent of individuals (Rydell & Mirenda, 1991). Echolalic children may repeat whole sentences in parrot-like fashion as if the sentence were unanalyzable into smaller components, as if they had learned the behaviour and stored it in memory ever since.

Play Behaviours

Closely related to language are play disorders. Young children with autism show significant delays in the development of all forms of play, especially symbolic play. Their play is less varied, sustained, and integrated than that seen in typical children. It is also quite different from that of intellectually disabled and other exceptional children. It is not delayed play, but play that differs in topography, pleasure, and complexity. Even when intellectual level is allowed for, the play of autistic children is often obsessive, mechanical, and repetitive, with a marked absence of both co-operative and innovative pretend play. For these youngsters, play as a vehicle for learning about objects and events—and especially for engaging in make-believe—does not appear to be intrinsically motivating (Lifter, Sulzer-Azaroff, Anderson, & Cowdery, 1993).

Perhaps because of the language deficits that invariably characterize infantile autism, the play of autistic children is striking in its lack of fantasy and sterile, repetitive, ritualistic, and solitary nature. These children do not seem to know how to use play forms. In a room full of toys, a child who is autistic is more likely to ignore the toys and engage in stereotypic self-stimulating body movements. If the child does play, toys are used in a deviant fashion. Unusual preoccupations (such as memorizing timetables) are characteristically pursued single-mindedly to the detriment of other activities.

Social and Emotional Development

Increasingly, impairments in social relatedness are considered to constitute some of the core symptoms of autism. Typically, children who are autistic live in their own isolated worlds, barely relating to others in the environment. Social development is minimal; even at their most developed, social interactions are limited in their quality and scope. Children with autism respond to other humans with aloofness and indifference, often becoming upset when interaction is demanded.

Children who are autistic often have great difficulty in interpreting and predicting the thoughts, feelings, and behaviours of others. This lack of intuition about the feelings and emotions of other people has been labelled as "theory of mind" (Baron-Cohen, 1998).

Severe social interaction deficits manifest as severely impaired relationships with parents, family members, and others in the environment. Children who are autistic do not attempt to gratify their needs through meaningful personal relationships; rather, they behave toward people as if they were inanimate objects. Indeed, children who are autistic often resent parents and others who try to show affection. As mentioned, they also show both aggressive and stereotypical self-stimulating behaviours that further interfere with social interactions.

Maladaptive Behaviours

Children with autism demonstrate maladaptive behaviours, which fall largely within two classes—aggressive behaviour, either self-directed (self-injurious behaviour) or directed toward others; or self-stimulating behaviour (discussed earlier). Some children who are severely disabled throw massive temper tantrums during which they bite, kick, scratch, and strike out at others. Such aggressive behaviour can sometimes cause serious physical harm to peers, parents, and teachers. Many children inflict serious injury upon themselves: they bang their heads against sharp corners, bite themselves, and gouge their own eyes. Some children hurt themselves so often they must be kept in restraints for their own safety.

Family Variables

Raising and training an autistic child can cause enormous stress for parents and family. A child is likely to ignore the presence of his or her mother or other family members, and the parents are continually faced with their child's failure to respond to interaction. The deviant gaze pattern, known as *gaze aversion* (the failure to look directly at another individual), is a conspicuous characteristic of autistic children and severely hinders parent–child interaction. In addition, children tend to show little response to their mother's voice, do not anticipate being picked up, and do not adapt their body postures to the people holding them. These behaviours inevitably have a deep effect on parental interaction and are compounded in later years by a child's lack of verbal responsiveness and bizarre and inappropriate behaviours.

Asperger's Syndrome

As we pointed out earlier, Asperger's syndrome is rather new in the North American catalogue of childhood disorders. Children with this syndrome appear to share many of the traits that we described in Chapter 5 under non-verbal learning disabilities.

Academics

Students with Asperger's syndrome have strong rote memory and visual memory skills and they appear to understand and prefer quantifiable information. Nevertheless, they can experience academic difficulties as a result of poor problem-solving and organizational skills; concrete and literal thinking; difficulty in differentiating relevant from irrelevant information; obsessive and narrowly defined interests; and low social standing among their peers (Linn & Myles, 2004).

Physical Development

Among people with Asperger's, you may see poor motor skills along with co-ordination and balance problems. There may be fine motor problems and gross motor clumsiness (Simpson & Myles, 1998; Wagner, 1999). Students may not be able to sit down in a chair without checking it first and may not know how to put a shirt on without watching themselves in a mirror. Many have problems balancing when walking or righting themselves when carrying heavy objects (Linn & Myles, 2004).

Language

In recent years, interest in the language development of persons with Asperger's syndrome has almost matched the focus on language in the area of autism. It is generally agreed that there is no clinically significant delay in language development for children with Asperger's. In general, these children possess good structural language skills that follow the same trajectory as their typical peers (Paul, 2003). Yet while individuals are often quite verbal, they also struggle with the pragmatics and semantics of language.

In the semantics domain, students will sometimes repeat the same word over and over and have a difficult time learning that words have multiple meanings. They struggle with language that uses abstract concepts such as metaphor, idiom, parable, allegory, and rhetorical questions (Linn & Myles, 2004).

Individuals with Asperger's also meet problems with pragmatic language in everyday environments. Their language may be stilted and formal and they are confused about the appropriateness of conversational topics. Speech is different from normal in rhythm, rate, and inflection, or may be much too loud (Safran, 2002). Voices are often monotone or show exaggerated inflections.

Sensory Differences

Sensory challenges are common in people with Asperger's syndrome. Children may be hypersensitive in sensory areas such as touch, smell, and vision. For example, fluorescent lights may cause agitation and behaviour problems (Linn & Myles, 2004).

Social Differences

To date, probably the major finding in the field of Asperger's syndrome is that the condition is first and foremost a social disorder. Linn and Myles (2004) write that for a child with Asperger's "situations and events are unpredictable, social interactions and relationships are obscure and complex, and everyday life seems confusing and unforgiving" (p. 3). The world is hostile and perplexing to these individuals. Barnhill (2001) points out that "Children with Asperger's syndrome are not only socially isolated but also demonstrate an abnormal range or type of social interaction that cannot be explained by other factors such as shyness, short attention span, aggressive behaviour, or lack of experience in a given area" (p. 261).

With average to superior intellectual capacity, the child with Asperger's seems typical but lacks the social awareness and skills needed to connect with the world. Many individuals with Asperger's go to great lengths to be accepted. Unfortunately, when they are not successful, they do not understand why. Further, children and youth with Asperger's do not acquire greater social awareness and skill merely as a function of age. As adolescents, they may experience increasing discomfort and anxiety in social situations.

The language differences that are characteristic of many persons with Asperger's seem to poorly equip them for interactive communication and socialization. Non-verbal deficits may translate as the child moving into others' personal space, and failing to recognize others' body language and even verbal cues warning that he or she has transgressed certain personal boundaries. Friends and new acquaintances may be acknowledged with overly tight and enthusiastic hugs.

Verbally, students with Asperger's show a lack of reciprocity in social interactions and conversations. Children will discuss at length a single topic or find it difficult to maintain an interaction that does not involve a narrowly defined one (Barnhill, 2001). For example, bypassing typical greetings such as "Hi, how are you?" the student may launch into a diatribe on the latest topic of concern (Safran, 2002). In this one-sided conversation, the child may give much more information than is desired and ignore the give-and-take of social interactions.

ASSESSMENT OF CHILDREN WHO HAVE AUTISM SPECTRUM DISORDERS

In the diagnosis of Autism Spectrum Disorders, we find interwoven currents of research and investigation. We also find that diagnosis has provoked unresolved controversy. Clinicians vary in their theoretical conceptions of the conditions and emphasize different aspects as essential for specific diagnostic labels.

The presence of co-occurring conditions further muddies clear identification. Children with autism, for example, display a wide range of behaviours, many of them similar to those found in children with other disorders. Before they are correctly diagnosed, children who are autistic may be falsely labelled as blind or deaf. Cognitive disability is often the initial diagnosis; however, as we saw, this is not an either-or category, as a high percentage of children with autism are also retarded.

Assessment of children with autism is so replete with difficulties that in the past this population was considered untestable through standardized tests. The complex and varied disabilities made such children exceptions to many of the rules by which psychoeducational tests are designed and administered and, as a result, standardized tests were seldom given. When they were, incomplete results were often interpreted on the basis of the examiner's intuitive sense of a child's peak skills.

There is now a growing recognition that broad and thorough assessment of children who are autistic is both possible and essential to provide the basis for educational and behavioural programming. DSM-IV provides five deficit areas to consider as diagnostic criteria for identifying children with Autism Spectrum Disorders—communication; socialization and social skills; restricted interests; sensory integration; and behaviour.

Evaluation must be multidisciplinary and incorporate a variety of procedures, tools, and adaptations. Procedures require flexibility in administration, appropriate means of communication, alternation of free and structured time, motivation and reinforcers, predictable routines, and tools that limit the use of language. See Chapter 12 on test adaptations, Chapter 15 on specialized tools and procedures.

Specialized instruments are often needed to explore particular diagnostic and treatment questions. For example, the Autism Screening Instrument for Educational Planning (Krug, Arick, & Almond, 1993) has five components: sensory relating, body and object use, language, social skills, and self-help skills. Many assessors adopt a functional approach to testing, which we discussed in Chapter 7 in relation to students with behavioural disorders. The aim is to find the purpose (function) of a behaviour that interferes with instructional objectives; take appropriate steps to reduce the behaviour; and reinforce and maintain a replacement behaviour.

According to DSM-IV, to receive a diagnosis of Asperger's an individual must exhibit some atypical repetitive patterns of behaviour, interest, and activities. Using the DSM-IV criteria, Asperger's needs two of the following to be diagnosed: marked delays in non-verbal behaviour such as gesturing, facial expression, and body posture; impairments in establishing peer relationships; absence of spontaneous seeking to share enjoyment, interests, or achievements with others; and delays in social reciprocity. As well, a child must show one of the following: preoccupation with one restricted area of interest; inflexibility or rigidity—sticking to a set, sometimes non-functional routine; stereotyped and repetitive motor movements; or preoccupation with parts or objects.

CHILDHOOD PSYCHOSES

psychoses

In general terms, **psychoses** are serious mental disorders in which the behavioural and thought processes of an individual become so disturbed that the person is out of touch with reality. More specifically, *childhood psychoses* refer to a heterogeneous group of clinical syndromes characterized by any number of maladaptive behaviours or clusters of behaviours that include severe disturbances in ego functioning. Such disturbances affect various aspects of adaptive behaviour, including the perception and ordering of experience, the assessment of reality, the control and channelling of impulses, and the success of interpersonal relations (Cummings & Finger, 1980).

Childhood Schizophrenia

Childhood schizophrenia is one of the childhood psychoses. To many people, schizophrenia brings to mind the condition of split personalities depicted in movies such as *The Three Faces of Eve*. In reality, adult schizophrenia is not commensurate with split personality. Nor are adult schizophrenia and childhood schizophrenia parallel conditions with only developmentally determined variations in symptomology. Early findings that presumed the childhood condition and the adult disorder to be the same have been replaced by research that sees childhood schizophrenia as a separate and identifiable condition.

Childhood schizophrenia is defined as

> a pervasive psychotic disorder involving a decline or arrest of ego development following a period of relatively normal development, occurring in children who demonstrate some degree of useful language and relatedness to others. Among children characterized as schizophrenic, there are wide variations in personality organization, clinical course, intellectual functioning, and identifiable etiological conditions. (Cummings & Finger, 1980, p. 510)

While the actual course of a schizophrenic illness in a child cannot be predicted, the development of the psychosis is usually gradual, without any abrupt onset or sudden break as is common in the adolescent or adult. This slow insidious onset of symptoms appears early in a child's development and increases in intensity over time. Cantor (1988) talks about the preschizophrenic infant who may be fearful and irritable from the very beginning and not like being touched or held. In older infants and toddlers, sensitivity to touch persists. The child may begin to withdraw and attend to only selected aspects of the environment. Children may become picky eaters and the introduction of anything new becomes more and more difficult.

The time of onset of the symptoms of schizophrenia seems to be an important variable in the outcome and course of the illness. The actual onset of schizophrenia is extremely rare before the age of six. Onset during middle childhood before age thirteen—*very early onset*—is quite rare. When it does occur, it is associated with an insidious and chronic outcome. Negative symptoms such as inattention, flat affect, apathy, and lack of interest in social relationships are more evident when the condition emerges very early and has been related to a more chronic progression of the illness (McClellan & Werry, 1992).

Onset between ages thirteen and eighteen is termed *early onset*. The outcomes and course of the condition at this age seem to have the same possibilities as adult schizophrenia, which could be anywhere from an acute onset with a better prognosis to a slower onset with poorer outcomes (McClellan & Werry, 1992).

Children who experience the onset of schizophrenia in early puberty escape early impairments of development in the realms of cognition, perception, and sensation. But when the condition does take hold, children regress dramatically in their behaviour and demonstrate extreme withdrawal from the real world. Their close relationships are severely disrupted and they experience an overall deterioration in work, social relations, and self-care. They often lack or lose daily living skills, including such basic self-care as grooming, dressing, using the toilet, and feeding.

Prevalence of Childhood Schizophrenia

Schizophrenia affects about 1 in every 100 adults, but is exceedingly rare in children under the age of eighteen. In fact, childhood schizophrenia is less than one-sixth as common as the adult type; probably less than one tenth of 1 percent (Lambert, 2001; McClellan & Werry, 2000). About 1 in 10 000 children will develop childhood schizophrenia (Tolbert, 1996). Of these, about 50 percent will develop serious neuropsychiatric symptoms (Taylor, 1998).

Childhood schizophrenia is considered more severe than the adult type. In rare childhood cases, twice as many boys as girls are schizophrenic. By adolescence, the ratio is equal between boys and girls (Wicks-Nelson & Israel, 1991). There is not a gender difference in average age of onset (Eggers & Bunk, 1997).

Etiology of Childhood Schizophrenia

Children who are schizophrenic display such a wide variety of symptom patterns and respond to so many different treatment modes that no one etiology seems sufficient to account for the disorder. A multifactorial etiology seems to be the best approach to causation. However, this means that the contributing factors are the subject of considerable debate.

Early investigations pinpointed environmental factors: maternal overprotection, maternal rejection, stimulus deprivation during infancy, inconsistent parenting, and severe and repeated emotional trauma. However, many children exposed to these factors do not develop schizophrenia, and it is moot whether family forces alone are enough to produce such a devastating condition.

While the significance of environmental factors has not been completely discounted, the weight of accumulating evidence points toward biology as the primary contributor to childhood schizophrenia. One consistent finding in support of biological factors is the high frequency of prenatal and perinatal complications among infants later diagnosed as schizophrenic. Pregnancy and birth complications include toxemias, vaginal bleeding, and maternal illness during pregnancy.

Investigators have also found a higher incidence of neurological symptoms in children who are schizophrenic, which leads to the suspicion that the condition may be a manifestation of subtle neurological damage, similar in origin to such disorders as minimal brain dysfunction. Moreover, neurological dysfunction is highly correlated with birth and pregnancy complications, further evidence that biological factors are responsible, at least to some degree, for childhood schizophrenia.

There is also convincing evidence for a hereditary predisposition (Plomin, 1989). Studies of monozygotic twins have found that if one twin is affected, the other, regardless of environmental variables, is more prone to the condition. Because fraternal twins do not correlate nearly as highly, a genetic determinant is indicated. Yet the chance that someone will develop schizophrenia is less than 50 percent even for those with the highest genetic risks—those whose identical twin or whose parents both have the disorder (Plomin, 1995).

Developmental Consequences

Childhood onset schizophrenia presents with loose associations, illogical thinking, and communication discourse deficits (Abu-Akel, Caplan, Guthrie, & Scott, 2000). As noted earlier, the behaviour of children with schizophrenia is extremely variable. As well, the behavioural patterns will be episodic rather than pervasive, as in autism.

Physical and Motor Development

Prior to the onset of the illness, children may show a different physical appearance and a negative affect compared to siblings and peers (Litter & Walker, 1993). Children tend to lag in physical and motor development. They show serious deficits in gross motor areas and milder problems in the fine motor areas. As children with schizophrenia regress, acquired toilet and grooming skills may disappear.

Cognitive Development

This population of children shows great variability in cognitive functioning. On the Weschler scales, most youngsters who are schizophrenic achieve higher scores on the performance than on the verbal subscales (Cantor, 1988). As the condition takes hold, there is an alteration in cognitive development, even though there is no intellectual impairment, causing the child to be unable to actualize knowledge (Taylor, 1998).

Language Development

Language is intimately related to cognition and social development. As children regress, their speech becomes limited and may reveal incoherent thinking. They show unpredictable changes in the topic of conversation (loose associations) and inadequate reasoning (illogical thinking). Schizophrenic children underutilize cohesive linguistic devices that link the content of one sentence to that of adjacent ones. For example, they use fewer conjunctions than typical children to tie together the ideas expressed in a series of clauses (sentences) and use fewer pronouns, articles, and demonstratives to refer to objects or persons in either the spoken text or the context (Abu-Akel et al., 2000).

Social and Emotional Development

Schizophrenia has its most profound effects on a child's ability to monitor and test reality and on the ability to initiate and sustain interactions with others in the environment. Those with schizophrenia show a blunting of emotional responsiveness so that social relationships are invariably disturbed. Their relations to people are sporadic and bizarre.

The condition results in extreme withdrawal from the real world. Children show a marked reduction in interests and human attachments; they appear to live in a fantasy world and show emotional apathy, indifference, and withdrawal. Yet apathy can quickly give way to uncontrollable excitement or an enraged temper tantrum.

Affected children display a wide variety of disturbances in mood, thought, and behaviour. Hallucinations and systematic delusions have been found consistently before the age of eighteen (McClellan & Werry, 1992). Delusions tend to reflect the day-to-day life of the child and exhibit themes of monsters, ghosts, or animals (Russell, 1994). Hallucinations tend to be auditory. One child with schizophrenia, for example, reported that a kitchen light said to do things and said to "Shut up" (Russell, Bott, & Sammons, 1989).

Assessment

DSM-IV notes that to be classified as schizophrenic, children must display at least two of the following symptoms. These are delusions, such as thinking one has special powers; hallucinations, such as hearing voices that no one else experiences; disorganized speech; grossly disorganized behaviour; and certain symptoms of social withdrawal.

INTERVENTION WITH CHILDREN WHO HAVE AUTISM SPECTRUM DISORDERS AND PSYCHOSES

Children with Autism Spectrum Disorders present huge challenges to those who attempt to help them develop more meaningful lives. The field has attracted many passionate devotees—teachers, clinicians, and researchers—with widely varied views and very different treatment regimes. In fact, there is often contentious debate about the best interventions. Simpson (2004) observes that "there is significant and often strident disagreement as to what constitutes an appropriate program for children and youth with an autism-related diagnosis" (p. 139). So much so that one mother of an autistic son poignantly asked, "How will I hear my son's voice if it's entangled in such legacy of wartime fear, cultural misogmy, and ideological posturing?" (Paradi, 2002, p. 70).

Medical Intervention

Drug therapy has shown inconclusive, unpromising results in the treatment of autism. There are no recognized psychopharmacological medications to treat autism directly. In general, stimulants or tranquilizers do not significantly enhance the functioning of children who are autistic, although there has been some recent clinical success with new drugs such as Naloxone.

Drugs are effective for children with schizophrenia and can be seen as an essential component of an overall treatment program for many, if not most, affected children (Forness, Walker, & Kavale, 2003). The new or atypical neuroleptic or antipsychotic drugs appear to be the most effective treatment. Antipsychotics used include haloperidol (Haldol), thioridazine (Mellaril), fluphenazine (Prolixin), and thiothixine (Navane) (Tolbert, 1996). For children and younger adolescents, SSRIs and atypical antidepressants are the drugs of first choice. They may diminish agitation almost immediately; they take longer to diminish hallucinations. However, side effects can be severe—sedation, and abnormal facial or motor movements (Forness, Kavale, & Walker, 2003). As well, the atypical antipsychotics often cause significant weight gain, particularly in adolescents. Stimulants and tranquilizers are also commonly administered. (See Table 8-2 on pages 268 and 269 for drug types.)

Therapy

Over the years, many different methods and approaches to therapy for children who are autistic and psychotic have been tried. These include psychotherapy, family therapy, speech therapy, residential treatment, psychiatric hospitalization, medication, megavitamin therapy, sensory stimulation, and sensory isolation. However, despite strong claims by individual researchers, no one method has been conclusively shown to substantially alleviate pervasive developmental disorders.

Technical Aids

For children who are not often interested in other people or comfortable with them, a computer may serve as a catalyst for social interaction. If children work in pairs, studies show that they spontaneously teach, help, and praise one another in computer environments, asking more questions of one another than of their teachers (Borgh & Dickson, 1986).

The internet can be attractive to students with Asperger's syndrome. The effort and anxiety associated with interpersonal connections is greatly reduced; students can get to the message unconstrained by their social limitations and deal only with the written word (Safran, 2002).

Educational Intervention

Historically, students presenting intensive educational challenges to our schools have been served outside the general classroom and, in many cases, outside the community school. Intervention was founded on psychodynamic principles and individual therapy designed to promote and sustain emotional growth. Treatment was usually conducted in a residential setting away from the parents and typically lasted several years. Today, the majority of children live at home with their families and a variety of educational settings are available. Children are enrolled in residential programs only when they are seriously delayed in feeding, toilet use, or other self-help skills; when their families badly need relief; or when they must be placed under extensive observation for assessment purposes.

David's story in the Case Study below is illustrative of the variety of placement options and a continuum of services. David began school in a segregated setting but is moving more toward an inclusive classroom.

CASE STUDY

David

David is our third child. Although the pregnancy was uneventful, he was born nearly a month early after a prolonged and arduous labour. When we brought David home he was fussy and distractible, and he cried almost constantly. He had feeding problems with breast and bottle, and could not be comforted by holding or rocking. Even with his feeding problems, David gained weight and developed into a beautiful child. However, his crying continued and worried the entire family.

By the time David was a year old, we were sure he had some problem or disorder. Most of the time, David lay in his crib. He never seemed to notice when anyone walked into the room. He never smiled and never liked to be picked up and held. Except for crying, he made almost no sounds, especially not the babbling sounds his two older sisters had made.

At first, we suspected David was deaf. For nearly a year, we went from doctor to doctor seeking help. One doctor said David might be hearing impaired,

and told us to come back in six months. Another suggested he was severely mentally retarded, and another said he was simply slow in developing.

One evening, a friend who taught special children was visiting the house. He tried to play with David, but could garner no responses. We discussed our frustration and growing sense of hopelessness. Our friend suggested we get in touch with a local society that helped the parents of troubled children. At this time, the word *autism* had still never been mentioned.

Within a month of being directed to the right facilities, David was diagnosed as autistic. In a way, the diagnosis was a relief. Although we had hoped that David was only slow to mature, we knew in our hearts that something was truly amiss. Professionals may rail against labels, but we badly needed a starting point, a direction in which to find help.

As a family, we now understand David's problems, although we sometimes find it very difficult to cope with them. He has developed only a few words of speech. His baby crying has given way to a high-pitched whine that goes on and on. David is extremely rigid in his attitudes and has massive temper tantrums if his routine is disrupted in any way. He has great difficulty dressing himself, although he is better at taking his clothes off. Food is an issue of concern in our daily lives. David will not eat different consistencies; he is very picky and prefers crunchy foods such as chips or cereals. But as soon as the food gets soft in his mouth, he tends to spit it out.

Service Delivery Models

Currently, a growing number of parents and educators are calling for the inclusion of all students within the mainstream of regular education, including those with severe disabilities. Most children with Asperger's syndrome participate in general education classes. However, there is acute disagreement within the field as to whether students with intensive educational needs belong in general education classrooms. In fact, one of the major placement issues of the day is whether such students should be based in general or special education classrooms or in neighbourhood or special schools.

Many argue for general school placement. Others contend that children who show extreme symptoms are probably not suitable for integration. Children with severe and multiple disabilities, they say, may be at odds with a system that has few resources and little inclination to meet their needs. Some students are seen to respond better in separate settings. For students with schizophrenia, for example, it appears that a highly structured individualized program provides a feeling of safety and allows them to keep symptoms in check as much as possible.

Although the tide is flowing very strongly toward inclusion, the norm within most North American schools is still for students who are intensively challenged to be educated in separate schools or classrooms. Arguments for and cautions about the inclusion of students with pervasive developmental disorders are shown in the Debate box.

A MATTER OF DEBATE

The Inclusion of Students with Pervasive Developmental Disabilities

INCLUSIVE PRINCIPLES

Pros	Cautions
All children should be educated in neighbourhood schools within general classrooms.	Inclusion implies substantive changes in classroom structures, the conceptualization of professional roles, and a continuous need for collaboration.
With support, general education teachers can include all students.	The diversity of needs among children with PDD is too great not to offer a wide variety of service options.

Pros	Cautions
Typical students become more accepting of human differences and show less discomfort interacting with people who have disabilities.	Intense needs challenge the boundaries of practitioner knowledge and organizational supports.
	Students may take up an inordinate amount of teachers' time.
	Teachers feel that they have limited resources and are not properly trained.
	Teachers require very specialized expertise.
	Generally, the more severe the disability, the more negative the attitudes teachers have toward inclusion.

ACADEMIC

Pros	Cautions
Curriculum can be modified.	Training often emphasizes early developmental skills usually thought of as too routine or too basic to be part of a regular instructional program.
	Children's educational rights must be at the forefront; students require education that prepares them for adult independence.
	For total functioning and future needs, children need access to alternative and specialized curricula and experiences.

SOCIAL

Pros	Cautions
Inclusion provides access to social relationships in normalized learning environments.	The gap between students may be too great for interaction to occur.
Typical peers accept students with severe disabilities. Inclusion removes the stigma associated with segregated placements.	Children with disabilities do not interact with peers unless they are supported and encouraged to do so.

Sources: Diamond & Carpenter, 2000; Westling & Fox, 2000; Hunt, Soto, Maier, & Doering, 2003.

Educational Approaches

It is almost impossible to describe current educational intervention for children identified as having PDD because the symptoms and educational needs of these students vary so greatly. The commonality is in the major goals of intervention—to decrease the behavioural symptoms that interfere with an individual's functioning and promote the development of skills in language, adaptive behaviour, social interaction, self-care, and independent living.

Various conceptual models have been used in the education and training of children with pervasive developmental disorders. Three major approaches have traditionally been applied—the psychodynamic, the psycho-educational, and the behavioural approach. Behavioural models are far and away the most popular. The principles and processes of psychodynamic and psycho-educational approaches were touched upon in Chapter 7. We stress behavioural models here.

Autism Spectrum Disorders

Children identified with Asperger's will receive the general curriculum, perhaps with adaptations and modifications. (Readers are urged to return to the ideas on non-verbal learning disabilities presented in Chapter 5.)

Individuals with diagnoses that fall along the autism spectrum continue to have among the poorest of prognoses compared to other groups with disabilities, and they frequently demonstrate poor responses to intervention efforts (Simpson, 2004). With their unresponsiveness and lack of communication skills, these children are very hard to train. Few receive academic training beyond basic levels.

At the outset, curriculum reflects all areas of development. Training may begin with the sensorimotor levels. (It clearly matches the curriculum we describe in Chapter 15 for children with multiple disabilities.) Many children need to be taught a wide range of basic daily living skills such as independent eating, dressing, and using the toilet. They must also learn how to relate effectively to others through training in social interaction and communication. Some students will need help to decrease inappropriate behaviours such as severe aggression or strong and persistent ritualistic and stereotyped behaviours.

Only 50 percent of children with autism will ever develop usable language. Therefore, communication is a focus. Speech and language development is related to general prognosis; the outcome appears to depend on the child's intellectual functioning at diagnosis and communicative speech development prior to the age of six (Gillberg & Steffenberg, 1987). Unless children achieve some use of spontaneous language by age five or six, the outlook is likely to be poor, even for those with a relatively high level of non-verbal skills.

Some examples of communication interventions are behavioural methods that stimulate communication focus by reinforcing a child's utterances and demanding closer and closer approximations to real words to obtain a reinforcer (see page 507 of Chapter 15 on Mand models). The child's echolalic speech can be decreased by non-attention, and food rewards can be used to gradually shape normal speech when he or she imitates the therapist's vocalizations (Lovaas & Smith, 1988). Another communication approach relies on the simultaneous use of speech and sign language. One study (Konstantareas, 1984) found that sign and speech produced better results than speech alone, possibly because sign language relies primarily on visual and kinesthetic modalities and circumvents the auditory ones.

For other children with autism who do not have functional verbal skills, teachers may introduce the Picture Exchange Communication System (PECS). Through the PECS, children are taught to communicate with pictures and symbols, allowing them to point to the things that are important to them; eventually, the PECS may help in acquiring functional speech. We see the use of the PECS in our Case Study about David.

The behaviour of children with PDD is often problematic. Teachers are perplexed when a student with Autism Spectrum Disorder does not respond favourably to a behavioural program that works with other children. The lack of effectiveness is often not due to the teacher's failure to manage the classroom. Instead, these children cannot handle typical behaviour management programs, especially those that involve removing points or tokens or not earning a

CASE STUDY

David (continued)

As soon as David was diagnosed, we contacted a local facility for autistic children. A therapist from the centre immediately began working with David in our home on an intense ABA therapy program. When David was just five years old, he attended a special preschool on a daily basis. All the children had some form of disability and the teachers were specially trained.

With David, the staff focused on trying to develop some social interactions, basic communication and language, and self-care skills, particularly toilet training. David did learn a few gestures to communicate his needs, but his progress was slow. He is still not fully toilet trained.

Since success in the preschool setting was very limited, at school age David first went to a special school with a program and goals contiguous with those at the preschool. Through a very structured behavioural program, the teachers worked on the same areas.

To help David relate to others in the environment, the teachers continued to teach some basic communication. They also worked on social skills training with the primary goal of helping David to get in touch and be more responsive to his environment and the people in it. They also stressed the self-help skills needed for independent functioning in relation to such basic needs as food, warmth, dressing, and toileting.

When he was nine years old, David moved from the special school into a special class in his local school. We did not feel that he was ready at that time for full inclusion, but he is slowly joining his peers in the general classroom for more activities. When

included in the general classroom, the major aim is social interaction and opportunities to hear and respond to normal language. There is some nice progress in the social domain. He seems to relate far more to his peers than in the past, is more co-operative with the teachers, and his temper tantrums have virtually disappeared when he is in the general classroom.

The Picture Exchange System (PECS) was introduced to David in the last year and by the end of the semester he had made significant improvements in his use of it. He can now use "I want/need" sentences to communicate by consistently selecting the photograph of the item he wants from a choice of sixteen, and then handing the photograph to his aide. The next step is "I see" sentences and learning to put the photograph in the "All done" box after completing an activity.

Each year, the school team reviews and revises David's IEP. The most recent IEP focused on goals for the general classroom. An extract is shown below.

EXTRACT FROM DAVID' IEP

Name: David
School: John Brown
Grade: 4

Present Levels of Functioning

David has been diagnosed as autistic. No IQ levels have been estimated, but he is functioning at pre-academic levels. David is just beginning to develop language; speech is not emerging yet.

Placement

David is in a special class but there is to be increasing integration into the general classroom for social and communication purposes.

Annual Goal (General Classroom)

To increase interactions with others in the environment, develop greater awareness of environmental stimulation, and use basic communication behaviour (greeting) with peers and teachers spontaneously and when prompted, and to communicate using the PECS with the paraeducator and teachers.

Long-Range Goals

- Improve language skills through the PECS program.
- Interact and respond more with peers and adults in the immediate environment.
- Learn to recognize his name in print.
- Work on fine motor development.
- Begin to use simple speech (single words) when it is modelled for him.

- Participate in art classes with peers on a daily basis.

Objectives

- When assisted to the correct hallway, David will locate and enter the art room independently.
- When given a visual cue by the teacher, he will sit in his assigned place.
- He will make eye contact when given the instruction, "Look at me."
- David will respond to communication at the beginning of the class by waving or saying "Hi" to a peer.
- When presented with a choice of paints and a gestural cue for each option, David will select the colours he wishes to use.
- At the end of the class before clean-up, David will tap the arm of a peer at the table and will point to his own artwork to show it to the peer.
- When prompted by other students, he will look at their artwork.
- When cued, David will place the finished work in his own folder.
- David will return to his own classroom with a peer.

Children who are autistic demonstrate severe self-isolation.

reinforcer. The response from the child may be dramatic. Not earning a reinforcer can become a "life and death" issue to a child who is rigid and inflexible. Or sometimes, even when children seem to be initially obsessed with earning a reinforcer, they will suddenly loose any interest in it. They will take the token if it is offered freely, but will not work to earn it. The reason for this is unclear.

For many students with Autism Spectrum Disorders, the best management strategies involve eliminating or significantly altering triggering events. This includes enhancing predictability and carefully organizing the daily schedule. A broad range of strategies and approaches is presented in Table 14-2.

Applied Behaviour Analysis

Although very difficult to treat and teach, children categorized as autistic do respond to behaviour modification techniques. So much so that the research literature is flooded with positive reports of the use of behaviour therapy and highly structured learning procedures. A promising model that is appearing right across Canada is **applied behaviour analysis** (ABA), a form of therapy based on the principles of behavioural psychology.

applied behaviour analysis

Table 14-2 Creating accessible classrooms

Accommodations

- Structure seating arrangements carefully. Locate desk in an area that will allow the student to adjust to changes.
- Delineate work areas and free time areas—use labels, room dividers, or tape.
- Set up a "chill" area, a quiet corner with perhaps a bean bag chair.
- Provide peer buddies.
- Provide an environment with little visual and auditory stimulation.
- Provide a personal workspace free from distractions.
- Children feel anxious and frustrated when confronted with unfamiliar experiences and variations in their routine. Be consistent and keep change to a minimum.
- Be consistent in classroom routines and rules.
- Prepare students for changes in routine.
- Display class schedules pictorially.
- Children may not understand that different teachers have different expectations. Provide separate rule sheets for each teacher. Laminate and keep them in the student's folder.
- Allow chew toys and water bottles at the children's desks.
- Allow students to change classes early accompanied by another student so they will not feel crowded in the hallways.
- Set up social skills groups in which students can learn practical social skills.
- Reduce anxiety by clearly designating classroom jobs, space, and time on the computer.

Adaptations, materials

- Provide plenty of visual support; for example, display visual listings of routines, behavioural expectations, and schedules. Use many colours to identify the different parts.
- Create a locator system on a bulletin board that shows students what they will do for the day and with whom they will do it. Use pictures where possible.
- Have pictures to accompany each classroom rule.
- Use a personal daily schedule that includes photographs, symbols, words, or some combination of these to teach a variety of skills (Downing & Peckham-Hardin, 2001).

Table 14-2 continued

Adaptations, instruction

social stories

- Use **social stories**—short stories that encourage children to behave positively in social situations. These are short, simple stories written from the perspective of the student that describe individual social situations for the child, identify difficult stressors, strategies for relieving the stress, and other appropriate responses. A simple example is, "In school, we sit on the carpet. The teacher reads a story. I walk to the carpet and sit down. I will be quiet and listen to the teacher. I will not touch my friends with my hands or feet. The teacher will say, `This is a good day.'"

- Speak using whispers.

- Use priming techniques. Familiarize students with material before it is introduced in class and show how new content fits into previous knowledge.

- Allow choice.

- Encourage use of word processing for written assignments and exams.

- Provide many layers of structure. Set up routines for class activities such as writing on the board an outline of what was covered the day before, what the class will do today, and where it will lead tomorrow.

ABA is defined as "the study of behavior and the manipulation of contingencies and setting events to increase or decrease specific behaviors" (Choutka, Doloughty, & Zirkel, 2004, p. 96). The regime includes predictable routines; supportive teaching arrangements; an intensive structured program that breaks lessons down into small elements; planned transitions; and family involvement.

Within this area, it is important to be aware of the varying terminology. Intensive Behavioural Intervention (IBI) can be used interchangeably for ABA. One subset of ABA methodology is discrete trial training (DTT). A further modification of DDT is Lovaas therapy, named after O. Ivor Lovaas.

Although ABA has become exceedingly popular in the past few years, it is not a new theory but one based on decades of scientific investigations. In fact, behavioral analysis dates back to Skinner, who in 1938 found that food rewards (for animals) led to behaviour changes. The application of behavioural techniques has burgeoned since the early 1960s; a whole host of approaches blossomed under the generic banner of behaviour modification. Today's behavioural analysis and its implications have evolved into a complex and refined corpus of knowledge (Fieber & Winzer, 2006).

From the research perspective, the work of Ivor Lovaas and his colleagues at the University of California, Los Angeles (UCLA), was groundbreaking in the area of behavioral intervention for autistic children. Lovaas (1987) published a study in which a group of 19 children received intensive behavioural treatment (40 hours per week, one-to-one). He reported that 47 percent of the sample achieved "normal intellectual and educational functioning." Then McEachin, Smith, and Lovaas (1993) published their research (a follow-up of the original Lovaas study) and documented remarkable gains in children with autism who received intensive behavioural treatment. Green (1991) wrote that no other treatment for autism offers comparable proof of effectiveness and that "there is abundant scientific evidence that Applied Behavioral Analysis . . . can produce comprehensive and lasting improvements in many important skill areas for most people with autism, regardless of their age" (p. 29). In concert, Smith (1999) noted that "strong evidence exists for the efficacy of behavior analytic approaches in ameliorating a wide range of problems displayed by children with autism" (p. 36).

The ABA program is intense—six or more hours a day. This type of immersion is essential because learning to clap, wave, or point can require hundreds of repetitions for a child with autism. Success is mediated by four variables. These are the age when treatment begins, the quantity of the therapy, the quality of therapy, and the intellectual potential of the child—whether, for instance, autism is coupled with intellectual disability.

The earlier treatments begin, the better the chances that a child will attain normal functioning levels. Numerous studies that have examined the effectiveness of early intervention programs for children with autism report positive outcome (e.g., Dawson & Osterling, 1997; McGee, Morrier, & Daly, 1999).

ABA has had several effects. First, in both Canada and the United States, increases in autism and the promises of ABA have led to mounting litigation by parents (see Nelson & Huefner, 2003). Second, the mounting optimism engendered by the approach has persuaded many schools and parents to opt for general classroom placement for children with Autism Spectrum Disorders as long as a paraeducator is in place (Fieber & Winzer, 2006).

Childhood Schizophrenia

There are a number of primary goals in the treatment of psychoses. These include regimes to decrease anxiety and its sources; ways to improve personal interaction skills; learning to find appropriate channels for affective expression; building of self-esteem and a sense of self; and learning adaptive mechanisms for dealing with stress.

The treatment for childhood schizophrenia needs to be multi-modal and should possibly include pharmacotherapeutics, family interventions, cognitive therapy, and environmental interventions. It is now clear that the longer psychosis continues untreated the worse the eventual long-term prognosis becomes, so early intervention is important (Birchwood, McGorry & Jackson, 1997).

SUMMARY

1. Different types of conditions, including childhood schizophrenia, Autism Spectrum Disorders, and severe and profound intellectual disabilities are found under the pervasive developmental disabilities umbrella. Many children display severe qualitative subnormalities that are not normal for any stage of development. However, individuals with PDD display unique combinations of symptoms with differing degrees of severity.

2. Children who are autistic present a shifting array of behaviours that seems to defy analysis. Autism reveals itself in fleeting eye contact, failure to form attachments, disrupted relationships, difficulty developing language skills, and stereotyped patterns of behaviour such as obsessive object spinning or light filtering. People with Asperger's syndrome are most clearly defined by social deficits. Childhood schizophrenia is variously characterized by qualitative changes in functioning, such as association disturbances, delusions, hallucinations, attention deficits, and inappropriate social interaction. In most cases, the first

symptoms are observed in people ranging from ages fifteen to forty-five, so schizophrenia is more common during adolescence.

3. Autism Spectrum Disorders can no longer be seen as a low-incidence disability; the conditions occur with far greater frequency than ever considered imaginable. The rate of about 1 in 10 000 from 20 years ago has mutated to suggest that as many as 1 in 150 children aged ten or younger may be affected. Certainly, rising prevalence rates point to broader definitions of the disorder, improved diagnostic techniques, and growing public awareness. Nevertheless, some epidemiologists see a real increase in absolute numbers.

4. The etiology of pervasive developmental disorders is a broadly researched area. It is also widely disputed. Even after intense research efforts, the etiology of childhood psychoses and ASD remains vague, the symptoms severe and complex, the diagnosis difficult, the treatments unclear, and the prognosis uncertain at best.

5. The preferred mode to assess children with pervasive developmental disorders is functional assessment. This is a method for identifying the variables that reliably predict and maintain problem behaviour. The focus is on environmental events and intervention that brings changes in the environment.

6. Children with pervasive developmental disorders pose a variety of complex management problems. Certainly, there have been successes, but they are not universally applicable and at present no one treatment method has proven notably effective with the entire group of children.

7. Although the theme of intervention remains relatively pessimistic, one promising and tantalizing approach has emerged. Most children respond best to structured behavioural techniques such as applied behaviour analysis (ABA), which has consistently achieved the most significant results in children with autism.

8. Controversy surrounds the placement of children with significant disabilities in general classrooms. Today students are found in a range of settings, with inclusion in general classrooms becoming much more common.

HISTORICAL NOTES

It was not until the closing decades of the 19th century that the psychotic child became an object of study. Psychiatrists and others initiated careful efforts to observe, describe, and classify the disordered behaviours demonstrated by child patients, and collected and organized the existing material in monographs on psychic disorders, mental diseases, and insanity in children. By 1900, there was an assortment of data demonstrating that children displayed psychotic disorders (see Winzer, 1993).

In 1906, Sante de Sanctis named the psychotic problems observed in youngsters *dementia praecoxissima* (dementia of childhood). Then in 1911, Eugen Blueler, a Swiss psychiatrist, renamed dementia praecox as *schizophrenia*. The work of de Sanctis and others contributed to the identification of a distinct condition known as childhood schizophrenia. By 1935 schizophrenia in children was well documented and distinguished, although not clearly, from the adult condition.

Credit for first identifying autistic behaviours in children and adults also goes to Eugen Blueler, who isolated specific non-verbal and non-relating behaviours in 1906. Blueler used the word *autistic* as an adjective. It was not until 1943 that Leo Kanner, a psychiatrist at Johns Hopkins University in Baltimore, identified an autistic syndrome and used *autism* as a noun.

One year later, Hans Asperger, a Viennese pediatrician, published "Die 'Autistischen Psychopathen' im Kindesalter." But Asperger's keen insights languished in Europe's postwar turmoil. Although his syndrome eventually became a popular research topic in Europe, it was not until 1981 that British psychiatrist Lorna Wing reintroduced Asperger's findings. In 1994, DSM IV acknowledged Asperger's syndrome.

In his 1943 work, Kanner described a number of symptoms that he found among a group of 11 children. In particular, he stressed the subjects' profound withdrawal from human contact and their obsessive desire for sameness in the environment. Kanner also identified similarities in the families of the 11 children. He found the parents to be highly intelligent and unusually high achievers, but also emotionally cold, aloof, and reserved in their interactions with their children.

Kanner himself did not reject biological factors as contributive causes of autism. However, the researchers who followed him chose to focus almost exclusively on psychogenic properties. They speculated that lack of adequate parenting was the primary factor in the onset of autism. Infants with autism were seen as withdrawing into isolation to escape a hostile world, deeply lacking in warmth, love, and nurturance.

Bruno Bettelheim, who established the Sonja Shankman Orthogenic School for severely emotionally disturbed children in 1944, adopted this line of thought. He interpreted autistic behaviour as a defence against a world perceived as hostile and rejecting. Bettelheim argued that children become autistic when their parents reject them or fail to respond to their attempts to influence their environment. Because children feel unable to exert any control over the external world, they withdraw into a private fantasy world and try to impose some order and consistency through an obsessive insistence on sameness. Bettelheim used the term "refrigerator mother" to characterize the mothers of autistic children. An even more devastating term, "the schizophregenic mother" laid direct responsibility for the child's condition on the mother's failure to provide love and nurturance.

Although researchers tended to agree that parents created a climate that encouraged autism, few attributed the condition exclusively to parental behaviour. Bettelheim did not deny the possibility that genetic or organic causes might also contribute to autism. Both Kanner and Asperger spoke to genetic footprints.

During the 1970s, environmental theories were largely abandoned as emerging evidence indicated that children from emotionally deprived settings were not at higher risk for autism and that mothers of children with autism also had non-disabled offspring. With little to support environmental theories, autism emerged as an ideal candidate for biological study. Researchers turned their attention to investigating a range of biochemical, sensorimotor, neurological, and cognitive defects.

Today the evidence for biological causes is widely accepted. At the outset, the recognition of psychoses in children and the formulation of methods for identification, diagnosis, and intervention were largely the bailiwick of psychiatrists and psychologists, not the school system. The behaviour of children with psychoses and autism placed them in the category of the uneducable. Well into the 20th century, such children were excluded from public school classes and often not accepted into residential settings.

It was not until the 1950s that services for disturbed children and youth really emerged. The preferred treatment was psychiatric in nature, based on the development of a therapeutic relationship between therapist and child. Institutionalization was the common mode, as many psychiatrists and other professionals believed that children who were autistic and psychotic could most effectively be treated away from their homes. (See also the Historical Notes in Chapter 7.)

In the 1960s, interest in returning many institutionalized children to the community mounted, and education began to assume responsibility for children with serious disturbances. For example, children with autism were integrated into classes in Toronto as early as 1956 (Lovatt, 1962). By the 1970s, the education of children with developmental disorders was firmly entrenched in the school system, and professionals began to encourage parents to keep their children at home. Today, some children with severe developmental disabilities are taught in special day schools or residential settings, but increasing numbers are attending classes in their neighbourhood schools.

CHAPTER 15

CHILDREN WITH SEVERE AND MULTIPLE DISABILITIES

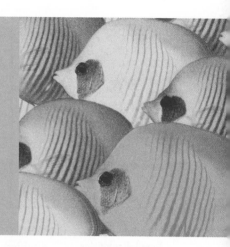

INTRODUCTION

Pervasive developmental disorders, as we discussed in the previous chapter, are complex and challenging conditions that affect every aspect of an individual's development. Subsumed within the broad category of *pervasive developmental disorders* are children with **severe and profound disabilities**. The term applies to those school-aged students who function intellectually within the lowest 1 percent of their particular age groups or have delays of two or three standard deviations in two or more areas of development (TASH, 1986). Many, if not most, of these students are also multiply disabled. Children with **multiple disabilities** show evidence of independent and interdependent deficits in two or more areas of functioning.

With definitions so broad, and people with severe or multiple disabilities such an extremely heterogeneous population, we cannot paint any general portrait of students with severe and multiple disabilities. The critical factor to note is that the more severe the disabilities, the more unique the child.

Children's development is integrated and organized across the various developmental domains—cognitive, language, physical, social, and emotional. With multiple disabilities, we cannot look at the impact of a single disability in isolation, but must instead realize that the interaction of disabilities results in the appearance of unique developmental and behavioural patterns. The conditions are not additive but cumulative and present a completely unique condition that may affect all the mind/body systems in different ways and to different degrees. For example, a deaf child with severe intellectual disabilities may have independent deficits in cognitive functioning, producing language, understanding language, and social interaction, as well as deficits resulting from a combination of these individual impairments.

Second, innumerable combinations of impairments are possible, although some appear more often than others, and some are more difficult to cope with. Individuals may suffer multisensory impairments such as deaf-blindness, or

**severe and pro-
found disabilities**

multiple disabilities

they may have conditions that combine sensory disorders with physical, neuro-logical, or mental disabilities. Impairments of vision or hearing occur much more frequently among children with multiple disabilities than among other children. It has been estimated that 1 in 5 can be expected to have impaired hear-ing and 2 in 5 impaired vision (Orelove & Sobsey, 1987).

Students with severe and multiple disabilities present a range of special educational and psychosocial needs. Because of their complex conditions, these children require the services of many disciplines, most importantly education, psychology, physiotherapy, occupational therapy, speech pathology, audiology, and medicine. As a result, a multidisciplinary approach to their treatment and education is essential. We can see this with Juanita, the child discussed in the Case Study below.

Many of the children we have met already in this text could be considered multiply disabled. For example, we encountered children with severe and profound intellectual disabilities in Chapter 6. Other instances are a child with Down syndrome who has a speech

CASE STUDY

Juanita

Juanita's mother had a difficult first pregnancy. The baby was born early after a contracted and arduous labour. Even though the mother was afraid that the child would suffer some adverse effects, she was stunned and frightened to soon find that the infant seemed to have a host of as-yet-unspecified develop-mental problems.

Consistent medical monitoring and assessment throughout the infant months confirmed the pres-ence of severe difficulties and it was soon found that Juanita had serious visual and hearing difficulties, probably joined to mental retardation. Although early assessments indicated that she was not totally deaf or completely blind, physicians could not pre-dict her future mental ability, the amount of resid-ual hearing or vision, or her functional potential with sight and hearing.

By the time she was a year old, further assess-ment found that Juanita had quite a lot of usable vision, although her hearing loss was in the severe to profound range. Both amplification and glasses were prescribed—not that Juanita took kindly to either the hearing aid or the glasses. Despite the intensity of

her disabilities, she had a mind of her own, and it took many months of perseverance on the part of her mother and many types of primary reinforcers before she would tolerate either appliance.

A home-visiting teacher came to the home to show the mother a range of activities to stimulate Juanita's mobility, communication, and interper-sonal interactions. The teacher demonstrated rein-forcement schedules to reinforce Juanita's use of the hearing aid and glasses.

At three years of age, Juanita began attending a local preschool class on a part-time basis. When she was ready for school, her mother enrolled her in the neighbourhood school, which had a special class for children with severe and multiple disabilities. For the first little while, Juanita remained in her special class, but soon the teacher worked to inte-grate her into a general classroom for increasingly longer periods of the day. The teacher facilitated a Circle of Friends to assist Juanita's integration and worked co-operatively with the classroom teacher on planning specific activities that Juanita could accomplish in a small-group setting.

disability, a youngster who is deaf and also emotionally disturbed, a child who is cerebral palsied with language disorders, and a child who is profoundly retarded and has autism.

These brief descriptions imply that multiple disabilities are usually severe disabilities. Often, they are. But do remember that few disabilities appear in any pure form, and children can suffer from combinations of minor disabilities that can be devastating to their learning and behaviour. In this chapter, however, our focus is on children with severe and profound disabilities and debilitating multiple impairments.

DEFINITIONS OF SEVERE AND MULTIPLE DISABILITIES

Terminology and definitions in this field are difficult and confusing. Together with the overarching *pervasive developmental disorders* and the somewhat more specific *severe and profound disabilities*, other descriptors are used. These include autistic or psychotic (see Chapter 14); physically disabled; multiply disabled; dual sensory impaired; deaf-blind; dependent multiply handicapped; and moderately, severely, or profoundly mentally retarded.

The significant and complex nature of severe and multiple disabilities means that the differences among students are far greater than the similarities. It also means that the formulation of precise definitions is a complex and virtually impossible task. With the heterogeneous nature of the population and the combinations of disabilities, we would have not one but dozens of definitions.

To overcome the problem, broad and encompassing generic definitions that attempt to include the entire range of possible combinations of conditions have evolved. Adding to the definition of severe disabilities presented in the chapter introduction is the definition from the American IDEA (1990). In this definition, *students with severe handicaps* are generically defined as

> those who may possess severe language and/or perceptual/cognitive deprivations, and evidence abnormal behaviour such as failure to respond to pronounced social stimuli; self-mutilation; self-stimulation; manifestation of intense and prolonged temper tantrums; and the absence of rudimentary forms of verbal contact. Students also have extremely fragile physiological conditions. (U.S. Federal definition 20 USC 1401(7))

The generic category of multiple disabilities is also found under the IDEA. It refers to

> a combination of impairments (such as mental retardation-blindness, or mental retardation-physical disabilities) that causes such severe educational problems that the child cannot be accommodated in a special education program solely for one of the impairments. The term does not include deaf-blindness.

Put together, the two definitions include children who are severely and profoundly retarded; deaf-blind; mentally retarded and deaf-blind; physically disabled; and severely emotionally disturbed. They focus on the combinations of problems possibly present as well as the range of interventions and allied disciplines necessary if children are to achieve their potential.

Criticisms of generic definitions abound, specifically because these definitions tend to use very broad parameters that may obscure the effects of particular disabilities, making it harder to clinically interpret the needs of an individual child. Moreover, generic definitions do not lead to precise programming. For example, children with visual or hearing impairments who are enrolled in generic programs do not have access to specialist services, such as orientation and mobility training, low-vision services, or communication training.

Critics argue that more appropriate definitions could be generic but worded in terms of children's behaviours and needs. When individuals who are severely or multiply disabled are defined by their service needs, they are people "who require ongoing support in several major life areas in order to participate in the mainstream of community life and who are expected to require such support throughout life" (Bellamy, 1985, p. 6).

Some educators avoid generic definitions altogether, preferring more specificity for particular broad groupings of individuals who are severely or multiply disabled. They use **multisensory impaired** to describe children with sight and hearing handicaps. Included here are children who may also be developmentally delayed or have neurological impairments. **Multiple dependent handicapped** refers to children who are severely mentally disabled and who also have sensory and/or other physical handicaps (see Orelove & Sobsey, 1987). *Multiply disabled* includes "those children who are so limited that they cannot develop a normal language system, nor can they provide adequately for their own survival needs" (Erin, Daugherty, Dignen, & Pearson, 1990, p. 16).

Dual sensory impairment refers to deaf-blind children—those whose disabilities are a complex of auditory, visual, communication, and language factors, often accompanied by other conditions that interfere with their learning. An individual who is deaf-blind is described under the IDEA (1990) as having

> a combination of hearing and visual impairments causing such severe communication, developmental, and educational problems that the child cannot be accommodated in either a program specifically for the deaf or a program specifically for the blind.

Under this definition, children who are deaf-blind suffer impairments in both vision and hearing, and will not have their needs met if they are placed in special education programs for students who are only deaf or only visually impaired, because children who are deaf-blind suffer deficits in both modalities. Programs for students who are deaf rely heavily on the use of vision, while instruction for students with visual impairment depends on auditory instruction. For many deaf-blind children, the sensory impairments also coexist with other challenging cognitive, physical, health, and behavioural characteristics.

multisensory impaired

multiple dependent handicapped

dual sensory impairment

CLASSIFICATION OF SEVERE AND MULTIPLE DISABILITIES

As we just explained, the complexity and variety of severe and multiple disabilities has spawned a number of definitions and descriptions. The heterogeneous population also means that classification systems and service delivery are beset with confusion. Generally, services have been administered on the basis of labels and discrete categories, and this tendency has resulted in the creation of a number of overlapping classification systems (see Table 13-1 on page 424).

The most common way to classify multiple disabilities is in primary and secondary terms. The major condition that causes a child to differ in learning or behaviour is referred to as the *primary disability*; other conditions that arise or are present are known as *secondary disabilities*. A child who is both visually impaired and intellectual disabled may be judged to suffer visual disabilities as the primary disabling condition, with intellectual disability being the secondary disability.

Approaches that focus on presumed primary and secondary disabilities have their own built-in set of problems. For one thing, many children have more than one set of pertinent characteristics, and the primary disability is often impossible to identify. Children who are both blind and retarded, for example, may be visually inattentive because they do not see or because they are intellectually unaware of the visual environment.

For another thing, and perhaps more importantly, viewing multiple disabilities as primary and secondary overlooks the cumulative nature of the conditions. Children cannot be appropriately classified under the category of a single impairment, because the combination of conditions creates an entirely new disability that requires access to special services for all the child's impairments, whether sensory, physical, mental, or behavioural. Children who suffer from visual impairments as well as intellectual disabilities, for example, cannot be appropriately accommodated in programs for mentally disabled children who don't have sight problems.

Sometimes children are classified and counted according to the agency that serves them. This also leads to problems, as the same child may be identified within the service delivery system of a number of agencies. Sometimes, too, children are simply classified by the type of educational program they attend.

PREVALENCE OF SEVERE AND MULTIPLE DISABILITIES

Estimating the true incidence and prevalence of almost any disability is an onerous, if not impossible, task. In the case of severe and multiple disabilities, a number of factors combine to hamper prevalence estimates. Difficulties arise because:

- Interpretations of the definition of certain populations have changed dramatically. For example, the number of persons with deaf-blindness has not increased substantially since 1974. Today, however, individuals categorized as deaf-blind can represent those with moderate to profound auditory and visual impairments with or without other educationally disabling conditions, who need services to increase independence; those with central processing problems that result in cortical blindness or central auditory dysfunctions; or those with progressive sensory impairments such as Usher's syndrome (Michael & Paul, 1991).

- As we mentioned earlier, children with combined disabilities may be registered for services with a variety of agencies, meaning that the same child might be identified within the service delivery systems of any of these agencies.

- Probably the greatest difficulty in obtaining prevalence figures arises when children are counted in terms of their primary disability. In some school districts, children who are severely or multiply disabled may be entered into classes designed for intellectually disabled, hearing-impaired, or visually impaired children, and are then defined and counted only by what is presumed to be the primary disability.

The prevalence rates are extremely low. Children with severe and multiple disabilities form less than 2 percent of the population of any given chronological age.

ETIOLOGY OF SEVERE AND MULTIPLE DISABILITIES

The major causes of childhood disabilities that we have outlined throughout this text are also causes of multiple disabilities in children. In fact, with the exception of rubella, the etiology of multiple disabilities almost parallels that of physical impairments. This is especially true for central nervous system damage that results in severe motor impairment.

In the past, rubella was the culprit in many childhood conditions. At its most devastating, rubella caused deaf-blindness and severe multiple disabilities. Today, rubella is well controlled. Chromosomal and genetic disorders account for only a tiny number of multiple disabilities. When they do appear, children often have complex disorders affecting several different body systems.

Injuries to the central nervous system account for significant numbers of multiple disabilities. Neurological impairments result from damage or dysfunction of the brain and/or the spinal cord incurred before, during, or after birth. Other nervous system disorders resulting in multiple disabilities stem from trauma, accident, or child abuse. Hydrocephalus is frequently associated; if treatment is unsuccessful or only partly successful, the child may have damage to the optic nerve as well as motor impairments.

New medical technology, intensive care nurseries, and lifesaving techniques are saving many infants who would have perished just a few years ago. Children who are premature, especially those with a birth weight of less than 1500 grams, are particularly vulnerable to insults of the central nervous system (see Chapter 3).

Meningitis contracted immediately after birth is a major cause of multiple disabilities. Fifty percent of infants who survive the disease suffer significant neurological impairments that include cerebral palsy, hydrocephalus, convulsive disorders, and hearing and visual handicaps (Fenichel, 1980).

The most commonly reported causes of deaf-blindness are multiple congenital anomalies such as Charge syndrome, Fetal Alcohol Syndrome, and hydrocephaly. Post-natal etiologies include asphyxia, encephalitis, head injury, stroke, and meningitis. Note, too, that the complexity of the disabilities seems to be on the rise. For example, deaf-blind children today have even more serious medical complications than those with the congenital rubella syndrome.

Syndromes

Usher's syndrome

Usher's syndrome, a condition of familial nerve deafness associated with pigment degeneration of the retina, is the most common etiology of deaf-blindness. The condition is transmitted through an autosomal recessive trait. The child is born deaf and gradually loses sight due to retinitis pigmentosa (RP). There is a high degree of variability in age of onset, severity, and speed of progression of the RP, but it is most often diagnosed in the early teen years (Miner, 1995).

Usher's syndrome accounts for more than half of the deaf-blindness found in adults. The incidence in the general population is no greater than 1 in 15 000 to 30 000 births. However, it accounts for 3 to 6 percent of all the profound prelingually deaf population, almost always born to hearing parents (Miller, 1985; Miner, 1995).

Briefly, there are three types of Usher's syndrome. The most severe—Type I—affects 90 percent of the Usher's population. These people have profound hearing loss with a gradual onset of RP. People with Type II have a mild to severe hearing impairment. Type III people have mild hearing impairment and a slow onset of visual disability.

Not all individuals who are genetically deaf-blind suffer from Usher's syndrome. As single conditions, deafness and blindness may be caused by different genes or infections. There are also other syndromes, such as Refsum's syndrome, Hallgren syndrome, and Laurence-Moon, that involve both deafness and visual impairment; however, additional pathologies such as obesity, retardation, diabetes, or scaly skin clearly distinguish these from Usher's. Other syndromes that may lead to deaf-blindness include rare hereditary syndromes such as Zellweger syndrome or Wolfram syndrome. Chromosomal anomalies such as Down syndrome and Trisomy 13 are also implicated.

DEVELOPMENTAL CONSEQUENCES OF SEVERE AND MULTIPLE DISABILITIES

As we have stressed, the variety and combinations of disorders presented by children who are severely or multiply disabled make generalizations about developmental consequences virtually impossible. These students may have orthopedic or health impairments, or hearing or speech disabilities. They may use unconventional behaviour to communicate a basic need or they may exhibit a combination of behaviours (Jones & Carlier, 1995).

Physical Development

Many domains of learning depend upon a child's ability to interact with the environment. During the period when typical children are developing most rapidly, multiple deficits prevent children with severe and multiple disabilities from interacting with the environment in ways that are critical for the subsequent development of social, motor, cognitive, and communication skills. As a result, many children with severe or multiple disabilities are very late in reaching developmental milestones. Walking, using first words, and toilet training may be quite delayed. In some children, they never emerge. This renders children doubly limited—by their delayed physical development and by their restricted ability to engage with the environment in ways that can stimulate development.

Students who are deaf-blind are particularly disadvantaged. Deprivation in one distance sense tends to increase reliance on the other. A lack in the senses of both vision and hearing place reliance on the near senses of taste, touch, and smell. Children who are deaf and blind therefore have an infinitely more complex task in gaining information about their environments.

Cognitive Development

Poor cognitive development characterizes students with severe and profound disabilities. Indeed, severe disabilities involving mental retardation imply, by definition, a low level of cognitive functioning. While depressed cognitive development is not a necessary concomitant of other multiple disabilities, these disabilities can be so severe that many children function in very low ranges. For example, although 94 percent of children who are deaf-blind have some usable vision and hearing, many of these children function in the severe to profound ranges of mental retardation as a result of their inability to perform basic skills (Chen & Haney, 1995).

Communication

For most children, the ready acquisition of their culture's language and speech is a natural part of early maturation. But for young children with disabilities, learning to communicate is not a simple or naturally occurring task. Communication demands so much of the human organism that language learning is vulnerable to all the problems that can and do affect children. Almost invariably, those with severe or multiple disabilities display serious developmental lags in speech and language.

Children lacking efficient communication are often divided into two groups. The first group, *presymbolic children*, do not use signs, words, or pictures for communication. They may not possess a recognizable communication system or may use gestures such as pointing, touching, or moving objects. The second group is made up of *minimally*

Students with multiple disabilities usually have a range of special educational and psychological needs.

symbolic children whose communication efforts may consist of intentional but idiosyncratic and non-conventional patterns such as reaching and leading.

Persons who are deaf-blind are diverse in their communication abilities. Some students retain some residual vision and hearing and can use speech. Some are non-verbal and rely on touch and gestures; still others combine the use of signs, speech, and gestures. Many children, however, find it very difficult to acquire the complex symbol system of language without enough sensory data to make language meaningful. They appear to have no awareness of linguistic symbols and may communicate only through body movements (Engleman, Griffin, Griffin, & Maddox, 1999).

Academic Achievement

The learning and educational attainments of children who are severely or multiply disabled depend upon a matrix of factors. Not the least of these are the quality of education, the age at which education begins, the age of onset of the conditions, the nature of the combination of disabilities, and the severity of each condition. Also important are factors such as the family's response to the child, the educational setting, the amount of integration with typical peers, the related services available for both the child and the family, and the amount of acceptance by the community.

By definition, children with severe disabilities are cognitively disabled and will require specialized services and modified curricula. Some children who are multiply disabled achieve well in school. But for most, the attainment and mastery of basic skills is tentative. Many children with severe and multiple disabilities function at pre-academic levels so that the academic competencies of general education are not within their purview. The needs of these students extend beyond but below the normal developmental curriculum.

Behaviour

Problem behaviours are the rule rather than the exception in the population of individuals with severe disorders. Stereotypic behaviours such as light gazing or hand flapping are prominent. Together with self-stimulation, we see self-injury, estimated to occur in about 8 to 19 percent of persons who are severely or profoundly retarded (Gedye, 1989). Behaviours include head banging, hair pulling, hand mouthing or biting, scratching, hitting parts of the body, face slapping, self-choking, kicking, and pinching. There are also aggressive acts, non-compliance, and other socially inappropriate behaviours that include frequent panic reactions, hyperkinesis, autism, withdrawal, frequent tantrums, and pica.

Pica is a recognized eating disorder and one of the most frequently observed eating dysfunctions among people with severe mental retardation. With pica, persons develop a pathological craving for abnormal food or substances not commonly regarded as food. Consuming non-edibles is a health problem that can be life threatening. It can result in such things as lead poisoning, intestinal blockages, and surgery to remove objects from the stomach.

In many cases the cause of problem behaviours is unknown. Some behaviours seem related to the type of brain damage a child has sustained; in other cases, behaviours may reflect the intense frustration caused by a child's inability to communicate. At other times, a student may engage in self-injury in order to escape an aversive task. When this happens, and the task is terminated in response to the injurious behaviour, the student is negatively reinforced and then likely to exhibit the behaviour when the activity or task is again presented (Evans & Stough, 2002).

Social and Emotional Development

The onset of attachment behaviours and social interactions may be very delayed from the very beginning of life. For one thing, a child's physical and behavioural deficits can disrupt the natural interchange between caregiver and child that is essential to early interactions. For another, the baby's first months may be dominated by periods of hospitalization, feeding problems, and an inability to maintain a wakeful state.

Play Behaviours

The play of children with severe and multiple disabilities is often limited. Sensory, motor, and language deficits restrict the normal progression, and the natural development that occurs, in play. Children who are deaf-blind characteristically display withdrawal and self-stimulating behaviours and rarely initiate social interactions or activities that are considered as part of play.

ASSESSMENT OF CHILDREN WHO HAVE SEVERE AND MULTIPLE DISABILITIES

Whether diagnosis is medical or psycho-educational, the assessment of children with severe or multiple disabilities taxes the ingenuity of clinicians. Because data generation is so difficult, a diverse range of measures is used. All tools and procedures attempt to assess a child's disabilities, the impact of the combination of disabilities, the possible etiology, the prognosis, and the strengths a child possesses.

Assessment of Hearing

It is often difficult to distinguish whether children fail to respond to an auditory stimulus because they do not hear it or because they are simply inattentive. This is particularly true of children with multiple disabilities, who require a wide range of sophisticated techniques for the assessment of auditory status. For these children, audiological assessment is divided into two major methods—electrophysiological and behavioural.

Electrophysiological procedures include electroencephalography-evoked (EEG) response audiometry (also known as *auditory brainstem evoked response*) and impedance audiometry. EEG assessment measures responses to auditory stimuli but requires no active participation on the part of the child. Electrodes are attached to the scalp and sounds of varying intensities are delivered through an earphone placed over the infant's ear. By evaluating the infant's brainwave patterns, an estimate of hearing, or hearing loss, can be made. Note that although these tests help to detect whether a child in fact hears sound, they do not provide information about the child's ability to interpret the auditory stimuli.

Acoustic *impedance audiometry* assesses conductive hearing losses by measuring the movement of the eardrum and middle ear muscles and bones in response to auditory stimulation. The audiologist can detect fluid in the middle ear, a sign of otitis media, for example.

Behavioural testing includes observation of behaviour, reflex audiometry, and play audiometry. Observations focus on the orienting responses infants show when they turn their heads toward the source of a sound. Diagnosticians can gain a crude measure of hearing status by observing infants' reactions to loud sounds.

When they are under the age of five or six months, infants also display reflexive behaviours that are useful for testing hearing (*reflex audiometry*). A startle movement, a reflex that affects face, arms, trunk, legs, and eyes, is present at birth and elicited by loud sound.

Play audiometry is used with children over two years of age who can understand the process. It involves an audiometer and a game in which the child performs an activity in response to the sound. The child may respond by building a stacking toy, dropping blocks into a box, or putting pieces into a puzzle.

Assessment of Vision

Determining whether a child with multiple disabilities has usable vision employs a number of procedures, particularly when children have neurological impairments and seem unable to establish normal visual contacts. A child who does not respond to conventional testing may be a candidate for several physiological tests that are administered by qualified clinical or medical personnel. Diagnosticians use electrophysiological procedures, behavioural measures, and functional tests.

Electrodiagnostic procedures assess the electrical activity of the optic pathway and occipital cortex of the brain. The presence of electrical activity indicates that an active pathway exists. Behavioural measures include field tests that use gross objects or lights. The Bailey-Hall Cereal Test for Visual Acuity (Bailey & Hall, 1983), for example, is a behavioural technique that uses picture cards including one of cereal; if the child selects the correct picture, he or she is rewarded with praise and a piece of cereal.

Functional tests assess the visual behaviour of an individual rather than just the physiological condition of the eyes. Things that are assessed are the ability to track objects, use visual fields, develop eye-hand coordination, and perform other functions that reflect visual development.

Psycho-educational Assessment

With their obvious disabilities, most students who have severe and multiple problems are not screened; assessment begins with diagnostic testing. Assessment is never a one-time affair; administration is on a regular basis, usually once or twice a year.

The psycho-educational assessment of children who are severely or multiply disabled has a number of separate but equally important goals, which include measurement of the overall level of intellectual function and exploration of the individual child's impairments and abilities. Assessment data are used to decide on the most appropriate educational placement and formulate an individual educational plan.

Assessing of children who are severely or multiply disabled is an arduous and challenging task requiring skilled practitioners, input from care providers, and many hours of observation and testing. Children may show limited or absent expressive and/or receptive language, limited hand use, and severe cognitive delays. Children are likely to withdraw from social interaction and have short attention spans and limited co-operation in testing situations. They may perform certain behaviours in one milieu but not during testing, and may perform tasks for a known person but not an unknown tester.

Diagnosticians need to first arrange the setting in order to enhance the assessment situation for both the child and the tester. Some environmental adaptations (which add to the procedural adaptations discussed in Chapter 13) are listed below.

- A natural environment is critical. Psychological and educational assessments of children with severe or multiple disabilities are best made in familiar surroundings using familiar tasks and materials.

- The foundation of an accurate and appropriate assessment is the establishment of rapport with the child and the family. During the assessment process, parents serve to enhance a child's feeling of security and as primary sources of information.

- No single assessment tool or procedure can meet all the needs of a population as diverse as that of children with severe or multiple disabilities. Specific instruments, administration, and procedures should vary according to the needs of the individual and the areas being assessed. However, many of the tasks that are used in tests must be eliminated because of motor difficulties, sensory impairments, and special problems present in the children being assessed.

Formal intelligence tests may be administered. However, for children with multiple disabilities, standardized assessment procedures are especially problematic and often yield information that is both inaccurate and biased (see Nelson, van Dijk, McDonnell, & Thompson, 2002).

When they do attempt to assess mental ability, diagnosticians usually select scales of infant development because the sensorimotor behaviours tapped are often in the repertoires of these children. Although infant scales are known to be poor predictors of later development in typical children, these measures with children who are severely disabled give IQs that have proven to be good predictors of later development (Fewell & Cone, 1983). Perhaps the most widely used test of cognition for children functioning in the sensorimotor period is the Ugiris and Hunt Scale of Infant Psychological Development or its adaptations (Dunst, 1980).

Equally important, if not more so, is the assessment of a child's functional skills and needs. That is, skills that are relevant to the child and family, and that occur in natural environments. Assessors use functional approaches that can include a combination of direct observation; informant interviews; adaptive behaviour scales; measures of prelinguistic communication behaviour and alternate methods of communication; and observational checklists.

Direct observation is a primary procedure because it permits assessment of a child's behaviour and achievements throughout a normal daily routine. For example, **activity-based assessment** measures the use of functional skills within the context of child-initiated, planned, and routine activities. It uses tools such as Transdiciplinary Play Based Assessment (Linder, 1993) and Assessment, Evaluation, and Programming System for Children (Bricker, 1993). **Arena testing** is an observational assessment approach in which people from several

activity-based assessment

arena testing

disciplines focus on their particular domains, such as motor skills or language, within the context of play. Arena assessment occurs at one point in time. In contrast, **collaborative ongoing assessment** follows a child through a day's activities.

collaborative ongoing assessment

A number of questionnaires and interview schedules have been constructed for use with parents, teachers, and other key informants who can provide important information about aspects of a child's progress. Parent interviews are strong indicators of a child's level of skills and awareness.

Language and communication assessment is critical. As we have stressed, many children are either prelinguistic or minimally linguistic: they meet problems in responding to interactions, imitating, and using basic communication. Informal language assessment focuses on three prelinguistic communication behaviours. First, it attempts to determine a child's understanding of sounds and gestures by observing his or her response to environmental sounds, speech sounds, and gestures, names, and requests. Second is communication use—how a child gains the attention of others; how he or she initiates play with caregivers and peers; whether the child anticipates and takes turns; and how the child interacts in routine communication events. Examiners also note the settings, people, and purposes for communication. These are assessed by looking at the reasons the child has to communicate, the objects and activities that he or she prefers, and when and with whom the most appropriate interactions occur.

Educational assessment focuses on functional areas of competence in the domains of communication, social behaviour, self-help, and independence skills. For some children, educational assessment also measures areas of academic competence, such as reading, writing, and mathematics.

INTERVENTION WITH CHILDREN WHO HAVE SEVERE AND MULTIPLE DISABILITIES

In the past, persons with severe and multiple disabilities were excluded from educational services. Over the last 40 years, education and treatment for this population has undergone considerable revision and expansion.

Treatment generally hinges on two major factors: etiology and the specific combination of disabilities. Although etiology is of less overall significance for educators, critical program modifications must be made for such secondary spinoffs as sensory problems and the psychological adjustments precipitated by conditions such as Usher's syndrome.

Medical Intervention

A medical examination is a routine part of the diagnostic process and is undertaken with the child who is severely or multiply disabled as early as possible. Procedures are used to determine the exact nature and sometimes the underlying causes of the disabilities.

Therapy

Physical and occupational therapists can help children to develop hand skills, body coordination, and other physical skills, and aid in gross motor development, muscle relaxation, and fine motor control. Speech and language therapy not only assists a child's development of speech and language but may also be used with children who have difficulty in controlling the fine motor muscles needed for eating. Therapists may also develop appropriate augmentative communication, discussed below, for children who cannot talk.

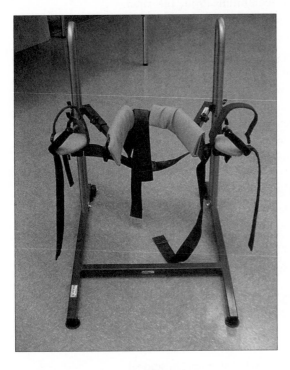

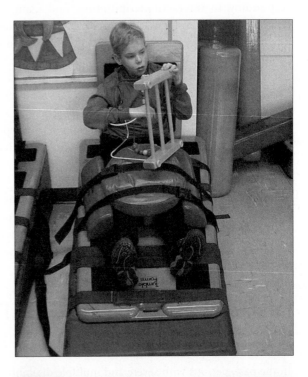

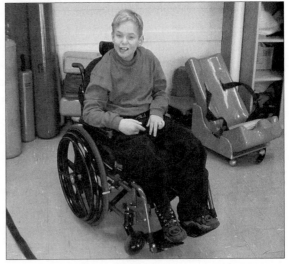

Standing frame; (top left); longsit-supplemental (top right); wheelchair (right).

Technical Aids

Improved equipment and adaptive devices have been developed to enrich education and improve the quality of life for individuals of all ages (see Chapter 13).

Educational Intervention

Children who are severely or multiply disabled take education beyond its traditional boundaries. These children may show different learning characteristics and developmental patterns. The instructional process may be hindered by maladaptive behaviour, the need to adapt technology and materials, and the difficulty in identifying appropriate reinforcers (Sisson, Van Hasselt, & Hersen, 1987).

Children's academic and social development is predicated on a set of related factors. They need a responsive environment capable of providing appropriate stimulation and opportunities for interaction. Further needs include sensory stimulation; well-planned, consistent habilitative and educational programs; and multiple treatment modalities. Older students require community-referenced instruction, social skills training, and supported employment (see Chapter 17).

Service Delivery Models

Children who are severely or multiply disabled need an extensive network of services to enable them to thrive and learn. The difficulties and potentialities resulting from each unique disability or combination of disabilities represent the decision point in placement and programming, so we find that students are educated in a variety of settings. Clinics, special schools, residential placements, special classes, or general classrooms are all in place.

The contemporary stress on inclusion equates with a movement away from the traditional residential school model. But while the reforms have opened up previously unavailable placement opportunities, a wide-scale movement toward general service delivery for all students with severe and multiple disabilities has not materialized (see the Debate feature in Chapter 14).

Policy in the United States is instructive in this regard. American courts have decided that residential programming is necessary when more than six hours of instruction are required to meet the child's educational needs; when the severity of the child's language deficiency precludes meaningful benefit from peer group learning and interaction with non-disabled peers in a mainstream setting; or when social and emotional adjustment are poor in the normal setting.

Children with mild physical or sensory impairments can thrive in general classrooms, where they participate in academic programs and benefit from interaction with typical peers. Additional support may come in the guise of speech therapists, physical therapists, audiologists, mobility and orientation specialists, and specialist teachers of the hearing or visually impaired.

As we discussed in Chapter 14, including children with more severe disabilities in general classrooms continues to be controversial. To briefly reiterate, the arguments for less restrictive environments are founded largely on the potential benefits for communication, social acceptance, self-esteem, and social skills (Kennedy, Shulka, & Fryxell, 1997; Mu, Siegel, & Allinder, 2000). Opposing voices speak against imprudent general education placement and point to the unique needs of students who are severely or multiply disabled. Needs include the expertise of specially trained staff, more intensive staffing allocations, community referenced curricula, and/or prosthetic techniques.

Educational Approaches

The learning characteristics and needs of children who are severely or multiply disabled vary widely. In general, these students require extensive ongoing support in more than one major area (mobility, communication, self-care, learning) in order to participate in school and the community.

A carefully task-analyzed Individual Education Plan (IEP) must be developed to show the modifications leading to educational, vocational, and psychosocial development. The more disabled the child, the more detailed and precise the task analysis and the goals and objectives need to be. Often progress is slow and the steps tiny, so the IEP will probably span five years, although there must be continuous assessment of a child's progress and detailed evaluations of the educational program. The IEP should arise from *team approaches* that rest on consultation and collaboration, as discussed below.

Team Approaches

The training and education of children with severe or multiple disabilities cannot rely on one person. Different disciplines bring unique skills and knowledge to intervention, and the nature of a particular child necessitates a partial blending of roles, skills, and knowledge across disciplines. When the expertise of different disciplines is shared, services are enriched, expanded, and made more comprehensive. Everyone involved can see the child as a total being rather than concentrating on one aspect of the child's development.

Typically, a team is composed of the family and professionals from a variety of disciplines, who collaborate in assessment and program planning. One individual, in consultation with other team members, works to carry out the individual program so that the case manager is both primary provider and service coordinator. Generally, in school settings the teacher assumes the role of service provider (Orelove & Sobsey, 1987).

Curricula

Curricula designed for children who are severely or multiply disabled must reflect all areas of development. Educational needs include language development, visual and auditory training, mobility training, and self-care skills. Psychosocial needs include adaptive behaviour, group activities, life skills, and a range of socialization experiences. Many students require pre-academic skills, which can include attention span, imitation skills, following instructions, perceptual motor skills, memory, the ability to formulate concepts, and premath skills. Children who are deaf-blind need a curriculum directed toward functional skills—specific self-care and independence skills that include drinking and pouring; dressing and undressing; using the toilet; personal care; kitchen preparation and cleanup; housekeeping; communication and language skills; and visual stimulation and visual perception skills.

Functional Skills

The key concept in teaching students with severe or multiple disabilities is functionality. The key skills are therefore **functional skills**—those that will help children to get along in their current and future environments; that have a high probability of being required at home, in school, at work, or in the community; and that will increase self-sufficiency in those environments. Skills are broad and first include **self-help skills**—the ability to care for oneself in order to achieve independence and self-sufficiency. Self-help skills are divided into those related to eating, dressing, bathing, grooming, and toileting; for example, independent eating, dressing, toileting, washing, combing hair, brushing teeth, and using a handkerchief.

functional skills

self-help skills

Together with the self-help skills, children need skills to participate in routine home and community activities such as playing with siblings, helping with simple chores, and eating at a fast-food restaurant. Students also learn simple homemaking skills, such as dusting, sweeping, setting and clearing a table, washing and drying dishes, washing and ironing clothes, sewing, using simple tools, and using the telephone. More advanced skills include functional math, such as telling the time, calendar use, and vending machine use; literacy skills that include reading maps, newspapers, and menus; mobility skills such as using public transportation or lockers; and other basic life skills such as personal hygiene, nutrition, and cooking. Personal and social skills include consideration for others, common courtesy, obedience, and self-judgment.

Within a functional approach, targets for instruction are selected by analyzing a child's environment. Teachers identify specific skills to immediately improve the child's ability to interact with the environment and to increase the probability that the child will perform functionally critical behaviours for success and survival in future environments. Important skills are then broken down into small, building steps in a task analysis. Skills are taught for generalization as well as for functional usefulness.

The skills presented must be generalizable, developmentally appropriate, and age appropriate. Teaching a child to grasp a toy may, for example, generalize to grasping a hairbrush or a toothbrush, both necessary self-help skills. Sorting shapes to corresponding pictures of shapes is not a skill that a child is likely to use during daily activities, whereas the child is likely to use the skill of matching various shaped lids to corresponding containers. While both skills involve matching, recognizing, and sorting shapes, the use of functional objects such as containers and lids enables the child to learn a necessary skill that will foster independence in real-life situations (Notari-Syverson & Shuster, 1995). Similarly, placing pegs in a board may aid in fine motor development, but is not really related to future needs. On the other hand, putting coins in a vending machine will develop the same motor areas and also provide a living skill. Or, if the objective is to teach students to operate a musical device during their leisure time, it is more functional and age appropriate for a fifteen-year-old to use a CD player than a gaily coloured Fisher-Price music box.

Some generic accommodations and modifications for students with severe and multiple disabilities are shown in Table 15-1.

Communication Training

Of all the needs of children with severe or multiple disabilities, the acquisition of communication skills is one of the greatest. The development of functional communication skills requires an approach that is focused, systematic, and individualized. Training may take

Table 15-1 Creating accessible classrooms

Accommodations

- Most training efforts should be conducted in natural environments.

- Encourage spontaneity by rewarding spontaneous behaviour.

- A school may elect one person, often a special education teacher, to act as a support facilitator. This person not only works with the severely disabled students but also helps regular classroom teachers adapt instruction and aids in facilitating peer acceptance (see Stainback & Stainback, 1988). Programs and models such as the Circle of Friends (Snow & Forest, 1987) and the McGill Action Planning Systems (MAPS) (Forest & Lusthaus, 1989) foster positive relationships and support networks to include individuals with severe disabilities in school and community life.

Modifications

- Children who are multiply disabled are often able to comprehend far more than they indicate; keep sentences short and use an expressive voice.

- For most deaf-blind children with other impairments, natural gestures offer the best foundation for communication. Natural gestures can easily be individualized.

- To stimulate speech, place your mouth on the child's cheek or hand when speaking so that he or she can feel your speech. Continue to hold your mouth against the child's cheek or hand between vocalizations so the child can feel the silence.

- Use much music and rhythm.

- Accompany communication with rhythmic body actions, touch sensations, or actions that engage a number of senses simultaneously.

- Reinforce vocalizations as consistently and frequently as possible. Provide vocal reinforcement for a short time after the child stops vocalizing. This offers a model dialogue, ensures that the child is not interrupted, and reinforces turn-taking patterns. Vocal reinforcement should include imitation of the child's sounds, whether verbal or pre-verbal.

- Improve the quality of language stimulation by interspersing short bursts of speech with short periods of silence. Use playful social routines, rhyming verses, and other communication games that are enjoyable for you and the child. For older students, try using rock and roll and other rhythmic patterns.

- Activities should contain multiple components that can provide numerous opportunities within a single activity. Painting, for example, would provide at least three opportunities for communication: obtaining access to the paint, the water, and the brush.

- Activities should lend themselves to repetitive action. If the child desires repeated actions, repeated opportunities exist for language use. Examples include playing catch and being pushed on a swing.

- Use experiential units in which instruction is modified to focus on tasks such as building things, setting up household tasks, or preparing food. This gives a child constant repetition of specific language, help with memory, and practice in living skills.

place in one-to-one, highly structured environments, but more generally it will take place in natural contexts such as the classroom.

Because language is the product of all aspects of development—physical, sensory, social, and neurological—the development of communication skills is a simultaneous activity. The major goal of language intervention is the initiation of effective communication. Two general strategies are used for presymbolic and minimally symbolic children, often in tandem. These are presymbolic training and communication-first approaches (Owens, 1991).

Presymbolic training is based on the belief that there are cognitive prerequisites for language acquisition. Skills are usually those characteristic of the sensorimotor stage of development, so training begins with the development of basic sensorimotor skills such as object permanence, causality, means-end behaviour, spatial relationships, schemas for relating to objects, and imitation.

A *communication-first* approach is functional in that it stresses nurturant and naturalistic language. Communication-first approaches place the initial emphasis on the establishment of a system that can later be expanded to symbol use. The progression of communication moves from signals (cries, for example), to the use of signs (systematic, consistent gesturing to indicate wants), to the use of increasingly complex linguistic forms, to the metalinguistic uses of language. The major skills taught are initial communication; turn-taking skills; generalized imitation skills; lexical growth and establishment of a basic vocabulary; early symbol communication rules; and participation in interactions that occur outside the training context (see Owens, 1991).

Because language training is usually undertaken in natural settings, the generic term is milieu language teaching methods. We find a number of tactics within milieu teaching such as transactional teaching, conversational teaching, and pragmatic intervention. As one specific example, the Mand-model procedure is a naturalistic technique used for teaching pre-academic skills involving language. The adult *mands* (as in demands or commands) that the child respond to a question. A correct answer is reinforced, repeated, and more information added. An incorrect answer gets a **prompt**—a verbal, physical, gestural, or modelling cue that helps the child to respond.

prompt

Not all children will acquire speech, especially those beginning at prelinguistic levels. They may need an alternative communication system, referred to as a **communication mode**. The selection of a communication mode and the strategies for teaching its use are ideally made in conjunction with family and therapists. Multiple factors must be considered: long-term linguistic needs; people with whom the child needs to communicate; and the most appropriate mode based on a child's mental ability, motivation, visual perception, motor control, and behavioural problems.

communication mode

Alternative Methods of Communication Alternative communication is a broad category that refers to symbols, aids, manual or electronic means, and strategies that serve to supplement any gestural, spoken and/or written communication abilities an individual may have (Beck, Thompson, Clay, Hutchins, Vogt, Romaniak, & Sokolowski, 2001). When alternative communication systems augment speech or accomplish communication function, they are termed *augmentative communication*.

Augmentative communication refers to a general group of procedures designed to support, enhance, or augment the communication of non-speaking individuals or utilize and supplement whatever vocal skills an individual possesses. The various procedures that

augmentative communication

Table 15-2 Methods of augmentative communication

Signal/code	Symbol	Manual
Yes/no	Rebus systems	Idiosyncratic gesturing
Audio-signalling	Blissymbolics	Amerind
Gesturing	Pictorial Ideographic Communcation (PIC)	American Sign Language (ASL)
Morse code	School-based manual systems	Unaided approaches

make up augmentative communication are used chiefly by individuals whose speech communication is impaired by hearing impairments; individuals with severe language deficits; individuals with severe neuromuscular or physical disabilities; and those with severe and multiple disabilities.

Augmentative communication both receives and transmits messages. There are two main types of augmentation: unaided and aided approaches. *Unaided approaches* rely on gestural communication; *aided approaches* depend on a device of some kind such as communication boards, mechanical or electrical devices, and computers. Table 15-2 outlines some alternative methods of communication.

Unaided Approaches. The major types of unaided approaches in augmentative communication are discussed below

- Signal communication includes the use of a simple yes/no system and audio-signalling. Yes and no signals may be indicated by movements of the head, hands, face, or eyes. A portable audio-oscillator that emits a loud tone has been used to teach four simple signals (need, help, yes, no).

- Code communication uses Morse code as a method of communication.

natural gestures

- Natural gestures are most often used with children who are deaf-blind, although they may also be part of communication training for children with severe or multiple disabilities who are not hearing impaired. **Natural gestures** are simple movements of one or both hands used to convey meaning to the child. For example, the word *eat* is indicated by tapping the lips with the fingertips of one hand.

- Tactile sign language is used with students who are deaf-blind. In this, the learner's hands are placed on top of the communicator's hands so that a gesture, sign, or finger spelling is felt.

- The Tadoma (vibration) method is also used with persons who are deaf-blind. The student places a thumb on the speaker's lips, an index finger on the speaker's jaw, and three fingers on the speaker's neck. This allows the learner to manually perceive the vibrations of the speaker's voice, the tension of the speaker's face, and the shape of the speaker's lips.

- Sign language, although typically associated with deaf people, may be beneficial to a much larger population in improving communication skills. In Chapter 14, we explained how sign language was used with children with autism. Used with prelinguistic children, it may stimulate language development and facilitate the onset and development of spoken language (Kouri, 1989).

- Amerind is a simpler system and more suitable for low-functioning individuals for whom sign language may prove too difficult. Amerind was adapted by Madge Skelly (1979), a speech and language pathologist and full-blooded Indian, from the system she learned from her grandfather. Amerind is built on the hand signals used by Native Americans and contains about 250 hand signals that can be arranged in any combination. (See the Case Study about Kent in Chapter 13 on pages 428 and 453–454.)

Aided Approaches *Augmentative devices* are operated by an individual to communicate basic needs. They can be easily activated by movement of the head or hand, or even by an eye blink. The Vocaid is an example of an augmentative device suitable for functional needs, such as a call for assistance. Some augmentative devices make use of speech synthesis. Children with good intellectual ability might use a system where the child spells a message on a grid using row-column scanning with an electronic device. Other high-technology aids include the use of pre-recorded messages, such as greetings or farewells, that users can select by striking a predetermined key.

Blissymbolics has been successful with children with severe motor disabilities. Charles Bliss, a refugee from Hitler's concentration camps, went to Shanghai, where he learned the Chinese writing system, in which each symbol stands for an idea rather than a sound. Based on this, Bliss developed an ideographic universal writing system. It was not popular until discovered by Shirley McNaughton at the Ontario Crippled Children's Centre in Toronto. Today, Blissymbolics is a complete language system. Even though it can be used for general conversation, the symbols are simple enough to be learned by children too young to read alphabetic writing. Bliss is used by 25 000 people in Canada, of whom one-quarter have cerebral palsy (Reich, 1986). Depending on a child's abilities, vocabularies of up to 400 terms may be learned. Figure 15-1 shows examples of Bliss symbols.

Bliss symbols are presented on a communication board. Other board systems designed to enhance oral communication among intellectually impaired non-verbal and limited-verbal individuals use pictures rather than the stylized symbols of Blissymbolics. Simple boards have clear pictures or photographs depicting basic needs and activities such as an item of food, a cup, a toilet or pot, a bed, and a toy. The child communicates by pointing to the appropriate pictures. Another example is the Pictorial Ideographic Communication (PIC), which is presented on a communication board and consists of pictures and symbols that represent objects and actions. Some communication boards are high-tech, with voice outputs that provide pre-recorded or programmed speech in the form of words, phrases, or sentences.

Orientation and Mobility Training Orientation and mobility training teaches individuals who have multiple disabilities that include blindness a basic knowledge of the environment and how to find their way to specific locations, such as the schoolroom or the workshop. The goals of orientation and mobility training are the same as for other children who are visually

Figure 15-1
Bliss symbols

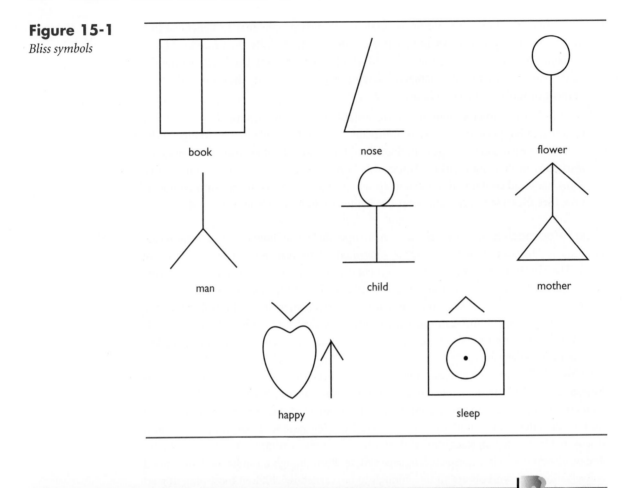

book

nose

flower

man

child

mother

happy

sleep

Juanita (continued)

Juanita is now nine years old. She still spends part of her time learning specific skills in the special class, but she is also comfortable and welcome in the general classroom and has a small group of friends who share with her both in and out of school.

Juanita's teacher looked at both formal and informal ways to provide multiple interactions daily in the classroom. She helped to develop informal peer supports and friendships for Juanita by fostering respect for individual differences and by providing a positive model. She stressed proximity through peer tutoring, co-operative learning, buddy systems, and involvement in extracurricular activities. Juanita's modified program kept her with the class but at her own developmental level. An extract from her IEP is shown below.

In one lesson, for example, the teacher read a book to the class. Juanita's objective was to sit on the floor in an assigned spot and direct her attention to the teacher. The second part of the lesson was to colour a picture from the story. The other children chose their colours, but a peer handed Juanita a marker and instructed her where to colour. After the other children wrote stories about their pictures, they read them aloud to Juanita and, using signs and natural gestures, prompted her to point to the pictures.

EXTRACT FROM JUANITA'S IEP

Present Levels of Functioning

Deaf, visually impaired, low cognitive functioning. Pre- to minimally linguistic. No intelligible speech and a few gestures for wants. Relies on her parents and caregivers for eating, dressing, and toileting. Developing many social skills and very interested in other children in the class.

Placement

Special class and general classroom part-time with paraeducator assistance.

Current Progress

Growing awareness of classmates. Will wave with assistance. Interest in signing as used by other class members.

Strategies for Inclusion

Paraeducator; simple signs used by all in environment; modified program stressing communication and life skills; out-of-class daily therapy.

Personnel

Classroom teacher, paraeducator, therapist.

Goals and Objectives

- Co-operate with others.
- Follow classroom directions.
- Adhere to the rules and routines of the classroom.
- Wave on command.
- Use basic sign communication.
- Develop life skills (special class).

impaired, but some of the teaching techniques may differ. Children who are multiply disabled often need alternative methods that provide safety and information and yet are within their capabilities. Some specialists introduce cane travel before the child is technically ready in the hope that he or she will develop greater confidence. This has proven very successful with low-functioning blind children.

SUMMARY

1. Pervasive developmental disorders are exceedingly complex conditions. Children with severe and multiple disabilities have a range of impairments.

2. A number of useful definitions for severe and multiple disabilities have evolved. Some attempt to offer comprehensive generic descriptions; others describe the parameters of types of disabling conditions. More specific definitions have developed for particular combinations of disabling conditions such as deaf-blindness.

3. The primary consideration when addressing severe or multiple impairments is the recognition that the conditions are not additive. Each multiple disability is an entirely new category of exceptionality, so that each child must be considered individually to an even greater degree than children with single disabilities. The special and diverse needs caused by the unique combinations of conditions challenge all those charged with training and educating severely or multiply-disabled children.

4. Treatment programs for children with developmental disabilities relate to the accuracy and specificity with which the problems and deficits are initially identified. However,

the assessment of children who are severely or multiply disabled is difficult for even the most experienced clinicians. As no one measure or battery of measures is suitable for all, a range of assessment measures must be employed.

5. The needs of children with severe and multiple disabilities are varied and complex; interventions involve a wide range of techniques and personnel. Education may take place in residential schools, special classes, clinics, or through school programs in hospitals. When the full inclusion of children with severe and multiple disabilities is considered, it entails substantial changes in the structure of the classroom, a different conceptualization of professional roles, and a continuous need for collaborative teaming.

6. A variety of services are needed to support students with severe or multiple disabilities, such as physical, occupational, and speech and language therapists. For the child who is deaf-blind, there may be an interpreter-tutor who acts as interpreter and facilitator. He or she needs skills in orientation and mobility, communication, and sign language.

7. When teaching students with severe or multiple disabilities, the most effective approach is a focus on functional skills. A functional approach ensures that the selection of objectives is based on their future usefulness.

8. Developing a communication system for these children should take precedence over all other interventions. Because there are cognitive prerequisites for language acquisition, some researchers suggest organizing teaching programs around the initial assessment of and subsequent training in cognitive skills such as object permanence, classification, imitation, and representational play with objects. Other researchers stress a communication-first approach. In the education of children who are deaf-blind, no aspect of language development can be ignored. The primary goal is to teach students to communicate in the easiest possible way.

9. Although communication is of paramount importance, it is important to acknowledge the parallel significance of instruction in self-care, mobility, problem-solving, and other skills.,

10. Children who are unable to acquire oral language may learn through various systems of augmentative communication that are used in place of speech.

HISTORICAL NOTES

History tells us very little about persons with multiple disabilities. Deaf-blindness is the condition we know the most about. In the middle of the 18th century, the Scots philosopher Dugald Stewart told of a deaf-blind lad named James Mitchell who responded to educational intervention. In Paris in the 1760s the Abbé de l'épée experimented with a system of raised-print blocks to use with individuals who were deaf-blind. In 1789 in Paris Victorine Morriseau was the first deaf-blind woman to receive education (Collins, 1995).

In 1837 Laura Bridgman was admitted to the Perkins Institution for the Blind in Boston, where Samuel Gridley Howe undertook her education. Laura had lost her sight, hearing, taste, and smell to scarlet fever at the age of two. Howe taught her the manual alphabet and eventually Laura read embossed books, did simple arithmetic, and mastered needlework and other kinds of handi-crafts. Howe's son-in-law, Michael Aganos, used Howe's directives when Helen Keller became a pupil at the Perkins Institution (Winzer, 1993).

Between 1900 and 1950 only a few programs opened. Most children with multiple disabilities were excluded from the residential schools; they had conditions that cut across several categories of impair-ment and tended to fall between the cracks. Public schools did not take the responsibility for providing education for these children, on the assumption that they were uneducable and could not learn.

The worldwide rubella epidemic between 1962 and 1964 left thousands upon thousands of children multiply disabled. While the needs of huge numbers meant that many programs were established, the historical legacy of special education meant that stu-dents with intense needs were chiefly served in some form of special placement, such as residential schools.

Educational practices for students with severe disabilities have changed markedly in the past 25 years. The definition of effective practice has moved from segregated services to general classrooms and neighbourhood schools. Even so, integration remains difficult and controversial, with a host of different opinions from professionals and parents. For example, dually-diagnosed children are among the least understood and most underserved of any group with disabilities. These children present such unique diagnostic and treatment challenges that they are at particular risk for long-term unfavourable outcomes (Baker, Blacher, Crnic, & Edelbrock, 2002).

SECTION 7

Infants, Preschoolers, Families, and Young Adults

Educators sometimes think of the critical years for learning as those between about ages five and eighteen—the time when children and adolescents are within the formal school system. But learning is a lifelong experience, of which an enormous amount takes place before children even reach school. By the time children are six years old, almost two-thirds of their ultimate cognitive ability is formed. And after the age of six, the child's potential for further intellectual growth is slowed (Bloom, 1964).

Educators should know "where children are coming from" as well as where they are going. They need to be aware of the experiences of the preschool years, as this period of development lays the groundwork for what we see in formal classrooms. They should also be knowledgeable about the special requirements of students at the other end of the age spectrum—young adults who are leaving the school system.

For very young children, the family is the central focus. All families face stresses and strains that are only multiplied when a child has a disability. Families may differ greatly in structure, cultural values, and economic status, but most families with a child who is disabled have to cope with additional emotional adjustments and care-giving demands.

Early childhood special education (ECSE) is a new discipline designed to ameliorate the effects of a disability in a very young child and assist the parents and family in dealing with the associated stress. Early identification and early intervention are essential elements of ECSE.

Just as ECSE is a new discipline, so interest in the needs of students nearing the end of their school careers is a relatively new development. Essentially, initiatives arose from data that showed that youths with disabling conditions were not faring well in the adult world, especially in the workforce.

Implicit in intervention with very young children and late adolescents with disabilities is the concept and practice of *transition*, an umbrella term for all activities and opportunities that prepare students for significant changes in their lives. For young children and their parents, transition is the movement from preschool to school. In older students, transition means the movement from elementary to junior high school or to secondary school.

The most important meaning of transition relates to adolescents who are moving to new environments, most often from school to work. Schools today are becoming involved in assisting young people to negotiate the transition to independent adult living.

This section addresses students with disabilities at both ends of the age spectrum. The discussion in Chapter 16 focuses on the manner in which a child affects the family, the influence the family has on the child's development and progress, types of early intervention that are available to help parents cope with their exceptional child and enhance prospects for his or her optimal development, parent involvement and parent training, and transition. The major focus of Chapter 17 is on the concepts and practices of transition for students at the end of their school careers.

Learning Outcomes

After reading this section, you should be able to

People and Foundations

1. Outline the development of early childhood special education.
2. Be aware of how transition programs for adolescents with disabilities evolved.

Issues

3. Differentiate among the models used to look at family functioning and understand how they influence intervention.
4. Understand the concepts and processes of early identification and early intervention.
5. Understand the link between early childhood education and education in the general school system.
6. Appreciate the need for transition services and understand the transition process and its major components, particularly for adolescents.

Knowledge

7. Understand the special needs of adolescents with disabilities.
8. Recognize how a family member with a disability impacts on family functioning, parent roles, sibling interactions, and the extended family.

Skills

9. Understand the processes of infant, preschool, kindergarten, and family needs assessment, as well as vocational evaluation.

CHAPTER 16

YOUNG CHILDREN WHO ARE EXCEPTIONAL AND THEIR FAMILIES

INTRODUCTION

All parents want their children to be born healthy, normal, and perfect, with sturdy bones, good vision, working organs, and the promise of growing into a normal, intelligent, and happy person. For most parents, the wish is fulfilled; the chances are huge that a child will be born in superlative condition.

While most children are born healthy and well formed, some parents must reduce the expectations they hold for their new infant. For them, the not-so-perfect child has been born. Their child is not like other children; it has problems that potentially threaten its physical, intellectual, social, or emotional functioning. When parents have a child who is exceptional, they face frustrations stemming from broken dreams; the goals and hopes for the child are no longer clear and the entire family functioning is affected.

No family, regardless of wealth, education, religious persuasion, race, or physical and mental health, is immune to having a child who is exceptional. About 3 percent of newborn infants have a condition that can be considered a developmental delay or developmental disability. Another 3 percent are born with significant conditions capable of causing medical or social disabilities (Berlin, 1983). For other children, problems appear later as a result of disease or accident. In all, between 5 and 20 percent of Canadian families have children with disabilities.

The child with a disability has a major impact on the family that usually requires modifications in family structure and roles. Only during the past few decades have professionals begun to fully appreciate the intricate facets that begin with the birth or diagnosis of a child with a disability. They now look at the parental pain and stress that accompany the diagnosis of a disabling condition in a child, the manner by which responses are mediated by contextual variables, and the degree of external support that parents need. Professionals now realize parents require assistance in areas such as understanding the nature and prognosis of the condition; handling the child; stimulating mobility, locomotion, and communication; responding appropriately to different or unexpected behaviours; and accessing schools, agencies, and support groups.

In the broadest terms, work with very young children with disabilities and their families is referred to as *early childhood special education*. It takes in two main processes. *Early identification* is designed to find the childhood disability as soon as possible. *Early intervention* includes a variety of educational, psychological, or therapeutic procedures aimed at infants and preschoolers.

You should be aware that early intervention within the context of special education fits under the umbrella of a universal trend in this area. Significant efforts to improve the lot of all children by providing a variety of childhood and family programs that support their development is a global agenda. Many researchers, practitioners, and parents argue that appropriate support for children's growth and development during the first years of life is a sound social investment. Early intervention affects cognitive development, nutrition, care, health, learning ability, and economic productivity.

Differences in economic development, social and educational policy, political systems, population, and geographical size, as well as within-country disparities have led to different national priorities in early childhood research, policy, and practice. Canada has embraced the general propensity so that early intervention for both normally developing young children and for those with disabilities is emerging as a priority of the federal, provincial, and territorial governments. More and more often, school systems are initiating early intervention. For example, in Alberta, children with severe disabilities are eligible for early childhood services at the age of two-and-a-half. From three-and-a-half years of age, children with mild or moderate disabilities are eligible for early education programs (Alberta Learning, 2000).

PARENTS AND FAMILIES

Parenting should be counted among the most esteemed professions. But while there are many apprenticeships available for professions and careers, none exist for that most difficult job: parenting. Few people study the art—or craft—and there are no courses to teach really practical methods of child-rearing, or to teach parents how to weather the crises, frustrated ambitions, and periods of high stress that are common to most families. Nonetheless, most parents manage to raise their children remarkably well. They willingly endure many trials, problems, and moments of despair, secure in the hope that one day their children will become self-sufficient adults.

Expecting parents have great dreams for their unborn child. They hope for intelligence and physical beauty and plan ahead for later accomplishments and successes. By the time the baby is born, parents are ready to provide for the infant's physical needs and have probably consulted one of the hundreds of volumes on child care and child rearing.

Typically, the birth of a child brings joy and excitement. When a parent holds a newborn close for the first time, feelings of belonging, togetherness, and attachment are cemented. The birth ends the period of expectations about the child and brings new challenges and responsibilities for parents as they adjust to the new family member.

The initial diagnosis of a disabling condition in a child elicits intense emotions in parents and other family members (Pochelmann, Clements, Abbesuto, & Farsad, 2005). Parental aspirations are shattered. The perfect child has died and in its place is a baby with apparent and frightening problems and unknown prospects for the future. When a disability is found, a void is created that is bridged only as the family reformulates its expectations to accommodate reality. The entire family undergoes a crisis but embarks on the road to *adaptation*—a complex, lifelong process involving ongoing challenges at multiple levels of family life.

The characteristics of the family—cultural background, socio-economic status, size, and religion—shape its ability to cope with a child who is exceptional. Each family's unique combination of strengths, stressors, vulnerabilities, and coping styles comes into play as the discovery of a disability in a child creates intense and conflicting feelings among the members of a family. Variance in family functioning seems to be associated with four factors: family hardiness, total functional support, parental age, and family stressors (Failla & Jones, 1991).

LOOKING AT FAMILIES

There are a number of ways to look at families and conceptualize the relationship between family members, the child with a disability, the care and treatment of the disabled member, the extended family, and the wider culture. Each of the theoretical frames used to view families is a little different, although they should be seen as a continuum with a different emphasis on certain factors and components of family functioning rather than different variables. Moreover, each of these ways of looking at families is important because these frameworks undergird the manner in which professionals present early intervention programs and interact with parents. Table 16-1 outlines ways of looking at families.

Stage Theories

Stage theories hold that parents pass through discrete stages before they can fully accept the condition of the child with a disability. Not all parents pass through all of these stages, and each person works through them at a different rate; however, most pass through similar stages before they accept the reality of their child's condition.

Stage theories represent the most traditional way of examining a family that includes a member with a disability. In general, these theories were based on early assumptions that focused on family pathology and saw the diagnosis of a disability in a child as a tragedy entraining lifelong hardship for the family. Although some of the ideas make intuitive sense, recent research has discarded stage theories in favour of other approaches that are more realistic, respectful of families, and more relevant to intervention practices.

Life-Cycle Approach

Instead of adopting a stage approach, it is more optimistic and contemporary to view a family and the impact of a member with a disability through a *life-cycle* or *lifespan approach*. A life-cycle perspective sees the family as a unit that is moving through time and experiencing a series of events, tasks, and transitions. By looking at the family life cycle, it can be seen that the impact of the child with a disability on the family changes over time. Families that provide the lifetime care of a child face unique stressors and demands over the life cycle, and family responsibilities and tasks shift in response to the child's changing needs.

Table 16-1 Looking at families

Model	Principles	Major focus
Stage theory	Parents pass through discrete stages from grief to acceptance	Parent counselling Parent therapy Parent self-help groups Information about the condition
Life-cycle theory	Families pass through cycles in which there may be crises, transition points	Transition support Liaison with other agencies Family support Intervention with the child
Systems theory	The family is a system within the larger social context	Priorities set by the family Stress on all family members Functional skills for the child Improved functioning within family needs
Social support theory	Families are systems of their own	Families helping themselves Families setting priorities Advocating for child

All families experience life-cycle transitions, and there seem to be specific periods that result in increased stress. These periods are the age at which the child should begin to walk; the age at which the child should begin to talk; entry into the public school system; onset of puberty; and the twenty-first birthday.

Having a child with a disability raises key questions that parents are likely to continue to revisit as their child matures and as the child and family undergo transitions in school and other life experiences. Stressful transitions may also include events such as the initial diagnosis of the disability; early childhood; school entry; when the development of a younger sibling surpasses that of the child who is disabled; when a child-management crisis occurs; adolescence; beginning adult life; maintaining adult life; and when guardianship issues are discussed. These events can serve to magnify a child's special needs to the family and create heightened stress.

Systems Approach

A systems approach is seen today as the most appropriate way to view families with a disabled member. Early intervention researchers, scholars, and practitioners have, in general, embraced the conceptual framework emerging from the systems approach. They use it as the basis of a family-centred approach to the development, delivery, and evaluation of services.

A systems theory or perspective sees a family as more than individuals bound by a biological relationship. It recognizes that actions in any part of the system affect the other parts and that solutions to problems can be found only when the problem is properly defined in its larger environmental context. That is, influences are multidirectional. Each adult and child influences every member of the household and each family relationship affects all the other family members. Therefore, whether the family is nuclear, single parent, or extended, it plays a powerful role in the child's social, emotional, behavioural, and academic development and progress. The factors that interact with child-rearing patterns include the child's age, sex, and temperament; the parents' personality, characteristics, personal history, and economic circumstances; the needs of family members; and the values of the culture.

Under a systems approach, the relationship between the child who is exceptional and the family is reciprocal; the child deeply affects the family climate, while the family, in turn, affects the child. Interaction with family members deeply influences the child's opportunities and barriers, challenges and expectations, ambitions and frustrations, and general quality of life.

Social Support Approach

In many ways, the *social support approach* overlaps the systems approach; the difference is mainly one of emphasis. Whereas a systems approach focuses chiefly on the social context of the family, a social support approach focuses on a family's functioning in four family subsystems: marital, sibling, parental, and extra-familial. The social support approach stresses families helping themselves and sees informal supports, such as the extended family and church, as more important than formal support.

Family support approaches include two major concepts—embeddedness and social networks influence. *Embeddedness* refers to the way that a developing child is enveloped within the family system, and the way that the family unit is embedded within broader social units consisting of relatives, friends, neighbours, church members, and so on. These people—the family's *social network*—directly and indirectly influence both the family and the child.

An interesting research thread within this approach follows the church and religious aspect of support. Hughes (1999) wrote that, "as parents attended church, they were more likely to receive support from church members. That support led to increased parental ability to endure" (p. 277). Others (e.g., Correa & Heward, 2000) found that the role of faith in God, more so than formal religious activities, appears to be important for families coping with a child with disabilities.

Social support networks may be more important for mothers than fathers. One study (McLinden, 1990) investigated the differences between mothers and fathers in the areas of social support and family satisfaction, and in their report, frequency-of-occurrence and degree-of-problem of events and feelings related to the presence of a child with special needs. The report found that mothers had a higher frequency of demands placed on their lives than fathers and also experienced more negative physical and emotional states.

Status of Disability

Another way to look at families is on the basis of the *type of condition* of the child. This is not a theoretical model or approach, but it does recognize that the nature of a child's disability can have a substantial impact on parental stress and levels of acceptance.

Most observers conclude that raising a child with a disability is often burdensome, tiresome, and frustrating. High levels of family stress may be created by a group of different factors. First of all, parents' discovery of their child's disability brings them into the orbit of a number of professional disciplines. Learning about the exceptionality is only the first of a lifelong series of interactions; many families are plunged into the world of infant stimulation, early intervention, preschools, respite services, medical intervention, and so on. Families will interact in some way with professionals from the disciplines of education, psychology, medicine, therapy, counselling, and allied public health and social work.

A major source of stress can be a particular child's slower progress, more difficult temperament, lack of social responsiveness, stereotypical behaviour patterns, or additional or unusual caregiving needs. Research on families with infants indicates that role confusion, social isolation, fatigue, financial worries, and lack of information on child development are cited by new mothers as primary causes of stress (Salisbury, 1987). The behaviours that parents of disabled infants have identified as most difficult, stressful, or uncomfortable are crying, resisting being held, being hard to soothe, passive non-responsiveness, tuning out, and emitting atypical motor responses.

Symptoms of stress are more evident among parents of children with delayed rather than prompt diagnoses and with unknown rather than specified etiologies (Goldberg, Marcovitch, MacGregor, & Lojkasek, 1986). Stress is also more evident among families when the child has a severe or profound rather than a mild or moderate condition. Studies have found greater stress reported by parents of boys and of children with limited communication skills (Frey, Greenberg, & Fewell, 1989). Parents of children with dual disabilities seem to be doubly stressed (Hintermaier, 2000).

Gifted children are advantaged in many ways, but they may cause disruption within the family.

Stress may occur from the outset if the attachment process between infants with disabilities and their parents is disrupted. Premature and disabled infants may be kept in neonatal intensive care for up to 12 weeks, depending on birth weight, gestational age, physical anomalies, respiration, and weight gain. Children who later show disturbed interactions include preterm, Down syndrome, blind, autistic, and failure-to-thrive infants. Such infants are less responsive than others, and parents need to work harder to focus their attention and generate smiles and contented vocalizations. Children with problems such as Fetal Alcohol Syndrome, Down syndrome, and cleft palate may have feeding problems and limited abilities to suck, bite, chew, or swallow. Feeding problems are common among infants who are autistic, beginning with poor nursing habits and continuing through infancy and childhood.

Some disruption may arise from the medical needs of a child. Children with chronic conditions such as cystic fibrosis require intense medical and therapeutic intervention. The age of the child may also be related to the condition. As children grow older, they become harder to manage. At the same time, the gap between the progress of children who are exceptional and their peers becomes more noticeable.

Accumulating data also suggest that parents of children with developmental disabilities experience deleteriously high levels of stress, higher frequencies of depression, and struggles with challenging behaviours. It is estimated that two-thirds of mothers of young children with developmental delays experience significant elevated stress levels. Parents of children with autism and behaviour disorders report higher levels of stress that parents of children with Down syndrome and parents of children without disabilities (Lessenberry & Rehfeldt, 2004).

Parents with children who are exceptional must also take on new roles: educator, lobbyist, advocate, therapist, and, of course, chauffeur. In addition, financial burdens can cause parents constant concern and frustration. The need for special equipment, special medical care, and special programs often brings financial hardship. Economic pressures can distort the family's emotional response to their child, particularly in families with limited financial resources.

In fact, the most significant and indirect cost associated with raising a child with a disability is the reduced employment opportunities for parents. According to a Canadian study (Roeher Institute, 2000), 68 percent of parents of children with disabilities do not work overtime, and 72 percent passed up promotions because of their competing demands with the care of their child. As well, 39 percent of parents of children with disabilities worked reduced hours and 46 percent worked alternative schedules. The study further found that the higher costs of raising a child with a disability meant there were a higher percentage of these families among the poor. Twenty-nine percent of families that had a child with a disability were in the lowest or lower-middle income brackets, as compared to 17 percent of families with typical children. Another Canadian study (Scorgie, Wilgosh, & McDonald, 1998) found consistent evidence that families of children with disabilities that had a higher income had more choices for help and support than families with lower incomes.

SIBLINGS

Brothers and sisters play important roles in the entire family drama. Siblings have a profound influence on each other's social and emotional development. Of the huge host of variables that affect sibling relationships, some of the most important are family size, birth order, gender, responsibilities and roles of all family members, temperaments, feelings and perceptions of self, personalities and their match, personal values and attitudes, and style (Atkins, 1987).

Parent roles change with the advent of a child with a disability, and it is obvious that sibling relationships will also change and take on special significance. Much of the research evidence about siblings is, however, inconclusive and underdeveloped (Hodapp, Glidden, & Kaiser, 2005). It simply tells us that the outcomes can range from very few effects to very positive or very negative ones. In other words, as in every family, there are joys and frustrations.

When the self-concept of siblings of children with disabilities is specifically addressed, the results are conflicting. Some research has found that children who have siblings with disabilities scored more poorly than children with non-disabled siblings on almost every measure of internalized adjustment problems; other research points to the beneficial consequences that may stem from the experience of having a brother or sister with a disability (Grisson & Borkowski, 2002).

With inconsistent research findings and family and sibling relationships that are so different, we must be hesitant about drawing conclusions. We can say:

- Siblings are important play partners for each other. When a child has a disability, the sibling roles are somehow altered. A child with a disability may not function as a playmate or a socializing agent for his or her siblings. Equality in relationships decreases as disability increases.

- There may be pressure on the typical child to "make up for" the deficits in the child who is disabled. Siblings may find themselves recipients of uneven expectation standards as compensation for parental disappointment. Sometimes, children are made to bear unrealistically high parental expectations. Or they may be expected to repress their abilities so that they do not perform better than the child who is special.

- Children may feel embarrassment in relating to the disabled sibling in the company of peers or in public. The presence of a sibling with a physical disability, for example, may lead to "de-identification" (see Neal & MacLean, 1995). Children may feel that they are viewed as flawed or weird by others because there is a disability in their family. One five-year-old asked, "Why does my baby sister have to go to school when the baby sister across the street gets to stay home and play?" A thirteen-year-old wanted to know, "Will my sister frighten my boyfriend away?" (Cramer, Erzkus, Mayweather, Pope, Roeder, & Tone, 1997).

- Parents may have different ways some of treating the normally developing children and the child with a disability. Because parents feel uncertainty regarding the care and management of a child who is disabled, they may subject that child to patterns of socialization that are significantly different from those that operate in the case of the other children. They may allow two quite different disciplinary systems to run side by side: one for the siblings and a more lenient, permissive one for the child who is disabled. Some parents treat their children with disabilities as though they were ill; they give them fewer responsibilities, place fewer restrictions on behaviour, and are more tolerant of undesirable behaviour, often at the expense of other siblings. Two different sets of rules intensify sibling rivalry. A twelve-year-old sister of a child with a hearing impairment complained, "I have to clean up my room and Mom cleans up Sherry's. That's just not fair. Her ears don't work, but her hands do" (Atkins, 1987, p. 38).

- Siblings may instinctively provide intervention as children and for years to come. Females, especially older sisters, are more likely to be involved in intervention. Older sisters with siblings who are intellectually disabled, for example, assume multiple caretaking responsibilities and frequently assume a teacher role (Brody, Stoneman, Davis, & Crapps, 1991).

Even though siblings may show nurturant and affectionate behaviour toward the disabled child, there may be heavy demands for caretaking responsibilities. Siblings may undertake activities such as teaching, feeding, babysitting, disciplining, and dressing (Hannah & Midlarsky, 2005). When siblings are required to supervise, care for, defend, and protect the child with a disability, resentment can develop. Excessive responsibility for caretaking is related to anger, guilt, increased sibling conflict, decreased opportunities for peer contacts and out-of-home activities and, quite possibly, subsequent psychological damage (Seligman, 1991).

THE EXTENDED FAMILY

Children with disabilities have a considerable influence on the extended family. And vice versa. The extended family may influence the development of children who are disabled through direct interactions and the nature of the support provided to their parents.

Relatively little research is available on the grandparents of normal children, much less the grandparents of children with disabilities. We do know that playing with and caring for young grandchildren supplies grandparents with a revitalized feeling of importance and purpose in life and may help soothe the increasing infirmities of advancing age and the approaching reality of death.

When a child is diagnosed as exceptional, more support is generally provided by the maternal than the paternal grandmother (Harris, Handleman, & Palmer, 1985). Such support is consistent with the maternal grandmother's understanding of her daughter's needs. On the other hand, some paternal grandmothers express their resentment toward their daughters-in-law. Pieper (1976) described how her mother-in-law lashed out in anger when presented with a grandchild with a disability. The grandmother blamed the daughter-in-law for having bad blood and burdening her husband with such a child.

PARENT SUPPORT

Before parents can effectively assist in the care and progress of their child with an exceptionality, they need to overcome their own emotional reactions. Many parents seek counselling or join self-help groups, especially during the period immediately following the initial diagnosis.

Counselling

Parent counselling differs from the usual conception of adult counselling, which is structured to facilitate changes in the client's behaviour. Parent counselling is not intended to change the personalities of family members; it is really closer to social work than to psychotherapy. The major aims are to help the family face continuing periods of grief and provide assistance in handling the special problems and environmental adjustments that having a child with a disability entails.

Counselling helps parents to understand the meaning of a child's diagnosis by focusing on information about the child, the nature and degree of the disability, educational planning, and future prognosis. Sessions also provide a forum in which parents can openly express and work through any feelings of anger, fear, and anxiety. They offer coping self-help skills, group relaxation, self-praise and self-instruction, and opportunities to favourably contrast participants with each other.

As siblings are an important aspect of family-centred practice, in many cases the counselling sessions will actively involve them. Problems are explained simply and honestly, with a fair assessment of how the child with a disability will affect family life.

Parent Self-Help Groups

Parents report that the people they most want to talk to are other parents of children with the same disabilities (Santelli, Turnbull, Marquis, & Lerner, 1997). Parent groups promote understanding and offer parents therapeutic involvement with people with similar problems; they provide a forum in which parents can discuss their concerns and exchange ideas with each other. It helps parents to talk about role changes, exhaustion, money problems, isolation, and so on with people who are going through the same experiences. Parents can channel their frustrations and anxieties into positive action for their children while gaining more realistic hopes for the future.

McMaster University researchers conducted a study of nine parent-run support groups in Ontario to explore the group's perceived effect in providing parents with support, reducing stress, and improving parents' ability to deal with disability issues. Results indicated substantial benefits for those belonging to the groups. Parents were seen to gain increased skills, a greater sense of power, and a sense of belonging. Participants were able to connect with each other and provide support and skills to deal with the day-to-day issues of raising a child with special needs ("Many roads … " 1999).

EARLY CHILDHOOD SPECIAL EDUCATION

We use the phrase *early childhood special education* (ECSE) to encompass two major processes: early identification and early intervention. These processes are not exclusive but natural corollaries. Early identification serves no purpose if it is not followed by early intervention, and appropriate early intervention rests on accurate identification.

ECSE is a relatively new field. Although efforts to intervene early actually date from preschool programs in the 1880s for children who were deaf, the term and concept were only formalized in 1986. This is explained in the Research Notes below.

RESEARCH NOTES

Early Childhood Special Education

In the late 1960s, the disciplines of regular early childhood education, special education, and ameliorative programs such as Head Start began to draw together. The result was an entirely new field, *early childhood special education*, formalized by federal legislation in the United States in 1986, Public Law

99–457, the Handicapped Children's Protection Act, an amendment of PL 94–142, and later amended as the IDEA of 1990. The IDEA contains three critical sections: Part H; Part B, section 619; and the Early Education Program for Children with Disabilities (EEPCD). These sections deal specifically with children with disabilities under the age of five and their families.

Of the many provisions in the legislation, one of the most important is the mandate for the full inclusion of families in any decisions relating to the preschool child or infant with a disability. To accomplish this, all intervenors must complete and comply with an Individual Family Services Plan (IFSP), which is akin to the IEP used for school-aged children.

PL 99–457 was described as "the most important legislation ever enacted for developmentally vulnerable young children" (Shonkoff & Meisels, 1990, p. 19). Some of the early optimism has become tempered by a recognition of the unusual complexity of the issues involved in both concept and practice. Nevertheless, in Canada and elsewhere, legislators and educators hearkened to the messages of PL 99–457. Today we see a burgeoning commitment and interest in ECSE and early intervention supported by a number of initiatives. Chief among these is a focus on literacy, founded on sustained and intensive research on early literacy instruction. Another strategy is moving from half-day to full-day programs, which seem to provide more consistent academic outcomes for all children. A third strategy is the continued and sustained involvement of teachers in professional development. A final strategy involves the reduction of class sizes.

Early Identification

Early identification refers to the practice of screening infants and young children in an attempt to identify those likely to experience problems in learning or behaviour. When compared to the practices used with school-aged children that we have discussed throughout the text, early identification is even broader. Involved personnel must be acquainted with procedures for assessing infants, toddlers, and preschoolers across a variety of domains, ways to assess family functioning, and ways to examine a child's environment.

early identification

The overarching aim of early identification is to collect data so as to target skills that will increase options for a child's participation in present and future environments. Lacking early assessment, a child may experience years of failure before a diagnosis is reached. Children may also develop secondary conditions, such as behavioural disorders.

The conventional testing that we have discussed throughout the categorical chapters in this text does not make much sense for infants and preschoolers. Tiny children do not wait, share, sit still, take turns, or follow directions, and are unlikely to cooperate with a strange adult (see Bagnato, 2005). A range of other procedures must be implemented.

Infant Identification

The chief purpose of infant assessment is to provide information regarding their strengths and weaknesses in order to plan intervention. Observation is the primary strategy. A trained observer may be able to distinguish signs of sensory or neurological problems, for example. Observation also provides an assessment of the child's strengths and needs related to a particular home and/or community activity that is identified as a concern to families, such as feeding behaviours or behaviour while shopping.

There are no tests available that adequately assess intelligence in the newborn or reliably predict later intellectual development. Measures designed to assess an infant's developmental state make use of sensorimotor tasks: gross motor behaviour, vocalization, and language behaviour. Generally, a six-month-old would be assessed on recognition of people and objects, motor coordination, alertness, awareness of the environment, and vocalization.

Preschool Assessment

In infants and preschoolers, screening is used to look for maturational lags and problems that can be improved through early intervention. Diagnosticians use developmental checklists, rating scales, readiness measures, basic concept inventories, and standardized measures.

Before examiners can employ these tools, they must know what behaviours they expect to observe. To test a three-year-old, they must focus on behaviour usually exhibited by two- to four-year-olds. These behaviours might include speaking in sentences of four to six words, building three-block pyramids, matching similar pictures, or buttoning. Problem behaviours might include poor attention span or failure to respond to oral language and visual symbols. A child who is out of touch with the environment may manifest poor motor control, low body image, and poor visual and auditory discrimination.

Observations of how a child functions in a setting such as a nursery school provide essential information about the child's progress and the effectiveness of the program. As well, they give information to others involved with the child. An audiologist, for example, needs data on how a child is responding with specific amplification.

Kindergarten Assessment

In kindergarten, as at the preschool level, the observation of behaviour serves as a valuable indicator of potential learning problems. Screening is used to identify children who do not possess the readiness skills needed to perform well in a structured school environment.

The concept of readiness is poorly defined and open to different interpretations. However, a range of available readiness tests attempt to assess a child's readiness for academic learning in specific areas of school achievement as well as potential academic difficulties. For example, reading readiness tests typically include subtests of letter recognition, shape perception, sound-symbol correspondences, and oral vocabulary.

Do remember our warning from Chapter 5 about children with maturational lags. Kindergarten screening procedures may identify maturational lags, but they should not be used to inappropriately label children early in their school careers.

Family Needs Assessment

The primacy of the decisions that families make about their children is at the heart of family-centred practices. To assist in determining family needs, a *needs assessment* is used to identify and examine both values and information.

Family needs refers to a family's expressed desire for services to be obtained or outcomes to be achieved (Bailey & Blanco, 1990, p. 196). A **family needs assessment** evaluates current conditions and needs in a family and provides information on what the parents' goals are for their child and for potential parent involvement in the early intervention program.

family needs assessment

Inclusion is particularly successful at the preschool level.

A parent interview is one mechanism used to determine family needs. Throughout the interview, an intervenor can explore child-rearing methods, discipline, the opportunities for learning in the home, and parental attitudes and perceptions about the child's behaviour and skills. Discussion questions may include topics such as: Are there specific home and/or community activities that are concerns for family members? What skills would family members like the child to learn or to use more often? What behaviours would family members like the child to exhibit less often? Which of these concerns are priorities for family members? (Cordesco & Laus, 1993).

Early Intervention

Early intervention should parallel or immediately follow early identification. The processes are not nearly as clear and coordinated as those within the school system. There are many types of intervention provided by different people in different settings under different agencies and jurisdictions. There are also quite a number of theoretical and practical issues surrounding early intervention.

The chief issue in early intervention is, "Why intervene early?" The answer is complex and includes the following:

- Research in child development clearly demonstrates that the early years are a time of rapid learning. After Benjamin Bloom (1964) summarized a plethora of studies on intellectual growth, he suggested that a stimulating environment is critical to optimal cognitive growth. Bloom proposed that intellectual development can be seen as following a negative growth curve; as the child grows older, a rich and diverse environment has a decreasingly positive effect. Thus, children at the age of three will benefit more from enrichment activities than children aged eight to ten.

- Early services can maximize skill development and reduce or alleviate the need for special services when a child enters school. Both developmental and educational intervention are likely to be more effective if they occur before the child's deficiencies become massive and are compounded by the numbing effects of extended school failure. In fact, the earlier intervention is started, the higher the rate of later educational attainment (Bloom, 1991).

- Intervention sustains growth. For children with Down syndrome, for example, early and sustained intervention halts the decline in cognitive development that typically occurs during the first twelve to eighteen months of life and appears to prevent further decreases throughout the remaining early childhood years. Similar outcomes have been observed for the motor development of children with cerebral palsy (Palmer, Shapiro, Wachtel, Allen, Hiller, Harryman, Master, Meinert, & Capute, 1988). For young children with behavioural disorders, early intervention is a decisive factor, as we explain in the Research Notes below.

RESEARCH NOTES

Early Intervention for Behavioural Disorders

Early intervention is often thought of in terms of the normative categories of disability—deafness, severe visual impairments, autism, and so on. However, it is also one of the most critical components of work with children with behavioural disorders, although early identification and early intervention remain unsolved problems. Turning the conceptions of early identification and early intervention into coherent, consistent, and sustained action presents a major challenge to educators (Kauffman, 2005).

The stability of children's behaviours once they reach elementary school illustrates the importance of early intervention. Behavioural disorders can actually be identified in very young children, and sustained action can ameliorate or eliminate many problems. On the other hand, festering problems will continue and even increase unless structured and systematic intervention occurs. It has been consistently documented that approximately half of the preschoolers who evidence behavioural problems continue to manifest problems several years later (Campbell, 1997). As we stress in Chapter 7, continued antisocial behaviour in childhood places a student at substantial

risk for a wide variety of negative outcomes. The continuation of antisocial behaviour in school is likely to lead to rejection and low levels of peer acceptance, increased risk of school failure, membership in deviant peer groups, dropping out of school, eventual delinquency, and poor adjustment and mental health in later years, especially for boys.

Of course, it is very difficult to measure behaviour in young children. But behavioural disorders may be seen even in infancy. Children who were identified as having hyperactive and aggressive behavioural problems were described by their mothers as infants as having more behaviour problems, such as being colicky, and a more difficult temperament, such as being irritable and difficult to manage at four months. Children with ADHD are often identifiable as toddlers or preschoolers. There is a mean onset age of four years for behavioural disorders or ADHD (Alderson, 1993; Barkley, 1998).

The correlations between early aggression and later antisocial behaviour may be as high as.92 (see Loeber & Stouthamer-Loeber, 1996, 1998). Highly aggressive three-year-olds are likely to become aggressive five-year-olds. Children's level of physical and verbal aggression at ages six through twelve are fairly good predictors of their tendency to threaten, insult, tease, and compete with peers at ages ten to fourteen. To complete the age ranges, Olweus (1987) found that children described as aggressive at thirteen and fifteen years of age were more likely at twenty-four to be engaged in criminal and antisocial activities. There are different manifestations of later violence including frequent fighting by age eighteen, partner abuse, and conviction for violent offences by age thirty-two.

In young children, future problems are indicated by frequent conflict with peers, extreme aggression or social withdrawal, and behaviour that is severe in intensity, high in rate, diverse in expression, and found over multiple settings. A combination of hyperactivity and aggression is highly predictable of future behaviour problems (see Stormont, 2001). But since young children's social and emotional behaviour is quite flexible, preventative efforts seem to have a good chance of success (Kamps, Tankersley, & Ellis, 2000). In fact, long-term follow-up data suggest that the life courses of children at risk for becoming aggressive and disruptive can be changed dramatically through early behaviour intervention (Strain & Timm, 2001).

Experts in the treatment of behavioural disorders argue that structured and systematic intervention needs to begin by age eight in order to prevent such problems from becoming chronic (see McConaughy, Kay, & Fitzgerald, 2000) and to alter behavioural patterns leading to more maladaptive conduct. The prime time for intervention is just prior to or at the point of formal school entry.

- For the family, early intervention serves as a support that enhances family functioning, provides crucial information for parents, and makes parents the primary players in their child's developmental progress. Activities are designed to support families to the greatest extent possible. These family-centred activities optimally include the siblings and the extended family as well as the parents.

- For the school-aged child, achievement levels in grade 3 seem to have particular predictive value. The prime time for intervention is before the end of this grade. We stressed in Chapter 5 that much current research emphasizes the need for intensive remedial reading instruction to begin before grade 3. Not only do young children embark on a cycle of frustration and failure, but they learn inappropriate strategies that soon become habitual and that can present an almost insurmountable obstacle to remediation. Teachers are well aware, for example, of how difficult it is to change the way children form letters once they have internalized incorrect formations.

Service Delivery Models

Infants and preschoolers with disabilities may be served in the home, in clinic settings, in separate specialized programs, or within the regular complex of child-care facilities. Increasing numbers of public school systems are implementing early childhood programs, especially programs for children who are considered to be at risk for school failure or those who have special needs. Those in the five to eight years of age range will be chiefly in regular schools and classrooms.

For infants and preschoolers, the contemporary philosophy is a family-based approach. It serves to broaden the scope of intervention services beyond the child to include family members and involves those family members in determining the goals of an early intervention program, based on the belief that children with disabilities and their families possess strengths that are as important as their needs. A principal objective of family-based practices is to enhance parents' confidence in their ability to parent and encourage their child's progress (Trivette & Dunst, 2004). Intervenors work to build on a family's existing strengths.

Infant Programs

Infants and toddlers are often served in centre-based (or clinic-based) programs, which are typically specialized. Families bring their infant or toddler to a program or an agency setting, where appropriate services are provided by professionals. Regular intervention sessions are scheduled either on an individual basis for infants or in small groups for toddlers. Most programs tend to follow developmental and therapeutic models in their curricula. A professional related to a discipline in the child's area of most significant need is the primary intervenor.

home visiting

Equally popular today is early intervention that takes place in the home and/or uses the home as a basis for curricular objectives. Programs are often referred to as **home visiting**, a process whereby a professional provides help over an extended period of time to a family in its own home (Wasik, Bryant, & Lyons, 1990).

In general, home-based early intervention involves consistent contact in the client's home between the child and the family and a representative of a formal agency. The appeal of home visiting is based on the opportunity to work with individuals within the family context. This enables professionals to learn first-hand about the conditions of life for children and parents and means that instructional recommendations are practical and realistic, because the teacher has the opportunity to observe the family's lifestyle and available resources.

Parents as Intervenors

Apart from teachers and other professionals, the primary intervenors in the early years are a child's own parents. *Parent involvement* does not mean that parents should do the job of professionals. Nor is parent involvement a specific set of activities such as parents' groups or teaching activities. Rather, parent involvement implies shared responsibility for a child's progress. As one worker said, "Effective parent involvement programs acknowledge the fact that parents are a child's earliest and most influential teachers. Trying to educate the young child without help and support from the home is akin to trying to rake leaves in a high wind" (Gough, 1991, p. 339).

Parents are trained to assist in program planning and/or teaching activities either at home or in a centre. They learn strategies for imparting specific skills and competencies in the belief that with instruction, modelling, and reinforcement, they can become more effective teachers of their own children. Some specific areas of parent training include understanding the nature and prognosis of the child's condition; physical management; managing self-care and daily living activities; guidance and behaviour management; handling the child; stimulating mobility, locomotion, and communication; and responding appropriately to different or unexpected behaviours. Daily routines such as caring for pets and grocery shopping are explained and modeled as rich experiences for development.

Treatment regimes depend on the special needs of a child. For example, parents of children with autism can learn how to manage their child and how to stimulate social, motor, and communicative development. For a child with a hearing impairment, parents may be instructed as to the nature of hearing impairment, the stages of normal language development, the use of a hearing aid, the various available modes of communication, and how to reinforce the child's early vocalizations by responding with pleasure and attention. For children with physical and health disorders, parents must be educated to promote their children's independence. This involves an acceptance of the disability, as well as recognition of the child's individual strengths and abilities.

Even though parent participation is highly valued, many difficulties remain. In fact, studies (e.g., Bricker, 1986) have found that only 20 to 40 percent of parents were actively involved in their child's early intervention program. The factors that influence parent involvement are diverse and difficult to document. The greater the number of unmet needs the parents have in their own lives, the less time, energy, and commitment they have to carry out educational and therapeutic interventions with their child. In other cases, parent intervention is hindered by limited knowledge bases, skill deficits, lack of self-confidence, impaired objectivity, economic considerations, and the needs of other family members. Sometimes parents are placed in an inappropriate, unrealistic, or overtly professionalized role.

The cultural background of the family is a major factor that can alter the intervention process, the role of professionals, and the amount of active parent participation. Culturally based beliefs affect the manner in which families adapt to the child, the family's willingness and ability to seek help, their communication styles with professionals, the level of trust given to caregivers and caregiving agencies, the amount and type of participation, the goals and outcomes they select for the child, and the family members who will participate in intervention activities. Factors that play a role in jeopardizing parent-intervenor collaboration include differences in language, dialect, values and belief systems; or insensitivity to religious beliefs, family traditions, or family pride. In British Columbia, for example, Lai and Ishiyama (2004) investigated the involvement of Chinese Canadian mothers of children with disabilities. Among other things, they found that limited English proficiency posed a first and major barrier to participation.

Even for those parents eager for involvement, the process may be neither cheap nor convenient. Parents enter programs with the expectation of getting help for their child. When the assistance carries with it high explicit or implicit expectations of parent participation and time-consuming commitments, not participating fully may make parents feel guilty. They feel that they are open to criticism for appearing not to have their child's interests at heart (Akerley, 1975).

Preschool Programs

Much remains unknown about how to achieve widespread, high quality programs for very young children, particularly in the context of early intervention. The current philosophy is that early childhood special education should not be separate from early childhood education. It should be thought of not as parallel care and education but as care and education that is embedded in and integral to general early childhood education.

Very young children who are exceptional usually receive their education in general classes.

The most appropriate settings for young children are comprehensive programs that promote regular contact with typical children.

The integration of children with disabilities into natural settings is predicated on the development of social interaction and friendship among children; the improvement in self-concept in children with disabilities; and opportunities for observation and imitation of the language, behaviour, and skills of normally developing peers. Children with special needs should be placed in a centre where they can achieve at their own level, where they are challenged to develop their potential but not swamped by a program beyond their grasp, where they can receive instruction in areas of need, and where they have opportunities to interact with other children.

Curriculum

Children with disabilities need the same skills as their peers, and they usually acquire the same skills in the same sequence. Therefore, it makes sense that the normal developmental processes of children provide the most critical reference for teachers of preschool children with mild disabilities. The regular early childhood curriculum includes communication, social and emotional development, self-care and physical development, the demands of the current environment, and the skills needed in the next environment. These curriculum objectives will be the same for young children with disabilities. Exceptions will probably be a somewhat expanded program to include early assessment, the development of an individualized program, the intervention of professionals and paraeducators, a range of teaching approaches and techniques, and adaptations to the environment.

TRANSITION

One common experience for each child and each family is the transition from a setting serving very young children to the formal school system. In early childhood special education, **transition** is the process of moving from one program to another, or from one service delivery mode to another.

transition

The child's transition from a preschool to a public school program is a time of change for both the child and the family. Preschool and public school programs differ on a number of dimensions, including location, personnel, transportation options, schedules, family support services, and methods of communication between home and teacher. Changing programs, systems, and personnel can be stressful for both child and parent.

For the parents, the public school brings changing roles and expectations. For example, in public school the child is often labelled officially for the first time as being different. For the child, the separation from a child-care or preschool program may be the most abrupt and permanent break with the past that he or she experiences before leaving home as a young adult. Transition means severing bonds with preschool staff, making new friends, generalizing old skills to new situations, acquiring new routines, and exploring new environments. Children face a group of strange people and inevitably experience separation fears along with the daunting tasks of learning the rules and consequences of an unfamiliar environment and their place in a new hierarchy.

The factors contributing to the success or failure of transitions are multiple and complex. They involve not only the child but also the quality of the sending and receiving programs, and the behaviour of the teachers, families, and communities. Especially important are the preparation, implementation, and follow-up that underlie the entire transition process. Preparing for transition involves a number of components—preparing children and family members for the move to a new program; minimizing the disruption caused by necessary changes in services; supporting children and family members as they adjust to the new program; making subsequent adjustments to new experiences for the child and the child's family; and providing the child with the skills to succeed in the new placement.

The success of transition is influenced by the child's skills and behaviours and the match between these skills and the expectations and requirements of the receiving program. Children who make the transition to kindergarten armed with the necessary survival skills and who use these skills in appropriate contexts are more likely to succeed in the regular classrooms than peers who lack the skills. But there can never be a universal list of transition skills, because classroom and teacher expectations differ too much. However, critical skills seem to include self-help, social interaction, and play, as well as the ability to function independently and respond to group instruction.

Service Delivery Models in Formal Schooling

One of the most difficult choices for many parents is the location of their child's schooling. A much-needed body of research has developed in recent years regarding parents' perceptions of location on a continuum of educational services. Parent attitudes, in tune with those of teachers, tend to be contradictory and inconclusive, but indicate a sustained movement toward inclusion in general classrooms.

SUMMARY

1. The presence of a child with a disability can be a difficult situation for all family members. This has led to a commitment to provide comprehensive, coordinated, and family-focused services to children with disabilities and their families.

2. The effects of stress on the families of very young disabled children are pervasive, multiple, and sometimes unsuspected. Families are as individual and unique as their children. With a child who is disabled, some families cope effectively and adaptively; others tend to feel helpless and to experience less personal gratification and more child-related problems.

3. Over the years, families, family functioning, the impact of a member with a disability, and the provision of treatment and services have been looked at in different ways. Researchers examine family functioning in terms of a *stage-theory approach*, a *life-cycle approach*, a *systems approach*, or its first cousin, a *social-support approach*. Each of these ways of viewing families translates into practical models for actually intervening and working with families.

4. The traditional stage theory suggests that the parents of children with disabilities pass through orderly stages before they accept the reality of their child's condition. The life-cycle approach sees families moving through time experiencing a series of events and tasks that include transitions. A family support system approach stresses how the family fits into the broader social context. Currently, the most common framework for understanding family assets, needs, resources, and perceptions is a systems approach or perspective that sees the family as a system. Any event involving a change in the life of a family that has a disabled child can cause stress to the whole system.

5. Each parent, each sibling, and each member of the extended family has a different reaction to the presence of a child with a disability in the family. However, studies on sibling relationships are contradictory and inconsistent, and those on the extended family sparse.

6. Both early intervention and its natural corollary, early identification, rest on the belief that children with disabilities can make positive gains if their problems are identified and diagnosed as early as possible and they receive educational and therapeutic services attuned to their special needs. Early intervention activities are directed toward ameliorating problems in children with established disabilities and toward intervention with children who are at risk, to prevent or hinder the development of conditions that impair learning or behaviour.

7. Early intervention is based on research evidence in child development, models of successful performance, the general observations of laypersons and experts, and the impetus from the 1986 American legislation, PL 99–452.

8. Early intervention allows treatment to begin; draws parents into the intervention process; may prevent the development of secondary conditions; and increases the chances that the child will achieve the greatest possible degree of independence. Parent involvement is critical. Research shows that early childhood special education is not as effective if parents are not involved and supported. Programs should be family-centred. They should establish the family as the focus of services, support and respect family decision making, and provide intervention services designed to strengthen family functioning.

9. Across Canada, policies affecting young children and their families are under the jurisdiction of a number of legislative frameworks and ministries. In general, infant and toddler programs offer parents intensive participation and usually continue until the child is about three years of age. Programs in which workers visit the home are a promising mechanism used to provide for a growing population of children under the age of three who are receiving special services.

10. Programs try to enhance a child's development by helping the parents to become effective intervenors. The goal of training is to enable family members to achieve desired outcomes and deal effectively with future concerns. For the child, the goal is optimal development in the motor, cognitive, language and communication, social, and self-help skill domains.

11. Today, many young children with disabilities are placed in normalized preschool settings (daycare or nursery school) under naturalistic curricula.

12. *Transition* is more than simply transferring records or relocating a child. It is a complex process, since it relates to both the family and the child.

HISTORICAL NOTES

For most of the 19th century, educators saw early adolescence, not early childhood, as the formative years for both normal and exceptional populations. Most educators agreed that a commitment to mental discipline was incompatible with children under the ages of six or seven and that school was physically, psychologically, and intellectually harmful to children younger than five or six years of age. The public schools catered to children from seven or eight years of age and up. Youngsters who were disabled went to institutional settings, where they were admitted much later, at ten or twelve years of age.

In the final three decades of the 19th century, the view of the incapacity of young children was revised as part of the emerging child study movement. Infancy was distinguished from childhood as a discrete period of development. Children from birth to about six years of age were now seen to be active beings who required play rather than formal lessons, but this could be presented within the confines of educational settings. Kindergarten care became a feature of American education in the 1880s.

Programs for young children with special needs were boosted early in the 1900s when Maria Montessori (1870–1962) began to work with retarded children in Italy. Montessori drew heavily on the sense training methods developed by Itard in his work with Victor (see Chapter 4).

Parent groups sprang up in the early decades of the 20th century. The first was the National Society for Crippled Children, formed in the United States in 1921. In 1933, an Ohio group of parents of children with mental disabilities established a parents' group to advocate the legal and educational rights of disabled children. The United Cerebral Palsy Association began in 1948.

Largely due to inadequate public and professional response to their children's educational and other needs, parents began to organize more formally on a local level in the 1940s and 1950s, and on a national level in the 1960s. Since then, parent organizations have had a tremendous impact on special education. Across Canada today, parent organizations exist at the local, provincial, and national level. Some of these groups are small, local, and casual; others are affiliated with professional organizations. Parent organizations have lobbied successfully for improved educational, social, recreational, and vocational services for their children.

However, in the actual delivery of services, parents tended to be ignored. Until the early 1970s, they were not invited to participate to any degree, but rather remained passive recipients of professional advice. Professionals made the major decisions about a child's needs and educational placement and then worked with other agencies to attain the prescribed goals. During the 1970s, professionals began to agree that parents could have a constructive impact, but involvement was typically limited to carrying out specific activities directed by the school. By the early 1980s, the traditional notion of professional expertise, which denied that parents were competent to take the initiative in regard to their child, began to change. Today, family-centred approaches emphasize that parents are the chief intervenors and advocates for their own children.

CHAPTER 17

ADOLESCENTS AND YOUNG ADULTS

INTRODUCTION

Recently, special education has begun to focus specifically on early childhood and late adolescence. Intense research is being directed toward very young children with special needs, and interest has grown dramatically in secondary-level students who are disabled and the schools' responsibilities to this population. Nevertheless, there remains a relative vacuum; the transition period from eighteen to twenty-six years of age has not received systematic study that incorporates educational, individual, and family perspectives.

As well, research in the area of adolescents with learning or behavioural disorders is strikingly deficient compared to the area of childhood groups. Elementary special education predominates the focus of research and also tends to be the main focus in undergraduate teacher preparation programs. Most program delivery models are found at elementary levels. Most inclusive projects occur at the preschool or elementary rather than high school or middle school level; efficacy studies to support inclusion have been conducted in elementary schools, and model programs described tend to be elementary.

The number of students with disabilities served in general classes decreases with the age of the students, and the number served in separate classes, separate schools, and residential facilities increases (Hobbs & Westling, 1998). Only one-third the number of students with severe disabilities who are included in the elementary years remain included in secondary school (see Peters Goessling, 2000).

There is much that we still do not know about educational and counselling needs and transition planning at secondary levels and the needs of young adults with disabilities. While there is a far greater focus on the post-school experiences of young adults than there was even 10 years ago, not enough is known about effective secondary-level programming, the experiences of young adults, and how schools can assist them as they enter the workforce or tertiary education.

We do know that many people who are disabled develop into productive and self-sufficient adults. They marry, have children, assume mortgages, hold down jobs, and participate in social activities. For a substantial proportion of young adults with disabilities, however, the transition from school to the adult world is difficult and trying. The school experience, though tainted with frustration and failure, nevertheless offers some predictability. The adult world does not have this predictability, and many people with disabilities tend to flounder in independent living. Occupationally, many never attain a satisfactory level of career development consistent with their capabilities.

In this final chapter, we discuss the needs of adolescents and young adults with disabilities. We focus particularly on the need for transition planning and specific transition programming that stresses academic achievement, social and personal adjustment, and post-school adjustment. This chapter also considers various types of post-secondary and employment options available to persons with disabilities.

ADOLESCENTS

In humans, the twenty-year developmental trajectory from birth on includes an extended and protracted childhood, which includes the period known as *adolescence*. Changes occur during adolescence within almost every domain of an individual's life—physical, social, educational, and familial. Many of these changes are gradual and have different timetables and magnitudes for different adolescents. Accompanying psychological, social, and physiological changes, and the biological capacity for adult relationships can cause confusion, uncertainty, social anxiety, and acute self-awareness. Adolescence brings a period of identity crisis, intense peer-group relationships, and sometimes rebellion against established order. As adolescent students develop their own identities and expectations of the future, they begin to think of themselves as independent individuals, not their parents' children. They become less compliant with teachers and parents, and more prone to question and criticize than younger children.

For the adolescent student, there is more to high school success than competency in academics. As students get older, the level of independence expected of them increases, and activities such as driving a car, attending school dances, and joining football teams become important. As well, the rapid body changes associated with the onset of adolescence and the transition from elementary to secondary school mean dramatic alterations in student peer-group composition and status. Social competence, peer acceptance, being popular with peers, and belonging to the right crowd are a vital part of growing up.

peers

Between the ages of six and twelve, children spend an average of 40 percent of their waking hours in the company of **peers**—children of their own age and status (Cole & Cole, 1989). As children grow older, their social networks become increasingly complex, containing friends and acquaintances unknown to their family members (Hay, Payne, & Chadwick, 2004). Adolescents spend large amounts of time with friends and place special emphasis on the qualities of intimacy, mutual understanding, and loyalty.

The characteristics specific to adolescents with disabilities simply exacerbate the normal difficulties of adolescence, so that fulfilling the multiple tasks of a teenager are far more tentative. Daily tests of personal competence against one's peers are the stuff of adolescence, but a disability can make an adolescent feel incompetent and unconfident; those who compete poorly meet a variety of problems in self-concept and interpersonal relation-ships. Low-achieving students, for example, are frequently judged in relation to high achievers, and feelings of inferiority, lack of motivation, and interpersonal hostility often result. Students with intellectual disabilities may not have the cognitive ability to cope with the new developments within themselves and the new demands of the environment. Or take the impulsive child. Even though this student likely experienced frequent teacher rep-rimands early in his school years, as an adolescent he now has to deal with social rejection and isolation and peer labels of "immature" and "weird" (Cherkes-Julkowski, Sharp, & Stolzenberg, 1997).

Adolescents are particularly vulnerable to the negative impact of having few or no friends, a situation that may be common for students with disabilities. One report (Polloway, Epstein, Patton, Cullinan, & Lueble, 1986) found that teacher ratings indicated that more than 20 percent of older students with mild intellectual disabilities were rejected by their peers. Siperstein and Bak (1989) found that, unlike typical children, children with intellec-tual disabilities generally nominated non-peers as friends. They found that 81 percent of adolescents with cognitive delays who were questioned mentioned someone outside of class as a friend. Almost half of the outsiders were adults—often paid tutors or friends of their parents.

For typical students, self-esteem increases steadily during adolescence and early adult-hood; on the average, eighteen-year-olds have higher self-esteem than thirteen-year-olds. Social, physical, and cognitive deficits hinder this process in adolescents with disabilities. Physical disabilities, for example, reduce the rate of self-concept formation (Lawrence, 1991).

Together with personal difficulties, the environmental demands related to the structure of secondary schools may prove problematic. Most middle and high schools are organized on a departmental or subject-matter basis, and secondary schools are generally large places in which students are expected to function independently. The instructional context changes. Classes become more demanding, requiring coverage of more course content. There is a heavier emphasis on grades and, of course, homework. As student bodies become larger, schedules become more complex and the system's ability to differentiate and indi-vidualize is compromised.

Adjusting to the school and its expectations, classroom routines, the pressures of daily life, peer groups, and a range of different teachers can be stressful for students with disabil-ities. They may have been successful in elementary school, where there is some continuity between instructional areas and teachers, but often have difficulty in high school dealing with several different teachers and compartmentalized instruction.

Students may lack the plethora of survival skills that include going to class every day; arriving at school on time; bringing pencils and other supplies to class; turning in work on time; talking to teachers politely; and reading and following directions. For example, school attendance is a problem for adolescents who are learning disabled: more secondary stu-dents with learning disabilities fail regular courses because of attendance than for any other reason (Kaplan, 1996).

The gap between students with disabilities and their peers continues to widen the fur-ther they progress in school. Teenagers who are disabled often become frustrated with their lack of progress; they may become caught in a spiral of failure and dissatisfaction, resign themselves to a poor view of their intelligence and their ability as a whole, and lose their self-esteem and motivation.

For teachers at the secondary level, the world of the adolescent raises issues that are far broader than those raised for the elementary-school child. These include the adolescent's emerging sexuality, vocational interests and talents, future expectations, range of leisure activities, and independent living skills.

Secondary teachers have different responsibilities and orientations than their peers at the elementary levels and may not offer students the same warm indulgence and social protection provided earlier. Secondary-level teachers are trained as content specialists, and a teacher can be involved in as many as 1000 to 1500 interactions with students each day. Secondary people tend to differ from elementary teachers on their views of integration and the kinds and numbers of accommodations they make (Olson, Chalmer, & Hoover, 1997). Findings show a tendency to be less accepting than others of students with special needs in general classrooms: when asked, secondary-level teachers usually display a less positive attitude toward educational inclusion than elementary teachers (Dev & Scruggs, 1997; Scruggs & Mastropoeri, 1996).

Teachers will find that student motivation and interest is different from that seen in elementary pupils. On average, the grades and attendance for all students, including those with special needs, decline after moving from elementary to junior high and high school (see Roderick & Camburn, 1999). Some teachers look at secondary programs for students with disabilities with "quiet resignation," and hold the view "that little, if anything, can be done for older students" (Schumaker, Deschler, Bulgren, Davis, Lenz, & Grossen, 2002, p. 2). They may feel that since students with disabilities show poor motivation and negative attitudes toward school and academic learning, remedial programming is not very realistic, and that these students are at the end of their school careers, anyway.

CONCEPTS OF TRANSITION

The transition from high school to adult life for adolescents with disabilities has gained considerable attention in the past 20 years or so. The development of transition initiatives is explained in the Research Notes below.

RESEARCH NOTES

The Concept and Practice of Transition for Adolescents

It was in the early 1980s that the need for transition activities became clear. Study after study indicated that many students with special needs, despite special education programs, still experienced major difficulties in bridging the gap between school and community work and living. They met difficulties in independent living, occupational stability, and status within their communities. They did not utilize community services and resources effectively, and tended to be isolated from peers, both disabled and non-disabled.

The secondary transition movement was grounded in the co-operative work/study programs of the 1960s and the career education initiative of the 1970s. For students with disabilities, the focus on transition emerged in the mid-1980s, when the U.S. Federal Office of Special Education Program's (OSEP) "Transition initiative" was articulated and implemented. It called for an "outcome- oriented process encompassing a broad array of services and experiences that lead to employment" (Will, 1984).

By 1990, the concept of transition had been made concrete in U.S. policy accompanied by federal discretionary grants. The Individuals with Disabilities Education Act (IDEA, 1990, PL 101–476) provided a clear definition. Under the amended IDEA of 2004, transition is

> a co-ordinated set of activities for a child with a disability that focus on improving the academic

and functional achievement of the child with a disability in order to facilitate the child's movement from school to post-school activities. The post-school activities can include post-secondary education, vocational training, and integrated employment (including supported employment), continuing and adult education, independent living, and responsible community participation. Transition services must be based on the individual child's needs, strengths, preferences, and interests. Transition services can also include instruction, related services, community experiences, the development of employment and other post-school adult living skills and functional vocational evaluation (IDEA 2004, Section 602 (34).

Simply defined, **transition** is "a systematic passage from school to adult life for students with disabilities" (Morningstar, Kleinhammer-Tramill, & Laltin, 1999, p. 1). **Transition planning** centres on "empowering and supporting young adults with disabilities to assume their rightful place in mainstream society as independent and contributing members" (Blanchett, 2001, p. 3).

When we confront the concept and practice of transition in relation to the needs of adolescents with disabilities, we find a set of intermeshed meanings and foci. These are

- *Transition as an ongoing experience.* Definitions of the term *transition* have in common the concept that a transition is a passage or an evolution, not simply a "here today, gone tomorrow" phenomenon. In other words, transitions are not a fleeting proposition but rather they represent recurrent, life-long processes that all individuals experience. For all students, the high-school experience represents a period of transition between the security of school and the complexity associated with the opportunities and risks of adult life. The quality of the secondary-school experience and the decisions made during high school have significant implications for the quality of life experienced after students leave school.

- *Transition as a movement.* The general concept of transition visualizes it as a movement from one service delivery system to another. For the adolescent with disabilities, this means moving from the school, with its services in education and counselling, to an adult world with community services and advocacy and self-help groups such as the Canadian Association for Community Living.

- *Transition as a school program focus.* Transition programs focus on the acquisition of life and vocational skills with the focus on the local community, and on both job preparation and job finding and maintenance. Programs seek the maximum development of intellectual, personal, social, and vocational skills necessary for independent functioning.

transition

transition planning

• *Transition as an appropriate response for families that sometimes feel abandoned.* As students near the end of their school careers, parents realize that special education services are ending but hold little certainty that community services will begin and provide needed support.

Transition programs rest on the premise that the quality of life and the extent to which youth with disabilities achieve the desired goals of employment, community living, and social and leisure opportunities are dependent upon the effectiveness and appropriateness of secondary-school experiences as well as on co-operative service planning and the availability of needed adult services. Educators must address specifically and directly the instructional requirements associated with school performance, secondary completion, and post-school preparation (Benz, Lindstrom, & Yovanoff, 2000). Students need skills in vocational pursuits and independent living; they need to be aware of career and post-secondary opportunities that match their interests and abilities; and they must possess strategies for pursuing opportunities in employment and post-secondary education.

When schools plan and implement transition programs, a number of salient points must be foregrounded. These are as follows:

• The transition process is a vehicle for alleviating the problems of youth with various disabilities through careful planning, instruction, placement, and the provision of ongoing support as and after they leave school.

• Transition is founded on the premise that all persons with disabilities can perform meaningful tasks and assume valued roles within normal community settings. However, enhancing the prospects for economic stability for persons who are exceptional by placing graduating students into jobs should not be considered an outcome in and of itself. Also important are **quality-of-life outcomes**—the tangible and intangible results of employment that contribute to the enhancement of students' lifestyles.

quality-of-life outcomes

• Effective transition planning is much more than the mere physical transfer of administrative responsibility for an individual's service program from the school to adult service agencies. Successfully negotiating the transition through and out of high school is a process that requires varying degrees of assistance from family and school personnel. It involves collaboration and coordination within a team approach. The likelihood of meaningful post-secondary outcomes is possible only when stakeholders work together. A transition team should include all those providing services in both school and community—special educators, family members, general and vocational educators, employers, community leaders, and adult service providers. The latter may include many different agencies, depending on the nature and severity of the disability.

  • The team should target skills that the student may need to be successful after The or she leaves school. It should also address the student's strengths, the family's critical concerns, and other needs related to broad skill domains (such as non-verbal communication, language, social relationships, self-management, academics, personal care, community living, home living, vocational skills, and recreational interests and skills).

• Parent participation in secondary programs has been traditionally underemphasized. For transition to be successful, parents must be involved.

- The transition component, to be developed not later than a student's 16th birthday, must be incorporated into the IEP planning process. Student participation in the IEP process will allow the individual to engage in self-evaluation, self-determination, student-identified post-school goals, and self-selected educational experiences (see the Case Study about Ben in Chapter 6).

- The IEP will include goals and objectives, timelines, and designations of responsible persons and agencies. Educationally, it will focus on a comprehensive curriculum that is functional in nature and includes community-based vocational instruction. It will identify and teach activities that will maximize an individual's participation in community settings, such as vocational training, personal management, and recreation/leisure activities. The plan will also identify the types of community services that will be necessary to support the individual's participation, and complete the steps required to access community services.

THE SCHOOL'S RESPONSIBILITIES IN TRANSITION

In transition, the school has two primary roles. First, it is its responsibility to develop and implement an effective program that will prepare students for life in their local communities. Second, the school must take the lead in coordinating the transition-planning process (see Figure 17-1). This involves secondary programs for transition, linkages to post-secondary environments, and post-secondary services.

Transition planning should start much sooner than high school; it should begin in the elementary grades. Career awareness can begin as early as the primary grades with discussions about what it means to work in a particular job (Bounds, 1997). Students also begin to learn the rudiments of community and vocational living skills in upper elementary school.

Service Delivery

For secondary students with mild disabilities, there are three essential components in senior programming: work preparation skills, functional academics, and life-skills training, which includes counselling and sex education. For students with severe disabilities, the curriculum should expose them to job options in the community in which they live; teach specific work skills such as using tools and equipment; and teach work-related skills, such as transportation and personal hygiene (McDonnell, Ferguson, & Mathot-Buckner, 1992).

It must be recognized that there is more evidence supporting the integration of younger children than there is for older students and that integration into general education options at the secondary levels is harder to implement than it is for young children. Various factors account for this:

- Younger children acclimatize more rapidly to integrated settings than older students.

- The mental gap between typical students and those with disabilities continuously widens with age.

Figure 17-1

The transition process

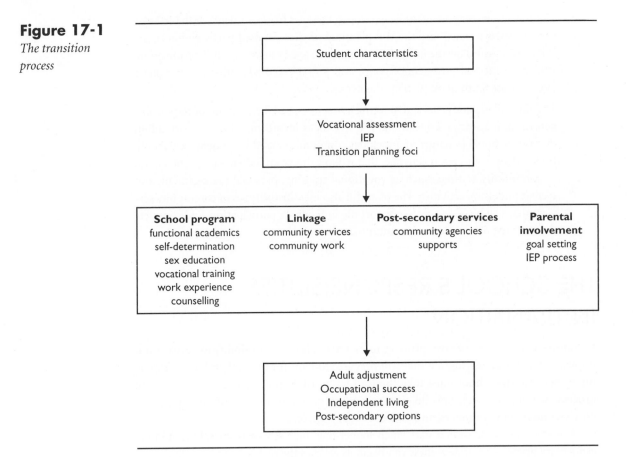

- The grade level of the class is a proxy for a number of variables. For example, primary grade students are more tolerant than those of junior high school age, who are more likely to ostracize a child.

- The instructional emphasis at the secondary levels is different from that of the elementary school. Curriculum in secondary schools is no longer focused on the acquisition of basic skills but on the use of skills to acquire content knowledge.

- Teachers at the elementary level are more student oriented than subject-matter oriented; the opposite goes for most high school teachers (MacMillan, Gresham, & Forness, 1996).

- Students lack skills. For example, by late adolescence, individuals with mild intellectual disabilities can be expected to develop academic skills at approximately the grade 6 level.

- The current needs and ultimate goals of students at the end of their school careers are different from those of younger children. As Figure 17-2 shows on page 548, the needs that must be addressed by secondary programming meld into after-school needs.

In many ways, inclusive practices are in direct conflict with what we know works for adolescent students with disabilities in terms of functional skill instruction and vocational training in the community. So it is not surprising that there is scepticism about whether

Planned and systematic opportunities to interact with non-disabled peers help prepare young people with disabilities to function independently in the general school.

inclusion is feasible or desirable for secondary students. The argument circles around three interrelated themes: the characteristics of adolescent students with disabilities, the content of the regular curriculum, and the future needs of students. We discuss each of these below.

Student Characteristics

Adolescents do not outgrow their learning difficulties, nor is simple maturation matched with an increase in motivation and achievement. On the contrary. Factors correlated with students with mild disabilities include physiological and neurological problems, deficits in cognitive processes such as memory and metacognitive awareness, disorders of attention, social behaviour problems, communication problems, and perceptual problems.

Learning disabilities offers a clear illustration. It is often assumed that learning disabilities can be cured and are not lifelong. This is not true. The disabilities change form as students get older, but even with appropriate intervention, learning disabilities do not just go away; they tend to endure into adulthood.

Secondary students classified as learning disabled often retain subtle manifestations of childhood traits, such as lack of coordination and hyperactivity. Academically, they tend to plateau at grade 4 or 5. The result: almost all of these students lack functional proficiency in language, reading, handwriting, spelling, and arithmetic. Students with learning disabilities enter secondary school severely deficient in basic reading and written expression skills; three or four years later they leave with little or no improvement in these areas (Espin & Foegen, 1996). They often cannot understand the abstract language of academic disciplines or comprehend the texts. By junior high or middle school, many students with learning disabilities have developed a special aversion to writing (Hallenbeck, 2002).

Figure 17-2

Needs of secondary-school students

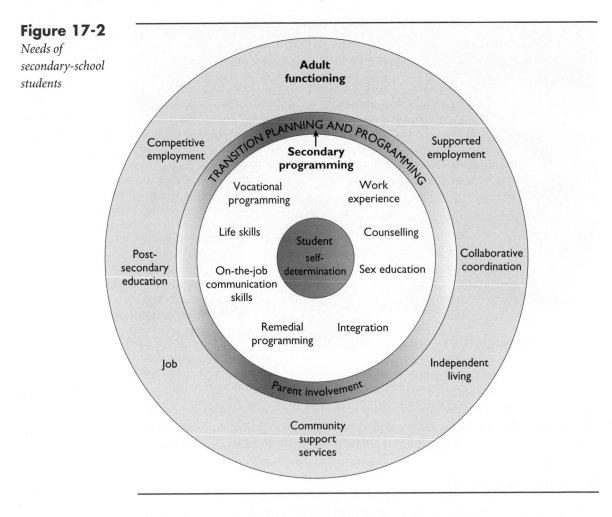

Academic failures create frustration, and students can become emotionally vulnerable and easily stressed. They tend to demonstrate a high degree of anxiety, low expectations of future success, poor adaptive strategies for coping with normal stress and solving everyday personal problems, reduced motivation, and poor self-concept.

As a further example, we can examine the adolescent experiences of students classified as having Attention Deficit Hyperactivity Disorder. While an estimated 50 percent of individuals experience a brain maturational spurt of unknown etiology and do outgrow the condition, the other 50 percent have difficulties that persist into adulthood and cause concentration and attention problems. In a longitudinal study, Lambert (1988) identified more than 100 hyperactive children in elementary school, tracked them until they were seventeen or eighteen years old, and then compared them with non-hyperactive peers. He found that the students in the hyperactive group were less likely to have graduated from high school and more likely to have run away from home or become delinquent. They were more aggressive than their peers and more likely to be receiving treatment for psychological problems.

Long-term prospects for students who are both hyperactive and aggressive are even more bleak. Students with ADHD or learning disabilities combined with aggression, inattention, and impulsivity are at elevated risk for violent and antisocial behaviour (Lynam, 1996).

Finally, persuasive evidence exists that students with behavioural disorders often cannot successfully follow and master the school curriculum. They demonstrate academic deficits, have lower grades, fail more courses, are often retained in one grade or more, and pass minimum competency tests at lower rates than students with other disabilities. Often beginning at an early age and frequently continuing for the rest of their lives, individuals with behavioural disorders have difficulty abiding by basic rules of conduct and relating appropriately to others. Their experiences are likely to be early school exit, unemployment, perhaps incarceration, and significant interpersonal problems.

Students with behaviour disorders perform poorly in relation to their peers with other disabilities and without disabilities on nearly every transition outcome. In the United States, less than 50 percent of these students graduate from high school (see Maag & Katsiyannis, 1998; Rylance, 1997). Few continue education after leaving high school and most do not link with services from community-based agencies, entering what "truly is an unwelcoming and cold world as adults" (Bullis & Cheney, 1999, p. 2).

Curriculum

Debates about school placement also centre on the content of the secondary school curriculum. Adolescents with disabilities who spend the majority of their school day in general education classes are expected to meet the same demands as their typical peers. Students must be able to listen to lectures and take notes; complete many written assignments; read content-area information, often from poorly organized textbooks; and take tests that frequently do not facilitate their responding.

In the general education classroom, students can experience success only when the teacher is able to meet their individual learning needs through appropriate curriculum adaptations. But curriculum adaptations are not a part of secondary classroom life. In general, secondary educators teach to single large groups and incorporate little or no differentiation based on student need. Few teachers make adaptations and, when they do, it frequently involves lowering their expectations of students rather than attempting to improve their programs (Fuchs, Fuchs, Hamlett, Phillips, & Karns, 1995). For example, a study of 60 social studies and science teachers who were seen as effective with students with learning disabilities by peers, principals, and self found that the teachers made few adaptations to meet special learning needs (McIntosh, Vaughn, Schumm, Haager, & Lee, 1994).

Future Needs

Finally, there are the future needs of students. In the educational mainstream, some of the necessary curricular elements are simply not present. The overall secondary curriculum is not congruent with the present needs of many senior students with disabilities; they have neither the interest nor the reading ability required for academic credit courses (Nesbit, 1990).

Traditional secondary school subjects are generally not related to the future needs of students; preparation for independent living requires much more than academic goals for adolescents who are disabled. Their hope is to work, not to continue schooling, and there is less likelihood that their career development needs will be met in general classrooms. By this stage, the major goal of education should not be to compensate for intellectual and physical deficiencies per se. Rather, instruction must be directed toward the development of critical skills necessary for adulthood, success in daily life, citizenship, and a future career.

What is needed is a comprehensive curriculum that leads to successful, satisfying employment. A variety of generic curriculum domains have been proposed during recent years as important components of secondary special education. The major areas of instruction are academic skills, specifically functional academics to remediate deficient basic skills; vocational skills, which include career exploration and occupational knowledge and skills, such as job-finding skills, work experience, and job maintenance; personal management skills, which include independent living knowledge and skills such as budgeting, home management, and social skills; and leisure skills.

Counselling

The needs of adolescents are quite different from those of younger children and, when the adolescent has a disability, these needs become even more intense. Many students who are exceptional need a personal relationship with a trusted adult "who will be available to encourage their efforts, validate their fears, and celebrate their accomplishments" (Benz, Lindstrom, & Yovanoff, 2000, p. 525). This person may be the counsellor.

Guidance Counselling

Guidance counselling assists students in selecting courses, adapting to their disability, and personal concerns. It may also slip over into the area of career plans, occupational choice, and job placement. Adaptation to the disability is a major thrust. Students need to understand that their disability need not impede their ability to work and embrace the idea that meaningful jobs and careers are within their reach.

Students may need instruction in social skills as they mature. As an example, many adolescents with visual impairments try to mask their disabilities because they perceive visual impairments as a negative attribute (Sacks & Corn, 1996). Students often need assistance in dealing with the implications of visual impairment; personal counselling and sex education to develop greater social awareness; and help with more pragmatic concerns such as dress codes and the use of cosmetics.

Vocational/Career Counselling

For all of us, career choices are limited by such factors as individual preferences, aptitude, and temperament. Many exceptional students are unaware of their strengths and weaknesses, which makes career and vocational education critical. Students need to assess the competencies required in specific occupations and identify realistic vocational goals that match their maximum vocational potential.

Few adolescents, disabled or not, know about available occupations in their geographic area, the content of people's work, or their earnings. Students with disabilities often have even fewer and less diverse career-related experiences and learning opportunities than their peers without disabilities. Individuals who are deaf, for example, know less than their hearing peers about different types of occupations (Schroedel, 1992).

Data suggest that students are aware of their lack of preparedness. A study of 106 students with severe physical disabilities (Liebert, Lutsky, & Gottlieb, 1990) found that graduates expressed a desire for more intensive guidance counselling (especially in the area of job placement), additional training in upgrading job skills, more help with transportation, and more access to social and recreational

Having some work experience before graduation helps adolescents with the transition to adult life.

programs. In another study of students with and without learning disabilities, the learning-disabled group had a far greater desire for more information about how to find a job, keep a job, and live independently than their non-disabled peers (Dowdy, Carter, & Smith, 1990).

For adolescents who are visually impaired, realistic career choices can be difficult. Those who are deaf need help in vocational training and counselling to assess their strengths, weaknesses, and interests. Counsellors can encourage students to consider a broad array of options and to take a major role in decision making.

Multipotential can be a mixed blessing; many youngsters who are gifted share a feeling of ambivalence about the future and their place in it. By ages thirteen or fourteen, some students are already conditioned to avoid failure at all costs. They are willing to pursue career choices far below their potential. Others cannot focus on career plans. (Talented children, on the other hand, often have fixed career goals prior to adolescence.) Gifted students need personal and career counselling, a networking system that links them to school and community resources, and appropriate role models.

For all students who are exceptional, a major aim of career counselling is a careful assessment and analysis of students' strengths and weaknesses, motivations and preferences, and performance in training programs. Counsellors need to establish students' present levels with regard to readiness for adult settings. For this, they employ **vocational evaluations**—comprehensive and systematic processes that utilize work (real or simulated) to assess the vocational potential of people with disabilities. The process incorporates data such as test scores, medical data, information on education and work experience, and the needs and interests of the individual in setting vocational goals and service requirements (Pruitt, 1986).

vocational evaluations

Vocational evaluation helps students identify their functional capacities and limitations, formulate realistic vocational goals, and determine their needs for rehabilitation

community-referenced assessment

programming (Power, 1984). Sometimes, the results of a vocational evaluation will suggest that the goals of the students (and sometimes their parents) are unrealistic. At other times, job choices may be below a student's capacity. For students with moderate and severe disabilities, an environmental inventory (**community-referenced assessment**) is typically used. This details the adaptations needed for the students to function in the community.

Sex Education

The major goal of normalization is a normal family and community life for all individuals, and sexual activity is a normal part of human life. It is a myth that individuals who are physically disabled do not have sexual needs or that persons with intellectual disabilities are asexual or oversexed. People with mental and physical disabilities have the same range of sexual needs and drives as everyone else.

Nevertheless, persons who are intellectually disabled are likely to face many conflicting stereotypes, including those that portray them as asexual, perpetually childlike, dependent or oversexed, and undiscriminating and easy (Olney & Kuper, 1998). The truth is that some people with intellectual disabilities develop a strong and normal interest in sex. But, as with non-disabled people, some seem to have little need for physical contact and some express more need than the average.

If physical development is normal, sexual development follows chronological rather than cognitive development. But psychosocial development may be reached at a later chronological age. Because of this, some individuals who are disabled are more likely to express experimentation overtly. They may also have trouble figuring out where the boundaries are and when to say no.

Writers and teachers have widely noted the importance of sex education for students with disabilities. Information and training is needed to

- Provide knowledge and skills. Adolescents with disabilities are less likely to have accurate information about sex and are more subject to fears and myths. Information helps them to overcome fears and develop a positive sexual identity.

- Prevent sexual abuse. Individuals with disabilities are more likely to be sexually exploited than their typical peers. The risk is most acute for individuals with intellectual disabilities in the community who are exposed to all the contingencies of sexuality, including situations that involve sexual coercion (Podell, Kastner, & Kastner, 1996). One study of people with intellectual disabilities (Stromsness, 1993) found that just under 80 percent of the subjects had been sexually abused. Toronto's Roeher Institute reports that 39 to 68 percent of girls and 16 to 30 percent of boys with intellectual disabilities will be the subject of sexual abuse before age eighteen (Roeher Institute, 1996).

- Prevent the spread of HIV and AIDS. Sex education must include instruction in social behaviour and self-protection. Effective AIDS education means talking about topics such as homosexuality, drugs, and condoms.

- Prevent unwanted pregnancies. Students do not learn easily from non-directed observations, books, or friends. They may be uninformed about the process of reproduction and birth control. Sex education programs should include explanations of bodily functions, the mechanics of reproduction, dating skills, and preparation for marriage and family.

Functional Academics

Despite special education programming often offered throughout their school careers, many adolescent students with disabilities continue to function far below grade level. They often require a functional skills approach to improve functioning in present environments and facilitate transition to and participation in age-appropriate future environments.

Adolescents with disabilities say that what they want is instruction in a challenging and relevant curriculum that will prepare them for life after school (Guterman, 1995). Rather than focusing solely on the traditional three R's, teachers of secondary students with disabilities must be concerned with targeting useful learning objectives. Students require functional skills and **functional academics**—that is, academics that have meaning and relevance to the learner who is soon to enter community work and life.

functional academics

Functional academics include intense remedial instruction for skill deficits, such as basic knowledge and skills in reading, computation, study skills, and strategy training to enable older students to gain knowledge of how to use skills to meet demands of the academic, occupational, and social environment. The curriculum may include **functional skills**—essentially all the components a student requires to successfully negotiate life as an adult. The myriad of skills include those in self-care, mobility training, communication, social interaction, health and safety, leisure time, vocational pursuits, and skills such as filling out applications, and improving job-related behaviour such as time on task, following directions, and dealing with authority (Maag & Katsiyannis, 1998).

functional skills

Vocational Education and Work Experiences

For adolescent students with disabilities, transition should focus on work personality (self-concept and motivation); work competencies (habits, physical and mental skills, and interpersonal skills); and work goals (career objectives). It should facilitate students' access to and participation in the receiving environment through job preparation that includes skills such as locating job openings in newspapers and displaying correct behaviour during a job interview. Particularly for students with severe disabilities, the school's vocational curriculum cannot be divorced from the community in which the child lives. Schools need to identify potential employment in early training conducted in the home community (Moon & Inge, 1993).

Students are given opportunities to learn a trade through high-school-sponsored vocational training and on-the-job training in the context of full- or part-time work-study programs. Course content includes a multitude of lessons about job search, job maintenance, and work-related interpersonal skills, such as obtaining documentation necessary to become employed; preparing a résumé; completing a job application; identifying jobs of interest; finding job leads; organizing a job search; contacting employers by telephone, in person, and in writing; interviewing for a job; and handling work-related paperwork such as timecards, paycheque stubs, work schedules, and tax returns. Students are taught about being a good employee and getting along with others on the job. This includes skills such as understanding instruction, asking a question, asking for help, accepting criticism, ordering job responsibilities, accepting assistance, giving instruction, offering assistance, apologizing, convincing others, being punctual, and practising good attendance.

Students also need practice in getting to and from work, which includes telephoning for bus route information, reading bus maps and schedules, and using appropriate and safe behaviour on public transit. There is also information on making positive job changes, setting realistic goals for the future, and being an effective self-advocate.

Work-study experiences, founded on the premise that there should be some cross-coordination between schoolwork and vocational experiences, play a major role in the secondary curriculum and link the preparatory employment to the receiving environment through **community-based instruction**; that is, instruction referenced directly to activities and performance demands in the local community. Students are placed in work situations in the community, and their academic programs are oriented to supplement the work experience.

For youth who are disabled, part-time jobs during school and enrolment in vocational classes correlate with increases in employability (Siegel, Robert, & Gaylord Ross, 1992). Students who have paid work as part of secondary school experiences are significantly more likely to have a competitive job than those without such experiences (62 percent

community-based instruction

Transition provides students with skills for adult employment.

versus 45 percent) (Bounds, 1997). For example, persons who are intellectually disabled and have been in school work-experience programs tend to respond better to occupational demands and are more employable than those who have not been in programs (Patton et al., 1989).

The reasons for this are fairly obvious. Work experiences allow individuals to try new things in an atmosphere that allows for a second chance. Students learn how to adapt to changes in the work environment and how to maintain acceptable levels of work performance. Training often gives students the boost they need to succeed in the work world. Not only do they learn specific job skills, but also they learn how to conduct themselves on the job, know the responsibilities that accompany employment, and gain a better idea of what it takes to succeed in a particular field (Bounds, 1997). Holding a paid job allows youth to hone their work skills and demonstrate their reliability to potential employers. Paid work experiences also provide students an opportunity to apply classroom learning in the real world, give meaning to their learning, and can be a great motivator (Bounds, 1997).

Social Skills Instruction

During adolescence, prosocial behaviours are being tested and refined based upon positive and negative social encounters that students experience daily. Compared to typical youth, those with high-incidence disabilities are more likely to show poor adaptive behaviour; experience delinquency, behavioural, and conduct problems; and display depression, anxiety, and poor social skills. Adaptive behaviour is predictive of certain aspects of future vocational performance, and the absence of effective social skills is considered to be a major cause of the less-than-successful adjustment of students who are disabled to the regular competitive workforce.

Wayne Nesbit from Memorial University noted that when senior students finish school, their personalities must be marketable. "The reality," observes Nesbit, "is that they will not receive an academic high school certificate nor will they earn a university degree. It is their personality and ability to work co-operatively which determines their acceptance and success in the work world" (1990, p. 5).

There is evidence that social skills training for adolescents has a profound impact in positively influencing their behaviour. For students with intellectual disabilities, for example, targeted social skills range from isolated non-verbal responses such as eye contact and gestures to complex skills involved in asking questions, expressing appreciation and praise, carrying on a conversation, and learning aspects of speech such as loudness, intonation, and intelligibility.

As another example, individuals with visual impairments tend to behave passively in social situations, so improving social skills becomes a need. Not only does assertiveness training have the potential to improve the social skills of persons who are visually impaired (Kim, 2003), but the level of social skills may be an important variable that distinguishes visually impaired adults who are employed from those who are not.

Self-management

Self-management refers to a multiplicity of skills needed for independence in the adult world: for example, apartment living, marriage, family responsibilities, budgeting, and community resources. Students with severe disabilities need instruction in life skills, which

self-management

include basic hygiene, grooming, and dressing, as well as mobility, money handling, shopping, housekeeping, and leisure skills. Even for those who can never achieve full independence, training contributes to feelings of confidence, self-reliance, and personal satisfaction.

self-determination

A subset of the self-management agenda is **self-determination**, which implies knowing what one wants in life and having the mechanisms to achieve the goal (Whitney-Thomas & Maloney, 2001). Self-determination is recognized as a critical outcome for students as they prepare to transition to the adult world. In fact, during the past decade, self-determination has become such a central topic in the special education literature that "promoting self-determination or teaching students to take control of their lives is becoming a hallmark of providing full and complete special education services" (Karnoven, Test, Wood, Browder, & Algozzine, 2004, p., 23).

Self-determination influences a person's ability to make choices and preferences about the future that are built on a realistic understanding of individual strengths and weaknesses. The most commonly identified components of self-determination are choice/decision-making; goal setting/attainment; self-evaluation/management; self-advocacy; person-centred planning for individualized education programs (IEPs and transition meetings); relationships with others; and self-awareness (Field & Hoffman, 1994; Wehmeyer, 1996).

Self-determination is associated with greater quality of life and more positive adult outcomes. Self-determined adults are more likely to be happy, have better lives, and have a better quality of life than those with similar disabilities who are not considered to be self-determined (Wehmeyer & Schwartz, 1997; Wehmeyer, Kelchner, & Richards, 1996).

Because the actions of self-determined people enable them to fulfill roles typically associated with adulthood, the development and acquisition of the various elements of self-determined behaviour should begin early in life. Because self-determination will not begin on its own but needs teaching and nurturing, it should be a component of classroom instruction. Teaching self-advocacy, such as communication and negotiation skills, can be accomplished through role play and direct instruction.

Futures Planning

Upon completion of their public schooling, many young people with disabilities still need additional assistance and support to negotiate the transition process successfully. Transition should ensure access to community support and continuity of services. The adult agency support component is designed to educate students and their family members about the procedures of becoming active clients of vocational rehabilitation or other agencies before graduation.

Parent Involvement

Although relatively little research exists on how families are involved in the transition process, the available evidence and collective experience of families suggests that current transition efforts are far from optimal. Parent involvement continues to be a major gap in successful transition services.

The experiences of parents of students with blindness are illustrative. Researchers (Houser, Moses, & Kay, 1987) found that families are not actively involved in the transition process. They are frequently isolated from information about available resources and possibilities for employment as well as from emotional support that other families with similar needs can supply. In many cases, they are unaware of their own resources; rely on professionals to plan and implement services for them; and may not understand the differences between education and rehabilitation services. Further, Nixon's (1991) interviews with 23 families of blind and visually impaired children revealed frustrations, uncertainties about the future, social concerns, and problems with stigma.

In one of the few studies on parents of students with severe mental retardation, parents were significantly less involved in the transition process than they desired to be. Seventy percent wanted involvement, but only 30 percent experienced it (McNair & Rusch, 1991). When Duquette and Stodel (2005) surveyed the parents of seven adolescent students with Fetal Alcohol Syndrome in eastern Ontario, the parents indicated that they had never been involved in their children's planning for transition from high school to the world of work.

POST-SCHOOL EXPERIENCES

A small but growing body of data addresses the experiences of youth with disabilities once they leave school. Outcomes are far more encouraging than they were even a decade ago. Today, many young people with disabilities move into post-secondary education or competitive employment with their regular peers. In fact, students with disabilities now represent "a significant cohort within the post-secondary student population" (Canadian Association of Disability Service Providers, 1999, p. 4).

This optimism is not untempered. A substantial number of other young people with disabilities still lag far behind their typical peers in graduation, post-secondary education, and post-school employment rates (Benz, Lindstrom, & Yovanoff, 2000). Israelite and her colleagues at York University in Toronto (2005) explored the experiences of nine university graduates with disabilities and their transition into the labour force. They found that participants experienced significant obstacles to employment, such as attitudinal and physical/sensory barriers in the workplace, limited access to public transit, and disincentives to work associated with government programs, which led to higher rates of underemployment and unemployment and lower work-related earnings.

Dropouts

From a sociological perspective, high school graduation may be seen as a rite of passage marking the successful movement of an individual from adolescence into adulthood. More pragmatically, high school graduation is the absolute minimum required for accessing many opportunities, including college, university, and many jobs, especially jobs that offer decent pay and working conditions (Statistics Canada, 2005).

A general definition used by researchers identifies a **dropout** as any person who has left secondary school for any reason prior to graduation (Sullivan, 1988). While dropouts voluntarily leave the system before completing their education, there is a widespread belief that many of these students are capable of graduating.

dropout

Local, provincial, and national studies show a multiplicity of definitions and methodologies for calculating dropout rates. Statistics Canada calculates the rate of twenty-year-olds. It reports that between 1991 and 1999 the high school dropout rate decreased from

18 to 12 percent; however, males continue to drop out of school at a higher rate than females. In 1999, 15 percent of twenty-year-old males did not complete high school, compared to 9 percent of females.

Dropout factors can be slotted into two broad, overlapping categories. First are factors that push students out of school: grade retention, low academic achievement, irrelevant curricula, attendance rate, low self-concept, and low need for self-development. Second are factors that pull students out. These include community type, pregnancy, marriage, having a job, institutionalization or incarceration, delinquency, drug use, and poor mental and physical health.

Students' self-reported explanations for dropping out tend to focus on the "push." Students tend not to view teachers and schools as supportive. They speak of low satisfaction with school, a sense of alienation, and feelings of not belonging that relegate them to the fringe, preventing them from fully participating in school experiences. For example, when Stuart (2003) interviewed 15 secondary-school-aged girls identified as behaviourally disordered, he found that they were not motivated to learn in school and felt that they were not in charge of their own learning. Many students believe that courses are irrelevant, which results in boredom and dampened motivation. There is also frustration born of poor academic concept, resulting in failure, grade retention, and poor self-concept.

Predicting who will drop out is not easy, although poor reading performance and retention in a grade seem to be primary. According to Robert Slavin and his colleagues (1990),

> Reaching the third grade on time with adequate basic skills may not provide a guarantee that a student will complete his education, but it appears that children who do not reach third grade on time with adequate skills have little chance of educational success, regardless of the remedial or special education resources invested in them later in their school careers.

Only a small amount of literature deals specifically with dropping out by students receiving special education. In the United States, approximately 38 percent of students who are disabled drop out (as compared to 25 percent of the general population (Schumaker et al., 2002); 29.4 percent of students with learning disabilities exit school without a diploma (United States Department of Education, 2000).

The dropout percentage for students with disabilities has decreased steadily over the past five years, and the graduation percentage has shown a general upward trend (see Blackorby & Wagner, 1996). More students go to college and have access to some form of vocational education that contributes significantly to the probability of competitive employment.

Nevertheless, special education must still address the fact that an unacceptable percentage of students with disabilities drop out of school, and a significant number of those students who do graduate do not secure employment later or retain secured jobs. When Lichenstein (1989) followed a population of students with mild disabilities beyond high school, he found that dropping out was a greater factor in unemployment than the disability itself. Other research findings consistently suggest that young adults at greatest risk for lifelong economic and social harm are those with disabilities who also dropped out of high school. These young people are seriously at risk because of their history of inadequate educational attainment, their chronic dependence on society, and their uncertain future in the job market (Edgar, Levine, & Maddox, 1985).

Competitive Employment

Competitive employment of persons with disabilities enhances feelings of self-worth and efficacy and increases the normalization of these persons, both in self-perception and the perception of society. The mere observation of individuals who are disabled engaging in functional, integrated, and age-appropriate activities appears to have effects on the development of a more respectful and optimistic attitude toward them from the public, one factor that contributes further to employment success.

According to Harris (1998), securing and maintaining employment continues to be the area that results in the largest negative discrepancy between those who have disabilities and those who do not. In the United States, it is estimated that approximately 25 percent of adults with severe disabilities and 8 percent with profound disabilities are employed (LaPlante, Kennedy, Kaye, & Wegner, 1996). According to a report from the Canadian Human Rights Commission, the situation of people with disabilities in the Canadian workforce is poor. Representation was 2.3 percent in 1997 in the federally regulated private sector ("Access denied … " 1999).

It is difficult to pinpoint the factors that contribute to failure for students with disabilities. Some problems certainly stem from conditions in the labour market, inadequate or inappropriate vocational and educational preparation, lack of transition support services, or other related factors, such as employer attitudes. Others relate to individual traits, work habits, and attitudes. As well, although employment rates and attendance at post-secondary institutions tend to be rising, they also tend to be category-specific. In other words, people with different disabilities have different experiences.

Many adults with learning disabilities, for example, are ill prepared to succeed in high school and beyond, and these adults do less well than peers (Levine & Mouse, 1998). When they do find jobs, people with learning disabilities often cannot keep them. It seems to be the subtle invisible aspects of learning disabilities that impede success in the work world. As we pointed out earlier, learning disabilities do not disappear; many adults retain subtle or overt manifestations. Some adults with learning disabilities learn to compensate for their attention problems and find occupations that allow them to utilize their strengths while minimizing their shortcomings.

For others, the disabling aspects of learning disabilities may become more firmly established in adulthood; they then contribute to the problems adults experience and may actually increase as the individual experiences new social and vocational expectations. Adults with learning disabilities continue to have reading problems and difficulties with written expression, and to need help with math skills. Individuals may exhibit low motivation, distractibility, self-concept problems, and lack of organization. They feel frustrated, have little self-confidence, and have difficulty controlling emotions and/or temper; depression often follows (Rogan & Hardman, 1990).

A growing body of data is available on adults with Attention Deficit Hyperactivity Disorder. It is estimated that up to 70 percent of children diagnosed with ADHD continue to have significant symptoms in adolescence and adulthood (Faraone & Doyle, 2001). The disorders manifest in different ways in adults and may vary considerably depending on task and content (Brown, 1995). For example, the hyperactivity component often dissipates in adults, but it is replaced by inner feelings of restlessness.

Compared to controls, adults who were diagnosed as ADHD as children receive fewer years of formal schooling and achieve lower overall occupational status. Studies report that they are more likely to have a range of psychiatric problems such as anxiety, depression, and antisocial personality disorder; are about twice as likely as the general population to abuse alcohol or become dependent on drugs such as cocaine; and have more employment problems and auto accidents than adults without ADHD (Biederman, Wilens, Mick, Spencer, & Faraone, 1999; Faraone, Biederman, Spencer, Wilens, Siedman, Mick, & Doyle, 2000; Rollins, Barkley, & DuPaul, 2000).

Youth who are behaviourally disordered experience challenges unlike those faced by other students with disabilities. These include poor social skills, social stigma, mental illness, and higher rates of academic failure, grade retention, and dropping out. It should come as little surprise that these students have more difficulty in adjusting to young adulthood than those who are learning disabled or intellectually disabled. Although they lack the basic skills needed for employment, many youth who are behaviourally disordered refuse school transition programs.

Those with behavioural disorders have higher unemployment. When they do obtain employment, only about 50 percent are likely to retain it for more than six months (Sitlington, Frank, & Carson, 1992). Negative factors include inappropriate strategies to solve conflicts and cope with frustration; these people often behave in ways that prevent them from being accepted, liked, and helped by employers and co-workers.

Rather than being characterized by successful work experiences, the post-school careers of these young people are characterized by unemployment, incarceration, and mental health problems. A number of investigations have shown that females with high-incidence disabilities have poorer post-school outcomes than males with the same disabilities (see Murray, 2003). The outcomes are far poorer still for women with behavioural disorders (Blackorby & Wagner, 1996; see Stuart, 2003).

Many adults who are mildly intellectually disabled are able to merge into the community and work at a variety of semi-skilled and service positions. They have varying degrees of success in attaining and retaining employment, but most can partially or totally support themselves. However, Toronto's Roeher Institute (1996) gathered data from Statistics Canada that showed that in this country only 31 percent of all persons with intellectual disabilities have competitive jobs. While 29 percent say that they are actively looking for work, they report that they have been refused a job because of their disability.

If not underemployed or unemployed, they are often the last hired and tend to hold unskilled and semi-skilled jobs. Adults who are intellectually disabled seem to be particularly susceptible to changes in the economy. Job success is a function of attitudes and personality, not IQ. On the job, persons with intellectual disabilities often have problems with job responsibility, task production competence, and/or social competence (Salzberg, Lignugaris-Kraft, & McCuller, 1988).

In contrast to other subgroups, the obstacles to obtaining and retaining employment for persons with visual impairments have been well addressed in the literature. Researchers conclude that the type and nature of employment is narrower for those with visual impairments than for other persons with disabilities so that these individuals are under-represented in the competitive labour market. Barriers include those related to transportation, public awareness of visual impairments, attitudes, difficulties with reading print, obtaining adaptive equipment, and accommodations (see Crudden & McBroom, 1999; Odolo & Sitlington, 2002). Employers worry about the complexity and expense of providing accommodations, delays in newly hired persons reaching full productivity, and expectations that it will be difficult to terminate an employee (Wolffe & Candela, 2002).

In the past 20 years, deaf youth have made strong gains in residential independence but are less likely to be involved in productive activities such as work or school. Unemployment and underemployment remain persistent problems, especially for women who are deaf (Schirmer, 2001). One factor accounting for this may be that the high degree of literacy and extensive education required for many current jobs are not within the purview of many deaf individuals. Deaf activists complain that students are often placed in vocational tracks where reading and math are de-emphasized; their lower skill levels then impose barriers to employment (Stewart & Kluwin, 2000).

It is important to assess all the above research on underemployment and unemployment in light of gender. Studies show that young women with disabilities are less likely than their male peers to enrol in vocational courses or participate in community work experience during high school. Post-school, women with disabilities are less likely to be employed than either young men with disabilities or young women without disabilities. Young women with disabilities who are employed are likely to work in lower-status occupations, such as service, clerical, or other helping jobs; earn lower wages than their male peers with disabilities; and have limited opportunity for promotion or career advancement (Lindstrom & Benz, 2002).

Supported Employment

The term **supported employment** describes a wide variety of work situations and vocational rehabilitation programs that range from adult day programs to highly automated production factories. Some essential features characterize all types of supported employment. First, programs are built on the belief that people with severe disabilities have the potential to work productively in a community of workers. Second, supported employment offers opportunities for paid productive work with ongoing support; training to ensure continued employment; and employment in a socially integrated environment. Additionally, supported employment offers much structure and ensures that people receive continuous help managing the routines of living and working.

supported employment

Specifically, supported employment experiences provide individuals who cannot be in competitive employment long-term support in a controlled and protected work environment. Workers have constant input and supervision; expectations are adjusted to each individual's ability; and personal differences are tolerated. Where possible, an individual is helped to progress to employment in the competitive labour market.

Post-secondary Education

As mentioned earlier, the dropout rate among students with disabilities has decreased. A parallel growth in the number of students with disabilities completing their high school and continuing their education at college or university is currently underway. Students with learning disabilities represent the largest segment. Cox and Klas (1996) estimated that in any Canadian college or university of 10 000 students, as many as 1000 may have some type of learning disability. When the Canadian National Education Association of Disabled

Students conducted a survey of 70 service providers, they found that the largest group of people with disabilities in post-secondary educational institutions was those with learning disabilities, a ratio of 36:1 to other groups with disabilities.

Despite their numbers, students with learning disabilities are less likely to persist in post-secondary education compared to students without disabilities (Horn & Babbitt, 1999). One U.S study (Murray, Goldstein, Nourse, & Edgar, 2000) found that, of the students with learning disabilities who attended post-secondary institutions, 80 percent had not graduated 5 years after high school; in 10 years, 56 percent of youth with learning disabilities had not graduated.

Many students with disabilities, including those who are learning disabled, are ill-prepared for the challenges of post-secondary education. Poor readiness manifests in the areas of academics, developing effective social networks, self-advocacy, and daily functional skills (Babbitt & White, 2002). Saskatchewan researchers (Burt, Parks-Charney, & Schwean, 2000) found that the organizational, study, and time management skills necessary in post-secondary education places students with ADHD at additional risk for dropping out and/or academic failure. For example, the enormous amount of reading and writing assigned can place tremendous pressure on individuals due to their difficulties with sustaining attention, concentrating, and completing tasks.

Universities and colleges across Canada have put accommodations in place to assist youth with disabilities on campus. Generally, faculty members seem willing to make accommodations (Cox & Klas, 1996). Typical approaches include modified tests, more time to complete tests, many short examinations rather than one long one, alternate assignments, and assistive devices such as computer access. Note-taking is the most frequently used support service for students who are deaf and hard of hearing.

SUMMARY

1. Consistent and structured programming for adolescents with disabilities has not traditionally been a prominent feature of special education. Few provisions have been made for students at secondary levels, party because individualizing instruction is particularly problematic in secondary school settings. Upper schools differ from elementary schools in their mission, staff development methods, the number of students taught by a given teacher, teachers' perceptions of their roles, and the limits on opportunities to meet individual needs.

2. Adolescence is a time of intense flux, emotionally, behaviourally and physically. The needs of adolescents are quite different from those of younger children; when the adolescent has a disability, his or her needs become even more intense. Adolescents and young adults with disabilities have complex support needs such as finding and keeping employment, living independently, planning post-secondary education, recreation, and friendships.

3. The concept and process of transition arose from data demonstrating negative outcomes for youth with disabilities. As currently proposed, transition focuses on the school-to-community scenario. Services are intended to provide young people with disabilities access to relevant post-secondary education opportunities, employment in competitive settings, residential independence, and future self-sufficiency.

4. School practices attempt to establish relationships between educational variables and better employment and independent living outcomes. Programs match the skills needed by individuals in the community so as to better prepare students for post-school life. Included are counselling, sex education, and functional academic skills—the tool skills needed for reading, writing, and math. Quality vocational programs include self-advocacy, self-determination, job placement, job maintenance, independent living, financial planning, transportation usage, and community agency support.

5. Research evidence does not point to any one service-delivery model to meet the needs of all secondary students. Because many adolescents with disabilities reach secondary school with severe deficits in the core areas of reading and math, there is often a mismatch between their abilities and the requirements of the system. A number of educators argue that despite the current emphasis on inclusion, the general classroom may not be the most suitable setting for late-secondary students. They contend that we need to pay more attention to bettering the lives of students than to their school address. The acquisition of requisite employment skills cannot be left to chance or viewed as a mere adjunct to mainstream curricula.

6. Students with disabilities experience a wide variety of post-secondary outcomes. Young people with disabilities may enroll in university or community college; enter competitive employment or military service; or be involved in more supported employment.

HISTORICAL NOTES

For most of the 19th century, special education catered to discrete age groups. Schooling was not designed for young children, although a high proportion of older students were instructed within the institutional complex. The Ontario Institution for the Deaf, for example, was established in 1870; by 1879, about 7 percent of the student population was between the ages of twenty-one and forty. In the schools for the blind, students were allowed to remain up to their thirtieth birthday (Winzer, 1993).

Adult attendance at school was voluntary and indicated the imperative need of disabled youth—getting a job and keeping it. Some adults were early school leavers who wanted more skills for the workforce; others had never before been offered the opportunity for education and training. Trade teaching held the paramount position so that young adults could obtain jobs in factories, manufacturing, and trades. When students were admitted for upgrading in trades, they received no wages for their work but were given free room and board (Winzer, 1993).

The adult experiences of persons with disabilities have not been of great interest to historians. Deaf communities are probably the most widely studied. It seems that wherever there were schools for the Deaf a community flourished, with deaf adults tending to marry other deaf people, send their children to residential schools for the Deaf, and confine their social relations to their community. There are some scattered indications of blind communities in the late 19th century, but they seem to have been short-lived.

Of course, there were studies carried out throughout the first half of the 20th century, but these tended to relate specifically to persons with intellectual disabilities and to be sporadic and also inconclusive. One reason, of course, was that while the school system was obsessed with children with mild disabilities, once they became adults, these persons simply melded into their communities and no longer carried a pejorative label. As well, the school experience and curriculum, while focused on trade teaching and then manual arts, was not often closely related to the opportunities in the actual work force and was often irrelevant to the future needs of students.

It was only in the early 1980s that educators became truly interested in adult experiences and the transition of persons with disabilities. As we pointed out throughout this chapter, transition programming is today a major thrust. At the same time, it is really still in its infancy, and much remains to be done in terms of research on outcomes and effective implementation.

GLOSSARY

Ability groupings: changing the environment to bring students who are gifted together.

Academic ability: intellectual ability measured by performance on IQ and standardized tests of academic achievement.

Academically endowed students: those scoring at the 95th percentile or higher on IQ and standardized tests of academic achievement.

Acceleration: students speed up their progress through the existing curriculum to complete a prescribed program in a shorter time period.

Accommodations: changes that assist a child's functioning in the environment; techniques that eliminate or minimize learning differences by offering alternate ways of handling a task.

Acoupedic (unisensory) approach: an oral method that aims to develop intelligible speech through the maximum development of listening skills.

Activity-based assessment: measures the use of functional skills within the context of child initiated, planned, and routine activities.

Adaptations: procedures, changes, or enhancements that enable a student who is exceptional to undertake tasks that he or she would not otherwise be able to accomplish easily.

Adaptive behaviour: how well a person is able to adapt to environmental demands according to the individual's age group and particular situation.

Adaptive (assistive) equipment: any device designed or modified to lead individuals with disabilities to independence.

Advocacy: the act of pleading a cause for another person.

Aggressive behaviour: behaviour—verbal, non-verbal, or physical—that injures another indirectly or directly and/or results in extraneous gains for the aggressor.

Albinism: a condition carried as an inherited autosomal recessive trait that results in lack of colouring.

Allergy (hypersensitivity): an abnormal and varied reaction that occurs following a contact with substances or agents that normally do not cause symptoms in other individuals.

Anoxia: deprivation of oxygen.

Anxiety: a fear with a future reference.

Aphasia: conditions that affect language reception and expression.

Aphonia: the condition where there is no voice.

Applied behavioural analysis: a form of therapy founded on structured principles of behaviourism, applied today to young children with serious Autism Spectrum Disorders.

Apraxia: the inability to program, position, and sequence the muscle movements involved in speech.

Arena testing: an observational assessment approach in which people from several disciplines focus on their particular domains such as motor skills or language within the context of play.

Arthritis: a common term for a variety of chronic systemic conditions involving inflammation of the joints.

Assessment: the process of gathering valid evidence to guide decisions about curriculum and instruction, and to evaluate the outcomes of instruction.

Assistive technology: various devices used to help students with disabilities function in their environments.

Asthma: a variable, reversible obstruction of the airway characterized by the narrowing of bronchial tubes, swelling of tissues, and clogging of mucus.

Astigmatism: a condition that results from an irregularity in the curvature of the cornea or lens of the eye.

Ataxia: problems with gait and ambulation.

At risk: a term that describes individuals who are more vulnerable to biological or environmental insult.

Attention disorders: difficulty in concentration, tuning in to sensory information, and engagement or active participation.

Attributions: the reasons that people give for what happens to them.

Atypical: a term that describes youngsters who do not reach the norm in some functional area or areas.

Audiogram: a chart on which hearing is recorded.

Audiology: the science of detecting and correcting hearing impairment.

Augmentative communication: a general group of procedures designed to support, enhance, or augment the communication of non-speaking individuals or utilize and supplement whatever vocal skills they possess.

Babbling: an almost universal response during infancy; random sound play of almost infinite variety.

Behaviour intervention plan: a written description of specific interventions for improving behaviour.

Behavioural phenotype: patterns of behaviour or the specific and characteristic behavioural repertoire exhibited by individuals with a certain condition.

Benchmark: the amount of progress a child is expected to make within a specified period.

Bibliotherapy: a procedure based on the concept that books serve a therapeutic purpose, especially for children with disabilities.

Biological risk: a term relating to infants and toddlers with a history of prenatal, perinatal, neonatal, or early developmental events resulting in biological insults to the developing nervous system.

Blindness: vision of 20/200 or less with correction.

Body image: a person's awareness of the body, its capabilities, the interrelationship of body parts, and the relationship of bodies to the environment.

Bullying: a specific form of verbal and physical aggression.

Cancer: a general term used to describe about one hundred conditions characterized by abnormal and uncontrolled cell growth.

Carrying: the way that a child with a physical or motor disability is moved.

Cataract: an opacity of the lens or its capsule that restricts the eye's ability to receive light and interferes with central and peripheral visual acuity.

Classroom management: the way in which teachers manipulate the classroom environment to minimize disruptions and give all children the optimum opportunity to engage in appropriate behaviour and reach learning and social goals.

Cochlea: a tiny, snail-shaped structure in the ear that is filled with a fluid similar to cerebral spinal fluid.

Cochlear implant: an electronic device that provides auditory information to individuals who have severe to profound sensorineural hearing losses in both ears and who receive limited or no benefit from conventional hearing aids.

Cognition: the process of recognizing, identifying, associating, and inferring meaning beyond the figural information provided by the environment that allows an understanding of a concept and application to new conditions.

Cognitive-behavioural processes: a conceptually related set of educational or therapeutic treatments.

Collaboration: any mutual effort to plan, implement, or evaluate educational programs for a student or students.

Collaborative ongoing assessment: a procedure that follows a child through a day's activities.

Colour blindness: a rare, sex-linked, hereditary disorder found almost always in males that arises from the absence or malfunctioning of the cone cells of the retina.

Communication: the process of exchanging information and ideas between participants.

Communication mode: the form in which the content of a message is expressed.

Communicative behaviour: the behaviour that conveys a social message from one person to another.

Communicative competence: knowing how to interact, communicate appropriately in various situations, and make sense of what others say and do in communicative interactions.

Community-based instruction: instruction referenced directly to the activities and performance demands of the local community.

Community-referenced assessment: assessment that details the adaptations needed for the students to function in the community.

Comorbidity: the simultaneous occurrence of two or more conditions.

Compulsions: repetitive behaviours or mental acts.

Conduct disorders: overt, aggressive, disruptive behaviour or covert antisocial acts that are repeated infractions of socially prescribed behavioural patterns and violate social norms and the rights of others.

Conductive hearing losses: hearing losses caused by problems in the mechanical transmission of sound waves through the outer and middle ear.

Congenital abnormalities: abnormalities present at birth.

Continuum of services: an ordered sequence of placements that vary according to the degree of restrictiveness.

Consultation: the process of two equals working together to discuss or solve a problem.

Co-operative learning: instructional arrangements where students learn together in heterogeneous groups.

Cornea: a transparent window covering the front of the eye, continuous with the sclera.

Co-teaching: collaboration between general and education teachers for an entire class of children.

Critical period: part of the life cycle during which the developing organism is particularly sensitive or responsive to specific environmental forces.

Curriculum-based assessment (CBA): a standardized measurement system used to monitor a student's academic growth and improve instructional programs.

Curriculum compacting (telescoping): bringing the content up to the level of the children and moving students through the curriculum far more rapidly.

Cystic fibrosis (CF): a genetically determined inborn error of metabolism characterized by pervasive dysfunction of the exocrine glands.

Deaf community: describes social and other associations of persons who are deaf and bound together by a common language and culture.

Deaf person: one whose hearing disability precludes successful processing of linguistic information through audition, with or without a hearing aid.

Decibel: the smallest difference in loudness intensity that can be perceived.

Developmental delay: a lag in reaching developmental milestones.

Developmental disability: a significant lag in development.

Developmental period: the period between conception and eighteen years of age.

Diabetes mellitus: an autoimmune illness that involves sugar metabolism.

Direct Instruction: activity-focused, teacher-directed classroom procedures that are systematic and usually conducted according to an individual plan.

Directionality: an awareness of left and right in the environment outside the body.

Disabilities: conditions that reflect the consequences of impairments in terms of functional performance and activity by the individual.

Discipline: helping children to learn to guide their own behaviour in a way that shows respect and caring for themselves, other people, and the physical environment.

Dropout: any person who has left secondary school for any reason prior to graduation.

DSM: a clinical manual that describes behavioural symptoms of all disorders currently recognized by the American Psychiatric Association (APA) and defines the symptoms and signs required for the diagnosis of each disorder.

Dually diagnosed: children with two disabilities such as deafness and blindness.

Dual sensory impairment: those whose disabilities are a complex of auditory, visual, communication, and language factors, often accompanied by other conditions that interfere with their learning.

Dysarthria: a group of speech disorders resulting from disturbed muscular control over the speech mechanisms.

Dysfluency: conditions in which the flow of speech is interrupted with blocking, repetitions, or prolongations of sounds, words, phrases, or syllables.

Dyslexia: a specific type of reading disability.

Dysnomia: forgetting words or word meanings.

Early identification: the practice of screening infants and young children in an attempt to identify those likely to experience problems in learning or behaviour.

Early intervention: a variety of educational, psychological, or therapeutic interventions provided for handicapped, at-risk, or disadvantaged infants and preschoolers to prevent or ameliorate developmental delays of disabilities or to provide support to children and families in cases where disabilities exist.

Echolalia: speech that is an immediate imitation of the speech of some other speaker.

Educational consultants: people who serve to assist classroom teachers throughout a school district to maintain children who are exceptional in their general school programs.

Educational setting: the place where students receive instruction.

Elective mutism: a condition found in emotionally disturbed children who do not speak or who speak only in certain circumstances.

Emergent literacy: the reading and writing knowledge and behaviour that precedes conventional literacy.

Emotional overlay: an adverse reaction to learning problems and academic failure.

Engagement: the amount of time spent involved with the environment or materials.

Enrichment: the provision of special activities in the regular classroom setting.

Environmental risk: a term that applies to families and their infants and toddlers who are considered biologically sound but whose early life experiences (including maternal and family care, health care, nutrition, opportunities for expression of language, adaptive behaviour, and patterns of physical and social stimulation) are sufficiently limited that there is a high probability of delayed development.

Epidemiology: the study of the distribution and determinants of diseases and handicapping conditions in a population.

Epilepsy: a convulsive disorder characterized by a sudden, excessive, disorderly discharge of neurons in the brain.

Established risk: a diagnosed medical disorder with a known etiology (cause) that bears relatively well known expectancies for developmental outcomes within varying ranges of developmental disabilities.

Etiology: the process of finding causes to explain how a particular problem came into existence.

Expressive disorders: those that affect the formulation of grammatic utterances.

Extra-familial influences: those agencies outside the family that influence a child's cognitive, social, and emotional development.

Family needs assessment: evaluates current conditions and needs in a family and provides information on what the parents' goals are for their child and for potential parent involvement in the early intervention program.

Fovea: the part of the eye that possesses a rich supply of light-sensitive nerve cells, the rods and cones, which convert the light into electrochemical impulses.

Functional academics: academics that have meaning and are relevant to the learner soon to enter community work and life.

Functional behavioural assessment: assessment that examines the function of a child's behaviour and plans how to reduce or eliminate it.

Functional language: the language that is useful in a child's daily activities and environment.

Functional skills: those skills that help children to get along in their current and future environments.

Gain: the amount of amplification provided by a hearing aid.

General uncoordination: lack of muscular control.

Glaucoma: a condition caused by interocular pressure on the eyeball.

Goal: a stated outcome desired as the result of some action.

Grammar: the rules and the word choices made; it formalizes the conventions of language so that communication is consistent throughout a certain society.

Habilitation: restoration of normal functioning.

Handicaps: the disadvantages experienced by individuals as a result of impairment or disability.

Haptic: encompasses touch, body movement, and position in space.

Hard-of-hearing person: one who, generally with the use of a hearing aid, has residual hearing sufficient to enable successful processing of linguistic information through audition.

Health impairments: limited strength, vitality, or alertness due to chronic or acute health problems.

Hearing impairment: a generic term indicating a hearing disability that may range in severity from mild to profound. It includes the subsets of deaf and hard-of-hearing.

Hertz: measurement of cycles of sound per second.

Holophrasic speech: a single word used to express a more complex idea.

Home visiting (home-based programs): a program in which a professional or paraprofessional provides help over an extended period of time to a family in its own home.

Horizontal enrichment: examining a certain curriculum area in greater depth.

Human central nervous system: the brain, the spinal cord, and the associated nerves and sense organs.

Hydrocephalus: a condition characterized by an excessive accumulation of cerebrospinal fluid in the brain due to an obstruction of flow.

Hyperactivity: failure to comply with age-appropriate situational demands for restrained activity, sustained attention, resistance to distracting influences, and inhibition of impulsive responses.

Hyperopia: farsightedness caused by too short an eye or too flat a corneal surface.

Impairments: abnormalities of body structure and system function resulting from any cause.

Impulsivity: difficulty in withholding active responses, such as blurting out statements or grabbing materials.

Incidence: the number of new cases of a particular condition ascertained over a given period of time, usually a year.

Incidental teaching: instruction that occurs within naturally occurring situations.

Independent studies: individualized learning experiences that allow students to select a topic, define problems or questions, gather and analyze information, apply skills, and create a product to show what has been learned.

Instructional discourse: the language that gives children information about the curriculum and feedback on their efforts in mastering it.

Instructional technology: various types of hardware and software.

Intelligence quotient (IQ): the relationship between a child's mental age (MA) and chronological age (CA).

Interpreter: a normally hearing person who facilitates the transmission of information between individuals who do not communicate with a common language or code.

Intervention: a general term for the application of professional skills to maintain or improve a child's potential and functioning; care and education aimed at influencing the direction and scope of children's developmental processes.

Iris: the membrane that gives the eye its colour and adapts the size of the pupil aperture in response to light intensity.

Itinerant teachers: specially trained educators who give individual assistance to a child for specific periods during the normal school schedule.

Labelling: the categorizing of children on the basis of their primary disability.

Language: a system of symbols organized into conventional patterns to communicate meaning.

Language delays: delays seen in children who demonstrate significant lags but whose language is still progressing according to the stages of normal language development.

Language disorders: impairment or deviant development of comprehension or use of a spoken, written, or other symbol system.

Language hierarchy: the four components of listening, speaking, reading, and writing.

Language problems: a range of difficulties with the linguistic code or with the rules and concentrations for linking the symbols and their sequences.

Laterality: an internal knowledge of the differences between left and right.

Leadership: the ability to effect positive and productive changes that are self-enhancing or group-enhancing.

Learning strategies: an individual's approach to tasks that are either generic or domain specific.

Least restrictive environment: the most appropriate placement in which a student can receive instruction and services.

Lens: a crystalline structure held in suspension by the iris.

Low vision: vision of 20/70 with correction.

Maturational lag: a child's delay in reaching some developmental milestones.

Medically fragile children: children with special health management needs, including those who demonstrate a wide range of chronic and progressive illnesses and severe disabilities.

Metacognition: the awareness of basic learning strategies and one's own awareness of how one learns.

Metalinguistics: the ability to think about and talk about language.

Mildly disabled: a term that traditionally included students with mild disabilities to learning and behaviour—learning disabled, mildly intellectually disabled, and mildly behaviourally disordered.

Mnemonic devices: rhymes, jingles, or images that order information to aid memory.

Mobility: negotiating space.

Modifications: learning outcomes that are substantially different from the prescribed curriculum. They generally apply to children with significant disabilities.

Morphology: the system of word building in a language.

Motivation: a force that energizes, sustains, and directs behaviour toward a goal.

Motor: a term used to denote muscular movement.

Motor assessment: an assessment that considers physical status, mobility, and functional aspects (how the child uses motor skills).

Motor development: the process through which a child acquires movement patterns and skills.

Multilevel instruction: instruction in which a main lesson is prepared and taught with variations included for individual student needs.

Multiple dependent handicapped: children who are severely mentally handicapped and who also have sensory and/or other physical handicaps.

Multiple disabilities: limitations so severe that children cannot develop a normal language system nor provide adequately for their own survival needs.

Multisensory impaired: a term that describes children with sight and hearing handicaps.

Muscular dystrophy: a group of inherited conditions characterized by degeneration of muscle fibres without neurological deficit.

Musculoskeletal impairments: specific disorders involving bones or muscles that impede bodily movements in the absence of damage to the central nervous system.

Myopia: nearsightedness; the greatest single cause of defective vision in children and young adults.

Myringotomy: a procedure in which ventilating tubes are placed in the eardrums to provide proper ventilation between the middle ear cavity and the outside environment via the external ear canal.

Natural gestures: simple movements used to convey meaning to a child.

Neologisms: non-words or words that are obviously peculiar.

Neurological impairments: conditions that result from damage or dysfunction of the brain and/or the spinal cord.

Neuromuscular diseases: acquired or inherited conditions that affect cells in the spinal cord or the peripheral motor nerves.

Non-compliance: failure to follow adult-delivered directions.

Normalization: the philosophical belief that all exceptional individuals, no matter what their level and type of disability, should be provided with an education and living environment that is as close to normal as possible.

Norm-referenced tests: tests that indicate a child's developmental level in relation to that of other children of the same age, the normative group.

Nystagmus: a rhythmic involuntary movement of the eyes.

Objective: a clear statement of exactly what a teacher wants a child to be able to do as a result of instruction; increments in the progress of learning from the present level of functioning to the child's annual goals.

Obsessions: persistent ideas, thoughts, impulses, or images.

Obsessive-compulsive disorders: recurrent obsessions or compulsions that are severe enough to interfere with daily living.

On-task behaviour: the amount of time a person is engaged with instruction or materials.

Oppositional defiant disorder: a condition in which children argue repeatedly with authority figures, show resentment, are touchy, angry, spiteful, and vindictive, and often throw temper tantrums, although physical aggression is limited.

Orientation: an individual's knowledge of his or her position in space.

Orthotic devices: devices that assist a limb's action.

Otitis media: a condition in which the mucosal lining of the middle ear becomes inflamed and the cavity filled with fluid.

Otosclerosis: a hereditary condition characterized by the destruction of the capsular bone in the middle ear and the growth of a web-like bone that attaches to and restricts the stapes.

Over-representation: when a group's membership in a program is larger than the percentage of the group in the educational system.

Passivity: disengagement from an activity.

Pediatric AIDS: AIDS contracted by children under thirteen years of age.

Peers: children of the same age and status.

Peer tutoring: an instructional arrangement where peers interact and teach other peers.

Perseverate: to repeat an activity purposelessly and sometimes disadvantageously.

Pervasive developmental disorders: a term that describes individuals who suffer from chronic disabilities that result in functional limitations in major life activities.

Phobia: an anxiety reaction that is specific to one stimulus; an intense fear with no rational basis.

Phonemic awareness: sensitivity to individual sounds within words and the ability to manipulate those sounds.

Phonetics: the description of the speech sounds of a language.

Phonological awareness: the ability to blend, segment, rhyme, or in other ways manipulate the sounds of spoken words.

Phonological difficulties: having a sound and pronouncing it correctly in some contexts but not others.

Phonology: the sound system of language; the rules for using the sounds of language.

Photophobia: a condition in which very bright light blinds the individual and thus decreases acuity.

Physical disabilities: disabilities that affect body systems; they include health disorders and problems related to mobility and motor skills.

Portfolio: a type of performance test made up of continuous collections of a student's work.

Positioning: the way in which a child with a physical or motor disability is seated or otherwise positioned.

Positive Behaviour Supports: proactive and systematic programs defined by many layers of prevention and support.

Post-lingual deafness: a condition shown by those who become deaf after the development of speech and language.

Pragmatics: the ways in which we use language; the role of context in communicative interactions.

Precocity: remarkable early development.

Prelingual deafness: a condition shown by those who are deaf prior to the development of speech and language.

Presbyopia: a condition in which the lens of the eye loses its ability to accommodate to near objects.

Presbycusis: deafness of age, the most common cause of auditory defect.

Prevalence: the total number of existing cases, old and new.

Preventative discipline: strategies and procedures that militate against any discipline problems arising.

Primary disability: the first or chief disability.

Primary prevention: procedures concerned with removing the causative factors that account for the initial occurrence of the disorder or strengthening the well-being of individuals in the population as a form of inoculation against the causes of subsequent problems.

Probes: brief samples of academic behaviour.

Prompt: a verbal, physical, gestural, or modelling cue that helps the child to respond.

Prosthetic devices: functional devices that substitute for missing body parts.

Psycho-educational assessment (direct testing): testing of children across a variety of domains relevant to social and educational performance.

Psychological processing (learning styles): the way an individual processes sensory information and puts it to meaningful intellectual use.

Psychoses: a heterogeneous group of clinical syndromes characterized by any number of maladaptive behaviours or clusters of behaviours that affect various aspects of adaptive behaviour and the success of interpersonal relations.

Quality-of-life outcomes: the tangible and intangible results of employment that contribute to the enhancement of lifestyle.

Receptive disorders: disorders that interfere with the comprehension of spoken language.

Rehabilitation: procedures that endeavour to restore an individual to normal or optimal functioning.

Remediation: helping a child to overcome, or compensate for, specific deficits in learning and development.

Replacement skills: a different way for a child to accomplish the same purpose without deviant behaviour.

Retina: a tissue-thin, intricate, and sensitive layer that is the actual seeing part of the eye.

Retinal detachment: damage that occurs when a hole or rip in the retina allows the inner retina layer to separate from the back portion.

Retinitis pigmentosa: a hereditary condition that causes degeneration of retinal tissues and loss of peripheral vision.

Retinoblastoma: a condition that results from a malignant tumour on the retina that may spread to the optic nerve and other areas.

Retinopathy of prematurity (retrolental fibroplasia): a condition that affects the retina and the vitreous humour.

Risk factors: the causes of potential disabilities.

Risk status: a mechanism for describing the likelihood that a particular individual will experience a specific outcome, given certain conditions.

Rubric: a generic scoring tool used to evaluate the quality of products and performance.

School culture: the beliefs, habits, and assumed ways of doing things among a school community.

School law: the legislation, regulations, by-laws, and judicial decisions that apply primarily to all or part of the public school system.

Screening: developmental and health activities that are intended to identify those children who have a high probability of exhibiting delayed or abnormal development.

Secondary prevention: ascertaining, as early as possible, the evidence of disorders that may cause disabilities as well as allied attempts to reduce, remove, or reverse substantially complex aspects of disabilities.

Selective mutism: a condition in which children speak rarely or only to certain people.

Self-concept: a person's description of him- or herself in relation to roles, attributes, or characteristics.

Self-determination: knowing what one wants in life and having the mechanisms to achieve the goal.

Self-directed learning: allowing students autonomous control of their own instruction.

Self-discipline: the ability to consider an outcome and select the behaviour that will achieve it.

Self-help skills: the skills necessary to care for oneself in order to achieve independence and self-sufficiency

Self-injurious behaviour: any self-inflicted, repetitive action that leads to laceration, bruising, or abrasions of one's own body.

Self-management: a set of procedures designed to develop the self-regulation of behaviour and the skills needed to assure adult independence.

Self-stimulating behaviour: persistent, stereotypic, repetitive mannerisms.

Semantics: word meaning.

Sensorineural hearing impairments: impairments that interfere with the conversion of sound waves to neural impulses for the brain.

Service delivery model: plans for bringing students, teachers, instruction, and learning together.

Severe and profound disabilities: disabilities of individuals who function intellectually within the lowest 1 percent of their particular age groups or have delays of two or three standard deviations in two or more areas of development.

Snellen chart: a screening tool for assessing visual acuity.

Social service delivery: giving assistance to people who need it.

Social skills: specific behaviours that people exhibit when interacting with others.

Social stories: short stories that encourage children to behave appropriately in social situations.

Special education: instruction that is specially designed to meet the unique needs of children and youth who are exceptional.

Special needs: an educational term to describe children with exceptionalities.

Speech: the mechanical production of language.

Speech disorders: problems encountered in the oral production of language; an impairment of verbal communication such that the intelligibility of spoken language is reduced.

Speech range: the range of pitch of most human speech.

Speech reading (lip reading): the skill of understanding speech through watching the lips and face.

Speech reception threshold (SRT): the level at which an individual actually understands speech.

Spina bifida: a congenital midline defect of the spinal column.

Strabismus: one of the most common oculomotor problems, resulting from inefficient ocular motor mobility.

Stuttering: speech flow disorder; a major category of dysfluency.

Supported employment: a wide variety of work situations and vocational rehabilitation programs that range from adult day programs to highly automated production factories.

Support services: services designed to assist a child with a disability and his or her teacher.

Syndrome: a constellation of findings similar from patient to patient.

Syntax: the network of organizational principles underlying linguistic expression.

Talent: a specific dimension of a skill in areas such as music or visual arts.

Task analysis: analyzing the behavioural components and prerequisite skills of a task; breaking skills down into their component parts.

Telegraphic speech: reduced speech that resembles a telegram in that only the essential aspects of the message, those possessing meaning, are included.

Tertiary prevention: intervention strategies used after a negative outcome has been attained.

Tests: controlled and structured procedures that attempt to elicit particular responses that the child might not demonstrate spontaneously.

Therapy: the treatment of an illness or disabling condition.

Transition: the process of moving from one program to another, or from one service delivery mode to another, and a systematic passage from school to adult life for students with disabilities.

Transition planning: helping students to plan so that they can assume their rightful places in society.

Traumatic Brain Injury (TBI): an insult to the brain caused by an external physical force that results in impairment of cognitive abilities or physical functioning and may result in disturbances of behaviour or emotional functioning.

Tympanic membrane: a tough, tightly stretched tissue that separates the outer from the middle ear.

Usher's syndrome: a condition of familial nerve deafness associated with pigment degeneration of the retina.

Vertical enrichment: a program in which students do additional independent work of their own choosing in the classroom, such as individual studies.

Visual acuity: the measure of the smallest image distinguishable by the eye.

Visual field: the entire area that can be seen when staring straight ahead, reported in degrees.

Visual functioning (visual efficiency): what a visually impaired person does with his or her residual vision.

Visual impairment: a generic term that includes mild visual impairments, low vision, and total blindness.

Visual system: the system that consists of the eye, which receives the light image; the nerve pathways, which transmit the image to the optical centres of the brain; and the brain itself, which interprets the image.

Vocational evaluation: a comprehensive and systematic process that utilizes work (real or simulated) to assess the vocational potential of people with disabilities.

Wraparound: an integrated plan that addresses the needs of a child or youth during and beyond the school day.

BIBLIOGRAPHY

Abang, T.B. (1980). *Teaching visually handicapped children in Nigeria*. Ibadan, Nigeria: Cleverianum Press.

Abbott, M., Walton, C., & Greenwood, C.R. (2002). Phonemic awareness in kindergarten and first grade. *Teaching Exceptional Children, 34*, 20–26.

Abroms, K.I., & Bennett, J.W. (1983). Current findings in Down's syndrome. *Exceptional Children, 49*, 449–450.

Abu-Akel, Ahmad, Caplan, R., Guthrie, D., & Scott, K. (2000). Childhood schizophrenia: Responsiveness to questions during conversation. *American Academy of Child and Adolescent Psychiatry, 39*, 779–786.

Access denied. (1999, May). Premiers' Council on the Status of People with Disabilities. Canadians with disabilities still lack equal opportunities, according to watchdog report. *Status Report: Quarterly Newsletter on Disability Issues in Alberta, 12*.

Adams, G.B. (2004). Identifying, assessing, and treating obsessive-compulsive disorder in school-aged children: The role of school personnel. *Teaching Exceptional Children, 37*, 46–53.

Adams, J.W., & Tidwell, R. (1989). An instructional guide for reducing the stress of parents of hearing impaired children. *American Annals of the Deaf, 134*, 323–328.

Adams, K., & Markham, R. (1991). Recognition of affective facial expressions by children and adolescents with and without mental retardation. *American Journal on Mental Deficiency, 96*, 21–28.

Agnew, J. (1986). Tinnitus: An overview. *Volta Review, 88*, 215–221.

Akamatsu, C.T., & Cole, E. (2000). Meeting the psychosocial needs of deaf immigrant and refugee children. *Canadian Journal of School Psychology, 15*, 1–18.

Akerley, M.S. (1975). Parents speak. *Journal of Autism and Childhood Schizophrenia, 5*, 373–380.

Alberta Education Response Centre. (1989). *A teacher's guide to allergies in the classroom*. Edmonton: Alberta Education.

Alberta Learning. (2000, November). *Shaping the future for students with special needs: A review of special education in Alberta—Final report*. Edmonton: Author.

Alberta Learning. (2002). *Standards for special education*. Edmonton: Author.

Alberta Teachers Association. (1993). *Trying to teach*. Edmonton: Author.

Alderson, D. (1993, February). Attention Deficit Disorder. *Keeping in Touch*, p. 2.

Aleman, S.R. (1991). *CRS report for Congress: Special education for children with attention deficit disorders: Current issues*. Washington, DC: Congressional Research Services.

Alper, S.K., Schloss, P.J., & Schloss, C.N. (1994). *Families of students with disabilities*. Boston, MA: Allyn and Bacon.

Alto, J.L., & Frankenberger, W. (1994). Effects of methylphenidate on academic achievement from first to second grade. *International Journal of Disability, Development and Education, 42*, 259–273.

Ambrose, N.G., Cox, N.J., & Yairi, E. (1997). The genetic basis of persistence and recovery in stuttering. *Journal of Speech, Language and Hearing Research, 40*, 567–580.

American Association on Mental Deficiency (1959). *A manual of terminology and classification in mental retardation*. Washington, DC: Author.

American Association on Mental Retardation. (1992). *Mental retardation: Definition, classification, and systems of support* (9th ed.). Washington, DC: Author.

American Medical Association (2002, May). *Educational forum on adolescent health: Youth bullying*. Chicago, IL: Author.

American Psychiatric Association (1968, 1982, 1987). *Diagnostic and statistical manual of mental disorders* (2nd ed., 3rd ed., 3rd ed.-Rev.). Washington, DC: Author.

American Psychiatric Association. (1994, 2000). *Diagnostic and statistical manual of mental disorders*. (4th ed., rev. ed). Washington, DC: Author.

American Speech-Language-Hearing Association. (1982). Definitions: Communicative disorders and variations. *ASHA, 24*, 949–959.

Anderson, J.A., Kutash, K., & Duchnowski, A.J. (2001). A comparison of the academic progress of students with EBD and students with LD. *Journal of Behavioral Disorders, 9*, 1–6–115.

Anderson, N.B., & Nickerson, K.J. (2005). Genes, race, and psychology in the genome era: An introduction. *American Psychologist, 60*, 5–8.

Archambault, F., & Hallmark, B.W. (1992). Regular classroom practices: Results of a national survey. In J.S. Renzulli (Chair), *Regular classroom practices with gifted students: Findings from the National Research Center on the Gifted and Talented Symposium conducted at the American Educational Research Association, San Francisco*.

Armstrong, E.M. (2003). *Conceiving risk, bearing responsibility: Fetal Alcohol Syndrome and the diagnosis of moral disorder*. Baltimore, MD: Johns Hopkins University Press.

Armstrong, T. (1995). ADD: Does it really exist? *Phi Delta Kappan, 77*, 424–428.

Arnold, K.M., & Hornett, D. (1990). Teaching idioms to children who are deaf. *Teaching Exceptional Children, 22*, 14–17.

Arthur, L., Gardner, F., & Murphy, L. (1990, September). "May I help you?" A business response to a deaf community. *Lifelong Learning*, 4–7.

Asperger, H. (1944). Die "Autistischen Psychopathen im Kindesalter". *Archiv für Psychiatrie und Nervenkrankheiten, 17*, 76–136.

The Association for Persons with Severe Handicaps (TASH). (1986). Definition of the people TASH serves. In L. Myer, C. Peck, & L. Brown (Eds.), *Critical issues in the lives of people with severe disabilities.* Baltimore, MD: Brookes.

Astley, S.J., & Clarren, S.K. (2000). Diagnosing the full spectrum of fetal alcohol exposed individuals: Introducing the 4-digit code. *Alcohol and Alcoholism, 35*, 400–410.

Atkins, D.V. (1987). Siblings of the hearing impaired: Perspectives for parents. *Volta Review, 89*, 32–45.

Atkinson, M.A., & MacLaren, N.K. (1990). What causes diabetes? *Scientific American*, 63–71.

Augoustinos, M. (1987). Developmental effects of child abuse: Recent findings. *Child Abuse and Neglect, 11*, 15–26.

Augusto, C.R., & McGraw, J.M. (1990). Humanizing blindness through public education. *Journal of Visual Impairment and Blindness, 84*, 397–400.

Autism Society Canada. (2004, March). Canadian autism research agenda and Canadian autism strategy: A white paper. Ottawa: Author. Retrieved June 12, 2004, from http://autismsocietycanada.ca/finalwhite-eng.pdf.

Babbit, B.S., & White, C.M. (2002). "R U ready?" Helping students assess their readiness for postsecondary education. *Teaching Exceptional Children, 35*, 62–66.

Badian, N.A. (1988). The prediction of good and poor reading before kindergarten entry: A nine-year follow up. *Journal of Learning Disabilities, 21*, 98–103.

Bagnato, S.J. (2005). The authentic alternative for assessment in early intervention: An emerging evidence-based practice. *Journal of Early Intervention, 28*, 17–22.

Bailey, D.B., Jr., Hatton, D., & Skinner, M. (1998). Early development trajectories of males with fragile X syndrome. *American Journal on Mental Retardation, 103*, 29–39.

Bailey, D.B., Jr., & Blanco, P.M. (1990). Parents' perspectives of a written survey of family needs. *Journal of Early Intervention, 14*, 196–203.

Bailey, D.B., Jr., & Brochin, H.A. (1989). Tests and test development. In D.B. Bailey & M. Wolery (Eds.), *Assessing infants and preschoolers with handicaps* (pp. 22–46). Columbus, OH: Merrill.

Bailey, I.L., & Hall, A. (1983). *Bailey-Hall Cereal Test for the Measurement of Visual Acuity in Children.* Berkeley, CA: Multimedia Center, School of Optometry, University of California.

Bailey, W.J. (1996, June 13). *Factline on nonmedical use of Ritalin.* http://www.drugs.indiana.edu/pubs/factline/ritalin.html.

Bain, D.A. (1980). Gifted and enriched education in Canada. In M. Csapo & L. Goguen (Eds.), *Special education across Canada: Issues and concerns for the '80s.* Vancouver: Centre for Human Development and Research.

Baird, S.M., Mayfield, P., & Baker, P. (1997). Mothers' interpretations of the behavior of their infants with visual and other impairments during interactions. *Journal of Visual Impairment and Blindness, 91*, 467–483.

Bak, J.J., Cooper, E.M., Dobroth, K.M., & Siperstein, G.N. (1987). Special class placements as labels: Effects on children's attitudes toward learning handicapped peers. *Exceptional Children, 54*, 151–155.

Baker, B.L., Blacher, J., Crnic, K.A., & Edelbrock, C. (2002). Behavior problems and parenting stress in families of three-year-old children with and without developmental delays. *American Journal on Mental Retardation, 167*, 433–444.

Baker, D. (1983). Justin Clark: Legal implications of the Mental Incompetency Act for Citizens of the World. *Canadian Journal on Mental Retardation, 33*, 14–20.

Baker, L. & Cantwell, D.P. (1982). Psychiatric disorders in children with different types of communication disorders. *Journal of Communication Disorders, 15*, 113–126.

Baker, L., & Cantwell, D.P. (1987). A prospective psychiatric follow-up of children with speech/language disorders. *Journal of the American Academy of Child and Adolescent Psychiatry, 26*, 546–553.

Ball, I. (1995, July). Drugs fear for unborn babies. *The Times*, p. 15.

Banarji, M., & Dailey, R. (1995). A study of the effects of an inclusion model on students with specific learning disabilities. *Journal of Learning Disabilities, 28*, 511–522.

Barden, R.C., Ford, M.E., Jensen, A.G., Rogers-Salyer, M., & Salyer, K.E. (1989). Effects of craniofacial deformity in infancy on the quality of mother–infant interactions. *Child Development, 60*, 819–824.

Barkley, R.A. (1998). *ADHD: A handbook for diagnosis and treatment.* New York: Guilford Press.

Barkley, R.A., Fischer, M., Edelbrock, C.S., & Smallish, L. (1990). The adolescent outcome of hyperactive children diagnosed by research criteria: An 8-year prospective follow-up study. *Journal of the American Academy of Child and Adolescent Psychiatry, 29*, 546–557.

Barnhill, G.P. (2001). What is Asperger syndrome? *Intervention in School and Clinic, 36,* 259–265.

Baron-Cohen, S. (1998). Autism and "theory of mind": An introduction and review. Retrieved from www.autism.net/html/baron-cohen.html.

Barringer, D.C., Strong, C.J., Blair, J.C., Clark, T.C., & Watkins, S. (1993). Screening procedures used to identify children with hearing loss. *American Annals of the Deaf, 138,* 420–426.

Barrington, K., Papageorgiou, A., & Usher, R. (2001, January 24). Better early than never. *The Globe and Mail,* p. A13.

Bates, J.E. (1987). Temperament in infancy. In J.D. Osofsky (Ed.), *Handbook of infant development* (pp. 1101–1149). New York: Wiley.

Batshaw, M.L., & Perrett, Y.M. (1986). *Children with handicaps: A medical primer.* Baltimore, MD: Brookes.

Bauer, A.M., & Shea, T.M. (1989). *Teaching exceptional students in your classroom.* Toronto: Allyn and Bacon.

Baum, C. (1989). Conduct disorders. In T.H. Ollendick & M. Hersen (Eds.), *Handbook of child psychopathology* (2nd ed.). New York: Plenum.

Baumeister, A.A., Kupstas, F., & Klindworth, L.M. (1990). New morbidity: Implications for prevention of children's disabilities. *Exceptionality, 1,* 1–16.

Beakley, B.A., & Yoder, S.L. (1998). Middle schoolers learn community skills. *Teaching Exceptional Children, 30,* 16–21.

Bearison, D.J., & Muhern, R.L. (Eds.) (1994). *Pediatric psychooncology: Psychological perspectives on children with cancer.* New York: Oxford University Press.

Beck, A.R., Thompson, J.R., Clay, S.L., Hutchins, M., Vogt, W.P., Romaniak, B., et al. (2001). Preservice professionals' attitudes toward children who use augmentative/alternative communication. *Education and Training in Mental Retardation and Developmental Disabilities, 36,* 255–271.

Beckman, P.J., & Lieber, J. (1994). The Social Strategy Rating Scale: An approach to evaluating social competence. *Journal of Early Intervention, 18,* 1–11.

Begley, S. (1996, February 19). Your child's brain. *Newsweek,* pp. 55–62.

Belcostas, F.P. (1987). Elementary pull-out programs for the intellectually gifted: Boon or bane? *Roeper Review, 9,* 41–55.

Bellamy, T. (1985). Severe disability in adulthood. *Newsletter for the Association for Persons with Severe Handicaps, 11,* 1–6.

Benbow, C.P. (1991). Meeting the needs of gifted students through use of acceleration. In M.C. Wang, M.C. Reynolds, & H.J. Walberg (Eds.), *Handbook of special education* (vol. 4, pp. 23–36). Elmsford, NY: Pergamon.

Bender, B.G. (1995). Are asthmatic children educationally handicapped? *School Psychology Quarterly, 1,* 274–291.

Bender, W.N., & Smith, J.K. (1990). Classroom behavior of children and adolescents with learning disabilities: A meta-analysis. *Journal of Learning Disabilities, 23,* 298–305.

Benner, G.J., Nelson, J.R., & Epstein, M.H. (2002). Language skills of children with EBD: A literature review. *Journal of Emotional and Behavioral Disorders, 10,* 43–59.

Bennett, B., & Smilanich, P. (1994). *Classroom management: A thinking and caring approach.* Ajax, ON: VISUTronx.

Bentley, K.M., & Li, A.K.F. (1995). Bully and victim problems in elementary schools and students' beliefs about aggression. *Canadian Journal of School Psychology, 11,* 153–165.

Benz, M.R., Lindstrom, L., & Yovanoff, P. (2000). Improving graduation and employment outcomes of students with disabilities: Predicting factors and student perspectives. *Exceptional Children, 66,* 509–529.

Beran, T.N., & Tutty, L.S. (2002). Children's reports of bullying and safety at school. *Canadian Journal of School Psychology, 17,* 1–14.

Berg, F. (1987). *Facilitating classroom listening: A handbook for teachers of normal and hard of hearing students.* Boston, MA: College-Hill.

Berglund, M., & Hoffbauer, D. (1996). New opportunities for students with traumatic brain injuries. *Teaching Exceptional Children, 28,* 54–56.

Berk, L. (1998). *Development through the lifespan.* Boston, MA: Allyn and Bacon.

Berkow, R. (Ed.) (1982). *The Merck manual of diagnosis and therapy.* Rahway, NJ: Merck, Sharp and Dohme.

Berkson, G., & Tupa, M. (2000). Early development of stereotypes and self-injurious behavior. *Journal of Early Intervention, 23,* 1–19.

Berlin, C.M., Jr. (1983). Biological causes of exceptionality. In R.M. Smith, J.T. Neisworth, & F.M. Hunt (Eds.), *The exceptional child: A functional approach.* New York: McGraw-Hill.

Bernard, H. (1973). *Child development and learning.* Boston, MA: Allyn and Bacon.

Bernthal, J., & Bankston, N. (1981). *Articulation disorders.* Englewood Cliffs, NJ: Prentice Hall.

Bessell, A.G. (2001). Children surviving cancer: Psychosocial adjustment, quality of life, and school experiences. *Exceptional Children, 67,* 345–359.

Betts, G.T. (1985). *Autonomous learner model for the gifted and talented.* Greeley, CO: Autonomous Learning Publications and Specialists.

Bianco, M. (2005). The effects of disability labels on special education and general education teachers' referrals for gifted programs. *LD Quarterly, 28,* 285–293.

Bickett, L., & Milich, R. (1990). First impressions formed of boys with attention deficit disorders. *Journal of Learning Disabilities, 23,* 253–259.

Bidwell, N. (1997). *The nature and prevalence of bullying in elementary schools.* Regina: Saskatchewan, Research Report 97–06, Saskatchewan School Trustees Association.

Biederman, J., Wilens, T., Mick, E., Spencer, T., & Faraone, S.V. (1999). Pharmacotherapy of attention-deficit/hyperactivity disorder reduces risk for substance abuse disorders. *Pediatrics, 104,* 20.

Bigelow, A. (1987). Early words of blind children. *Journal of Child Language, 14,* 47–56.

Bigge, L., Best, S.J., & Heller, K.W. (2001). *Teaching individuals with physical, health, or multiple disabilities* (4th ed.). Upper Saddle River, NJ: Prentice Hall.

Bin, J.L. (2001). Language development in children with attention deficit disorder. *Dissertation Abstracts International, 61.*

Birchwood, M., McGorry, E., & Jackson, H. (1997). Early intervention in schizophrenia. *British Journal of Psychiatry, 170,* 2–5.

Bird, R. (2002). *Report to the Legislature on the principal findings from the epidemiological study of autism in California: A comprehensive pilot study.* California: University of California at Davis.

Biriamah, K. (2005). Achieving equitable outcomes or reinforcing societal inequalities? A critical analysis of UNESCO's Education for All and the United States' No Child Left Behind programs. *Educational Practice and Theory, 27,* 25–34.

Bishop, V. (1986). Identifying the components of success in mainstreaming. *Journal of Visual Impairment and Blindness, 80,* 939–946.

Blackorby, J., & Wagner, M. (1996). Longitudinal postschool outcomes of youth with disabilities: Findings from the national longitudinal transition study. *Exceptional Children, 62,* 399–413.

Blanchett, W.J. (2001). Importance of teacher transition competencies as rated by special educators. *Teacher Education and Special Education, 24,* 3–12.

Bleck, E.L., & Nagel, D.A. (1982). *Physically handicapped children: A medical atlas for teachers.* New York: Grune and Stratton.

Bloom, B.S. (Ed.) (1956). *Taxonomy of educational objectives: Handbook 1: Cognitive domain.* New York: David McKay.

Bloom, B.S. (1964). *Stability and change in human characteristics.* New York: Wiley.

Bloom, B.S. (1985). *Developing talent in young people.* New York: Ballantine Books.

Bloom, B.S., & Sosniak, L.A. (1981). Talent development vs. schooling. *Educational Leadership, 39,* 86–94.

Bloom, D.T. (1991, Winter). Mainstreaming remains the goal. *Day Care and Early Education, 18,* 44–45.

Bluestone, D.C. (1982). Otitis media in children: To treat or not to treat. *New England Journal of Medicine, 306,* 1399–1404.

Bogie, H. (1997, Fall). Eaton vs. Brant County Board of Education: The Supreme Court of Canada decision, released Feb. 6, 1997. *Keeping in Touch, 6.*

Bonn, D. (1998). Tune in early for best results with cochlear implants. *Lancet,* pp. 352–362.

Bono, K.E., Bolzani Dinehart, L.H., Claussen, A., Scott, K.G., Mundy, P.C., & Katz, L.F. (2005). Early intervention with children prenatally exposed to cocaine: Expansion with multiple cohorts. *Journal of Early Intervention, 27,* 268–284.

Borgh, K. & Dickson, W.P. (1986). Two preschools sharing one microcomputer: Creating prosocial behavior with hardware and software. In P.F. Campbell & G.G. Fein (Eds.), *Young children and microcomputers* (pp. 37–44). Englewood Cliffs, NJ: Prentice Hall.

Borland, J.H. (1989). *Planning and implementing programs for the gifted.* New York: Teachers College Press.

Bornstein, M.H., Selmi, A.M., Hayes, O.M., Painter, K.M., & Marx, E.S. (1999). Representational abilities and the hearing status of child/mother dyads. *Child Development, 70,* 833–852.

Bos, C.C., & Vaughn, S. (1998). *Strategies for teaching students with learning and behavior problems.* Boston, MA: Allyn and Bacon.

Bouchard, D., & Tetrault, S. (2000). The motor development of sighted children and children with moderate and low vision aged 8–13. *Journal of Visual Impairment and Blindness, 94,* 564–574.

Bounds, B. (1997, April/May). Should special education students be paid for vocational training? *CEC Today,* 14.

Bourque, J., & Li, A.K. (1987). Perceived competence, social adjustment and peer relations of intellectually gifted children in segregated versus regular-classroom settings. *Canadian Journal of Special Education, 3,* 191–200.

Boyle, R., & Yeager, N. (1997). Blueprints for learning: Using cognitive frameworks for understanding. *Teaching Exceptional Children, 29,* 26–31.

Bracken, B.A., & Newman, V.L. (1994). Child and adolescent interpersonal relations with parents, peers, and teachers: A factor analytic investigation. *Canadian Journal of School Psychology, 10,* 108–122.

Bradley, C. (1937). The behavior of children receiving Benzedrine. *American Journal of Psychiatry, 94,* 577–585.

Bransky, T. (1987). Specific program information: A key to attitudes about the gifted education program. *Gifted Child Quarterly, 31,* 20–24.

Bray, I., Wright, D.E., Davies, C., & Hook, E.B. (1998). Joint estimation of Down syndrome risk on ascertainment rates: A meta-analysis of nine published data sets. *Prenatal Diagnosis, 18,* 9–20.

Breslau, N., & Davis, G.C. (1986). Chronic stress and major depression. *Archives of General Psychiatry, 43,* 309–314.

Bricker, D.D. (1986). *Early education of at-risk and handicapped infants, toddlers and preschool children.* Glenville, IL: Scott Foresman.

Bricker, D.D. (1993). *Assessment, evaluation, and programming system for children: AESP measurement for birth to three years* (Vol. 1). Baltimore, MD: Brookes.

Brinthaupt, G.P. (1991). Cystic fibrosis and parental adjustment. In M. Seligman (Ed.), *The family with a handicapped child* (2nd ed., pp. 295–336). Boston, MA: Allyn and Bacon.

British Columbia, Ministry of Education (1995). *Special education services: A manual of policies, procedures and guidelines.* Victoria: Author.

Brody, G.H., Stoneman, Z., Davis, C.H., & Crapps, J.M. (1991). Observations of the role relations and behavior between older children with mental retardation and their younger siblings. *American Journal on Mental Retardation, 95,* 527–536.

Brook, U., Watemberg, N., & Geva, D. (2000). Attitude and knowledge of attention deficit hyperactivity disorder and learning disability among high school teachers. *Patient Education and Counseling, 40,* 247–252.

Brown, A.L. (1978). Knowing when, where, and how to remember: A problem of metacognition. In R. Glaser (Ed.), *Advances in instructional psychology* (vol. 1, pp. 77–165). Hillsdale, NJ: Erlbaum.

Brown, M. B. (2000). Diagnosis and treatment of children and adolescents with attention deficit/hyperactivity disorder. *Journal of Counseling and Development, 78,* 195–203.

Brown, T.E. (1995). Differential diagnosis of ADD versus ADHD in adults. In K.G. Nadeau (Ed.), *A comprehensive guide to attention deficit disorder in adults: Research, diagnosis, treatment* (pp. 93–108). New York: Brunner/Mazel.

Bryan, T., Burnstein, K., & Ergul, C. (2004). The social-emotional side of learning disabilities: A science-based presentation of the state of the art. *LD Quarterly, 27,* 45–51.

Bryan, T.H., & Sullivan-Burstein, K. (1997). Homework how-to's. *Teaching Exceptional Children, 29,* 32–37.

Bryan, W.H., & Jeffrey, D.L. (1982). Education of visually handicapped students in the regular classroom. *Texas Teachers Journal of Education, 9,* 125–131.

Bullis, M., & Cheney, D. (1999). Vocational and transition intervention for adolescents and young adults with emotional or behavioral disorders. *Focus on Exceptional Children, 31,* 1–24.

Burt, K.L., Parks-Charney, R., & Schwean, V.L. (2000). The AD/HD skills and strategies program: A program for AD/HD adults in postsecondary education. *Canadian Journal of School Psychology, 12,* 122–134.

Bussing, R., Faye, G. A., Leon, C. E., Garvan, C.W., & Reid, R. (2002). General classroom teacher's information and perceptions of attention deficit hyperactivity disorder. *Behavioral Disorders, 27,* 327–339.

Butterworth, J. (2002). From programs to supports. In R.L. Schalock, P.C. Baker, & M.D. Croser (Eds.), *Embarking on a new century: Mental retardation at the end of the 20th century* (pp. 83–100). Washington, DC: AAMR.

Caffey, J. (1946). Multiple fractures in the long bones of infants suffering from chronic subdural hematoma. *American Journal of Roentgenology, 56,* 163–173.

Calfee, R.C. (1987). The school as a context for assessment of literacy. *The Reading Teacher, 40,* 738–743.

Campbell, M. (1997, August 9). A pill before lunch at Camp Ritalin. *The Globe and Mail,* p. C30.

Canadian Association for Community Living (1987). *Community living 2000: A time of change, a time of challenge.* Toronto: Author.

Canadian Association of Disability Service Providers in Post-Secondary Education (1999). Toward developing professional standards of service: A report on support for students and graduates with disabilities in post-secondary education in Canada. Retrieved from www.cadsppe.cacuss.ca/english/standards.htm.

Canadian Council on Social Development. (1999). *The progress of Canada's children into the millennium 1999–2000.* Ottawa: Author.

Canadian Education Association. (1975). *Notes on the use of auxiliary personnel in some Canadian school systems.* Toronto: Author.

Canadian Hard of Hearing Association. (2000). *Working with hearing loss: A guide for employees, employers and entrepreneurs.* Ottawa: Author.

Canadian Institute of Child Health. (1994). *The health of Canada's children: A CICH profile.* Ottawa: Author.

Canadian Institute of Child Health (2000) *The health of Canada's children* (3rd ed). Ottawa: Author.

Canadian Lung Association. (1997). *Asthma.* Toronto: Author.

Canadian National Institute for the Blind (CNIB). (1980). [Brochure]. Toronto: Author.

Canadian Office for Disability Issues. (1997). *Global Applied Disability Research and Information Network on Employment and Training.* Retrieved from www.gladnet.org.

Cantor, S. (1988). Childhood schizophrenia. *American Journal on Mental Retardation, 94,* 688–690.

Carney, A. (1986). Understanding speech intelligibility in the hearing impaired. *Topics in Language Disorders, 6,* 47–59.

Cartledge, G.T, Tillman, L.C., & Johnson, C.T. (2001). Professional ethics within the context of student discipline and diversity. *Teacher Education and Special Education, 24,* 25–37.

Casby, H.W. (1997). Symbolic play of children with language impairment: A critical review. *Journal of Speech, Language, and Hearing Research, 40,* 468–479.

Case, R.E., & Taylor, S.S. (2005). Language difference or learning disability? Answers from a linguistic perspective. *Clearing House, 78,* 127–130.

Caspi, A., Elder, G.H., & Bern, D.J. (1987). Moving against the world: Life-course patterns of explosive children. *Developmental Psychology, 23,* 308–313.

Cassidy, W. (2005). From zero tolerance to a culture of care. *Education Canada, 45,* 40–42.

Cassidy, W., & Bates, A. (2005). "Drop-outs" and "push-outs:" Finding hope at a school that actualizes the ethic of care. *Education, 112,* 66–102.

Cataracts: Some facts you should know. (1990). Alberta: CNIB.

Catts, H.W. (1993). The relationship between speech-language impairments and reading disorders. *Journal of Speech and Hearing Research, 36,* 948–958.

Cawley, J.F., Parmer, R.S., Shephard, T., & Smith, M. (1997). Item complexity and computational performance of students with disabilities. *Learning Disabilities: A Multidisciplinary Journal, 8,* 97–107.

Cazden, C.B. (1988). *Classroom discourse: The language of teaching and learning.* Portsmouth, NH: Heinemann.

Celeste, M. (2006). Play behaviors and social interactions of a child who is blind: In theory and practice. *Journal of Visual Impairment and Blindness, 100,* 75–90.

Center for Assessment and Demographic Studies. (1991). *Stanford Achievement Test, eighth edition: Hearing-impaired norms booklet.* Washington, DC: Gallaudet University.

Center for Disease Control. (2004). About autism. Retrieved from www.cdc.gov/ncbddd/dd/aic/about/default.htm.

Chall, J.S., Jacobs, V., & Baldwin, L. (1990). *The reading crisis: Why poor children fall behind.* Cambridge MA: Harvard University Press.

Challman, R.C. (1939). Personality maladjustments and remedial reading. *Journal of Exceptional Children, 6,* 7–11, 35.

Chang, F., Early, D.M., & Winton, P.J. (2005). Early childhood teacher preparation in special education at 2- and 4-year institutions of higher education. *Journal of Early Intervention, 27,* 110–124.

Chapman D.A., Scott, K.G., & Mason, C.A. (2002). Early risk factors for mental retardation: Role of maternal age and maternal education. *American Journal of Mental Retardation, 107,* 46–9.

Chen, D., & Haney, M. (1995). An early intervention model for infants who are deaf-blind. *Journal of Visual Impairment and Blindness, 89,* 213–221.

Cheney, D. & Muscott, H.S. (1996). Preventing school failure for students with emotional and behavioral disorders through responsible inclusion. *Preventing School Failure, 40,* 109–116.

Cherkes-Julkowski, M., Sharp, S., & Stolzenberg, J. (1997). *Rethinking attention-deficit disorders.* Cambridge: Brookline Books.

Chernos, S. (1999). ADHD and Ritalin. *Education today, 11,* 23–25.

Children with communication disorders. (1995). *ERIC Digest, H 470.* Reston, VA: Council for Exceptional Children.

Chomsky, N. (1965). *Aspects of the theory of syntax.* Cambridge, MA: MIT Press.

Choutka, P.M., Doloughty, P.T., & Zirkel, P.A. (2004). The "discrete trials" of applied behavior analysis for children with autism: Outcome-related factors in the case law. *The Journal of Special Education, 38,* 95–103.

Clark, B. (1988). *Growing up gifted* (3rd ed.). Columbus, OH: Merrill.

Clarke, G., & Zimmerman, E. (2001). Identifying artistically talented students in four rural communities in the United States. *Gifted Child Quarterly, 45,* 104–114.

Cleaver, R.L., & Whitman, R.D. (1998). Right hemisphere, white-matter learning disabilities associated with depression in an adolescent and young adult psychiatric population. *The Journal of Nervous and Mental Disease, 186,* 561–565.

Coggins, T.E., & Morrison, J.A. (1981). Spontaneous imitations in Down syndrome children: A lexical analysis. *Journal of Speech and Hearing Research, 24,* 303–308.

Coie, J. (1985). Fitting social skills intervention to the target group. In R.H. Schnider, K.H. Rubin, & J.E. Ledingham (Eds.), *Peer relationships and social skills in childhood: Issues in assessment and training.* New York: Springer-Verlag.

Colangelo, N. (1989). Moral dilemmas as formulated by gifted students. *Understanding Our Gifted, 1,* 10–12.

Cole, E. (1992). Depression and the risk for suicide in children and adolescents. In S. Miezitis (Ed.), *Creating alternatives to depression in our schools.* Toronto: Hogrefe and Huber.

Cole, E., & Brown, R. (1996). Multidisciplinary school teams: A five-year follow-up study. *Canadian Journal of School Psychology, 12,* 155–168.

Cole, H. & Sarnoff, D. (1980, June). Interactive creativity: Explorations of basic meanings and their implications for teaching and counselling. Paper at the Twenty-sixth Annual Creative Problem Solving Institute, Buffalo.

Cole, M., & Cole, S.R. (1989). *The development of children.* San Diego, CA: Scientific American Books.

Coleman, M.R. (2001). *Conditions of teaching children with exceptional learning needs. The bright futures report.* ERIC Ed. Doc. No.455 660.

Coleman, M.R. (2005). Academic strategies that work for gifted students with learning disabilities. *Teaching Exceptional Children, 38,* 28–32.

Collins, B. (1995). The integration of students with severe or profound disabilities from segregated schools into regular public schools: An analysis of changes in parent perceptions. *Journal of Development of Physical Disabilities, 7,* 51–65.

Comings, D.E., & Comings, B.G. (1987). A controlled study of Tourette syndrome. 1. Attention-deficit disorder, learning disorders, and school problems. *American Journal of Human Genetics, 4,* 701–741.

Conn-Blowers, E.A., & McLeod, H.J. (1989). Special education in Alberta. In M. Csapo & L. Goguen (Eds.), *Special education across Canada* (pp. 19–27). Vancouver: Centre For Human Development and Research.

Conners, C.K. (2002). Forty years of methylphenidate treatment in attention deficit hyperactivity disorder. *Journal of Attention Disorders, 6,* 527–530.

Conrad, P. (2004). The discovery of hyperkenesis: Notes on the medicalization of deviant behavior. In S. Danforth & S.G. Taft (Eds.). *Crucial readings in special education* (pp. 18–24). Upper Saddle River, NJ: Pearson.

Conte, R., Andrews, J., Loomer, M., & Hutton, G. (1995). A classroom-based social skills inventory for children with learning disabilities. *Alberta Journal of Educational Research, 41,* 84–102.

Cook, B.G. (2002). Inclusive attitudes, strengths, and weaknesses of pre-service general educators enrolled in a curriculum infusion teacher preparation program. *Teacher Education and Special Education, 25,* 262–277.

Cook B.G., Semmel, M., & Gerber, M.M. (1999). Attitudes of principals and special education teachers toward inclusion: Critical differences of opinion. *Remedial and Special Education, 20,* 199–207, 256.

Cooper, H., & Nye, B. (1994). Homework for students with learning disabilities: The implications of research for policy and practice. *Journal of Learning Disabilities, 27,* 470–479.

Copeland, M.E., & Kimmel, J.R. (1989). *Evaluation and management of infants and young children with developmental disabilities.* Baltimore, MD: Brookes.

Cordesco, L.K., & Laus, M.K. (1993). Individualized training in behavioral strategies for parents of preschool children with disabilities. *Teaching Exceptional Children, 25,* 43–47.

Corn, A.L. (1980). Optical aids in the classroom. *Education of the Visually Handicapped, 12,* 114–121.

Cornwell, A., & Bawden, H.N. (1992). Reading disabilities and aggression: A critical review. *Journal of Learning Disabilities, 25,* 281–289.

Correa, V., & Heward, W. (2000). Special education in a culturally diverse society. In W. Heward (Ed.), *Exceptional children: An introduction to special education* (6th ed., pp. 82–114). Upper Saddle River, NJ: Merrill/Prentice Hall.

Cox, D.H., & Klas, L.D. (1996). Students with learning disabilities in Canadian colleges and universities: A primer for service provision. *Journal of Learning Disabilities, 29,* 93–97.

Craig, W.M., & Peplar, D.J. (1997). Observations of bullying and victimization in the schoolyard. *Canadian Journal of School Psychology, 13,* 41–60.

Cramer, S., Erzkus, A., Mayweather, K., Pope, K., Roeder, J. & Tone, T. (1997). Connecting with siblings. *Teaching Exceptional Children, 30,* 46–51.

Cramond, B., & Martin, C.E. (1987). Inservice and preservice teachers' attitudes toward the academically brilliant. *Gifted Child Quarterly, 31,* 15–19.

Cratty, B. (1986). *Perceptual and motor development in infants and children* (3rd ed.). Englewood Cliffs, NJ: Prentice Hall.

Crawford, L.V. (Ed.) (1982). *Pediatric allergic diseases.* Garden City, NY: Medical Examination Publishing Company.

Crealock, C. (1983). Teacher and student behaviours in regular and special education settings. *BC Journal of Special Education (British Columbia), 7,* 321–330.

Crealock, C. (1996). Issues in Canadian legislation applied to students with special needs. *International Journal of Special Education, 11,* 13–20.

Crick, N.R., Casas, J.F., & Nelson, D.A. (2002). Towards a more comprehensive understanding of peer maltreatment: Studies of relational victimization. *Current Directions in Psychological Science, 11,* 98–101.

Crockenberg, S.R., & Litman, C. (1990). Autonomy as competence in two-year-olds: Maternal correlates of child defiance, compliance, and self-assertion. *Developmental Psychology, 26,* 961–971.

Cropley, A. (2006). Creativity: A social approach. *Roeper Review, 28,* 125–130.

Crudden, A., & McBroom, L. (1999). Barriers to employment: A survey of employed persons who are visually impaired. *Journal of Visual Impairment and Blindness, 93,* 341–350.

Csapo, M. (1981). The emotionally disturbed child in Canada's schools. *Behavior Disorders, 6,* 139–149.

Csapo, M. (1988). Sexual abuse of children. *BC Journal of Special Education, 12,* 121–159.

Culross, R.D. (1997). Concepts of inclusion in gifted education. *Teaching Exceptional Children, 29,* 24–26.

Cummings, S.T., & Finger, D.C. (1980). Emotional disorders. In H.E. Rie & E.D. Rie (Eds.), *Handbook of minimal brain dysfunction.* New York: Wiley.

Cunningham, C.E. (2004). COPEing with selective mutism: Ten stages in the emergence of speech at school. McMaster University website: www.psychdirect.com/children/selectivemutism.htm.

Curci, R.A., & Gottlieb, J. (1990). Teachers' instruction of noncategorically grouped handicapped children. *Exceptionality, 1,* 239–248.

Curlee, R.F., & Yairi, E. (1997). Early intervention with early childhood stuttering: A critical examination of the data. *American Journal of Speech-Language Pathology, 6,* 8–18.

Dao, M. (1991). Designing assessment procedures for educationally at-risk southeast Asian-American students. *Journal of Learning Disabilities, 24,* 594–601, 629.

Darwin, C. (1859). *On the origin of the species.* London: Murray.

Dauber, S.L., & Benbow, C.P. (1990). Aspects of personality and peer relations of extremely talented adolescents. *Gifted Child Quarterly, 34,* 10–14.

David, J. (Ed.) (1990). *Our forgotten children: Hard of hearing pupils in the schools* (2nd ed.). Washington: Self Help for the Hard of Hearing.

Davis, G.A., & Rimm, S.B. (1985). *Education of the gifted and talented.* Englewood Cliffs. NJ: Prentice Hall.

Davis, G.A., & Rimm, S.B. (1994). *Education of the gifted and talented* (3rd ed.). Boston, MA: Allyn and Bacon.

Davis, L.J. (1997). Universalizing marginality: How Europe became deaf in the eighteenth century. In L.J. Davis (Ed.), *The disability studies reader* (pp. 110–127). New York: Routledge.

Dawson, G., & Osterling, J. (1997). Early intervention in autism. In M.J. Guralnick (Ed.), The effectiveness of early intervention (pp. 307–326). Baltimore, MD: Brookes.

Dawson, G., Metzoff, A.N., Osterling, J., & Rinaldi, J. (1998). Neurophysiological correlates of early symptoms of autism. *Child Development, 69,* 1276–1285.

de Bettencourt, L.U. (1987). Strategy training: A need for clarification. *Exceptional Children, 54,* 24–30.

Decker, S.N., & DeFries, J.C. (1980). Cognitive abilities in families with reading disabled children. *Journal of Learning Disabilities, 13,* 517–522.

Decker, S.N., & DeFries, J.C. (1981). Cognitive ability profiles in families of reading disabled children. *Developmental Medicine and Child Neurology, 23,* 217–227.

De La Paz, S., & Graham, S. (1997). Strategy instruction in planning efforts on the writing performance and behavior of students with learning disabilities. *Exceptional Children, 63,* 167–181.

de Mause, L. (1975). Our forefathers made childhood a nightmare. *Psychology Today, 8,* 85–88.

DePaepe, P., Garrison-Kane, L., & Doelling, J. (2002). Supporting students with health needs in schools: An overview of selected health conditions. *Focus on Exceptional Children, 35,* 1–24.

De Pompei, R., & Blosser, J. (1987). Strategies for helping head-injured children successfully return to school. *Language, Speech and Hearing Services in the Schools, 18,* 292–300.

Derevensky, J., & Coleman, E. (1989). Gifted children's fears. *Gifted Child Quarterly, 33,* 65–68.

DeRuiter, J.A., & Wansart, W. (1982). *Psychology of learning disabilities.* Rockville, MD: Aspen Systems.

Destad, L. (1987). A personal legacy. *Phi Delta Kappan, 68,* 744–745.

Dev, P.C., & Scruggs, T.E. (1997). Mainstreaming and inclusion of children with learning disabilities: Perspectives of general educators in elementary and secondary schools. In T.E. Scruggs & M.A. Mastropieri (Eds.), *Advances in learning and behavioral disorders* (vol. 11, pp. 135–178). Greenwich, CT: JAI Press.

De Witt, K. (1991, May 12). How best to teach the blind: A growing battle over braille. *The New York Times,* pp. 1, 18.

Diabetic retinopathy. (1990). Alberta: Canadian National Institute for the Blind.

Diamond, K.E., & Carpenter, C. (2000). The influence of inclusive preschool programs on children's sensitivity to the needs of others. Cited in S. Sandall & M. Ostrosky, *Journal of Early Intervention, 23,* 81–94.

Diller, L. (1998). *Running on Ritalin: A physician reflects on children, society, and performance in a pill.* New York: Bantam Books.

Dimitrovsky, L., Spector, H., Levy-Shiff, R., & Vakil, E. (1998). Interpretation of facial expressions of affect in children with learning disabilities with verbal or nonverbal deficits. *Journal of Learning Disabilities, 31,* 286–292, 312.

Dishion, T.J., Andrews, D.W., & Crosby, L. (1995). Antisocial boys and their friends in early adolescence: Relationship characteristics, quality, and interactional process. *Child Development, 66,* 139–151.

Dodge, K.A., Bates, J.E., & Pettit, G.S. (1990). Mechanisms in the cycle of violence. *Science, 250,* 1678–1683.

Dodge, K.A., Pettit, G.S., & Bates, J.E. (1994) Socialization mediators of the relation between socioecononic status and child conduct problems. *Child Development, 65,* 649–665.

Dodge, K.A., Pettit, G.S., McCloskey, C.L., & Boron, M.M. (1986). Social competence in children. *Monographs of the Society for Research in Child Development, 51,* 2. Serial 213.

Doherty, S.L., Frankenberger, W., Fuhrer, R., & Snider, V. (2000). Children's self-reported effects of stimulant medication. *International Journal of Disability, Development and Education, 47,* 39–54.

Dokecki, F., Baumeister, A.A., & Kupstas, F.D. (1989). Biomedical and social aspects of pediatric AIDS. *Journal of Early Intervention, 13,* 99–113.

Dolmage, W.R. (1999). Lies, damned lies and statistics: The media's treatment of youth violence. *Education and Law Journal, 10,* 4–46.

Don, A.J., Schellenberg, E.G., & Rourke, B.P. (1999). Music and language skills of children with Williams syndrome. *Child Neuropsychology, 5*, 154–170.

Dote-Kwan, J. (1995). Impact of mothers' interactions on the development of their young visually impaired children. *Journal of Visual Impairment and Blindness, 89*, 46–58.

Douvanis, G., & Hulsey, D. (2002). *The least restrictive environment mandate: How has it been defined by the courts?* ERIC Clearinghouse on Disabilities and Gifted Education. Arlington, VA: CEC.

Dowdy, C.A., Carter, J., & Smith, T.E.C. (1990). Differences in transitional needs of high school students with and without learning disabilities. *Journal of Learning Disabilities, 23*, 343–348.

Down, J.L. (1866). Observations on ethnic classification of idiots. *London Hospital Report, 3*, 229–262.

Downey, G., & Walker, E. (1989). Spatial cognition and adjustment in children at risk for psychopathology. *Developmental Psychology, 25*, 835–845.

Downing, J., and Peckham-Hardman, K. (2001). Daily schedules: A helpful learning tool. *Teaching Exceptional Children, 53*, 62–69.

Drew, C.J., Logan, D.R., & Hardman M.L. (1992). *Mental retardation: A life cycle approach* (5th ed.). New York: Macmillan.

Dunn, N.L., McCartan, K.W., & Fugura, R.W. (1988). Young children with orthopedic handicaps: Self-knowledge about their disability. *Exceptional Children, 55*, 249–252.

Dunn, W. (1989). Integrated related services for preschoolers with neurological impairments. *Remedial and Special Education, 10*, 31–39.

Dunst, C.J. (1980). *A clinical and educational manual for use with the Uzgiris and Hunt Scales of Infant Psychological development.* Baltimore, MD: University Park Press.

DuPaul, G., & Stoner, G. (2003). *ADHD in the schools* (2nd ed.). New York, NY: Guilford.

Dupre, A.P. (1997). Disability and the public school: The case against "inclusion." *Washington Law Review, 72*, 775–858.

Duquette, C., & Stodel, E.J. (2005). School experiences of students with fetal alcohol spectrum disorder. *Exceptionality Education Canada, 15*, 51–75.

Dworet, D., & Bennett, S. (2002). A view from the north: Special education in Canada. *Teaching Exceptional Children, 34*, 22–27.

Dykens, E. (1996). DNA meets DSM: The growing importance of genetic syndromes in dual diagnoses. *Mental Retardation, 34*, 125–127.

Dykens, E. (2001). Introduction to the special issue on behavioral phenotypes. *American Journal on Mental Retardation, 106*, 1–3.

Dykens E., & Kasari, C. (1997). Maladaptive behavior in children with Prader-Willi syndrome, Down syndrome,

and nonspecific mental retardation. *American Journal on Mental Retardation, 102*, 228–237.

Dykens, E., Leckman, J., Paul, R., & Watson, M. (1988). Cognitive, behavioral and adaptive functioning in fragile X and non–fragile X retarded men. *Journal of Autism and Developmental Disorders, 18*, 41–52.

Dykens, E.M., Rosner, B.A., Ly, T., & Sagun, J. (2005). Music and anxiety in William's syndrome: A harmonious or discordant relationship? *American Journal of Mental Retardation, 110*, 346–358.

Easterbrooks, S. (1999). Improving practices for students with hearing impairments. *Exceptional Children, 65*, 537–554.

Eber, L., Nelson, C.M., & Miles, P. (1997). School-based wraparound for students with emotional and behavioral challenges. *Exceptional Children, 63*, 539–555.

Eber, L., Sugai, G., Smith, C.R., & Scott, T.M. (2002). Wraparound and positive behavioral interventions and supports in the schools. *Journal of Emotional and Behavioral Disorders, 10*, 171–181.

Ecklund, J. (2000, February 26). Number of "difficult kids" on the rise. *Lethbridge Herald*, p. A3.

Edgar, E., Levine, P., & Maddox, M. (1985). *Washington State follow-up data of postsecondary special education students.* Seattle: Networking and Evaluation Team, University of Washington.

Edlind, E.P., & Heansly, P.A. (1985). Gifts of mentorship. *Gifted Child Quarterly, 29*, 55–60.

Edmunds, A.L. (2003). The inclusive classroom: Can teachers keep up? A comparison of Nova Scotia and Newfoundland and Labrador teachers' perceptions. *Exceptionality Education Canada, 13*, 29–48.

Edmunds, A.L., & Edmunds, G.A. (2005). Sensitivity: A double-edged sword for the pre-adolescent and adolescent gifted child. *Roeper Review, 27*, 69–77.

Edmunds, A.L., Halsall, A., MacMillan, R.B., & Edmunds, G.A. (2000). *The impact of government funding cuts on education: Report from a teacher survey.* Nova Scotia: Nova Scotia Teachers' Union.

Eggers, C. & Bunk, D. (1997). The long-term course of childhood-onset schizophrenia: A 42-year follow up. *Schizophrenia Bulletin, 23*, 105–117.

Elbaum, B., Vaughn, S., Hughes, M., Moody, S.W, & Schumm, J. (2000). How reading outcomes of students with disabilities are related to instructional grouping formats: A meta-analytic review. In R. Gershen, E. Schiller, & S. Vaughn (Eds.), *Contemporary special education research* (pp. 105–135). Mahwah, NJ: Erlbaum.

Elementary Teachers' Federation of Ontario (ETFO) (2002). *Fulfilling the promise: Ensuring success for students with special needs.* Toronto: Author.

Elias, M. (2005, May 24). Teen girls with ADHD at higher risk of mental illness. USA Today. Retrieved from USATODAY.comRSS.

Elksnin, L.K. (1997). Collaborative special education language services for students with learning disabilities. *Journal of Learning Disabilities, 30*, 414–426.

Elliott, J.G. (2006). Dyslexic diagnoses, debates, and diatribes. *Education Canada, 46*, 14–17.

Elliott, L. (1993, 18 May). Mainstreaming opposed by deaf community. *ATA News*, p. 11.

Engleman, M.D., Griffin, H.C., Griffin, L.W., & Maddox, J.I. (1999). A teacher's guide to communicating with students with deaf-blindness. *Teaching Exceptional Children, 31*, 64–70.

Englert, C.S., & Mariage, T. (1991). Making students partners in the comprehension process: Organizing the reading POSSE. *Learning Disabilities Quarterly, 14*, 123–138.

Englert, C.S., & Mariage, T. (2003). The sociocultural model in special education interventions: Apprenticing students in higher-order thinking. In L.H. Swanson, K. Harris, & S. Graham (Eds.) *Handbook of learning disabilities* (pp. 45–467). New York: Guilford.

Epanchin, B.C., & Paul, J.L. (1986). *Emotional problems of children and adolescents. A multidisciplinary perspective.* Columbus, OH: Merrill.

Epilepsy Canada Scientific Council. (1994). *Statistics.* Ottawa: Author.

Erickson, M.T. (1992). *Behavior disorders in children and adolescents* (2nd ed.). Englewood Cliffs, NJ: Prentice Hall.

Erin, J., & Koenig, A. (1997). The student with a visual impairment and a learning disability. *Journal of Learning Disabilities, 30*, 309–320.

Erin, J., Daugherty, W., Dignen, K., & Pearson, N. (1990, January). Teachers of visually handicapped students with multiple disabilities: Perspectives of adequacy. *Journal of Visual Impairment and Blindness*, 16–20.

Erting, C.J., Prezioso, C., & Hynes, M. (1990). The interactional content of deaf mother–infant communication. In V. Volterra & C.J. Erting (Eds.), *From gesture to language in hearing and deaf children* (pp. 97–106). New York: Springer-Verlag.

Espin, C.A., & Foegen, A. (1996). Validity of general outcome measures for predicting secondary students' performance on content-area texts. *Exceptional Children, 62*, 497–514.

Etscheidt, S. (2002). Psychotherapy services for students with emotional and behavioral disorders: A legal analysis of issues. *Behavioral Disorders, 27*, 386–399.

Evans, R.A., & Stough, L.M. (2002). SIB: Suggested functions and interventions. *Beyond Behavior, 12*, 3–7.

Evans, S., Tickle, B., Toppel, C., & Nichols, A. (1997). Here's help for young children exposed to drugs. *Teaching Exceptional Children, 29*, 60–62.

Evenson, B. (1999, August 7). Schoolyard bullies are victims, too: Researchers. *National Post*, pp. A1, A2.

Exceptional and homeless (2003, March). *CEC Today*, pp. 1–2, 7, 13, 15.

Faerstein, L.M. (1986). Coping and defence mechanisms of mothers of learning disabled children. *Journal of Learning Disabilities, 19*, 8–11.

Failla, S., & Jones, L.C. (1991). Families of children with developmental disabilities: An examination of family hardiness. *Research in Nursing and Health, 14*, 41–50.

Famularo, R., Stone, K., Barnum, R., & Wharton, R. (1986). Alcoholism and severe child maltreatment. *American Journal of Orthopsychiatry, 56*, 481–485.

Faraone, S.V., & Doyle, A.E. (2001). The nature and heritability of attention-deficit/hyperactivty disorder. *Child and Adolescent Psychiatric Clinics of North America, 10*, 299–316.

Faraone, S.V., Biederman, J., Spencer, T., Wilens, T., Siedman, L.J., Mick, E., et al. (2000). Attention-deficit/hyperactivity disorder in adults: An overview. *Biological Psychiatry, 48*, 9–20.

Farmer, T.W., & Hollowell, J.H. (1994). Social networks in mainstream classrooms: Social affiliations and behavioral characteristics of students with EBD. *Journal of Emotional and Behavioral Disorders, 7*, 143–155, 163.

Farrington, D.P. (1983). Offending from 10 to 25 years of age. In K.T. Van Dusen & S.A. Mednick (Eds.), *Prospective studies of crime and delinquency* (pp. 17–37). Boston, MA: Kluwer-Nijhoff.

Farrington, D.P. (1987). Early precursors of frequent offending. In J.Q. Wilson & G.C. Loury (Eds.), *From children to citizens* (Vol. 3). *Families, schools, and delinquency prevention* (pp. 27–51). New York: Springer Verlag.

Farrington, D.P., Gallagher, B., Morley, L., St. Ledger, R., & West, D.J. (1986). *Cambridge study in delinquent development: Long term follow-up.* Cambridge, England: Cambridge Institute of Criminology.

Feldhusen, J.F. (1989). Why the public schools will continue to neglect the gifted. *Gifted Child Today, 12*, 55–59.

Feldhusen, J.F., & Clinkenbeard, P.A. (1987). Creativity instructional materials: Review of research. *Journal of Creative Behavior, 20*, 1153–1182.

Feldhusen, J.F., & Hoover, S.M. (1986). A conception of giftedness: Intelligence, self-concept and motivation. *Roeper Review, 8*, 140–143.

Feldman, D. (1993). Child prodigies: A distinctive form of giftedness. *Gifted Child Quarterly, 37*, 188–193.

Feldman, R. (2000). *Development across the lifespan* (2nd ed.). Upper Saddle River, NJ: Prentice Hall.

Fenichel, G.H. (1980). *Neonatal neurology.* New York: Churchill Livingstone.

Fenson, L., Dale, P., Reznick, S., Bates, E., Thal, D., & Pethick, S. (1994). *Variability in early communicative development.* Monographs of the Society for Research in Child Development, 59 (5, Serial No. 242).

Fewell, R.R., & Cone, J.D. (1983). Identification and placement of severely handicapped children. In M. Snell (Ed.), *A systematic approach for instruction of moderately, severely and profoundly handicapped children* (pp. 46–73). Columbus, OH: Merrill.

Fichten, C.S., Judd, D., Tagalikis, V., Amsel, R., & Robillard, K. (1991). Communication cues used by people with and without visual impairments in daily conversations and dating. *Journal of Visual Impairment and Blindness, 85,* 371–377.

Fidler, D.J., Hodapp, R., & Dykens, E.M. (2002). Behavioral phenotypes and special education: Parent report of educational issues for children with Down syndrome, Prader-Willi syndrome, and Williams syndrome. *Journal of Special Education, 36,* 80–88.

Fieber, N., & Winzer, M. (2006). Confronting autism spectrum disorders: A case study from Alberta, Canada. *Journal for the Humanization of Education, 1,* 100–110.

Field, S., & Hoffman, A. (1994). Development of a model for self-determination. *Career Development for Exceptional Individuals, 17,* 159–169.

Field, T. (1984). Play behaviors of handicapped children who have friends. In T. Field, J.L. Roopnarine, & M. Segal (Eds.), *Friendships in normal and handicapped children* (pp. 153–163). Norwood, NJ: Ablex.

Fink, A.H., & Janssen, K.N. (1992). The management of maltreated adolescents in school settings. *Preventing School Failure, 36,* 32–36.

Finn, C.A., Heath, N.L., Petrakas, H., & McLean-Haywood, D. (2002). A comparison of school service models for children at risk for emotional and behavioral disorders. *Canadian Journal of School Psychology, 17,* 61–68.

Fisher, C., Berliner, D., Filby, N., Marliave, R., Cahen, L., & Dishaw, M. (1980). Teaching behaviors, academic learning time, and student achievement: An overview. In C. Denham & A. Lieberman (Eds.) (pp. 7–32). *Time to learn* (pp.7–32). Washington, DC: National Institute of Education.

Fisher. D., Grove, K.A., & Sax, C. (2000). The resilience of changes promoting inclusiveness in an urban elementary school. *Elementary School Journal, 100,* 213–227.

Fitzgerald, R. (1996). *Assaults against children and youth in the family, 1996.* Ottawa: Statistics Canada, Canadian Centre for Justice Statistics.

Fitzgerald, R. (1999). *Family violence in Canada: A statistical profile.* Ottawa: Statistics Canada, Canadian Centre for Justice Statistics.

Flavell, J. (1976). The metacognitive aspects of problem solving. In L.B. Resnick (Ed.), *The nature of intelligence.* Hillsdale, NJ: Erlbaum.

Flaxbeard, R., & Toomey, W. (1987). No longer deaf to their needs. *British Journal of Special Education, 14,* 103–105.

Fletcher, J.M., Dennis, M., Northrup, H., Barnes, M.A., Hannay, H.J., Landry, S.H. et al., (2004). Spina bifida; Genes, brain, and development. In L.M. Glidden (Ed.), *Handbook of research in mental retardation* (Volume 28, pp. 63–117). San Diego, CA: Academic Press.

Folstein, S.E., & Rutter, M.L. (1988). Autism: Familial progression and genetic implications. *Journal of Autism and Developmental Disorders, 18,* 3–29.

Fombonne, E. (2003). The prevalence of autism. *Journal of the American Medical Association, 289,* 87–89.

Fondacaro, D.M. (2001). Asperger syndrome: *A qualitative study of successful educational interventions.* ERIC Ed. Doc. No.454 658.

Ford, T., Goodman, R., & Meltzer, H. (2004). The relative importance of child, family, school, and neighborhood correlates of childhood psychiatric disorder. *Society of Psychiatry and Psychiatric Epidemiology, 39,* 487–496.

Forest, M., & Lusthaus, E. (1989). Promoting educational equality for all students: Circles and maps. In S. Stainback, W. Stainback, & M. Forest (Eds.), *Educating all students in the mainstream of regular education* (pp. 43–57). Baltimore, MD: Brookes.

Forgan, J.W., & Gonzales-DeHass, A. (2004). How to infuse social skills training into literacy instruction. *Teaching Exceptional Children, 36,* 24–30.

Forness, S.R. & Kavale, K.A. (2002). Impact of ADHD on school systems. In P.S. Jensen & J.R. Cooper (Eds.) *Attention deficit hyperactivity disorder: State of the science best practices* (pp. 1–20, 24). Kingston, NJ: Civic Research Institute.

Forness, S.R., Kavale, K.A., & Crenshaw. T.M. (1999). Stimulant medication revisited: Effective treatment of children with ADHD. *Journal of Emotional and Behavioural Disorders, 7,* 230–233.

Forness, S.R., Kavale, K.A., Sweeney, D.P., & Gresham, F.M. (1999). The future of research and practice in behavioral disorders: Psychopharmacology and its school implications. *Behavioral Disorders, 24,* 305–318.

Forness, S.R., Kavale, K.A., & Walker, H.M. (1999). Identifying children at risk for antisocial behavior: The case for comorbidity. In R.G. Gallimore, C. Bernheimer, D.L. MacMillan, & D. Speece (Eds.), *Developmental perspectives on children with high incidence disabilities* (pp. 135–155). Mahwah, NJ: Erlbaum.

Forness, S.R., Walker, H.M., & Kavale, K.A. (2003). Psychiatric disorders and treatments: A primer for teachers. *Teaching Exceptional Children, 35,* 42–49.

Foster, S.L., & Ritchey, W.L. (1979). Issues in the assessment of social competence in children. *Journal of Applied Behavior Analysis, 12,* 625–638.

Fox, C.L., & Boulton, M.J. (2005). The social skills problems of victims of bullying: Self, peer and teacher problems. *British Journal of Educational Psychology, 75,* 313–328.

Frankenberger, W., & Cannon, C. (1999). Effects of Ritalin on academic achievement from first to fifth grade. *International Journal of Disability, Development and Education, 46,* 199–221.

Frankenberger, W., Farmer, C., Parker, L., & Cermak, J. (2001). The use of stimulant medication for treatment of attention-deficit/hyperactivity disorder: A survey of school psychologists' knowledge, attitudes, and experience. *Developmental Disabilities Bulletin, 29,* 132–151.

Franklin, M.E. (1992). Culturally sensitive instructional practices for African-American learners with disabilities. *Exceptional Children, 59,* 107–114.

Freeland, A. (1989). *Deafness: The facts.* Oxford: Oxford University Press.

French, D.B., & MacDonnell, B.M. (1985). A survey of questions posed by regular classroom teachers integrating hearing impaired students in Nova Scotia and New Brunswick. *ACEHI Journal, 11,* 12–33.

Freund, J., Casey, P.H., & Bradley, R.H. (1982). A special education course with pediatric components. *Exceptional Children, 48,* 348–351.

Frey, K.S., Greenberg, M.T., & Fewell, R.R. (1989). Stress and coping among parents of handicapped children: A multidimensional approach. *American Journal on Mental Retardation, 94,* 240–249.

Friesen, J.W. (1997). The concept of giftedness in First Nations context. *Multicultural Education Journal, 15,* 26–35.

Frodi, A.M. (1981). Contributions of infant characteristics to child abuse. *American Journal on Mental Deficiency, 85,* 341–349.

Froese-Germain, B. (2004). We're all born 'in': Perspectives on inclusive education. *Perspectives, 4,* 1, 3–12.

Frymier, J., & Gansneder, B. (1989, October). The Phi Delta Kappa study of students at risk. *Phi Delta Kappan, 71,* 142–151.

Fuchs, D., & Fuchs, L.S. (1995, January). Sometimes separate is better. *Educational Leadership,* pp. 22–24.

Fuchs, L.S., Fuchs, D., Hamlett, C.L. Phillips, N.B., & Karns, K. (1995). General educators' specialized adaptations for students with learning disabilities. *Exceptional Children, 61,* 440–459.

Futrell, M., Gomez, J., & Bedden, D. (2003). Teaching the children of a new America. *Phi Delta Kappan, 84,* 381–385.

Gadd, J. (1997, March 28). 10,000 child abuse cases tallied: Toronto police investigated an average of 10 incidents a day in past 3 years. *The Globe and Mail,* p. A1.

Gadow, K. (1986). *Children on medication (vol 1.): Hyperactivity, learning disabilities, and mental retardation.* Boston, MA: College Hill.

Gagné, F. (1985). Giftedness and talent: Reexamining an examination of the definitions. *Gifted Child Quarterly, 29,* 103–112.

Gagné, F. (1989). Peer nominations as a psychometric instrument: Many questions asked but few answered. *Gifted Child Quarterly, 33,* 53–58.

Gagné, F. (1991). Toward a differential model of giftedness and talent. In N. Colangelo & G.A. Davis (Eds.), *Handbook of gifted education* (pp. 65–80). Needham Heights, MA: Allyn and Bacon.

Gagné, F. (2005). An imperative, but, alas, improbable consensus! *Roeper Review, 27,* 12–14.

Gagné, F. & Schader, R.M. (2006). Chance and talent development. *Roeper Review, 28,* 88–90.

Gallagher, J.J. (1975). *The gifted child in the elementary school.* Washington, DC: American Educational Research Foundation.

Gallagher, J.J. (1998). Accountability for gifted students. *Phi Delta Kappan, 79,* 739–742.

Gallagher, J.J. (2000). Unthinkable thoughts: Education of gifted students. *Gifted Child Quarterly, 44,* 5–12.

Galligan, B. (1990). Serving people who are dually diagnosed: A problem evaluation. *Mental Retardation, 28,* 353–358.

Gallimore, L., & Woodruff, S. (1996). The bilingual-bicultural (bi-bi) approach: A professional point of view. In S. Schwartz (Ed.), *Choices in deafness: A parents' guide to communication options* (2nd ed.). Bethesda, MD: Woodbine House.

Galt, V. (1997, 28 August). Teachers support disabled in classes: Fiscal, social realities prevent student integration. *The Globe and Mail,* pp. A1, A10.

Garcia, E.E. (1988). Attributes of effective schools for language minority students. *Education and Urban Society, 20,* 387–398.

Gardner, H. (1983). *Frames of mind: The theory of multiple intelligences.* New York: Basic Books.

Gardner, H. (1997, March). *Expanding our concept of intelligence: What's missing and what could we gain.* ERIC Doc. No. ED 303 052.

Gardner, H., & Hatch, T. (1989). Multiple intelligences go to school. *Educational Researcher, 18,* 4–10.

Gardynik, U.M., & McDonald, L. (2005). Implications of risk and resilience in the life of the individual who is gifted/learning disabled. *Roeper Review, 27,* 206–214.

Gearheart, B., Mullen, R.C., & Gearheart, C.J. (1993). *Exceptional individuals: An introduction.* Pacific Grove, CA: Brooks/Cole.

Gedye, A. (1989). Extreme self-injury attributed to frontal lobe seizure. *American Journal on Mental Retardation, 94,* 20–26.

George, A.L., & Duquette, C. (2006). The psychosocial experiences of a student with low vision. *Journal of Visual Impairment and Blindness, 100,* 152–163.

Gerard, J.A., & Junkula, J. (1980). Task analysis, handwriting, and process- based instruction. *Journal of Learning Disabilities, 13,* 49–58.

Gerber, M.M. (1988). Tolerance and technology of instruction: Implications for special education reform. *Exceptional Children, 54,* 309–314.

Gerber, M.M., & Solari, E.J. (2005). Teaching effort and the future of cognitive-behavioral interventions. *Behavioral Disorders, 30,* 289–299.

Gersh, E.S. (1991a). What is cerebral palsy? In E. Geralis (Ed.), *Children with cerebral palsy.* New York: Woodbine.

Gersh, E.S. (1991b). Medical concerns and treatment. In E. Geralis (Ed.), *Children with cerebral palsy.* New York: Woodbine.

Getch, V.Q., & Newharth-Pritchett, S. (1999). Children with asthma: Strategies for educators. *Teaching Exceptional Children, 31,* 30–36.

Gilger, J.W., Pennington, B.F., & De Fries, J.C. (1992). A twin study of the etiology of comorbidity: Attention-deficit-hyperactivity disorder and dyslexia. *Journal of the Academy of Child and Adolescent Psychiatry, 31,* 343–348.

Gillberg, C., & Steffenburg, S. (1987). Outcomes and prognostic factors in infantile autism and similar conditions: A population-based study of 45 cases followed through puberty. *Journal of Autism and Developmental Disorders, 17,* 273–287.

Ginsberg, G., & Schlossberg, M. (2002). Family-based treatment of childhood anxiety disorders. *International Review of Psychiatry, 14,* 143–154.

Glass, C. S., & Wegar, K. (2001). Teacher perceptions of the incidence and management of attention deficit hyperactivity disorder. *Education, 121,* 412–420.

Glassberg, L.A., Hooper, S.R., & Mattison, R.E. (1999). Prevalence of learning disabilities at enrollment in special education students with behavioral disorders. *Behavioral Disorders, 25,* 9–21.

Gleason, J.B. (1985). *The development of language.* Columbus, OH: Merrill.

Goebe, J., Kassow, D., May, D., & Kundert, D. (2003). Parental opinions about facial plastic surgery for individuals with Down syndrome. *Mental Retardation, 41,* 29–34.

Gogel, E.M., McCumsey, J., & Hewitt, G. (1985, November/December). What parents are saying. *Gifted/Talented/Creative,* 7–9.

Goguen, L. (1993). Right to education for the gifted in Canada. In K.A. Keller, F.J. Monks, & A.H. Passow (Eds.), *International handbook of research and development of giftedness and talents* (pp. 771–777). New York: Pergamon.

Goldberg, S., Marcovitch, S., MacGregor, D., & Lojkasek, M. (1986). Family responses to developmentally delayed preschoolers: Etiology and the father's role. *American Journal on Mental Deficiency, 90,* 610–617.

Golden, J. (2005). *Message in a bottle: The making of fetal alcohol syndrome.* Cambridge, MA: Harvard University Press.

Goldring, E.B. (1990). Assessing the status of information on classroom organizational frameworks for gifted students. *Journal of Educational Research, 83,* 313–326.

Goodman, R. (1987). Infantile autism: A syndrome of multiple primary deficits. *Journal of Autism and Developmental Disorders, 19,* 409–424.

Goodrich, C., & Bailey, I. (2000). A history of the field of visual rehabilitation from the perspective of low vision. In B. Silverman, M. Lang, B. Rosenthal, & E. Faye (Eds.), *The Lighthouse handbook on visual impairment and visual rehabilitation* (pp. 675–708). New York: Oxford University Press.

Goreau, M., Kennedy, C., & Sawalzty, D. (1996). "Conquering heroes": A study of childhood cancer survivors. *Early Childhood Education, 29,* 67–73.

Gottlieb, J., Alter, M., Gottlieb, B.W., & Wishner, J. (1994). Special education in urban America: It's not justifiable for many. *Journal of Special Education, 27,* 453–465.

Gough, P.B. (1991). Tapping parent power. *Phi Delta Kappan, 75,* 339.

Gray, C.D. (1989). Opening comments on the conference on developmental disabilities and HIV infection. *Mental Retardation, 27,* 199–200.

Green. G. (1991). Evaluating claims about treatment for autism. In C. Maurice, G. Green, & E. Luce (Eds.), *Behavioral intervention for young children with autism: A manual for parents and professionals.* Austin, TX: Pro-Ed.

Gregory, S., Bishop, J., & Sheldon, L. (1995). *Deaf young people and their families.* Cambridge: Cambridge University Press.

Gresham, F.M. (1995). Best practices in social skills training. In A. Thomas & J. Grimes (Eds.), *Best practices in school psychology* (pp. 1021–1030). Washington, DC: NASP.

Gresham, F.M. (1997, November/December). We need a better way to identify students with learning disabilities. *CEC Today,* 14.

Gresham, F.M. (1998). Noncategorical approaches to K–12 emotional and behavioral difficulties. In S. Reschley, W. Tilly, & J. Grimes (Eds.), *Functional and noncategorical identification and intervention in special education* (pp. 165–180). Des Moines, IO: Iowa Department of Education.

Gresham, F.M., Lane, K.L., & Lambros, K. (2000). Comorbidity of conduct and attention deficit hyperactivity problems: Issues of identification and intervention with "fledgling psychopaths." *Journal of Emotional and Behavioral Disorders, 8,* 83–93.

Gresham, F.M, & MacMillan, D.L. (1996). Learning disabilities, low achievement, and mild mental retardation: More alike than different? *Journal of Learning disabilities, 29*, 570–582.

Griffin, H.C., Williams, S.C., Davis, M.L., & Engleman, M. (2002). Using technology to enhance cues for children with low vision. *Teaching Exceptional Children, 35*, 36–42.

Griffiths, P., Smith, C., & Harvie, A. (1997). Transitory hyperphenylalaninaemia in children with continuously treated phenylketonuria. *American Journal on Mental Retardation, 102*, 27–36.

Grisson, M., & Borkowski, J.G. (2002). Self-efficacy in adolescents who have siblings with or without disabilities. *American Journal on Mental Retardation, 107*, 79–90.

Gross, J. (2003, April 13). Nudging toward normal: Step by step, skill by skill, applied behavior analysis taught Ben to talk. *The New York Times*, pp. 27–28, 32.

Grossman, H. (Ed.) (1977). *Manual on terminology and classification in mental retardation.* Washington, DC: American Association on Mental Deficiency.

Grossman, H. (1995). *Special education in a diverse society.* Boston, MA: Allyn and Bacon.

Grover, R., Shahidi, S., Fisher, B., Goldberg, D., & Wethers, D. (1983). Current sickle cell screening program for newborns in New York City, 1979–1980. *American Journal of Public Health, 73*, 249–252.

Groves, P.M., & Rebec, G.V. (1988). *Introduction to biological psychology* (3rd ed.). Dubuque, IA: Brown.

Growing challenge for teachers—Providing medical procedures for students. (1998). *CEC Today, 5*, 1, 5, 15.

Gualtieri, G.J., Koriath, U., Van Bourgondien, M., & Saleeby, N. (1983). Language disorders in children referred for psychiatric services. *Journal of the American Academy of Child Psychiatry, 22*, 165–171.

Gubbins, E.J. (1991, April). Research needs of gifted and talented through the year 2000. In J. Renzulli (Chair), *The National Research Center on the Gifted and Talented: Present activities, future plans, and an invitation for input and involvement.* Chicago: American Educational Research Association.

Guerra, N.G., & Slaby, R. (1990). Cognitive mediators of aggression in adolescent offenders, 2. Intervention. *Developmental Psychology, 26*, 269–277.

Guilford, J.P. (1988). Some changes in the Structure of Intellect model. *Educational and Psychological Measurement, 48*, 1–4.

Guitar, B. (1998). *Stuttering: An integrated approach to its nature and treatment.* Baltimore, MD: Williams and Wilkins.

Gunter, P.L., Hummel, J.H., & Conroy, M.A. (1998). Increasing correct academic responding: An effective intervention strategy to decrease behavior problems. *Effective School Practices, 17*, 36–54.

Guralnick, M. (1981). Programmatic factors affecting child–child social interactions in mainstreamed preschool programs. *Exceptional Education Quarterly, 1*, 71–91.

Guralnick, M. (1990). Social competence and early intervention. *Journal of Early Intervention, 14*, 3–14.

Guralnick, M., & Bricker, D. (1987). The effectiveness of early intervention for children wih cognitive and general developmental delays, In M. J. Guralnick & C. Bennett (Eds.), *The effectiveness of early intervention for at-risk and handicapped children* (pp. 115–173). New York: Academic Press.

Guralnick, M.J. & Hammond, M.A. (1999). Sequential analysis of the social play of young children with mild developmental delays. *Journal of Early Intervention, 22*, 243–256.

Guralnick, M.J., & Neville, B. (1997). Designing early intervention programs to promote children's social competence. In M.J. Guralnick (Ed.), *The effectiveness of early intervention* (pp. 579–610). Baltimore, MD: Brookes.

Guterman, B.R. (1995). The validity of categorical learning disabilities services: The consumer's view. *Exceptional Children, 62*, 111–124.

Hagerman, R.J. (1988). Fragile X syndrome: An overview. *Early Childhood Update, 4*, 1, 6.

Hagerman, R.J., & Sobesky, W.E. (1989). Psychopathology in fragile X syndrome. *American Journal of Orthopsychiatry, 59*, 142–152.

Hall, A.S., & Gushee, A. G. (2002). Medical interventions for ADHD youth: A primer for school and mental health counsellors. *Journal of Mental Health Counselling, 24*, 140–153.

Hallahan, D.P., & Kauffman, J.M. (2003). *Exceptional learners: Introduction to special education* (9th ed.). Boston, MA: Allyn and Bacon.

Hallahan, D.P., Kauffman, J.M., & Lloyd, J.W. (1999). *Introduction to learning disabilities.* Boston, MA: Allyn and Bacon.

Hallenbeck, M.J. (2002). Taking charge: Adolescents with learning disabilities assume responsibility for their own writing. *Learning Disabilities Quarterly, 25*, 227–246.

Hamm, E.M. (2004). Managing asthma in the classroom. *Childhood Education, 81*, 16–19.

Hammer, E. (October, 1984). *Quality of life for the multiply handicapped child.* Paper prepared for the Helen Keller Seminar on the Multiply Handicapped, New York City.

Handel, R.D. (1983). Teachers of gifted girls: Are there differences in classroom management? *Journal for the Education of the Gifted, 6*, 86–97.

Hannah, M.E., & Midlarsky, E. (2005). Helping by siblings of children with mental retardation. *Journal on Mental Retardation, 110*, 87–99.

Harber, J.R. (1980). Issues in the assessment of language and reading disorders in learning disabled children. *Learning Disability Quarterly, 3,* 20–28.

Hardman, M.L., Drew, C.J., Egan, M.W., & Wolf, B. (1993). *Human exceptionality: Society, school, and family* (4th ed.). Boston, MA: Allyn and Bacon.

Harrington, F. (2000). Sign language interpreters and access for deaf students to university curricula: The ideal and the reality. In R.P. Roberts, S.E. Carr, D. Abraham, & A. Dufour (Eds.), *The critical link 2: Interpreters in the community* (pp. 219–273). Amsterdam: John Benjamins.

Harrington, M.L., & Powers, A.R. (2004). Preparing teachers to meet the needs of children who have cochlear implants. *Teacher Education and Special Education, 27,* 360–372.

Harris, K.R., Friedlander, B.D., Scaller, B., Frizzelle, R., & Graham, S. (2005). Self-monitoring of attention versus self-monitoring of academic performance: Effects among students with ADHD in the general education classroom. *Journal of Special Education, 39,* 145–156.

Harris, L., & Associates Inc. (1998). *The NOD/Harris Survey on employment in people with disabilities.* New York: Author.

Harris, S.L., Handleman, J.S., & Palmer, C. (1985). Parents and grandparents view the autistic child. *Journal of Autism and Developmental Disorders, 15,* 127–137.

Harrison, T.R. (1980). *Harrison's principles of internal medicine* (9th ed.). New York: McGraw-Hill.

Harry, B., Kalyanpur, M., & Day, M. (1999). *Building cultural reciprocity with families.* Baltimore, MD: Brookes.

Hastings, P., & Noone, S.J. (2005). Self-injurious behavior and functional analysis: Ethics and evidence. *Education and Training in Developmental Disabilities, 40,* 335–342.

Hastings, R., Sonuga-Barke, E.J., & Remington, B. (1993). An analysis of labels of people with learning disabilities. *British Journal of Clinical Psychology, 32,* 463–465.

Hatton, D.D., Bailey, D.B., Burchinal, M.R., & Ferrell, K.A. (1997). Developmental growth curves of preschool children with vision impairments. *Child Development, 68,* 788–806.

Hauser-Cram, P., Warfield, M., Shonkoff, J., Krauss, M., Lipshur, C.C., & Sayer, A. (1999). Family influences on adaptive development in young children with Down syndrome. *Child Development, 70,* 979–989.

Hay, D.F., Payne, A., & Chadwick, A. (2004). Peer relations in childhood. *Journal of Child Psychology and Psychiatry, 45,* 84–108.

Haywood Gear, G. (1976). Accuracy of teacher judgment in identifying intellectually gifted children: A review of the literature. *Gifted Child Quarterly, 20,* 478–487.

Healey, W. (1999). Focus on disability—Williams syndrome. *CEC Today, 6,* 11.

Hearing loss and surgery. (1982). *Lifeline Magazine, 4,* 8–10.

Heath, N. (1996). The emotional domain: Self-concept and depression in children with learning disabilities. *Advances in Learning and Behavioral Disabilities, 10,* 47–75.

Heath, N.L., & Ross, S. (2000). The prevalence and expression of depressive symptomology in children with and without learning disabilities. *Learning Disabilities Quarterly, 23,* 24–26.

Heflin, L.J., & Bullock, L.M. (1999). Inclusion of students with emotional/behavioral disorders: A survey of teachers in general and special education. *Preventing School Failure, 43,* 103–111.

Heinze, T., & Leyser, Y. (1998). Variables associated with stress and adaptation in families of children with visual disabilities. *International Journal of Special Education, 13,* 1–17.

Helfer, R.E. (1987). The developmental basis of child abuse and neglect: An epidemiological approach. In R.E. Helfer & R.S. Kempe (Eds.), *The battered child* (4th ed.). Chicago, IL: University of Chicago Press.

Heller, K.W. (1997). The critical need for physical/health disability certification. *Physical Disabilities: Education and Related Services, 16,* 1–5.

Heller, K.W., Frederick, L.D., Dykes, M., Best, S., & Cohen, E.T. (1999). A national perspective on competencies for teachers of individuals with physical and health disabilities. *Exceptional Children, 65,* 219–234.

Henderson, R.A. (1989). PKU and maternal PKU: The cure and the problem. *BC Journal of Special Education, 13,* 253–257.

Herronkohl, R.C., Egolf, B.P., Ellen, C., & Herrenkohl, E.C. (1997). Preschool antecedents of adolescent assaultive behavior: A longitudinal study. *American Journal of Orthopsychiatry, 67,* 422–432.

Hessler, G., & Kitchen, D. (1980). Language characteristics of a purposive sample of early elementary learning disabled students. *Learning Disability Quarterly, 3,* 36–41.

Hetherington, E.M., & Parke, R.D. (1986). *Child psychology: A contemporary viewpoint* (3rd ed.). New York: McGraw-Hill.

Hewison, J. (1988). The long-term effectiveness of parental involvement in reading: A follow-up to the Haringey Reading Project. *British Journal of Educational Psychology, 58,* 184–190.

Hicks, L. (1987). Unpublished paper. St. John's: Memorial University of Newfoundland.

Higgins, E.C., & Raskind, M.H. (2000). Speaking to read: The effects of continuous vs. discrete speech reception systems on the reading and speech of children with learning disabilities. *Journal of Special Educational Technology, 15,* 19–30.

Hill, S.A. (1997). The relevance and value of music therapy for children with Rett syndrome. *British Journal of Special Education, 24,* 124–128.

Hinshaw, S. (2002). Preadolescent girls with attention-deficit/hyperactivity disorder: 1. Background characteristics, comorbidity, cognitive and social functioning, and parenting practices. *Journal of Consulting and Clinical Psychology, 70,* 1086–1098.

Hinshelwood, J. (1917). *Congenital word blindness.* London: H.K. Lewis.

Hintermaier, M. (2000). Children who are hearing impaired with additional disabilities and related aspects of parental stress. *Exceptional Children, 66,* 327–332.

Hipp, K.A., & Huffman, J.B. (2000, April). How leadership is shared and visions emerge in the creation of learning communities. Paper presented at AERA, New Orleans.

Hobbs, N. (Ed.) (1975). *Issues in the classification of children: A sourcebook of categories, labels, and their consequences.* San Francisco: Jossey Bass.

Hobbs, T., & Westling, D.L. (1998). Inclusion, inclusion, inclusion: Promoting successful inclusion. *Teaching Exceptional Children, 31,* 12–19.

Hobson, R.P. (1988). Beyond cognition: A theory of autism. In G. Dawson (Ed.), *Autism: New perspectives on diagnoses, nature and treatment.* New York: Guilford.

Hodapp, R.M., & Fidler, D.J. (1999). Special education and genetics: Connections for the 21st. century. *Journal of Special Education, 33,* 130–137.

Hodapp, R.M., Glidden, L.M., & Kaiser, A.P. (2005). Siblings of persons with disabilities: Toward a research agenda. *Mental Retardation, 43,* 334–338.

Holahan, C. K. (1991). Lifetime achievement patterns, retirement and life satisfaction of gifted aged women. *Journal of Gerontology, 36,* 741–749.

Holden-Pitt, L., & Diaz, J.A. (1998). Thirty years of the annual survey of deaf and hard-of-hearing children and youth: A glance over the decades. *American Annals of the Deaf, 142,* 72–76.

Holder, H.B., & Kirkpatrick, S.W. (1991). Interpretation of emotion from facial expressions in children with and without learning disabilities. *Journal of Learning Disabilities, 24,* 170.

Holland, A.L., Swindell, C.S., & Ruinmuth, O.M. (1990). Aphasia and related adult disorders. In G.H. Shames & E.H. Wiig (Eds.), *Human communication disorders* (3rd ed.) (pp. 424–462). Columbus, OH: Merrill.

Holmgren, R.A., Eisenberg, N., & Fokes, R.A. (1998). The relation of children's situational empathy-related emotions to dispositional prosocial behavior. *International Journal of Behavioral Development, 22,* 169–194.

Hoover, J., & Stenhjem, P. (2003). Bullying and teasing of youth with disabilities: Creating positive school environments for effective inclusion. National Center on Secondary Education and transition, 2, www.ncset.org/publications/print-resource.asp?id = 1332.

Horn, L., & Babbitt, L. (1999). *Students with disabilities in postsecondary education: A profile of preparation, participation, and outcomes.* Washington, DC: National Center for Education Statistics.

Houser, L., Moses, E., & Kay, J.L. (1987). A family orientation to transition. *Education of the Visually Handicapped, 19,* 109–119.

Howe, M.J.A. (1999a). *Genius explained.* Cambridge: Cambridge University Press.

Howe, M.J.A. (1999b). *The psychology of high abilities.* New York: New York University Press.

Howse, H. (1988). Asthma in children. Unpublished paper, St. John's: Memorial University of Newfoundland.

Huebner, K.M. (1985). The challenges in providing appropriate educational services to rural visually impaired children and their families. *Rural and Special Education Quarterly, 6,* 2–4.

Huessman, L.R., Eron, L.D., & Yarmel, P.W. (1987). Intellectual functioning and aggression. *Journal of Personality and Social Psychology, 52,* 232–240.

Hughes, M., Dote-Kwan, J., & Dolendo, J. (1998). A close look at the cognitive play of preschoolers with visual impairments in the home. *Exceptional Children, 64,* 451–462.

Hughes, R.S. (1999). An investigation of coping skills of parents of children with disabilities: Implications for service providers. *Education and Training in Mental Retardation and Developmental Disabilities, 34,* 271–280.

Hugh-Jones, S., & Smith, P.K. (1999). Self-reports of short- and long-term effects of bullying on children who stammer. *British Journal of Educational Psychology, 69,* 141–158.

Human Resources Development Canada (2000). Job futures. http://jobfutures.ca/doc/jf/index/shtml

Human Resources and Labour Canada (1993). *Leaving school.* Ottawa: Queen's Printer.

Hunt, P., Soto, G., Maier, J., & Doering, K. (2003). Collaborative teaming to support students at risk and students with severe disabilities in general education classrooms. *Exceptional Children, 69,* 315–332.

Hunter, A. (2000). Outcomes of the routine assessment of patients with mental retardation in a genetic clinic. *American Journal of Medical Genetics, 90,* 60–68.

Hutchinson, J. (1997, September). Is your child safe at school? *Readers Digest, 151,* 46–53.

Hysert, L. (1993, Fall). Voiceprint presents the information age to the blind. *Disability Today,* 41–42.

Immen, W. (1995, April 19). The truth about selective vision. *The Globe and Mail,* p. A8.

Ingalls, L., & Hammond, H. (1996). Prereferral school-based teams: How effective are they? *Rural Special Education Quarterly, 15,* 9–18.

Injuries at a glance. (1994, Fall). *Disability Today,* 73–74.

Innes, J.J. (1994). Full inclusion and the deaf student: A deaf consumer's review of the issue. *American Annals of the Deaf, 139,* 152–156.

Isabell, R.A., & Barber, W.H. (1993). Respiratory disorders: An update and status report for educators. *BC Journal of Special Education (British Columbia), 17,* 244–255.

Isrealite, N., Swartz, K., Huynh, J., & Tucco, A. (2005). Post-secondary students and graduates with disabilities; the transition from university to work. *Exceptionality Education Canada, 15,* 5–26.

Iverson, G., & Osman, A. (1998). Behavioral intervention for children and adults with brain injuries: A guide for families. *Journal of Cognitive Rehabilitation, 16,* 14–23.

Jackson, L., & Panyan, M.V. (2002). *Positive behavioral support in the classroom: Principles and practices.* Baltimore, MD: Brookes.

Janney, R.E., Snell, M.E., Beers, M.K., & Raynes, M. (1995). Integrating students with moderate and severe disabilities into regular education classrooms. *Exceptional Children, 61,* 425–439.

Johnsen, S.K., Ryser, G., & Dougherty, E. (1993). The validity of product portfolios in the identification of gifted students. *Gifted International: A Talent Development Journal, 8,* 40–43.

Johnson, D.G. (1989). An unassisted method of psychological testing for visually impaired individuals. *Journal of Visual Impairment and Blindness, 83,* 114–118.

Johnson, G.M. (1998). Principles of instruction for at-risk learners. *Preventing School Failure, 42,* 107–113.

Jones, B.E., Clark, G.M., & Soltz, D.F. (1997). Characteristics and practices of sign language interpreters in inclusive education programs. *Exceptional Children, 63,* 257–268.

Jones, C.S. (1987). Cerebral palsy. In C.E. Reynolds (Ed.), *Encyclopedia of special education* (pp. 293–296). New York: Wiley.

Jones, M.H. (1983). Cerebral palsy. In J. Umbriel (Ed.), *Physical disabilities and health impairment: Assessment, treatment, education.* Baltimore, MD: University Park Press.

Jones, M.M., & Carlier, L.L. (1995). Creating inclusionary opportunities for learners with multiple disabilities: A team-teaching approach. *Teaching Exceptional Children, 27,* 23–27.

Jones, V.J. (1996). "In the face of predictable crisis": Developing a comprehensive treatment plan for students with emotional or behavioral disorders. *Teaching Exceptional Children, 29,* 54–59.

Joony, P., & Ridler, O. (2005). School violence: Perception and reality. *Education Canada, 45,* 61–63.

Joseph, B., Egli, M., Koppekin, A., & Thompson, T. (2002). Food choice in people with Prader-Willi syndrome: Quantity and relative preference. *American Journal on Mental Retardation, 107,* 128–135.

Juel, C. (1988). Learning to read and write: A longitudinal study of fifty-four children from first through fourth grade. *Journal of Educational Psychology, 80,* 437–447.

Kadesjo, B., Gillberg, C., & Nagberg, B. (1999). Autism and Asperger syndrome in seven-year-old children: A total population study. *Journal of Autism and Developmental Disorders, 29,* 327–332.

Kahn, J.V. (1985). Evidence of the similar-structure hypotheses controlling for organicity. *American Journal of Mental Deficiency, 89,* 372–378.

Kaiser, A.P., Cai, X., Hancock, T.B., & Foster, E.M. (2002). Teacher-reported behavior problems and language delays in boys and girls enrolled in Head Start. *Behavioral Disorders, 28,* 23–39.

Kamps, D.M., Tankersley, M., & Ellis, C. (2000). Social skills intervention with young at-risk students: A 2-year follow-up study. *Behavioral Disorders, 25,* 310–324.

Kanner, L. (1943). Autistic disturbances of affective contact. *Nervous Child, 2,* 217–250.

Kanter, J., & Streissguth, A. (1997). *The challenge of Fetal Alcohol Syndrome: Overcoming secondary disabilities.* Seattle, WA: University of Washington Press.

Kaplan, P.S. (1996). *Pathways for exceptional children: School, home, and culture.* Minneapolis/St. Paul, MN: West Publishing.

Kaplan, R.M., & Saccuzzo, D.P. (1993). *Psychological testing: Principles, applications, and issues* (3rd ed.). Pacific Grove, CA: Brooks/Cole.

Karnes, M.B., & Strong, P.S. (1978). *Nurturing leadership talent in early childhood.* Urbana, IL: Institute for Child Behavior and Development, University of Illinois.

Karnoven, M., Test, D.W., Wood, W.M., Browder, D., & Algozzine, B. (2004). Putting self-determination into practice. *Exceptional Children, 71,* 23–41.

Kasten, E.F., Coury, D., & Heron, T. (1992). Educators' knowledge and attitudes regarding stimulants in the treatment of attention deficit hyperactivity disorder. *Developmental and Behavioural Pediatrics, 13,* 215–219.

Kauffman, J.M. (1993). How we might achieve the radical reform of special education. *Exceptional Children, 60,* 6–16.

Kauffman, J.M. (1999). How we prevent the prevention of emotional and behavioral disorders. *Exceptional Children, 65,* 338–468.

Kauffman, J.M. (2005). *Characteristics of emotional and behavior disorders in children and youth* (7th ed.). Upper Saddle River, NJ: Merrill Prentice Hall.

Kauffman, J.M., Lundrum, T., Mock, D, R., Sayeski, B., & Sayeski, K.L. (2005). Diverse knowledge and skills require a diversity of instructional groups. *RASE, 26,* 2–6.

Kauffman, J.M., Mostert, M.P., Trent, S.C., & Hallahan, D.P. (2002). *Managing classroom behavior: A reflective case-based approach* (3rd ed.). Boston, MA: Allyn and Bacon.

Kaufman, F.A, & Sexton, D. (1983, September). Some implications for home-school linkages. *Roeper Review,* 49–51.

Kaufman, J., & Zigler, E. (1989). The intergenerational transmission of child abuse. In D. Cicchetti & V. Carlson (Eds.), *Child maltreatment: Theory and research on the causes and consequences of child abuse and neglect* (pp. 129–151). New York: Cambridge University Press.

Kavale, K.A., & Forness, S.R. (1996). Social skills deficits and learning disabilities: A meta-analysis. *Journal of Learning Disabilities, 29,* 226–237.

Kavale, K.A., & Forness, S.R. (1997). Defining learning disabilities: Consonance and dissonance. In J.W. Lloyd, E. Kameenui, & D. Chard (Eds.), *Issues in educating students with disabilities* (pp. 3–25). Mahwak, NJ: Erlbaum.

Kavale, K.A., & Forness, S.R. (2000). What definitions of learning disabilities say and don't say: A critical analysis. *Journal of Learning Disabilities, 33,* 239–256.

Kavale, K.A., Holdnack, J.A., & Mostert, M.P. (2005). Responsiveness to intervention and the identification of specific learning disabilities: A critique and alternative proposal. *LD Quarterly, 28,* 2–16.

Kaye, K., Elkind, L., Goldberg, D., & Tytum, A. (1989). Birth outcomes for infants of drug abusing mothers. *New York State Journal of Medicine, 89,* 256–261.

Kazdin, A.E. (1989). *Behavior modification in applied settings* (4th ed.). Pacific Grove, CA: Brooks/Cole.

Keating, D.P. (1980). Four faces of creativity: The continuing plight of the intellectually underserved. *Gifted Child Quarterly, 24,* 56–61.

Keller, H. (1933). *Helen Keller in Scotland.* London: Methuen.

Kemp, M. (1998). Why is learning American Sign Language a challenge? *American Annals of the Deaf, 143,* 255–259.

Kempe, C., Silverman, F., Steele, B., Droegemueller, W., & Silver, H. (1962). The battered child syndrome. *Journal of the American Medical Association, 181,* 17–24.

Kennedy, C.H., Shukla, S., & Fryxell, D. (1997). Comparing the effects of educational placement on the social relationships of intermediate school students with severe disabilities. *Exceptional Children, 64,* 31–47.

Kennedy, G.H., & Meyer, K.A. (1998) The use of psychotropic medication for people with severe disabilities and challenging behavior: Current status and future directions. *Journal of the Association for Persons with Severe Handicaps, 23,* 83–97.

Kerr, B., Colangelo, N., & Gaeth, J. (1988). Gifted adolescents' attitudes toward their giftedness. *Gifted Child Quarterly, 32,* 245–247.

Keyser-Marcus, L., Brid, L., Sherron-Targett, P., Yasada, S., Johnson, S., & Wehman, P. (2002). Enhancing the schooling of students with traumatic brain injury. *Teaching Exceptional Children, 34,* 62–67.

Khatena, J. (1982). *Educational psychology of the gifted.* New York: Wiley.

Khoury, J.T., & Appel, M.A. (1979). Gifted children: Current trends and issues. In A. Lane (Ed.), *Readings in human growth and development of the exceptional individual.* Connecticut: Special Learning Corporation.

Kim, Y. (2003). The effects of assertiveness training on enhancing the social skills of adolescents with visual impairments. *Journal of Visual Impairment and Blindness, 97,* 285–297.

King, E.W. (2005). Addressing the social and emotional needs of twice-exceptional students. *Teaching Exceptional Children, 38,* 16–20.

King, N.J., Heyne, D., & Ollendick, T.H. (2005). Cognitive-behavioral treatments for anxiety and phobic disorders in children and adolescents: A review. *Behavioral Disorders, 30,* 241–257.

Kirk, S. (1963, April 16). Behavioral diagnosis and remediation of learning disabilities. In Proceedings of the Conference on Exploration into the Problems of the Perceptually Handicapped Child: First annual meeting (vol. 1). Chicago.

Klien, R.G., & Last, C.G. (1989). *Anxiety disorders in children.* Newbury Park, CA: Sage.

Klesner, H. (1994). *ESL achievement project: Development of English as a second language achievement criteria as a function of age and residence in Canada.* North York, ON: North York Board of Education.

Klinger, J.K., Vaughn, S., Hughes, M.T., Schumm, J.S., & Erlbaum, B. (1998). Academic outcomes for students with and without disabilities in inclusive classrooms. *Learning Disabilities Research and Practice, 13,* 153–160.

Kluwin, T.N., & Stewart, D.A. (2000, Winter/Spring). Interpreting in schools: A look at research. *Odyssey,* 15–17.

Koger, S.M., Schetter, T., & Weiss, B. (2005). Environmental toxicants and developmental disabilities. *American Psychologist, 60,* 243–255.

high incidence disabilities: Parental perspectives. Exceptional Children, 69, 163–179.

Kohn, A. (2004, April). Test today, privatize tomorrow. *Phi Delta Kappan.* Retrieved from www.alfiekohn.org/articles.html

Kolata, G. (1988, January 5). New treatments may aid women who have miscarriages. *The New York Times,* p. C5.

Konstantareas, M.M. (1984). Sign language as a communication prosthesis with language-impaired children. *Journal of Autism and Developmental Disorders, 14,* 9–25.

Kooistra, L., Crawford, S., Dewey, D., Cantell, M., & Kaplan, B.J. (2005). Motor correlates of ADHD: Contributions of reading disability and oppositional defiant disorder. *Journal of Learning Disabilities, 38,* 195–206.

Korbin, J.E. (1987). Child abuse and neglect: The cultural context (4th ed.). In R.E. Helfer & R.S. Kempe (Eds.), *The battered child* (pp. 23–41). Chicago, IL: University of Chicago Press.

Kouri, T. (1989). How manual sign acquisition relates to the development of spoken language: A case study. *Language, Speech and Hearing Services in the Schools, 20,* 50–62.

Kovacs, M. (1989). Affective disorders in children and adolescents. *American Psychologist, 44,* 209–215.

Kristensen, H. (2001). Multiple informants' report of emotional and behavioral problems in a nation-wide sample of selective mute children and controls. *European Child and Adolescent Psychiatry, 10,* 135–142.

Krug, D.A., Arick, J.R., & Almond, P.J. (1980). Behavior checklist for identifying severely handicapped individuals with high levels of autistic behavior. *Journal of Child Psychology and Psychiatry, 21,* 221–229.

Krug, D.A., Arick, J.R., & Almond, P.J. (1993). *Autism Screening Instrument for educational planning.* Austin, TX: Pro-Ed.

Krupp, M.A., & Chatton, M.J. (1983). *Current medical diagnosis and treatment.* Los Altos, CA: Lange Medical Publications.

Kuder, S.J. (2003). *Teaching students with language and communication disorders* (2nd ed.). Boston, MA: Pearson.

Kuhne, M., & Wiener, J. (2000). Stability of social status of children with and without learning disabilities. *Learning Disabilities Quarterly, 23,* 64–75.

Kulik, J.A. (1992). *An analysis of the research on ability grouping: Historical and contemporary perspectives.* Storrs, CT: National Research Center on the Gifted and Talented, University of Connecticut.

Kulik, J.A., & Kulik, C. (1991). Research on acceleration. In N. Colangelo & G.A. Davis (Eds.), *Handbook of gifted education* (pp. 190–191). Boston, MA: Allyn and Bacon.

Kulik, J.A., & Kulik, C.C. (1992). Meta-analytic findings on grouping. *Gifted Child Quarterly, 36,* 73–78.

Kulik, J.A., & Kulik, C.C. (1997). Ability grouping. In N. Colangelo & G.A. Davis (Eds.), *Handbook of gifted education* (pp. 230–242). Boston, MA: Allyn and Bacon.

Kuzemko, J.A. (1978). *Allergy in children.* Kent, England: Pittman Medical.

Kyger, M.M. (1999). Fix it before it breaks: Training teachers to use precorrection procedures. Cited in J.M. Kauffman (2001). *Characteristics of emotional and behavior disorders in children and youth* (7th ed.). Upper Saddle River, NJ: Merrill Prentice Hall.

Lagercrantz, H., & Slotkin, T.A. (1986, April). The "stress" of being born. *Scientific American,* 100–107.

Lago-Delello, E. (1998). Clasroom dynamics and the development of serious emotional disturbance. *Exceptional Children, 64,* 479–492.

Lahey, B.B., Hammer, D. Crumrine, P.L., & Forehand, R.L. (1980). Birth order & sex interactions in child development problems. *Developmental Psychology, 16,* 608–615.

Lai, Y., & Ishiyama, F.I. (2004). Involvement of immigrant Chinese Canadian mothers of children with disabilities. *Exceptional Children, 71,* 97–108.

Lambert, L.T. (2001). Identification and management of schizophrenia in childhood. *Journal of Child and Adolescent Psychiatric Nursing, 14,* 73–84.

Lambert, N. (1988). Adolescent outcomes for hyperactive children: Perspectives on general and specific patterns of childhood risk for adolescents' educational, social, and mental health problems. *American Psychologist, 43,* 786–799.

Landau, B. (1983). Blind children's language is not "meaningless." In A.E. Mills (Ed.), *Language acquisition in the blind child* (pp. 62–76). San Diego, CA: College Hill Press.

Landau, S., Milich, R., & Diener, M.B. (1998). Peer relations of children with attention-deficit hyperactivity disorders. *Reading and Writing Quarterly: Overcoming Learning Difficulties, 14,* 83–105.

Lane, D.A. (1989). Bullying in school. *School Psychology International, 10,* 211–215.

Lane, H., & Bahan, B. (1998). Ethics of cochlear implantation in young children: A review and reply from a Deaf World perspective. *Otolaryngology: Head and Neck Surgery, 119,* 297–308.

Lane, K.L. (2003). Identifying young students at risk for antisocial behavior: The utility of "teachers as tests." *Behavioral Disorders, 28,* 360–89.

Langlois, S. & Morrison, P. (2002). *Suicide deaths and suicide attempts.* Ottawa: Small Business and Special Surveys Division.

La Plante, M.P., Kennedy, J., Kaye, S.A., & Wegner, B. (1996). *Descriptive statistics abstract, No. 11.* Washington, DC: US Department of Education, National Institute on Disability and Rehabilitation Research.

Larrivee, B. (2005). *Authentic classroom management: Creating a learning community and building reflective practice.* Boston, MA: Pearson.

Lawrence, B. (1991). Self-concept formation and physical handicap: Some educational implications for integration. *Disability, Handicap, and Society, 6,* 139–146.

Learning Disabilities Association of Canada (LDAC)(2002). Official definition of learning disabilities. Retrieved from www.doc-taac.ca/english/defined.htm.

Lecavalier, L., Tasse, M.J., & Levesque, S. (2001). Assessment of mental retardation by school psychologists. *Canadian Journal of School Psychology, 17,* 97–107.

Lederberg, R.A. (1991). Social interaction among deaf preschoolers. *American Annals of the Deaf, 136,* 53–59.

Lee, D.J. (2002). More than ability: Gender and personal relationships influence science and technology involvement. *Sociology of Education, 75,* 349–373.

Lee, T.H., Blasey, C.M., Dyer-Friedman, J., Glaser, B., Reiss, A.L., & Eleiz, S. (2005). From research to practice: Teacher and pediatrician awareness of phenotypic traits in neurogenetic syndromes. *American Journal on Mental Retardation, 110,* 100–106.

Lefebrue, A. (1983). The child with physical handicaps. In P.D. Strenhauser & Z. Rae-Grant (Eds.), *Psychological problems of the child in the family* (2nd ed.). New York: Basic Books.

Leffert, J.S., Siperstein, G.N., & Millikan, E. (2000). Understanding social adaptation in children with mental retardation: A social-cognitive perspective. *Exceptional Children, 66,* 530–545.

LeFever, G.B., Villers, M.S., Morrow, A.L. & Vaughn, E. (2002). Parental perceptions of adverse educational outcomes among children diagnosed and treated for ADHD: A call for improved school/provider collaboration. *Psychology in the Schools, 39,* 63–71.

Lemon, L.A., & Barber, W.H. (1991). Gilles de Tourette syndrome: A review and implications for educators. *BC Journal of Special Education, 15,* 146–158.

Lerner, J. (1981). *Learning disabilities: Theories, diagnosis and teaching strategies.* Boston, MA: Houghton Mifflin.

Lerner, J. (2000). *Learning disabilities: Theories, diagnosis, and teaching strategies* (3rd edition). Boston, MA: Houghton Mifflin.

Lerner, J., Mardell-Czudnowski, C., & Goldenberg, D. (1981). *Special education for the early childhood years.* Englewood Cliffs, NJ: Prentice Hall.

Le Roy, C.H., Powell, T.H., & Kelber, P.H. (1994). Meeting our responsibilities in special education. *Teaching Exceptional Children, 26,* 37–44.

Lessenberry, B.M., & Rehfeldt, S.A. (2004). Evaluating stress levels of parents of children with disabilities. *Exceptional Children, 70,* 231–244.

Leuenberger, J., & Morris, M. (1990). Analysis of spelling errors by learning disabled and normal college students. *Learning Disability Focus, 5,* 103–118.

Levine, E. (1981). *The ecology of early deafness: Guides to fashioning environments and psychological assessments.* New York: Columbia University Press.

Levine, P., & Mouse, S.W. (1998). What follow-up studies say about postschool life for young men and women with learning disabilities: A critical look at the literature. *Journal of Learning Disabilities, 31,* 212–233.

Levy, S., Coleman, M., & Alsman, B. (2002). Reading instruction for elementary students with emotional/behavioral disorders: What's a teacher to do? *Beyond Behavior, 11,* 3–10.

Lewis, M. (2000). Hearing parental voices: An opinion survey on the use of plastic surgery for children with Down syndrome. www.bio.brandeis.edu/downsyndrome

Lewis, S., & Tolla, J. (2003). Creating and using tactile experience books for young children with visual impairment. *Teaching Exceptional Children, 35,* 22–28.

Lewis, T.J., & Bullock, L. (2004). Scientifically supported practices in emotional and behavioral disorders: A proposed approach and brief review of current practices. *Behavioral Disorders, 29,* 247–259.

Li, A. (2004). Classroom strategies for improving and enhancing visual skills in students with disabilities. *Teaching Exceptional Children, 36,* 38–46.

Li, A.K. (1985). Changing preservice teachers' attitudes toward emotionally disturbed children. *Canadian Journal of Special Education, 1,* 73–82.

Lichenstein, S. (1989). Post-school employment patterns of handicapped and nonhandicapped graduates and dropouts. *International Journal of Educational Research, 15,* 501–513.

Lieberman, L., & McHugh, E. (2001). Health-related fitness of children who are visually impaired. *Journal of Visual Impairment and Blindness, 95,* 272–288F.

Liebert, D., Lutsky, L., & Gottlieb, A. (1990). Postsecondary experiences of young adults with severe physical disabilities. *Exceptional Children, 57,* 56–63.

Lifter, K., Sulzer-Azaroff, B., Anderson, S.R., & Cowdery, G.E. (1993). Teaching play activities to preschool children with disabilities: The importance of developmental considerations. *Journal of Early Intervention, 17,* 139–159.

Lin, S.L. (2000). Coping and adaptation in families of children with cerebral palsy. *Exceptional Children, 66,* 201–218.

Linder, T. (1993). *Transdisciplinary play-based assessment: A functional approach to working with young children* (rev. ed.). Baltimore, MD: Brookes.

Lindfors, J. (1987). *Children's language and learning* (2nd ed.). Englewood Cliffs, NJ: Prentice Hall.

Lindsay, G., & Dockrell, J. (2000). The behavior and self-esteem of children with specific speech and language difficulties. *British Journal of Educational Psychology, 70,* 583–601.

Lindstrom, L.E., & Benz, M.R. (2002). Phases of career development: Case studies of young women with learning disabilities. *Exceptional Children, 69,* 67–83.

Links, P.S., Stockwell, M., Abichandani, F., & Simeon, E. (1980). Minor physical anomalies in childhood autism. Part II: Their relationship to maternal age.

Journal of Autism and Development Disorders, 10, 287–292.

Linn, A., & Myles, S.B. (2004). Asperger syndrome and six strategies for success. *Beyond Behavior, 14*, 3–9.

Lipp, M. (1988, May). Educating gifted students. Paper presented at Canadian Education Association Meeting, Fredericton.

Lipp, M. (1992, Spring). An emerging perspective on special education: A development agenda for the '90s. *The Special Education Leadership Review, 1*, 19–29.

Litter, J., & Walker, E. (1993). Interpersonal behavior of preschizophrenic children: A study of home movies. *Child Psychiatry and Human Development, 23*, 283–295.

Lloyd, J.W., Kauffman, J.M., Lundrum, T., & Roe, D.L. (1991). Why do teachers refer pupils for special education? An analysis of referral reports. *Exceptionality, 2*, 115–126.

Lochman, J.E., & Lampran, L.B. (1986). Situational and social problem-solving skills and self-esteem of aggressive and nonaggressive boys. *Journal of Abnormal Child Psychology, 14*, 605–617.

Lochman, J.E., White, K.J., & Wayland, K.K. (1990). Cognitive-behavior assessment and treatment with aggressive children. In P.C. Kendall (Ed.), *Cognitive-behavior therapy with children and adolescents.* New York: Guilford.

Loeber, R. (1990). Developmental and risk factors of juvenile antisocial behavior and delinquency. *Clinical Psychology Review, 10*, 1–41.

Loeber, R., & Stouthamer-Loeber, M. (1996). Family factors as correlates of juvenile conduct problems and deliquency. In M. Tonry & N. Morris (Eds.), *Crime and justice* (vol. 7). Chicago, IL: University of Chicago Press.

Loeber, R., & Stouthamer-Loeber, M. (1998). Development of juvenile aggression and violence: Some common misconceptions and controversies. *American Psychologist, 53*, 242–259.

Logan, K.R., Bakeman, R., & Keefe, E.B. (1997). Effects of instructional variables on engaged behavior of students with disabilities in general classrooms. *Exceptional Children, 63*, 481–497.

Longmuir, P.E., & Bar-Or, O. (2000). Factors influencing the physical activity levels of youths with physical and sensory impairments. *Adapted Physical Activity Quarterly, 17*, 40–53.

Louis, B., & Lewis, M. (1992). Parental beliefs about giftedness in young children and their relationship to actual ability level. *Gifted Child Quarterly, 36*, 27–31.

Lovaas, O.I. (1987). Behavioral treatment and normal educational and intellectual functioning in young autistic children. *Journal of Consulting and Clinical Psychology, 55*, 3–9.

Lovaas, O.I., & Smith, T. (1988). Intensive behavioral treatment for young autistic children. In B.B. Lahey &

A.E. Kazdin (Eds.), *Advances in clinical child psychology* (vol. 2). New York: Plenum.

Lovatt, M. (1962). Autistic children in a day nursery. *Exceptional Children, 29*, 103–108.

Lowenbraun, S., & Thompson, M.D. (1982). Hearing impairments. In N.G. Haring (Ed.), *Exceptional children and youth* (3rd ed.). Columbus, OH: Merrill.

Lowey, M. (1993, Summer). 3-D image and laser camera improving prostheses for amputees. *Disability Today,* 7–9.

Lowman, D.K. (1998). Preschoolers with complex health care needs in preschool classrooms. *Young Exceptional Children, 1*, 2–6.

Lue, S.L. (2001). *A survey of communication disorders for the classroom teacher.* Boston, MA: Allyn and Bacon.

Luotomen, M., Uhari, M., & Aitola, L. (1996). Recurrent otitis media during infancy and linguistic skills at the age of nine years. *Pediatric Infectious Disease Journal, 15*, 854–858.

Lynam, D. (1996). Early identification of chronic offenders: Who is the fledgling psychopath? *Psychological Bulletin, 120*, 209–234.

Lyon, G.R. (1995). Research initiatives in learning disabilities: Contributions from scientists supported by the National Institute of Child Health and Development. *Journal of Child Neurology, 10*, 5120–5126 (Supplement 1).

Lyon, G.R. (1996). Learning disabilities. *The Future of Children, 6*, 54–76.

MacAnally, P., Rose, S., & Quigley, S. (1987). *Language learning practices with deaf children.* Boston, MA: College Hill Press.

MacCuspie, P.A. (1993). Short-term placements: A crucial role for residential schools. *Journal of Visual Impairment and Blindness, 87*, 193–198.

MacCuspie, P.A. (1996). *Promoting acceptance of children with disabilities: From tolerance to inclusion.* Halifax: Atlantic Provinces Special Education Authority.

MacDonald, I.M. (1995). *Junior high school student perceptions on the nature and extent of school violence.* Masters thesis, Edmonton: University of Alberta.

MacDougall, J. (1989). Deaf Canadians in revolt. In E. Wolf-Schein & J.D. Schein (Eds.), *Post-secondary education for deaf students* (pp.79–88). Edmonton: University of Alberta.

MacMillan, D.J., & Siperstein, G.N. (2001, August). *Learning disabilities as operationally defined by schools.* Paper at LD Summit, Washington, DC. Cited in Hallahan and Kauffman, 2003.

MacMillan, D.L., Gresham F.M., & Forness S.R. (1996). Full inclusion: An empirical perspective. *Behavioral Disorders, 21*, 145–159.

McBride, H., & Seigel L.S. (1997). Learning disabilities and adolescent suicide. *Journal of Learning Disabilities, 30*, 652–659.

McCabe, J.R., Jenkins, J.R., Mills, P.E., Dale, P.S., Cole K.N., & Pepler, L. (1996). Effects of play group variables on language use by preschool children with disabilities. *Journal of Early Intervention, 20,* 329–340.

McCarthy, M.M. (1994). Inclusion and the law: Recent judicial developments. *PDK Research Bulletin*, 13.

McClellan, J.M. & Werry, J.S. (1992). Schizophrenia. *Psychiatric Clinics of North America, 15,* 131–147.

McClellan, J. & Werry, J. (2000). Summary of the practice parameters for the assessment and treatment of children and adolescents with schizophrenia. *Journal of the American Academy of Child and Adolescent Psychiatry, 39,* 1580–1582.

McConaughy, S.H., Kay, P.J., & Fitzgerald, M. (2000). How long is long enough? Outcomes for a school-based prevention program. *Exceptional Children, 67,* 21–34.

McConnell, J. (1999). Parents, adolescents, and career plans of visually impaired students. *Journal of Visual Impairment and Blindness, 93,* 498–515.

McCrindle, K. (1995, Summer). War on words: Label vs. euphemism. *Disability Today*, 16–22.

McDonnell, J., Ferguson, B., & Mathot-Buckner, C. (1992). Transition from school to work for students with severe disabilities: The Utah community employment placement project. In F. Rusch, L. De Stefano, J. Chadsey-Rusch, L.A. Phelps, & E. Szymanski (Eds.), *Transition from school to adult life: Models, linkages, and policy* (pp. 33–50). Sycamore, IL: Sycamore Publishing.

McEachin, J.J., Smith, T., & Lovaas, O.I. (1993). Long-term outcomes for children with autism who received early intensive behavioral treatment. *American Journal on Mental Retardation, 97,* 359–372.

McFadden, M., & Ellis, J. (2000). What happens to gifted education within inclusive schooling? In M. Winzer & K. Mazurek (Eds.), *Special education in the 21st century: Issues of inclusion and reform* (pp. 142–162). Washington, DC: Gallaudet University Press.

McGee, G.G., Morrier, M.J. & Daly, T. (1999). An incidental approach to early intervention for toddlers with autism. *Journal of the Association for Persons with Severe Handicaps, 24,* 133–146.

McGee, L.M., & Richgels, D.J. (1990). *Literacy's beginnings: Supporting young readers and writers.* Boston, MA: Allyn and Bacon.

McIntosh, K. (1984). Viral infections of the fetus and newborn. In M. Avery & H.W. Taeusch Jr. (Eds.), *Schaffer's diseases of the newborn* (5th ed.). Philadelphia, PA: Saunders.

McIntosh, R., Vaughn, S., Schumm, J.S., Haager, D., & Lee, O. (1993). Observations of students with learning disabilities in general education classrooms. *Exceptional Children, 60.*

McKinley, A.M., & Warren, S.F. (2000). The effectiveness of cochlear implants for children with prelingual deafness. *Journal of Early Intervention, 23,* 252–263.

McKinney, J.D., McLure, S., & Feagans, L. (1982). Classroom behavior of learning disabled children. *Learning Disabilities Quarterly, 5,* 45–51.

McKinney, J.D., Montague, M., & Hocutt, A.M. (1993). Educational assessment of students with attention deficit disorders. *Exceptional Children, 60,* 125–131.

McLaren, J., & Bryson, S.E. (1987). Review of recent epidemiological studies of mental retardation: Prevalence, associated disorders, and etiology. *American Journal on Mental Retardation, 92,* 243–254.

McLaughlin, M., & Henderson, K. (2000). Defining US special education into the twenty-first century. In M. Winzer & K. Mazurek (Eds.), *Special education in the 21st century: Issues of inclusion and reform* (pp. 41–61). Washington, DC: Gallaudet University Press.

McLeskey, J., Henry, D., & Hodges, D. (1999). Inclusion: What progress is being made across disability categories? *Teaching Exceptional Children, 31,* 60–64.

McLeskey, J., & Waldron, N.L. (2002). Inclusion and school change: Teacher perceptions regarding curricular and instructional adaptations. *Teacher Education and Special Education, 25,* 41–54.

McLinden, S. (1990). Mothers' and fathers' reports of the effects of a young child with special needs on the family. *Journal of Early Intervention, 14,* 249–259.

McNair, J., & Rusch, F.R. (1991). Parent involvement in transition programs. *Mental Retardation, 29,* 205–216.

McNeill, J., & Fowler, S. (1996). Using story reading to encourage children's conversations. *Teaching Exceptional Children, 28,* 44–46.

McWilliams, B., Morris, H., & Shelton, R. (1990). *Cleft palate speech* (2nd ed.). Philadelphia, PA: B.C. Decker, Inc.

Ma, X. (2001). Bullying and being bullied: To what extent are bullies also victims? *American Education Research Journal, 38,* 351–370.

Ma, X., Stewin, L.L., & Mack, D.L. (2001). Bullying in school: Nature, effects and remedies. *Research Papers in Education, 16,* 247–270.

Maag, J.W. (2001). Rewarded by punishment: Reflections on the disuse of positive reinforcement in schools. *Exceptional Children, 67,* 173–186.

Maag, J.W., & Katsiyannis, A. (1998). Challenges facing successful transition for youths with E/BD. *Behavioral Disorders, 23,* 209–221.

Maag, J.W., & Reid, R. (2006). Depression among students with learning disabilities: Assessing the risk. *Journal of Learning Disabilities, 39,* 3–10.

Maccini, P., McNaughton, D., & Ruhl, K. (1999). Algebra instruction for students with learning disabilities: Implications from a research review. *Learning Disability Quarterly, 22,* 113–126.

Maddux, C. (2000). Technology and special education. In M. Winzer & K. Mazurek (Eds.), *Special education in the 21st century: Issues of inclusion and reform* (pp. 83–105). Washington, DC: Gallaudet University Press.

Maheady, L. (1997). Preparing teachers for instructing multiple ability groups. *Teacher Education and Special Education, 20*, 322–339.

Main, M., & George, C. (1985). Responses of abused and disadvantaged toddlers to distress in agemates: A study in the day care setting. *Developmental Psychology, 21*, 407–412.

Maker, J.C. (1993). Creativity, intelligence, and problem solving: A definition and design for cross-cultural research and measurement related to giftedness. *Gifted Education International, 9*, 68–77.

Makin, K. (1997, February). Classroom exclusion acceptable, court says. *The Globe and Mail*, p. A7.

Maloney, J. (2002, July/August). Washington update. *LDA Newsbriefs, 37* (no. 4), pp. 5–6.

Manitoba Department of Education (1998). *Manitoba Special Education Review*. Manitoba: Proactive Information Services.

Manitoba Education Training and Youth (2002). Educational planning. Retrieved from www.edu.gov.mb.ca/metks4/instruct/specedu/eduplan.html.

Manitoba Ministry of Education, Training and Youth (2001). *Supporting inclusive schools: A handbook for student services*. Winnipeg: Author.

Many roads to one place: Clear benefits of parent support groups: Status report (1999, May). *The Quarterly Newsletter on Disability Issues in Alberta*, 10.

Mar, H.H., & Sall, N. (1995). Enhancing social opportunities and relationships of children who are deaf-blind. *Journal of Visual Impairment and Blindness, 89*, 280–286.

Marano, H.E. (1995, September/October). Big bad bully. *Psychology Today*, 50–57, 62–70, 74–82.

Mark, R., Beal, A.L., & Dumont, R. (1998). Validation of a WISC-III short-form for the identification of Canadian gifted students. *Canadian Journal of School Psychology, 14*, 1–10.

Marland, S.P., Jr. (1972). *Education of the gifted and talented: Report to the Congress of the United States by the Commission of Education*. Washington, DC: US Government Printing Office.

Marschark, M. (1993). *Raising and educating a deaf child: A comprehensive guide to the choices, controversies, and decisions faced by parents and educators*. New York: Oxford University Press.

Marschark, M. (2001). *Language development in children who are deaf and hard of hearing: A research synthesis*. Washington, DC: National Association of State Directors of Special Education.

Marston, D. (1996). A comparison of inclusive only, pull-out only, and combined service models for students with mild disabilities. *Journal of Special Education, 30*, 121–132.

Martin, A.J., Linfoot, K., & Stephenson, J. (1999). How teachers respond to concerns about misbehavior in their classroom. *Psychology in the Schools, 36*, 347–358.

Matthews, J., & Frattali, C. (1994). The professions of speech-language pathology and audiology. In G.H. Shames, E.H. Wiig, & W.A. Secord (Eds.), *Human communication disorders: An introduction* (4th ed., pp. 2–33). New York: Merrill/Macmillan.

Mattison, R.E., Hooper, S.R., & Glassberg, L.A. (2002). Three-year course of learning disorders in special education students classified as behavioral disorder. *Journal of the American Academy of Child and Adolescent Psychiatry, 41*, 1454–1461.

Maurer, H., & Newbrough, J. (1987). Facial expressions of mentally retarded and nonretarded children: 1: Recognition by mentally retarded and nonretarded adults. *American Journal on Mental Deficiency, 91*, 505–510.

Mayberry, R., Woodlinger, Cohen, R., & Goldwin-Meadow, S. (1987). Symbolic development in deaf children. In D. Cicchetti & M. Beeghly (Eds.), *Symbolic development in atypical children* (pp. 109–126). San Francisco, CA: Jossey Bass.

Mayer, C. (1999). Shaping at the point of utterance: An investigation of the composing processes of deaf student writers. *Journal of Deaf Studies and Deaf Education, 4*, 37–49.

Mayne, A., Yoshinaga-Itano, C., Seday, A.L., & Carey, A. (2000). Expressive vocabulary development of infants and toddlers who are deaf or hard of hearing. *Volta Review, 100*, 1–28.

Mazurek, K., & Winzer, M. (1994). *Comparative studies in special education*. Washington, DC: Gallaudet University Press.

Meadow, K.P. (1980). *Deafness and child development*. Berkeley, CA: University of California Press.

Meadows, N.B., Neel, R.S., Scott, C.M., & Parker, G. (1994). Academic performance, social competence, and mainstreaming: A look at mainstreamed and non-mainstreamed students with serious behavior disorders. *Behavioral Disorders, 19*, 170–180.

Meents, C.K. (1989) Attention deficit disorder: A review of the literature. *Psychology in the Schools, 26*, 168–178.

Meichenbaum, D. (1979). *Cognitive-behavior modification*. London: Plenum.

Mellon, N. (2000). Language acquisition. In J.K. Niparko, K.I. Kirk, N.K. Mellon, A.M. Tobbins, D.L. Tucci, & B.S. Wilson (Eds.), *Cochlear implants: Principles and practices* (pp. 291–315). Philadelphia, PA: Lippincott, Williams and Wilkins.

Mercer, C.D. (1987). *Students with learning disabilities* (3rd ed.). Columbus, OH: Merrill.

Mercer, J.R. (1973). *Labelling the mentally retarded: Clinical and social system perspectives on mental retardation.* Berkeley, CA: University of California Press.

Metcoff, J., Cristiloe, P., Crosby, W.M., Sandstread, H.H., & Milne, D. (1989). Smoking in pregnancy: Relation of birth weight to maternal plasma carotene and cholesterol levels. *Obstetrics and Gynecology, 102,* 302–308.

Meyer, A., & Rose, D.H. (2000). Universal design for individual differences. *Educational Leadership, 58,* 39–43.

Meyer, M.S., & Felton, R.H. (1999). Repeated reading to enhance fluency: Old approaches and new directions. *Annals of Dyslexia, 49,* 283–306.

Meyers, E. (1984). A study of concerns of classroom teachers regarding a resource room program for the gifted. *Roeper Review, 7,* 32–36.

Michael, M.G., & Paul, P.V. (1991). Early intervention for infants with deaf-blindness. *Exceptional Children, 57,* 200–210.

Milberger, S., Biederman, J., Faraone, S.V., Chen, L., & Jones, I. (2002). Is maternal smokimg a risk factor for attention deficit hyperactivity disorder? American Family Physician. www.aafp.org/afp/20020615.html

Miller, C.A. (1985). Infant mortality in the United States. *Scientific American, 235,* 31–37.

Miller, D. (2006). Students with fetal alcohol syndrome. *Teaching Exceptional Children, 38,* 12–18.

Miller, M. (2005). Using peer tutoring in the classroom: Applications for students with emotional/behavioral disorders. *Beyond Behavior, 15,* 25–30.

Miller, M.S., & Moores, D.F. (2000). Bilingual/bicultural education for deaf students. In M. Winzer & K. Mazurek (Eds.), *Special education in the 21st century: Issues of inclusion and reform* (pp. 221–237). Washington, DC: Gallaudet University Press.

Miller, S.P., Butler, F.M., & Lee, K. (1998, September). Validated practices for teaching mathematics to students with learning disabilities: A review of the literature. *Focus on Exceptional Children,* 1–24.

Mills, J.R., & Jackson, N.E. (1990). Predictive significance of early giftedness: The case of precocious reading. *Journal of Educational Psychology, 82,* 410–419.

Miner, I.D. (1995). Psychosocial implications of Ushers Syndrome Type 1 throughout the life cycle. *Journal of Visual Impairment and Blindness, 89,* 287–296.

Mira, M.P., & Tyler, J.S. (1991). Students with Traumatic Brain Injury: Making the transition from hospital to school. *Focus on Exceptional Children, 23,* 1–6.

Moffitt, T. (1993). "Life course persistent" and "adolescent limited" antisocial behavior: A developmental taxonomy. *Psychological Review, 100,* 674–701.

Moline, S., & Frankenberger, W. (2001). Use of stimulant medication for treatment of attention-deficit/hyperactivity disorder: A survey of middle and high school students' attitudes. *Psychology in the Schools, 38,* 569–584.

Monkman, H., & Baskind, S. (1998). Are assistants effectively supporting hearing-impaired children in mainstream schools? *Deafness and Education, 22,* 15–22.

Monroe, E. (1991). Who's the teacher? *ATA Magazine, 71,* 25–26.

Montagu, A. (1977). *Life before birth.* New York: Signet Books.

Moon, M.S., & Inge, K. (1993). Vocational preparation and transition. In M.E. Snell (Ed.), *Instruction of students with severe disabilities* (4th ed., pp. 556–588). New York: Merrill.

Mooney, S., & Smith, P.K. (1995). Bullying and the child who stammers. *British Journal of Special Education, 22,* 24–27.

Moore, K.L., & Persaud, T.V.N. (1993). *Before we are born.* Philadephia, PA: Saunders.

Moore, P. (1986). Voice disorders. In G. Shames & E. Wiig (Eds.), *Human communication disorders* (2nd ed., pp. 183–229). Columbus, OH: Merrill.

Moores, D.F. (1982). *Educating the deaf: Psychology, principles and practices* (2nd ed.). Boston, MA: Houghton Mifflin.

Moran, M.J., & Pentz, A.L. (1995). Helping the child with a cleft palate in your classroom. *Teaching Exceptional Children, 27,* 46–48.

Morningstar, M.E., Kleinhammer-Tramill, P., & Laltin, D.L. (1999, May). Using successful models of student-centered transition planning and services for adolescents with disabilities. *Focus on Exceptional Children,* 1–20.

Mossish, R. (1997). Gambling with discipline. *Keeping in Touch, 1,* 4.

Mount, R.H., Hastings, R.P., Reilly, S., Cass, H., & Charman, T. (2003). Towards a behavioral phenotype for Rett syndrome. *American Journal on Mental Retardation, 108,* 1–12.

Mrug, S., Hoza, B., & Gerdes, A. C. (2001). Children with attention-deficit/hyperactivity disorder: Peer relationships and peer-oriented interventions. *New Directions for Children and Adolescents, 91,* 51–77.

Mu, K., Siegel, E.B., & Allinder, R.M. (2000). Peer interactions and sociometric status of high school students with moderate or severe disabilities in general education classrooms. *Journal of the Association for Persons with Severe Handicaps, 25,* 142–152.

Munby, H., Hutchinson, N.L., & Chin, P. (1999). "I know how to do it": Research priorities for co-operative and career education in Canada's secondary schools. In Y. Lenoir, W. Hunter, D. Hodgkinson, P. de Broucker, &

A. Dolbec (Eds.), *A pan-Canadian research agenda* (pp. 37–54). Ottawa: Canadian Society for Studies in Education.

Munson, L.J., & Hunt, N. (2005). Teachers grieve! What can we do for our colleagues and ourselves when a student dies? *Teaching Exceptional Children, 37,* 48–50.

Murphy, E., Grey, I.M., & Honan, R. (2005). Co-operative learning for students with difficulties in learning: A description of models and guidelines for implementation. *British Journal of Special Education, 32,* 157–164.

Murphy, J., & Slorach, N. (1983). The language development of pre-school hearing children of deaf parents. *British Journal of Disorders of Communication, 18,* 118–126.

Murphy, K.R., & Barkley R.A. (1996). Parents of children with attention deficit-hyperactivity disorder: Psychological and attentional impairment. *American Journal of Orthopsychiatry, 66,* 93–102.

Murphy-Brennan, M.G., & Oei, T. (1999). Is there evidence to show that fetal alcohol syndrome can be prevented? *Journal of Drug Education, 29,* 5–24.

Murray, C. (2003). Risk factors, predictive factors, vulnerability, and resilience: A framework for understanding and supporting the adult transitions of youth with high-incidence disabilities. *Remedial and Special Education, 24,* 16–26.

Murray, C., Goldstein, D.E., Nourse, S., & Edgar, E. (2000). The postsecondary school attendance and completion rates of high school graduates with learning disabilities. *Learning Disabilities Research, 15,* 119–127.

Myers, G., Cerone, S., & Olson, A. (1981). *A guide for helping the child with spina bifida.* Springfield, IL: Charles C. Thomas.

Myers, P., & Hammill, D.D. (1990). *Learning disabilities: Basic concepts, assessment practices and instructional strategies* (4th ed.). Austin, TX: Pro-Ed.

Myles, B.M., & Simpson, R.L. (2001). Effective practices for students with Asperger's syndrome. *Focus on Exceptional Children, 34,* 1–16.

Naeyaert, K.M., & Grace, G. (1990). Prevalence and causes of blindness and visual impairment in Canada. *Journal of Visual Impairment and Blindness, 84,* 361–363.

Naggs, T. (1999). Hunter's syndrome: Description and educational considerations. *Journal of the International Association of Special Education, 2,* 25–37.

Nash, J.M. (2002, May 6). The secrets of autism. *Time,* 36–46.

National Advisory Committee on Dyslexia and Related Reading Disorders (1969). *Reading disorders in the United States.* Washington, DC: Department of Health, Education and Welfare.

National Association. (1991). *Liaison Bulletin, 17,* 2.

National Commission on Excellence in Education (1983). *A nation at risk: The imperative for educational reform.* Washington, DC: US Government Printing Office.

National Institute of Mental Health (2003). *Attention deficit disorder with hyperactivity.* Retrieved from www.nimh.nih.gov.

National Joint Committee on Learning Disabilities (2001). Collective perspectives on issues affecting learning disabilities: Position paper, statements, and reports. Austin, TX: Pro-Ed.

National Population Health Survey, Canada (1996–1997). Ottawa: Statistics Canada, Health Statistics Division.

Naylor, C. (2002, June). BC teachers' views of special education issues: BCTF research report, section 111, 2002-WLC-01. Victoria: BCTF.

Neal, S., & MacLean, W. (1995). Disrupted lives: Siblings of disturbed adolescents. *American Journal of Orthopsychiatry, 65,* 274–281.

Nealis, J.T. (1983). Epilepsy. In J. Umbriel (Ed.), *Physical disabilities and health impairments: An introduction* (pp. 74–85). Columbus, OH: Merrill.

Neihart, M. (1999). The impact of giftedness on psychological well-being: What does the empirical literature say? *Roeper Review, 22,* 10–17.

Neilson, S.L., & McEvoy, M.A. (2004). Functional behavioral assessment in early education settings. *Journal of Early Intervention, 26,* 115–131.

Nelkin, D., & Tancredi, L. (1989). *Dangerous diagnostics: The social power of biological information.* New York: Basic Books.

Nelson, C., & Huefner, D.S. (2003). Young children with autism: Judicial responses to the Lovaas and discrete trial training debates. *Journal of Early Intervention, 26,* 1–19.

Nelson, C., van Dijk, J., McDonnell, A.P., & Thompson, K. (2002). A framework for understanding young children with severe multiple disabilities: A van Dijk approach to assessment. *Research and Practice for Persons with Severe Disabilities, 27,* 97–111.

Nelson, J.R., Benner, G.J., & Cheney, D. (2005). An investigation of the language skills of students with emotional disturbance served in public school settings. *Journal of Special Education, 39,* 97–105.

Nelson, J.R., Benner, G.J., Lane, K.M., & Smith, B.W. (2004). An investigation of the academic achievement of K-12 students with emotional and behavioral disorders in public school settings. *Exceptional Children, 71,* 59–73.

Nelson, J.R., & Roberts, M.L. (2000). Ongoing reciprocal teacher–student interactions involving disruptive behavior in general-education classrooms. *Journal of Emotional and Behavioral Disorders, 8,* 27–37.

Nelson, J.R., Stage, S.A., Epstein, M.H., & Pierce, C.D. (2005). Effects of a prereading intervention on the literacy and social skills of children. *Exceptional Children, 72,* 29–45.

Nelson, K.B., & Ellenberg, J.H. (1986). Antecedents of cerebral palsy: Multivariate analysis of risk. *New England Journal of Medicine, 315,* 81–86.

Nelson, L.H., & Johnston, S.S. (2003). Children with cochlear implants. *Young Exceptional Children, 7,* 2–10.

Nesbit, W. (1990, March). The efficacy of integrated senior programs. *Keeping in Touch,* 3–4.

Nevins, M.E., & Chute, P.M. (1996). *Children with cochlear implants in educational settings.* London: Singular Publishing.

New Brunswick Department of Education (2002). *Guidelines and standards: Education planning for students with exceptionalities.* Fredericton, NB: Author

Newacheck, P.W., & Taylor, W.R. (1992). Childhood chronic illnesses: Prevalence, severity, and impact. *American Journal of Public Health, 82,* 364–371.

Nicholls, A.C., & Martin, Y.M. (1983). Judicial decisions and the public schools. *Canadian Journal of Education/Revue canadienne de l'education, 8,* 97–116.

Nielson, M.E., & Higgins, L.D. (2005). The eye of the storm: Services and programs for twice-exceptional learners. *Teaching Exceptional Children, 38,* 8–15.

Niles, W.J., & Marcellino, P.A. (2004). Needs-based negotiation: A promising practice in school collaboration. *Teacher Education and Special Education, 27,* 419–432.

Nirje, B. (1979). Changing patterns in residential services for the mentally retarded. In E.L. Meyen (Ed.), *Basic readings in the study of exceptional children and youth.* Denver, CO: Love Publishing.

Nixon, H.L. (1991). *Mainstreaming and the American dream: Sociological perspectives on parent coping with blind and visually impaired children.* New York: American Foundation for the Blind.

Notari-Syverson, A.R., & Shuster, S.L. (1995). Putting real-life skills into IEP/IFSPs for infants and young children. *Teaching Exceptional Children, 27,* 29–32.

Nova Scotia (1996). Department of Education and Culture. *Special education policy manual.* Halifax: Author.

Odolo, N.S., & Sitlington, P.L. (2002). What does the future hold? A follow-up study of graduates of a residential school program. *Journal of Visual Impairment and Blindness, 96,* 842–851.

Ollendick, T.H., & King N.J. (1999). Child behavior assessment and cognitive-behavior intervention in schools. *Psychology in the Schools, 36,* 427–436.

Olmeda, R.E., Thomas, A.R., & Davis, C.P. (2005). An analysis of sociocultural factors in social skills training studies with students with attention deficit/hyperactivity disorder. *Multiple Voices, 6,* 58–72.

Olney, M.F., & Kuper, E.V. (1998). The situation of women with developmental disabilities: Implications for practitioners in supported employment. *Journal of Applied Rehabilitation Counselling, 29,* 3–11.

Olson, M.R., Chalmer, L., & Hoover, J.H. (1997). Attitudes and attributes of general education teachers identified as effective inclusionists. *Remedial and Special Education, 18,* 28–35.

Olweus, D. (1987, Fall). Schoolyard bullying: Grounds for intervention. *School Safety,* pp. 4–11.

Olweus, D. (1993). *Bullying at school: What we know and what we can do.* Cambridge, MA: Blackwell.

O'Melia, M.C., & Rosenberg, M.S. (1994). Effects of cooperative homework teams on the acquisition of mathematics skills by secondary students with mild disabilities. *Exceptional Children, 60,* 538–548.

Orelove, F.P., and Sobsey, D. (1987). *Educating children with multiple disabilities: A transdisciplinary approach.* Baltimore, MD: Paul Brooks.

Orenstein, P. (2000). Schoolgirls: Young women, self-esteem, and the confidence gap. In J.M. Isake-Barnes & N.N. Wane (Eds.), *Equity in schools and society* (pp. 239–251). Toronto: Canadian Scholars' Press.

Orton, S. (1927). Studies in stuttering. *Archives of Neurology and Psychology, 18,* 671–672.

O'Shea, D.J., Hammitte, D., Mainzer, R., & Crutchfield, M. (2000). From teacher preparation to continuing teacher development. *Teacher Education and Special Education, 23,* 71–77.

Osher, D., Osher, T., & Smith, C. (1994). Toward a national perspective on emotional and behavioral disorders: A developmental agenda. *Beyond Behavior, 61,* 6–17.

Osofsky, J.D., & Thompson, M.D. (2000). Adaptive and maladaptive parenting: Perspectives on risk and protective factors (2nd ed.). In J.P. Shonkoff & S.J. Meisels (Eds.). *Handbook of early childhood intervention* (pp. 54–75). New York: Cambridge University Press.

Office of Technology Assessment (OTA), U.S. Congress. (1987). Technology dependent children: Hospital vs. home care—a technical memorandum. *OTA-TM-H-38.* Washington, DC: Author.

Otis-Wilborn, A., Winn, J., Griffin, C., & Kilgore, K. (2005). Beginning special educators' forays into general education. *Teacher Education and Special Education, 28,* 143–152.

Overton, T. (2003). *Assessing learners with special needs: An applied approach* (4th ed.). Upper Saddle River, NJ: Prentice Hall.

Owens, R.J., Jr. (1991). *Language disorders: A functional approach to assessment and intervention.* New York: Merrill.

Owens, R.J., Jr. (1996). *Language development: An introduction* (4th ed.). Boston, MA: Allyn and Bacon.

Ozanne, A.E., Kaimmer, H., & Murdoch, B.E. (1990). Speech and language skills in children with early treated phenylketonuria. *American Journal on Mental Retardation, 94,* 625–632.

Pagliaro, L.A. (1995). Adolescent depression and suicide: A review and analysis of the literature. *Canadian Journal of School Psychology, 11,* 191–201.

Palinscar, A.S., & Brown, A.L (1984). Reciprocal teaching of comprehension: Fostering and comprehension monitoring activities. *Cognition and Instruction, 2,* 117–175.

Palmer, B., & Sellars, M. (1993). The integration of hearing-impaired people in ordinary schools. *Education Today, 43,* 28–31.

Palmer, F.B., Shapiro, B.F., Wachtel, R.C., Allen, M.C., Hiller, J.E., Harryman, S.E., et al. (1988). The effects of physical therapy on cerebral palsy. *New England Journal of Medicine, 318,* 803–808.

Paradi, V. (2002). *Elijah's cup: A family's journey into the community and culture of high-functioning autism and Asperger's syndrome.* New York: Free Press.

Pardeck, J.T. (1990). Children's literature and child abuse. *Child Welfare, 69,* 83–88.

Parker, W.D. (1997). An empirical typology of perfectionism in academically talented children. *American Educational Research Journal, 34,* 545–562.

Pastor, P.N., & Rueben, C.A. (2002). *Attention deficit disorder and learning disabilities, United States, 1997–1998.* National Center for Health Statistics, Vital Health (stat 19 206).

Patten, B.M. (1973). Visually mediated thinking: A report of the case of Albert Einstein. *Journal of Learning Disabilities, 6,* 415–420.

Patterson, D. (1987, August). The causes of Down syndrome. *Scientific American,* 52–57, 60.

Patterson, G.R. (1980). Mothers: The unacknowledged victims. *Monographs of the Society for Research in Child Development, 45,* no. 5.

Patterson, G.R. (1982). *Coercive family process.* Eugene, OR: Castalia Press.

Patterson, G.R., De Baryshe, B.D., & Ramsey, E. (1989). A developmental perspective on antisocial behavior. *American Psychologist, 44,* 322–335.

Paul, R. (2003). Promoting social communication in high functioning individuals with autism spectrum disorders. *Child and Adolescent Psychiatric Clinics of North America, 12,* 87–106.

Paulesu, E., Demonet, J.F., Fazir, F., McCrory, E., Charroine, V., Brunswick, N., et al. (2001). Dyslexic-cultural diversity and biological unity. *Science, 291,* 2165–2167.

Pearl, R. (1987). Social cognitive factors in learning disabled children's social problems. In S.J. Ceci (Ed.), *Handbook of cognitive, social, and neurological aspects of learning disabilities* (vol. 2). Hillsdale, NJ: Erlbaum.

Peckham, V.C. (1993). Children with cancer in the classroom. *Teaching Exceptional Children, 26,* 26–32.

Pennington, B.F. (1990). *Diagnosing learning disorders: A neuropsychological framework.* New York: Guilford.

Perkins, W.H. (1990). What is stuttering? *Journal of Speech and Hearing Disorders, 55,* 370–382.

Perks, B. (1984). *Identification of gifted children.* Ed.D. thesis, University of British Columbia.

Peters Goessling, D. (2000). From tolerance to acceptance and celebration: Including students with severe disabilities. In M. Winzer & K. Mazurek (Eds.), *Special education in the 21st century: Issues of inclusion and reform* (pp. 175–197). Washington, DC: Gallaudet University Press.

Pettito, L.A., & Marenette, P.F. (1991). Babbling in the manual mode: Evidence for the ontogeny of language. *Science, 251,* 1493–1495.

Pfeffer, C.R. (1984). Clinical aspects of childhood suicidal behavior. *Pediatric Annals, 13,* 56–57, 60–61.

Pfeiffer, S.I. (2003). Challenges and opportunities for students who are gifted: What the experts say. *Gifted Child Quarterly, 47,* 161–169.

Pfeuti, M. (1997). Asthma: A chronic illness in the classroom. Unpublished paper, University of Lethbridge.

Pfiffner, L., & Barkley, R.A. (1990). Educational placement and classroom management. In R.A. Barkley (Ed.), *Attention Deficit Hyperactivity Disorder: A handbook for diagnosis and treatment* (pp. 498–539). New York: Guilford Press.

Phelp, M. (2000, November 11). The promise of hope. *The Globe and Mail,* pp. A14–15.

Picard, A. (2006, June 2). Winning the battle on injuries. *The Globe and Mail,* p. A13.

Pieper, E. (1976). Grandparents can help. *Exceptional Parent, 6,* 7–10.

Pierce, B.A. (1990). *Family genetic sourcebook.* New York: Wiley.

Piirto, J. (1994). *Talented children and adults: Their development and education.* New York: Merrill.

Pilecka, A. (1995, July). Childhood allergies. Lecture presented at University of Lethbridge.

Pinel, P.J. (2000). *Biopsychology* (4th ed.). Boston, MA: Allyn and Bacon.

Pirro, J.F. (1993, September). Gallaudet football: "The difference is in the hear" for the up-and-down Bisons. *Mainstream,* 16.

Pivik, J., McComas, J., & Laflamme, M. (2002). Barriers and facilitators to inclusive education. *Exceptional Children, 69,* 97–107.

Planta, R.C. (1990). Widening the debate on educational reform: Prevention as a viable alternative. *Exceptional Children, 56,* 306–313.

Plomin, R. (1989). Environment and genes: Determinants of behavior. *American Psychologist, 44,* 105–111.

Plomin, R. (1995). Genetics and children's experiences in the family. *Journal of Child Psychology and Psychiatry, 36,* 33–68.

Plomin, R., De Fries, J.C., & McClearn, G.E. (1990). *Behavioral genetics: A primer* (2nd ed.). New York: Freeman.

Pober, B.R., & Dykens, E.M. (1993). Williams syndrome: A novel view of medical, cognitive, and behavioral features. *Mental Retardation, 5,* 929–943.

Pochelmann, J., Clements, M., Abbesuto, L., & Farsad, V. (2005). Family experiences associated with a child's diagnosis of fragile X or Down syndrome: Evidence of disruption or resilience. *Mental Retardation, 43,* 255–267.

Podell, D.M., Kastner, J., & Kastner, S. (1996). Adolescents with mental retardation: Perceptions of sexual abuse. *American Journal of Orthopsychiatry, 66,* 103–110.

Pollack, D. (1980). Acoupedics: An approach to early management. In G.T. Mencher & S.E. Gerber (Eds.), *Early management of hearing loss.* New York: Grune and Stratton.

Polloway, E.A., Epstein, M.H., Patton, J.R., Cullinan, D., & Lueble, J. (1986). Demographic, social, and behavioral characteristics of students with educable mental retardation: A survey of the field. *Education and Training of the Mentally Retarded, 21,* 27–34.

Pope, A.M., & Tarlov, A.R. (Eds.) (1991). *Disability in America: Toward a national agenda for prevention.* Washington, DC: National Academy Press.

Porter, G.L. (2004, Winter). Meeting the challenge: Inclusion and diversity in Canadian schools. *Education Canada, 44,* 48–50.

Powell, S., & Dalley, M. (1995). When to intervene in selective mutism: The multimodel treatment of a case of persistent selective mutism. *Psychology in the Schools, 32,* 114–123.

Powell, S.E., Welch, E., Ezell, D., Klein, C.E., & Smith, L. (2003). Should children receive medication for symptoms of attention deficit hyperactivity disorder? *Peabody Journal of Education, 78,* 107–115.

Power, P.W. (1984). *A guide to vocational assessment.* Austin, TX: Pro-Ed.

Praisner, C.L. (2003). Attitudes of elementary school principals toward the inclusion of students with disabilities. *Exceptional Children, 69,* 135–145.

Prasher, V.P., Chowdhury, T.A., Rowe, B., & Bain, S.C. (1997). ApoE genotype and Alzheimer's disease in adults with Down syndrome: Meta-analysis. *American Journal on Mental Retardation, 102,* 103–110.

Prewitt, K. (2005, April). Demography and democracy. Presented at AERA, Montreal.

Prince, M. (2001). *Governing in an integrated fashion: Lessons from the disability domain.* Ottawa: Canadian Policy Research Networks.

Pruitt, W. (1986). *Vocational evaluation* (2nd ed.). Menomonie, WI: Walt Pruitt Associates.

Pyryt, M.C. (2003, Summer). Special education on Alberta's screen. *Keeping in Touch,* p. 4.

Quay, H.C. (1972). Patterns of aggression, withdrawal, and immaturity. In H.C. Quay & J.S. Werry (Eds.), *Psychopathological disorders of childhood.* New York: Wiley.

Quay, H.C. (1986). Classification. In H.C. Quay & J.S. Werry (Eds.), *Psychopathological disorders in childhood* (3rd ed.). New York: Wiley.

Quinsland, L.K., & Vanginkel, A. (1990). Cognitive processing and the development of concepts by deaf students. *American Annals of the Deaf, 135,* 280–284.

Rathus, S. (1988). *Understanding child development.* New York: Holt, Rinehart and Winston.

Rea, P.J., McLaughlin, V.L., & Walther-Thomas, C. (2002). Outcomes for students with learning disabilities in inclusive and pullout programs. *Exceptional Children, 68,* 213–222.

Reading difficulties versus learning disability. (1997, November/December). *CEC Today,* pp. 1, 9, 13.

Reading summit sheds new insights on teaching reading to students with disabilities. (1999). *CEC Today, 5,* pp. 1, 9, 15.

Reagan, T. (1988). Multiculturalism and the deaf: An educational manifesto. *Journal of Research and Development in Education, 22,* 1–6.

Reich, P.A. (1986). *Language development.* Englewood Cliffs, NJ: Prentice Hall.

Reid, R., Gonzales, J.E., Nordness, P.D., Trout, A., & Epstein, M.H. (2004). A meta-analysis of the academic status of students with emotional/behavioral disturbance. *Journal of Special Education, 38,* 130–144.

Reid, R., Maag, J.W., & Vasa, S.F. (1993). Attention deficit hyperactivity disorder as a disability category: A Critique. *Exceptional Children, 60,* 198–214.

Reid, R., Trout, A.L., & Schwartz, M. (2005). Self-regulation for children with attention deficit/hyperactivity disorder. *Exceptional Children, 71,* 361–377.

Reis, S., Schader, R., Milne, H., & Stephens, R. (2003). Music and minds: Using a talent development approach for young adults with Williams syndrome. *Exceptional Children, 69,* 293–313.

Reis, S.M. (1989). Reflections on policy affecting the education of gifted and talented students: Past and future perspectives. *American Psychologist, 44,* 399–408.

Reis, S.M., & O'Shea, A.A. (1984). An innovative enrichment program: The Enrichment Triad/Revolving Door Model. *Special Education in Canada, 58*, 135–138.

Reis, S.M., & Purcell, J. (1992). *An analysis of content elimination and strategies used by elementary classroom teachers in the curriculum compacting process.* Storrs, University of Connecticut, National Research Center on the Gifted and Talented.

Reis, S.M., & Westberg, K.L. (1994). The impact of staff development on teachers' ability to modify curriculum for gifted and talented students. *Gifted Child Quarterly, 38*, 127–135.

Reiss, A.L., & Freund, L. (1990). Fragile X syndrome. *Biological Psychiatry, 27*, 223–240.

Remine, M.D. (1996). *Entering and maintaining play interactions: Hearing impaired preschoolers in an integrated setting.* Masters thesis, University of Melbourne.

Rempel, R.G. (1992, Winter). Let the buyer beware: Integration is more than just a word. *Disability Today,* 46–48.

Renzulli, J.S. (1978). What makes giftedness? Reexamining a definition. *Phi Delta Kappan, 60*, 180–184, 261.

Renzulli, J.S. (1979). *What makes giftedness?* Los Angeles: National/State Leadership Training Institute on the Gifted and Talented, Brief no. 6. Report (1981).

Renzulli, J.S., & Reis, S.M. (1991). The schoolwide enrichment model: A comprehensive plan for the development of creative productivity. In N. Colangelo & G. Davis (Eds.), *Handbook of gifted education* (pp. 111–141). Boston, MA: Allyn and Bacon.

Renzulli, J.S., & Reis, S. (2000). The schoolwide enrichment model. In K.A. Heller, T.J. Monks, R.J. Sternberg, & R.F. Subotnik (Eds.), *International handbook of gifted and talented* (2nd ed., pp. 367–382). Amsterdam: Elsevier.

Renzulli, J.S., & Smith, L.H. (1984). Revolving door: A truer turn for the gifted. *Learning, 9*, 91–93.

Resistance and acceptance: Educator attitudes to inclusion of students with disabilities. (1997, Fall). *Keeping in Touch,* pp. 1, 4.

Rest, M.C. (1990, July). The shadow children: Preparing for the arrival of crack babies in school. *Phi Delta Kappan Research Bulletin,* 1–6.

Reynolds, M.C., Wang, M., & Walberg, H.J. (1987). The necessary restructuring of special and regular education. *Exceptional Children, 53*, 391–398.

Richards, C.M., Symons, D.K., Greene, C.A., & Szuskiewicz, T. (1995). The bidirectional relationship between achievement and externalizing behavior problems and students with learning disabilities. *Journal of Learning Disabilities, 28*, 8–17.

Rimm, S., & Lowe, B. (1988). Family environments of underachieving gifted students. *Gifted Child Quarterly, 32*, 353–359.

Rimm-Kaufman, S.E., & Kagan, J. (2005). Infant predictors of kindergarten behavior: The contribution of inhibited and uninhibited temperament types. *Behavioral Disorders, 30*, 331–347.

Ripley, K., & Yuill, N. (2005). Patterns of language impairment and behaviour in boys excluded from school. *British Journal of Educational Psychology, 75*, 37–50.

Roach, V. (1995). Supporting inclusion: Beyond the rhetoric. *Phi Delta Kappan, 77*, 295–299.

Robbins, J.H., Ugnat, A.M., & Waters, C. (2005). Trends in mortality from diabetes mellitus in Canada, 1986–2000. *Chronic Diseases in Canada, 26*, 25–29.

Robert, L.J. (1995). *An epidemiological study of behaviour disorders in the Saskatoon Tribal council student population.* M.Ed. thesis, University of Saskatchewan.

Roberts, C., Pratt, C., & Leach, D. (1991). Classroom and playground interactions of students with and without disabilities. *Exceptional Children, 57*, 212–224.

Roberts, C.D., Stough, L.M., & Parrish, L.A. (2002). The role of genetic counseling in the elective termination of pregnancies involving fetuses with disabilities. *Journal of Special Education, 36*, 48–55.

Roberts, J. (2000). Pediatric HIV/AIDS: A review of neurological and psychosocial implications of infection. *Canadian Journal of School Psychology, 15*, 19–34.

Roberts, K. (1997). A preliminary account of the effects of otitis media on 15-month-olds' categorization and some implications for early language learning. *Journal of Speech, Language and Hearing Research, 40*, 508–518.

Roberts, S.B., Brown, P.M., & Rickards, F.W. (1996). School pretend play entry behaviors of preschoolers with and without impaired hearing. *Journal of Early Intervention, 20*, 52–83.

Robins, L.N. (1986). The consequences of conduct disorders in girls. In P. Olweus, J. Block, & M. Radke-Yanow (Eds.), *Development of antisocial and prosocial behavior: Research, theories and issues.* New York: Academic Press.

Robins, L.N., & Earls, F. (1985). A program for preventing antisocial behavior for high-risk infants and preschoolers: A research prospectus. In R.L. Hugh, P.A. Gongla, V.B. Brown, & S.E. Goldston (Eds.), *Psychiatric epidemiology and prevention: The possibilities* (pp. 73–84). Los Angeles, CA: Neuropsychiatric Institute.

Robinson, D.O., Allen, D.V., & Root, L.P. (1988). Infant tympanometry: Differential results by race. *Journal of Speech and Hearing Disorders, 53*, 341–346.

Robinson, G.A., Palton, J.R., Polloway, E.A, & Sargent, L.R. (Eds.). (1989). *Best practices in mental retardation.* Reston, VA: Council for Exceptional Children.

Rock, E.E., Fessler, M.A., & Church, R.P. (1997). The concomitance of learning disabilities and emotional/behavioral disorders: A conceptual model. *Journal of Learning Disabilities, 30*, 245–263.

Rockefeller, N.A. (1976, October 16). Don't accept anyone's verdict that you are lazy, stupid or retarded. *TV Guide*, 12–14.

Roderick, M., & Camburn, E. (1999). Risk and recovery from course failure in the early years of high school. *American Educational Research Journal, 36*, 303–343.

Rodger, N.W., & Hunt, J.A. (1980). *Research horizons*. Toronto: Canadian Diabetic Association.

Rodin, D. (1989). Prognosis of cognitive function in children with epilepsy. In B.P. Hermann & M. Seidenberg (Eds.), *Childhood epilepsies: Neurophysiological, psychosocial and intervention aspects* (pp. 33–50). New York: Wiley.

Rodriguez, A., & Bohlin, G. (2005). Are maternal smoking and stress during pregnancy related to ADHD symptoms in children? *Journal of Child Psychology and Psychiatry, 46*, 246–254.

Roeher Institute (1996). *Disability, community and society*. Toronto: Author.

Roeher Institute (2000). *Count us in: Overview of childhood disability*. Toronto: Author.

Rogan, L.L., & Hardman, L.D. (1990). Adult outcome of learning disabled students 10 years after initial follow-up. *Learning Disability Focus, 5*, 91–102.

Rogers, S.J. (1988). Cognitive characteristics of handicapped children's play: A review. *Journal of the Division for Early Childhood, 12*, 161–168.

Rojas, N.L., & Chan, E. (2005). Old and new controversies in the alternative treatment of ADHD. *Mental Retardation and Development Disabilities Research Reviews, 11*, 116–130.

Rollins, S.H., Barkley, R.A., & DuPaul, G.J. (2001). Use and management of medications for children diagnosed with attention deficit hyperactivity disorder. *Focus on Exceptional Children, 33*, 1–16.

Rose, D.H., & Meyer, A. (2002). *Teaching every student in the digital age: Universal design for learning*. Alexandria, VA: Association for Curriculum Development.

Rosenblith, J.F., & Sims-Knight, J.E. (1985). *In the beginning: Development in the first two years*. Monterey, CA: Brooks/Cole.

Rosenblum, L.P. (2000). Perceptions of the import of visual impairment on the lives of adolescents. *Journal of Visual Impairment and Blindness. 94*. 434–445.

Ross, D.P., & Roberts, P. (1999). *Income and child well-being: A new perspective on the poverty debate*. Ottawa: Canadian Council on Social Development.

Ross, R. (1979). A program model for altering children's consciousness. *Gifted Child Quarterly, 23*, 109–117.

Rovet, J.F., Erlich, R.M., & Hoppe, M. (1988). Specific intellectual deficits in childhood with early onset diabetes mellitus. *Child Development, 59*, 226–234.

Ruppert, E.S., & Buhrer, K. (1992). Ohio's infant hearing screening and assessment program. *Clinical Pediatrics, 31*, 19–22.

Russell, A.T. (1994). The clinical presentation of childhood-onset schizophrenia. *Schizophrenia Bulletin, 20*, 631–646.

Russell, A.T., Bott, L., & Sammons, C. (1989). The phenomonology of schizophrenia occurring in childhood. *Journal of the American Academy of Child and Adolescent Psychiatry, 28*, 399–407.

Ryan, J.B., Reid, R., Epstein, M.H., & Evans, J.H. (2005). Pharmacological intervention research for academic outcomes for students with ADHD. *Behavioral Disorders, 30*, 135–154.

Rydell, P.J., & Mirenda, P. (1991). The effects of two levels of linguistic constraint on echolalia and generative language production in children with autism. *Journal of Autism and Developmental Disorders, 21*, 131–157.

Rylance, B.J. (1997). Predictors of high school graduation or dropping out for youths with severe emotional disturbance. *Behavioral Disorders, 23*, 5–17.

Sabornie, E.J., Cullinan, D., Osborne, S.S., & Brock, I.B. (2005). Intellectual, academic, and behavioral functioning of students with high-incidence disabilities: A cross-categorical analysis. *Exceptional Children, 72*, 47–63.

Sacks, S.Z., & Corn, A.L. (1996). Students with visual impairments: Do they understand their disability? *Journal of Visual Impairment and Blindness, 90*, 412–422.

Sadker, D. (1999). Gender equity: Still knocking on the classroom door. *Educational Leadership, 56*, 22–26.

Sadler, C. (2000). Effective behavior support implementation at the district level: Tigard-Tualatin School District. *Journal of Positive Behavior Interventions, 2*, 241–243.

Safer, D.J., & Zito, J.M. (2000). Pharmacoepidemiology of methylphenidate and other stimulants for the treatment of attention deficit hyperactivity disorder. In L. Greenhill & B. Osmon (Eds.) *Ritalin: Theory and practice* (2nd ed., pp. 7–26). Larchmont, NY: Liebert.

Safran, S.P. (2002). Supporting students with Asperger's syndrome in general education. *Teaching Exceptional Children, 34*, 60–66.

Safran S.P., & Oswald, K. (2003). Positive behavior supports: Can schools reshape disciplinary practices? *Exceptional Children, 69*, 361–373.

Safran, S.P., & Safran, J.S. (1987). Teachers' judgment of problem behaviors. *Exceptional Children, 54*, 240–244.

Safran, S.P., & Safran, J.S. (1996). Intervention assistance programs and prereferral teams: Directions for the twenty-first century. *Remedial and Special Education, 17*, 363–369.

Saigh, P.A. (1997). Post-traumatic stress disorders. In R.J. Morris & T.R. Kratochwill (Eds.), *The practice of child therapy* (3rd ed., pp. 390–418). Boston, MA: Allyn and Bacon.

Salend, S.J., & Garia, M. (1995). Increasing the homework completion rates of students with mild disabilities. *Remedial and Special Education, 16*, 271–278.

Salend, S.J., & Longo, M. (1994). The roles of the educational interpreter in mainstreaming. *Teaching Exceptional Children, 26*, 22–28.

Salisbury, C.L. (1987). Stressors of parents with young handicapped and nonhandicapped children. *Journal of the Division for Early Childhood, 11*, 154–160.

Salisbury, C.L. (1991). Mainstreaming during the early childhood years. *Exceptional Children, 58*, 146–155.

Salisbury, C.L., Evans, I.M., & Palombaro, M.M. (1997). Collaborative problem-solving to promote the inclusion of young children with significant disabilities in primary grades. *Exceptional Children, 63*, 195–209.

Salkind, N. (1990). *Child development* (6th ed.). Fort Worth, TX: Holt, Rinehart and Winston.

Salzberg, C.L., Lignugaris-Kraft, B., & McCuller, G.L. (1988). Reasons for job loss: A review of employment termination studies of mentally retarded workers. *Research in Developmental Disabilities, 9*, 153–170.

Samson, G.E. (1985). Effects of training in test-taking skills on achievement test performance: A quantitative synthesis. *Journal of Educational Research, 78*, 261–266.

Samuels, C.A. (2006, February 22). Cardiac cases raise concerns over drugs for ADHD. *Education Week.*

Sancilio, M.F.M, Plumment, J.M., & Hartup, W.W. (1989). Friendships and aggressiveness as determiners of conflict outcomes in middle children. *Developmental Psychology, 25*, 812–819.

Sanders, D. (1971). *Aural rehabilitation.* Englewood Cliffs, NJ: Prentice Hall.

Sandoval, J. (1998). Neuromuscular diseases. In L. Phelps (Ed.), *Health-related disorders in children and adolescents: A guidebook for understanding and educating* (pp. 463–473). Washington, DC: American Psychological Association.

Sanghavi, D. (2005, April 26). Time to calm down about Ritalin. *The Boston Globe* online.

Santelli, B., Turnbull, H., Marquis, J., & Lerner, E. (1997). Parent-to-parent programs: A resource for parents and professionals. *Journal of Early Intervention, 21*, 73–83.

Santos, K.E. (1992). Fragile X syndrome: An educator's role in identification, prevention, and intervention. *Remedial and Special Education, 13*, 32–37.

Santrock, J. (1999). *Life-span development* (7th ed.). Boston, MA: McGraw-Hill.

Sarouphen, K.M. (1999). Discovering multiple intelligences through a performance-based assessment: Consistency with independent ratings. *Exceptional Children, 65*, 151–161.

Saunders, S. (1999). Teaching children with fragile X syndrome. *British Journal of Special Education, 26*, 76–79.

Savage, R.C. (1988). Introduction to educational issues for students who have suffered traumatic brain injury. In R.C. Savage & G.F. Wolcott (Eds.), *An educators' manual: What educators need to know about students with traumatic brain injury.* Scarborough, MA: National Head Injury Foundation.

Sax, L., & Kautz, K.J. (2003). Who first suggests the diagnosis of attention deficit/hyperactivity disorder? *Annals of Family Medicine, 1*, 171–174.

Scarborough, H. (1989). Prediction of reading disability from familial and individual differences. *Journal of Educational Psychology, 81*, 101–108.

Scarborough, H. (1990). Very early language deficits in dyslexic children. *Child Development, 61*, 1728–1743.

Scaringi, M. (1994, fall). A study in pediatric brain injury. *Disability Today*, 75–77.

Schein, J.D. (1989). *At home among strangers: Exploring the deaf community in the United States.* Washington, DC: Gallaudet University Press.

Schein, J.D. (1994). Deafness in Canada and the United States. *Deaf American Monographs*, 93–99.

Schiff, N.B., & Ventry, I.M. (1976). Communication problems in hearing children of deaf parents. *Journal of Speech and Hearing Disorders, 41*, 348–358.

Schildroth, A.N., & Hotto, S. (1996). Annual survey of hearing impaired children and youth: 1991–92 school year. *American Annals of the Deaf, 138*, 163–171.

Schirmer, B.R. (2001). *Psychological, social, and educational dimensions of deafness.* Boston, MA: Allyn and Bacon.

Schneider, H., & Eisenberg, D. (2006). Who receives a diagnosis of attention deficit/hyperactivity disorder in the United States elementary school population? *Pediatrics, 117*, 601–609.

Schneller, R. (1989). Intercultural and intrapersonal processes and factors of misunderstanding: Implications for multicultural training. *International Journal of Intercultural Relations, 13*, 465–483.

Schorr, L.B. (1988). *Within our reach.* New York: Doubleday.

Schreibman, L., & Charlop, M.H. (1989). Infantile autism. In T.H. Ollendick & M. Hersen (Eds.), *Handbook of child psychopathology* (2nd ed.). New York: Plenum.

Schroedel, J. (1992). Helping adolescents and young adults who are deaf make career decisions. *Volta Review, 93*, 37–46.

Schroeder, F.K. (1996). Perceptions of braille usage by legally blind adults. *Journal of Visual Impairment and Blindness, 90*, 210–218.

Schumaker, J.B., Deschler, D.D., Bulgren, J.A., Davis, B., Lenz, B.K., & Grossen, B. (2002). Access of adolescents with disabilities to general education curriculum: Myth or reality? *Focus on Exceptional Children, 35*, 1–16.

Schunk, D.H. (1987). Peer models and children's behavioral change. *Review of Educational Research, 57,* 149–174.

Schwartz, L.L. (1980). Advocacy for the neglected gifted: Females. *Gifted Child Quarterly, 24,* 113–117.

Schwartz, M.H., Wolfe, J.N., & Cassar, R. (1997). Predicting teacher referrals of emotionally disturbed children. *Psychology in the Schools, 34,* 51–61.

Scorgie, K., Wilgosh, L., & McDonald, L. (1998). Stress and coping in families of children with disabilities: An examination of recent literature. *Developmental Disabilities Bulletin, 26,* 22–42.

Scott, T.M. (2003). Making behavior intervention planning decisions in a schoolwide system of positive behavioral support. *Focus on Exceptional Children, 36,* 1–18.

Scruggs, T.E., & Mastropieri, M.A. (1989). Reconstructive elaborations: A model for content area learning. *American Educational Research Journal, 26,* 311–327.

Scruggs, T.E., & Mastropieri, M.A. (1990). The case for mnemonic instruction: From laboratory investigations to classroom applications. *Journal of Special Education, 24,* 7–32.

Scruggs, T.E., & Mastropieri, M.A. (1996). Teacher perceptions of mainstreaming/inclusion: A research synthesis. *Exceptional Children, 63,* 59–74.

Scruggs, T.E., & Mastroprieri, M.A. (2002). On babies and bathwater: Addressing the problems of the identification of learning disabilities. *Learning Disabilities Quarterly, 25,* 155–168.

Seidenberg, P.L. (1997). Understanding learning disabilities. In D.K. Bernsteinad & E. Tiegerman-Farker (Eds.), *Language and communication disorders in children* (4th ed.). Boston, MA: Allyn and Bacon.

Seligman, M. (1991). Siblings of disabled brothers and sisters. In M. Seligman (Ed.), *The family with a handicapped child* (2nd ed.). Boston, MA: Allyn and Bacon.

Shames, G.H., & Wiig, E. (1990). *Human communication disorders* (3rd ed.). Columbus, OH: Merrill.

Shaw, A.K., Morrison, H.I., Spechley, K.N., Maunsell, E., Berrera, M., Schanzer, D., et al. (2004). The late effects study: Design and subject representativeness of a Canadian multi-centre study of late effects of childhood cancer. *Chronic Diseases in Canada, 25,* 119–126.

Shaywitz, S.E., & Shaywitz, B.A. (1987). *Attention deficit disorder: Current perspectives.* Paper presented at the National Conference on Learning Disabilities. Bethesda, MD.

Shea, B., & Wiener, J. (2003). Social exile: The cycle of peer victimization for boys with ADHD. *Canadian Journal of School Psychology, 18,* 55–90.

Shippen, M.E., Crites, S.A., Houchins, D.E., Ramsey, M.L., & Simon, M. (2005). Preservice teachers' perceptions of including children with disabilities. *Teacher Education and Special Education, 28,* 92–99.

Shonkoff, J., & Meisels, S. (1990). Early childhood intervention. In S. Meisels & J. Shonkoff (Eds.), *Handbook of early intervention* (pp. 3–32). New York: Cambridge University Press.

Shore, B., & Tsiamis, A. (1986). Identification by provision: Limited field test of a radical alternative for identifying gifted children. In K. Heller & J. Feldhusen (Eds.), *Identifying and nurturing the gifted* (pp. 93–102). Toronto: Hans Huber.

Shores, D., & Wehby, C.H. (1999). Analysing the social behavior of students with emotional and behavioral disorders in classrooms. *Journal of Emotional and Behavioral Disorders, 7,* 194–199.

Siegel, L., Lam., D.C., & Ladyman, S. (2000). *A review of special education in British Columbia.* Victoria: Province of British Columbia.

Siegel, S., Robert, M., & Gaylord Ross, R. (1992). A follow-along study of participants in a longitudinal transition program for youths with mild disabilities. *Exceptional Children, 58,* 346–356.

Siegle, D., & McCoach, D.B. (2005). Making a difference: Motivating gifted students who are not achieving. *Teaching Exceptional Children, 38,* 22–27.

Siegler, R.S., & Kotovsky, K. (1985). Two levels of giftedness: Shall ever the twain meet? In R.J. Sternberg & J.E. Davidson (Eds.), *Conceptions of giftedness* (pp. 417–435). New York: Cambridge University Press.

Sigafoos, J., Pidden, R., & Curfs, L.M. (2000). Educational implications of Prader-Willi syndrome. *The Journal of the International Association for Special Education, 3,* 3–16.

Sigelman C.K., & Shaffer, D.R. (1991). *Lifespan human development.* Pacific Grove, CA: Brooks/Cole.

Silberman, R. (1981). A comparison of visual functioning in hearing-impaired children and normally hearing children. *Volta Review, 83,* 95–104.

Silva, P.A. (1980). The prevalence, stability and significance of developmental language delays in preschool children. *Developmental Medicine and Child Neurology, 22,* 768–777.

Silverman, L.K. (1989). Invisible gifts, invisible handicap. *Roeper Review, 12,* 37–42.

Simen, R.J., & Rogers, R.C. (1989). School psychology and medical diagnosis: The fragile X syndrome. *Psychology in the Schools, 26,* 380–388.

Simpson, R.L. (2004). Inclusion of students with behavior disorders in general education settings: Research and measurement issues. *Behavioral disorders, 30,* 19–31.

Simpson, R.L. (2005). Evidence-based practices and students with Autism spectrum disorders. *Focus on Autism and Other Developmental Disorders, 20,* 140–149.

Simpson, R.L., & Myles, B.S. (1993). Successful integration of children with autism in mainstreamed settings. *Focus on Autistic Behavior, 7,* 1–13.

Simpson, R.L. & Myles, B. (1998). Aggression among children and youth who have Asperger's syndrome: A different population requiring different strategies. *Preventing School Failure, 42,* 149–153.

Singer, J.D. (1988). Should special education merge with regular education? *Educational Policy, 2,* 409–424.

Siperstein, G.N., & Bak, J.J. (1989). Social relationships in adolescents with mild mental retardation. *Mental Retardation, 27,* 5–10.

Siperstein, G.N., & Leffert, J.S. (1997). Comparisons of socially accepted and rejected children with mental retardation. *American Journal on Mental Retardation, 101,* 339–351.

Sisson, L.A., Van Hasselt, V.B., & Hersen, M. (1987). Psychological approaches with deaf-blind persons: Strategies and issues in research and treatment. *Clinical Psychology Review, 7,* 303–328.

Sitlington, P.L., Frank, A.R., & Carson, R. (1992). Adult adjustment among high school graduates with mild disabilities. *Exceptional Children, 59,* 221–233.

Sivin-Kachala, J., & Bialo, E.R. (1995). *Report on the effectiveness of technology in schools, 1990–1994.* Washington, DC: Software Publishers Association.

Skelly, M. (1979). *Amer-Ind gestural code based on universal American Indian hand talk.* New York: Elsevier.

Skiba, R. (2002). Special education and school discipline: A precarious balance. *Behavioral disorders, 27,* 81–97.

Skotko, B.G., Koppenhaver, D.A., & Erickson, K.A. (2004). Parent reading behaviors and communication outcomes in girls with Rett syndrome. *Exceptional Children, 70,* 145–166.

Slavin, R., Karweit, N., & Madden, N. (Eds.). (1989). *Effective programs for students at risk.* Needham Heights, MA: Allyn and Bacon.

Slavin, R.R., Madden, N.E., Kariviet, N.L., Liverman, B.J., & Dolan, L. (1990). Success for all: First year outcomes of a comprehensive plan for reforming urban education. *American Education Research Journal, 27,* 255–278.

Sleeter, C.E., & Grant, C.A. (1994). *Making choices for multicultural education: Five approaches to race, class, and gender.* New York: Merrill.

Smith, A.J., Del'aunne, W., & Geruschat, D.R. (1992). Low vision mobility problems: Perceptions of O and M specialists and persons with low vision. *Journal of Visual Impairment and Blindness, 86,* 58–62.

Smith, D. (2003, May). Cultivating otherwise untapped potential. *Monitor on Psychology,* 62–64.

Smith, D.D., & Luckasson, R. (1995). *Introduction to special education: Teaching in an age of challenge* (2nd ed.). Needham Heights, MA: Allyn and Bacon.

Smith P. (1999). Drawing new maps: A radical cartography of developmental disabilities. *Review of Educational Research, 69,* 117–144.

Smith, P.K., & Thompson, D. (1991). *Practical approaches to bullying.* Great Britain: David Fulton.

Smith, S.D., & Pennington, B.F. (1987). Genetic influences. In K.A. Kavale & S.R. Forness (Eds.), *Handbook of learning disabilities* (vol. 1): *Dimensions and diagnosis* (pp. 49–75). San Diego, CA: College-Hill.

Smith, W.J. (1994). *Equal educational opportunity for students with disabilities: Legislative action in Canada.* McGill University, Office of Research on Educational Policy.

Smulker, D. (2005). Unauthorized minds: How "Theory of mind" theory misrepresents autism. *Mental Retardation, 43,* 11–24.

Snider, V.E., Busch, T., & Arrowood, L. (2003). Teacher knowledge of stimulant medication and ADHD. *Remedial and Special Education, 24,* 45–56.

Snider, V.E., Frankenberger, W., & Aspenson, M. (2000). The relationship between learning disabilities and attention deficit hyperactivity disorder: A national survey. *Developmental Disabilities Bulletin, 28,* 18–38.

Snow, C.E., Burns, M., & Griffin, P. (1998). *Preventing reading difficulties in young children.* Washington, DC: National Academy of Sciences.

Snow, J., & Forest, M. (1987). Circles. In M. Forest (Ed.), *More educational intervention* (pp. 169–176). Downsview, ON: G. Allan Roeher Institute.

Southern, W.T., Jones, E.D., & Fiscus, E.D. (1989). Practitioner objections to the academic acceleration of gifted children. *Gifted Child Quarterly, 33,* 29–35.

Spafford, C., & Grosser, G. (1996). *Dyslexia: Research and resource guide.* Boston, MA: Allyn and Bacon.

Speltz, M.L., Endriga, M.C., Fisher, P.A., & Mason, C.A. (1997). Early predictors of attachment in infants with cleft lip and/or palate. *Child Development, 68,* 12–25.

Spencer, P. (2002). Language development of children with cochlear implants. In J. Christiansen & I. Leigh (Eds.), *Cochlear implants in children: Ethics and choice.* Washington, DC: Gallaudet University Press.

Sprague, J., & Walker, H. (2000). Early identification and intervention for youth with antisocial and violent behavior. *Exceptional Children, 66,* 367–379.

Sprinthall, N.A., & Sprinthall, R.C. (1990). *Educational psychology: A developmental approach* (5th ed.). New York: Random House.

Sridhar, D., & Vaughn, S. (2000). Bibliotherapy for all: Enhancing reading comprehension, self-concept, and behavior. *Teaching Exceptional Children, 33,* 74–82.

Stainback, S., & Stainback, W. (1988). Educating students with severe disabilities. *Teaching Exceptional Children, 21,* 16–19.

Stanley, J.C., & Benbow, C.P. (1986). Extremely young college graduates: Evidence of their success. *College and University, 58,* 361–371.

Stanovich, K. (1994). Annotation: Does dyslexia exist? *Journal of Child Psychology and Psychiatry, 35,* 579–595.

Statement of policy approved for bilingual/bicultural program Ontario (1993). *Deaf Education, 2,* 1–2.

Statistics Canada (2000). Divorces, 1998. Retrieved from www.statscan.ca/Daily/English/000928/d000928b.htm.

Statistics Canada (2005). The gap in achievement between boys and girls. Retrieved from www.statscan80/English/freepub/81-004-XIE/200410/mafe.htm.

Steele, B.F. (1986). Notes on the lasting effects of early child abuse throughout the life cycle. *Child Abuse and Neglect, 10,* 283–291.

Steere, D.E., & Cavainolo, D. (2002). Connecting outcomes, goals, and objectives in transition planning. *Teaching Exceptional Children, 34,* 54–59.

Stephens, O. (1989). Braille: Implications for living. *Journal of Visual Impairment and Blindness, 83,* 288–289.

Sternberg, R.J. (1987). A unified theory of intellectual exceptionality. In J.D. Day & J.G. Borkowski (Eds.), *Intelligence and exceptionality: New directions for theory, assessment and instructional practices* (pp. 135–172). Norwood, NJ: Ablex.

Sternberg, R.J. (2005). WICS: A model of giftedness in leadership. *Roeper Review, 28,* 37–44.

Sternberg, R.J., & Lubart, R. (1995). *Defying the crowd.* New York: Free Press.

Stevens, D.D., & Englert, C.S. (1993). Making writing systems work. *Teaching Exceptional Children, 26,* 34–39.

Stevens, V., DeBourdeuadhuji, I., & Van Oost, P. (2002). Relationship of the family environment to children's involvement in bully/victim problems at school. *Journal of Youth and Adolescence, 31,* 419–428.

Stewart, D.A. (1984). Mainstreaming deaf children: A different perspective. *The ACHEI Journal, 10,* 91–104.

Stewart, D.A., & Kluwin, T. (2001). *Teaching deaf and hard of hearing students: Content, strategies, and curriculum.* Boston, MA: Allyn and Bacon.

Stokoe, W.C., Jr., & Battiston, R. (1975). *Sign language, mental health and satisfactory interaction.* Linguistic Research Laboratory, Gallaudet College, Washington, DC.

Storch, E.A., & Esposito, L.E. (2003). Peer victimization and posttraumatic stress among children. *Child Study Journal, 33.*

Stormont, M. (2001). Preschool family and child characteristics assessment with stable behavior problems in children. *Journal of Early Intervention, 24,* 241–251.

Stormont, M., & Stebbins, M.S. (2005). Preschool teachers' knowledge, opinions, and educational experiences with Attention Deficit/Hyperactivity Disorder. *Teacher Education and Special Education, 28,* 52–61.

Stough L.M., & Baker L. (1999). Identifying depression in students with mental retardation. *Teaching Exceptional Children, 31,* 62–66.

Strain, P.S., & Timm, M.A. (2001). Remediation and prevention of aggression: An evaluation of the Regional Intervention Program over a quarter century. *Behavioral Disorders, 26,* 297–313.

Stram, P.S., & Stram, R.D. (2005). Cyberbullying by adolescents: A preliminary assessment. *The Educational Forum, 70,* 21–32.

Stromsness, M.M. (1993). Sexually abused women with mental retardation: Hidden victims, absent resources. *Women and Therapy, 14,* 139–152.

Strong, K., & Sandoval, J. (1999). Mainstreaming children with neuromuscular disease: A map of concerns. *Exceptional Children, 65,* 353–366.

Strouse, J.H. (1997). *Exploring themes of social justice in education: Readings in social foundations.* Upper Saddle River, NJ: Prentice Hall.

Stuart, S.K. (2003). Choice or chance: Career development and girls with emotional or behavioral disorders. *Behavioral Disorders, 28,* 15–161.

Subsotnik, R. (1997). Teaching students in a multicultural society. In J. Banks & C. Banks (Eds.), *Multicultural education: Issues and perspectives* (3rd ed., pp. 361–382). Boston, MA: Allyn and Bacon.

Sugai, G., & Horner, R. (1994). Including students with severe behavioural problems in general education settings: Assumptions, challenges, and solutions. In J. Marr, G. Sugai, & G. Tindel (Eds.), *The Oregon Conference Monograph* (vol. 6, pp. 109–120). Eugene, OR: University of Oregon.

Sugai, G., & Horner, R. (1999). Discipline and behavioral support: Preferred processes and practices. *Effective School Practices, 17,* 10–22.

Sullivan, A.K., & Strang, H.R. (2002–2003). Bibliotherapy in the classroom: Using literature to promote the development of emotional intelligence. *Childhood Education, 79,* 74–80.

Sullivan, M. (1988). *A comparative analysis of dropouts and non-dropouts in Ontario secondary schools.* Toronto: Ontario Ministry of Education.

Sutherland, K.S. (2000). Promoting positive interactions between teachers and students with emotional/behavioral disabilities. *School Failure, 44,* 110–115.

Sutherland, K.S., Wehby, J.H., & Copeland, S.R. (2000). Effects of varying rates of behavior-specific praise on the on-task behavior of students with EBD. *Journal of Emotional and Behavioral Disorders, 8,* 2–8.

Sutherland, K.S., Wehby, J.H., & Yoder, P.J. (2002). Examination of the relationship between teacher praise and opportunities for students with EBD to respond to academic requests. *Journal of Emotional and Behavioral Disorders, 10,* 5–13.

Swanson, H.L. (1999). *Interventions for students with learning disabilities: A meta-analysis of treatment outcomes.* New York: Guilford.

Swanson, H.L., & Hosbyn, M. (1998). Experimental intervention research on students with learning disabilities: A meta-analysis of treatment outcomes. *Review of Educational Research, 68,* 277–321.

Swanson H.L. & Sanche-Lee, C. (2000). A meta-analysis of single- subject design intervention research for students with LD. *Journal of Learning Disabilities, 38,* 114–136.

Swanwick, R.A. (1998). Learning English as a second language: Opportunities and challenges for sign bilingual deaf children. *Deafness and Education, 22,* 3–9.

Sweeting, H., & West, P. (2001). Being different: correlates of the experience of teasing and bullying at age 11. *Research Papers in Education, 16,* 225–246.

Swiatek, M.A., & Benbow, C.P. (1991). Ten-year longitudinal follow-up of ability-matched accelerated and unaccelerated gifted students. *Journal of Educational Psychology, 83,* 528–538.

Sylvester, R. (1997, February). The neurobiology of self-esteem and aggression. *Educational Leadership, 54,* 75–79.

Szabo, L. (2006, 14 February). Mixed messages on ADHD. Retrieved February 23, 2006, from www.usatoday.com/news/health/2006–02–14-adhd-x.htm.

Tannenbaum, A.J. (1962). *Adolescent attitudes toward academic brilliance.* New York: Bureau of Publications, Teachers College, Columbia University.

Tannenbaum, A.J. (1986). The enrichment matrix model. In J.S. Renzulli (Ed.), *Systems and models for developing programs for gifted and talented* (pp. 391–428). Mansfield Center, CT: Creative Learning Press.

Taylor, E.H. (1998). Advances in the diagnosis and treatment of children with serious mental illness. *Child Welfare, 77,* 311–332.

Taylor, R.L., Richards, S.B., Goldstein, P.A., & Schilit, J. (1997). Teacher perceptions of inclusive settings. *Teaching Exceptional Children, 29,* 50–54.

Taylor, S., & Hefle, S.L. (2001). Food allergies and other food sensitivities. *Food Technology, 55,* 68–83.

Taylor-Greene, S.J., & Kartub, D.T. (2000). Durable implementation of school-wide behavior support: The High Five Program. *Journal of Positive Behavior Interventions, 2,* 233–235.

Teeter, P.A. (1988). *Interventions for ADHD: Treatment in developmental context.* New York, NY: Guilford.

Telford, C.W., & Sawrey, J.M. (1981). *The exceptional individual* (4th ed.). Englewood Cliffs, NJ: Prentice Hall.

Telzrow, C.F., & Bonar, A.M. (2002). Responding to students with nonverbal learning disabilities. *Teaching Exceptional Children, 34,* 8–13.

Teplin, S.W. (1995). Visual impairment in infants and young children. *Infants and Young Children, 8,* 18–51.

Terman, L.M. (1926). *Genetic studies of genius: Mental and physical traits of a thousand gifted children* (2nd ed.). Stanford, CA: Stanford University Press.

Terman, L.M., & Oden, M.H. (1951). The Stanford studies of the gifted. In P. Witty (Ed.), *The gifted child.* Lexington, MA: D.C. Heath.

Thomas, G., & Loxley, A. (2001). *Deconstructing special education and constructing inclusion.* Philadelphia, PA: Open University Press.

Thompson, L.J. (1971). Language disabilities in men of eminence. *Journal of Learning Disabilities, 4,* 34–44.

Tiessen, J. (1996, winter). Orthotics and prosthetics: Fit and fashion join a tradition of function. *Disability Today,* 23–25.

Tolbert, H.A. (1996). Psychosis in children and adolescents: A review. *Journal of Clinical Psychiatry, 57,* 4–8.

Torgesen, J.K. (1998 Spring–Summer). Catch them before they fall. *American Educator,* pp. 32–41.

Torgesen, J.K., Morgan S.T., & Davis, C. (1992). Effects of two types of phonological awareness training on word learning in kindergarten classrooms. *Journal of Educational Psychology, 84,* 364–370.

Torrance, E.P. (1966). *The Torrance Tests of Creative Thinking: Norms and technical manual.* Princeton, NJ: Personnel Press.

Torrance, E.P. (1969). Creative positives of disadvantaged children and youth. *Gifted Child Quarterly, 13,* 71–81.

Tournaki, N., & Criscitiello, E. (2003). Using peer tutoring as a successful part of behavior management. *Teaching Exceptional Children, 36 (2),* 22–29.

Traxler, C.B. (2000). The Stanford Achievement Test, 9th edition: National norming and performance standards for deaf and hard-of-hearing students. *Journal of Deaf Studies and Deaf Education, 5,* 337–348.

Treffinger, D. (1986). Research on creativity. *Gifted Child Quarterly, 30,* 15–19.

Trief, E., Duckman, R., Morse, A.R., & Silberman, R.K. (1989). Retinopathy of prematurity. *Journal of Visual Impairment and Blindness, 83,* 500–504.

Trivette, C. & Dunst, C. (2004). Evaluating family-based practices: Parenting Experience Scale, *Young Exceptional Children, 7,* 12–19.

Turnbull, A.P., Turnbull, R., Shank, M., & Leal, D. (1999). *Exceptional lives: Special education in today's schools.* Columbus: OH: Prentice Hall.

Tyler, J.S., & Colson, S. (1994, December). Common pediatric disabilities: Medical aspects and educational implications. *Focus on Exceptional Children,* 1–16.

Ulster, A.A., & Antle, B.J. (2005). In the darkness there can be light: A family's adaptation to a child's blindness. *Journal of Visual Impairment and Blindness, 99,* 209–218.

UNICEF (2005). *Children and disability in transition in CEE/CIS and Baltic states.* Florence, Italy: Author.

United States, Department of Education (1987). *Ninth annual report to Congress on the implementation of the Education of the Handicapped Act.* Washington, DC: US Government Printing Office.

United States, Department of Education (2000). *Twenty-second annual report to Congress in the implementation of the Individual with Disabilities Education Act.* Washington, DC: Author.

United States National Research Council (2001). *Educating children with autism.* Washington, DC: National Academy Press.

United States, *PL 101–476, Sec. 602* (a)(19)), IDEA, 1990.

Urquhart, I. (2005, November 9). Special education debate returns to haunt Ontario. Retrieved from the *Toronto Star*, www.the star.com.

Valentine, F. (2001). *Enabling citizenship: Full inclusion of children with disabilities and their parents.* Ottawa: Canadian Public Policy.

Valentine, F., & Vickers, J. (1996). "Released from the yoke of paternalism and charity": Citizenship and the rights of Canadians with disabilities. *International Journal of Canadian Studies, 14*, 155–177.

Van Dyke, D.C., & Fox, A.A. (1990). Fetal drug exposure and its possible implications for learning in the preschool and school age population. *Journal of Learning Disabilities, 23*, 160–163.

Van Osdol, W.R., & Shane, D.B. (1982). *An introduction to exceptional children.* Dubuque, IA: William C. Brown.

Vanpoelvoorde, L., & Shaughnessy, M.F. (1991). Parental reactions to cleft palate children. *BC Journal of Special Education (British Columbia), 15*, 276–283.

Van Rijn, N. (2000, July 14). Guidelines suggest limited use of behaviour-altering drug in kids. *Lethbridge Herald*, p. A15.

Van Riper, C., & Emerick, L. (1990). *Speech correction: An introduction to speech pathology and audiology* (8th ed.). Englewood Cliffs, NJ: Prentice Hall.

Van Tassel-Baska, J. (1987). The ineffectiveness of the pull-out model in gifted education: A minority perspective. *Journal for the Education of the Gifted, 10*, 255–264.

Van Tassel-Baska, J. (1989). Appropriate curriculum for gifted learners. *Educational Leadership, 4*, 13–15.

Van Tassel-Baska, J. (1994). *Comprehensive curriculum for gifted learners* (2nd ed.). Denver, CO: Love.

Van Tassel-Baska, J. (1995). The development of talent through curriculum. *Roeper Review, 18*, 98–102.

Van Tassel-Baska, J., & Brown, E.F. (2000). An analysis of gifted education curriculum models. In F.A. Karnes & S.M. Bean (Eds.), *Methods and materials for teaching the gifted* (pp. 93–131). Waco: TX: Prufrock Press.

Van Tassel-Baska, J., Landau, M., & Olszewski, P. (1985). Toward developing an appropriate math/science curriculum for gifted learners. *Journal for Education of the Gifted, 7*, 257–272.

Vaughn, S., Bos, C., & Schumm, J.S. (1997). *Teaching mainstreamed, diverse, and at-risk students in the general education classroom.* Boston, MA: Allyn and Bacon.

Vaughn, S., Gersten, R., & Chard, D.J. (2000). The underlying message in learning disabilities intervention research: Findings from research syntheses. *Exceptional Children, 67*, 99–114.

Vaughn, V.L., Feldhusen, J.F., & Asher, J.W. (1991). Meta-analyses and review of research on pull-out programs in gifted education. *Gifted Child Quarterly, 35*, 92–98.

Vedantam, S. (2006). 300,000 children in US found to have autism. Retrieved from *The Washington Post*, www.washingtonpost.com/wp-dyn/content/article/2006/05/04/AR2006050501724-pfhtml.

Vergason, G.A., & Anderegg, M.L. (1997). The ins and outs of special education terminology. *Teaching Exceptional Children, 29*, 34–39.

Verhaaran, P., & Connor, F.P. (1981). Physical disabilities. In J.M. Kauffman and D.P. Hallahan (Eds.), *Handbook of special education* (pp. 248–289). Englewood Cliffs, NJ: Prentice Hall.

Volk, H.E., Neuman, R.J., & Todd, R.D. (2005). A systematic evaluation of ADHD and comorbid psychopathology as a population-based twin sample. *Journal of the American Academy of Child and Adolescent Psychiatry, 68*, 768–775.

Vorhees, C.V., & Mollnow, E. (1987). Behavioral teratogenesis: Long-term influences from early exposure to environmental agents. In J.D. Osfosky (Ed.), *Handbook of infant development* (pp. 913–972). New York: Wiley.

Wagner, S. (1999) Focus on disability–Asperger's syndrome. *CEC Today, 6*, p. 11.

Walberg, H.J. (1991). Improving school science in advanced and developed countries. *Review of Educational Research, 61*, 25–69.

Walker, H.M., Ramsey, E., & Gresham, F.M. (2004). *Antisocial behavior in school: Evidence-based practices* (2nd ed.). Bellmont, CA: Woodsworth/Thomson Learning.

Walker, N., & Wrigglesworth, G. (2001). The effect of conductive hearing loss on phonological awareness, reading and spelling of urban Aboriginal students. *Australian Journal of Audiology, 23*, 37–51.

Walz, N., Beebe, D., & Byars, K. (2005). Sleep in individuals with Angleman syndrome: Parent perceptions of patterns and problems. *American Journal on Mental Retardation, 110*, 243–252.

Warren, P. (1988). *Teachers and the law.* St. John's, NL: Memorial University of Newfoundland.

Warren, W., & Hasenstab, S. (1986). Self-concept of severely to profoundly hearing-impaired children. *Volta Review, 88,* 289–295.

Wasik, B.H., Bryant, D.M., & Lyons, C.M. (1990). *Home visiting: Procedures for helping families.* Newbury Park, CA: Sage.

Webber, J., & Scheuermann, B. (1997). A challenging future: Current barriers and recommended action for our field. *Behavioral Disorders, 22,* 167–178.

Wechsler, D. (1974). *Wechsler Intelligence Scale for Children–Revised.* New York: Psychological Corporation.

Wehmeyer, M. (1996). Self-determination in youth with severe cognitive disabilities: From theory to practice. In L.E. Powers, G.H.S. Singer, & J. Sowers (Eds.), *On the road to autonomy: Promoting self-competence for children and youth with disabilities* (pp. 17–36). Baltimore, MD: Brookes.

Wehmeyer, M., & Schwartz, M. (1997). Self-determination and positive adult outcomes: A follow-up study of youth with mental retardation or learning disabilities. *Exceptional Children, 63,* 248–255.

Wehmeyer, M., Kelchner, K., & Richards, S. (1996). Essential characteristics of self-determined behavior of individuals with mental retardation. *American Journal on Mental Retardation, 100,* 632–642.

Weiner, L. & Septimus, A. (1991). Psychosocial consideration and support for the child and family. In P.A. Pizzo & C.M. Wilfert (Eds.) *Pediatric AIDS: The challenge of HIV infants, children and adolescents* (pp. 577–594). Baltimore, MD: Williams and Wilkins.

Weishaar, M.K., & Boyle, J.R. (1997, Fall). Note-taking for students with disabilities. *CEC Today, 12.*

Weiss, G., & Hechtman, L.T. (1986). *Hyperactive children grown up.* New York: Guilford.

Weiss, J.B., & Weiss, J. (1981). Use of the talking calculator to improve mathematical skills. *Journal of Visual Impairment and Blindness, 75,* 61–63.

Wenar, C. (1994). *Developmental psychopathology* (3rd ed.). New York: McGraw-Hill.

Wender, P.H. (2000). *ADHD: Attention-deficit hyperactivity disorder in children and adults.* New York, NY: Oxford University Press.

Wenz-Gross, M., & Siperstein, G.N. (1997). Importance of social support in the adjustment of children with learning problems. *Exceptional Children, 63,* 183–193.

Wesanko, E. (1990, June). Long-term consequences of communication disorders. *Keeping in Touch, 2.*

Westat Inc. (1994). *Issues and options in outcome-based accountability for students with disabilities.* College Park, MD: Center for Policy Options in Special Education.

Westling, D.L., & Fox, L. (2000). *Teaching students with severe disabilities* (2nd ed.). Upper Saddle River, NJ: Prentice Hall.

Whalen, C.K. & Henker, B. (1980). *Hyperactive children: The social ecology of identification and treatment.* New York, NY: Academic Press.

Whitmore, J.R. (1988). Gifted children at risk for learning difficulties. *Teaching Exceptional Children, 20,* 10–14.

Whitney-Thomas, J., & Maloney, M. (2001). "Who I am and what I want": Adolescents' self-definition and struggles. *Exceptional Children, 67,* 375–389.

Wicks-Nelson, R., & Israel, A.C. (1991). *Behavior disorders of childhood* (2nd ed.). Englewood Cliffs, NJ: Prentice Hall.

Widom, C.S. (1989). Does violence beget violence? A critical examination of the literature. *Psychological Bulletin, 106,* 3–28.

Wiener, J. (2004). Do peer relationships foster behavioral adjustments in children with learning disabilities? *Learning Disabilities Quarterly, 27,* 21–30.

Wiener, J., Harris, P.J., & Shirer, C. (1990). Achievement and social behavioral correlates of peer status in LD children. *Learning Disabilities Quarterly, 13,* 114–127.

Wiig, E.H., & Semel, E. (1976). *Language disabilities in children and adolescents.* Columbus, OH: Merrill.

Wilbur, R. (2000). The use of ASL to support the development of English and literacy. *Journal of Deaf Studies and Deaf Education, 5,* 81–104.

Wilde, J. (2006). Teachers' and counselors' knowledge and experience related to Attention Deficit Hyperactivity Disorder. M. Ed thesis, University of Lethbridge.

Will, G. (1999, December 5). Don't just reach for Ritalin: New research finds old truth—sometimes, boys will be boys. *Calgary Sunday Sun,* p. C6.

Will, M. (1984). *OSERS programming for the transition of youth with disabilities: Bridges from school to working life.* Washington, DC: Office of Special Education and Rehabilitation Services, US Department of Education.

Willard-Holt, C. (1998). Academic and personality characteristics of gifted students with cerebral palsy: A multiple case study. *Exceptional Children, 65,* 37–50.

Williams, B.F., Howard, V.F., & McLaughlin, T.F. (1994). Fetal alcohol syndrome: Developmental characteristics and directions for further research. *Education and Treatment of Children, 17,* 86–97.

Williams, D.F. (1999). The child who stutters: Guidelines for the educator. *Our Young Exceptional Children, 2,* 9–14.

Williams, J., Sharp, G., Bates, S., Griebel, M., Lange, B., Spence, G.T., et al. (1996). Academic achievement and behavioral ratings in children with absence and complex partial epilepsy. *Education and Treatment of Children, 19,* 143–152.

Williamson, P., McLeskey, J., Hoppey, D., & Rentz, T. (2006). Educating students with mental retardation in general classrooms. *Exceptional Children, 72,* 347–361.

Willig, A.C., & Greenberg, H.F. (1986). *Bilingualism and learning disabilities: Policy and practice for teachers and administrators.* New York: American Library.

Wilson, E.O. (1998). *Consilience: The unity of knowledge.* New York: Vintage.

Wilson, G.L. (2004). Using videotherapy to access curriculum and enhance growth. *Teaching Exceptional Children, 36 (6),* 32–37.

Winebrenner, S. (2000, September). Gifted students need an education, too. *Educational Leadership,* 52–56.

Wing. L. (1981). Asperger's syndrome: A clinical account. *Psychological Medicine, 11,* 115–130.

Wingert, P., & Kantrowitz, B. (1997, October 27). Why Andy couldn't read. *Newsweek,* 56–64.

Winzer, M.A., Altieri, E., Jacobs, T., & Mellor, E. (2003). Reform in special education: Case studies from Australia, Canada, and the United States. *Journal of the Academy for the Humanization of Education, 1,* 96–118.

Winzer, M.A., Rogow, S., & David, C. (1987). *Exceptional children in Canada.* Toronto: Prentice Hall.

Winzer, M.A. (1993). *The history of special education: From isolation to integration.* Washington, DC: Gallaudet University Press.

Winzer, M.A. (1995). *Educational psychology in Canadian classrooms* (2nd ed.). Toronto: Allyn and Bacon.

Winzer, M.A. (1997). *Special education in early childhood: An inclusive approach.* Toronto: Allyn and Bacon.

Winzer, M.A. (in press). *A history of special education: From integration to inclusion.* Washington, DC: Gallaudet University Press.

Winzer, M.A., & Mazurek, K. (1998). *Special education in multicultural contexts.* Columbus, OH: Merrill.

Wolffe, K.E., & Candela, A.R. (2002). A qualitative analysis of employers' experience with visually impaired workers. *Journal of Visual Impairment and Blindness, 96,* 622–634.

Wolke, D., Woods, S., Stanford, K., & Schultz, H. (2001). Bullying and victimization of primary school children in England and Germany: Prevalence and school factors. *British Journal of Psychology, 92,* 673–696.

Wood, J.G. (2004). Ongoing psychopharmacological treatment of emotional and behavioral disorders: Helping students address transition needs. *Beyond Behavior, 123,* 15–16.

World Health Organization (2001). *International classification of functioning, disability, and health.* Geneva: Author.

Worling, D., Humphries, T., & Tannock, R. (1999). Spatial and emotional aspects of language inferencing in nonverbal learning disabilities. *Brain and Language, 70,* 220–239.

Wotherspoon, T., & Schissel, B. (2001). The business of placing Canadian children and youth "at-risk." *Canadian Journal of Education, 26,* 321–339.

Wright, D., & Bray, I. (2000). Estimating birth prevalence of Down's syndrome. *Journal of Epidemiology and Biostatistics, 5,* 89–97.

Yairi, E., & Ambrose, N. (1992). A longitudinal study of stuttering in children. *Journal of Speech and Hearing Research, 35,* 755–760.

Yell, M.L., & Shriner, J.G. (1997). The IDEA amendments of 1997: Implications for special and general education teachers. *Focus on Exceptional Children, 30,* 1–19.

Yewchuk, C. (1984). Gifted education in Alberta: Current developments. *Special Education in Canada, 58,* 142–143.

Ylvisaker, M. (1986). Language and communication disorders following pediatric injury. *Journal of Head Trauma Rehabilitation, 1,* 48–56.

Yoder, P., Camarata, S., & Gardner, E. (2005). Treatment effects on speech intelligibility and length of utterance in children with specific language and intelligibility impairments. *Journal of Early Intervention, 28,* 34–49.

Yoshingata-Itano, C. (1994). Language assessment of infants and toddlers with significant hearing losses. *Seminars in Hearing, 15,* 128–147.

Ysseldyke, J.E., & Algozzine, B. (1990). *Introduction to special education* (2nd ed.). Boston, MA: Allyn and Bacon.

Ysseldyke, J.E., Algozzine, B., & Thurlow, M.L. (2000). *Critical issues in special education* (3rd ed.). Boston, MA: Houghton Mifflin.

Zammitt, N.O., Hare, A., Mason, J., & Elliott, G. (1999). Use of low vision aids by children attending a centralized multidisciplinary visual impairment service. *Journal of Visual Impairment and Blindness, 93,* 351–359.

Zeesman, A. (2001). HRDC research on children and youth at risk. In Canadian Education Statistics council (Ed.), Pan-Canadian education research agenda 2000 symposium report (p. 5). Toronto: Canadian Education Statistics council catalogue No. 81–589.

Zemlin, W.R. (1990). Anatomy and physiology of speech. In G.H. Shames & E.H. Wiig (Eds.) *Human communication disorders* (3rd ed.) Columbus, OH: Merrill.

Zentall, S.S. (1993). Research on the educational implications of attention deficit hyperactivity disorder. *Exceptional Children, 60,* 143–153.

Zetlin, A., & Murtaugh, M. (1988). Friendship patterns of mentally handicapped and non-handicapped high school students. *American Journal on Mental Retardation, 92,* 447–454.

Zetlin, A. & Murtaugh, M. (1990). Whatever happened to those with borderline IQS? *American Journal on Mental Retardation, 94,* 463–469.

Zigmond, N., Jenkins, J., Fuchs, L.S., Deno, S., Fuchs, D., Baker, J.N., et al. (1995). Special education in restructured schools: Findings from three multi-year studies. *Phi Delta Kappan, 76,* 531–540.

Zirpoli, T.J. (1990). Physical abuse: Are children with disabilities at greater risk? *Intervention in School and Clinic, 26,* 6–11.

Zirpoli, T.J., & Melloy, K.J. (1997). *Behavior management: Applications for teachers and parents* (2nd ed.). Columbus, OH: Merrill.

Zito, J., Safer, D., dos Reis, S., Gardner, J., Boles, M., & Lynch, F. (2000). Trends in the prescribing of psychotropic medication to preschoolers. *Journal of the American Medical Association, 283,* 1025–1030.

Zoccolillio, M., Tremblay, R., & Vilano, F. (1996). DSM-III-R and DSM-III criteria for conduct disorders in preadolescent girls: Specific but insensitive. *Journal of American Academy of Child and Adolescent Psychiatry, 35,* 461–470.

Zwolen, T.A. (2000). Selection criteria and evaluation. In S.B. Waltzman & N.L. Cohen (Eds.), *Cochlear implants* (pp. 63–77). New York, NY: Thieme-McKinley.

AUTHOR INDEX

SUBJECT INDEX

Photo Credits